AN INTRODUCTION TO COGNITIVE BEHAVIOUR THERAPY

PRAISE FOR THE BOOK

PRAISE FOR THE THIRD EDITION

'Want to learn to practice CBT with an expert CBT therapist at your side? Then immerse yourself in the third edition of Kennerley et al.'s *An Introduction to Cognitive Behaviour Therapy*, the most complete and up-to-date introductory CBT text available. Each chapter offers clear guidance for management of common clinical dilemmas. Video links demonstrate skills and help therapists really understand CBT as a living, breathing therapy. Even experienced therapists can benefit. This book offers a comprehensive and sophisticated view of CBT in practice.'

Dr Christine A. Padesky, co-founder of the Center for Cognitive Therapy and co-author of *Mind over Mood*

'There are many books that give us the basics of CBT. This one gives us the basics and beyond – what to do, when to do it, how to do it, and why we need to do it. Its mix of case material, techniques and illustrations (including truly enlightening videos of therapy in practice) make the book hard to put down. Whatever the disorder, whatever the age group, whatever the complexity – this book will help you to improve your practise. Consider it mandatory reading for any trainee, supervisor or clinician who takes patient care seriously.'

Professor Glenn Waller, University of Sheffield

'*An Introduction to Cognitive Behaviour Therapy* has been a core text for learners, novice and experienced practitioners, and CBT educators alike since its first edition in 2007. All reputable CBT training programmes have this text on their essential reading lists. The third edition with its comprehensive new features such as the inclusion of videos, new case studies, additional exercises, and a focus on the cultural context of CBT will make what is already a great book indispensable.'

Pamela Myles, University of Reading

'This book is not just an introduction to CBT; it is *the* introduction to CBT. The depth of the authors' expertise as therapists, supervisors and trainers shines through and their knowledge is shared in an accessible way. The new edition includes several contemporary themes and also provides a companion website with video links. Quite simply, new students of CBT should start here.'

Dr Stephen Barton, Newcastle University

'This third edition contains all of the conciseness and clarity of the earlier editions, but with greater depth and scope. Any questions about how to use it in practice can be answered by using the demonstration videos and companion website. Comprehensive, authoritative, practical and friendly, this remains the essential guide to CBT.'

Dave Roberts, Oxford Brookes University

PRAISE FOR THE SECOND EDITION

'This text seeks to genuinely enable therapists' understanding, providing how-to guides, case examples and route maps to learning. The authors' proficient understanding of the breadth and complexity of CBT shines through.'

Professor Willem Kuyken, Mood Disorders Centre

'It is great to see an already outstanding book brought right up to date. As ever, for these authors, excellence begets excellence.'

David Richards, Professor of Mental Health Services Research, University of Exeter

HELEN KENNERLEY,
JOAN KIRK &
DAVID WESTBROOK

AN INTRODUCTION TO COGNITIVE BEHAVIOUR THERAPY

SKILLS & APPLICATIONS

Los Angeles | London | New Delhi
Singapore | Washington DC | Melbourne

SAGE Publications Ltd
1 Oliver's Yard
55 City Road
London EC1Y 1SP

SAGE Publications Inc.
2455 Teller Road
Thousand Oaks, California 91320

SAGE Publications India Pvt Ltd
B 1/I 1 Mohan Cooperative Industrial Area
Mathura Road
New Delhi 110 044

SAGE Publications Asia-Pacific Pte Ltd
3 Church Street
#10-04 Samsung Hub
Singapore 049483

First edition published 2007. Reprinted 2007 (twice), 2008 (twice), 2009
Second edition published 2011. Reprinted 2012, 2013, 2014 (twice), 2015 (twice), 2016

This third edition first published 2017

Editor: Susannah Trefgarne
Editorial assistant: Edward Coats
Production editor: Rachel Burrows
Copyeditor: Solveig Gardner Servian
Proofreader: Andy Baxter
Indexer: Adam Pozner
Marketing manager: Camille Richmond
Cover design: Wendy Scott
Typeset by: C&M Digitals (P) Ltd, Chennai, India
Printed in the UK

Library of Congress Control Number: 2016938705

British Library Cataloguing in Publication data

A catalogue record for this book is available from the British Library

ISBN 978-1-4739-6256-9
ISBN 978-1-4739-6258-3 (pbk)

At SAGE we take sustainability seriously. Most of our products are printed in the UK using FSC papers and boards. When we print overseas we ensure sustainable papers are used as measured by the PREPS grading system. We undertake an annual audit to monitor our sustainability.

Dedicated to Joan Kirk (1945–2016)
and David Westbrook (1950–2013)

CONTENTS

LIST OF FIGURES AND TABLES

FIGURES

TABLES

ABOUT THE AUTHORS

Helen Kennerley is a Consultant Clinical Psychologist working in the NHS and a Senior Associate Tutor with the University of Oxford. Most of her time is dedicated to the Oxford Cognitive Therapy Centre (OCTC), where she is the Director of its Supervision and Training course, and where she carries out CBT training and supervision herself. Her clinical work has been predominantly with survivors of childhood trauma. She has practised CBT for over 30 years, having trained in Oxford and the US. She was a founder member of OCTC and has written several popular cognitive therapy self-help books. In 2002 she was shortlisted for the British Association for Behavioural & Cognitive Psychotherapies (BABCP) award for most influential female cognitive therapist in Britain and in 2015 her book, *Overcoming anxiety: a self-help guide using cognitive and behavioural techniques*, was highly commended in the BMA medical book awards. She is BABCP-accredited as a therapist, supervisor and trainer.

Joan Kirk was a Consultant Clinical Psychologist for over 40 years, having trained in Liverpool, Edinburgh and Oxford. Her original behavioural orientation gradually changed in the 1970s to a cognitive-behavioural position. She was keen to spread the word and so supervised and taught enthusiastically, as well as doing research and writing. She was Head of Adult Clinical Psychology Services in Oxford for many years, and from there she developed the Oxford Cognitive Therapy Centre, and was its first Director. She left the NHS in 2004, to work independently. Joan was a Fellow of the British Psychological Society, and a BABCP-accredited therapist.

David Westbrook was a Consultant Clinical Psychologist, former Director of Oxford Cognitive Therapy Centre and a Senior Associate Tutor with the University of Oxford. Before training as a clinical psychologist he was a psychiatric nurse, eventually becoming the nurse in charge of a specialist behaviour therapy unit in London. This led on to an interest in cognitive therapy, which included training from many of the world's leading CBT therapists. He practised CBT for over 25 years and was involved in training, supervision and research as well as being an NHS clinician, providing a service for clients with severe and complex problems. He was BABCP-accredited as a therapist, supervisor and trainer.

ACKNOWLEDGEMENTS

No text is ever completed without the support, and even sacrifice, of many whose names do not appear on the cover. This is certainly true of *An Introduction to Cognitive Behavioural Therapy*: the generosity of others has been immense and we cannot possibly list everyone by name.

Suffice to say that this book would never have materialised had we not been approached and so very well supported by SAGE and the editorial staff there. It would not have been possible to commit the time to writing it if our family members had not been prepared to tolerate the absences and stresses that we imposed. We would have been unable to conceive of the book had we not already been privileged to learn from wise tutors and colleagues. And this type of text, in particular, can only be written because so many students have given us useful feedback and because so many clients have shared their experiences with us.

So, thank you.

PREFACE

Updating this third edition was a very bitter-sweet task. For years I had worked closely with Joan Kirk and David Westbrook both in the Oxford Department of Clinical Psychology and later in the Oxford Cognitive Therapy Centre (OCTC). Most recently we had collaborated on this introduction to CBT text and had grown used to sharing thoughts, debating ideas and pulling something together that was 'ours'. Sadly, by the time Joan and I began this edition, David had died and by the time I submitted it Joan had passed away after a long illness.

Their deaths have left a significant gap in the CBT world.

Joan was an extraordinary person, a clever, innovative and energetic clinical psychologist who led by wise example and inspired those around her. An early pioneer of CBT, she founded OCTC to promote CBT excellence 25 years ago. In collaboration with the University of Oxford she helped establish one of the UK's earliest CBT Diplomas. She also co-edited one of the best-selling early CBT texts (*Cognitive behavior therapy for psychiatric problems*: Hawton et al., 1989). Joan's professional life is rich with achievements and she was, deservedly, made a Fellow of the British Psychological Society. However, those of us lucky enough to know her will best remember her unstinting generosity, warmth, humour and her love of parties.

David was, in the words of our friend Gillian Butler, 'a big man with a big brain and a big heart.' Like Joan, he was talented and versatile: he was a clinician, manager, researcher and innovator. Like Joan, he was motivated by the desire to offer the very best to both clients and practitioners. He achieved this through his clinical work, his training of others and his research and writing. He co-edited the very successful *Oxford guide to behavioural experiments in cognitive therapy* (Bennett-Levy et al., 2004) and he was writing and publishing right up to his death. He was a Founding Fellow of OCTC and became its Director when Joan retired. Yet despite his many accomplishments and renown, his personal style was always informal. He was ever down to earth and approachable.

As I read and re-read passages in the book I could 'hear' the voices of Joan and David and this was both delightful and sad. Such is the nature of memory that I was transported back to the first edition when we sat around various kitchen tables with various vintages of wine, discussing our ideas, our perspectives and the 'OCTC way'. Some turns of phrase in this text were – and are – undeniably theirs, and I continue to smile at the wry humour of Joan and feel a deep satisfaction in hearing the logical clarity of David. This book is still bursting with their wisdom and sensitivity and I hope you enjoy sharing that.

Helen Kennerley, Oxford, 2016

HOW TO USE YOUR BOOK AND ITS COMPANION WEBSITE

An Introduction to Cognitive Behaviour Therapy, Third Edition comes with a companion website. Visit **https://study.sagepub.com/kennerley3e** to access a wealth of online resources that will enhance your understanding of the subject.

VIDEOS

Over **40 videos** are provided online and are referred to throughout your book. Just look out for the video icons in the margins and then visit the website to watch.

Showing how CBT skills and techniques can be applied to common mental health problems, and how key theories and concepts translate into real-life practice, the videos cover a wide range of skills including:

- Eliciting feedback from your client
- Dealing with signs of problems in the therapeutic relationship
- Measuring CBT's effectiveness
- Developing positive imagery
- Setting an agenda

Take a look at the following pages for the full list of videos.

DEVISING A SPONTANEOUS BEHAVIOURAL EXPERIMENT

INTRODUCING THOUGHT DIARIE

CONSTRUCTING A SIMPLE FORMULATION

A man with health anxiety believed that if he became short of breath, he could pass out and die; he therefore made sure that he always stayed within reach of a doctor's surgery. During therapy in the clinic, he had questioned this belief and had begun to develop two new possibilities: that he would not pass out if he became breathless and that it was okay to move beyond the reach of a doctor's surgery. With his agreement, the therapist then drove him into the countryside where neither of them knew the whereabouts of doctors' surgeries. They then ran up and down the road so that he became breathless (an activity he had been avoiding). This meant that he could test out his new belief that he would not pass out, whilst dropping the safety-seeking behaviour of being near a doctor's surgery.

Case Studies and Examples are highlighted in blue throughout the book. Read these to get a sense of how real-life therapy works and to better understand practice.

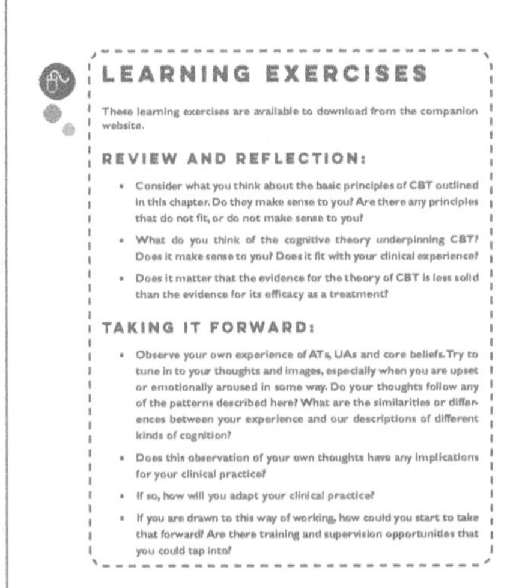

LEARNING EXERCISES

These learning exercises are available to download from the companion website.

REVIEW AND REFLECTION:

- Consider what you think about the basic principles of CBT outlined in this chapter. Do they make sense to you? Are there any principles that do not fit, or do not make sense to you?
- What do you think of the cognitive theory underpinning CBT? Does it make sense to you? Does it fit with your clinical experience?
- Does it matter that the evidence for the theory of CBT is less solid than the evidence for its efficacy as a treatment?

TAKING IT FORWARD:

- Observe your own experience of ATs, UAs and core beliefs. Try to tune in to your thoughts and images, especially when you are upset or emotionally aroused in some way. Do your thoughts follow any of the patterns described here? What are the similarities or differences between your experience and our descriptions of different kinds of cognition?
- Does this observation of your own thoughts have any implications for your clinical practice?
- If so, how will you adapt your clinical practice?
- If you are drawn to this way of working, how could you start to take that forward? Are there training and supervision opportunities that you could tap into?

Learning Exercises can be found both at the end of each chapter and online and are marked by the mouse icon. Complete these to review and reflect on what you have just read.

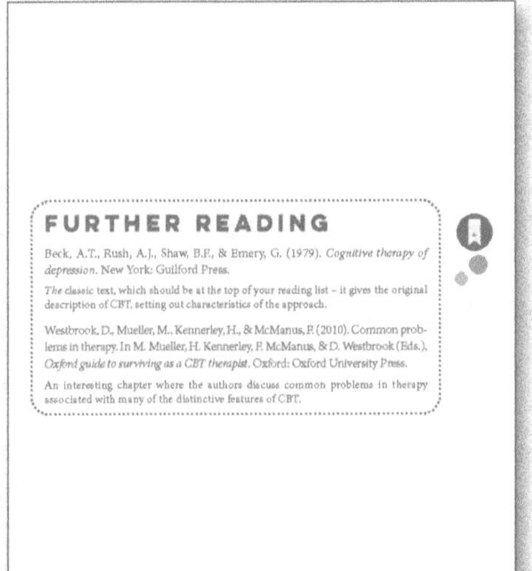

FURTHER READING

Beck, A.T., Rush, A.J., Shaw, B.F., & Emery, G. (1979). *Cognitive therapy of depression*. New York: Guilford Press.

The classic text, which should be at the top of your reading list – it gives the original description of CBT, setting out characteristics of the approach.

Westbrook, D., Mueller, M., Kennerley, H., & McManus, F. (2010). Common problems in therapy. In M. Mueller, H. Kennerley, F. McManus, & D. Westbrook (Eds.), *Oxford guide to surviving as a CBT therapist*. Oxford: Oxford University Press.

An interesting chapter where the authors discuss common problems in therapy associated with many of the distinctive features of CBT.

Further Reading suggestions are included in each chapter and are signposted by the bookmark icon. Use these to help you deepen your knowledge and reinforce your learning of key topics.

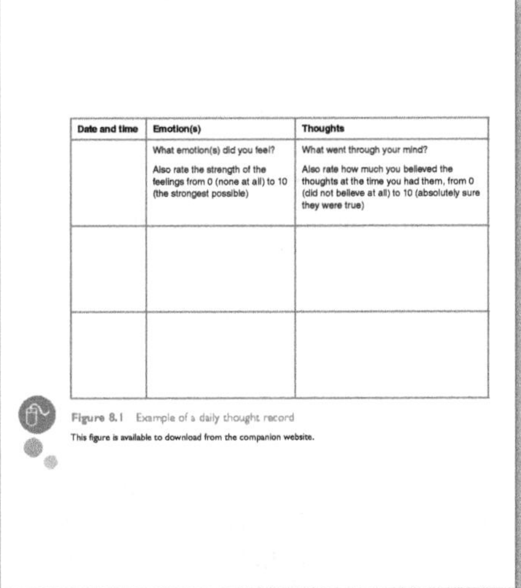

Date and time	Emotion(s)	Thoughts
	What emotion(s) did you feel? Also rate the strength of the feelings from 0 (none at all) to 10 (the strongest possible)	What went through your mind? Also rate how much you believed the thoughts at the time you had them, from 0 (did not believe at all) to 10 (absolutely sure they were true)

Figure 8.1 Example of a daily thought record

This figure is available to download from the companion website.

Reproducible figures are available to download from the companion website:

- an example daily thought record (Figure 8.1)
- a behavioural experiment record sheet (Figure 9.2) and
- a weekly activity schedule (WAS) (Figure 12.2)

LIST OF VIDEOS

1

BASIC THEORY, DEVELOPMENT AND CURRENT STATUS OF CBT

- Introduction
- A brief history of CBT
- Some basic principles
- 'Levels' of cognition
- Automatic thoughts (ATs)/Negative automatic thoughts (NATs)
- Core beliefs
- Underlying assumptions
- Characteristic cognitions in different problems
- Generic CBT model of problem development
- The current status of CBT
- CBT competences
- The empirical evidence about CBT
- Summary
- Learning exercises
- Further reading

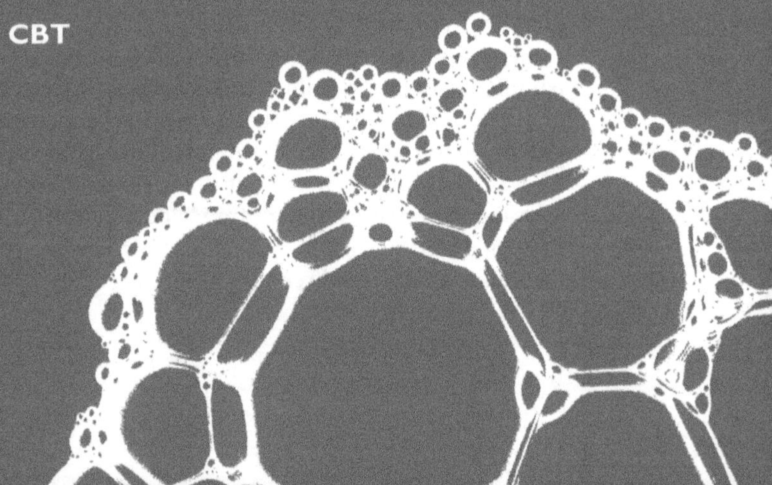

INTRODUCTION

In this chapter we will introduce you to the fundamentals of cognitive behaviour therapy (CBT), including the basic theory and the development of the approach. We start here because CBT is sometimes criticised for being a rather simple-minded 'cookbook' approach to therapy: if the client has *this* problem then use *that* technique. However, the approach taken in this book is based not on the mechanical application of techniques but on *understanding*: understanding your client, understanding CBT theory, and bringing the two together in a formulation (see Chapter 4). You should already have some ideas about understanding people, based on your clinical and personal experience. This chapter will start you on the road to understanding CBT theory: CBT 'first principles' if you like.

One further clarification. Talking about CBT as if it were a single therapy is misleading. Modern CBT is not a monolithic structure, but a broad movement that is still developing, and full of controversies. The approach we take in this book is based on the 'Beckian' model, first formulated by A.T. Beck in the 1960s and 1970s (Beck, 1963, 1964; Beck, Rush, Shaw & Emery, 1979). This model has been dominant in the UK for well over 30 years, and we would therefore see ourselves as being in the mainstream of CBT in this country. However, other CBT theorists and clinicians might differ, in major or minor ways, with some of the approaches expounded here. We should also say that although we think that some of the later developments in CBT, such as the 'Third Wave' therapies (Hayes, 2004), are exciting developments that have the potential to enrich CBT greatly, our aim here is primarily to provide a foundation for 'basic' CBT. We therefore restrict our consideration of those developments to a separate chapter (Chapter 17).

A BRIEF HISTORY OF CBT

Just as some knowledge of a person's background can be helpful in understanding his current state, an appreciation of how CBT developed can help us to understand its modern form. Modern CBT has two main influences: first, behaviour therapy as developed by Wolpe and others in the 1950s and 1960s (Wolpe, 1958); and second, the cognitive therapy approach developed by A.T. Beck, beginning in the 1960s but becoming far more influential with the 'cognitive revolution' of the 1970s.

Behaviour therapy (BT) arose as a reaction against the Freudian psychodynamic paradigm that had dominated psychotherapy from the nineteenth century onwards. In the 1950s, Freudian psychoanalysis was questioned by scientific psychology because of the lack of empirical evidence to support either its theory or its effectiveness (Eysenck, 1952). BT was strongly influenced by the behaviourist movement in academic psychology, which took the view that what went on inside a person's mind was not directly observable and therefore not amenable to scientific study. Instead behaviourists looked for reproducible associations between observable events, particularly between *stimuli* (features or events in

the environment) and *responses* (observable and measurable reactions from the people or animals being studied). Learning theory, a major model in psychology at that time, looked for general principles to explain how organisms learn new associations between stimuli and responses.

In this spirit, BT avoided speculations about unconscious processes, hidden motivations and unobservable structures of the mind, and instead used the principles of learning theory to modify unwanted behaviour and emotional reactions. For instance, instead of trying to probe the unconscious roots of an animal phobia, as Freud famously did with 'Little Hans' (a boy who had a fear of horses: Freud, 1909), behaviour therapists constructed procedures, based on learning theory, which they believed would help people learn new ways of responding. The BT view was that someone like Little Hans had learned an association between the stimulus of a horse and a fear response, and the task of therapy was therefore to establish a new, non-fearful, response to that stimulus. The resulting treatment for anxiety disorders, known as *systematic desensitisation*, asked clients to repeatedly imagine the feared stimulus whilst practising relaxation, so that the fearful response would be replaced by a relaxed response. Later developments often replaced *imaginal* exposure (e.g. thinking about a mental picture of the horse) with *in vivo* exposure (approaching a real horse).

BT rapidly became successful, especially with anxiety disorders such as phobias and obsessive-compulsive disorder (OCD), for two main reasons. First, in keeping with its roots in scientific psychology, BT had always taken an empirical approach, which soon allowed it to provide solid evidence that it was effective in relieving anxiety problems. Second, BT was a far more economical treatment than traditional psychotherapy, typically taking 6–12 sessions.

Despite this early success, there were limitations of a purely behavioural approach. Mental processes such as thoughts, beliefs, interpretations, imagery and so on, are such an obvious part of life (and problems) that it began to seem absurd for psychology not to deal with them. During the 1970s this dissatisfaction developed into what became known as the 'cognitive revolution', wherein ways were sought to bring cognitive phenomena into psychology and therapy whilst still trying to maintain an empirical approach that would avoid ungrounded speculation.

Beck had trained as a psychiatrist and as a psychodynamic psychotherapist, but he increasingly felt that there was more that he could offer the clients who did not respond to a psychodynamic intervention. During the 1950s and early 1960s, he and others had already begun to develop ideas about cognitive therapy (CT) and considered the fusion of insight with BT, but their ideas became increasingly influential from the 1970s onwards. The publication of Beck's book on CT for depression (Beck et al., 1979), and research trials showing that CT was as effective a treatment for depression as antidepressant medication (e.g. Rush, Beck, Kovacs & Hollon, 1977), fuelled the revolution. Over the succeeding years, BT and CT grew together and influenced each other to such an extent that the resulting amalgam is now most commonly known as 'cognitive behaviour therapy' – CBT.

SOME BASIC PRINCIPLES

So, what elements of BT and CT have emerged to form the foundation of modern CBT? Here we set out what we see as the most basic principles and beliefs on which our model of CBT is based, so that you can decide for yourself whether you think they make sense – or at least enough sense to be worth giving CBT a try. Below are what we consider to be the fundamental beliefs about people, problems and therapy that are central to CBT. We are not suggesting that these beliefs are necessarily unique to CBT – many of them may be shared by other approaches – but the combination of these principles goes some way towards characterising CBT.

THE COGNITIVE PRINCIPLE

The core idea of any therapy calling itself 'cognitive' is that people's emotional reactions and behaviour are strongly influenced by *cognitions* (in other words, their thoughts, mental images, beliefs and interpretations about themselves or the situations in which they find themselves – fundamentally the *meaning* they give to the events of their lives). What does this mean?

It may be easiest to start from a 'non-cognitive' perspective. In ordinary life, if we ask people what has made them sad (or happy, or angry, or whatever), they often give us accounts of *events* or *situations*: for example, 'I am fed up because I have just had a row with my girlfriend'. However, it can't be quite that simple. If an event automatically gave rise to an emotion in such a straightforward way, then it would follow that the same event would have to result in the same emotion for anyone who experienced that event. What we actually see is that to a greater or lesser degree, people react *differently* to similar events. Even events as obviously terrible as suffering a bereavement, or being diagnosed with a terminal illness, do not produce the same emotional state in everyone: some may be completely crushed, whilst others cope reasonably well. So it is not just the event that determines emotion: there must be something else. CBT says that the 'something else' is cognition: that is, the interpretations people make of the event. When two people react differently to an event it is because they are seeing it differently, and when one person reacts in what seems to be an unusual way, it is because he has unusual thoughts or beliefs about the event: it has an idiosyncratic *meaning* for him. Figure 1.1 illustrates this.

Let's look at a simple example of this process. Suppose you are walking down the street and you see someone you know coming the other way, but she does not seem to notice you.

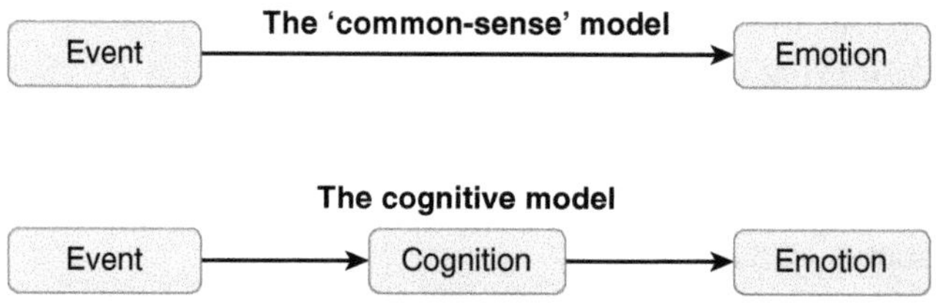

Figure 1.1 The basic cognitive principle

Here are a number of possible thoughts about this event – note how the possible emotional responses arising from those interpretations vary:

- 'I can't think of anything to say to her, she'll think I'm really boring and stupid.' (Leading to anxiety)
- 'Nobody would ever want to talk to me anyway, no one seems to like me.' (Causing depression)
- 'She's got a nerve being so snooty, I've not done anything wrong.' (Triggering anger)
- 'She's probably still hung over from that party last night!' (Resulting in amusement)

This illustrates the fundamental cognitive principle, that different cognitions give rise to different emotions. It also shows the association between certain kinds of cognition and corresponding emotional states: for instance, that thoughts about others being unfair, or breaking rules that we hold dear, are likely to be associated with anger. We will return to this idea later.

There is, of course, nothing new about the notion that meaning is important. The ancient Greek Stoic philosopher Epictetus said over 1,800 years ago that 'Men are disturbed, not by things, but by the principles and notions which they form concerning things.' Yet as we shall see in the rest of this book, the ramifications and elaborations of this simple idea have led to the development of a powerful approach to helping people in distress. By helping people to review their cognitions, we may be able to help them change the way they feel.

THE BEHAVIOURAL PRINCIPLE

Part of the inheritance from BT is that CBT considers behaviour (what we *do*) as crucial in maintaining – or in changing – psychological states. Consider the above example again. If you had either the first or second cognition, then your subsequent behaviour might have a significant effect on whether your feelings of anxiety or depression persisted. If you approached your acquaintance and chatted, you might discover that she was actually friendly towards you. As a result, you might be less inclined to think negatively in future. On the other hand, if you pretended not to see her, you would not have a chance to find out if your thoughts were inaccurate, and negative thoughts and associated emotions might persist. Thus, CBT believes that behaviour can have a strong impact on thought and emotion, and, in particular, that changing what you do is often a powerful way of changing thoughts and emotions.

THE CONTINUUM PRINCIPLE

In contrast to some more traditional medical approaches, CBT believes that it is usually helpful to see mental health problems as arising from exaggerated or extreme versions of normal processes, rather than as pathological states that are qualitatively different from, and inexplicable by, normal states and processes. In other words, psychological problems are at one end of a continuum, not in a different dimension altogether. Related to this belief are the further ideas that (a) psychological problems can happen to anyone, rather than being some freakish oddity; and (b) that CBT theory applies to therapists as much as to clients.

THE HERE-AND-NOW PRINCIPLE

Traditional psychodynamic therapy took the view that looking at the symptoms of a problem (e.g. the anxiety of a person with a phobia) was superficial, and that successful treatment must uncover the developmental processes, hidden motivations and unconscious conflicts that were supposed to lie at the root of a problem. BT took the view that the main target of treatment was the symptoms themselves and that one could tackle the anxiety (or whatever) directly, by looking at what processes currently maintained it and then changing those processes. Psychoanalysis argued that treating symptoms rather than the supposed 'root causes' would result in *symptom substitution*: that is, the unresolved unconscious conflict would result in the client's developing new symptoms. In fact, a wealth of research in BT showed that such an outcome, although possible, was rare: more commonly, tackling symptoms directly actually resulted in more global improvement.

Modern CBT has inherited BT's approach. The main focus of therapy, at least most of the time, is on what is happening in the present, and our main concerns are the processes currently maintaining the problem, rather than the processes that might have led to its development many years ago. Having said that, CBT does not dismiss the past, far from it, and Chapter 4 on assessment and formulation discusses this further.

THE INTERACTING SYSTEMS PRINCIPLE

This is the view that problems should be thought of as interactions between various 'systems' within the person and in their environment, and it is another legacy from BT (Lang, 1968). Modern CBT commonly identifies four such 'internal' systems:

- cognition;
- affect, or emotion;
- behaviour;
- physiology.

These systems interact with each other in complex feedback processes and also interact with the environment – where 'environment' is to be understood in the widest possible sense, including not just the obvious physical environment but also the social, family, cultural and economic environment. Figure 1.2, based on Padesky and Mooney's five-system framework (Padesky & Mooney, 1990), illustrates these interactions.

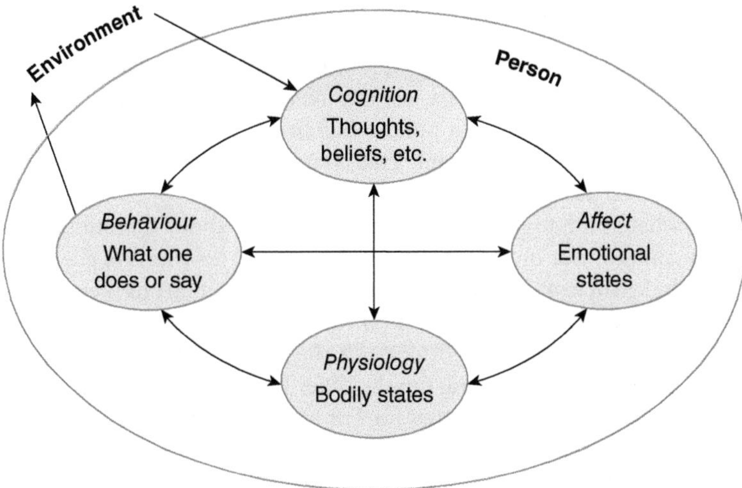

Figure 1.2 Interacting systems

This kind of analysis helps us to describe problems in more detail, to target specific and dynamic aspects of a problem and to gain a richer understanding of its maintenance. We can also consider times when one or more systems are not correlated with the others. For example, 'courage' could be said to describe a state where a person's behaviour is not correlated with emotional state: although a woman is feeling fearful, her behaviour is not overtly fearful. Clinically it can be crucial to identify mis-matches between clients' thoughts, feelings and actions so that we can better understand a person's strengths, needs and perceptions.

THE EMPIRICAL PRINCIPLE

CBT believes we should evaluate theories and treatments as rigorously as possible, using scientific evidence rather than just clinical anecdote. This is important for several reasons:

- Scientifically, so that our treatments can be founded on sound, well-established theories. One of the characteristic features of CBT is that, in contrast to some schools of therapy that have remained little changed since they were first devised, it has developed and made steady advances into new areas through the use of scientific research.
- Ethically, so that we can have confidence in telling people who are receiving and/or purchasing our treatments that they are likely to be effective.
- Economically, so that we can make sure that limited mental health resources are used in the way that will bring most benefit.

THE INTERPERSONAL PRINCIPLE

As Beck's early psychodynamic training taught him, CBT takes place in the context of a dynamic relationship. In CBT this is a *working alliance* as CBT is not 'administered' or 'done to' a client. Instead, we foster a milieu that enables us to work with a person, who engages with full knowledge and consent. This is such an important principle that we have dedicated Chapter 3 to its exploration.

Contrary to what some might expect, we hypothesise about intention and unspoken feelings and we monitor our own cognitive and emotional reactions to clients. Sometimes there is much to be learnt from this and we formulate its impact on our therapy. For example, we might hypothesise that a fleeting look of discomfort during a session is significant and usefully explored because it might reveal a client's relevant but shameful secret, one which serves to maintain the problem. On the other hand it might simply reveal a bout of cramp – so we should always be prepared for our hypotheses to be refuted!

SUMMARY OF CBT PRINCIPLES

These then are what we would take as the basic principles at the heart of CBT. To summarise:

- *The cognitive principle*: it is interpretations of events, not events themselves, that are crucial.
- *The behavioural principle*: what we do has a powerful influence on our thoughts and emotions.
- *The continuum principle*: mental health problems are best conceptualised as exaggerations of normal processes.
- *The here-and-now principle*: it is usually more fruitful to focus on current processes rather than the past.
- *The interacting systems principle*: it is helpful to look at problems as interactions between thoughts, emotions, behaviour and physiology and the environment in which the person operates.
- *The empirical principle*: it is important to evaluate both our theories and our therapy empirically.
- *The interpersonal principle*: we work with an informed and active person and we consider and formulate dynamic aspects of our relationship.

Let us now turn to an elaboration of the fundamental cognitive principles.

'LEVELS' OF COGNITION

So far we have talked about 'cognition' as if it were a single concept. In fact, CBT usually distinguishes between different kinds or 'levels' of cognition. The following account of

levels of cognition is based on what has been found clinically useful; a later section will briefly consider the scientific evidence for some of these ideas.

When we talk of cognitions, we refer not only to thoughts – which can readily be put into words – but to images, too. This convention is rather confused by CBT therapists' widespread use of terms such as 'automatic thoughts' (ATs) and 'negative automatic thoughts' (NATs) as we seem to be excluding images. Be assured that images are relevant cognitions just as thoughts are.

It is worth noting that different CBT practitioners might categorise cognitions differently, and although the following classification is commonly used, it is not the only one.

AUTOMATIC THOUGHTS (ATs)/ NEGATIVE AUTOMATIC THOUGHTS (NATs)

Automatic thoughts (ATs) is a term used to describe a stream of thoughts that almost all of us can notice if we try to pay attention to them. They can be positive, neutral or negative in content. Negative automatic thoughts (NATs), as first described by Beck in his work with depressed clients, are often fundamental to CBT. These are negatively tinged appraisals or interpretations – *meanings* we take from what happens around us or within us. Any of us might experience them.

Think of a recent time when you became upset: anxious, annoyed, fed up or whatever. Put yourself back in that situation and remember what was going through your mind. Most people can fairly easily pick out NATs. For example, if you were anxious, you might have had thoughts about the threat of something bad happening to you ('Oh no – now I'm messing up …') or people you care about ('He's not going to manage this alone …'); if you were annoyed, you might have had thoughts about others being unfair, or not following rules you consider important ('Come on – that's so out of order!'); if you were fed up, there might have been thoughts about loss or defeat, or negative views of yourself ('Here I go again – there's just no point …').

ATs (and therefore NATs) are thought to exert a direct influence over mood from moment to moment, and they are thus of central importance to any CBT therapy. They have several common characteristics:

- As the name suggests, one does not have to *try* to think ATs – they just happen, automatically and without effort (although it may take effort to pay attention to them and notice them).
- They are specific thoughts about specific events or situations. Although they may become stereotyped, particularly in chronic problems, they may also vary a great deal from time to time and situation to situation.
- They are, or can easily become, conscious. Most people are either aware of this kind of thought, or can soon learn to be aware of them with some practice in monitoring them.

- They may be so brief and frequent, and so habitual, that they are not 'heard'. They are so much a part of our ordinary mental environment that unless we focus on them we may not notice them, any more than we notice breathing most of the time.
- They are often plausible and taken as obviously true, especially when emotions are strong. Most of the time we do not question them: if I think 'I am useless' when I am feeling fed up about something's having gone wrong, it seems a simple statement of the truth. One of the crucial steps in therapy is to help clients stop accepting their ATs in this way, so that they can step back and consider their accuracy. As a common CBT motto has it, 'Thoughts are opinions not facts' – and like all opinions, they may or may not be accurate.
- Although we usually talk about ATs as if they were verbal constructs (e.g. 'I'm making a mess of this'), it is important to be aware that they may also take the form of images. For example, in social phobia, rather than thinking in words, 'Other people think I'm peculiar', a person may get a mental image of himself looking red-faced, sweaty and incoherent.
- Because of their immediate effect on emotional states, and their accessibility, ATs are usually tackled early on in therapy.

CORE BELIEFS

At the other end of the scale from ATs, core beliefs represent a person's 'bottom line' (a term coined by Fennell, 1997), their fundamental beliefs about themselves, others, the world in general or the future. Characteristics of core beliefs are:

- Most of the time they are not immediately accessible to consciousness. They may have to be inferred by observation of characteristic thoughts and behaviours in many different situations.
- They manifest as general and absolute statements (e.g. 'I am bad' or 'Others are not to be trusted'). Unlike ATs, they do not typically vary much across times or situations but are seen by the person as fundamental truths that apply in all situations.
- They are usually learned early on in life as a result of childhood experiences, but they may sometimes develop or change later in life (e.g. as a result of adult trauma).
- They are generally not tackled directly in short-term therapy for focal problems such as anxiety disorders or major depression (although they may change anyway). Tackling them directly may be more important in therapy for chronic problems like personality disorders (see Chapter 17).

UNDERLYING ASSUMPTIONS

Underlying assumptions (UAs) can be considered as bridging the gap between core beliefs and ATs. They develop as a response to the core belief and are often referred to as dysfunctional assumptions (DAs) when they backfire and hinder rather than help a person.

Core beliefs give us our fundamental (and often thematic) perspectives whilst UAs can be thought of as 'rules for living', more specific in their applicability than core beliefs but more general than ATs. They often take the form of conditional 'If … then …' propositions, or are framed as 'should' or 'must' statements. They often represent attempts to live with negative core beliefs. For example, if I believe that I am fundamentally unlovable, I may develop the assumptions that

- 'If I always try to please other people then they will tolerate me, but if I stand up for my own needs I will be rebuffed,' or
- 'If I keep a low profile, no-one will see the real me and never know that I am unlovable,' or
- 'I must always put other's needs first, otherwise they will reject me.'

Such UAs offer hope that I can contain the situation and provide a guide to how to live my life so as to overcome some of the effects of the core belief, but it is always a fragile truce: if I fail to please someone, then I am in trouble. When one of my UAs is violated, then NATs and strong emotions are likely to be triggered. Characteristics of UAs are:

- Like core beliefs, they are not as obvious as ATs and may not be easily verbalised. They often have to be inferred from actions or from patterns of common ATs.
- They are usually conditional statements, taking the form of 'If … then …', or 'should/must … otherwise …' statements.
- Some may be culturally reinforced: for example, beliefs about putting others first, or the importance of success, may be approved of in some cultures.
- They become 'dysfunctional' when they are too rigid and over-generalised, not flexible enough to cope with the inevitable complications and setbacks of life.
- They are usually tackled later on in therapy, after the client has developed some ability to work with ATs. It is thought that modifying UAs may be helpful in making clients more resistant to future relapse (Beck et al., 1979).

Figure 1.3 illustrates these levels of cognitions for one kind of belief and also shows some of the dimensions along which the levels vary.

It is easy to assume that core beliefs are 'at the root' of the problem, or are the 'underlying' cause, and that therefore they must be tackled directly for therapy to be effective. Although

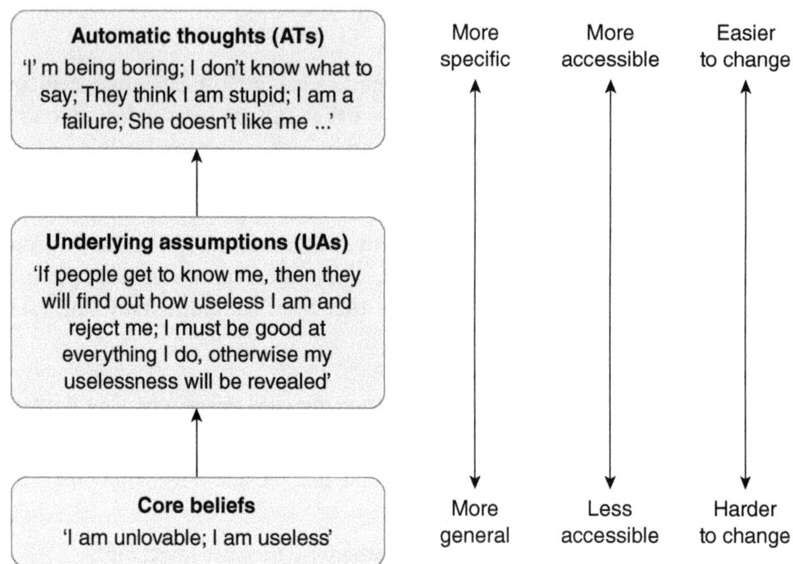

Figure 1.3 Illustration of levels of cognition

this can be the case, we would question this blanket assumption. Core beliefs are certainly more *general* than ATs, but that does not necessarily mean that they are more important. Most successful CBT research to date targets ATs, but that does not make the therapy ineffective or short-lived. This is probably for two reasons:

- People with common mental health problems such as anxiety or depression have a *range* of core beliefs, not just negative and unhelpful ones. Through the process of therapy they can bring their more positive or functional beliefs back into operation.
- Reviewing and building evidence that tests ATs can have an impact, a 'knock-on effect', on core beliefs so we don't need to target core beliefs directly.

Although there is not yet much research evidence, working with core beliefs may be more important in lifelong problems such as very chronic difficulties and personality disorders, where clients may never have formed much in the way of longer-term functional beliefs. So often a child or young person evolves a 'rule for living' that helps them at the time. For example, 'If I please everyone and keep out of trouble no-one will hurt me' would be protective for a bullied and abused child but would hold back the adult. In adulthood it would have lost its usefulness and become dysfunctional, it would need to be reviewed and revised, and because of its long-standing and unchallenged status a therapist might well need to focus on it.

CHARACTERISTIC COGNITIONS IN DIFFERENT PROBLEMS

We mentioned earlier that modern CBT theories see characteristic forms of cognition associated with particular kinds of problem. These characteristic patterns involve both the *content* of cognitions and the *process* of cognition. If we take depression as an example, then the thoughts of depressed people are likely to contain characteristic *contents* (e.g. negative thoughts about themselves or others). Depressed people are also likely to show characteristic general biases in the *way* that they think (e.g. towards perceiving and remembering negative events more than positive ones; or tending to see anything that goes wrong as being their fault; or over-generalising from one small negative event to a broad negative conclusion). Here, we briefly consider some examples. (See also later chapters on specific problems.)

DEPRESSION

As first described by Beck, the characteristic cognitions in depression form the *negative cognitive triad*, namely negatively biased views of *oneself*, of the *world in general* and of the *future*. In other words, the typical depressed view is that I am bad (useless, unlovable, incompetent, worthless, a failure, etc.); the world is bad (people are not nice to me, nothing good happens, life is just a series of trials); and the future is also bad (not only am I and the world bad, but it will always be like this and nothing I can do will make any difference).

ANXIETY

The general cognitive process here is a bias towards *the over-estimation of threat*, (i.e. perceiving a high risk of some unwanted outcome) and/or the *underestimation of ability to cope* (i.e. perceiving oneself as lacking necessary skills). The exact nature of the threat, and therefore the content of cognitions, is different in different disorders. For example:

- In *panic*, there is catastrophic misinterpretation of harmless anxiety symptoms as indicating some imminent disaster (e.g. dying or 'going mad').
- In *health anxiety*, there is a similar misinterpretation of harmless symptoms as indicating illness, but on a longer time scale (e.g. I might have a disease that will kill me sometime in the future).
- In *social anxiety*, thoughts are about being negatively evaluated by others (e.g. 'They will think I am stupid/boring/peculiar').
- In *OCD*, thoughts are about being responsible for, and/or needing to prevent, some harm to oneself or others.

ANGER

In anger, the thoughts are usually about others' behaviour being *unfair*, breaking some implicit or explicit rule, or having hostile intent: 'They ought not to do that, it's not fair, they're trying to put me down'. Just as we saw with anxiety, rapid and extreme conclusions are drawn, thus illustrating the cognitive process and content that leads to anger. In both anxiety and anger this is fuelled by adrenaline, reminding us of the interacting systems of psychological experiences.

GENERIC CBT MODEL OF PROBLEM DEVELOPMENT

Now we can put together the ideas introduced so far to develop a broad picture of how CBT sees the development of problems (see Figure 1.4). This generic model proposes that through experience (most commonly childhood experience, but sometimes later experience), we

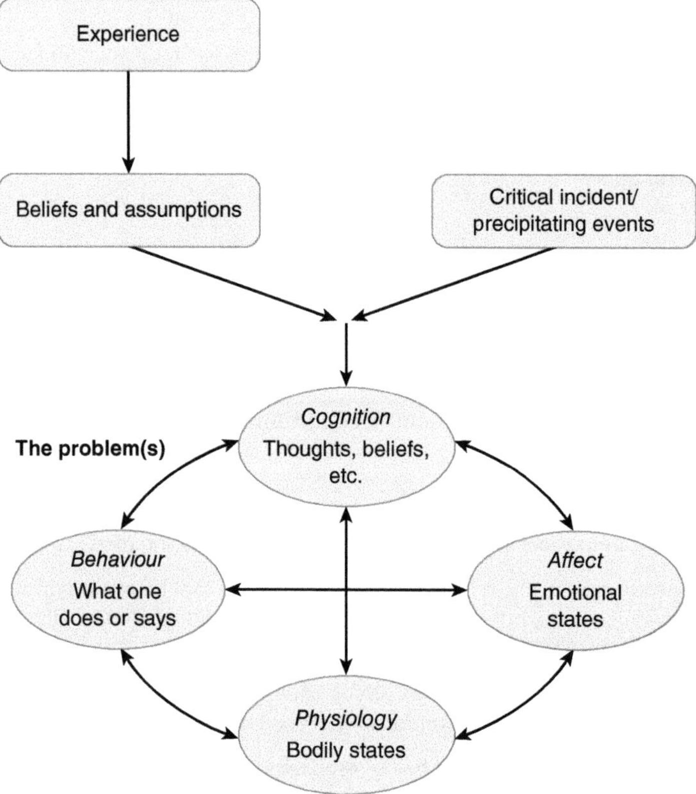

Figure 1.4 Generic problem development model

develop core beliefs and assumptions which are, to a greater or lesser extent, functional and which allow us to make sense of our world and find a way through it. There is nothing inherently pathological about this, it simply recognises that we all learn from things that happen to us. As a result of our experiences, most of us have a mixture of functional and dysfunctional beliefs, with the functional ones allowing us to cope reasonably well most of the time. Even quite dysfunctional beliefs may not cause any particular problems for many years, if at all.

However, if we encounter an event (or series of events) that violates a core belief or assumption and cannot be handled by our more helpful beliefs (sometimes called a *critical incident*), then unhelpful assumptions can become more active, negative thoughts evoked, and unpleasant emotional states such as anxiety or depression can result. The problem has been 'switched on'.

Subsequent interactions between negative thoughts, emotions, behaviour and physiological changes may then result in persisting dysfunctional patterns, and we get locked into vicious cycles or feedback loops that maintain the problem. This prevents the problem from 'switching off' once circumstances change. This is where CBT therapists look to understand the persistence of difficulties and to generate ideas about recovery through breaking cycles.

THE CURRENT STATUS OF CBT

Having earlier reviewed the history of CBT, in this section we review its current status and important contexts.

IMPROVING ACCESS TO PSYCHOLOGICAL THERAPIES (IAPT)

Perhaps the most significant development in the wider landscape of CBT since the first edition of this book, at least in England and Wales, is the explosive growth of the government's Improving Access to Psychological Therapies (IAPT: see www.iapt.nhs.uk) programme. This programme resulted from planning and lobbying led by a prominent economist and adviser to the government, Lord Layard, who became convinced that (a) mental health problems are a major source of unhappiness and loss of economic activity, and (b) that CBT could make a difference to many of the most common mental health problems (Centre for Economic Performance, 2006). He and others, especially Professors David Clark and David Richards, persuaded the government that a major investment in psychological therapy would make an impact on health, and also that such an investment would be largely self-funding, since improvements in mental health would allow a proportion of clients to return to work, thus saving on unemployment benefits.

After some pilot work in 2006, the government announced in 2007 that the IAPT programme would receive a large amount of funding, amounting to over £170 million annually by the third year. This enabled a massive increase in the provision of evidence-based psychological therapies, mainly aimed at treating anxiety and depression in primary care: the goal was to train and put into NHS services several thousand new therapists. The first of the new services and training courses were up and running by the autumn of 2008.

IAPT's first wave involved two types of CBT, because it was thought that although CBT has a strong evidence base (see later in this chapter), there was a particular shortage of qualified CBT therapists. The first category of IAPT CBT (involving 60 per cent of the new therapists) was known as 'high intensity' therapy (HI), and it offered a 'traditional' form of CBT. The second group (40 per cent of therapists) were 'low intensity' (LI) workers (since re-titled 'psychological wellbeing practitioners' or PWPs) who offered guided self-help, very brief psychological interventions, behavioural activation and exercise. Both groups' training was initially funded by the government, and consisted of a one-year in-service training course. To give you an idea of what was considered possible in a relatively short time, the HI course comprised around 65 training days over the year, whilst LI training comprised around 25 days. HI workers were already professionally qualified (nurses, psychologists, etc.), but PWPs did not need a professional mental health qualification and were expected to match their local communities more closely in terms of education, class and so on.

IAPT has adopted a stepped care approach to mental health care – a model that integrates it into existing mental health services and which is relevant beyond IAPT provisions. This is reviewed in Chapter 11. Over the last few years the IAPT approach has been extended to supporting a wider population than just those with anxiety and depressive disorders. Programmes now address child and adolescent problems, mental health problems associated with chronic physical conditions and severe mental illnesses, for example.

The impact of IAPT has been rigorously evaluated and preliminary data from the pilot sites supported the effectiveness of the programme (Clark, Layard, Smithies, Richards, Suckling & Wright, 2009) and a more recent – and highly readable – overview of outcome can be found in Layard and Clark's text (2014).

The main focus of our book is traditional CBT, or HI therapy in IAPT terms, but in many ways the LI services are the most radical part of the IAPT programme, as they deliver therapy in ways quite different from our established concept of CBT. We briefly consider some of the features of LI CBT in Chapter 16, but for more detail see Richards (2010), Bennett-Levy et al. (2010) and Papworth, Marrinan, Martin, Keegan and Chaddock (2013).

CBT COMPETENCES

Another important development since this book's first edition is the publication of the 'CBT competences framework'. This initiative, funded by the UK Department of Health, was linked to the IAPT programme and had the goal of identifying what skills a therapist needs in order to provide good-quality CBT for anxiety and depression: if we are going to train the many more CBT therapists that IAPT proposed, what exactly should we be training them to do? Roth and Pilling (2007), in consultation with an expert reference group, produced a useful mapping of competences for both LI and HI interventions. Their approach was to identify important competences through a close examination of the treatment manuals for CBT interventions that have been shown to be effective for different disorders. It seemed reasonable to suppose that since treatment based on these manuals works, then if other therapists follow the same strategies they will be providing effective treatment. Roth and Pilling produced a 'map' of competences divided into five domains:

- *Generic competences in psychological therapy*: These are the basic competences needed by a therapist from *any* school of therapy (e.g. knowledge of mental health, ability to relate to clients and so on).
- *Basic CBT competences*: Skills related to the basic structure of CBT therapies, such as agenda-setting or use of homework.
- *Specific CBT techniques*: The core treatment strategies, such as using thought records and identifying and testing thoughts and beliefs.
- *Problem-specific competences*: Approaches used in treatment programmes for particular disorders, such as Beckian CT for depression, or exposure and response prevention for OCD.
- *Meta-competences*: The 'higher level' skills that allow a therapist to make effective judgements about when to use which specific treatment strategy. This includes using the formulation to adapt treatment to an individual, dealing with difficulties during treatment and so on.

This framework is too detailed to reproduce here, but see Roth and Pilling (2007), and the CORE website cited in 'Further reading' at the end of the chapter, for more detailed information about the competences framework.

In this book we aim to introduce you to CBT skills in all these domains, with some chapters mapping particularly closely onto specific domains as follows:

- generic competences in psychological therapy – Chapters 3 and 19
- basic CBT competences – Chapters 1, 2, 5, 6 and 11
- specific CBT techniques – Chapters 7–10
- problem-specific competences – Chapters 12–15
- meta-competences – Chapters 4 and 11.

THE EMPIRICAL EVIDENCE ABOUT CBT

Finally, since we have talked about CBT's commitment to empiricism, we should consider the empirical status of CBT. Just what is the evidence that CBT is effective? And what is the evidence that CBT theory is an accurate model of human functioning?

EVIDENCE REGARDING CBT TREATMENT

Roth and Fonagy (2005), in the second edition of *What works for whom?* (their landmark summary of psychotherapy efficacy), report evidence showing that CBT is strongly supported as a therapy for most of the psychological disorders in adults that they studied, and has more support in more kinds of problem than any other therapy. Table 1.1 summarises this.

Table 1.1 Summary by the current authors (adapted from Roth & Fonagy, 2005, Ch. 17)

	Cognitive/ behaviour therapies	Interpersonal therapy	Family Interventions	Psychodynamic psychotherapy
Depression	✓	✓	❍	?
Panic/agoraphobia	✓	❍	❍	❍
Generalised anxiety disorder	✓	❍	❍	❍
Specific phobias	✓	❍	❍	❍
Social phobia	✓	❍	❍	❍
Obsessive-compulsive disorder	✓	❍	❍	❍
Post-traumatic stress disorder	✓	❍	❍	?
Anorexia	?	❍	?	?
Bulimia	✓	✓	❍	❍
(Some) personality disorders	✓	❍	❍	✓
Schizophrenia	?	❍	✓	❍
Bipolar disorder	?	❍	❍	❍

Key to summary:

✓ = Clear evidence of efficacy

? = Some limited support for efficacy

❍ = Not currently well validated (NB this indicates a lack of sufficient evidence to support efficacy; it does not necessarily imply that there is good evidence of *in*effectiveness)

In addition to this evidence of CBT's *efficacy* (i.e. that it works in tightly controlled research trials), there is also some useful evidence demonstrating its *effectiveness* (i.e. that it can also work well in ordinary clinical practice, outside specialist research centres). See, for example, Merrill, Tolbert and Wade (2003), Stuart, Treat and Wade (2000) and Westbrook and Kirk (2005).

A second useful source of evidence is the UK National Institute for Health and Clinical Excellence (NICE). This is an agency charged by the government with the task of surveying the evidence for the effectiveness of different treatments and making recommendations

about which treatments ought therefore to be made available in the National Health Service (NHS). Its guidelines on mental health conditions are periodically updated and so it is wise to visit the NICE website (www.nice.org.uk/guidance/conditions-and-diseases/mental-health-and-behavioural-conditions, accessed 22 May 2016).

NICE has produced guidelines on several major mental health problems, which include the following recommendations:

- *Depression* (NICE, 2009):
    - 'For people with persistent subthreshold depressive symptoms or mild to moderate depression, consider offering one or more of … individual guided self-help based on the principles of cognitive behavioural therapy (CBT); computerised cognitive behavioural therapy (CCBT)' (p. 9);
    - 'For people with moderate or severe depression, provide a combination of antidepressant medication and a high-intensity psychological intervention (CBT or IPT)' (p. 9);
    - 'People with depression who are considered to be at significant risk of relapse … or who have residual symptoms, should be offered one of the following … individual CBT; … mindfulness-based cognitive therapy for people who are currently well but have experienced three or more previous episodes of depression' (p. 10).
- *Generalised anxiety disorder* (GAD) *and panic disorder* (NICE, 2011a): The 2004 guidelines recognised that 'interventions that have evidence for the longest duration of effect, in descending order, are: [first] cognitive behavioural therapy;' (p. 6). The 2011 guidelines recommend low intensity interventions for mild GAD and CBT/applied relaxation for established GAD.
- *Post-traumatic stress disorder* (PTSD) (NICE, 2005a): 'All people with PTSD should be offered a course of trauma-focused psychological treatment (trauma-focused cognitive behavioural therapy [CBT] or eye movement desensitisation and reprocessing [EMDR])' (p. 4).
- *Obsessive compulsive disorder* (OCD) *and body dysmorphic disorder* (BDD) (NICE, 2005b): people with OCD or BDD should be offered CBT (including exposure and response prevention), either in group or individual format and, depending on severity and preference, also consider SSRI medication; it also says that 'when adults with OCD request forms of psychological therapy other than cognitive and/or behavioural therapies as a specific treatment for OCD … they should be informed that there is as yet no convincing evidence for a clinically important effect of these treatments' (pp. 18–21).
- *Eating disorders* (NICE, 2004b): 'Cognitive behaviour therapy for bulimia nervosa … should be offered to adults with bulimia nervosa' (p. 4); 'Cognitive behaviour therapy for binge eating disorder … should be offered to adults with binge eating disorder'(p. 5).
- *Psychosis and schizophrenia* (NICE, 2014a): Offer cognitive behavioural therapy (CBT), with or without family intervention, to those at risk and to all people with psychosis or schizophrenia. This can be in conjunction with medication.

NICE also recommends CBT in the management of other conditions such as chronic fatigue syndrome (2007), alcohol-use disorders (2011b), antenatal and post-natal mental health problems (2014b).

In summary then, at the time of writing, CBT is a psychological therapy with a most solid and wide evidence base for efficacy and effectiveness.

EVIDENCE REGARDING CBT THEORY

It is a fallacy to think that demonstrating the efficacy of a treatment proves the truth of the theory on which that treatment is based. The treatment's efficacy could be due to some combination of factors not imagined in the theory. Thus, for most of us, even a randomised controlled trial (RCT) showing that a treatment based on traditional witchcraft was effective for depression would not necessarily convince us that depression was in fact caused by evil spirits; instead we might investigate whether there was a powerful placebo effect, or perhaps whether the herbal potions used in the treatment contained a psychoactive substance. In the same way, the efficacy of CBT as a treatment does not show that CBT theory is true. In fact, the evidence for some of the fundamental theoretical ideas of CBT is more patchy than the evidence for the treatment's efficacy. Clark, Beck and Alford (1999) present a detailed consideration of the balance of scientific evidence in the case of the cognitive theory of depression. In summary, they conclude that regarding the supposed patterns of negative thinking in depression, there is evidence that there is:

- an increase in negative thinking about oneself, the future and (less clearly) the world;
- a reduction in positive thinking about the self, but this change is less marked and may be less specific to depression (in other words, the same thing also happens in other problems);
- a specific increase in thoughts and beliefs about loss and failure (more so than in people who suffer from anxiety problems).

Regarding the proposed *causal* role of negative thoughts (i.e. the suggestion that negative thinking can provoke low mood), Clark et al. (1999) conclude that there is some experimental evidence that negative self-referent thinking can indeed induce subjective, behavioural, motivational and physiological features similar to mild to moderate depression. If we experimentally provoke negative thoughts about themselves in non-depressed people, we can produce temporary states quite similar to depression.

There is also some evidence that the proposed cognitive processing biases can be identified in experiments, with evidence that in depressed people there is:

- a bias towards processing negative information relevant to themselves (but no such bias for neutral or impersonal information);
- enhanced recall of negative events, and increased negative beliefs.

Furthermore, there is evidence that these changes in processing can occur at an automatic, pre-conscious level.

The least well-supported part of the theory is the suggestion that people are vulnerable to depression because of negative beliefs that are still present in 'latent' form even when they are not depressed. Clark et al. (1999) suggest that there is a little supportive evidence for this idea, but that it has proved difficult to get clear evidence (perhaps not surprisingly, when one considers the difficulties of identifying such 'latent' beliefs experimentally).

A similar picture is found for specific CBT models for other disorders: in some areas there is good solid research support and in others the evidence is equivocal. Overall, then, the evidence is:

(a) that CBT is undoubtedly an effective treatment for many problems; and

(b) that there is support for CBT theory but that there is still room for exploring and developing this approach further in some areas.

SUMMARY

- Modern CBT is derived from the legacy of BT (with its emphasis on the importance of *behaviour change* in overcoming mental health problems) and CT (with its emphasis on understanding and changing the *meaning* of events), and Beckian CBT is also coloured by his experience of psychodynamic training (so there is recognition of the importance of the therapeutic relationship and developmental factors).
- Problems can usefully be described in terms of the interactions between four 'systems' that interface with a fifth system, namely the environment:
    - the *cognitive* system – what a person thinks, imagines, believes;
    - the *behavioural* system – what they do or say that can be directly observed by others;
    - the *affective* system – their emotions;
    - the *physiological* system – what happens to their body, such as autonomic arousal or changes in appetite.
- We distinguish three 'levels' of cognition:
    - automatic thoughts (ATs) – specific thoughts that arise spontaneously in various situations, which can have a negative effect on mood, and which are relatively accessible to consciousness;
    - underlying assumptions (UAs) – 'rules for living' that guide behaviour and expectations in a variety of situations, and which are often in *conditional* (if … then …) form;
    - core beliefs – very general beliefs about oneself, other people or the world in general, and the future, which operate across a wide range of situations but which are often not immediately conscious.

- Different kinds of psychological problem have different characteristic cognitions, in content, style or both (e.g. in anxiety there is a preoccupation with threat, and associated biases towards perceiving threat).
- There is considerable evidence that CBT can be an effective way of helping various mental health problems; and less clear, but still significant, evidence for the theories lying behind the treatment.

LEARNING EXERCISES

These learning exercises are available to download from the companion website.

REVIEW AND REFLECTION:

- Consider what you think about the basic principles of CBT outlined in this chapter. Do they make sense to you? Are there any principles that do not fit, or do not make sense to you?
- What do you think of the cognitive theory underpinning CBT? Does it make sense to you? Does it fit with your clinical experience?
- Does it matter that the evidence for the theory of CBT is less solid than the evidence for its efficacy as a treatment?

TAKING IT FORWARD:

- Observe your own experience of ATs, UAs and core beliefs. Try to tune in to your thoughts and images, especially when you are upset or emotionally aroused in some way. Do your thoughts follow any of the patterns described here? What are the similarities or differences between your experience and our descriptions of different kinds of cognition?
- Does this observation of your own thoughts have any implications for your clinical practice?
- If so, how will you adapt your clinical practice?
- If you are drawn to this way of working, how could you start to take that forward? Are there training and supervision opportunities that you could tap into?

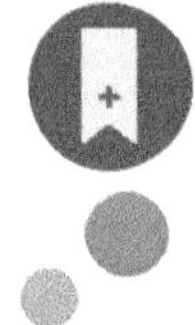

FURTHER READING

Beck, A.T., Rush, A.J., Shaw, B.F., & Emery, G. (1979). *Cognitive therapy of depression.* New York: Guilford Press.

Although now over 30 years old, the book that started the cognitive revolution is still a classic, with a real feel for the clinical realities of working with depressed clients.

Greenberger, D., & Padesky, C. (2015). *Mind over mood* (2nd ed.). New York: Guilford Press.

A well-established and best-selling self-help book now in its second edition. It is designed to assist the general public, but it is also a clear and simple introduction to CBT that many new therapists find very useful, whether or not they plan to use it with clients!

House, R., & Loewenthal, D. (Eds.). (2009). *Against and for CBT: towards a constructive dialogue?* Ross-on-Wye: PCCS Books.

A mixture of (mostly highly critical) views on the philosophy, science, ethics and politics of CBT (and by association, the IAPT programme). Often coming from a post-modernist stance, and containing some of the jargon so often associated with that approach, many of the chapters are not easy reading – but interesting if you want a different perspective.

The Centre for Outcomes Research and Effectiveness (CORE) website at University College, London, under whose auspices the CBT Competences framework was developed: www.ucl.ac.uk/clinical-psychology/CORE/CBT_Framework.htm (accessed 22 May 2016).

The CORE site contains more detailed descriptions of the CBT competences for anxiety and depression, and a self-assessment tool to allow clinicians to evaluate how well their own skills match the competences.

2

DISTINCTIVE CHARACTERISTICS OF CBT

- Introduction
- Collaboration
- Structure and active engagement
- Time-limited and brief
- Empirical in approach
- Problem-oriented in approach
- Guided discovery
- Behavioural methods
- *In vivo* work
- Summaries and feedback
- Myths about CBT
- Summary
- Learning exercises
- Further reading
- Video links
    - 2.1 Capsule summaries (i)
    - 2.2 Capsule summaries (ii)
    - 2.3 Eliciting feedback (i)
    - 2.4 Eliciting feedback (ii)

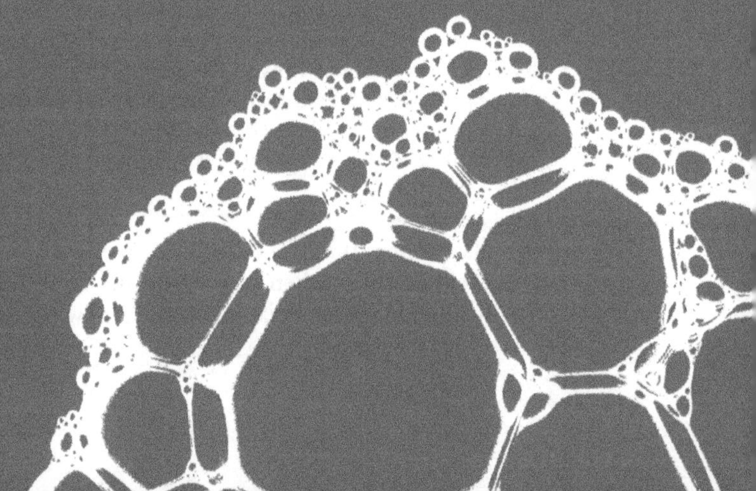

INTRODUCTION

CBT has many features in common with other psychotherapies, but it is also different in important respects. In this chapter we describe the fundamental characteristics of the CBT approach, and we also explore some of the myths about CBT. We hope this is helpful for you, as well as for your clients: giving them accurate information about therapy allows them to make an informed choice about whether they want to proceed (Garfield, 1986) and it may also improve outcome (Roth & Fonagy, 2005).

CBT is distinguished by a combination of characteristics, which can be summarised as:

- collaborative;
- structured and active;
- time-limited and brief;
- empirical;
- problem-oriented.

CBT also frequently employs the techniques of guided discovery, behavioural methods, *in vivo* work, summaries and feedback. Other psychotherapies might well embrace such techniques and approaches but they are particularly prominent in CBT.

COLLABORATION

CBT is fundamentally a *collaborative* project between therapist and client or patient. Both are active participants, with their own areas of expertise: the therapist has knowledge about effective ways to solve problems, and the client has expertise in his own experience of his problems. This collaborative emphasis may be different from what the client expected of therapy, and so it is important to clarify what he is anticipating so that you can establish a shared view from the outset. Part of the initial introduction to therapy would include a statement about the client's crucial role. For example, you might say:

> We each have an important role in the treatment. I know quite a lot about CBT, and about how particular sorts of problem can present difficulties for people. However, you know very much more than I do about the details of how your problem affects you, and it is this knowledge that will allow us to understand and gradually change the situation for you. This really is a joint enterprise.

This also implies that you cannot be expected to know all of the answers all of the time. There will be times when you are unsure, and then you can always ask your client for clarification, more information, or their view of the situation.

A woman described a vivid dream to her therapist and asked, 'What am I supposed to make of that?' The therapist was not confident in his ability to interpret dreams but he was curious to understand what lay behind the question, so he said: 'I can't interpret your dream or speculate on its meaning, but I can help you understand how it affected you.'

Remember that CBT encourages openness and honesty between therapist and client: be overt about what you are doing and why, and ask for honest feedback about what is helpful and what is not.

Following the conversation above, the therapist simply enquired: 'How does that sound to you?' and he discovered that his client was a little disappointed not to be told what her dream meant but she was prepared to go along with him to see if it was helpful. He then posed questions to explore the personal impact of the dream: 'What do you think was important about your having that dream?' and 'How did it leave you feeling?' and so on. Afterwards they debriefed this exploration and the therapist asked: 'How did you feel about our looking at your view of the dream, rather than my answering your initial question directly?' and 'What did you learn from doing this?' The client fed back that she had found it surprisingly enlightening – this experience then helped to support the collaborative way of working.

Collaboration should develop as treatment proceeds. Encourage your client gradually to take a more active role in setting agendas, devising homework and giving feedback. Enhance this by being genuinely respectful and by fostering the sense that he is becoming his own therapist. The hope is that clients will leave therapy as skilled CBT practitioners, so they are encouraged to use the approach independently, and to be prepared should a relapse occur in the future (see Chapter 6).

STRUCTURE AND ACTIVE ENGAGEMENT

The problem-focused and structured nature of CBT requires the therapist to work with the client to maintain structure in the sessions. For example, at the beginning of each session, we set an explicit, shared agenda, and then largely stick to it (see Chapter 11, which elaborates on the process of agenda-setting).

CBT therapists are *actively* engaged with the client and may talk more than in some other therapies – perhaps as much as 50 per cent of the time in the early stages. This can feel onerous to new therapists. However, much of your input is in the form of questions, and the way the session develops is the result of a joint effort. In the early stages of therapy, the content of sessions will be directed to a greater extent by the therapist, but responsibility is increasingly picked up by the client as sessions progress. For example, homework tasks are likely to be devised by you at first, but as treatment proceeds, your clients will have a greater role in setting up assignments for subsequent meetings.

A woman had obsessional problems focused on sticking to the rules, not falling foul of authority, and complying absolutely with official requirements. She had more generalised beliefs about always needing to do the right thing, and the likelihood of rejection if she stepped out of line. She had had eight treatment sessions and was taking more responsibility for the content of sessions when the following discussion took place:

Therapist:	You say that doing something for yourself, particularly for pleasure, would be very difficult for you. How do you think you might take this forward, so that we could find out more about how you feel, and what beliefs are operating in situations like that? [*therapist setting stage for experiment*]
Client:	Well, my friend has twice invited me to go to a jewellery class with her, and I would love to go, but both times I said that I had too much on ... and I did, but I would have found it difficult to say yes, even if I'd got nothing to do. So I suppose I could go with her, and see what happened.
Therapist:	For our purposes, what do you think you could look out for?
Client:	Well, I would need to know what feelings I had, and what beliefs seemed to be relevant.
Therapist:	Anything else that would be useful to look out for?
Client:	I suppose what I felt like afterwards, because that is when the guilt is likely to kick in.
Therapist:	Let's include that then. What sort of diary form shall we set up?

The extent to which the client determines the content of sessions is partly a function of timing and his personality, beliefs and attitudes. An autonomous person might assume control from early in treatment, whereas a more dependent person will benefit from a slower handover of responsibility and will probably need more coaching.

TIME-LIMITED AND BRIEF

Both clients and commissioners of services find CBT attractive partly because it is often relatively brief. In this context, 'brief' means somewhere between six and 20 sessions. The number of sessions is guided by treatment trials concerning the target problem but is also influenced by the specifics of the problem and the client, as well as available resources. As resources are often scarce, it is important to help people efficiently, and the structure and focus of CBT contribute to achieving that. Table 2.1 gives some suggestions about possible lengths of treatment for different types of problem.

Evidence does not suggest that long treatments necessarily do better than shorter ones (Baldwin, Berkerjon, Atkins, Olsen & Nielson, 2009), and neither do clients who have been on long waiting lists necessarily require an equally lengthy treatment. For therapists used to other treatment approaches, the rapid move from one or two sessions of assessment and formulation into a six- or eight-session therapy may feel uncomfortably rushed, but this is likely to become less difficult as you become more familiar with the approach.

Table 2.1 Guidelines on length of treatment

Type of problem	Number of sessions
Mild	Up to 6
Mild to moderate	6–12
Moderate to severe *or* moderate problems with co-existing personality disorder	12–20
Severe problems with co-existing personality disorders	>20

It is helpful to give an indication of how long treatment is likely to last and to build in regular progress reviews. It is essential to review progress each session but, in addition, more major reviews can be carried out every three to six sessions. Therapy is not always effective: CBT doesn't suit everyone all of the time. There are those who will never find it beneficial and those who might not find it beneficial right now. You need to prepare your client for this and be prepared to spot a mis-matching of client and CBT as early as possible. Clients shouldn't feel that they have 'failed' – maybe the timing or the choice of therapy was not appropriate for them.

> As you know, the therapy that we offer here is CBT. It has a very good track record for many psychological problems and I'm hopeful that it will help you. However, I will be checking in regularly to see if it is making a difference, to see if it is meeting your needs. The fact is that no single therapy works for every problem or with every person, so we'll need to monitor how well it suits you. If it does suit you that's great, but if it seems that it's not meeting your needs I'd like us to spot that as soon as possible so that we can begin to plan an alternative way forward.

Having said this, we can give CBT the best chance by making it clear that it requires active practice and collaboration to be effective.

If it appears that the therapy is not helpful, or if progress has reached a plateau, it is easier to bring treatment to a close if review points have been pre-established. If progress is made but residual problems are still present, then it is probably worth continuing with treatment. At this point, your client's problem(s) need to be clearly re-formulated (see Chapter 4) so that you can both appreciate what CBT can help with and what needs to be dealt with elsewhere. It is worth considering the benefits of encouraging your client to manage some difficulties independently. This is generally best done by gradually increasing the length of time between sessions, so that the client takes increasing responsibility for dealing with residual problems and setbacks, while there continue to be opportunities for review with the therapist.

There is no commitment within CBT to a standard '50-minute hour', or any other standard session length. A session involving *in vivo* experiments, for example with someone with agoraphobia, may last two or three hours. On the other hand, a review session towards the end of treatment may last only 20 minutes. Bear in mind that if relevant and productive homework assignments have been set up, then the majority of treatment can be considered to be taking place outside the 'therapy hour'. Indeed, Professor Glenn Waller (Waller et al., 2007) reminds his clients that they will be getting not one hour a week therapy but '168-hours-a-week-therapy' (p. 9) and by this he means that the client will be active between sessions.

EMPIRICAL IN APPROACH

There is a strong emphasis within CBT on using empirical psychological knowledge. For example, it is established that early loss of a parent predisposes one to depression in adult life (Brown, Harris & Bifulco, 1986); that people with generalised anxiety disorder (GAD) are intolerant of uncertainty (Ladouceur, Dugas, Freeston, Leger, Gagnon & Thibodeau, 2000); and people who are depressed have a reduced ability to access specific memories, especially of positive events, that is, they have an 'over-general memory' (Williams, Teasdale, Segal & Soulsby, 2000). There is also an emphasis on referring to contemporary research on treatment efficacy and efficiency. Therapy rests on this type of knowledge base.

Furthermore, CBT has borrowed from behaviour therapy a commitment to establishing the efficacy of treatment in individual clinical cases (see Chapters 5 and 18) and to training our clients to be empirical in their approach to managing their problems – we encourage critical data collecting and review.

As a therapist, you need to keep informed about the evidence from research trials and use this to guide interventions in individual cases. It is sometimes claimed that the samples studied by research teams are atypical of those found in clinical settings and therefore trial data are not relevant. However, unless you have good evidence to demonstrate why another approach would be likely to be more successful, then it is fairer to the client if the available empirical evidence is given appropriate weight. This is not to discount therapist intuition about what is likely to be helpful, merely to suggest that such insights should be built into a formulation that is consistent with evidence about psychological processes. None of us should be cavalier about discounting well-described and apparently relevant data, and we need to be aware that there is some indication that therapists tend to switch too early from treatment protocols, and that this is detrimental to therapeutic outcome (Schulte & Eifert, 2002), although the evidence is not conclusive (Ghaderi, 2006).

Within individual therapy, the client is also encouraged to tackle his problems in an empirical way. For example:

- *Thoughts, images and beliefs are considered as hypotheses to be investigated*: for example, a woman who thought, 'I am a useless mother' was encouraged to see this as one possible view among other possibilities and to look at the evidence supporting each view.
- *Data can be collected to test out ideas*: for example, a man who feared spiders because he believed that they would run towards him was encouraged to collect data about how often a spider on a tray ran towards a (therapist's!) hand, rather than away from it (see Chapter 9 for a discussion of behavioural experiments like this).

- *New beliefs can be formulated in the light of evidence and subsequently tested out*: there is an emphasis on 'discovering how it is' by trying out new behaviours, new ways of thinking, new ways of interacting, and not simply relying on verbal discussion or new insights for changes in feelings and beliefs. It is always important to be guided by the client about what new evidence would be helpful (again, look at Chapter 9 for more detail about such interventions).

Following discussions with her therapist, a woman who was chronically depressed revealed a belief that 'You must always try to make the most of your potential' (underlying assumption). As part of therapy, she was working on a new belief set that 'Things can be done for their own sake, and still feel satisfying and enjoyable. You do not need to be making the most of your potential.'

To test this out, she chose to join a non-auditioned choir for the fun of it, and she began to learn French so that she could 'get by', with no intention of becoming fluent.

In choosing strategies to address your clients' difficulties, you might well find that you draw on other strategies in addition to those laid out in this text. For example, interventions such as skills training (assertiveness, time management, etc.), or grief work, or couple therapy, may also be relevant. Whatever interventions are used, they should be formulation driven, well planned and evaluated so that you can review the efficacy of your treatment.

PROBLEM-ORIENTED IN APPROACH

A person's problem may be a dysphoric mood, a relationship difficulty, an unhelpful behaviour (e.g. a repetitive habit like hair-pulling), or an occupational problem (e.g. frequent loss of jobs). CBT identifies what *problems* are pertinent for the client, and then focuses on resolving or reducing them. Problems are described in specific terms, not at the general level of diagnosis. For example, if someone was suffering from depression, you would want to know how this was actually affecting him and what specific aspects of the problem he wanted help with: such as for one person, this may be self-critical thoughts, low mood, social withdrawal, reduced interests, while for another it may be impaired concentration, poor sleep, tearfulness and irritability.

Once you have agreed what problems will be tackled, goals are set for each problem and these goals provide the focus for treatment. The process of goal-setting explicitly focuses the client on where he hopes to be at the end of treatment, and in what ways he wants to be different from how he is now (see Chapter 11).

GUIDED DISCOVERY

The therapist uses a form of enquiry and exploration often described as 'Socratic' in a process of guided discovery. This particular approach helps clients clarify thoughts, images and beliefs and generate alternative perspectives and plans (see Chapter 7). Therapists use carefully constructed questions and tasks, to help clients understand *for themselves* the idiosyncratic meanings of situations, alternative ways of looking at things and ways of testing out the usefulness of new perspectives.

BEHAVIOURAL METHODS

Behavioural interventions are a necessary element of CBT, and many assignments include behavioural tasks and experiments. These are used to test out new possibilities and perspectives derived in treatment sessions, to enhance learning and also to encourage generalisation from treatment sessions to everyday life – where the changes really need to be made. There is a wide variety of possible behavioural interventions (see Chapter 9 for a thorough review of behavioural strategies), and some of the principles of behaviour therapy have been directly adopted by CBT: for example, taking a graded approach to new tasks and breaking them down into manageable chunks.

IN VIVO WORK

CBT therapists often take therapy out of the office and into the real world, in order to help with assessment or to carry out a behavioural experiment. Such real-life *in vivo* work can be invaluable. For example, a person with long-standing OCD may have become unaware of the detail of his obsessional rituals, and you may underestimate his problems unless you directly observe them. Similarly, it is important to check out that changes in belief in a clinic setting are translated into real-life settings, so it may be helpful to do experiments *in vivo*, possibly with the therapist accompanying the client.

A man with health anxiety believed that if he became short of breath, he could pass out and die; he therefore made sure that he always stayed within reach of a doctor's surgery. During therapy in the clinic, he had questioned this belief and had begun to develop two new possibilities: that he would not pass out if he became breathless and that it was okay to move beyond the reach of a doctor's surgery. With his agreement, the therapist then drove him into the countryside where neither of them knew the whereabouts of doctors' surgeries. They then ran up and down the road so that he became breathless (an activity he had been avoiding). This meant that he could test out his new belief that he would not pass out, whilst dropping the safety-seeking behaviour of being near a doctor's surgery.

If someone is trying out a difficult new behaviour, it may be helpful for you to be there to offer encouragement and support. In some instances, therapist modelling of behaviours may be useful, although you should withdraw as soon as possible, and allow the client to continue alone in such experiments.

A woman with agoraphobia had catastrophic concerns about the consequences of becoming anxious, particularly that she would be publicly ridiculed if she were to soil herself. To test this out, she accompanied her therapist to a local shopping centre and observed from a distance the responses of members of the public to an obvious brown stain on the back of the therapist's skirt – responses best described as studied indifference.

It is often possible to draw on the assistance of relatives or friends for *in vivo* work, but this must be planned carefully, with an eye to detail, and it may be necessary to help the aide identify and tackle unhelpful thoughts of their own. For example, a spouse may believe that exposing their loved one to panic is harmful; such a belief would be counterproductive in a behavioural experiment about the consequences of panic.

SUMMARIES AND FEEDBACK

CBT makes frequent use of summaries and feedback during sessions, which is one way of keeping the agenda in focus. You might pause to summarise the main points under discussion approximately every 10 minutes, and more frequently than that in the early stages of therapy. Summaries should include the emotions that the client has described, and the meaning of the event or situation for him. This is not supposed to be an *interpretation* of what the client has said. Indeed, it is better to use the client's own words as far as possible, rather than substitute your own. The latter may significantly change the meaning for the client, especially if he has used a metaphor or some idiosyncratic phrasing.

It can be equally helpful to ask your client to summarise the discussion, by saying, for example: 'Can you feed back to me what you think the main points of our discussion are so far? I would just like to check out that I am on the same track as you.'

This provision of summaries helps to ensure a shared understanding of key points. It is sometimes startling to learn how misunderstood the client or the therapist has been.

After discussing why it is helpful to write down NATs, the therapist mentioned that it was really helpful that the client was readily able to identify his thoughts. When asked for feedback, the client said that he now understood that, as he was aware of his NATs but still felt bad, it was unlikely that he would benefit from CBT.

Summaries can also be enlightening for the client. For example:

Therapist: It sounds as if the qualities that attracted you to your partner are now the things that you find most upsetting. Is that right?

Client: Yes, but I had not thought about it like that before.

It is particularly useful to summarise the key points at the end of the session and to ask the client what is the 'take-home' message for him – again, this will reduce misunderstandings. It is also important to gather feedback on the session, for example what has been helpful, unhelpful or upsetting:

Therapist: It would be helpful if you would let me know if I say anything that is difficult to understand, or indicates that I am barking up the wrong tree, or is upsetting in any way. It is sometimes hard for people to mention things that they do not like, or that imply that there is a misunderstanding. Yet it can be very helpful if you let me know if there are things that are unhelpful, because we can then sort it out, or clarify what we meant. Have I said anything today which will play on your mind, or was upsetting?

Therapist: I will ask you a similar question at the end of each session. Do not hesitate to let me know if there is any comment you would like to make.

Therapist: What are the main points that you will take away from today?

Clients are more likely to give genuine feedback if you take time early in treatment to explain why feedback is valuable and give honest encouragement when you receive it.

Each session can also begin with a request for feedback on the previous one – what had been helpful or whether the client had any new ideas about the previous discussion. Again, it is more likely that your client will review the session and give feedback if you have discussed the advantages of thinking about therapy between sessions, and taken seriously the client's feedback on this.

A depressed man said that he did not like to think about sessions when he was not with the therapist. Exploration revealed that he struggled with negative thoughts about being overwhelmed, thoughts that could then be dealt with.

See Videos 2.1 and 2.2: Sharing capsule summaries, and Video 2.3: Eliciting feedback from your client during a session (i) and Video 2.4: Eliciting feedback from your client at the end of a session (ii).

MYTHS ABOUT CBT

In this section, we will identify and explore some of the common myths surrounding CBT.

THE THERAPEUTIC RELATIONSHIP IS NOT IMPORTANT IN CBT

The therapist qualities that are valued in other therapies are equally important within CBT. Warmth, empathy and unconditional regard, which were identified by Rogers (1951) as important for successful psychotherapeutic work, have been promoted by Beck (Beck et al.,

1979), and have been found to be typical of CBT therapists (e.g. Wright & Davis, 1994) and to be valued by clients (Ackerman & Hilsenroth, 2003). This contrasts with the mistaken view that CBT is impersonal and not concerned about the therapeutic relationship. At the most basic level, if a client is to be willing to reveal personally significant material, to carry out frightening and difficult new behaviours and to feel safe, then he has to be able to trust the therapist. Therefore, although CBT does not see the relationship as the major therapeutic tool, it is nevertheless seen as an essential foundation for effective therapy. It is recognised that the therapist must pay attention to any emerging difficulties in the therapeutic relationship and must attempt to understand what client beliefs may have been triggered to produce them (see Chapter 3).

It is sometimes believed that CBT therapists have no interest in the client's feelings about the therapist. However, there has been an increasing recognition over the past 30 years of the importance of relationship factors – but construed in cognitive rather than psychodynamic terms (see Orlinsky, Grawe & Parks, 1994). It is also sometimes assumed that the therapeutic alliance is neglected with shorter-term interventions, however Chaddock (2013) has proposed that attending to interpersonal factors is even more important in brief therapies such as the IAPT PWP-led interventions.

The therapeutic relationship in CBT is enmeshed with the working alliance (Kennerley, 2014a) and much of Beck et al.'s consideration of the working alliance was generated from a psycho-dynamic perspective (1979). From the outset Beck stressed that in order to achieve fruitful 'therapeutic collaboration' (p. 45), attending to the therapeutic relationship was crucial.

CBT IS MECHANISTIC – JUST APPLY TECHNIQUE X TO PROBLEM Y

CBT is based on an explicit model that links emotion, behaviour, cognition and physiology, and this model underpins the therapeutic strategies that have been shown to work effectively. At a clinical level, there is often a specific model for the problems presented by a client. For example, there is a model for panic disorder that highlights the role of catastrophic misinterpretation of benign physical or mental symptoms and avoidance; there is a different model for depression that focuses on the client's negative view of the self, other people and the world and behavioural withdrawal. There may also be a fairly detailed protocol derived from such models – clear guidelines for treating clients with a specific kind of problem. In that case, a formulation informed by the model would be developed for the individual client, but the treatment would not be technique-driven (e.g. 'I think he needs some anxiety management training'), but would instead be based on an understanding of what psychological processes are maintaining *a particular person's* problem and the specific relationships between emotions, thoughts, behaviours and physiological features which are important in *his* case. This is discussed further in Chapter 4.

CBT IS ABOUT POSITIVE THINKING

It is sometimes suggested that CBT is not concerned with the client's circumstances or interpersonal situation but is only interested in getting someone to see things positively. This is a misunderstanding: CBT aims to promote *realistic* evaluation of cognitions. We don't aim to show that people are 'wrong' or that things are actually positive. When people have problems, their thinking may be excessively negative, but sometimes it is accurate – your client may think his partner is not interested in him because his partner is not interested in him! The formulation should take account of interpersonal and socio-economic circumstances and not assume that the client's thoughts are distorted.

A woman presented with low mood following redundancy from her job in a hotel. This was the third job that she had lost: the first two through redundancy, and the last after interpersonal difficulties with her boss. She was feeling low because however hard she tried, it seemed that luck was against her, and things went wrong. She felt hopeless about being able to improve things. Rather than assuming that her view was distorted, the therapist helped the client to review the evidence, to see what had contributed to each of the job losses and what responsibility she might have for the outcomes. Therapy may have needed to focus on her interpersonal skills, or her occupational standards, or possibly a tendency to attribute blame to others. In the event, it appeared to be much as she had initially thought: luck had been against her, and treatment therefore focused on helping her to tolerate the intrinsic unfairness of events and to problem solve.

CBT also acknowledges that some unhelpful thoughts may have been accurate in the past but are no longer so. For example, a child growing up in an emotionally deprived home may accurately have believed that 'No one is there for me', but this may no longer be true in her adult world even though the belief is still strong. CBT would help her appreciate the origin of the belief, why it was understandable that she still held it, and CBT would support her in discovering that it was no longer valid all of the time.

In short, the aim of treatment is to understand and resolve problems, not to simply promote positive thinking.

CBT DOES NOT DEAL WITH THE PAST

Most CBT sessions focus on the here and now, because most therapy is concerned with tackling current problems and hence what is currently maintaining them. This is not to say that CBT cannot work with past history when necessary, nor that it discounts the importance of past experiences in accounting for problem development (see Chapter 4). The main reason for focusing on the here and now is that the factors that account for the development of a problem are often different from the ones that are maintaining it, and so relatively greater attention is paid to the present situation (maintenance of the problem, which we can often do something about) than to the past (origin of the problem, which we can't change).

A 16-year-old girl with anxiety about wetting herself had had an experience as a young child when she felt humiliated after wetting herself in front of her friends on a school trip. She had not been able to 'hold on' when instructed to do so by her teacher and had been teased by her friends. Now she was older, she knew she was capable of 'holding on' for many hours and no longer had friends who would tease her. The problem now was largely maintained by avoidance of situations where she would not have easy access to a lavatory, by not drinking before going out, and by a range of other 'safety-seeking behaviours' like wearing long thick socks under her trousers so that urine would be absorbed if she did have an accident. For this girl, the problem had been precipitated by one set of factors, but was being maintained by different ones.

CBT DEALS WITH SUPERFICIAL SYMPTOMS, NOT THE ROOTS OF PROBLEMS, SO ALTERNATIVE 'SUBSTITUTE' SYMPTOMS ARE LIKELY TO OCCUR

As noted in Chapter 1, there used to be concern that simply 'removing symptoms' would result in the emergence of other manifestations of an underlying problem. However, a number of studies show that CBT clients are, if anything, protected against relapse, rather than developing further problems (e.g. Durham & Turvey, 1987; Williams, 1997; Hollon et al., 2005).

The strategies taught in CBT are often readily generalised to other problems, and practitioners strive to encourage this. In addition, the CBT formulation of problems aims to throw light on the psychological *processes* maintaining them, and to intervene in ways that impact on these processes. In doing so it addresses fundamental maintaining patterns, patterns that can affect several presenting difficulties. This is discussed in more detail in Chapter 4.

A woman with agoraphobic symptoms had a number of other difficulties, including obsessive-compulsive problems about harm coming to her relatives, depression, worries about being rejected and abandoned by loved ones, and lack of assertiveness. The agoraphobic problem was successfully dealt with at the beginning of treatment, as the client identified this as a priority because, in her view, it prevented her from functioning effectively as a wife and mother. She was able to travel around independently, even though the issues concerning being abandoned were at that stage intact. Her depression lifted spontaneously and her obsessional symptoms were subsequently dealt with using many of the strategies that she had developed to combat agoraphobia. Finally, attention was paid to the more generalised concerns about self-worth and her lack of assertiveness, although her view of herself had already improved enormously through her learning to conceptualise and manage her other difficulties.

CBT IS ADVERSARIAL

It is sometimes suggested that the CBT therapist tells the client what is wrong with his thinking and how he ought to think. As one mental health information centre leaflet put it, 'Cognitive therapy takes the form of an argument between client and therapist. As such, it is only suitable for the robust.' In reality, only *bad* CBT looks like an argument! You should aim to approach your client open-mindedly. Be curious and be prepared to be wrong so that your pre-judgement doesn't cloud your assessment. In this way you can get a sense of what it is to be him, to experience the problem as he does. You can also prompt him to question his beliefs for *himself*. There are good psychological reasons for encouraging him, via enquiry, to work out new perspectives for himself. If he reviews the evidence for a belief, and then draws his own conclusions, he is more likely to be convinced and he is more likely to remember his new conclusions (see Chapter 7).

CBT IS FOR SIMPLE PROBLEMS: YOU NEED SOMETHING ELSE FOR COMPLEX PROBLEMS

CBT is a wide-ranging and flexible approach to therapy, which skilful practitioners can apply to many psychological problems, provided the client is at least minimally engaged in the process. Within Axis I disorders (as defined by the American Psychiatric Association in the *Diagnostic and Statistical Manual* (DSM-IV-TR; APA, 2000), clients with very severe and chronic difficulties have been helped by this approach (Haddock, Barrowclough, Shaw, Dunn, Novaco & Tarrier, 2009), and there is now increasing evidence of its efficacy for those with personality disorders and other complex problems (see Chapter 17).

CBT IS INTERESTED IN THOUGHTS AND NOT EMOTIONS

CBT is indeed interested in helping people modify cognitions (not just thoughts, but images too) but usually as a means to an end, not an end in itself. Most clients want help with mood, feelings or behaviour: they ask for help in managing their depression, their fear or their eating disorder, for example, rather than requesting help with 'dysfunctional thinking'. Cognitive change is a means of helping people change in those other systems, but therapy is rarely fruitful if it is a purely intellectual discussion of abstract thoughts. If a person is experiencing no emotion during the process, it is very unlikely that he will achieve a shift in emotion or behaviour (Safran, 1998).

A depressed woman who was socially isolated described a situation when she met some friends but perceived herself to be on the edge of the group, and insignificant as far as other people were concerned. She described the scene and her negative thoughts in a calm and measured way, and although she could identify evidence that she was valued by the others (they included her in plans for the evening, they chatted as though they assumed she would join them on a weekend trip), this had no impact on her view that she was peripheral. She was asked to talk about the scene again, but while describing her negative thoughts this time, she was asked to bring to mind and engage with how she was feeling during the distressing situation. Only then, when she had elicited her emotional reaction to being valued by others, did the strength of her negative thoughts begin to weaken.

CBT IS ONLY FOR THE PSYCHOLOGICALLY MINDED

Typically, CBT requires a person to be able to recognise and talk about cognitions and emotions, and to distinguish between them. It is also advantageous if a client can relate to psychological models – a vicious cycle or a preliminary formulation, for example. However, if someone has difficulty in reflecting in this way, the therapist can help him to increase his capacity to do that (see Butler & Surawy, 2004), and it is worth offering a trial of a few sessions to see if the client can take to the approach. You can make it clear that CBT is on trial to see if it's the right therapy for this person at this time – don't let the client feel that he has failed if CBT is not for him.

CBT IS QUICK TO LEARN AND EASY TO PRACTISE

CBT has some powerful strategies that are *relatively* easy for a therapist to learn and apply, and this book introduces you to the basic skills. However, using the approach in a creative and flexible way is as difficult as any other therapy, and you are reminded that you will need to receive regular supervision (see Chapter 19) and keep yourself updated on developments in CBT.

CBT IS NOT INTERESTED IN THE UNCONSCIOUS

CBT does not use the concept of the unconscious in the Freudian sense but certainly recognises that cognitive processes may not be conscious. In many instances, you and your client are attempting to clarify the meanings of experiences that may initially be out of awareness. This is not generally interpreted as repressed material but is taken to be at a pre-conscious level, available on reflection to consciousness. Many people need training to increase their awareness of, for example, images, ATs or assumptions. Socratic enquiry is used to help them identify such cognitions and subsequently to establish the meaning of them. Therapists might hold hypotheses (and these might be explored with the client), however, they never offer an interpretation; the client is by and large considered to be the expert. This is discussed further in Chapter 7.

There are instances when thoughts or images may be actively blocked by the client. For example, someone who has been sexually abused as a child might dissociate from an experience or memory that is extremely distressing; in OCD, many clients never confront the disturbing thoughts that motivate their ritualistic behaviour, by avoiding situations that would trigger the thoughts. Generally, the CBT techniques described in Chapters 8 and 9 are used to help clients identify the nature of these unconscious thoughts or beliefs.

CBT DEMANDS HIGH INTELLIGENCE

CBT makes no greater demands on intelligence than any other therapy and, indeed, has for some time been adapted for use with people with learning difficulty (Stenfert-Kroese, Dagnan & Loumidis, 1997). Similarly, CBT has been adapted for use with children and young people (Graham, 1998), and with very elderly adults (Wilkinson, 2002).

SUMMARY

The basic characteristics of CBT make this a fascinating and satisfying way of working with clients, as you help them develop strategies for managing problems, and guide them as they work out new, more adaptive perspectives on their world.

Some of the key characteristics include:

- *collaboration*, where client and therapist each bring their expertise to bear on the problem;
- *a structured and active format*, with agenda-setting and goals for treatment contributing to a structured therapy, in which therapist and client actively engage in the therapeutic process;

- *time limits*, with most therapy lasting between 6 and 20 sessions;
- *an empirical basis* relying on psychological evidence, and emphasising measurement of problems, and empirical estimates of outcome;
- *problem-orientation*, with treatment addressed via a detailed formulation of the problems;
- *guided discovery* as the cardinal mode of exploring difficulties and solutions;
- *behavioural awareness*, with many behavioural tasks and assignments;
- *summaries and feedback* frequently used, to make sure that therapist and client are on track.

LEARNING EXERCISES

These learning exercises are available to download from the companion website.

REVIEW AND REFLECTION:

- If you are currently working with psychological therapies, how do the characteristics set out here compare with what you are used to? Can you see advantages to CBT for your clients? If so, how could you introduce the concept of CBT to them? Do you have any misgivings about the structure or other aspects of CBT?
- If you have read things about CBT that have surprised you, what were they? Did you buy into the myths about CBT? If so, how strongly did you believe each of them? What impact has this chapter had on your beliefs about CBT?
- Are there any aspects of CBT that you anticipate would make you feel uncomfortable? Is there somewhere that you can explore your discomfort – a colleague or supervisor with whom you might talk? If you decide to use CBT but feel uncomfortable, might you tackle this in a graded way?

TAKING IT FORWARD:

- If you look back at the last five clients you have seen, in how many sessions did you collaboratively agree homework that involved a

behavioural task of some kind? Could you identify any sessions where it would have been helpful to include between-session tasks? What could they have been?

- **If there were any myths that you bought into (e.g. that CBT is adversarial), check out whether this was borne out in practice in your sessions with clients. If so, think about how you could make the sessions more typical of CBT, and try this out.**
- **Work out how you could explain to your client that feedback is helpful and welcome, and practise this with two clients. How could you ask them whether your request made them feel uncomfortable in any way?**

FURTHER READING

Beck, A.T., Rush, A.J., Shaw, B.F., & Emery, G. (1979). *Cognitive therapy of depression*. New York: Guilford Press.

The classic text, which should be at the top of your reading list – it gives the original description of CBT, setting out characteristics of the approach.

Westbrook, D., Mueller, M., Kennerley, H., & McManus, F. (2010). Common problems in therapy. In M. Mueller, H. Kennerley, F. McManus, & D. Westbrook (Eds.), *Oxford guide to surviving as a CBT therapist*. Oxford: Oxford University Press.

An interesting chapter where the authors discuss common problems in therapy associated with many of the distinctive features of CBT.

VIDEO LINKS

- **2.1 Sharing capsule summaries (i)**
- **2.2 Sharing capsule summaries (ii)**
- **2.3 Eliciting feedback from your client during a session (i)**
- **2.4 Eliciting feedback from your client at the end of a session (ii)**

3

THE THERAPEUTIC RELATIONSHIP

- Introduction
- The therapeutic relationship as an essential foundation of therapy
- The role of the therapist
- Ways of building a positive and collaborative client–therapist relationship
- Ruptures in the therapeutic alliance
- Working with diversity and difference
- Boundary issues
- Maintaining treatment boundaries
- Summary
- Learning exercises
- Further reading
- Video links
    - 3.1 Setting the scene
    - 3.2 Problems in the relationship
    - 3.3 Therapist dilemma (i)
    - 3.4 Therapist dilemma (ii)

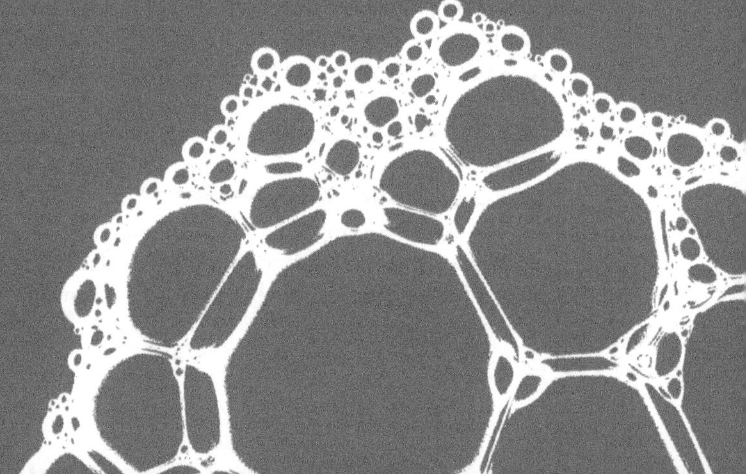

INTRODUCTION

This chapter reviews the importance of the therapeutic relationship in CBT. We will look at:

- the extent to which the therapeutic relationship is an essential foundation for therapy;
- the role of the therapist in CBT and the importance of non-specific therapist factors;
- ways of building collaborative client–therapist relationships – and of repairing ruptures in the therapeutic alliance;
- working with clients from different cultural backgrounds;
- boundary issues.

THE THERAPEUTIC RELATIONSHIP AS AN ESSENTIAL FOUNDATION OF THERAPY

An effective therapist–client relationship is important for treatment, with good evidence relating quality of relationship to therapeutic outcome (Orlinsky et al., 1994). Its relevance has long been recognised by the British Association for Behavioural & Cognitive Psychotherapies (BABCP) as one of its accreditation criteria stipulates that a practitioner should: 'Demonstrate knowledge and understanding of the therapeutic relationship and competence in the development, maintenance and ending of such relationships.' However, within CBT the therapeutic relationship is seen as necessary but not sufficient for a good treatment result, and in treatment trials there is typically a beneficial effect from CBT over and above that of being in a therapeutic relationship (Roth & Fonagy, 2005).

Moreover, the evidence indicates that it may be the nature of the *client's* participation in treatment that is the strongest predictor of outcome. For example, a man is more likely to do well if he is engaged with the therapeutic task, offers suggestions about treatment, warmly interacts with the therapist and is trusting of the therapist; and a client who consistently completes homework will do better than one who does not (Kazantzis, Whittington & Dattilio, 2010). Furthermore, in so far as therapist characteristics are related to outcome, it is the client's *perception* of those characteristics, and not the behaviours themselves that predicts outcome (Wright & Davis, 1994). For example, if a therapist's empathic skills are assessed by both her client and by an independent observer, the client's perception of empathy is a better predictor of outcome. This highlights the importance of the client as an active contributor to the therapy process.

The term 'working alliance' or 'therapeutic collaboration' was used by Beck et al. in their 1979 text (p. 45), and describes a particular interpersonal dynamic within CBT that is an active partnership of collaboration and discovery. They promoted the notion of therapist and client working as a team, each bringing their own expertise and sharing responsibility for change – but it was more than a businesslike, practical arrangement as it required 'the same subtle therapeutic atmosphere that has been described explicitly in the context of psychodynamic psychotherapy … [the] relationship involves both the patient and the therapist and is based on trust, rapport and collaboration' (p. 50). Empathic collaboration was viewed as key to establishing a working alliance in CBT.

The therapeutic relationship can be viewed as a useful laboratory for working on problems, providing an opportunity to acquire new skills that can then be transferred to situations in real life. For example, the client may learn to evaluate a 'hot' thought in a therapy session with coaching from the therapist, before generalising the same technique to 'real life'. The client may also use sessions to review and modify unhelpful beliefs as they are played out with the therapist in the clinical setting. Safran and Muran (1995) suggest that the therapist can act in ways that provide new, constructive interpersonal experiences for the client, with the client and therapist stepping back together from the interaction and examining what is currently going on between them.

A client's formulation included beliefs about others failing to be there for him when he was in trouble. In a session where difficulties in the relationship seemed to be emerging, the therapist used her own feelings as the cue for a discussion, saying 'I am feeling rather uncertain of where to take things just now and perhaps a bit defensive too, and I wonder why. It's my difficulty, I know, but could we explore this together?' The discussion revealed that the client was uncertain whether or not the therapist could help him so he had been disinclined to engage in CBT and he also predicted that the therapist would 'sack him' if he didn't do well. They were then able to understand the tension in their relationship and went on to look at whether the therapist would be likely to withdraw if things became difficult, or whether she would want to find ways of hanging in there even in the face of difficulty, a discussion that was highly relevant to the client's fears, and which led to the therapeutic relationship becoming a 'laboratory' for testing out those fears.

Within this model, the ways in which the client responds to the therapist may be influenced by beliefs developed early in life (possibly modified by subsequent experience), as well as by characteristics and behaviour of the therapist herself. However, the therapeutic relationship is not construed in terms of 'transference', in the psychoanalytic sense that it is a representation of another relationship from early life, but instead is considered as *a relationship in its own right*, with the potential for providing new evidence about the range of possibilities for relationships; for example, a new belief like 'People may stay with you even if difficulties emerge between you' may be strengthened. The extent to which any corrective interpersonal experience in therapy will colour other relationships should be considered empirically. If the issues are being openly discussed, it is easier to check out whether there is indeed any generalisation to everyday life.

Bordin's (1979) analysis of the therapeutic relationships as a *working alliance* is useful. He suggested that three components are necessary for a successful working alliance:

- *Agreement on the task*: what needs to be done in therapy, what the process of change (cognitive? behavioural?) will be, what activities and techniques will be used.
- *Agreement on therapy goals*: what is being sought from therapy in the short and long term (e.g. 'to leave the house having checked the cooker only once', 'to complete tax returns without checking with my accountant'), with client and therapist each contributing personal commitment to the goals.
- *A positive therapist–client bond*, typified by mutual liking, respect, trust and commitment.

It is clear that a good working alliance is necessary for a good outcome (Krupnick et al., 1996). At its most basic, you cannot carry out effective therapy with a client who drops out because he finds you cold and unempathic. The alliance needs to be established within the first three or four sessions (Horvarth, 1995), but this is not to say that the quality of the relationship remains fixed. It varies as treatment progresses, and it may be necessary to attend to breakdowns in the alliance in order for therapy to succeed. Thus, the quality of your therapeutic relationship should continue to be a focus of concern throughout the course of treatment.

Although it is not clear whether effective CBT is typified by a particular kind of alliance, it appears from a number of studies (e.g. Raue & Goldfried, 1994) that whatever the therapeutic modality, clients consider similar qualities of the working alliance to be important. These include being:

- helped to understand their problems;
- encouraged to face whatever situations cause them distress;
- able to talk to an understanding person;
- at ease with the personality of the therapist.

Some of these features map onto central features of CBT: for example, sharing a formulation of the client's problems for him to comment on, designing behavioural experiments to test out unhelpful beliefs. Some of the factors relate to the qualities of the therapist, and these will now be considered.

THE ROLE OF THE THERAPIST

One of the guiding principles of CBT is that, as therapist, you work empathically and collaboratively to engage the client in therapy (Ackerman & Hilsenroth, 2003). This aspect of therapy is developed further in the chapter on Socratic methods (see Chapter 7), but the general approach is that you function as a guide and mentor rather than as an instructor. You are 'walking alongside' your client as he explores new options for feeling and behaving, and your role is to open up new opportunities for exploration, by asking questions or giving information that may lead him into previously unexplored areas. You need to have a good understanding of his current bearings in order to do this, so you need to adopt an open-minded curiosity and respect about your client's beliefs, emotions and behaviours, and not to assume that you know how he feels or thinks.

This demands a lot of active enquiry on your part, and the tone of the interaction is crucial: it should not be accusatory ('You can't really mean you think that!'), nor persuasive or haranguing ('Do you think it is possible that most people respond in this way and that you are not picking up the cues?'). You should reflect a genuine, concerned interest in your client's current perspectives or feelings. This is a fine balance because, while you are trying to get a detailed sense of what it is like to be him in the current situation, you also need to maintain a measure of scepticism about what he is saying, since it is possible that he is making cognitive errors that will significantly distort the picture he presents.

Although the therapist's role as guide is paramount, it may be appropriate to adopt an educative, information-giving role from time to time:

> A young man was troubled by intrusive ideas about stabbing other people. He was very reassured when he was given the information that the vast majority of people from time to time have unpleasant intrusive thoughts which they find repellent in some way. This was supplemented by appropriate reading. (Rachman & de Silva, 1978)

Another important role for the therapist is *practical scientist*, providing a model for the client to adopt in relation to both current and future problems. Hypotheses about problems and experiences are set up and tested, and new conclusions are drawn if appropriate. The adoption of an open-minded approach is relevant throughout therapy, and the importance of looking for evidence that contradicts your initial hypotheses is particularly important – and this is as true for the therapist's initial formulation as it is for the client's initial beliefs. Evidence inconsistent with your ideas is the royal road to new perspectives!

The *collaborative* nature of the therapeutic relationship means that you relate to your client in an adult-to-adult way as far as possible. Thus you are open about your ideas concerning his problems and share your take on the formulation in a way that allows him to give feedback on its relevance or accuracy; you may disclose information about yourself *if this is in the client's interest*; and you are free to say 'I don't know' or 'Can I just think that over for a minute', without needing to appear all-knowing. It is acceptable for you and your client to problem solve together. The only occasional exceptions to this openness are when it is clearly in the client's interest not to be open: for example, you might choose not to disclose early in treatment your ideas about a possible final weight for a woman with an eating disorder lest you jeopardise her motivation to return to therapy and at least engage in weight stabilisation; you might not yet share your knowledge (gleaned from medical notes) of a childhood of abuse in case your client is not ready to explore this as bringing it up might risk his disengagement.

Within the complex web of interactions between therapist, client and techniques, it is clear that a good cognitive therapist also needs the characteristics identified by Rogers as necessary for other therapies, namely warmth, empathy, genuineness and unconditional regard for the client (Beck et al., 1979). Therapists who act in this way have been shown in many studies to achieve better outcomes (Lambert & Bergin, 1994; Orlinsky et al., 1994).

Furthermore, in a survey by Wright and Davis (1994), they found that clients wanted their therapists to:

- offer a physically safe, private, confidential setting, comfortable and free from distraction;
- be respectful;
- treat client concerns seriously;
- prioritise client interests over their own;
- be competent;
- share practical information about how to make life improvements;
- permit the client to make personal choices when using information and therapist suggestions;
- be flexible in evaluating the client – not assume that the client fits a theory or is now totally understood;
- review how the client gets on if therapist recommendations are followed;
- pace herself well, not rush, or keep changing appointments.

A different survey of women who had successfully completed a course of CBT distinguished between those who had disclosed histories of childhood sexual abuse and women who stated that they had not been sexually abused. The researchers found that the latter group prioritised competence in CBT skills, while the former particularly wanted their therapists to show acceptance of them and commitment to the therapy (Middle & Kennerley, 2001). This reminds us that different clients have different therapeutic needs – in this case the survivors of abuse wanted a more overtly supportive therapeutic alliance.

Although none of the qualities that we have noted are specific to CBT, they nevertheless give a useful checklist of general rules to follow. Many of them are consistent with the general approach of CBT (e.g. are implied by a collaborative approach), and many would fall under the general rubric of treating one's clients in a respectful and empathic way.

WAYS OF BUILDING A POSITIVE AND COLLABORATIVE CLIENT–THERAPIST RELATIONSHIP

The general principles of the cognitive behavioural approach provide a sound foundation for building a good client–therapist relationship. For example:

- careful listening to get a real sense of how it is to be the client;
- taking time to set a shared agenda;
- making it clear that feedback is welcome; and
- carefully establishing the client's goals for treatment;

all contribute to an effective alliance.

People differ in what they bring to therapy, and consideration of these factors can also ease the development of a good relationship. For example, some may be at a relatively early stage in their 'preparedness to change' (Prochaska & DiClemente, 1986), and the therapist needs to be aware of this. A client with an eating disorder may be willing to think about extending the range of food she is eating only if she can be assured of no weight gain; or a client with OCD may be unwilling to consider limiting hand-washing just yet. In such cases, collaboration might be better achieved through initial motivational work (Miller & Rollnick, 2002) rather than active CBT.

See Video 3.1: Setting the scene and engaging your client.

It seems that inexperienced therapists are able to create a good working relationship with their clients, but that more experienced clinicians are better able to spot potential ruptures in an alliance. We will now consider how to deal with ruptures when they occur, bearing in mind that an experienced supervisor is invaluable in this area (see Chapter 19).

RUPTURES IN THE THERAPEUTIC ALLIANCE

Do not be surprised that ruptures in the working alliance occur: your client's problems have often become so well entrenched that he is unable to deal with them independently, and this means that change is likely to be difficult. As a result, he may experience a range of unhelpful emotions and thoughts in the session while he is struggling to deal with his problems.

SIGNS OF A RUPTURE IN THE THERAPEUTIC ALLIANCE

These may be reflected in non-verbal cues from your client related to emotional states such as discomfort, anger or mistrust; or feelings experienced by you as therapist. There may also be outward signs, such as not carrying out homework tasks, expressing scepticism about the approach, or high levels of expressed emotion. The important issue is to be mindful of the quality of the interaction between you and your client, so that you can take early steps to intervene when difficulties arise. Do not ignore it and hope that it will go away.

See Video 3.2: Dealing with signs of problems in the therapeutic relationship.

HOW TO DEAL WITH RUPTURES IN THE ALLIANCE

Watson and Greenberg (1995) point out that ruptures can be related to:

- the goals or tasks of therapy (e.g. the client does not understand or agree with the goals or strategies used in treatment);
- the client–therapist bond (e.g. the client is not collaborative, or does not trust or respect the therapist).

They argue for dealing with the former problems by approaching them directly, such as by clarifying the rationale for treatment, or possibly changing the approach. For example, if the client believes that reducing avoidance is important but does not believe that reducing safety-seeking behaviours (see Chapters 4 and 13) would be helpful, it may be best to switch in the short term to reducing avoidance, possibly moving on to a behavioural experiment to investigate the role of safety-seeking behaviours once he has exhausted the contribution of avoidance (if there is a remaining problem!).

If the rupture in the alliance seems to be related to your bond with the client, first deal with this within your current therapeutic relationship, without assuming that the problem is a reflection of your client's characteristic interpersonal relationships.

A woman became very irritated when the therapist had to change an appointment. The therapist commented on this, and sought to clarify what had triggered the angry feelings. It transpired that the client was feeling let down, because it seemed to her that she must be of very low priority to the therapist. When she was asked to consider other possibilities, she asked the therapist to explain why she could not make the original appointment time. At this point, the therapist chose to reveal that she was going to a family funeral, and that it was only in such circumstances that she would change an appointment. They then discussed what the woman could take away from this experience, and if it told her any more about how to respond to unpleasant feelings. She said that she would continue to try to check out whether her initial responses were likely to be accurate, or whether other explanations could be relevant.

If such work is unsuccessful, or if the formulation indicates that the client may, for example, find it difficult to trust *anyone*, then it may be necessary to consider the rupture as a characteristic pattern and to use the therapeutic relationship to provide the client with a corrective emotional experience (Safran & Muran, 1995).

Newman (1994) makes the point that you should consider what contribution you are making to any therapeutic impasse, rather than assume that the problem always resides within the client.

A woman with health anxiety was making little consistent progress, despite a formulation that apparently accounted well for her problem, and despite her commitment to homework tasks. The therapist could see that she frequently had moist eyes, but she always denied that she was upset when asked about it. In supervision, the therapist became aware that he was reluctant to discover that his client had the potential for becoming very upset, because the client was slightly histrionic in style, and the therapist had ATs about being 'washed away' by the woman's distress. As a result, he always asked about her feelings in a neutral voice, and never reflected his own perception of the woman's sadness. Not surprisingly, she did not feel able to share her feelings with the therapist, and denied that she was upset.

If it seems that the therapeutic relationship is being affected by your own issues or blindspots, then you can discuss this with a supervisor; if this is not immediately available, then take the opportunity to do some work yourself: for example, listen to recordings of your treatment sessions, keep a thought record of your ATs and images in session, look for your own 'hot cognitions'. This can be interesting and enlightening; self-supervision is discussed in more detail in Chapter 19.

If it seems that the impasse is related to your client's issues, then, rather than viewing this as an indication of poor motivation or ambivalence, it is more useful to formulate the issue in the same way as any other problem. For example, you could consider:

- what function the behaviour may have (e.g. if the client is hostile, he may be protecting himself against feared rejection);
- what idiosyncratic beliefs may be fuelling the impasse (e.g. the client may believe that a competent therapist would be able to read his mind);
- what fears the client may have about complying (e.g. if he were to change, he may be faced with challenges he could not tackle);
- what skills he may lack (e.g. he may be unable to reflect on his emotional experience);
- what environmental features may be contributing (e.g. he may be exhausted through caring for an elderly mother).

The problem can then be tackled in CBT in the same way as other problems. This could include:

- revisiting the formulation and rationale;
- using Socratic methods to clarify the issues;
- collaborating and providing choices, while providing structure, limits and guidance;
- reviewing the pros and cons of change versus no change;
- communicating with the client's language, metaphors or images;
- gently persisting when the client subtly avoids – don't take 'I don't know' for an answer;
- maintaining an empathic attitude, and avoiding blaming or making negative interpretations of your client's behaviour.

See Videos 3.3: Presenting the therapist dilemma: a simple issue (i), and 3.4: Presenting the therapist dilemma: a more complex issue (ii).

Again, we remind budding CBT therapists that effective clinical supervision (see Chapter 19) will be as invaluable for them in tackling this kind of problem as it would be for the highly experienced. If a supervisor is not available at the time, then reflect on the issue by yourself, as discussed above.

WORKING WITH DIVERSITY AND DIFFERENCE

Another important area to consider is broadly that of diversity and difference. Here we shall think about some general aspects of working with clients whose backgrounds and experiences might differ from the therapist's. Many of the same principles can be applied when working with people who differ in physical ability, ethnicity or sexual orientation, as well as age and social class. An excellent recent guide is El-Leithy's chapter 'Working with diversity in CBT' (2014).

Although approximately 10 per cent of the UK population belongs to an ethnic minority group, there is a marked homogeneity among therapists, who are predominantly from the dominant white culture. As a therapist you need to be mindful that your perspectives and beliefs are probably grounded in that culture. It is therefore important that you try to learn about the beliefs of clients from other groups, so that you do not fail to consider issues and questions potentially important for them.

It is worth bearing in mind that the dominance of a western perspective in CBT is not limited to therapists, but it is often shared with the society in which we practise. It is easy to take for granted the emphasis on the autonomy of the individual rather than on the value of collectivism, or on assertiveness rather than on compromise or subjugation of one's own needs; but if you are working with someone from a different cultural group, then you need to be aware that they may hold different views, which would be supported by others in their community although they may vary from yours. It is especially important that you are aware of your own blind spots and areas of prejudice. For example, is the trouble at work, which your client is describing, an accurate description of racism, rather than the distorted thinking that you were planning to guide him through? Is this woman's submissive attitude towards her family a reflection of cultural norms rather than low self-esteem?

There are many ways of gaining information about different cultures. There are an enormous number of books about ethnic and cultural minority groups (Hays, 2006, gives an extensive bibliography), but there are many other ways to gain relevant knowledge, for example:

- read newsletters and suchlike from the groups themselves;
- seek supervision from someone from the relevant group;
- attend cultural celebrations and other events organised by different communities;
- read the historical accounts of the arrival and integration of any ethnic groups, and about legal decisions concerning them.

The dominant cultural message will otherwise colour our understanding of the experiences of members of other groups, and we shall maintain our ignorance of how it is for them.

Is it worth the effort? There is disappointingly little research about the efficacy of CBT with groups other than western white ones, but there is a growing body of evidence about how cross-cultural competence in the therapist may facilitate psychotherapy and improve assessment (Hays, 2006). We will first consider issues of engagement at the assessment stage, and then go on to think about more general ideas about modifying CBT for use in different client groups.

ENGAGING YOUR CLIENT

During an assessment, it is essential that you begin to engage your client. An important bridge in building a good working relationship is demonstrating your respect for his culture. If you bear in mind that the dominant culture will often by implication denigrate alternative views of the world, it will be apparent that you need to pay explicit attention to, and genuinely value, the positive aspects of the different culture; this could be, for example, spirituality, sense of humour, or the involvement of children in family events within the group.

Acknowledgement of the environmental setting in which the client finds himself will contribute to this. Your client's problems may present in an adverse environmental setting (e.g. poor housing or difficulties accessing benefits), but there may also be positive features (e.g. an active church/mosque or community facility) which you should overtly note. Interpersonal supports may be very strong, and different from those in the dominant culture; or there may be an important extended family, possibly including aunts and uncles from a broader base than blood relatives, whose views about, and response to, his problem may be more important in its maintenance than would be typical in the dominant culture. Furthermore, if the client has a positive racial or ethnic identity, this is often associated with positive self-esteem, lower levels of loneliness, anxiety and depression, and improved mastery, optimism and coping, and this may be worth including in the formulation if it is indeed an asset for your client.

On the other hand, distress caused by racism and discrimination figures highly in the reasons that people from minority groups seek help (see e.g. Kelly, 2006), and may also contribute to low self-esteem. It is therefore important to acknowledge what the experiences are, and not to assume that the distress is a result of distorted perception or other cognitive error. As far as your working alliance is concerned, your client's previous experiences may, for example, result in her being reluctant to see a white therapist or a male therapist or in being hostile if she does; acknowledging this as an understandable position may be a necessary step in forming a working alliance.

It is also important to understand how the client's background will have been crucial in the development and maintenance of assumptions and beliefs: for example, the client's beliefs about the importance of personal privacy as opposed to the value of openness about one's feelings may be shared by most people in his community.

Clearly, no ethnic or other minority group is homogeneous, and the idiosyncratic experiences and beliefs of the individual are as important as for people of the dominant culture. For example, skin colour may partly determine the kind of racism suffered by someone, but may also contribute to self-esteem and status within the minority group. More specific experiences of discriminatory behaviour may account for beliefs that have a direct impact on therapy: for example, a woman may repeatedly turn up late for sessions because she believes that the therapist would not hesitate to keep her waiting as others do; a man might be reluctant to fully discuss his sexuality because professionals have ridiculed or dismissed him in the past and now he expects this.

An important dimension to consider with someone from an ethnic minority group is acculturation, the extent to which the client has adopted the dominant culture (including beliefs about self and the world), or remains within his indigenous culture. It is as important as ever, throughout the assessment, to listen to the idiosyncratic detail of what the client is reporting, and not to be blinkered by pre-conceived beliefs of your own.

It is helpful to be open about the issues of race/ethnicity/minority status. Questions like 'Are there aspects of your race and culture that are important for me to know in order for us to work together?' or 'Are there any religious or spiritual beliefs that are important for you to tell me about?' can demonstrate your interest and potential respect.

The client's understanding of the nature of his problem and what he expects of the therapeutic relationship may be different from yours, and ways of modifying how you work with this will now be considered.

WAYS OF MODIFYING CBT

ENHANCING THE THERAPEUTIC RELATIONSHIP

Many of the distinctive characteristics of CBT mean that it is easily generalisable to clients from different cultures and backgrounds, and it allows a good working relationship to be maintained. For example, CBT aims to adopt a non-judgemental stance; there is an emphasis on tailoring treatment to the individual; it is a collaborative approach where the client's perspectives on and knowledge about his problems are respected and valued; and it aims to be empowering and to equip the client with transferable skills.

However, in working with diversity, it is important that the therapist demonstrate her credibility for the client. This can partly be achieved by showing respect for the client and his culture or sub-culture, but it will also be useful to demonstrate that she has something to offer – which may mean that it is important that she begins to work on a goal where a good outcome could be quickly expected.

Having a therapist who validates their experiences will help clients maintain a good working relationship, and may reduce the high drop-out rate which may otherwise bedevil working with minority groups (Hays & Iwamasa, 2006). It is therefore important, for example, not to discount reports of discrimination as necessarily distorted, whether arising from ethnicity, sexuality, physical disability or other group difference. By the same token, by developing a genuine curiosity about the value of differences between groups, you will be showing respect for the other culture, and increasing the strength of your relationship.

DEALING WITH DIFFERENT BELIEF SYSTEMS

Although CBT is generalisable to other cultural groups, there are no grounds for complacency; there are limitations in the approach. CBT is non-judgemental as long as the therapist is aware of the frames of reference that he is operating in, and is not blind to his own underlying beliefs. For example, the approach is predicated on empiricism and rationality, which implicitly devalues the spirituality that may be central to the world view of other groups. However, as idiosyncratic beliefs about oneself and the world have primacy within CBT, it should be ideally placed for working across cultural boundaries.

When a client and therapist have different beliefs about the nature of the problem, it is helpful to acknowledge the differences, and if possible work with the CBT model in parallel with the client's model, hopefully demonstrating the usefulness of the CBT approach.

An Asian man who was highly educated and had lived in UK for 25 years presented with reduced motivation and enjoyment, social withdrawal, inactivity, neglect of himself and his work, and self-criticism and hopelessness. Although he had been diagnosed as depressed, he did not agree with this diagnosis, and would not take medication. He believed that the problem was that he had fallen out of love with his wife of 20 years, and that without a woman behind him, life had no meaning and he could have no motivation. This understanding of the problem was shared by his uncle and a friend, and so appeared to be culturally acceptable.

It was agreed with the therapist that he would work on increasing his social activity, and on pleasure and enjoyment of everyday activities, in order to improve his chances of finding a new partner. The therapist explained that in CBT terms this approach might lead to improvement in his mood and level of motivation. As his social activity improved, his general level of activity increased. Time was also spent on identifying NATs about being unable to initiate action on his own behalf, and he reported that he was feeling better in himself. It was important for the therapist to give the client's theory the benefit of the doubt, and to try to test out its usefulness using a well-developed CBT strategy.

Similarly, in clients who present with somatic complaints, it can be helpful to adopt a two-stage approach, where the focus in the first stage is on the presenting physical symptoms. When you have a clear understanding of the nature of the problem, you can move on to stage two, which involves linking the physical complaint to the other three systems familiar in CBT – emotions, cognitions and behaviour. Naeem, Phiri, Rathod and Kingdon (2010) described this approach with a woman who had headaches: once the therapist had made it clear in the first two sessions that he understood the nature of the headache, he then linked it to the emotional and physiological changes that can be associated with headaches, and how they might be tackled, for example using relaxation.

In addition to differences in belief about the nature of the problem, the same can be true of beliefs about the therapeutic process and relationship. For example, be aware that some cognitive biases, such as 'all or nothing' thinking, or perfectionism, may be unfamiliar to your client. As usual, check out with your client whether you are making sense and whether what you are doing fits with his experience.

Some may find the collaborative nature of the therapeutic relationship surprising and unwelcome, and may expect (and prefer) the therapist as expert. Asking questions, or challenging you (as a perceived authority figure), may be unacceptable in some cultural groups, and you may need to take special care when trying to get feedback, or to find out if the formulation or homework makes sense. You can in this instance ask positive questions, such as 'What did you find helpful about today?', 'Are there particular things that you would like to focus on more?', which do not imply criticism of the therapist. The more general point is that it is important to look out for any ruptures in the therapeutic relationship, and to bear in mind that a belief about the therapeutic process may be implicated.

PRACTICAL DIFFICULTIES

At a more concrete level, there are a number of practical difficulties that may interfere with psychotherapeutic effectiveness. These include ones relating to language and literacy, non-verbal social behaviours and the need for interpreters.

As CBT relies so heavily on unpicking the meaning of experiences, it is crucially important that differences in language between client and therapist, and their relation to experience, do not lead to misunderstanding. The ways in which concepts relate to each other differ from language to language, and the straightforward translation of ideas might not be possible. For example, the Greek language has three different words for love (sexual love, brotherly love and unconditional love), which are less finely differentiated in English (Iwamasa, Hsia & Hays, 2006). It is particularly important therefore to check out with your client that you seem to have understood what was being said. The preference for using the client's own words when summarising what she has said is therefore particularly germane in cross-cultural work.

It may sometimes be necessary to involve an interpreter in therapy sessions, though this merits careful consideration.

Ana could get by with lip reading but she wanted to do more than just 'get by' in therapy and so she secured funding for an interpreter. Her therapist thought this a good idea; he encouraged Ana and said that he would happily accommodate another person in the session. He thought that this was all that would be necessary. Shockingly quickly the quality of therapy suffered because he had not spent time with Ana discussing the implications of involving an interpreter. All too late he discovered that it was customary to have two, not one, interpreters (and this made the office uncomfortable), that the interpreters were not dedicated to Ana and sometimes changed; that they had little psychological briefing so they struggled to grasp and share some of the concepts and they were sometimes visibly upset by the content of the session. The therapist had not considered the practicality of additional time being necessary because the signed conversation had to be repeated verbally and vice versa. He repeatedly forgot to look at Ana when he spoke, instead turning to the interpreters who then felt awkward having to re-direct him to address Ana. What had seemed like a brilliant and simple solution to Ana's difficulties in using therapy had resulted in poor treatment.

It is easy to fall into some of these traps and by way of guiding us through them, Ardenne and Farmer (2009) recommend that any of us working via interpreters ensure the following:

- The interpreter is sufficiently psychologically minded to provide a psychological interface between therapist and client.
- There is opportunity for minimal training in CBT working, for example to clarify that summaries, as opposed to a more detailed translation of what the client has said, are not adequate.
- Protection for the interpreter from vicarious traumatisation/despair.

- Acceptability of the interpreter to the client. This can be an issue if there are few people locally who speak the client's language, but care should be taken to establish acceptability, particularly if a family member, or other known member of the client's community, is being offered as interpreter.
- The interpreter understands the importance of confidentiality.

Reading and writing skills may not be well-developed in some groups, so be creative. For reading, make as much use as possible of translated material, or audio recordings. Mobile phones or digital recorders can be used to record cognitions, and to record sessions. Beads or counters are commonly used in counting in some cultures, and may be more familiar than a knitting or golf counter for monitoring intrusive thoughts, for example. You may find that your client is more familiar with new technology than you are, so do not be reluctant to suggest cutting-edge strategies, but ask for his help when devising measures or homework aids.

Non-verbal and social behaviours differ between groups, and it would be worthwhile becoming familiar with typical behaviours if you were working frequently with one cultural group. For example, smiling can have very different meanings in different groups.

There are suggestions for reading some more detailed material at the end of the chapter, which gives specific information about different ethnic minority groups. The most important sources of information, however, probably lie in your local communities.

We will now turn to considering issues about boundaries in CBT.

BOUNDARY ISSUES

> [Keep] far from all intentional ill-doings and all seduction, and especially from the pleasures of love with women and men.
>
> The Hippocratic Oath

The relationship between therapist and client is different from other social relationships, and boundary issues need careful and serious consideration in CBT, just as they do in other approaches. Treatment boundaries provide a framework for appropriate roles for the therapist and client, and include structural components – such as where, when and at what cost – as well as what happens in the therapy between the therapist and client. The main governing principles are common to all therapeutic encounters:

- The client's needs must have primacy.
- Gratification of the therapist's needs (beyond professional satisfaction) is excluded from consideration in the therapeutic setting.

Therapeutic boundaries are set in such a way that the client can:

- feel safe;
- trust the therapist to act in his interest;

- feel free to disclose material of deep personal significance;
- be confident that he understands the therapist.

In addition, the therapist must also feel safe, by ensuring that there are sensible policies about the kinds of referral accepted; assessments include a consideration of risk; and the physical location and arrangement of the clinic/sessions takes account of safety.

The following guidelines for appropriate boundaries within CBT may be useful:

- Refrain from self-seeking or personal gratification.
- Maintain confidentiality unless it involves a significant risk to the safety of the client or others.
- Evaluate the effect of a boundary violation on the client. Rather than adopting an absolute rule like 'never accept a gift', consider the impact of such behaviour on the client and the therapeutic relationship.

A gift of a jar of home-made chutney from one client could mean that a further attempt was being made to identify the therapist as a family friend, while for another it may mean that the client was at last beginning to see himself as an independent adult, equal in the relationship.

- Make choices about boundaries that minimise the risk of harm to the client. This means only departing from ordinary clinical practice when it will clearly benefit the client.

A behavioural experiment with a socially anxious man took place in a coffee shop. Part of the experiment involved complaining that the coffee was too cold. The therapist did the task initially, and as part of this, he had to disclose to the client how self-conscious and anxious he felt. Although that was crossing the more usual boundary re. disclosure of feelings, it was definitely in the interests of the client.

- Do not express opinions about, or otherwise interfere in, aspects of the client's life other than those relevant to the formulation and goals of therapy. If your client sought help for his panic attacks, bear that in mind when he begins to tell you about the way his child's school is dealing with the child's frequent absences – unless it relates to his panic attacks, do not give your advice or opinion, or share similar experiences.
- Seek to increase the client's independence and autonomy, hence increasing his freedom to explore and the choices available to him.

MAINTAINING TREATMENT BOUNDARIES

The therapeutic relationship is non-reciprocal in a number of ways, putting the therapist in a powerful role, even in the relatively collaborative mode of CBT. This non-reciprocity includes:

- extensive self-disclosure by the client, with almost total non-disclosure of significant material by the therapist;
- the emotional neediness of the client, compared with the exclusion of any of the therapist's emotional needs;
- the power attributed to healers in many societies in order for them to reduce suffering and restore health.

Crucially, maintaining appropriate boundaries is the responsibility of the therapist: it is never reasonable to blame the client for infringements. The maintenance of boundaries is unequivocally your responsibility, whatever the behaviour of the client, so it is incumbent on you to seek sufficient supervision and support if you are concerned about boundaries. In rare cases (such as clients with sociopathy) it may be necessary to terminate therapy if the client cannot maintain reasonable boundaries even with coaching and encouragement.

Although the power differential between therapist and client is generally acknowledged, some therapists have felt exploited by their clients. For example, Smith and Fitzpatrick (1995) described reports of clients with severe or borderline personality disorders forming 'special' relationships with their therapists, where contact outside the therapy became established. Some therapists have blamed clients for 'leading' them into flagrant boundary violations. You might find yourself potentially over-involved with, and feeling manipulated by, your client; but you must be alert to this and be prepared to discuss the situation with both the client and other professionals.

It is sometimes argued that the nature of the transference relationship means that the client may seek the fulfilment of needs arising from unresolved conflicts, and that boundaries must therefore be very strictly enforced and contained by the therapist. Transference in this psychoanalytic sense is not part of CBT theory, so although some boundaries are important (as discussed in this section and below), such strict adherence to inflexible boundaries is not necessary in all aspects of therapy. For example, if a client has to postpone a session for some reason, this would usually be accepted by the therapist and would only be considered to be resistance if it happened repeatedly, with no other explanation.

Effective CBT may mean that you need to visit your client at home, possibly at unusual times of the day. For example, a man with obsessional rituals that are preventing him from starting the day may need visiting first thing in the morning. Do not undertake this lightly. Consider whether you should put safeguards in place to reduce the possibility of misinterpretations of your behaviour: for example, an assistant could be taken along for a home visit or a relative included in the setting-up of the session.

You might need to accompany clients into a range of everyday situations, for example in order to do behavioural experiments. Personal feelings may even be disclosed, *if this is appropriate* to the ongoing task.

A socially anxious man had fears about sweating heavily, particularly in cafés and bars with bright lights. The therapist arranged to have a couple of treatment sessions in a bright café. The therapist wet his face, his back and armpits to look as though he was sweating heavily, and the anxious man sat nearby, observing the responses of the waitress and other people to the therapist. The client then asked the therapist what thoughts were going through his head, and how he felt in the situation.

It is helpful to make the aims of such sessions very explicit, by spending time agreeing what predictions are being tested out, how the experiment will be carried out and so on (see Chapter 9). This makes good technical sense and it also sets boundaries for the session, making it clear that this is a treatment session with a specific purpose, and not a social event. This can be difficult for some clients to understand, especially if the therapist contact is the only social event of the week.

A woman with obsessional problems was finding it difficult to test out the effects of exposure and response prevention on her fears of pushing people off the pavement into the path of cars. The therapist and client therefore spent two lengthy sessions walking in crowded streets, busy with cars. Although they planned what specific 'tasks' she should do as they walked along, and discussed changes in her distress level as she walked past people near the edge of the pavement, they nevertheless had quite long periods of time when they were not specifically addressing the problem. The therapist then discussed general topics of a non-emotional and relatively non-personal nature, like annual holidays, but continued to be mindful of the nature of any disclosure and its possible impact on the client.

Finally, the open, collaborative style of CBT can sometimes be compromised if the therapist is involved in a compulsory admission to an institution. The repercussions can be minimised if you discuss it openly with the client, including what it meant to him, and any associated misperceptions, either beforehand or after the crisis has resolved.

KINDS OF BOUNDARY VIOLATION

Although there is a continuum of boundary violations, *any* straying over boundaries should be done in awareness of the principles sketched out earlier in this chapter. There are particular kinds of violation that are worth specific consideration, namely dual relationships, self-disclosure, non-sexual physical contact and sexual relationships, which are discussed in detail below.

Dual relationships, where the therapist and client are in a second relationship in addition to the therapeutic one: for example, being school governors together. Although therapists are usually advised against such dual relationships, it is sometimes difficult to avoid them. If a therapist lives in a small community, for example a rural setting or an academic group, then barring her from treating all those with whom she had an existing relationship might mean that they have no access to treatment at all. Similarly, if you are involved in groups related to your political, religious, ethnic or sexual identity, then dual relationships may be inevitable as people tend to seek out a therapist with similar values to themselves. In addition, despite ethical guidelines prohibiting dual relationships for therapists, it is not uncommon for therapists to accept invitations to, for example, a client's special event.

It may be possible to differentiate those dual relationships that are harmful to the client or therapy from those that are innocuous. Gottlieb (1993) suggested that the therapist should consider the other (non-therapeutic) relationship along three dimensions – power, duration and whether the other relationship had a planned finite end – with risk to the client increasing with augmenting values on any of the three dimensions. You should be mindful of such factors before entering into a dual relationship.

A therapist decided to join the only choir in her small local town, even though she knew that a current client was in the choir. This meant that the client would see her with her friends, possibly being picked up by her husband, and with opportunities for casual interactions in the 10 weeks that the choir was planned to rehearse. This was deemed to be acceptable, given there was no other choir available and that the therapist was a musical enthusiast. It would probably not have been acceptable had the client been the conductor, for example, where role reversal could have become an issue.

Self-disclosure would almost always be seen as inappropriate in psychodynamic therapy or counselling, but there is a less rigidly drawn line within CBT. Self-disclosure can be useful if it is done with the client's interests in mind. For example, a therapist could disclose information about a past problem of her own that she had overcome, in order to increase the client's hope for improvement and confidence in the proposed method. Beck et al. (1979) suggested that it may be appropriate to use self-disclosure with the more severely depressed, as this may facilitate their engagement in treatment. It would probably never be helpful to describe current problems, whether psychological or financial, social or sexual, to a client: he can reasonably expect that the focus should be on his own problems.

It may sometimes be necessary to disclose personal details to a client (e.g. illness in the therapist or her family, or pregnancy) if the circumstances are likely to have an impact on the delivery of treatment. But judgements of this kind may be less clear-cut than they seem, and you should make use of supervision if you have concerns about sharing such information.

A young woman in her twenties was discussing whether to try to forgive her emotionally abusive mother. Her therapist had been recently bereaved, and was grieving for the close supportive relationship that she had had with her own mother. In the course of the session, the client said to the therapist, 'I feel that you really want me to make moves towards my mother', and the therapist became aware that she had too much emotional involvement in the client achieving that closeness for herself. Supervision confirmed that disclosure would not be in the client's interest, as the therapist's own issues were not resolved.

Non-sexual physical contact may feel comfortable to some therapists, who would give a distressed or frightened client a reassuring pat, but they may still confine this to clients of the same gender as themselves. However, never underestimate the potential for clients to misinterpret such actions. Departures from normal practice should not be made casually – always be aware and mindful of your client's formulation. For example, a touch on the arm could be alarming to someone with a history of abuse, who has rules about maintaining her distance from people; while a gentle pat could be misinterpreted as sexual by a client longing for physical closeness to another person, especially someone showing unconditional warmth and empathy. A useful way to deal with this is to find a time when your client is calm and to ask him how he would like you to react when he is highly distressed. For example, you could say 'You were obviously very distressed when we were talking earlier. I wonder how I could be most help at times like that? Some people like to simply express the feelings, and to deal with it themselves; others may find a pat on the hand or arm comforting. Some people ask for a hug, although that is something that I don't do as a therapist. Can we talk through how you might like me to respond? Is there any particular way you would like me to react?'

Obviously such discussion must be constrained by what you feel is right for your own therapeutic boundaries.

Pope, Tabachnick and Keith-Spiegel (1987) reviewed three kinds of physical contact between therapists and clients and found that a sizeable minority of therapists had experience of each kind of touching. According to a survey of therapists, the least unacceptable was shaking hands with the client; that was practised often by 76 per cent of therapists and was generally seen as ethically acceptable. Hugging was considered acceptable in some circumstances by 44 per cent, but was only practised regularly by 12 per cent. Kissing was seen as unacceptable or rarely acceptable by 85 per cent of therapists, and was practised only infrequently by 24 per cent and never at all by 71 per cent.

The distinction between erotic and non-erotic physical contact falls along a continuum: it is not 'all or nothing'. Cultural influences are relevant here: in many European and South American cultures, kissing on both cheeks is a customary form of greeting and may be only rarely interpreted as erotic, even in a therapy situation. Holding back from kissing could be seen by some clients as distant and aloof. In other words, the therapist has to draw boundaries flexibly and sensitively and cannot simply use rules about proscribed behaviour.

Sexual relationships between therapist and client are the most harmful kind of boundary violation, with possible negative impacts on vulnerable individuals, as well as damage to the therapeutic relationship. It is difficult to get data on the frequency of such behaviour, and estimates of the number of therapists who have had sexual intercourse with at least one client range from 1 per cent to 12 per cent, but these are likely to be underestimates because of the compelling reasons for therapists to conceal the behaviour. There is an extensive literature on the harmful effects on clients of such boundary transgressions (Pope & Bouhoutsos, 1986), and some authors have suggested that in such cases the therapist should be charged with rape, since the client could not be capable of informed consent within that relationship.

Therapists who engage in sexual behaviour with clients tend to gradually blur boundaries rather than suddenly descend into inappropriate behaviour. Inappropriate self-disclosure, rather than other boundary violations, tends to precede sexual transgressions (Simon, 1991). Sexual violation of boundaries appears to be more common among middle-aged male therapists who are professionally isolated and currently experiencing personal problems, often including marital problems. They typically begin to cross appropriate boundaries by discussing their own problems with younger, female clients (Gabbard, 1991).

It is therefore incumbent on you as therapist to be aware of any gradual change in boundaries with any particular client, and to raise this with your supervisor if it seems that your relationship may be subtly changing. It may seem that your client's needs may be best met via a relationship different from a typical clinical one, but in that case, discuss it openly with your supervisor, to protect both yourself from allegations by a client who may possibly misinterpret your motivation, and your client from possible abuse. Another sensible rule is that in situations where there is a grey area, it is probably in the interests of both client and therapist to err on the side of caution.

SUMMARY

A good working alliance between you and your client is an essential component of successful CBT, without which the sophisticated models of CBT would be irrelevant. The following principles are useful:

- Establish a good relationship early in therapy, then be aware of the quality of the relationship throughout treatment, and attend to any developing problems between you and your client.
- The therapeutic relationship can be seen as a laboratory where problems can be worked on.
- Many of the cardinal features of CBT, such as collaboration, active participation, use of guided discovery and so on, contribute to the development of a good working relationship.
- The therapist's role in CBT is to be a guide, who is genuinely curious and respectful about the client's perspectives, aiming to broaden the range of possibilities open to him.

- The Rogerian characteristics that typify good therapy in other approaches are equally important in CBT.
- If there are disruptions in the therapeutic relationship, these are construed in cognitive behavioural terms, and dealt with in the here and now, in terms of the immediate situation; only if this is unsuccessful is the disruption dealt with as a more enduring characteristic.
- Consider your own possible contribution to a breakdown in the relationship with our client.

When working with clients from different cultural backgrounds:

- Remember that your perspectives on events are likely to be grounded in the dominant culture, and different from those of other groups.
- Find out about the different groups with whom you work.
- Be aware of your blind spots as far as your beliefs are concerned.
- Focus on engagement and developing a good therapeutic alliance with an emphasis on:
  - showing respect for your client's culture;
  - acknowledging the difficulties he may face through discrimination;
  - being open about issues to do with race/minority status.

In order to work cognitive behaviourally with different groups:

- Remember that CBT translates well to different belief systems.
- Demonstrate your credibility early on.
- Acknowledge if there are differences in belief about the nature of the client's problems.
- Be aware that there may be differences in beliefs about the therapeutic relationship, and also about cognitive processes.

There may be practical difficulties, for example in language and literacy, which may need to be creatively tackled.

Boundary issues need careful consideration in CBT, particularly as clinical contact may be in unusual places, at unusual times. The major principle is that the client's needs are of prime importance.

- Three specific boundary issues were considered. These were:
  - dual relationships;
  - self-disclosure;
  - physical contact.

Make use of supervision if you are concerned about a boundary issue.

LEARNING EXERCISES

These learning exercises are available to download from the companion website.

REVIEW AND REFLECTION:

- What are your reactions to reading about the therapeutic relationship in CBT? Are you surprised or reassured by anything you have read?
- If you have worked in other ways, in what ways do you behave differently in CBT therapy compared with your work in other modalities? In what ways are there similarities? In what ways would it be helpful to change?
- If you notice a disruption in your relationship with a client, what physiological or cognitive cues in yourself alerted you to it?
- Do you feel that you are responsive enough to diversity and difference in your clients? If not, what steps could you take to remedy this?

TAKING IT FORWARD:

- Find a client who is not very actively engaged in the session, for example, frequently responding 'I don't know'. Think about the pros and cons of commenting directly on this, as opposed to trying to encourage him to be more active, without explicitly addressing the issue. Try to explicitly follow up the issue of inactivity, in order to test out whether the pros and cons that you listed were relevant.
- Find a client with whom you feel that boundaries are an issue. Reflect on the ways in which they are being stretched, and on what has contributed to the difficulties in maintaining more typical boundaries. Discuss this in your supervision.
- When you are working with someone who has a culturally different background from you, ensure that your formulation truly reflects your client's inner world and is not biased by prejudices that you might have.
- If this chapter has raised issues for you, discuss them with your supervisor.

FURTHER READING

Beck, A.T., Rush, A.J., Shaw, B.F., & Emery, G. (1979). *Cognitive therapy of depression*. New York: Guilford Press.

This classic text describes clearly a style of therapeutic relationship which, as they say, facilitates effective treatment.

Gilbert, P., & Leahy, R. (Eds.). (2007). *The therapeutic relationship in the cognitive behavioural psychotherapies*. Hove: Routledge.

The most comprehensive collection of CBT views on the therapeutic relationship.

Hays, P.A., & Iwamasa, G.Y. (Eds.). (2006). *Culturally responsive cognitive behaviour therapy: assessment, practice and supervision*. Washington, DC: American Psychological Association.

This book has detailed advice about working with different cultural groups. All of the examples are American, but they give a good feel for the dimensions of difference.

Safran, J.D., & Segal, Z.V. (1990). *Interpersonal process in cognitive therapy*. New York: Basic Books.

An interesting book with interesting ideas about addressing difficulties in the therapeutic relationship.

Padesky, C.A., & Greenberger, D. (1995). *Clinician's guide to mind over mood*. New York: Guilford Press.

This book has some specific ideas on working with minority groups of different kinds.

El-Leithy, S. (2014). Working with diversity in CBT. In A. Wittington & N. Grey (Eds.), *How to become a more effective CBT therapist: mastering metacompetence in clinical practice*. Chichester: Wiley

This is an excellent chapter, giving a contemporary overview of working with diversity in CBT and refers the reader to several very useful source references.

VIDEO LINKS

- **3.1 Setting the scene and engaging your client**
- **3.2 Dealing with signs of problems in the therapeutic relationship**
- **3.3 Presenting the therapist dilemma: a simple issue (i)**
- **3.4 Presenting the therapist dilemma: a more complex issue (ii)**

4

ASSESSMENT AND FORMULATION

- **Introduction**
- **Formulation in CBT**
- **Formulation: art or science?**
- **Focus on maintenance processes**
- **The process of assessment**
- **Assessing current problems**
- **Maintaining processes**
- **Assessing past history and problem development**
- **The order of assessment components**
- **'Non-specific' factors and the therapeutic relationship**
- **Making formulations**
- **Sample formulation**
- **Suitability for CBT**
- **Setting the scene for the assessment**
- **Possible problems during assessment**
- **Possible problems in making formulations**
- **Summary**
- **Learning exercises**
- **Further reading**
- **Video links**
  - **4.1 Exploring the client's fear**
  - **4.2 Modifiers**
  - **4.3 Getting more detailed information**
  - **4.4 Teamwork in conceptualisation**
  - **4.5 'Blobby' formulation**
  - **4.6 Vicious flower formulation**

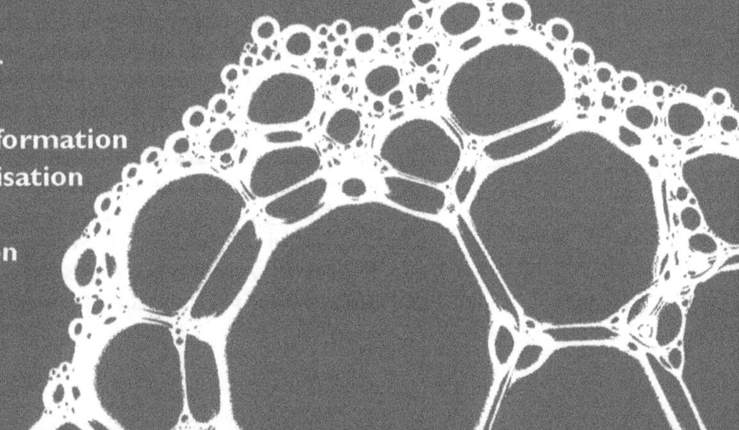

INTRODUCTION

Central to the successful use of CBT is developing a *formulation* (sometimes known as a *case conceptualisation*): an individualised picture that helps us to understand and explain a person's problems. This chapter describes the role of formulations, the assessment process that is used to develop them, how to construct formulations and some of the common pitfalls in this phase of treatment.

FORMULATION IN CBT

Definitions and approaches differ, and there is no one 'correct' way of devising formulations (see e.g. Persons, 1989; Bruch & Bond, 1998; Butler, 1998; Kuyken, Padesky & Dudley, 2009). However, most approaches share core features (Bieling & Kuyken, 2003).

Our working definition of a CBT formulation is that a CBT formulation uses the CBT model to develop:

- a description of the current problem(s);
- an account of why and how these problems might have developed;
- an analysis of the key maintaining processes hypothesised to keep the problems going.

There are a number of the benefits of making a formulation like this:

- The formulation helps both client and therapist understand the problems, so that what may present as a baffling collection of random symptoms moves from chaotic confusion to something that *makes sense*. This process can begin to combat the demoralisation that is common in clients at initial presentation (and sometimes in therapists, when faced with difficult and complex problems).
- The formulation acts as a bridge between CBT theories about problem development and maintenance and the individual client's experience. It is 'the lynch pin that holds theory and practice together' (Butler, 1998). CBT theories are necessarily pitched at a general level: they describe typical clients who have panic attacks, or depression, or whatever; and they describe the processes involved in each disorder in general terms and at a somewhat abstract level – as is appropriate for scientific theories. But to apply those theories to an individual in a clinical setting, we need to move from these generalisations to the specific experience of *this* person in front of us. One important function of the formulation is to bridge this gap.
- The formulation provides a shared rationale and guide for the therapy that may follow. If we have a reasonable understanding of the processes causing and maintaining problems, then we can more easily see what interventions might be useful to overcome them. A good formulation therefore makes it easy to establish what therapy needs to do, at least in broad terms, and helps clients understand why particular strategies may be useful.

- The formulation begins the process of opening up new ways of thinking – a key part of CBT – by giving clients a different way of understanding their symptoms. Many come to the initial assessment with a view of their problems which is either threatening, or self-critical, or both. For example, in OCD, clients often see the fact that they have unpleasant thoughts as meaning that they must be evil or immoral; or in health anxiety, they may see bodily symptoms as indicating that they are seriously ill. The process of constructing a formulation can be a first step in combating hopelessness, considering alternative views of the symptoms, and this can free clients to see different ways of tackling them.
- The formulation can help the therapist to understand, or even predict, difficulties in therapy or in the therapeutic relationship. For example, if low self-esteem and self-critical thoughts are important elements in the formulation, we can predict that this client may have difficulties in doing homework, because he will be worrying about not doing it 'well enough' or worrying that the therapist will disapprove of his thoughts. By taking account of such predictions from the formulation, we may be able to avoid difficulties or manage them better.

FORMULATION: ART OR SCIENCE?

Although the benefits described above might seem obvious, the scientific status of formulation in CBT is actually far from clear. For example, there is a relative lack of research evidence indicating whether formulations are reliable, that is, whether different therapists agree on a formulation for the same client (Bieling & Kuyken, 2003); there is also little evidence about whether treatment based on formulation is more effective than purely protocol-driven therapy (i.e. therapy given in a standardised way so that all clients with a particular problem get essentially the same treatment). In fact, there is one fascinating study which suggests that BT based on an individual formulation may sometimes result in worse outcomes than completely standardised therapy (Schulte, Kuenzel, Pepping & Schulte, 1992), although a later study found some evidence of superiority for CBT based on an individual formulation in bulimia nervosa (Ghaderi, 2006). It is not our intention to explore these controversies in detail, but we think it is worth describing our position on some of them.

First, as noted above, one of the roles of formulation is to act as a bridge between CBT theories and the experience of an individual. In fulfilling this role, it seems to us inevitable that the process of formulation lies somewhere in the no man's land between science and art (or at least craft). On the one hand, we are attempting to use empirically validated and evidence-based CBT models, derived using scientific principles, to help people. On the other hand, we have to apply these theories to the unique individuals with whom we are working, and we therefore need to work with their idiosyncratic thoughts and feelings. Such a process cannot be completely described in objective and generalisable terms: the ideal formulation is not just 'true' in a scientific sense, it must also 'make sense' to the client at the level of subjective meaning – and that is a task which involves as much craft as science.

Second, even the most rigid treatment protocol needs some individualising: no treatment manual can or should prescribe the therapist's every word. There is, therefore, a need to translate general guidelines into what is appropriate for *this* client at *this* time, which is one of the roles of the formulation.

Third, clinical practice inevitably brings us clients who do not 'fit' the models, those for whom an intervention according to the protocol does not work, or clients for whom there simply is no clearly recommended protocol (either from CBT or any other form of treatment). In such instances, the only thing we can do – other than giving up – is to build an individual formulation and develop a course of therapy based on that formulation.

Our view is, therefore, that CBT practitioners should start by assessing the problem of the person in front of them, then to see whether there is some well-established treatment model that 'fits' their presentation and a protocol that has been shown to be effective for that particular difficulty. If there is, this model should be used to inform the formulation and the protocol used as a basis for treatment. *However*, protocols should always be applied within the framework of a formulation that can guide its application to the individual client, and therapists also need to know when to leave the protocols behind and develop an idiosyncratic treatment plan. An individual formulation is the best tool we have for achieving both those ends.

FOCUS ON MAINTENANCE PROCESSES

The main focus for CBT formulations and treatment plans is usually on current maintenance processes. Several linked beliefs contribute to this focus:

- The processes that start a problem are not necessarily the same as the processes that keep it going. Once a problem has begun, maintenance processes can take on a life of their own and maintain a problem, even if the original cause has long since disappeared.
- It is generally easier to get clear evidence about current processes than it is about original causes, which may have happened many years ago.
- It is easier to change maintenance processes that are happening here and now than to change developmental processes, which by definition are in the past. In any case, if past events are indeed still having important effects, then they must be doing so through some current psychological process and so they will be addressed.

Thus, the main focus of CBT, most of the time, tends to be on the here and now, and the main focus of assessment and formulation tends to be the same. A client described the key role of maintenance processes versus original causes to one of the authors thus:

Imagine you're walking along a crumbly and unstable cliff-top. Whilst you're walking near the edge, a seagull flies down and lands near to your feet, and the weight of the seagull is enough to make the edge of the cliff crumble. You fall over the edge, but you just manage to grab on to a branch 20 feet down, so you're left hanging there, clinging to the branch. Now if you're dangling there, and you want to get out of this situation and get safely back up to the top of the cliff ... then it's no use looking for the seagull!

A more prosaic analogy which makes the same point is that if you want to put out a fire then you had better tackle what keeps it going (heat, fuel, oxygen, etc.) rather than look for the match that started it.

This is not to say that history or development are irrelevant. We are talking about what is *usually* the *main* focus of CBT, not about what is *always* the *only* focus. There are several reasons why developmental history can be important:

- Information about the past is essential if one is to answer the question 'How did I get here?', which is often important to clients. They want some understanding of what led to their problems, and we should help them achieve that goal (although not always possible in practice – sometimes the developmental causes of a problem remain mysterious despite our best efforts).
- It may be useful to identify original causes in order to prevent their operating again in the future. Following the analogy above, once the fire is out then it may well be a good idea to find out where the match came from, so that we can avoid future fires from the same cause.
- There are some difficulties where an important part of the problem is inherently about the past. PTSD, or the consequences of childhood trauma, are obvious examples where it is clear that past events might need to be a focus of therapy. When 'schema-focused' therapy is used (e.g. with people with personality disorders or other complex problems), then the past is often closely reviewed. But even in these applications of CBT, the main focus is often on how the past is operating in the present.

Thus, CBT assessment and therapy neither can, nor should *exclude* the exploration of past events and their implications, but the main focus is typically more biased towards the present than the past, and towards specific examples rather than general rules.

THE PROCESS OF ASSESSMENT

The aim of CBT assessment is primarily to arrive at a formulation which is agreed as satisfactory by both client and therapist, and which will serve the purposes outlined above.[1] Assessment within this framework is not a simple matter of ticking off a checklist

[1] Of course, in many service contexts an assessment may have other, more generic, purposes as well, such as risk assessment, establishing urgency, or screening for particular treatments. However, here we emphasise a typical CBT assessment, which has the goal of devising a CBT formulation.

of symptoms or completing a standard life history. Rather, it is an active and flexible process of repeatedly building and testing hypotheses.

The therapist is constantly trying to make sense of information from the client, and he builds up tentative ideas (hypotheses) about what processes might be important in the formulation. He asks further questions to test these hypotheses. If the client's responses seem to support a hypothesis, it may become part of the formulation; if not, then it will need to be modified and explored further. This process continues until the therapist feels that there is enough of a formulation – enough of an understanding of the problem – to begin discussing it with the client. This might begin as a modest understanding, but one which gradually builds into something more complex. For example, preliminary discussions might begin with outlining simple maintaining patterns:

- 'So when you get anxious, you get light-headed and this makes you even more anxious?'
- 'It sounds as if you do less when your mood is low and that this can make you feel even more miserable.'

Eventually, more detail (more hypotheses) will furnish the formulation and a more comprehensive working draft will be agreed. This might capture the origin and the trigger for the problem along with one or more maintaining cycles that embrace cognitive and behavioural elements, for example. But even after that point, further information emerging during treatment may lead to modifications or additions to the formulation. Most of the time such modifications will be minor 'tweaks', but sometimes new information will emerge that demands a significant reformulation of the problem.

Figure 4.1 illustrates this cycle and you can see just how the therapist moves from data gathering to generating hypotheses to testing hypotheses (which is also a point of data gathering) – it really is an active *process*, and this continues throughout therapy. A good formulation is never static.

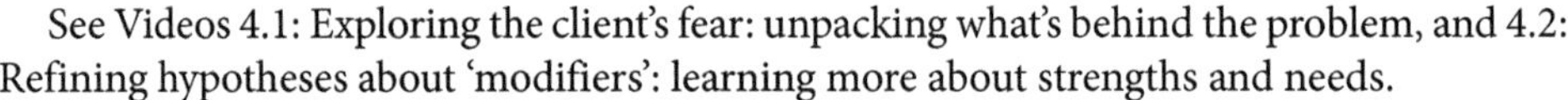

See Videos 4.1: Exploring the client's fear: unpacking what's behind the problem, and 4.2: Refining hypotheses about 'modifiers': learning more about strengths and needs.

ASSESSING CURRENT PROBLEMS

In keeping with the centrality of maintenance processes in CBT, relatively more time tends to be spent on exploring details of current experience than in some other approaches to therapy. This is an aspect of CBT that beginning therapists can find uncomfortable, perhaps partly because it involves an unfamiliar degree of structured questioning. Information about history and problem development may be obtained from a fairly ordinary narrative. However, the kind of information and level of detail about current problems that we need for a CBT formulation cannot usually be obtained without careful, sometimes probing and repetitive, questioning at interview (and perhaps from other sources of information as well, as discussed in the next chapter). Of course it is crucial that you also pay attention to building rapport and a constructive therapeutic relationship (see below).

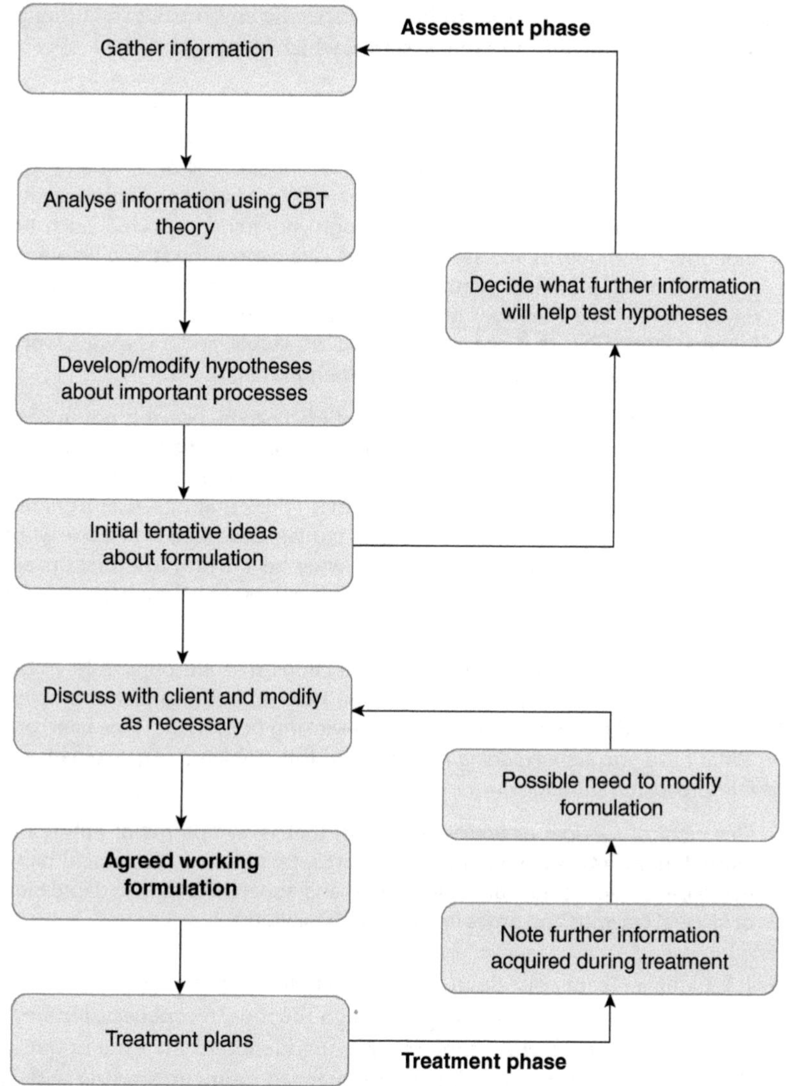

Figure 4.1 The process of assessment

PROBLEM DESCRIPTION

The first step is to develop a description of each aspect of the presenting problem. Your aim is to get a clear picture of its exact nature, at the level of specific patterns of cognitions, behaviour, emotions and so on. Note that a 'problem' in this sense is not a diagnostic label. Terms such as 'depression' or 'social anxiety' may be useful shorthand but are not enough in themselves for our purposes. We need to be more specific and break presenting problems or diagnostic labels into the four 'internal systems', which comprise:

- *Cognitions*: that is, words or images that go through the client's mind when he has the problem. A good question to get at these is 'What goes through your mind when … ?' (e.g. '… when you're feeling anxious' or '… when you're feeling low'). It can also be useful to look out for changes of emotion during a session and to ask 'What went through your mind just now?'. Such 'hot thoughts' (i.e. thoughts accessed whilst they are generating strong emotions) are often much more informative than thoughts reported in calm moments days or weeks later. Thought records as part of homework can also be useful here. Remember that not all cognitions are verbal, and it is always worth checking whether clients have upsetting mental images.
- *Emotions or affect*: that is, the client's emotional experience. It is not uncommon for clients to have difficulty in distinguishing between thoughts and emotions. The distinction is not helped by the fact that in English we often say 'I feel that …' when what we really mean is 'I think that …'. A useful guide is that in general an emotion can be at least crudely described in just one word: 'depressed', 'anxious', 'angry' and so on. If what he is trying to express needs significantly more than one word (e.g. 'I felt that I might have a heart attack'), then it is probably a thought, not an emotion.
- *Behaviour*: that is, what the client does: actions that are outwardly visible. Useful questions to ask are 'What do you now *do* because of the problem which you did not use to do?' (e.g. safety-seeking behaviours – see later) and 'What have you *stopped doing* as a result of the problem?' (e.g. avoidance of fear-provoking situations).
- *Physiological changes or bodily symptoms*: that is, symptoms of autonomic arousal in anxiety, such as increased heart rate, sweating, aches and pains, nausea, and so on; or loss of sexual interest and appetite for food in depression; or visceral cravings and urges in addictive behaviours.

See Video 4.3: Using a recent episode to get more detailed information.

A good strategy is to ask your client to go through the most recent occasion he can recall when he experienced the problem symptoms. Having identified the time in question, you then take him through what happened, from moment to moment, starting with whatever change he first noticed: perhaps a dip in mood, perhaps a worrying physiological symptom, or perhaps a frightening thought. Elicit what happened in each of the four systems: 'What went through your mind when that happened? How did it make you feel? Did you notice any changes in bodily sensations? What did you do? And what was the next thing that happened …' and so on.

As we recognised earlier, there is indeed a 'fifth system', namely the environment. This also merits scrutiny during the assessment of presenting problems as the reactions of others, the stresses of particular domestic circumstances, the pressures of a work or institutional setting can impact on problems.

TRIGGERS AND MODIFYING FACTORS

Another line of enquiry establishes the factors currently affecting the problem, in two areas:

- *Triggers*: what factors make the problem more or less likely to occur.
- *Modifiers*: what contextual factors make a difference to how *severe* the problem is when it does occur.

As a simple example, a spider phobia by definition will be *triggered* by seeing a spider but may also be triggered by seeing pictures of spiders, by seeing anything in the environment that looks even vaguely like a spider, or even by the word 'spider' (some clients make up different terms for spiders because the word itself is so distressing to them). When the phobia is triggered by such situations, the severity of the fear is likely to be *modified* by other factors: for example, the spider's size, length of its legs, its speed, how close it is to the person, whether escape is easy and so on.

Be aware that many factors can operate as triggers or modifiers. Amongst those to consider are:

- *Situational variables*: Are there specific situations, objects or places that make a difference?
- *Social/interpersonal variables*: Are there particular people who make a difference? The number of people around? Particular kinds of people?
- *Cognitive variables*: Are there particular kinds or topics of thought which tend to trigger problems?
- *Behavioural variables*: Does the problem occur when the client or other people are doing specific activities?
- *Physiological variables*: Is the problem affected by taking alcohol or drugs? Are the problems more likely when the person is tense, tired or hungry? Does a woman's menstrual cycle affect the problem?
- *Affective variables*: Is a problem worse when the person is depressed, bored or upset? Some clients may react badly to any kind of strong emotion, even positive emotion, because it makes them feel out of control.

Some clients will respond to this line of questioning by saying that they are *always* anxious or depressed and nothing makes any difference. Although this is how it might feel, this is almost never true. Such responses often arise because a person has become so distressed and overwhelmed by the problem that he has lost the ability to 'step outside' and think about it objectively. Careful, gentle questioning will usually bring out some factors that do make a difference. You can prompt your client to recall and consider various situations in the session and to dwell on them in an attempt to evoke their problem feelings and thoughts. By doing this you might establish that different circumstances promote different reactions. If you feel comfortable in asking it, one question that can offer insights is:

'What situation would be your worst nightmare?' It goes without saying that this question must be timed sensitively, particularly as many clients will have avoided considering this, but by noting what dimensions the client uses to describe this worst situation, you may get clues as to what variables are important. Another useful approach is to use self-monitoring in the session or as homework to spot differences that the client may not recall retrospectively.

Information about triggers and modifiers is useful in two ways. First, it starts to give the therapist helpful clues about possible beliefs and maintaining processes, by considering what themes might lie behind the variables discovered. If someone is especially anxious in situations where his behaviour might be observed by others, perhaps there is some element of fear of negative evaluation; if he is particularly depressed when he perceives others as rejecting him, perhaps there are some beliefs about being unlovable or unworthy. These clues can then prompt further questions that can help to confirm or refute the initial hypotheses. Later chapters will give you ideas about the kind of beliefs that are frequently found in different disorders.

The second benefit of this information is that it can be useful in treatment. It can be used to identify targets for treatment (e.g. if the client feels anxious in restaurants or supermarkets, those might be areas he wants to work on), or to plan interventions (e.g. when planning a behavioural experiment on what happens if the client panics, it is helpful to know that he is more likely to panic in crowded shops and less likely to panic if accompanied by a trusted person).

CONSEQUENCES

The last major area of investigation of the current problems is what happens as a result of them. Consider four main aspects:

- What impact has the problem had on the client's life? How has his life changed because of the problem?
- How have important others (friends, family, doctors, work colleagues, etc.) responded to the problem?
- What coping strategies have been tried, and how successful have they been?
- Are prescribed medications or other substances being used to help him cope?

The first question is important to help us get a picture of what has been lost (or, occasionally, gained) as a result of having the problem. The next questions may give important clues about maintaining processes. Many maintaining processes arise from perfectly reasonable 'common-sense' attempts by the client or others to manage the problem. Unfortunately such responses may sometimes backfire and maintain the problem instead. For instance, it is human nature to avoid or escape from a situation perceived as threatening – indeed, it is an entirely functional response in many situations (e.g. if threatened with physical attack). It just happens that escape and avoidance may also fuel unnecessary fears by denying us the opportunity to learn that we can cope, we can deal with the fear in some situations. Another quite natural response is to ask for (and to give) reassurance in response to worries.

Again it is unfortunate that this can sometimes be at best ineffective and at worst can exacerbate the problem if it stops us from learning to assure ourselves, if it makes us dependent on others. There are many other examples where such natural responses to a problem turn out to be unhelpful in the long run and, in our assessments, we must ask detailed questions to discover the longer-term impact of certain behaviours – the outcome just might be persistence of a problem.

Having said this, we are not suggesting that people are motivated (even unconsciously) to hold on to their problems, it's just that sometimes 'coping' goes awry (see notes on possible problems, below).

Another reason for exploring coping is that sometimes people have developed quite good strategies that we can build on. With a bit of shaping up – perhaps being more consistent or taking things further – these coping attempts can provide effective treatment strategies. It is always worth asking clients what they think helps: often they have good ideas!

MAINTAINING PROCESSES

A crucial focus of assessment and formulation is identifying maintenance patterns: that is, the psychological processes that keep a problem going. These are often in the form of vicious circles, or feedback loops: cycles in which the original cognition, behaviour, affective or physiological response gives rise to effects that ultimately feed back to the original symptom and maintain or even worsen it. In later chapters we will look at some of the specific processes that CBT theories suggest may be important in different disorders. In this section we simply summarise some of the most common vicious circles you will meet repeatedly in many different disorders. This should serve as a guide to some of the things to look for during an assessment.

The concept of safety-seeking behaviours (often simply referred to as 'safety behaviours') has assumed a central place in many current theories of anxiety disorders since it was outlined by Salkovskis (1991). Anxious clients frequently do something that they believe protects them from the threat they fear. For example, someone who fears collapsing in a supermarket may cling tightly on to the shopping trolley so as not to fall over; someone who fears being seen as boring and dislikeable may take care not to reveal anything about himself. People are endlessly inventive, and no matter how many clients you see, you will still encounter safety behaviours that you have never met before. Although this kind of response is easily understandable, it can have an unnoticed and unintended side effect. It blocks the threat beliefs from being disconfirmed, because when nothing happens, the 'lucky escape' is attributed to the success of the safety-seeking behaviour instead of resulting in a decreased perception of threat (see Figure 4.2).

There are several popular stories that illustrate this concept to clients. One concerns a man who comes across a friend standing in the street waving his arms up and down. When he asks the friend what he is doing, the answer is, 'Keeping the dragons away.' 'But there are no dragons around here,' the man replies. To which his friend says, 'See, that's how well it works!'

Stories like this can naturally lead on to therapeutic strategies by helping clients to think about how the dragon-fearing man might learn that actually there are no dragons.

Figure 4.2 Safety-seeking behaviours

Most people will easily come up with the answer that he needs to stop waving his arms so that he can see that there are still no dragons. They can then be asked to consider whether that might have any lessons for their own problems and thus build on the formulation (see also Chapters 13 and 14 on anxiety disorders).

ESCAPE/AVOIDANCE

Avoidance (or escape) can be considered as a particularly common form of safety-seeking behaviour. However, it is worth identifying avoidance separately, partly because of its near-universal prevalence in anxiety problems and partly because its unhelpfulness is immediately clear to clients in a way other safety behaviours may not be. This is perhaps because the notion is part of 'folk psychology', as shown in the advice that if you fall off a horse, the best thing to do is to get straight back on it (see Figure 4.3).

Avoidance is not necessarily as obvious as running away when one meets an anxiety-provoking situation, it can be subtle. For example, someone who gets anxious in social situations might accurately report that he does not avoid such situations. However, careful exploration might reveal that although he talks to people, he never looks them in the eyes, or he never discusses himself, or he busies himself being helpful in checking that other guests have drinks. In other words, he engages in subtle rather than obvious avoidance.

REDUCTION OF ACTIVITY

This maintaining process, illustrated in Figure 4.4, is as common in depression as avoidance is in anxiety. For psychological and neurological reasons, low mood leads to reduced activity, which then leads to the loss of most of what used to give positive feelings such as the pleasure of achievement, purposeful activity or social acceptance. Lack of positive feedback in turn fuels low mood and the cycle closes.

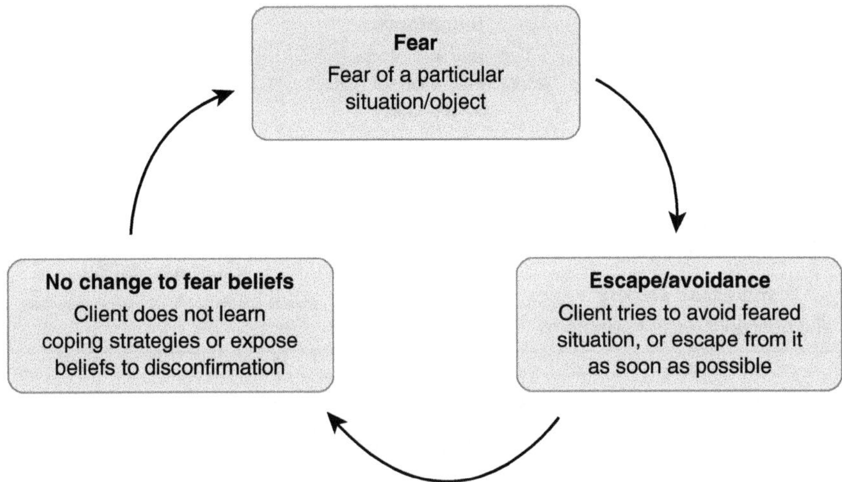

Figure 4.3 Escape/avoidance

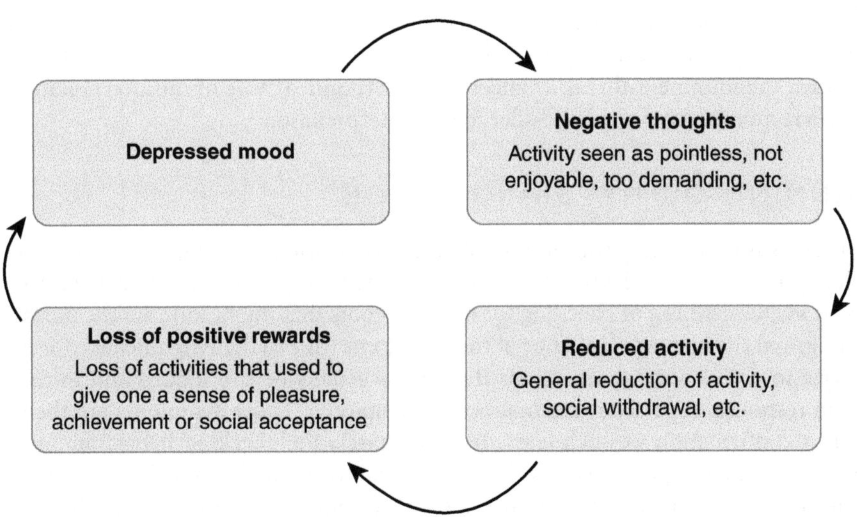

Figure 4.4 Reduction of activity

CATASTROPHIC MISINTERPRETATION

Originally conceived by Clark (1986) as the central cognitive process in panic disorder, this cycle (see Figure 4.5) can also be important in other problems such as health anxiety or OCD. The central idea in panic disorder is that bodily or cognitive changes – most often symptoms caused by anxiety, such as increased heart rate, breathing difficulties or other

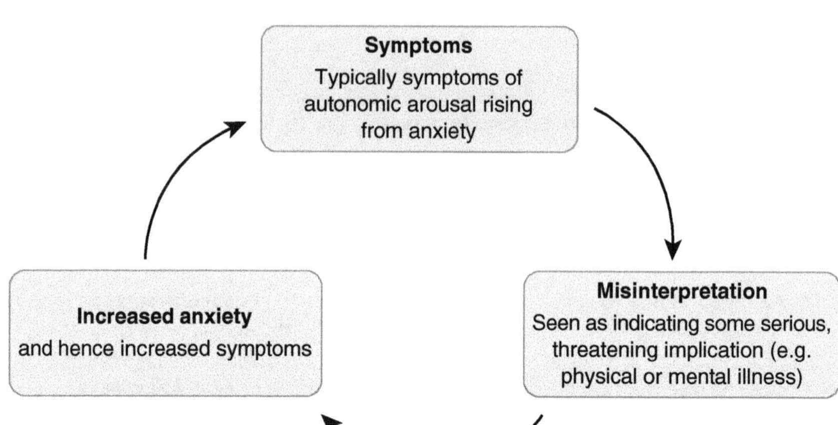

Figure 4.5 Catastrophic misinterpretation

signs of autonomic arousal – are interpreted as indicating some immediate and serious threat: that I am about to have a heart attack, or a stroke, or that I am 'going mad'. Naturally enough, such a thought causes yet more anxiety, and hence more symptoms, which seems to confirm the imminent threat … and so it goes round, a cycle of misinterpretation promoting a response that provides fodder for misinterpretation.

SCANNING OR HYPERVIGILANCE

This process is particularly common in phobia and health anxiety but is also seen in other problems such as PTSD. Figure 4.6 shows how the worry that one might have a serious illness leads to scanning or checking for the symptoms that might indicate the illness. This scanning, and the increased salience of the symptoms (due to their significance for health), leads one to notice normal sensations that might usually be overlooked and to think the worst in response to perfectly normal bodily symptoms. Those symptoms are then interpreted as confirmation of one's fears. In some cases, the checking behaviour may even *produce* worrying symptoms. For example, a woman who feared that her throat would close up, causing her to choke, would frequently and strenuously try to clear her throat with a loud 'Ahem'. As a result, she produced unpleasant feelings and irritation in her throat, which she then took as proof that there was indeed something wrong.

A useful metaphor to illustrate this kind of process is to ask clients to remember a time when they have been thinking about buying a particular model of car. They may have noticed that at such times it seemed as if suddenly the roads were absolutely full of that kind of car. What can we make of this? Most will readily concede that it is unlikely that the owners' club for that particular car has decided to follow them around. Those cars were actually always there, but they went unnoticed until they became important or relevant. Now that they have become relevant, they seem to be everywhere.

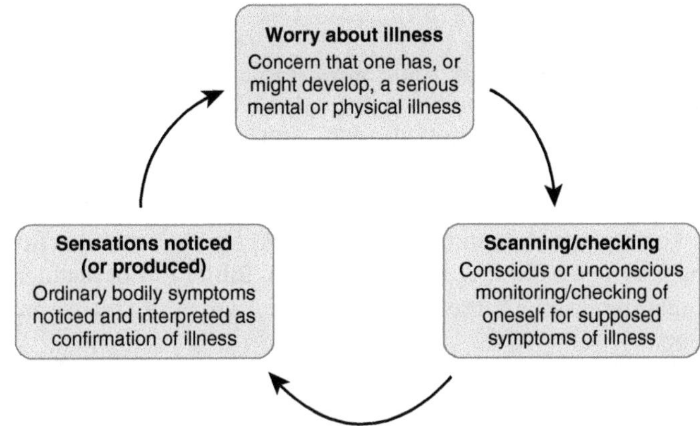

Figure 4.6 Scanning or hypervigilance

SELF-FULFILLING PROPHECIES

This refers to a process through which people with negative beliefs find that their behaviour results in confirmation of those beliefs. Figure 4.7 illustrates this process for two examples: socially anxious and hostile behaviour. In the first case, the expectation of rejection by others leads to withdrawing from social interactions: for example, declining invitations to social events, or not joining in attempts at conversation. Over time this behaviour may lead to others ceasing to make such social approaches – which of course serves to prove to the person that other people do not like them.

A similar pattern can be seen in some forms of hostile or aggressive behaviour. The expectation of hostility from others can lead to aggressive behaviour, for example in order to show that one is not to be intimidated. The aggression may then elicit hostile behaviour from others, thus confirming the prediction.

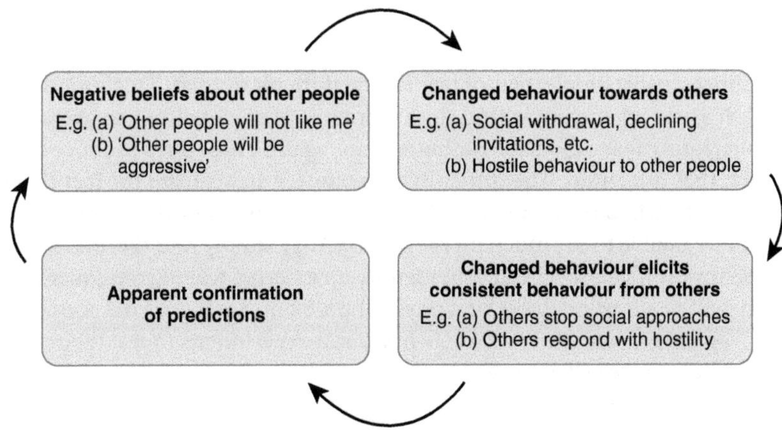

Figure 4.7 Self-fulfilling prophecies

PERFORMANCE ANXIETY

This pattern (see Figure 4.8) is in some ways similar to self-fulfilling prophecy and is common in social anxiety, when there is difficulty in carrying out some action. It is also seen in those with psychological difficulties in public speaking, swallowing, in male erectile dysfunction, and in 'shy bladder syndrome', for example. Worry that one is not going to be able to perform 'adequately' (talk coherently, swallow, maintain an erection or urinate) leads to anxiety, which then may indeed disrupt performance, resulting in hesitant speech, an inability to swallow, erectile difficulties, inhibition of bladder release and so on. This, of course, strengthens the negative beliefs about performance and the unhelpful pattern is set up.

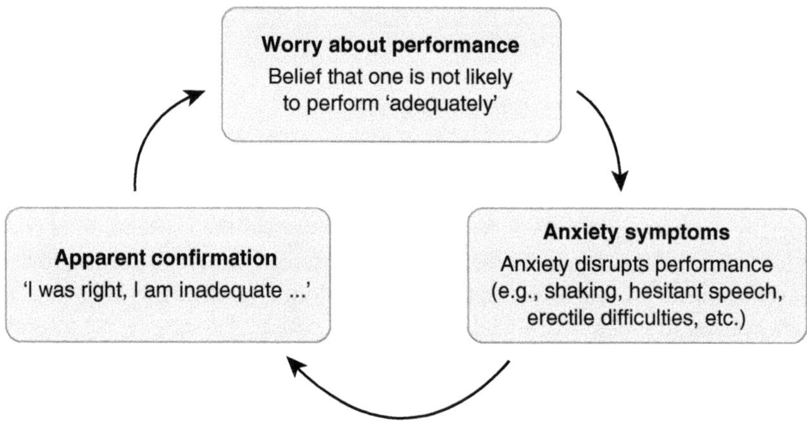

Figure 4.8 Performance anxiety

FEAR OF FEAR

Although conceptually simple, fear of fear can be difficult to treat. This process, illustrated in Figure 4.9, arises when people find the experience of anxiety itself so aversive that they develop anticipatory fears about becoming anxious again. These fears produce the very anxiety of which they are afraid. The difficulty in treatment stems from the fact that this cycle can become so detached from outside influences that there is nothing tangible to focus on: some clients are unable to say much more than that they simply find the anxiety intolerable. Sometimes, however, you will be able to identify an external feared consequence – perhaps that anxiety will result in madness or a physical problem. Such external consequences can give you a way in, for example by doing behavioural experiments to test the reality of these feared consequences (see Chapter 9).

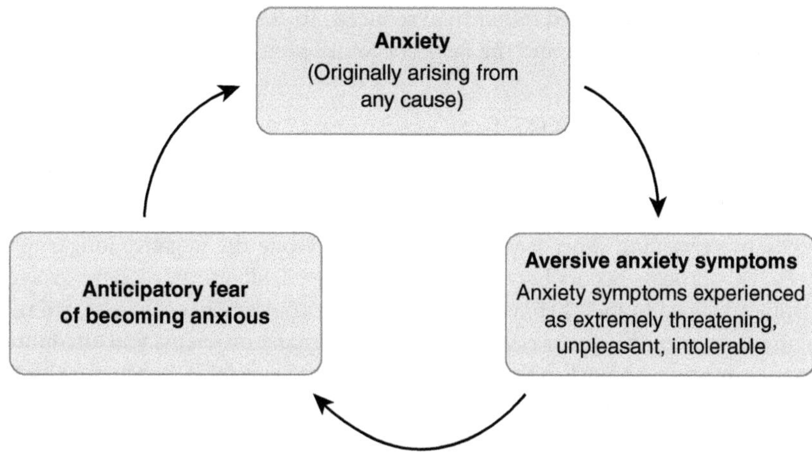

Figure 4.9 Fear of fear

PERFECTIONISM

A common pattern in clients with rigid rules and high standards or people with negative beliefs about their own capacity or worth is the cycle involving perfectionism shown in Figure 4.10. The desire to fulfil high standards (e.g. in achieving a low weight) or to prove oneself not completely worthless or incapable results in such high and inflexible demands that they can never be attained all of the time. Therefore, a sense of disappointment, failure

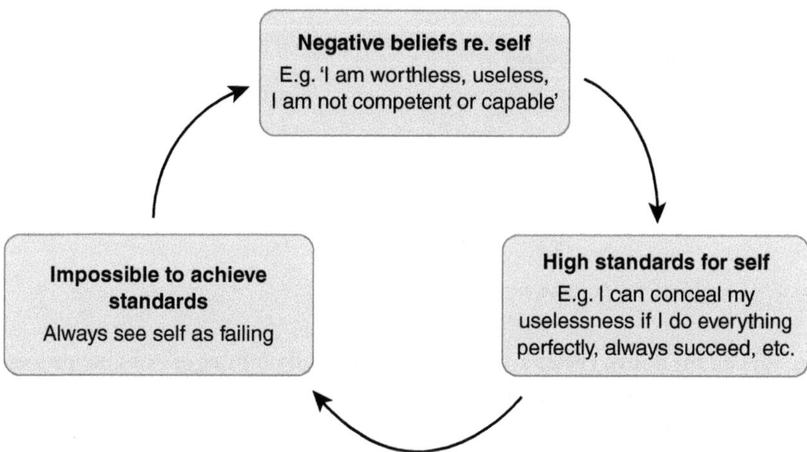

Figure 4.10 Perfectionism

and worthlessness is maintained rather than reduced. To compensate for this, standards are sometimes raised even further and the target becomes even less attainable.

SHORT-TERM REWARDS

We end with one of the most basic maintaining processes, going right back to the days of learning theory and operant conditioning. Figure 4.11 shows the process of behaviour being maintained by rewarding short-term consequences, despite the negative longer-term consequences. This process occurs because humans – indeed, all animals – have evolved to be more strongly shaped in their behaviour by short-term consequences than long-term ones.

The importance of this process will be obvious in many problems you encounter, such as substance misuse, some forms of eating disorder, aggressive behaviour, escape and avoidance behaviour, reassurance seeking and so on. Appreciating the potency of short-term reinforcement can help us better understand the drive behind behaviours that clearly do not help our clients in the longer term, and this can help us retain the compassionate, non-judgmental position so crucial to CBT.

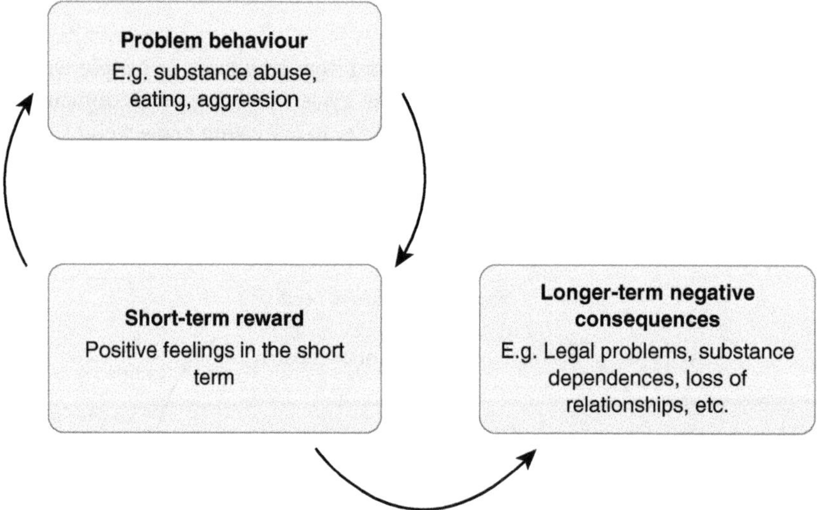

Figure 4.11 Short-term reward

Do note that all the above cycles are intended as general outlines of possible processes, not universal laws: use them as ways to start your thinking, to generate hypotheses for the formulation, and adapt them as necessary.

Before we move on to elaborating the assessment process, this is probably a good point to introduce the concept of the *mini-formulation*. A mini-formulation is simply a very pared-down understanding of a problem and it often takes the form of the key vicious cycle that maintains a particular difficulty. That is why we mention it here, at the end of the section on maintaining patterns.

Lea sought help for panic attacks. After hearing her account of them, her therapist was able to help her understand why they were so powerful by sharing a simple cycle of: giddiness triggering the thought that 'I'm going to pass out and hurt myself' which fuelled anxiety and this worsened the giddiness. Even at this early stage in therapy, this mini-formulation helped Lea enormously. She immediately realised that she was not losing control of her life and that there was a pattern to her problem – a pattern that she could see might be broken.

Enzo could not recall a time when he had felt confident and now his mood and self-esteem were at an all-time low. In his view he had a character flaw and things were just going to get worse. His therapist helped him see a simple but repeating pattern of hopeless thoughts leading to him giving up (occupationally and socially), which then brought down his mood and this drove more hopeless thoughts. This simple vicious cycle helped Enzo appreciate that there was a reason for him feeling as though he was 'trapped' by his thoughts and misery and his therapist was able to introduce the idea that they could break out of this trap using CBT.

Here you see a simple maintaining cycle helping Lea, who had a relatively straightforward and recent-onset problem, and also helping Enzo who suffered long-standing difficulties. In both instances the client was feeling overwhelmed and hopeless, and in both cases, teasing out a fundamental pattern underlying the problem gave an explanation and hope. When you share maintaining cycles it is crucial that you quickly introduce the idea that these patterns can be broken, otherwise a person might grow even more hopeless because they feel that they are simply trapped by their problems. It is also important to be sensitive to your clients' views of the complexity of their difficulties. Although Enzo found it helpful and clarifying to see his long-standing mood problems summarised very parsimoniously, another person might feel that this oversimplified things and worry that the therapist wasn't really understanding him.

ASSESSING PAST HISTORY AND PROBLEM DEVELOPMENT

Having considered common current maintenance patterns, we move on to looking at the past: the history and the development of the problem. This part of the assessment aims to identify vulnerability factors, precipitating factors and modifying factors.

VULNERABILITY FACTORS

Under this heading, we look for anything in the person's history that might have made him vulnerable to developing a problem, but which does not by itself *necessarily* mean that he will develop a problem. For example, we know from Brown and Harris's classic work (1978) that factors such as the loss of a parent in childhood make a person vulnerable to depression, but that does not mean that *everyone* who has lost a parent will inevitably become depressed. For depression to develop, other events need to come into play (in Brown and Harris's model, 'severe life events' – or what we have called 'precipitants' below).

In CBT terms, the main factor believed to contribute to such vulnerability is the development of particular beliefs, either in the form of assumptions or core beliefs (see Chapter 1). A multitude of such beliefs may be relevant, and their exact form is highly idiosyncratic to particular clients, but common examples are: 'I must succeed at everything I do'; 'If you are nice to others then they ought to be nice to you'; 'I can only cope with life if I have a partner to help me'; or 'I am worthless'. Although a pervasive sense of worthlessness is fairly obviously unhelpful, many of these beliefs may enable a person to function well for long periods of time because they promote useful qualities such as drive and friendliness, for example. It is only when a situation resonates with the belief in an unhelpful way that problems may result. The people in the examples above may do well until they fail to succeed, or do not get the respect they crave, or do not have a partner. At that point, frustrations, self-recriminations, panic and despair might kick in and precipitate a problem.

Later chapters will look more specifically at beliefs commonly thought to be linked to particular problems.

PRECIPITANTS

The events or situations that actually provoke the onset of a problem are known as the precipitants. In the standard cognitive-therapy model they are also known as 'critical incidents'. Precipitants are factors that seem to be closely associated with the actual onset of a problem or with a significant worsening of a long-standing problem. Although there may be a single significant event which does this (perhaps a trauma in PTSD or a loss event in depression), it is often the case that there is no single event, but rather a series of more minor stresses, any one of which the person might have coped with but which are overwhelming when they occur together in a relatively brief time. When there *is* a single event, we often find that the event in some sense 'matches' a pre-existing belief: for example, the person who feels it is essential to be in a relationship loses an important relationship, or the person who believes he must always be coping and in control comes up against something uncontrollable.

People sometimes get confused between precipitants (which provoke the onset of a problem, as defined above) and triggers (which trigger a problem now, as described above). Both refer to factors that elicit a problem, but the differences are:

- precipitants happened in the past, whilst triggers are continuing to operate in the present;
- precipitants typically happened once, or at least a limited number of times, whilst triggers can happen many times even within a single day.

For example, think about someone who has developed a fear of driving in cars. Then the *precipitant* for this fear might have been having a car crash, or a near miss, five years ago: the precipitant happened once, and it happened in the past. On the other hand their fear may now be *triggered* any time this person has to go in a car, and perhaps also when they see TV programmes or other media showing 'dangerous' driving: the triggers are happening now, and they may happen relatively frequently.

MODIFIERS

Just as we look for modifying factors in the current problems, so it may also be useful to look at modifying factors across time. We often hear reports that the problems have just slowly grown worse, but sometimes careful exploration reveals that there have been times of improvement or of rapid worsening. Common modifying factors include changes in relationships; major role transitions such as leaving home, getting married or one's children leaving home; and changes in responsibilities such as a promotion at work or having a child. This retrospective review of modifiers can help us better understand a person's strengths and vulnerabilities.

THE ORDER OF ASSESSMENT COMPONENTS

In what order should you explore these different aspects of problems in your assessment? We do not believe there is any one 'right' way of doing this, for the simple reason that both clients and therapists vary. Some clients have little idea of what to expect from a psychological assessment and no strong preferences about how to proceed and are happy to follow a structure largely set by the therapist. Other clients may be set on telling their story in chronological order, from birth to the present day. Yet others may at first want nothing more than a space to express their distress. Therapists need to be responsive to these differences.

That said, all other things being equal, our preference is to begin an assessment by exploring the current problems. Starting here is relatively easy for most people, and it helps to orient the therapist in later stages of the assessment. You know quite a bit about the problem and, therefore, have some hypotheses about what kind of area may be important to explore when looking at problem development and personal history.

At first, you may prefer to take a structured approach to assessment, keeping the focus fairly tightly on one area at a time. Later on, as you gain experience and the structure becomes second nature, you may find that you can 'loosen up' and allow the conversation to wander around more, whilst still retaining in your mind the structure and how different aspects of the problem fit together.

'NON-SPECIFIC' FACTORS AND THE THERAPEUTIC RELATIONSHIP

We noted in Chapter 3 that one of the common myths about CBT is that it has little interest in the therapeutic relationship, and we hope it is clear that this is not true. Whilst CBT does not generally give the therapeutic relationship a central curative role, it still regards the relationship as an essential vehicle for change. This is particularly important during the assessment, when that relationship is being established. Although we have talked about some of the technical aspects of assessment, we want to make it clear that paying attention to the human relationship between client and therapist is just as important – indeed, probably even more important. If you forget to ask a particular question you can always come back to it later, whereas if you fail to respond with warmth and humanity to your clients, they may not come back at all! It is therefore crucial not to get so absorbed in the pursuit of information that you stop genuinely listening or fail to notice and respond to distress.

Newcomers to CBT sometimes worry that asking the number of questions a CBT assessment demands must automatically mean that the client feels harassed and intruded upon. Our experience is that this is not usually so. If questions are asked with warmth and empathy, in a genuine spirit of curiosity and desire to understand, most clients will see the assessment as a positive experience with someone who is interested in, and wants to understand, their way of looking at the world. But don't just take our word for it – ask your client. As you assess a person's difficulties check on how they feel about the process, ask them if they are comfortable, if your line of enquiry makes sense, if there is anything that they think you are missing and so on. This is a good opportunity to establish collaboration.

A good technique, throughout therapy but perhaps especially during assessment, is to pause frequently to summarise your understanding of what the client has told you and to ask for their feedback on whether you've got it right. This has several benefits. It gives you time to reflect and to think about where to go next. It helps reduce the risk of misunderstanding, by giving the client a chance to correct differences between your summary and what they meant to convey. And the request for feedback gives the message that the client is an active partner and that the therapist is not necessarily all-wise and all-knowing.

MAKING FORMULATIONS

NOT TOO FAST; NOT TOO SLOW

The process of assessment and formulation is worth spending time on, because developing a good formulation will pay dividends in more efficient and focused therapy. But how much time? You may feel two opposing pressures. Sometimes, there is an urge to 'get stuck in' and get into treatment as quickly as possible. On the other hand, therapists sometimes feel that they cannot come up with a satisfactory formulation until they know absolutely everything about their client's history, from the moment of birth to the present day. The best answer is probably somewhere in the middle.

In general we would recommend a two-session assessment, at least until you are familiar with the CBT approach. In the first session, aim to get as much as you can of the necessary information. You then have the time between sessions to try to make sense of the information and develop a preliminary formulation. Trying to construct a formulation will very quickly highlight any important gaps in the assessment. You can then go into the second session with a clear idea of what else you need to know and, in most cases, develop the formulation in discussion with the client by the end of the second session. This is not a hard and fast rule. In some cases, perhaps with very complex problems or with clients with whom you find it difficult to form a relationship, the process of assessment may take longer. On the other hand, as you become more experienced in CBT you will probably find that with clients with straight-forward problems you can develop at least a rough formulation within one session. But the two-session approach works well for most beginners most of the time.

DIAGRAMS

Some people find that the best way of communicating formulations is through diagrams rather than words. There are two common approaches to drawing formulations: white-board and paper. Many CBT therapists have a whiteboard in their office and use this, while others just draw them onto paper. The whiteboard has the advantage of being larger and therefore easier to see and also easier to rub out as changes are made. Photographs can be taken of the whiteboard as a reference. Paper formulations can be photocopied for the client to take away.

In either case, it is helpful to make the process of drawing up a formulation as collaborative as possible. Don't just produce a beautiful formulation like a rabbit out of a hat. Involve your client in the process, asking him what should go where: 'From what we have discussed so far, what do you think might have led to the problem starting?', 'What do you think the effect is when you do that?' and so on. Kuyken, Padesky and Dudley's (2009) book is a really useful source of ideas about what they term 'collaborative case conceptualisation'.

See Video 4.4: Collaborative construction of the formulation: teamwork in conceptualisation.

Figure 4.12 shows a possible template for formulations. This is not meant to be prescriptive. There are many different ways of showing formulations, and you will probably develop your own style. This is just one possible approach, which does at least give a clear picture of the most important elements in any formulation.

SAMPLE FORMULATION

Figure 4.13 shows an example of a formulation for someone who presented with a fear of becoming incontinent of faeces whilst driving. This had led to his being unable to drive more than a mile or two from home. That was just far enough for him to continue to get to work but was only achieved by plotting an intricate route that kept him in easy reach of a public toilet. The relevant information summarised in the formulation is as follows.

VULNERABILITY

Two factors seemed important. First, that he had been brought up in a family where going to the lavatory was of more than average concern: in his words, his family were 'obsessed by bowels'. He recalled that as a child he would be asked every day whether he had opened his bowels, and if he had not, he would be given laxative medication.

Second, and probably more important, he recalled with some distress an incident when he was 11 or 12 years old when, whilst he had a stomach bug, he had in fact been faecally incontinent on the school bus on the way home. Not surprisingly, he remembered this as an extremely shameful and humiliating experience.

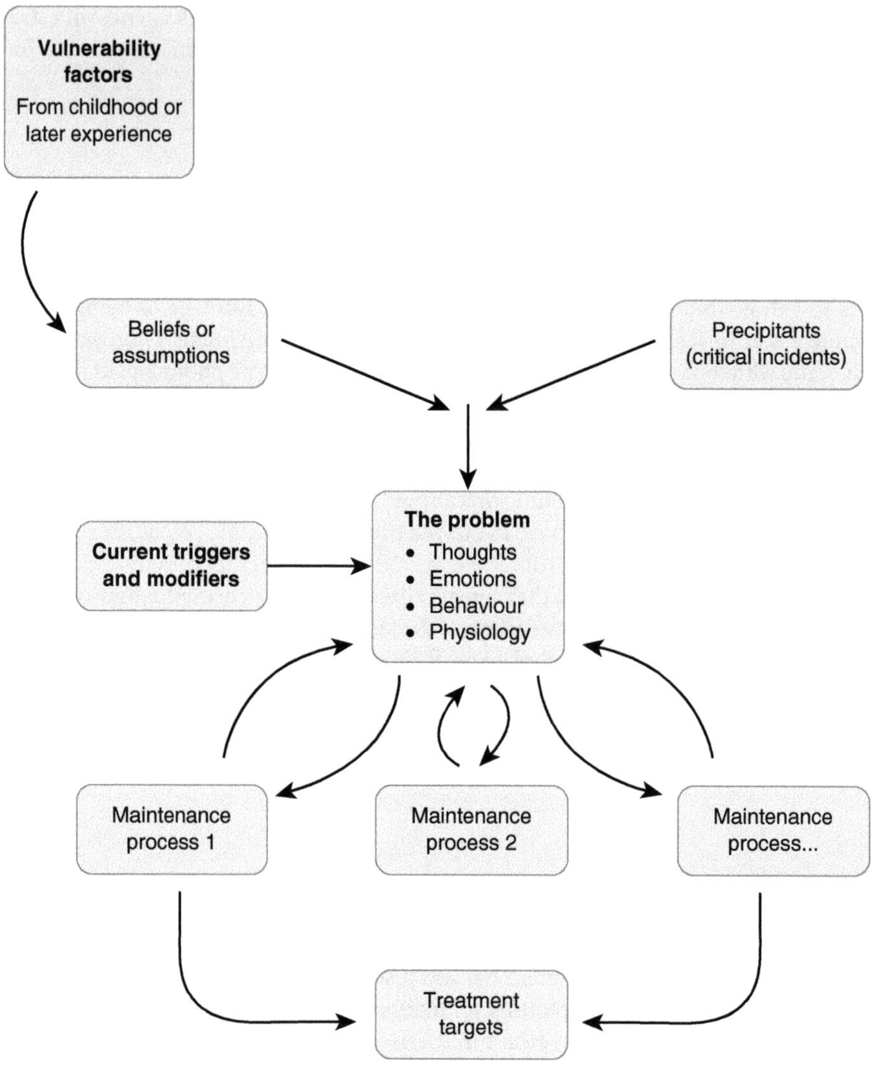

Figure 4.12 A template formulation

BELIEFS

It was hypothesised that these earlier experiences had led to beliefs that he could suffer incontinence of faeces and the result would be catastrophic. Perhaps related to this, he reported that he had always felt a slight association between his bowel function and anxiety: when he felt anxious, he would tend to want to go to the lavatory, and when he felt an urge to open his bowels, there was some degree of anxiety.

PRECIPITANTS

This man's history is an interesting illustration of the earlier point about the 'fit' between precipitants and pre-existing beliefs. Some years before the incident that precipitated his problem, he had suffered what would seem a far more 'traumatic' experience, when he had killed someone in a road traffic accident. The accident was not his fault – the other person had run out into the road –nevertheless it was obviously upsetting. However, despite significant temporary distress, it did not lead to persisting problems.

What did lead to the presenting problem seems a much more objectively trivial event, but because it linked with his beliefs, it proved more powerful as a precipitant. The incident occurred at a time when he was under a great deal of stress at work, due to conflict within the company. During this time, whilst driving to work and feeling a bit under the weather, he had a sudden urge to open his bowels and he became very anxious that he would lose control. Nothing disastrous actually happened. He found a place to pull over, went behind a hedge and then carried on driving to work. However, this immediately led to further anxiety, which increased steadily over the next few months.

THE PROBLEMS

He became anxious (*emotion*) at the thought of driving more than a short distance from home. He had typical anxiety symptoms, including increased heart rate, muscle tension, feeling hot and so on, but particularly an unsettled stomach (*physiology*). He believed that if he did not reach a toilet within a few minutes of getting an urge to use the lavatory, he would lose control (*cognition*). He avoided driving almost entirely except for getting to work and coped with that only by his safety behaviour of staying within range of public toilets (*behaviours*). He also focused a great deal of attention on his intestines (*cognition*), checking both before and during any journey whether he needed to go to the toilet and always trying to open his bowels before he set off (*behaviour*).

MAINTENANCE

Three maintenance processes were identified. First, his avoidance of driving outside 'safe' areas was a safety behaviour that blocked testing his beliefs about his lack of control. Second, his anxiety created gut symptoms that were interpreted as proof of losing control. And third, his constant checking of intestinal sensations constituted 'scanning', which led to his noting bowel sensations that were actually perfectly normal.

SIMPLE FORMULATIONS

Figure 4.13 illustrates a relatively simple formulation. This is excellent as we aim to keep shared formulations simple so that they are as understandable as possible. There are two more simple alternative templates that you might also find useful: one is endearingly referred to as the 'blobby formulation' and the other the more elegantly named 'vicious flower' framework.

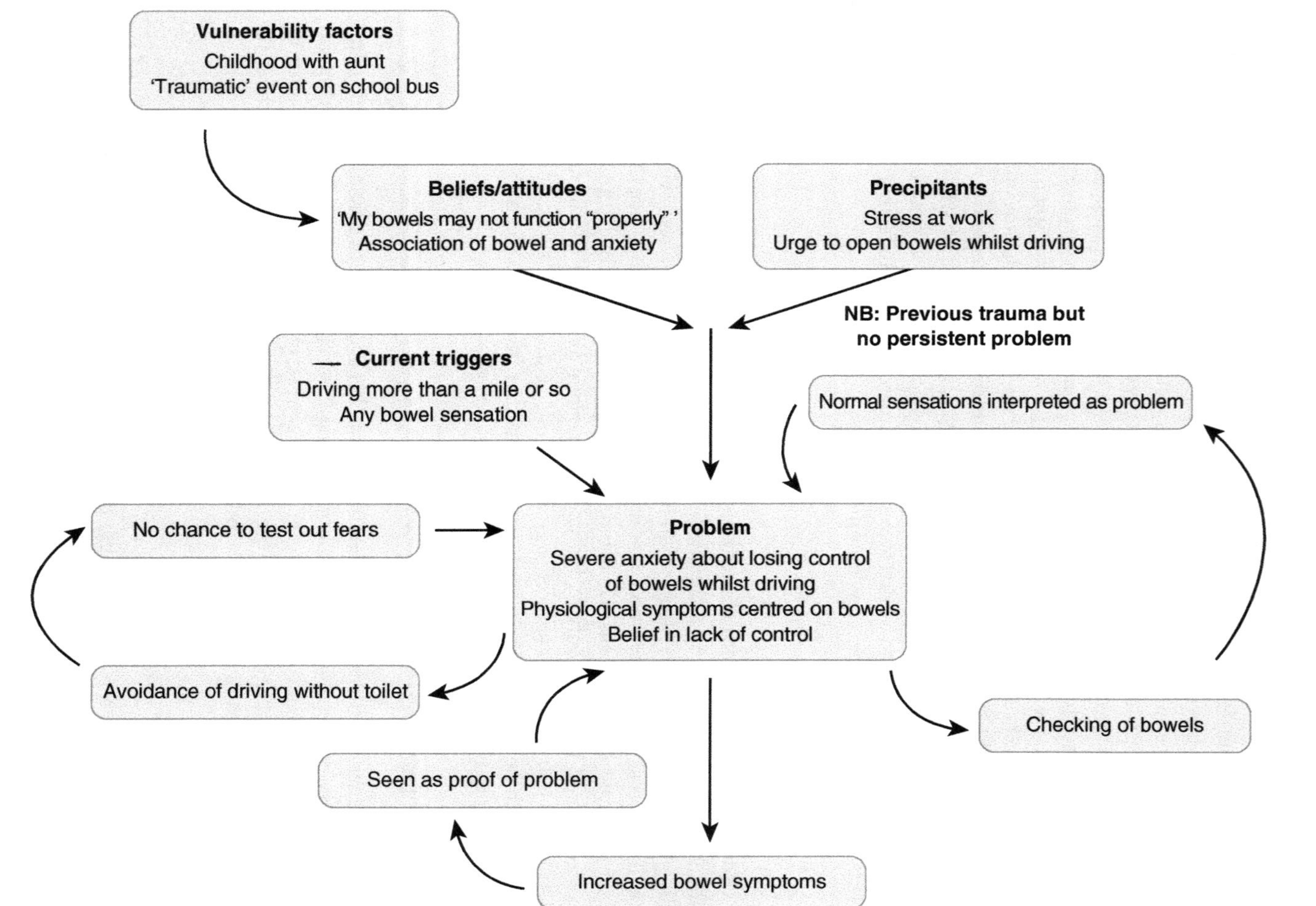

Figure 4.13 An example formulation

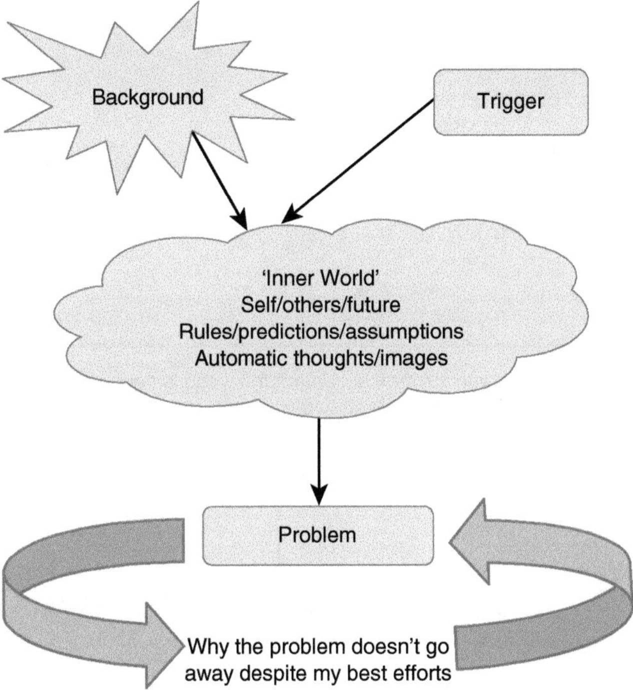

Figure 4.14 The 'blobby' formulation

The term 'blobby formulation' (Kennerley, 2015) reflects the simplicity of a conceptualisation framed as two or three 'blobs' of information, just enough to convey that it is understandable why this person developed this problem and why it isn't going away (see Figure 4.14).

Alice was referred for therapy when she was in her late-twenties. She had difficulty going back into work after a brief period of bullying which had been resolved within her organisation. She was very critical of herself and couldn't understand why she was still wracked with anxiety despite the incident having been dealt with professionally and to her satisfaction. She kept repeating that she was 'foolish' and 'silly' but she continued to avoid returning to work. Her therapist wanted to share a compassionate explanation as soon as possible so that Alice could start to ease up on the self-criticism that only made her stress levels worse. Her therapist learnt that Alice had a long history of neglect and bullying and that she had developed a strong belief that the world was a dangerous place and that she should do whatever was necessary to keep herself safe. Using this information, she and her therapist were able to share a preliminary formulation that enabled Alice to appreciate that it was 'no wonder' that she was so very sensitive following the recent bullying incident and she could see how her coping strategy was backfiring. (This scenario is illustrated in Figure 4.15.)

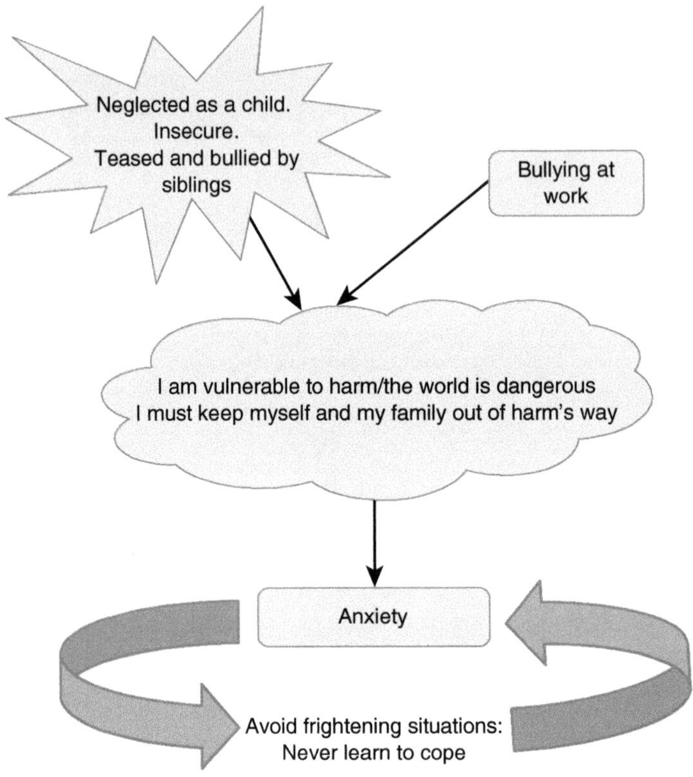

Figure 4.15 The 'blobby' formulation: Alice

See Video 4.5: Constructing a simple formulation with your client: the 'blobby' formulation.

The 'vicious flower', another parsimonious framework, illustrates a central core problem with various maintenance processes, which looks a bit like a flower with petals – hence the name (Salkovskis, Warwick & Deale, 2003; Butler, Fennell & Hackmann, 2008). This framework is particularly useful when there is an obvious core concern driving several different maintenance processes; the framework allows you to draw together different aspects of a complex problem in a way that facilitates movement back and forth between the more generalised core problems and the specific examples of how the problem shows itself (see Figure 4.16 for an example). Moorey (2010) has also developed a useful vicious flower for conceptualising the key processes in depression.

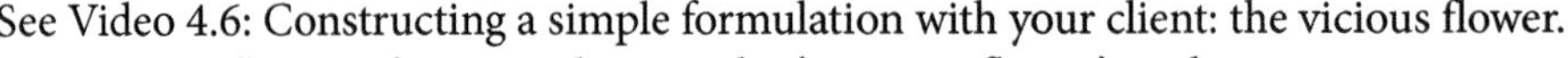

See Video 4.6: Constructing a simple formulation with your client: the vicious flower.

The vicious flower often morphs into the 'virtuous flower' as therapy progresses and each petal is addressed, negative cycles being replaced by positive, functional cycles. Ultimately, your client has a summary of coping, which is very enabling in the longer term. This is relevant to our next section: using 'positive' formulations.

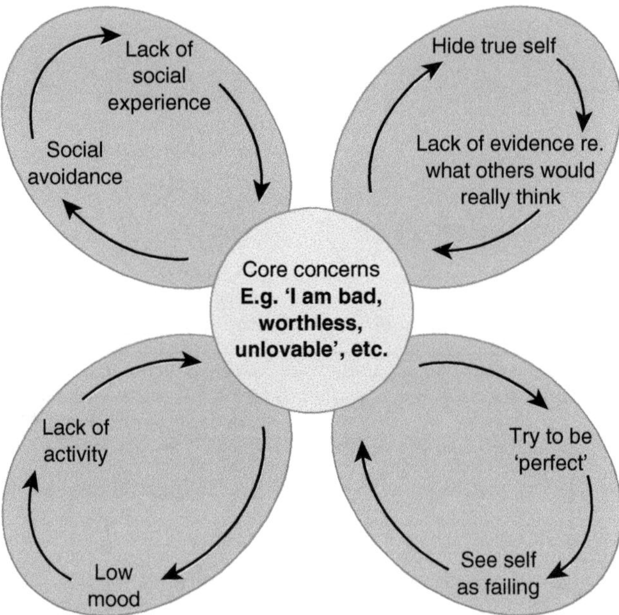

Figure 4.16 Example of 'vicious flower' formulation

POSITIVE FORMULATIONS

Formulations do not have to be pure frameworks of pathology. They should provide a 'snapshot' of a person's difficulty within their personal context. This means that we can often find helpful attributes, resources and virtuous cycles that remind us of our client's strengths – these can be built upon (Kuyken et al., 2009).

Howard had been abused during his childhood. He had managed to cope until his job stress became extreme and his negative beliefs about himself and others were revived. This was why he now believed that he was bad and unlovable and had to please people to protect himself from hurt; why he had difficulty trusting others; why he was prone to depression. His formulation captured all this along with the key vicious cycle of depression and social avoidance. However, there was more to Howard than his problem. He had a steadfast social network and although he had difficulty trusting, people seemed to like him and he was socially skilled. He was extremely self-sufficient (sometimes rather too self-sufficient) and he had built a career and a home for himself. Because he was ostensibly so competent, people turned to him for advice. He also recalled that he had a loving grandmother who often cared for him and in this relationship he had felt loved and safe, and he recalled that in the not so distant past he'd managed his dips in mood by keeping active and looking to his own needs. His formulation depicted this (see Figure 4.17) and Howard said that this comprehensive overview helped him keep a balanced view of who he was and his capabilities. This alone eased his pessimism and hopelessness.

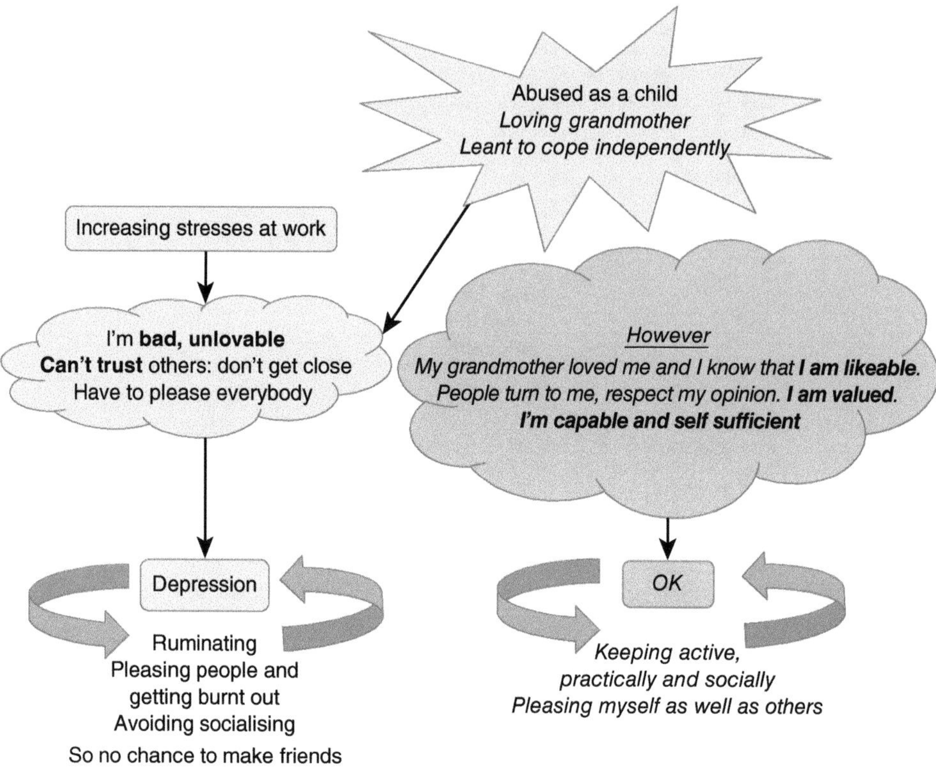

Figure 4.17 Howard's formulation of pathology and strengths

As clients make progress, the formulation should reflect this. Formulations are dynamic, changing as people develop new outlooks and behaviours. This means that formulations might begin with an emphasis on problems but they should evolve into a summary of strengths and coping.

At the beginning of her CBT for depression, Chase didn't believe that there were positive aspects to her life and her initial formulation was indeed one of pathology. However, as she progressed in therapy and the formulation was reviewed and updated, she and her therapist built up a coping framework reflecting the advances she had made. This captured her progress and ultimately she had a new view of her strengths and abilities, which she could recognise even though she had suffered adversity. This very much helped her in her long-term coping by reminding her of her inner resources and the behaviours that worked for her rather than against her. Thus her end-of-therapy positive formulation contributed to her long-term coping. (This scenario is illustrated in Figure 4.18.)

Padesky and Mooney (2012) take positive formulations a step further. Having helped clients build a understanding of their strengths, Padesky and Mooney aim to enhance resilience by

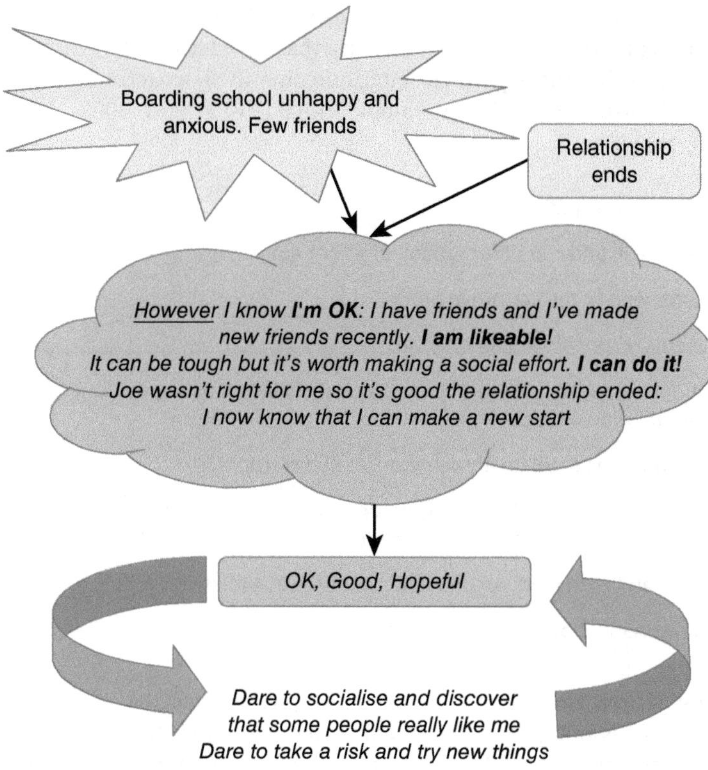

Figure 4.18 Chase's end-of-treatment formulation

encouraging a conceptualisation of 'possibilities'. Clients are invited to imagine their hopes and how it will be for them when they can manage their difficulties and are feeling and behaving differently. Thus, the person in therapy projects how things could be and mentally and emotionally rehearses the state of recovery and coping. This is a sophisticated variation on positive formulations and if you are drawn to the idea, then Padesky and Mooney's paper (2012) is a good starting point.

One final word about including positive information in the formulation: this has to be explored sensitively. Some people – like Chase – just can't believe that there is anything positive to record and pushing her on this might have seemed unempathic and might have strained the therapeutic alliance.

SUITABILITY FOR CBT

Virtually all psychological problems can be formulated, but being able to formulate a person's problems does not necessarily mean that they can benefit from CBT. So a crucial question is: 'Who is suitable for CBT?' The truth is that there is not much solid evidence about how we should match clients to therapies – whether CBT or any other therapy. Safran and colleagues developed a set of criteria that have been widely discussed, and two studies have found that these predict better outcome in short-term CBT (Safran, Segal, Vallis, Shaw & Samstag, 1993; Myhr, Talbot, Annable & Pinard, 2007). A client will do better (on average) if he:

- can access cognitions in session;
- is aware of, and can differentiate, different emotions;
- relates well to the cognitive model;
- accepts responsibility for change;
- can form a good collaborative therapeutic alliance (using evidence from previous relationships);
- has problems of relatively acute onset and history;
- does not show unhelpful 'security operations' (i.e. attempts to control anxiety to such a degree that therapy is difficult);
- shows ability to work on one issue at a time in a relatively focused way;
- is reasonably optimistic about therapy.

However, these factors are not well established empirically and the strength of the association with outcome is not great, so use them as a guide rather than a rigid set of criteria. Furthermore, they were devised to assess suitability for short-term CBT – one may be able to overcome less positive factors in longer-term work.

Faced with the lack of evidence about suitability, many therapists offer clients a trial period – perhaps five or six sessions – during which both can evaluate how well CBT fits for this individual. As we said earlier, this is genuinely a trial period to see if CBT suits the client as sometimes the approach or simply the timing of it is wrong. It is as well to be explicit about this:

> As you know, CBT has a good track record in treating many problems, but there are times when it might not be the optimum choice, and there are some problems for which a different approach might be better. In our first few sessions we will be keeping this in mind and considering if CBT is indeed the best therapy for your difficulties right now. If we decide that it's not, then we will still have carried out a useful assessment and we can discuss other options. How does that sound to you?

Although five or six sessions may not be long enough to resolve the presenting problems, it usually is long enough to get an idea of whether CBT seems to be useful. If it is, then the therapy can continue. If not, you will probably have a good enough conceptualisation to enable you both to consider other possible treatment plans.

SETTING THE SCENE FOR THE ASSESSMENT

Creating the right milieu for the assessment is crucial. Get it right and there is a good chance that you will engage your client and he will open up enough for you to complete a preliminary formulation and you can set the scene for the collaborative and empirical therapy that will follow.

'Getting it right' involves making your work together feel safe from the outset, so that's your starting point. We are usually open and interested in making things comfortable:

> In this session, I will be trying to get a better understanding of your difficulties so that we can both decide if CBT is the right therapy for you – if it will offer you what you need. This means that I shall be asking lots of questions. If this gets a bit too much for you, just let me know and we can take a break. It is important that you feel as comfortable as possible so it would be helpful for me to know a couple of things before we start. One is how will I recognise that you are upset? – people express this differently and sometimes I'm not sure what's going on, so I would really appreciate you telling me what to notice. The second thing is what do you prefer me to do if you are upset? Some people ask me to acknowledge tears, for example, while others ask that we don't draw attention to them; some people ask me to change the subject for a short while until they feel better and some people ask if they can leave the room for a few minutes. I'm pretty flexible, so if you explain to me what will make you feel most comfortable, we can make a plan and I can try to accommodate it.

In this way, you are maximising the likelihood that your client will open up and share necessary information, whilst you are giving the message that this is a collaborative endeavour and the client's experience and perspective matter.

Another way of ensuring that you gather relevant information is to be overt about your strategy. We usually outline a simple formulation, often drawing up a simple framework on a whiteboard whilst saying something along the lines of:

> Just so you know where I'm coming from when I ask you various questions, let me show you how cognitive therapists try to understand problems. I usually begin by asking about the difficulty that brought you here [*starts drawing on the whiteboard indicating a central problem*] and then I'll probably ask some questions to help me understand why the problem didn't resolve itself [*draws a 'maintaining cycle' arrow from the central problem*] – what's maintaining the problem. When we know what's keeping the problem going, we can start to develop ideas about changing things. How does that sound? Is this what you expected? Is this an approach that you can relate to?

Or:

> As a cognitive behavioural therapist I'm interested in what's driving your difficulties in terms of what you do and what goes through your mind. So I'll be asking you about the behaviours that help or hinder the situation, and we

will be exploring the thoughts, images, rules, predictions and so on that run through your mind. All this will help us understand what fuels the problem and when we have a handle on that we'll have an idea about how best to take things forward. How does this sound to you? It does mean that I will be directing a lot of questions your way – how do you feel about that?

This simple interchange sets up a collaborative and hopeful basis for the assessment. The client knows what the therapist will be doing and why, he has a rationale for this particular interrogative part of CBT, his views have been sought and the therapist has made it clear that he thinks that change is possible.

POSSIBLE PROBLEMS DURING ASSESSMENT

As previously noted, a common difficulty for beginners in CBT is getting sufficient detailed information about the problems. This may be due to therapist or client issues.

PROBLEMS FOR THE THERAPIST

For therapists, the difficulty may lie partly in not yet knowing what information is important. With more experience with a range of psychological problems, you will develop a sense of what areas are likely to be important in particular problems. You should also read about CBT models, so that you know what theorists see as important (we hope that the rest of this book will help!). One of the skills that experienced therapists demonstrate is not so much always asking the right questions but recognising quickly when they are asking the *wrong* question and rapidly moving on to try a different angle.

It is important to try to get the balance between giving up too easily and persisting too long. In most cases, if your client is not managing to tell you much about an area of questioning, it is worth persisting for at least a while and trying different approaches. Clients often find one question easier to answer than another, and what initially seems a totally fruitless line of enquiry may suddenly open up in a more productive way. However, do not be *so* persistent that the client feels as if it is an interrogation rather than an assessment! In general, our experience is that when you are first learning it is worth persisting slightly beyond the point that feels completely comfortable to you; it will usually be acceptable to the client.

PROBLEMS FOR THE CLIENT

For clients, there may be several difficulties that make it hard for them to answer your questions. In any particular case, it is important to understand what is causing the difficulty, but there are two common classes: those where the client genuinely does not know the answer to your question; and those where he does know, but is reluctant to answer.

Not knowing the answers:

- The client has become so used to the problem (or so demoralised by it) that he no longer notices the factors you are trying to assess. Often, further gentle questioning can begin to elicit variations and thus reveal more information. Another useful technique is self-monitoring (see Chapter 5), either done close to the time of emotional upsets so as to increase the accessibility of thoughts or done hourly to pick up variations in mood.
- Avoidance or other safety-seeking behaviours have become so widespread or so effective that the client no longer experiences negative thoughts or engages in certain behaviours and thus cannot report them.
- A particular cognition can become so familiar and overused in certain situations that we unconsciously bypass it. A useful metaphor for understanding this is the reaction of an experienced driver seeing a red traffic light. He would not consciously think 'Red light – that means I had better stop, because if I don't a car coming the other way might crash into me, and that could be very disastrous ...'. He would just automatically brake on seeing the red light. This is a good thing as it makes his actions more rapid and thus makes him a safer driver. The cognitions are still there, however: if he put his foot on the brake and nothing happened, then his thoughts (and emotions) concerning road danger would be easily accessible in this novel situation. A useful strategy, therefore, can be to try a small *behavioural experiment* (see Chapter 9), used as an assessment strategy. If the client is willing to see what happens if he creates a novel situation and does not avoid or does not perform his usual safety behaviour, then the thoughts and emotions are likely to become much more apparent.
- The client is amongst that small proportion of people who simply find it very difficult to access or report thoughts and emotions. Some people are better with images and 'felt sense', so routinely ask 'What runs through your mind, what words or pictures?' and 'Where is it in your body – how does it feel, physically?'. Some people simply get better with practice, so it is worth persisting for a while, for example via homework, as above. A few people never do get comfortable with cognitions and feelings. In such cases, a more traditional behavioural approach may prove more fruitful.

Knowing the answers but being reluctant to report them:

- Fear of the therapist's reactions. For instance, a man may think that you will disapprove of his thoughts or behaviour, or find his symptoms 'silly', or laugh at him. Always try to discover the reason behind the reluctance before trying to do anything about it. Most clients will be able gradually to talk about the obstructing thoughts, even if they do not yet feel able to talk about the original thoughts themselves. It may also be helpful to offer the client suggestions about the kind of worries other clients have reported, so that he realises that the therapist has heard this kind of thing before (but without putting words into the client's mouth, of course).

- Other feared consequences are of reporting the symptoms openly. A client may fear she will be diagnosed as 'mad' and locked away, or that the therapist will contact the police or social services and have her arrested or have her children taken away. Someone with profound feelings of badness may fear that he will morally contaminate his therapist. A PTSD sufferer might anticipate that talking about a trauma will trigger intolerable flashbacks. Some people with obsessive-compulsive problems report fearing that their protective rituals, particularly those involving 'magical thinking', will no longer work if they reveal the full details, thus putting themselves or others at serious risk. Again, it can be helpful to offer clients examples of common fears and also perhaps to clarify the differences between different kinds of mental health problem (e.g. that OCD is different from schizophrenia).

POSSIBLE PROBLEMS IN MAKING FORMULATIONS

EFFECT IS NOT PURPOSE

It is important to avoid the assumption that clients or their relatives necessarily *intend* (even unconsciously) the consequences of their behaviour. The fact that one of the effects of the behaviour of a woman with agoraphobia is that her husband always has to accompany her does not by itself prove that she is behaving like that *in order* to have her husband always with her. Similarly, a client's husband reassuring her in a way that seems to maintain an obsessional problem does not show that he is doing that *in order* to keep her obsessional. This is not to say that such motivation (sometimes called *secondary gain*) does not exist; just that it is not universal. Some independent evidence is needed, beyond the mere effect, to show that it is important in any particular case. Freud himself is supposed to have said in relation to Freudian symbolism, 'Sometimes a cigar is just a cigar.' We might perhaps extend this to '*Most of the time* a cigar is just a cigar.' Most clients and their families want to get rid of their problems: they just get trapped in patterns of thought and behaviour that do not help them to achieve that goal.

CENSORING THE FORMULATION

Therapists sometimes ask whether there is any element of a formulation that should *not* be shared with the client. As a general rule, the answer is 'No.' As part of the collaborative approach of CBT, the formulation should be open. A possible, but rare, exception to this is if the full formulation would contain some element that might threaten the therapeutic relationship. Discussions about the formulation will typically happen fairly early on in the relationship, when there may not yet be sufficient trust and confidence to contain conflicts. An obvious example would be if you thought you had sufficient evidence to assume secondary gain as part of the formulation (see above). Even with strong evidence for that kind of process, the client might be offended by such a suggestion early on in therapy. It might be wise not to make it part of the formulation until the relationship has strengthened and such issues can be openly discussed.

SPAGHETTI JUNCTION

It is not necessary for a working formulation to contain *every* piece of information you have about a person. Including too much in a formulation can result in a nightmare of criss-crossing lines and boxes that is confusing rather than clarifying. Remember, the aim of the formulation is to make sense of the information gathered to explain the key processes involved in the maintenance of the problem. A degree of filtering and simplification is necessary and desirable to make the formulation reasonably easy for both client and therapist to grasp. A good motto is the saying attributed to Einstein: 'Everything should be made as simple as possible – but no simpler.'

TUNNEL VISION

Sometimes we may fix too early on a hypothesis and then get 'stuck', only paying attention to information that confirms the hypothesis and not looking for other information (Kuyken, 2006). It is important to remember that in order to test a hypothesis adequately, we have to look for evidence that would *refute* that hypothesis, not just evidence that supports it.

We can also sometimes try to force clients into fitting the formulation, rather than making the formulation fit the client. It is crucial that you are responsive to what they tell you and that the formulation is idiosyncratic to your client.

FORMULATIONS DON'T MAKE SENSE

A common problem is a formulation that has boxes and interlinking arrows that look fine but which, and on closer examination, make no logical sense. This can happen as a result of careless use of a conceptualisation heuristic. For example, the elegantly simple five-part model (Padesky & Mooney, 1990: see Figure 4.19) is often misused in this way.

Although this framework is popular and can be very useful as an accessible reminder of the multiple interconnections between the systems, it needs to be made more specific if it is to form the basis of a useful formulation. Used without enough consideration, it can lead to lumping together miscellaneous thoughts in one box; putting equally disparate collections of behaviours, emotions and bodily changes in other boxes; drawing arrows between the boxes; and then sitting back, satisfied that the problems have been explained. But they have not, because the arrows do not represent any comprehensible process. Instead of being specific about what behaviour is linked to what thought or what emotion, we just have one big arrow linking all thoughts to all behaviours, all emotions and so on. Although each one of these links might make sense when taken individually, they make no sense at all when they are all massed together. As a result, the therapist (not to mention the client) is likely to struggle to explain just *how* these supposed links operate.

Always think critically about your formulations and ask yourself what psychological process the arrows and boxes represent. Make sure you can explain *how* a specific thought in one box leads to a particular behaviour in another box, or *how* that behaviour has an effect on a specific belief. In short, make sure your formulations make sense.

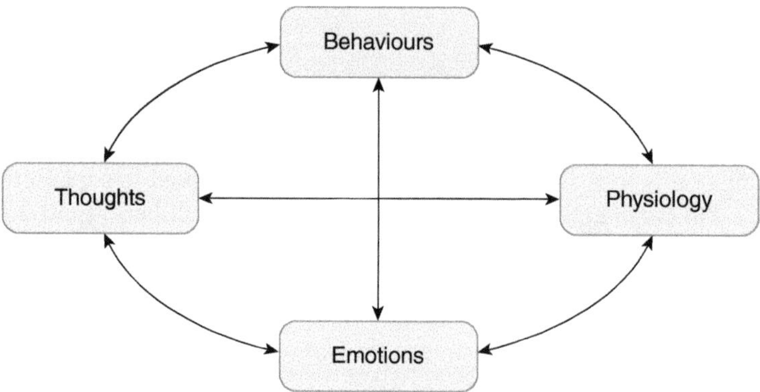

Figure 4.19 Interacting systems (based on Padesky & Mooney's five-part model, 1990)

FORMULATION IS NOT USED!

It may seem obvious that a formulation cannot help if it is not used, but it can be forgotten. Having constructed the formulation, therapists sometimes file it away as a task completed and never think about it again. Remember that the point of the formulation is to guide both therapist and client throughout treatment. Try to get into the habit of referring back to the formulation frequently: 'How does this experience fit with the formulation?'; 'What would our formulation suggest might be a good way forward here?'; 'Is this work [in session or as homework] going to make a difference to an important maintaining process?'.

FORMULATION IS NOT UPDATED

If a therapy is working, a client's problems will ease as their cognitions and behaviours change. This needs to be reflected in the formulation. If a formulation isn't changing, then therapy is not working. If therapy is helping, then we should see strengths, resources and virtuous cycles becoming ever more prominent. By the end of a successful course of CBT, the formulation should be a summary of what works for the client and a guide for the future.

CORE BELIEFS AND SCHEMATA

Finally, a note of caution about the transition from the formulation to treatment plans. There is sometimes a belief that if your formulation contains core beliefs or schemata, then (a) those must be the primary targets for treatment, because they are more 'fundamental' or 'deeper' than ATs or behaviour; and (b) you should therefore begin by modifying them. This is rarely true. Core beliefs and schemata are certainly broader in their applicability than a typical AT, but that does not necessarily render them more important or more fundamental and certainly does not imply that working with ATs and behaviours is 'superficial'. On the contrary, almost all the evidence currently available for the effectiveness of CBT is based on working primarily at the level of specific ATs and their associated behaviours. There is also evidence that working at that level actually results in changes at the wider

belief level as well (see e.g. the fascinating 'dismantling' study of Jacobson et al., 1996). Our approach is to keep things as simple as possible and work with more general beliefs and assumptions only when it is clearly necessary because we have got as far as we can with more specific thoughts and behaviours.

SUMMARY

- CBT formulations aim to provide a concise description of the key features of a problem, how it started and what keeps it going.
- CBT assessments are used to gather the information for, and to test out the key hypotheses of, a CBT formulation, so that we end up with a framework that is based on evidence and makes sense to both client and therapist.
- The formulation should, whenever possible, be informed by an established treatment model that has an evidence base for its efficacy; when clients do not easily fit an established model, then you need to develop a formulation by applying basic CBT theory to your individual client.
- CBT formulations mainly (but not exclusively) focus on the current maintenance processes. As well as helping both client and therapist to understand the important processes, they provide the foundation for treatment plans (which will typically aim to disrupt the identified maintenance processes).
- Formulations can take different formats, but are often in the form of diagrams, so as to make clear the 'vicious circle' maintenance processes.

LEARNING EXERCISES

These learning exercises are available to download from the companion website.

REVIEW AND REFLECTION:

- **What do you make of the comparative lack of research evidence to show that formulation-based therapy has any advantage over completely standardised therapy? Does this mean we should give up formulations, or does it show that the research up to now is too limited? How could we find out more about the scientific status of formulation?**

(Continued)

(Continued)

- In your view, what are the pros and cons of diagnosis-based models?
- What kind of evidence is needed for one to conclude that 'secondary gain' is operating in a particular case? If there is such evidence, how would you go about discussing it with your client?
- What is your view of the place and relevance of simplified formulations?
- What is your view of the place and relevance of positive formulations?

TAKING IT FORWARD:

- Try to draw up a formulation diagram for a couple of your clients and see how far you can get. Try to embrace pathology and strengths. What problems do you run into? How could you overcome those problems?
- Try to simplify your client's formulation and see if you can reduce it to a meaningful minimum.
- Take these formulations to supervision and discuss with your supervisor how well they work and what you could do to test out whether they are accurate.
- Practise drawing up formulations collaboratively with your clients and eliciting their reactions. Do any of your clients find the formulation unhelpful? If so, in what way?
- Review your client's formulation regularly and update it!

FURTHER READING

Grant, A., Townend, M., & Mill, J. (2009). *Assessment and case formulation in cognitive behavioural therapy*. London: Sage.

Contains interesting discussions of some of the key theoretical and empirical controversies around case formulation, but also has fascinating extended accounts of individual clients and their formulations.

Kuyken, W., Padesky, C., & Dudley, R. (2009). *Collaborative case conceptualization: working effectively with clients in cognitive-behavioural therapy*. New York: Guilford Press.

A creative and inspiring book on different kinds of case conceptualisation (i.e. formulation in our terms) and how to use them collaboratively with clients through all stages of therapy.

VIDEO LINKS

- **4.1 Exploring the client's fear: unpacking what's behind the problem**
- **4.2 Refining hypotheses about 'modifiers': learning more about strengths and needs**
- **4.3 Using a recent episode to get more detailed information**
- **4.4 Collaborative construction of the formulation: teamwork in conceptualisation**
- **4.5 Constructing a simple formulation with your client: the 'blobby' formulation**
- **4.6 Constructing a simple formulation with your client: the vicious flower**

5

MEASUREMENT IN CBT

- Introduction
- The empirical nature of CBT
- During and at the end of treatment
- Why bother with measurement?
- Psychometric aspects of monitoring
- Obtaining useful and accurate measures
- What sorts of information to collect
- Other sources of information
- Making the most of the data
- Problems when using measurements
- Summary
- Learning exercises
- Further reading
- Video links
  - 5.1 Questionnaires (i)
  - 5.2 Questionnaires (ii)
  - 5.3 Self-monitoring task

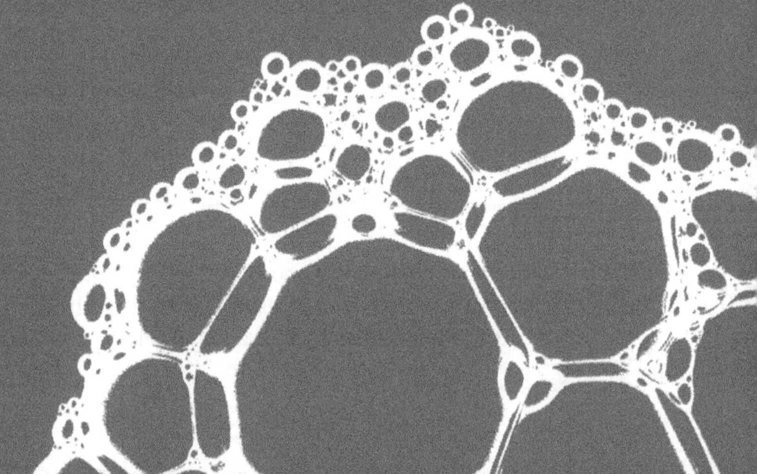

INTRODUCTION

We have already discussed the commitment within CBT to an empirical approach in establishing the effects of treatment, both for groups and for individuals, and this issue will be considered in more detail in Chapter 18. This chapter will describe how to translate this empirical approach into action with individual clients. We will look at how measurement can be used to increase your understanding of problems at the assessment stage and during treatment. We will also consider why it is worthwhile using measures in this way, how to devise them and we will give examples of the kinds of measures that might be useful.

THE EMPIRICAL NATURE OF CBT

From the start, we want to encourage clients to view treatment as an experiment, in which thoughts, feelings and behaviour, and the relationships between them, can be investigated during both assessment and treatment. We want them to be curious, bold and empirical.

ASSESSMENT AND FORMULATION

At assessment, it is helpful to ask clients to collect data about the nature of their problem, to supplement and fine-tune what they report in this initial interview. Such data may contribute to two main goals:

- To elaborate the formulation: for example, it may be helpful to look at triggers for particular thoughts, feelings or behaviours, and how these relate to each other, so that tentative ideas about a formulation can be explored further.
- To provide a baseline against which the problem can be compared in the future: for example, measuring the frequency or severity of the problem.

A depressed client believed that she was ruining her children's lives by continually 'going on' at them, shouting inappropriately and being unable to regain control once she had 'lost it'. She agreed that it would be useful to keep a diary to find out how frequently this occurred, and when it happened (see Figure 5.1). The main thing that she learned at this stage was that in fact she did it rarely, only twice in a week. This was very helpful information, as she had misperceived herself as *always* angry and nagging, presumably as a result of selectively noticing and then remembering situations that were consistent with her belief about herself.

DURING AND AT THE END OF TREATMENT

Once your client has a good description of his problem, what triggers and maintains it, he can begin to try out new ways of behaving, thinking and interacting and then assess what effect this has on the problem. Regular measures allow both client and therapist to evaluate

Date	Triggers
2nd May	—
3rd May	—
4th	Dan said it was my fault he had forgotten his football boots, and we had to drive back for them
5th	—
6th	Emma doing her hair for so long she missed the bus
7th	—
8th	—

Figure 5.1 Rating scale for how often a woman 'lost it' with her children, and what triggered it ('losing it' meant shouting for more than a minute)

the impact of interventions, and it is particularly important to gather data at the end of treatment so that overall progress can be assessed.

A client with OCD recorded how long it took her to leave her house if she planned to go out, and how long it took her to get away from work at the end of the day. As she introduced response prevention into a number of tasks (see Chapter 14), she could clearly see the effect of this intervention on the length of time it took her to leave home and work (see Figure 5.2).

Date	Place	Time taken (mins)
Before response prevention		
5th Jan	home	23 mins
5th Jan	work	37 mins
7th Jan	home	25 mins
7th Jan	home	18 mins
After response prevention		
6th Feb	home	8 mins
7th Feb	home	7 mins
7th Feb	work	11 mins
9th Feb	home	9 mins

Figure 5.2 Length of time spent leaving places when disrupting OCD rituals

Event	How early or late	Comments made by others	Anxiety beforehand, 0–10*
London train	45 mins early	Nil	7
Board meeting	On time	Nil	2
Guildford train	10 mins early	Nil	3

*0 = not at all anxious; 10 = as anxious as I could possibly be

Figure 5.3 Chart of arriving on time (or late) at events and the effect on others and anxiety levels

To take another example of evaluating treatment changes:

A man who was very anxious away from home realised that arriving early for trains was a safety-seeking behaviour when travelling. It kept in place his belief that 'only by staying 100 per cent in control will I be safe, and not be rejected.' He experimented with arriving at places either just on time, or even late, in order to find out whether there were catastrophic results, and found that no one commented or appeared to notice. To his surprise, he found that he was slightly less anxious on the days that he reduced his punctuality, not more anxious, as he had predicted (see Figure 5.3).

Although very simple measures were used in each of these cases, they provided helpful data about the nature of the problems and their responses to straightforward interventions.

WHY BOTHER WITH MEASUREMENT?

You may need to be creative and ingenious in devising useful monitoring to assess problems and evaluate the effects of different interventions. However, this begs the question of why you should use measures at all. There are a number of reasons why it is helpful to gather data to supplement information derived from interviews:

- Regular measures allow you to obtain a baseline of important aspects of the problem and then to use this to assess the effects of future intervention.
- Observations of behaviours, thoughts or feelings made at the time they occur are more reliable than retrospective estimates (Barlow, Hayes & Nelson, 1984).
- Direct observations by the client in real life can have therapeutic effects in themselves, for example by providing accurate information about the scale of the problem or about its progress. (They can also have anti-therapeutic effects, which need to be understood and carefully managed.)

A client assiduously produced thought records each week and carefully picked the most distressing examples for consideration in the session. This significantly coloured her assessment of how the previous week had been, as her attention was focused on the difficult times (an anti-therapeutic effect). To counteract this, she began to give herself a global mood rating three times daily (eventually reducing this to once daily when her mood was more stable) and was very surprised to find that on many days her mood was considerably lighter than she was retrospectively reporting – and simply gathering these data lifted her mood. This was very encouraging for her as this exercise illustrated beautifully that if she focused on NATs she felt worse, but also that she could manipulate her attention and improve her mood. Initially she had been doubtful that CBT was the right approach for her, but her therapist's curiosity and creativity had helped her devise assessments that engaged her.

- Once they have begun to improve, many clients lose awareness of how disabling the problem was initially. Baseline measures of the problem can help the client to assess his progress more accurately.

As a client's agoraphobic symptoms improved, he focused on his difficulty driving to nearby market towns, claiming that going into his local town had never really been a problem. This was dispiriting for him, as it seemed that he was making little progress. However, a review of his early diaries was sufficient to reassure him that he had once found going to his local town very difficult and that indeed he had made enormous progress. He saw that tasks he now took for granted had initially presented real problems for him.

- If an intervention does not have the impact that the formulation would predict, measurement can help you and the client to work out why. For example, it may be that the treatment is not being delivered appropriately.

A client was feeling out of control and overwhelmed by everyday domestic tasks. As a first step in trying to break the cycle of feeling inundated, giving up and then feeling out of control and overwhelmed, she decided to spend 20 minutes on three days each week tidying up papers that covered the surfaces in her kitchen. She, rated how overwhelmed she felt when attempting this task. This intervention appeared to have little impact on her feelings or her behaviour. She also kept a daily log, and as this indicated that she was only managing to complete the task once a week she was taking this as further evidence that she was overwhelmed. However, the routine log also revealed other information that allowed the therapist and client to trouble-shoot and work out how to increase the probability that she would carry out the task: it was apparent that she was most productive when she was alone in the morning, so they scheduled tidying papers during this time period. She was then able to complete the task at least three times a week, she broke the cycle and not only learnt that she could take control of certain aspects of her life but that her best time for doing this (whatever the task) was in the morning. By looking beyond the information gleaned from the task itself, therapist and client were able to transform what could have been a 'failure' to a sophisticated understanding of this woman's strengths and needs.

There are therefore sound reasons for using measures as part of routine clinical practice. We shall now consider how to do this in ways that will provide information that will be genuinely helpful for therapy, beginning with a note on the psychometric qualities of measures.

PSYCHOMETRIC ASPECTS OF MONITORING

REACTIVITY OF MEASUREMENT

The process of monitoring can have a positive or negative effect on whatever is being measured. In habits such as smoking, a beneficial reduction may occur if the client becomes aware of triggers and responds to the beginning of a potential cycle by inhibiting a response. On the other hand, change can be in the opposite direction. For example, some clients' response to the initial monitoring of NATs is an increased preoccupation and/or frequency of negative thoughts, which may increase anxiety or depression in the short term. It is helpful to explain that a temporary exacerbation of the problem is possible and to encourage persistence with monitoring long enough to see its longer-term advantages.

VALIDITY AND RELIABILITY

When standardised measuring instruments such as questionnaires are developed, an enormous amount of attention is paid to psychometric qualities, particularly *validity* and *reliability*:

A *valid* measure is one that measures what it purports to measure and not some irrelevant feature: for example, a questionnaire of social anxiety should measure just that and not be couched in language so complex that responses to it are affected by a person's verbal ability, or by the differing norms of his social group.

A *reliable* measure achieves the same result or score when repeated under the same conditions at another time, or with another assessor: it is repeatable. A measure low in reliability is affected by extraneous features and so produces inconsistent findings.

Standardised measures, such as a well-developed mood questionnaire, will usually have been tested for validity and reliability. However, in many cases you need ingenuity to devise more idiosyncratic measures, and it is then important to try to make them as reliable and valid as possible in the circumstances. The following section suggests how this can be achieved.

OBTAINING USEFUL AND ACCURATE MEASURES

Most of the principles that will be described here are easy to apply but can make an enormous difference to the value of the measures used.

SIMPLICITY

Do not overburden your client. Try to resist the temptation of downloading detailed schedules from internet sites (or photocopying them from books) and simply asking your client to try to complete them. Not all of these schedules will seem relevant and some will be far too demanding – either way you could lose collaboration. Begin with a limited and meaningful task that does not ask too much. As your client becomes more persuaded of the value of information obtained through monitoring, and becomes more skilled, you may increase the demands on him, but still keep in mind the difficulty of observing and recording.

A depressed man began treatment by going out each day for a short walk, and he recorded how long he walked (in minutes), and how much he enjoyed it (on a 10-point scale of enjoyment). This was just about manageable given his depressed state but as treatment progressed and his mood and motivation improved, he also began to record ATs, to rate how critical his wife was (on a 10-point scale), and to record the three best things he had done that day (a simple list). In addition, he was soon able to monitor specific activities/tasks for particular purposes. This was quite onerous for him, but he felt it was all relevant and because the tasks had been introduced gradually, he felt that they were doable.

It is important to continue monitoring only while the measures continue to be useful. On the other hand, bear in mind that it is helpful to have some measures (e.g. a mood rating or questionnaire) that are continued throughout treatment so that you can look at variations over the course of treatment.

CONSIDER MEASURES IN MORE THAN ONE SYSTEM

Although it is important to limit demands on your client, you should bear in mind that different aspects of the problem may change in different ways, and that this detail may need to be tracked in records that persist beyond the initial data collection.

A woman with anxieties about her health focused on reducing the amount of time that she discussed her worries with her husband and mother, or asked for reassurance (i.e. a behavioural aspect). She kept records (see Figure 5.4) which included information about behavioural, cognitive and emotional aspects of the problem. In the first two weeks, her success in effecting behavioural change had little impact on her anxiety or on the strength of her beliefs that she may have something seriously wrong with her health. Nonetheless she persisted with the behavioural change and self-monitoring and before long her recordings showed that her anxiety was falling and her beliefs shifting.

RELEVANCE

Only ask for information that you will use and that will make a difference to treatment. It is unlikely that the anyone will go to the trouble of monitoring unless he sees its relevance, and it may also jeopardise the therapeutic relationship if you ask for information merely 'out of interest'.

Behavioural: Each time you ask for reassurance, or discuss your symptoms with your husband or mother, please put a tally:

Date	Tally	Total
14th	///////////	11
15th	/////	5
16th	//	2
17th	///	3
18th	///////	7
19th	//	2

Cognitive: Rate (daily) how strongly you believe the following statement, from 0–100: 'My eyes are normal, and work as well as most people's'.

Date	Rating
14th	55
15th	45
16th	43
17th	50
18th	43
19th	45

0 = not at all; 100 = totally believe

Emotional: Rate (daily) from 1–10, the most anxious you have felt, and how anxious you have felt on average, where 0 = not at all anxious, and 10 = as anxious as I could possibly feel.

Date	Peak anxiety	Average anxiety
14th	8	4
15th	7	5
16th	8	4
17th	9	6
18th	7	5
19th	8	5

Figure 5.4 Records of different aspects of health anxiety

SPECIFIC, CLEARLY DEFINED TARGETS

In order to improve the reliability of your measures, try to ensure that two observers engaged in the same task would agree on their observations. This means spelling out in detail what you want to be recorded.

If you were asking someone to record the frequency with which they 'lose their temper' you could refine this by saying, 'Let's try and be specific about what we mean. For the purposes of this exercise, what would you want to include in "losing your temper"? What would you be doing that would mean that you had lost it?' You then might discover that 'losing your temper' included shouting loudly, saying unkind and inappropriate things, banging doors; but not talking across someone or feeling angry but not shouting.

The advantage of *operationalising* in this way is that, should an incident occur, the client would not have to make a judgement at the time about whether what had happened was included in the definition, it would be clear from the agreed criteria.

It is not uncommon that an internal state is the focus of measurement, in which case it is not possible to use the criterion of agreement by two observers. Nevertheless, you should take care to minimise ambiguities in what is being recorded.

One client became dissociated in a number of situations and was recording where this happened. It was agreed in advance that she would look for instances where she had been unaware of her surroundings but that she would not include occasions when she felt unpleasantly vague and light-headed but was still aware of where she was.

PROVIDE CLEAR, SIMPLE AND RECORDED INSTRUCTIONS

Do not expect your client to remember what the task entails, because he may either forget it altogether, or his memory may distort the task: write it down (or, even better, get him to do so) in a notebook or on smartphone for example.

USE SENSITIVE AND MEANINGFUL MEASURES

In some cases, measures that are most sensitive to change, and therefore helpful in plotting progress, may not capture the characteristics of the problem that are most important for the client. Both sensitive *and* meaningful measures are important but for different reasons: the first because they allow you to look at the effects of interventions relatively quickly, and the second because they focus on what the client believes to be the central, meaningful aspects of the problem.

A depressed woman was most interested in whether *her mood* was improving in response to treatment. As part of therapy, she was trying to increase the number of pleasurable and satisfying activities she engaged in, and she kept a daily record of how many hours she managed to work, and how many social contacts she had, and these were totalled each week. She also kept a daily mood rating. Although her activity ratings were directly related to an aspect of the formulation (reduced activity), she was more interested in her daily mood scores and her weekly Beck Depression Inventory score, as she felt this best captured how she was getting on.

PROVIDE AIDS TO RECORDING

Minimise demand by providing as much support as possible for the practical task of monitoring, at least in the early stages of therapy. Rating forms or diaries should be drawn up with your client, with as many copies as will be required. The record sheets should be as simple and discreet as possible, bearing in mind that many clients would be embarrassed to be seen recording personal information. For example, a small index card might usefully record daily information, dedicated pages could be inserted into a diary, or a phone memo pad could be used.

TRAIN CLIENTS TO USE MEASURES

Even if the task appears to be straightforward, always ask your client to go through a recent example and carry out the recording process with you. This will ensure that the task is clear and will allow you to discuss difficulties that crop up. For example, suppose you asked a woman to complete a three-column record of the situation, her feelings and her thoughts: you might take her through this task like this:

Therapist: Can we think about the last time that you felt panicky, and fill in the record about that? What would you put in this column here, where it says 'Situation'?

Client: I was out shopping.

Therapist: That's interesting, just where were you, and when? It might be important to discover just which places are difficult for you and when.

Client: OK, well it was in the village. I wasn't actually in a shop but I was planning to go to the 'Coffee Bean' to buy some coffee. It was mid-day when there are all these queues of people. Just the thought of it was upsetting. I stood outside, dreading going in. I was so nervous and I was cross with myself, too.

Therapist: That's really helpful because now I'm getting a much clearer idea of what was going on. So, in the 'Situation' column, why don't you write what you just said about being in the village at mid-day, standing outside a busy 'Coffee Bean'. [*Client does so*] That's great. Now, you've actually started to move on ahead of me and given me information for the 'Feelings' and 'Cognitions' columns, so why don't we tease out just how you felt and what was going through your mind when you say 'it was upsetting'.

In this example, you see how the therapist is encouraging and takes the lead in detailing and organising the information. As therapy progresses the client would be able to do this for herself. You should also spend some time clarifying rating procedures, as they may be unfamiliar to your client. For example, you might say:

> That's interesting; people often experience several feelings, which is why the column is labelled 'Emotions'. You could note down that you felt dread and that you were nervous and that you were also cross: three emotions. You might have noticed that there is a 1–10 scale for you to rate the strength of

> the emotions. This is so we can see how different situations affect the levels of your emotions, and this helps us better understand your particular experiences. Let's go over that now. [*Looking at the record and the scale together*] Zero on this scale means that you are not feeling an emotion at all, and 10 means 'as bad as you could possibly imagine feeling it'. Can you think of a time when you have felt like that, a 10? ... and what about a 5; can you think of a time when you felt moderately anxious, halfway between these two? .... and what about a 7? Can you think of a time when you have felt quite a bit more than 'moderate', but not as extreme as a 10?

In this conversational way, the client is tutored in making distinctions concerning the intensity of emotion. This is vital, as we all become rather 'all or nothing' in our judgement when we get distressed and it becomes hard to discriminate levels of feeling. In coaching and tutoring your clients, remember that you are anticipating that they will learn the *skill* of self-monitoring and be able to use this to manage problems in the future, so make sure that you are preparing to pass on the responsibility for this.

COLLECT DATA AS SOON AS POSSIBLE AFTER THE EVENT

If records are not completed until some time after the event, it is likely that recall will be less vivid and/or will be biased by the client's mood at the time he completes the record. It may not be possible for him to record an experience as soon as it happens, particularly if he is with other people, but he should be encouraged to go over in his mind what he will record and to complete the task as soon as it is practically possible. Alternatively, it may be possible for him to make a brief note at the time and to complete the full monitoring when it is more convenient.

PAY ATTENTION TO THE MONITORING

We should never fail to take notice of information that has been collected. If the information is truly valuable, then the next session should to some extent rely on it; but in any case, it is important that the client's efforts are rewarded by genuine interest, so that he will be willing to continue monitoring in future. Ensure that feedback on any such homework is part of your shared agenda for the session.

WHAT SORTS OF INFORMATION TO COLLECT

There are many different ways of recording useful information, and the following examples give a flavour of this variety. There will be other examples in later chapters, and many academic papers and books will also give measures for specific problems that can be adopted for clinical use.

FREQUENCY COUNTS

A useful guide is that if there is something relevant that you can count, then count it! Counting is potentially the most reliable measurement method, even though it may appear very simple. The variety of features that can be counted is almost boundless, and it is worth trying to think of aspects of the problem that could be measured in this way. Examples include:

- number of self-critical thoughts;
- number of times of checking (that the house is locked, that there are no spider's webs, etc.);
- number of eye-lashes pulled out (in trichotillomania);
- number of toilet rolls used in a week (to assess OCD problems);
- number of phone calls received;
- number of times of swearing;
- number of times clothes changed;
- number of urges to binge.

Therapist and client creativity is the only limit to the variety of possible frequency counts.

It is important to have an idea of what the frequency might be before monitoring; it is not helpful to ask someone to record the number of intrusive thoughts in a day if the total is likely to be a few hundred! Should the frequency be very high, then the client can be asked to take a sample at a relevant time of day (e.g. a half-hour period when the thoughts are at their most troubling) or, if there is no reason to focus on a particular time, an arbitrary time (e.g. between 5 and 6 o'clock).

DURATION OF EVENT/EXPERIENCE

The duration of an event or experience may also be relevant, and is also likely to be a reliable measure. Examples include:

- time spent washing for a client with obsessions;
- time spent body-checking for someone with health anxiety;
- time spent travelling alone for a man with agoraphobia;
- time able to concentrate on reading for a depressed client.

Again, use your imagination.

SELF-RATINGS

These are amongst the most commonly used measures, as they can capture the quality of internal events such as emotions and cognitions. They are less reliable than frequency

Whenever you are away from home, rate:

- *How anxious you feel before you go to the lavatory:*
  0 = not at all anxious; 10 = as anxious as you could possibly feel
- *How strong was your urge to go:*
  0 = no urge at all; 10 = very strong urge
- *How much urine you pass:*
  0 = none, 1 = a little, 2 = a moderate amount, 3 = a lot, 4 = a great deal

Date and time	Anxiety 0–10	Urge 0–10	Amount 0–4
23rd July, 9.15	6	5	2
23rd July, 11.00	7	4	1
23rd July, 12.15	6	6	1
23rd July, 15.20	5	5	2

Figure 5.5 Diary for a man anxious about micturition

counts or measures of duration, but their reliability can be improved if the simple guidelines outlined above are followed. Although they are more reliable than a simple description of the experience, they remain subject to shifts in 'anchor points', in the sense that a rating of 'moderate', or 5 on a 10-point scale, may mean something different at the beginning of treatment compared with the end, as the individual gradually comes to have fewer highly distressing experiences.

If a discrete event is being monitored, then the client can be asked to rate it each time it occurs. For example, a man with anxiety about micturition rated how anxious he felt before going to the lavatory and also rated how much urine he passed (see Figure 5.5).

However, if the phenomenon being measured is continuous (as anxiety may sometimes be) or occurs very frequently, then it may be necessary for the person to choose a time to rate (as described above under 'Frequency counts'). An alternative is to take an average rating for a period of time: for example, to rate average anxiety during the morning, afternoon and evening; more detailed information can then be obtained, for example using the level of anxiety as a cue to begin to look at triggers (see Figure 5.6).

DIARIES

You will have noticed that we've been combining frequency and duration counts and self ratings with diaries. Diaries can combine the kinds of measure described above *and* allow you to look at the links between different aspects of problems, such as the relationship between the problem and particular triggers, safety-seeking behaviours and modulating

Rate how anxious you have felt *on average* each morning, afternoon and evening. If you have a rating greater than 5, note what you were doing at the time.

	Anxiety 0–10	**Situation if anxiety > 5**
Monday a.m.	4	
p.m.	7	In meeting with seniors
evening	2	
Tuesday a.m.	6	Planning presentation
p.m.	7	Presentation
evening	2	
Wed. a.m.	4	
p.m.	4	

Figure 5.6 Diary of anxiety about work

variables. As diaries are more multi-faceted, it is even more important to pay attention to setting up the recording and training the client in their use. Unless care is taken, the client may return with information that is inconsistently collected and difficult to analyse. Get feedback from the client about what is relevant, whether the recording sheet seems sensible and whether there are ambiguities that would make it difficult to use. Also, do be diligent in pacing this increase in data collection so that your client never feels overwhelmed.

Figure 5.7 shows a diary from a woman with a phobia about vomiting, which prevented her from carrying out a range of social and domestic activities. The diary included aspects of the problem that she felt were important, particularly her sense of achievement, which compensated for the anxiety she experienced in the short term.

Two diaries in common use are described later: the Dysfunctional Thought Record or Daily Thought Record (DTR) in Chapter 8, and the Activity Schedule in Chapter 12.

QUESTIONNAIRES

There is an enormous range of questionnaires available for clinical use, many of them originally developed for use in research trials (see Chapter 18 for some questionnaires commonly used in clinical practice). A major advantage of many questionnaires is that they will provide you with the scores of relevant groups (e.g. the normal population, or a group of depressed out-patients) so that you can compare your client's score to others. However, a questionnaire may not be as sensitive a measure as a simpler record focused on the client's own problem. In other words, questionnaires are different from rating scales or frequency

Date	Situation	Safety behaviours dropped	Anxiety 0–10	Sense of achievement 0–10
23rd June	Made ill friend a cup of tea and drank with her	Did not disinfect tea-cup; held the cup afterwards and drank from it; drank on 'her' side; did not wipe the work surface; took dog for walk so did not sit and think it all through	8	10
26th June	Walked down passage where someone had been sick	Did not go to the far side; went back the same way, though knew it was there; did not hold my breath; wore same clothes in the evening	9	10
27th June	Ate yoghurt on day date expired	Kept busy in evening and did not sit and ruminate to check whether I felt sick; did not stay up late in case I felt sick in bed	6	9

Figure 5.7 Diary recording success in dropping safety behaviours

counts, but not necessarily better: it depends on what information you need. In any event, it is important to use questionnaires that are well standardised and validated, otherwise the results of the questionnaire may be unreliable and not meaningful.

See Video 5.1: Questionnaires (i): introducing questionnaires, giving the rationale and checking the client's understanding; and Video 5.2: Questionnaires (ii): feeding back the results of questionnaires.

OTHER SOURCES OF INFORMATION

Although the majority of the information used in therapy is provided by the client, different data sources can be relevant: these might include other informants, live observations of behaviour and physiological data.

OTHER INFORMANTS

It may be helpful to interview others for several reasons:

- They may have information unavailable to the client: for example, a client may believe he behaves oddly in social situations, and someone else's view can provide useful information to confirm or contradict; or a relative may report that their spouse is very quiet and initiates little conversation whether at home or out socially, and this may not be obvious to the client.

- The problem may have an impact on another person, which can exacerbate a difficulty: for example, a client with obsessional problems may involve relatives or other significant people in his rituals, thus stressing them. This in turn could create an environmental tension worsening the obsessional problem. Consider also a client who would not allow anyone into the kitchen for the rest of the day after she had rigorously cleaned it: this resulted in a strained family who pressured her and then she felt harassed and compelled to exert even more control over the situation.
- The way someone else helps the client deal with problems may be relevant to its maintenance: for example, an elderly husband was very loathe to let his wife go out for even a short walk to begin building up her self-confidence following an RTA, as he feared that she might become unsteady or lose her way. And of course, reassurance-giving is a classic example of the interpersonal maintenance of a problem.
- The other person's beliefs about the problem may be important as they might influence the beliefs of the client: for example, that medication is likely to be the only effective solution; that the client is a bad person; that avoidance is always the best solution.

Other informants should be approached in a similar way to the client, recognising that they will need to be engaged, to be given hope and, possibly, to be educated about CBT. The reasons for using Socratic enquiry will also apply to them just as much as to the client (see Chapter 7).

Although an interview is the most common way of obtaining information from other informants, they can be asked to provide more directly observed material in the same way as the client. Frequency counts, ratings, diaries and questionnaires may all be useful in some circumstances.

The issue of confidentiality should be discussed with both the client and the other informants, to establish whether there are things that either party does not wish to be disclosed. It is worth checking out whether the reasons for this are well founded or perhaps based on an erroneous belief. For example, a relative may be concerned that mentioning worries about suicidal ideas might put such ideas into the client's head, when in fact this is not a risk.

LIVE OBSERVATION AND ROLE PLAY

Observing your client at the time the problem occurs can provide significant information that the client has forgotten or of which he was unaware. For example, a woman with a complex hand-washing ritual took for granted some of the details involved in the ritual, including that she washed the soap and put it back on the sink after completing each stage in the ritual; a man with social phobia was unaware of the extent to which he averted his gaze in casual social interactions. Live observation means that you, the therapist, can judge for yourself the extent of a problem and you can discover important details that may be outside your client's awareness.

Sometimes, you can observe behaviour in naturalistic settings: for example, a therapist accompanied a man with social anxiety into shops and observed his interactions when he asked for goods or presented items for purchase. At other times, you might contrive a situation: for example, the therapist asked a teenager with OCD to briefly 'contaminate' herself during a session by touching a doorknob with her bare hands (which she usually avoided) and then to carry out her usual ritual to make things safe.

Sometimes you can recreate a relevant situation in session using role play: a young man was nervous about asserting himself at work, quite convinced that he spoke unclearly and looked 'odd' when he tried to ask for something for himself. Through role play his therapist was able to observe his interpersonal skills and to properly appreciate just how difficult he found the situation. She was also able to give him some useful feedback – namely, that he was actually rather fluent and did not look odd at all in her view.

You can, of course, use the full range of measures while observing the client, including frequency count and rating scales.

PHYSIOLOGICAL MEASURES

Many research reports, particularly those involving anxiety, include measures of physiological state, and indeed, it may be the physiological symptoms that are the most upsetting for the client as, for example, in panic disorder. Although there are simple, portable instruments for measuring (e.g. heart rate or galvanic skin response), these are rarely used in routine clinical practice. Often, the client's perception of the physical changes, and their meaning to him, are sufficient indices of change within that response system.

A client feared fainting when anxious, and in order to give him information about the state of his blood pressure (BP), he was asked to focus on his heart rate (HR). This was raised, and the therapist questioned him about the relationship between HR and BP, and then explained to him that fainting results from a decrease in BP.

Thus, the focus was on an indirect measure of a physiological variable and did not demand direct physical recording.

MAKING THE MOST OF THE DATA

Time and energy go into collecting information, so you should ensure that you make good use of it. First, examine it carefully to see what it says about the hypothesis it was designed to test. This may involve *collating* the data in some way. For example, if your client has produced a series of questionnaires over a number of weeks, graph the results and look for variations. This is something that people can be encouraged to do for themselves. Figure 5.8 shows a graph for a series of Beck Depression Inventory (BDI) scores from someone being treated for depression.

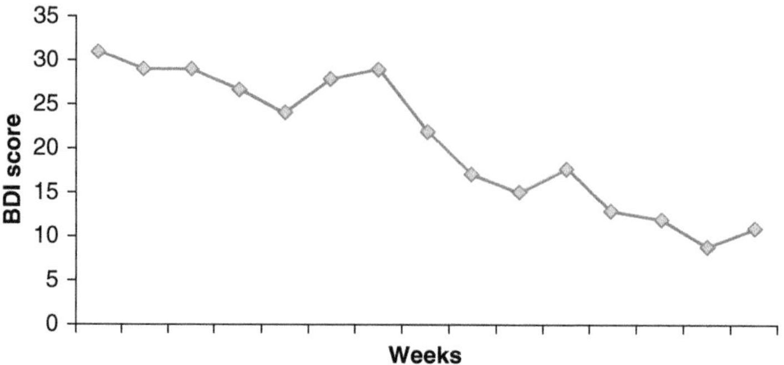

Figure 5.8 Graph of the BDI scores over treatment

However, a series of *diaries* may be more difficult to summarise because the information is not categorised easily. You might find that asking your client to review 'What this is telling me' a useful way forward, particularly as this targets shifts in cognitions. This exercise also helps your client develop the skill of 'reading' a diary and getting the most out of data collection.

Therapist: Looking over your diaries from the past week, what have you learnt? What changes can you see?

Client: I can see that there is a theme of 'get active–feel less depressed' and there is a pattern of things being worse in the morning. Mornings give me a 'back to square one' feeling. I can see that going out with Heather cheers me more than anything – that's why I've been doing that more often.

Therapist: On our 1–10 scale, how do you feel in the morning?

Client: Between 2–3. If you look at the diary, it's pretty much the same for each morning (although it used to be all 1–2 when I first came to therapy). Actually there is one rating of 4 – after Heather and I had been out all day before.

Therapist: Hm. What do you make of that?

Client: Things are getting a bit better and I should keep up my contact with Heather?

Therapist: Very possibly. How does it feel if you've been active, particularly if you've met up with Heather?

Client: If I just go for a walk then I get up to a 5 (but it doesn't last very long); if I do some exercise then I get up to a 6 and it lasts longer; if I meet up with Heather I get 8s and it lasts for a few hours.

Therapist: So, what do you make of that?

Client: The more active I am the better I feel and the best activity is social – having contact with Heather.

Therapist: Indeed – now if we consider everything that you've gleaned from your diary today, there really is *a lot* of useful information there. A lot. I wonder if it might be helpful to summarise it. How would you sum up your progress from looking at your diaries?

Client: It's still very hard: every day is a challenge but I now know that there are things I can do to shift my mood and the mornings just might be getting easier because of what I'm doing.

Therapist: When we started therapy your said 'There's no point in trying, I'll never feel better,' and you believed that 90 per cent. How does what you've just said fit with that?

Client: I'm slowly changing my mind. I am making progress, but it is slow.

Therapist: How about writing that down as your summary of the week and giving it a rating?

Client: Okay – and I'd give it a 60 per cent rating right now (but it might not be so good in the morning).

Here the therapist has used a gentle series of enquiries to help the client explore the information in the diary and to arrive at an authentic new conclusion about progress – a Socratic approach that we will revisit in Chapter 7.

A common stumbling block when anxiety levels are being reviewed is the static or worsening anxiety scores that actually represent improvement! It represents improvement because the client is actually doing more, taking more risks, pushing himself despite the anxiety. The lack of improvement in anxiety scores can be demoralising, so it needs to be reviewed and discussed. As we have already noted, avoidance is the common response to anxiety and this will often keep anxiety ratings low. Once someone starts to tackle their fear, their anxiety scores might not decline (or they might even increase) as more and more difficult tasks are attempted. Figure 5.9 shows data from a client who was severely claustrophobic. It may be helpful to ask him, in the session, to group *tasks* by their difficulty level. He could then look at behavioural improvements in anxiety ratings for *activities* at each difficulty level.

Date	Situation	Anxiety 0–10*	Difficulty 1–5**
12th November	Small room, door open	5	1
14th November	In lift, up one floor	7	2
15th November	End of row, back of hall	4	2
16th November	Small room, door closed	7	3
17th November	Small room, door closed, smoky air	8	4
19th November	Small room, door open	3	1
21st November	Middle of row, back of hall	4	3
23rd November	Small room, door closed	5	3

*0 = not at all; 10 = as anxious as I could possibly be

**1 = imagined being able to do this; 5 = thought I would never manage this

Figure 5.9 Diary of anxiety scores rising with increasingly difficult tasks

As the treatment progresses, data collecting assignments will evolve from the session and the responsibility for collating and interpreting information can increasingly be handed over to your clients. You can ask them to review their own diaries and identify themes or the most important incident to discuss. This helps them develop the ability to review and prioritise, which is necessary for effective problem solving.

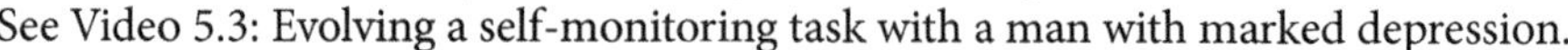

See Video 5.3: Evolving a self-monitoring task with a man with marked depression.

PROBLEMS WHEN USING MEASUREMENTS

THE CLIENT DOES NOT APPRECIATE ITS POTENTIAL VALUE

It is important to elicit and discuss your client's doubts and, if necessary, to get agreement to do some measurement as an experiment.

THE CLIENT CANNOT READ OR WRITE

If a person cannot read or write, you will need ingenuity to find other modalities for recording relevant data, for example using a mobile phone. It is helpful to get the client's advice about how to circumvent the problem, as he will probably have tackled other situations like this.

POOR RELIABILITY OR VALIDITY OF A QUESTIONNAIRE

Always check that a questionnaire has data on reliability and validity and that its normative data are relevant for your client. An adult version of a depression scale might not be the best questionnaire for a teenager; a western anxiety scale might not be relevant to an Asian population. The best questionnaires have often been reviewed and developed for wider use across age range and culture, so do investigate this.

Also, be aware that clients can invalidate the results from the questionnaire or render them unreliable. This is sometimes unintentional: the client has simply misunderstood what to do, and we are again reminded of the advantage of rehearsing questionnaire completion in session. Sometime the results are invalid because a self-report measure can be manipulated to give the response that your client wants to give. For example:

Josh believed that no-one really understood just how dreadful he felt so he exaggerated his anxiety scores to try to impress upon his therapist that he really needed help.

Kat had gained a certain amount of tranquillity now that she had decided to kill herself and she certainly didn't want to let her therapist sabotage her plans. Therefore she made sure that she did not endorse the obvious 'suicide' questions on the BDI.

Ron coped by being brave, telling himself that he was 'strong – can deal with things'. He certainly was not going to dwell on the questionnaire items that asked him about anxiety and misery – he didn't dare go there and he didn't want his therapist to go there either.

Zena found this therapist the best yet and so wanted to please him that she rated progress in the areas she thought he'd want to see improvement in. She was careful, however, never to rate herself feeling too well as she did not want to be discharged.

These examples highlight how essential it is to review questionnaire and other self-report measures really closely. Talk through them with your client, note if their affect in the session is consistent with their self-report accounts, and dare to use Socratic exploration if you feel that all is not what it seems. You can see how crucial this would be with someone like Kat. For clients such as Ron, who have difficulty expressing problems and needs, you could first introduce standardised measures or simple self-ratings of strengths and aptitudes. This might ease him into feeling more confident in himself and thus later enable him to use reports of pathology and need.

Poor reliability can arise from over-using a self-report measure as this can lead to a familiarity that undermines accuracy. For example:

Dino completed the PHQ-9 before every session. He became so familiar with the items that he'd stopped really reading each question and he became careless in completing the whole questionnaire. If he felt that things were relatively OK, he would simply check an entire left-hand column of responses and if things were difficult for him he'd shift over and check a right-hand column. This was less taxing for him but it meant that his therapist lost sight of subtle fluctuations in his mood state.

Some standardised measures have parallel forms that you can use to avoid this problem, but the majority of assessments that we tend to use in CBT don't. So you will find yourself administering the same form over (and over) again. Once more, it is clear that you need to review the responses with your client to establish how true they are, but you also could ask yourself if you really need to collect such detailed information so frequently. For example, in Dino's case it might have been more useful to administer the questionnaire only at the beginning of treatment, at review sessions and on discharge. If you want to keep a closer eye on session-to-session changes, then you might negotiate a simple 3-, 4- or 5-point scale of wellbeing to be completed at the start of each meeting (which is how Dino had begun to use the PHQ-9 anyway).

SUMMARY

- Measuring the qualities of the problems presented by the client, and then assessing changes as treatment progresses, are crucial aspects of CBT. It can be an interesting, creative and collaborative part of therapy, as you use your ingenuity to design measures. Although much useful information is gleaned from the clinical interview, it can be helpful to have supplementary information, both at assessment and during and at the end of treatment. There are a number of reasons for this including:

  - to allow you to assess the effects of intervention;
  - to capitalise on the more reliable there-and-then observations of the problem;
  - to benefit from any possible therapeutic effects of measurement;
  - to allow the client to compare baseline with subsequent measures, so as to more accurately plot progress;
  - to reinforce the idea that treatment can be seen as an empirical exercise.
- It is important to bear in mind the psychometric properties of measures, such as reactivity, reliability and validity. The latter two can be maximised by following some straightforward rules, which are described in the text.
- The measures you collect should be integral to subsequent sessions, and it is very important that you always show genuine interest in the data your client produces.
- Measures differ in their level of complexity, ranging from simple counts, through ratings and diaries, to questionnaires. Think carefully about what information you want, and be creative with your client in devising relevant measures.
- Bear in mind that there are other sources of information – relatives, friends, other staff, psychophysiology – in addition to that provided by your client.
- Make as much use as you can of whatever data your client brings – graph it if that would be helpful, try to relate different aspects to each other, and to whatever hypotheses are thrown up by the formulation.

LEARNING EXERCISES

These learning exercises are available to download from the companion website.

REVIEW AND REFLECTION:

- There are suggestions in the chapter about how to maximise the validity and reliability of any measures that you devise. Think about those suggestions: are there any that you would have problems with? If so, how could you tackle the difficulty?
- It is sometimes claimed that the important aspects of the problems that people present cannot be measured. Consider three clients' problems, and think about what aspects of their problems seem to be difficult to measure. What would you be forfeiting or ignoring if you tried to measure them? What would you gain if you devised a measuring scheme and collected some data?
- Review a sample of your caseload: look at the measures that you have used and consider the validity and reliability of your clients' responses.

TAKING IT FORWARD:

- It can be instructive to carry out some monitoring for yourself, to get an idea of how enlightening and onerous it can be. You could, for example, do a thought record (see Chapter 8) for a day; or you could keep records about the frequency of a behaviour that worries you – snapping at people, scratching your head – and what triggers it on each occasion. Note the challenges that such monitoring presents, and consider how these could be minimised for your clients.
- Review your clients' notes and try to identify missed opportunities for data collection and evaluation. Consider how you might now do something about that. Plan just how you will collect more relevant information and how you will share the rationale for doing so.

FURTHER READING

Hayes, S.C., Barlow, D.H., & Nelson-Gray, R.O. (1999). *The practitioner: research and accountability in the age of managed care.* Boston, MA: Allyn & Bacon.

These authors have consistently argued for therapists to adopt the role of scientist practitioner for the benefit of clients, and this book gives a good resumé of this approach.

VIDEO LINKS

- 5.1 Questionnaires (i): introducing questionnaires, giving the rationale and checking the client's understanding
- 5.2 Questionnaires (ii): feeding back the results of questionnaires
- 5.3 Evolving a self-monitoring task with a man with marked depression

6 HELPING CLIENTS BECOME THEIR OWN THERAPISTS

- **Introduction**
- **Helping the client learn and remember**
- **Relapse management: a skill for life**
- **'Self-help' reading (bibliotherapy)**
- **Possible problems**
- **Summary**
- **Learning exercises**
- **Further reading**
- **Video links**
    - **6.1 The learning cycle**
    - **6.2 Relapse management**

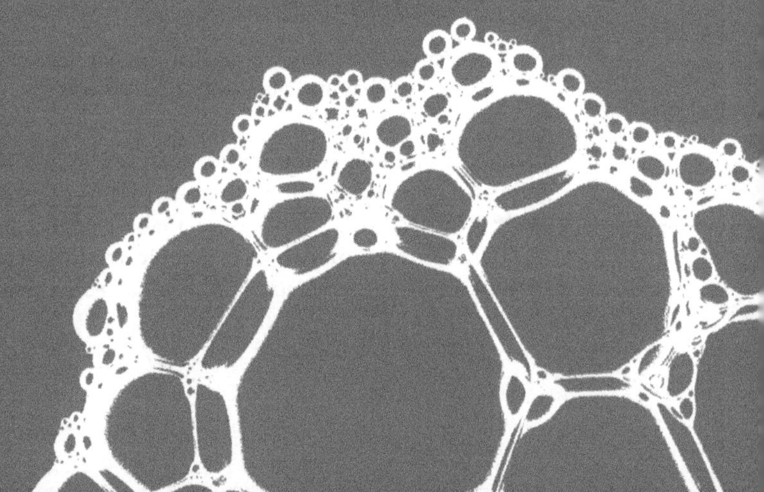

INTRODUCTION

> One of the most powerful components of the learning model of psychotherapy is that the patient begins to incorporate many of the therapeutic techniques of the therapist. (Beck et al., 1979: 4)

In CBT we teach our clients to become their own therapist, with the skills to manage relapse. Essentially, the cognitive therapist aims to make herself redundant, and this means thoroughly educating clients in the model and methods of CBT. There is more to this than simply sharing the cognitive model and strategies: there are ways in which we can make therapeutic techniques more accessible and more memorable and ways in which we can prepare people for independent long-term coping. In Chapter 3 we described how the therapeutic relationship is crucial in helping a client to explore and learn, and how collaboration is fundamental to learning the skills of CBT, so you can see that this is relevant to helping clients become their own therapists. This chapter will build on this and focus on ways in which learning and independence can be further enhanced and relapse management established.

HELPING THE CLIENT LEARN AND REMEMBER

Clients cannot take on the role of therapist unless they can recall the model and methods of CBT. Human beings are good at forgetting. As far back as the 1880s, the psychologist Ebbinghaus demonstrated that we quickly forget *the majority* of information that we attend to, so therapists need to strive to make facts and practical skills memorable.

A starting point is to ask people if they have any particular learning issues. This will help you consider how best to present and frame crucial information. Another pragmatic step is to simply encourage them to:

- keep notes of key learning points;
- review their notes (!);
- make plans to practise skills so that both explicit and procedural knowledge (the 'what' and the 'what to do') is not lost.

Create the right environment for learning by minimising distraction, using visual aids, giving time for information to be processed, and keeping stress levels optimum. These are easily achieved goals and they can make a significant difference to retention.

There are many models to explain learning, but perhaps one of the most relevant (and simple) for us as therapists is the adult learning theory of Lewin (1946) and Kolb (1984).

ADULT LEARNING THEORY

This model emphasises the importance of experiential learning and the value of reflection: learning through experiencing *and* reflecting *and* doing. It comprises four necessary stages in effective learning:

- experience;
- observation;
- reflection;
- planning.

These form a cycle as illustrated in Figure 6.1. For learning to be effective, one needs to move through all the stages of the cycle.

This understanding of the elements of effective learning can help therapists in many ways: for example, in deciding when to provide information and when to use Socratic method and in creating assignments to make learning more memorable. The next chapter focuses on the Socratic method, but it is worth noting here that the Socratic method contains elements of the learning cycle. When using it, we cue people to share their experiences (observation); use this to develop new understandings of their problems (reflection); then synthesise new possibilities and ways forward (planning new experiences). Similarly, Chapters 8 and 9 focus on cognitive and behavioural techniques respectively, and you will again see how these crucial elements of CBT are linked by the learning cycle: cognitive techniques help develop new insights and possibilities (observation–reflection–planning) which are tested 'in the field' (experience).

As an example of the learning cycle, you could present the model of CBT or illustrate the interactions of feelings, thoughts and actions in a way that takes your client around all four elements.

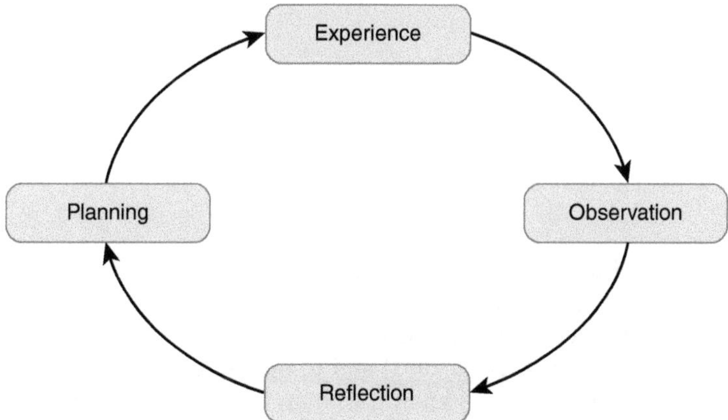

Figure 6.1 The adult learning cycle (adapted from Lewin, 1946 and Kolb, 1984)

EXPERIENCE, OBSERVATION

Therapist: How did you feel?

Client: Pretty anxious: I was scared.

Therapist: And what was running through your mind?

Client: I thought that I would embarrass myself – look like a fool.

Therapist: So what did you do?

Client: I told my boss that I couldn't do the presentation because I would be on annual leave – I then booked in annual leave.

Therapist: So you got out of doing the presentation: how did that leave you feeling and what was going through your mind then?

Client: After the initial relief, I felt even worse. I still hadn't faced my anxiety of public speaking and now I had the fear that my boss would realise that I'd lied to her.

Therapist: It seems that you felt scared and you thought that you would embarrass yourself; so you avoided what frightened you but soon regretted it.

Client: Well, yes.

REFLECTION

Therapist: So, what might you learn from this?

Client: I suppose it's obvious really: if I get scared, I should face up to my fears. Running away is only making me feel worse about myself and I think that it makes me more anxious.

PLANNING

Therapist: Facing up to your fears … do you have any thoughts on how you might go about doing that?

This could then lead to planning a behavioural experiment that would provide an experience that could be reviewed, and so on. This incorporation of experience and cognition has been shown to promote greater cognitive, affective and behavioural change than purely verbal interventions (Bennett-Levy, 2003) and to help to bridge the 'thinking–believing gap' that clients often experience ('I know it with my head but I just don't *feel* that it is so') (Rachman & Hodgson, 1974).

It has been suggested that we each have preferences in the way that we use information and learn from it. Honey and Munford (1992) mapped these preferences on to the learning

cycle and identified four preference types: activist, reflector, theorist and pragmatist. As you can see, they use the descriptive labels differently from Lewin and Kolb, which can be confusing, but the labels are less important than the concepts. As you read through the descriptions of each stage in the cycle consider your own preferences.

EXPERIENCE (ACTIVIST)

The time of action, engagement, 'doing'. This is the preferred quadrant of the *activist*, who enjoys being engaged in something tangible. Within therapy this might include role play or setting a behavioural assignment or accompanying a client during a behavioural task.

OBSERVATION (REFLECTOR)

The part of the cycle where there is reflection upon what has happened: the preferred position of the *reflector*, who takes time to digest events and mull them over. In sessions this could include the process of reviewing a client's thought diary or collecting feedback at the end of a meeting.

REFLECTION (THEORIST)

Making sense of what happened by relating it to previous experiences and knowledge. This analytical phase is preferred by the *theorist*, who enjoys searching for understanding and links. In therapy, this might be the process of reflecting back on the formulation of a problem, generalising from an experience or abstracting principles.

PLANNING (PRAGMATIST)

The phase when practical implications of a new understanding are considered, preferred by the *pragmatist*. This marks the time when plans are made, thus creating the basis for further experience. In therapy this is the time of preparing the next step, setting goals and tasks based on a new understanding.

Personal preferences (of client or therapist) can result in the under- or over-emphasising of elements of the cycle. For example:

- The *activist* might dwell disproportionately on the 'doing' part of the task, for instance engaging in a behavioural assignment but then failing to review it thoroughly. This means that it is difficult to appreciate the implications of the experience and to take it forward. At worst, the experience is wasted.
- The *reflector* might review the assignment in some detail but fail to make links with previous experiences or to generalise to develop principles. In this case, planning would be impaired as it could lack a theoretical basis and would be unlikely to make links with the client's problem formulation.
- The *theorist* will make links, but if observation is weak there will be little to work with. If the phase of planning is also weak, then meaningful future opportunities for learning can be lost.

- Finally, the *pragmatist* will focus on creating concrete plans, but these will be less effective without proper engagement in the active phase and the stages of observation and theorising. Unless all four phases are involved, even the best planning is unlikely to result in new skills being learnt or remembered.

Be aware that your own preferences might interact unhelpfully with the preferences of your client. For example, two reflector-theorists might have an agreeable and stimulating time philosophising but not be sufficiently active in therapy, so that experiential learning does not occur. Problems can also arise from an antagonistic combination, such as the activist–theorist therapist frustrated by the reflector or the pragmatist client, who might seem frustratingly slow or obsessive. Thus, in some instances, difference in preferences can underpin problems in the therapeutic alliance (see Chapter 3). On the other hand, different preferences and styles can complement each other. An activist client can be encouraged to reflect and plan by a therapist with different preferences just as the activist–pragmatist therapist can build on the theorising of the 'armchair' client and help him better engage in behavioural experiments.

See Video 6.1: Taking your client around the learning cycle using clinical material.

We hope that it is now clear that learning style is relevant to communicating CT, and to the development of the therapeutic alliance. It really is worth taking time to reflect on it. As a therapist, try to stand back and appreciate how your style and preference can complement your client's preferred way of learning and working.

REMEMBERING

Learning is not just about *acquiring* knowledge; information also has to be *retained* and it has to be *retrievable*. Since clients need to be able to remember salient points from therapy, an understanding of memory and how we might enhance it can be a valuable adjunct to our work. There are several useful resources for understanding more about memory and information processing, but one of the most informative and readable books is still Alan Baddeley's *Your memory: a user's guide* (2004). This section owes much to his text.

The main systems involved in remembering are:

- *Short-term memory (STM)*: This is the 'temporary holding point' for information (20–30 seconds). The information will be forgotten if it is not relevant or rehearsed enough to be transferred to long-term memory.
- *Long-term memory (LTM)*: This is the 'depot', where information may be held indefinitely. Contrary to some beliefs, memory is not held like a recording that gets replayed when we recall something. It is more like a jigsaw puzzle, with the pieces being stored in different parts of the brain waiting to be reconstructed when we remember. This is an important point because it makes memory susceptible to distortion.

Is this relevant to clinical practice? Yes: the following example illustrates how understanding something about learning and memory can help a person get the most out of treatment.

Whilst learning a relaxation technique, a man reclines in a chair in his therapist's office. His sensory memory processes verbal instruction, the tone of his therapist's voice and the physical sensation of relaxing a body part or breathing slowly. This will be held in STM while he carries out instructions and reflects on the effects of relaxation. If the exercises are considered relevant, they are then more likely to be stored in LTM.

If the exercises are not considered relevant, or are poorly attended to, they will be lost.

Let us assume that the rationale for introducing relaxation exercises was initially persuasive and this man attended to the instructions, practised at home and returned to the session giving feedback on the experience. However, it emerged that his practice was not as the therapist expected. Although some elements of the regime had been remembered, parts had been forgotten and parts had been mixed up with other exercise instructions. Overall, the exercises had not been helpful. Discussion revealed what might have contributed to this:

1. He did not remember the rationale for the exercises and so struggled to appreciate their relevance.
2. The exercise had only been practised once in session, there had been little debriefing and nothing written down: thus he had formed a poor memory of the exercise.
3. In trying to recall the relaxation exercise the client had unwittingly drawn on memories of yoga techniques learned years earlier, which disrupted his recollection.
4. Both therapist and client tended towards the 'activist' quadrant of the learning cycle and were light on planning.

How might the client's recall have been improved?

- *Relevance*: material that is perceived as important or meaningful is more likely to be remembered. This is why sharing a rationale – and checking that the client understands and agrees with the rationale – is so important in therapy.
- *Focus*: distractions impair memory, so clients benefit from being focused. Therapists should minimise distraction and keep clients directed towards the task.
- *Repetition*: repeating information and experiences will render them more memorable. In this case, the therapist might usefully run through the relaxation exercise more than once.
- *Active engagement*: getting feedback would also have helped. This would have prompted rehearsal of the information and encouraged the formation of personal links: subjectively relevant material is always more memorable than information that does not have personal associations.
- *Memory aids*: we all forget things, so we all benefit from notes, lists and so on. It might have been helpful to have given this man a handout restating the rationale and the techniques of relaxation, or to have recorded the exercise.

- *Familiarity*: we tend to 'reorganise' our memories in the light of previous experiences and beliefs (Bartlett, 1932). Therefore, it is useful if the therapist checks out the client's responses to, and associations with, a particular technique. Often, previous experiences can helpfully be incorporated – in this example, familiar yoga techniques could have been structured into the exercises, making them more memorable.
- *Working through the learning cycle*: the client would have benefited from being cued to reflect on the exercise, consider what he had learnt and how he might take that forward. The conceptualisation and planning stages of the learning cycle offer an opportunity for trouble-shooting and for making concrete plans to practise.

Principles of effective learning apply to each of the cognitive and behavioural techniques we introduce, from simple diary-keeping through to complicated behavioural experiments. By using them you can help clients better learn the skills of symptom management; but we also want our clients to be able to manage their difficulties in the longer term, and so they must become skilled in relapse management, too. We turn to this now.

RELAPSE MANAGEMENT: A SKILL FOR LIFE

As stated earlier, clients must become independent of the therapist, and that means they need to remember the techniques of CBT *and* to be able to use them in difficult situations *and* to draw on them after a setback. It is crucial to long-term success that clients are able to tackle setbacks productively, to learn from them and build on them. You might wonder why this section is called relapse *management* rather than *prevention*. Although some treatment approaches might aim to have no relapses, it can be almost impossible to prevent some degree of relapse in some disorders and with some clients. Those who anticipate that they can completely prevent relapse (client or therapist) are likely to be disappointed. However, it is possible to learn how to *manage* such events and to regain progress that has been lost.

Our recommendation is that relapse management is introduced early on in therapy so that it is developed as a skill that can be refined over the course of treatment. The most basic form of relapse management comprises three questions asked following a setback:

- 'How can I make sense of this?'
- 'What have I learnt from it?'
- 'With hindsight, what would I do differently?'

Following a setback or lapse or relapse (however it is experienced), people are often too distressed to engage in a demanding recovery procedure, but these three simple questions are 'mentally portable' and will give swift direction for recovery. You can first work through them in session and later they can prompt your clients 'in the field' – in this way, they develop the habit of analysing and profiting from setbacks.

Carol struggled with an eating disorder and had periods of binge-eating. One evening she bought quite large quantities of her favourite foods, went home alone and consumed them, only spitting out chewed mouthfuls when she became over-full, but unable to stop eating. During this time she could not stop herself. Such an evening would usually have marked the beginning of a significant decline. She would have woken the next day feeling physically unwell and uncomfortable, she would have concluded that she was a hopeless failure and her mood would certainly have been depressed. As a 'hopeless failure' she would have felt powerless to resist the urge to comfort eat. However, on this occasion, she asked herself:

- How can I make sense of this lapse? She realised that she had been feeling stressed at work for several days but had kept pushing herself in order not to think about her troubled relationship. In addition, she had begun to resume her old habit of starving throughout the day in an attempt to lose weight. Once she had reflected on her situation, she was then able to say: 'It's no wonder that I fell off the wagon. Not only was I stressed to breaking point but I set myself up for a binge by not eating during the day.'
- What have I learnt from it? 'I realise that, for me, it is dangerous to starve as a means of weight control – it backfires. Also, I need to keep a check on my stress level: when it gets too high I am vulnerable to comfort eating.'
- With hindsight, what would I do differently? 'Hard as it is, I would try to eat 'sensibly' and avoid starving. Looking back, I made a mistake in trying to pretend that I did not have problems in my relationship and then throwing myself into my work as a distraction. If I had that time over again I would acknowledge my problems, or maybe even talk to someone about them rather than ignoring them.'

Not only does this give Carol a plan for coping in the future, but she has learnt more about her particular needs and vulnerabilities. With each setback she will be able to continue to 'fine-tune' her understanding of her difficulties and develop a wider and more individually tailored repertoire of coping responses.

The pioneers of relapse work in CBT are Marlatt and Gordon (1985), who first developed their model and strategies in the treatment of addictive behaviours. However, their understanding of relapse risk and management has proven to be relevant across psychological disorders (Witkiewitz & Marlatt, 2007). They identified several factors that rendered people vulnerable to relapse. A particularly potent one was a dichotomous, or 'all or nothing' interpretation of a setback. They observed that those who perceived themselves as *either* being in control *or* having failed tended to relapse at the first sign of difficulty: these clients flipped from feeling in control to feeling as though they had failed completely. Once in the 'failure' mindset, they tended to be dominated by a sense of hopelessness which drove unhelpful behaviours such as continuing to drink for comfort. Instead, Marlatt and Gordon encouraged a continuous notion of being in control and slipping out of control, which could accommodate minor and even significant setbacks without automatically assuming failure (see Figure 6.2).

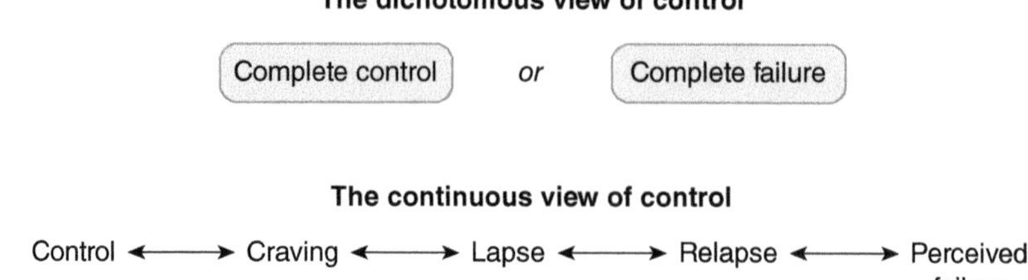

Figure 6.2 The dichotomous and the continuous views of control

Holding onto this model of a *spectrum* of experiences between control and perceived failure increased the likelihood that a slip or a setback would be perceived as a temporary aberration that could be corrected. To further encourage resilience, clients would be urged to consider the different stages along the continuum and to ask:

- 'When will I be at risk of this happening?'
- 'What are the signs?'
- 'What could I do to avoid losing control?'
- 'What could I do if I did lose control (damage limitation)?'

In this way, 'early warning signs' can be detected and steps taken to avert a lapse, whilst there is a well-considered backup plan in place. Thus, a lapse can be construed as an anticipated event for which there is a solution.

What factors besides dichotomous thinking predispose a person to relapse? Marlatt and Gordon identified a sequence of events that systematically increased the likelihood of relapse:

- *Being in a high-risk situation*: for example, a depressed person being socially isolated, or someone with an eating disorder not having eaten for too long.
- *Having poor or no coping strategies*: for example, poor mood management skills or no helpful ideas for dealing with hunger pangs in a controlled way.
- *The sense of loss of self-efficacy*: for example, thinking 'I'm hopeless. It's my fault that I'm depressed,' or 'There's no point in trying to resist. I just can't.' Such thoughts give a person 'permission' to let go or give in. This step can be exacerbated by substance misuse.
- *Engaging in unhelpful behaviours*: for example, withdrawing further or binge-eating.

In Marlatt and Gordon's view, the worst was still to come: they recognised that many clients who were striving to remain abstinent from problem behaviours became caught up in a powerful cycle of unhelpful thoughts and behaviours once they ceased to be abstinent. They called this the 'abstinence violation effect' (AVE) and saw this as marking true relapse – a state of not being able to break away from the problem behaviours because of compelling negative thoughts (see Figure 6.3).

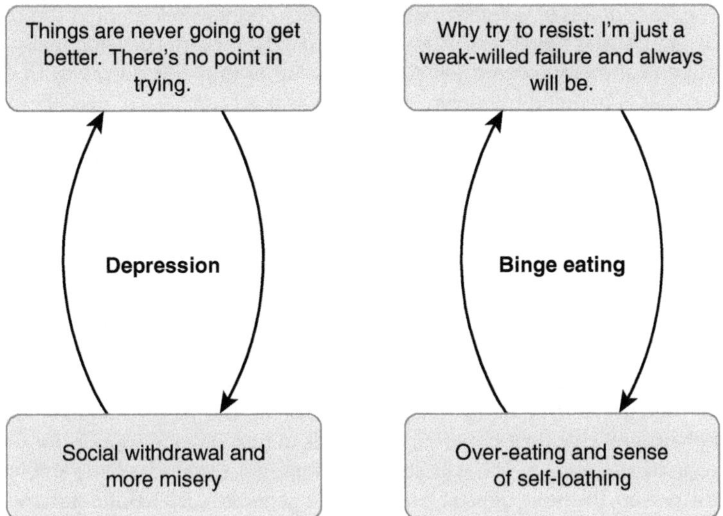

Figure 6.3 The relapse cycle

An advantage of identifying the steps en route to the AVE is that they offer clear points for interventions, which can then interrupt progress towards relapse. As memory and performance are often impaired in distress, it is advisable to encourage your clients to write down their personal plan for minimising relapse and to make sure that they have easy access to it, of course. Below we lay out some strategies for each of the steps towards relapse:

- *Being in a high-risk situation*: The key is to identify (through monitoring), predict and, where possible, avoid high-risk situations. For example, if a depressed person learns he is at risk of becoming miserable when socially isolated, he needs to strive to maintain social contacts; if a woman with an eating disorder is at risk of binge-eating when over-stressed or hungry, she needs to avoid getting into those situations. However, difficult circumstances are sometimes unavoidable, so vulnerable clients may find themselves in a high-risk situation. This does not make relapse inevitable, although it is more likely if the client has poor coping strategies or has grown increasingly ambivalent about change (in which case it may be helpful to try to re-motivate clients by using a motivational interviewing approach: see Miller & Rollnick, 2002 or Rollnick, Miller & Butler, 2008).
- *Having poor or no coping strategies*: Clients are encouraged to develop appropriate cognitive and behavioural coping strategies and to plan how they would put the strategies into action. Although this is a routine part of their CBT, it is helpful for them to keep reminders of what works for them, which they can access at times of need when their memory might be impaired by their emotional state. Someone prone to depression might list all the social activities and contacts he could try if he felt vulnerable; the woman at risk of binge-eating might keep a reminder of the activities that curb her urge to binge.

- *The sense of loss of self-efficacy*: This is a very cognitive element in the course of relapse, and therefore CBT is well placed to help clients develop realistically hopeful and empowered self-statements. For example: 'It is my way of thinking that is bringing me down, but tough as it is I can "coach" myself out of it again. Furthermore, there are a lot of friends out there who want to support me,' or 'I can resist. I have resisted in the past. I am not saying that it is easy but I know that it's possible for me.' Again, clients need to anticipate when they are likely to use such statements, and it can be helpful to rehearse using them either in role play or in imagination. This also affords the therapist an opportunity to check that the self-statements are not unhelpfully bullying or critical.
- *Engaging in the unhelpful behaviour*: for example, withdrawing further from social activity, or binge-eating. As you saw in Figure 6.3, people can get locked in a powerful and unhelpful cognitive-behavioural cycle. You can use techniques of cognitive restructuring (Chapter 8) to break the pattern and to support behavioural change (Chapter 9), which will in turn provide support for further cognitive reappraisal. This is illustrated in Figure 6.4. Clearly the more ambivalent the person, the more difficult it might be to generate such helpful statements.

It is worth noting that ambivalence about change (which is discussed more fully in Chapter 11, on the course of therapy) can render a person even more vulnerable to lapses and relapse, and you need to keep track of your client's motivation to change.

See Video 6.2: Sharing the principles of relapse management and teaching the skill.

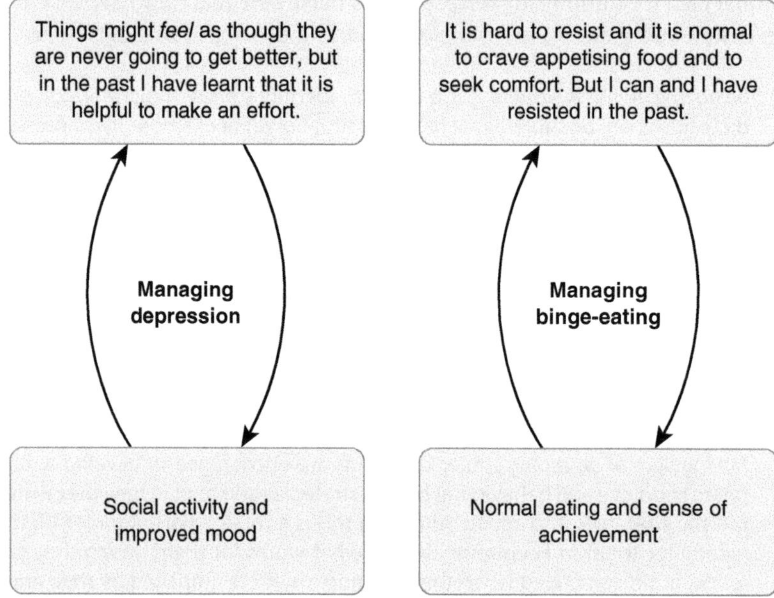

Figure 6.4 Breaking the relapse cycle

'SELF-HELP' READING (BIBLIOTHERAPY)

Your clients' progress and maintenance can be enhanced by their reading relevant literature. Chapter 16 reviews different methods of delivery of CBT, amongst which is bibliotherapy.

There is a wide range of very good CBT texts for the public, some of which are general (e.g. Butler & Hope, 2007; Greenberger & Padesky, 2015) some of which are specific to particular problems (e.g. *Overcoming social anxiety and shyness:* Butler, 2008; *Overcoming depression:* Gilbert, 2009; *Overcoming anxiety:* Kennerley, 2014b; *Overcoming low self-esteem:* Fennel, 2016).

If you are intending to supplement CBT with such literature, do make sure that you have read the booklets or books yourself, so that you can evaluate the quality or demands of the text before you recommend them.

POSSIBLE PROBLEMS

THERAPIST MAINTAINS ROLE OF EXPERT; CLIENT STRIVES TO REMAIN A PATIENT

First, discover what assumptions might be relevant to this problem: what makes sense of it? For example, perhaps you are thinking: 'I have to know more than the client in order be competent'; or the client believes, 'I can never help myself, so there's no point in trying'. The obvious next step is evaluating and testing such assumptions. Use supervision (self, peer or expert) to help clarify and rectify this type of impasse.

COURSE OF THERAPY NOT REFLECTING THE LEARNING CYCLE

Review your and your client's learning styles and preferences. Share the cycle with your client and discuss the mutual advantage to working your way around it. If appropriate, use supervision to discuss the possible impact on your work and ways of overcoming problems.

THE CLIENT WANTS TO BE 'FIXED' OR 'PARENTED'

Some clients do not readily take to the idea of collaboration and self-help. Sometimes, a few sessions of socialising your client into the ways of CBT will be sufficient to shift expectations of passivity or long-term care. However, there will be those who continue to find the goal of self-help unappealing, or even frightening. Try to uncover the assumptions that explain this attitude – assumptions that might have to be tackled before your client can engage in CBT. This can take some time, and you need to ask yourself if you have the time and the skill needed to do this (see Chapter 17 for more discussion of working with complex clients). In any case, an essential guideline is to review regularly. Clarify unhelpful patterns, and if it is not possible for you to help your client with CBT, then consider referral to a therapy that better meets their needs at this stage. For example, supportive counselling might be better for some or a more obviously interpersonally focused therapy, such as cognitive analytic therapy (CAT).

RELAPSE MANAGEMENT IS RESERVED UNTIL THE END OF TREATMENT

Awareness of personal vulnerability and its management is relevant from the outset of therapy. Try to build this into early sessions by asking 'When can you imagine struggling with this?' or 'When do you see yourself being at risk of having a setback?'. If your client has a lapse, use the opportunity to review this *thoroughly* (setting aside enough time to do so), encouraging your client to learn from setbacks early on in your work together.

THERAPIST FEELS PRESSURED AND SKIMPS ON RELAPSE MANAGEMENT

Relapse management is an investment of time, but it is a worthwhile investment as it can save your client the distresses of relapse and it can save your organisation the cost of offering further treatment. If your client cannot see trouble coming or handle it when it arrives, then he will be vulnerable to relapse – even if he is otherwise skilled in cognitive and behavioural techniques.

SUMMARY

An over-arching goal of the cognitive therapist is to ensure that the client becomes his own therapist. We aim to make ourselves redundant by communicating the knowledge and skills necessary to maintain progress and minimise relapse. We can do this most effectively if we attend to the principles of adult learning and memory formation, and if we invest time in addressing relapse management.

- Adult learning theory reminds us to attend to the strengths and preferences both we and our clients show when encountering new information. It also reminds us to be conscientious in encouraging clients to spend time in each 'quadrant' of the learning cycle:
  - observing;
  - reflecting and making links with previous knowledge and developing new ideas;
  - problem solving and thinking how to take things forward;
  - creating active experiences.
- Models of memory remind us of the importance of maintaining focus, encouraging rehearsal of new material, emphasising its relevance, using memory aids and exploiting familiarity with previous experiences and knowledge.
- Relapse management is the key to continued progress and its concepts really need to be introduced from the beginning of treatment so that clients have good opportunity to develop the ability to learn how to learn from their setbacks.

LEARNING EXERCISES

These learning exercises are available to download from the companion website.

REVIEW AND REFLECTION:

- Note what strikes you as being particularly interesting or important in this chapter. How you are going to remember this?
- How do learning theory or memory processes fit with *your* understanding of CBT – do they make sense when you consider them in the context of your work? How do they fit with *your* experiences of having to remember procedures and protocols or the difficulties your clients have in recalling things from one session to the next?
- How does relapse management fit with your experience of dealing with setbacks, either personally or with your clients? Does it seem like a valid approach?

TAKING IT FORWARD:

- Learn more about your learning style, perhaps by completing a learning styles questionnaire (see Honey & Mumford, 1992), or by recording your sessions and observing how you interact with different clients.
- Learn more about memory by reading more on this topic (e.g. Baddeley, 2004) or by signing up for a relevant course or a workshop.
- Plan your clinical sessions in order to enhance memory (both yours and your client's!) and to get the most out of your learning style.
- If relapse management is a particularly pertinent section for you, update your reading (see below); you could introduce it in your sessions and evaluate its impact on client progress. Review with your supervisor your attention to helping your client become his own therapist, to ensure that you keep this in mind.

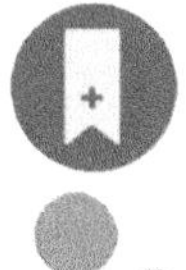

FURTHER READING

Baddeley, A. (2004). *Your memory: a user's guide* (2nd ed.). London: Carlton.

An excellent introduction to memory, written by a leading expert who knows how to communicate with the lay person as well as the specialist. It is a classic work, really well researched and informed yet not at all difficult to read and highly relevant to our work as client coaches and trainers.

Honey, P., & Mumford, A. (1992). *The manual of learning styles*. Maidenhead: Peter Honey.

This is the manual that explains and helps you evaluate your learning style. It has been in use now for over 20 years, which gives you an idea of how helpful it has been. It is rather expensive though, and perhaps only for those who need a detailed analysis of their learning style.

Witkiewitz, K., & Marlatt, G.A. (2007). *Therapist's guide to evidence-based relapse prevention*. Burlington, MA: Elsevier.

This is one of the few relapse prevention texts that cover a range of psychological problems, rather than simply substance misuse. Invited authors address eating disorders, mood disorders and PTSD, for example. Marlatt was key in developing relapse prevention models and methods over 25 years ago, so he brings a huge amount of knowledge and experience to this edited text.

VIDEO LINKS

- **6.1 Taking your client around the learning cycle using clinical material**
- **6.2 Sharing the principles of relapse management and teaching the skill**

7 SOCRATIC METHODS

- Introduction
- Why choose Socratic methods?
- When do we use Socratic enquiry?
- How do we use Socratic methods effectively?
- When not to opt for Socratic methods
- Problems when using the Socratic approach
- Summary
- Learning exercises
- Further reading
- Video links
  - 7.1 Downward arrowing
  - 7.2 Stages in Socratic method
  - 7.3 Socratic applications

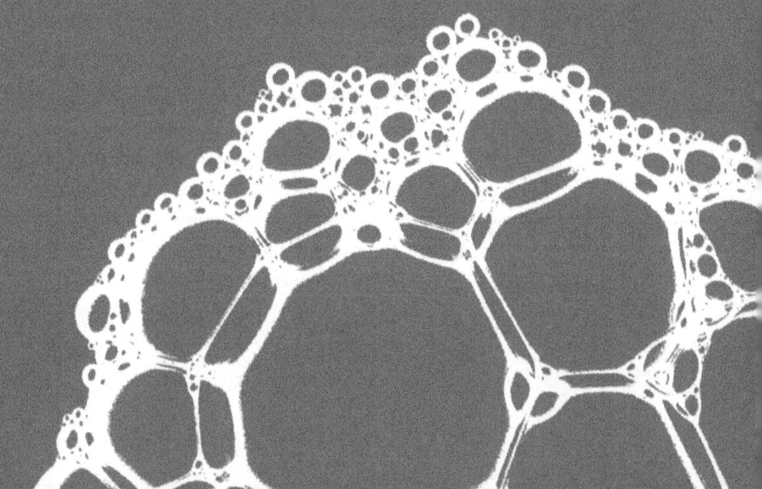

INTRODUCTION

Socratic methods embrace a range of interventions to help clients learn how to help themselves, and the approach is seen as fundamental to good CBT. Beck himself has stated clearly that 'Cognitive therapy uses primarily the Socratic method' (Beck, Emery, & Greenberg, 1985: 177). Although there remains some dispute as to the precise definition (Carey & Mullan, 2004), it is generally accepted that the Socratic approach is a 'cornerstone of cognitive therapy' (Padesky, 1993). So, in this chapter we look at why it is considered so invaluable, how you can develop your skill in using it and, crucially, when it is better not to.

By far the most commonly used Socratic strategy is the Socratic question – so that's where we start.

What is a 'Socratic question'? A cognitive therapist uses many types of question (see James, Morse & Howarth, 2009 for a review). For example, we use direct, information-gathering questions, which can range from a simple 'What is your address?' to a far more challenging 'Have you made plans to kill yourself?'. At other times we ask social questions to put our clients at ease ('How was the trip to Wales at the weekend?', 'Did your son's exams go well?' etc.) or we make enquiries to clarify confusion such as 'Just what was it that she said to you?'. However, the single type of question most strongly associated with CBT is the Socratic question.

Socratic enquiry derives from Socrates, a philosopher living in Athens around 400 BC. He spent his time in the marketplace, encouraging the young men of Athens to question the truth of popular opinion. His unique approach was in using questions to help his students reach a conclusion without directly instructing them. In this way, he supposedly elicited from a totally untutored slave boy the basic principles of geometry.

A Socratic question was one that the student had the ability to answer – although he might not yet realise it – and which would enlighten the student in some way. Socrates encouraged students to make use of their own knowledge base, to form their own opinions and to see new possibilities, which they could act on. Within CBT, Socratic questions are not aimed at proving the questioner's point – the intention is to encourage the other person to query their view and to develop new outlooks. Socratic questioning affords the therapist and client opportunities to reveal what clients already know but have not yet considered, or have forgotten. Through sensitive enquiry, clients are encouraged to use existing knowledge, to discover alternative views and solutions for themselves, rather than the therapist suggesting them.

We will come back to the 'Socratic question' per se, but let us now widen our own perspectives and consider the 'Socratic *method*', which can encompass so much more than enquiry. You will recall that our primary aim is to direct attention to possibilities that had previously been outside client awareness, and there are means other than questioning to achieve this. For example, we can reflect dilemmas to prompt a new perspective:

Therapist: So it sounds as if you criticise yourself if you do X, and you give yourself a hard time if you do Y.

Client: It is rather 'no win'. I hadn't thought of it that way – no wonder I feel bad.

We can simply summarise:

Therapist: Let me see if I can sum up, then. You are the person that fixes the family's problems and no-one seems to help you when you struggle.

Client: That sounds rather harsh, but I suppose if I'm honest that is how it is. I can see now that there never is anyone there for me and that's probably why I feel the way I *do*.

We can offer information:

Therapist: I ran a clinic yesterday. Five of my five clients had been abused as children. How does that strike you?

Client: That I am not the only one – I am not so weird.

We also set up behavioural experiments, role plays or encourage surveys and log-keeping that can yield new possibilities and perspectives. Simply by facilitating such activities, we can encourage discovery. Clients often return to sessions and summarise what they have learnt for themselves:

Phaedra took part in an active experiment on public transport: 'It was really hard to take that first step onto the train but when I stepped off at the other end I just knew I could do this again; I knew that I'd be fine.'

The therapist took on the role of the client whilst Becky played the teenage son who had been so cruel to her. After the role play, without prompting, Becky said that she'd begun to realise how frustrated and confused her son must be and this helped her to feel empathy rather than hurt.

Jake carried out a survey: 'By the time I'd asked the fifth person about their sleep pattern, I realised that I was well within the normal population.'

Karim completed a weekly activity schedule: 'Although I was sure that I simply felt low all of the time, by day four I could see that it was always worse in the morning and my mood did improve as the day went on – not much, but there was a change.'

This self-driven discovery is particularly important in engendering the self-confidence that our clients need if they are to become independent of us.

We supplement experiential activities with the verbal Socratic method of debriefing, especially if our client has difficulty in developing a new view. Following a behavioural experiment, we typically ask 'And what have you learnt?', 'What will you do differently as a consequence?' so that we can be sure that there has been new learning and that this will manifest in new behaviour. In reviewing diaries or other logs we might ask 'Are there any patterns here?' in order to prompt exploration and new learning. But do remember that not all Socratic interventions require verbal methods.

As you can see, there are different ways to achieve the goal of encouraging new perspectives, but what is 'good' Socratic technique?

Your technique is 'good' if the experience that you have created (be this via a question or via a behavioural experiment or via some other CBT intervention) is one where:

- your client can engage, he can work out an answer to the question or she can carry out the assignment;
- the experience reveals new, relevant perspectives.

A 'good' intervention draws attention to information relevant to the issue being discussed but outside current focus. This can be helpful in clarifying the meanings of problems, and it can also be used to draw on the new information in order to re-evaluate previous conclusions and to construct new plans.

However, a good Socratic intervention for one person at one time is not necessarily good for a different person, or at a different time. Take our earlier question: 'What is a good Socratic question?' Clearly, this would not be useful if I asked it of a person who could not possibly know the answer, but what if I asked it of a colleague who could come up with a response? Would that make it good?

It would not be good if I asked a colleague who readily answered the question, but simply thought, 'So what?': she already knew that she knew the answer and so learnt nothing from the exercise. However, imagine that my colleague had lost confidence in her ability to teach CBT and had told me that she knew nothing of worth and could contribute very little to our training programme. In that context, answering the question might help her realise that she had specialist knowledge and could contribute to training. In this case, the enquiry provoked an answer that illuminated the issue.

WHY CHOOSE SOCRATIC METHODS?

Why do cognitive therapists strive to develop a repertoire of good Socratic questions and other methods? There are several compelling reasons:

- Socratic methods are effective in encouraging a personal review of a situation and, where relevant, a shift in attitude, feeling and behaviour *that feels authentic*.
- Socratic methods enhance learning so that new perspectives are better retained.
- Self-generated conclusions will often have more credibility than will advice from a therapist.

In his self-help book, David Burns (1980) wrote: 'Through a process of thoughtful questions, you discover on your own the beliefs that defeat you. You unearth the origin of your problems by repeating the following questions over and over: "If that negative thought were true, what would it mean to me? Why would it upset me?" *Without introducing some therapist's subjective bias* or personal beliefs or theoretical leanings, you can *objectively* and systematically go right to the root of your problems' (p. 239; emphasis in the original). Here we see how Socratic methods can minimise therapist bias (and we therapists can be wrong in our hypotheses, no matter how experienced we are) and personalise the process of exploration and conclusion. But that's not all: here you see Burns promoting a self-help strategy, and that is always the end goal in CBT. We want to make ourselves superfluous by skilling the client. Socratic methods do not rest on advice giving or reassuring, so the client learns how to review experiences independently – they develop a skill for life.

Although didactic teaching has value in CBT, and it really does, Socratic methods encourage clients to sift through data and draw their own conclusions – conclusions that are more likely to be memorable and convincing.

The pedagogical world has long argued that *enduring* learning requires more than just exposure to fact or experience or instruction or modelling; it requires deeper cognitive processing. A typical perspective is that of Wittrock (1978) who states that

> learning with understanding from instruction is a generative process. Effective instruction does not teach, in the usual sense of the word. Instead, it facilitates the learner's ability to construct meaning from experience. (p. 1)

and

> instruction involves the stimulation of relations between the stimuli and stored memories by inducing verbal or imaginal elaborations. (p. 25)

This has been established empirically in a particularly elegant study by Erdelyi, Buschke and Finkelstein back in 1977. They looked at memory for Socratic stimuli by studying three types of information input, representing different levels of cognitive processing. One experimental group was presented with a 40-item word list; a second group was shown the same items but in pictorial form so that processing would be at both a verbal and a visual level. A third group (referred to as 'the Socratic subjects') solved 40 riddles, which generated the same 40 items. On testing, the 'Socratic' group members (who had engaged in a greater depth of cognitive processing by generating their own items) had the best recall, followed by the group who had viewed pictures.

This phenomenon applies even to clients suffering from dementia. Barrett, Crucian, Schwartz and Heilman (2000) showed that clients with dementia preferentially retained 'self-discovered' or internally generated material over material that had been simply presented to them.

Why might this be? Neuroscientists link memory to alterations within neural networks within the brain, and the more complex the alterations, the more lasting the memory – be it for facts, experiences, plans or procedures. The harder the brain works, the more active are the neural networks. The brain has to work much harder to *generate* a response than to just listen to, or look at, something, so the learning is more enduring. Quite simply, Socratic methods require more neurological activity than just listening to or looking at something, thus they promote deeper learning.

In the light of all this, it is rather disappointing that we have to acknowledge that the empirical status of Socratic method within CBT remains poor (see Clark & Egan, 2015 for an excellent review). However, there does seem to be an increasing interest in evaluating its impact, with a recent study showing that the skilful use of Socratic questions predicted recovery from depression (Braun, Strunk, Sasso & Cooper, 2015).

Finally, we consider the proposal that Socratic methods generate conclusions that might have more credibility than the therapist's advice or perspectives. We see this in the empirically established motivational interviewing (MI) approach developed by Bill Miller (1983). This is a goal-directed counselling approach, not referred to as 'Socratic' by Miller but sharing many of its characteristics. In an article by Miller and his colleague Rollnick (Rollnick & Miller, 1995), they summarise the 'spirit of motivational interviewing'(p. 325) as:

- Motivation to change is elicited from the client, and not imposed from without.
- It is the client's task, not the counsellor's, to articulate and resolve his or her ambivalence.
- Direct persuasion is not an effective method for resolving ambivalence.
- The counselling style is generally a quiet and eliciting one.
- The counsellor is directive in helping the client to examine and resolve ambivalence.
- Readiness to change is not a client trait, but a fluctuating product of interpersonal interaction.
- The therapeutic relationship is more like a partnership or companionship than expert/recipient roles.

It is easy to see the commonalities between MI and a Socratic method: clients generate their own notions to address ambivalence and the therapist is their partner encouraging this. There is a body of excellent research showing the efficacy of MI in creating solutions that are experienced as authentic and are carried through.

In summary, then, we have seen that there is a range of Socratic methods at our disposal and that there are good reasons for incorporating these approaches throughout a therapy session and over a course of therapy. Of course, there will be times when direct questioning or didactic teaching is a better therapeutic option, but here we illustrate how the Socratic approach can be helpful in many areas of therapy.

1 ASSESSMENT AND FORMULATION

In identifying the cognitions, affect, behaviours and sensations pertinent to a client's difficulties, Socratic dialogue can elaborate something that might 'cross a client's mind' but was not previously fully acknowledged. Simple questions such as 'How do you feel?' or 'What went through your mind?' can help a person clarify and articulate feelings and thoughts. Other examples of useful assessment questions are:

- Did you 'see' anything in your mind's eye?
- What did you do when that happened?
- What did it mean to you when you thought/did that?
- When was the first time that this thought occurred to you/this image cros: your mind?
- Did you have any other feelings?

You can also further inform the formulation by asking questions that help you continue to elaborate and to check out hypotheses generated by the preliminary formulation, such as:

- And when that happens, just how do you feel, what's it like in your body?
- Remind me – what goes through your mind when you feel like that?
- What do you tend to do at those times, let's go through this in detail?
- How does that fit with this cycle here?

Socratic questions are part of a Socratic *process* of enquiry and some of your questions will not be overtly 'Socratic' in that they will simply gather information, setting the scene and fuelling hypotheses that then drive more obviously 'Socratic enquiry'. Some of your statements will be didactic, filling gaps in knowledge so that you can then return to a Socratic review. Thus you would expect to use a mix of direct questions and information giving to create the necessary foundation for a fruitful Socratic intervention.

Sometimes an informational question is the most appropriate way to test a hypothesis, sometimes a Socratic one is better. Consider the following example:

Therapist: So what is your main difficulty at present? [*Direct, information-gathering question*]

Client: It's my mood, I'm so depressed. I can't shake it off and I can't see it ever getting better.

Therapist: When did your mood start to be a problem for you? [*Direct, information-gathering question*]

Client: It's always been a problem – at least since I was a teenager, but I just got on with it. Since I retired I've not been able to shake off this heavy misery.

Therapist: [*Hypothesis: marked to severe depression, worsened by the life event of retirement*] Can I ask you a little more about your mood? [*Direct question, setting the scene for further exploration and giving the message that the client has choices, thus encouraging the client to be more open to Socratic enquiry*]

The therapist can now begin to explore the validity of the hypothesis by asking Socratic questions which give more insight into the nature of this client's depression. In this example, the therapist then poses a question that refines the hypothesis:

Therapist: And what else goes through your mind? [*This is one of several Socratic questions that have built up an understanding of the client's inner world*]

Client: That there is no point in carrying on .... [*falls silent*]

Therapist: [*Hypothesis: marked to severe depression, suicidal*] Can you say more? [*Direct question to discover if the client is able to elaborate, and also to convey to him that he isn't under pressure to do more than he can tolerate*]

Client: Well, I might as well be dead.

Therapist: I'm beginning to understand just how bad you must be feeling and I'm sorry to hear that you are so distressed. How often do you feel so low that you believe that?

Client: Pretty much all the time.

Therapist: [*Hypothesis: marked to severe depression, suicidal, at risk*] I see. Have you made plans? [*Thus begins a series of direct questions to establish risk*] ... have you ever made an attempt on your life? ... do you live with someone or alone? *[and so on]*

From this example, you can see that we need to consider our entire interaction and the role that different verbalisations play. To go back to our question, 'What is a good Socratic question?' – one answer is that it is embedded within other types of enquiry that will engender trust and encourage explorations whilst always attending to safety.

2 EDUCATION

An essential part of CBT is teaching our clients the model and the skills of CBT. Sometimes this is best achieved didactically and we can simply direct them to reading material and videos or we can tell them what they need to know. This didactic foundation is essential if your client does not yet have knowledge that they need to draw new conclusions or try out new ways of being. Our colleague, Dr Gillian Butler, always reminded therapists in training to 'mind the gap', namely ask questions until we establish a gap in knowledge and then fill the gap didactically.

Therapist: When you have these vivid sensations and night terrors, what do you think is happening?

Client: I've no idea. I think I must be losing it, going mad.

Therapist: Have you heard of the term 'flashback'?

Client: Yes. It's a military thing, nothing to do with my problems.

Therapist: Let me tell you a bit about flashbacks ... [*the therapist explains the phenomenon of flashbacks and shares some printed information, then continues*] In the light of what we've just talked about, what do you think might be happening when you have these sensations and night terrors?

Client: I think that I could be having flashbacks to trauma.

Therapist: And if you consider that possibility, how do you feel about the situation you are in right now?

Client: I feel more hopeful, not so scared that I'm going mad.

Here you see the fluid process of direct, information gathering revealing a gap in knowledge, didactic information filling the gap followed by Socratic exploration to personalise relevance of this new knowledge: a 'good' Socratic question is not a stand-alone question, but part of a 'good' process.

Some psycho-education is best achieved experientially (e.g. teaching assertiveness skills or breathing techniques) and this can combine didactic and Socratic methods. For example, a therapist might model being assertive and the client would observe (didactic) whilst being involved in the exercise. The therapist would then prompt her to draw her own conclusions from the experience (Socratic) and to try this out for herself and reflect on what she had learned (Socratic).

The precise links between cognitions and feelings, and their impact on motivation and behaviour, are often fruitfully explored collaboratively using Socratic enquiry. A standard means of examining these links is to encourage the client to engage in a hypothetical exercise and imagine the consequences of different thoughts. For example:

Therapist: Imagine that you believed that dogs were dangerous and you saw a dog: what would go through your mind?

Client: That dog could bite me!

Therapist: How would you feel?

Client: Nervous, anxious.

Therapist: What would you do?

Client: I'd avoid the dog – I might even run away.

Therapist: Now imagine that you believed dogs were cuddly and safe: what would go through your mind?

Client: I suppose I'd think – Oh, he looks sweet.

Therapist: How would you feel?

Client: I imagine that I'd feel rather nice. I'd feel relaxed and pleased, especially if the dog was friendly.

Therapist: What would you do?

Client: In that case, I'd probably approach it and stroke it.

Therapist: What does that suggest about the links between thoughts and feelings, or thoughts and actions?

Client: Well, I guess that this shows me that my thoughts make a difference to my feelings. My attitude towards something affects the way I feel about it. I suppose it also shows that the way I feel about a situation can make a difference to how I respond. Is that what you wanted me to say?

Therapist: It's not about what I wanted you to say, but rather about the conclusion *you* draw. What you just said – did you mean it? Did it seem true for you?

Client: Well, yes, I can see that it's true – but it seems a bit simple, doesn't it?

This particular technique can be elaborated if necessary. Further questions can be added, such as: '… and what might happen if you avoided/approached the dog? … what might you learn about dogs? … what might you learn about yourself?', thus encouraging the development of other scenarios that can facilitate further exploration of the linkages.

3 REVIEWING UNHELPFUL COGNITIONS

The Socratic method is an ideal 'review tool' for prompting people to consider a range of possibilities that lie outside their current perspective and so construct alternative views of a situation or event. Several types of question can be used for this purpose:

- 'evidence for' questions;
- 'evidence against' questions;
- 'alternative view' questions;
- 'consequences of' questions.

You will see examples of each in the next section. You might note that some of the questions prompt a shift in perspective by asking the client to consider changes in time or in person, for example: 'If we fast-forwarded a year and this was no longer a "hot" issue at work, how would you feel?' or 'How would someone else see this?'. This can help your client make the crucial shift from a negative, distressed mindset to a more realistic and bearable one: we will elaborate on this later in the chapter.

It might seem odd that we ask questions to elicit evidence supporting the problem cognition, but these are important in building up a *balanced* view of a situation; they enable the client to see that 'it's no wonder that I have this thought' and therefore minimise the likelihood of self-criticism, such as 'I am stupid for thinking like this'. Questions here include:

- 'In your experience, what fits with this belief, what makes it seem true?'
- 'Why might any of us have that thought at some time?'

In searching for evidence that is inconsistent with the problem cognition, you direct the client's attention to incidents or experiences that provide alternative possibilities and which begin to test the original belief, thus reviewing the validity of unhelpful cognitions. You might ask:

- 'I'm just wondering, do you have any experience of this not being the case?'
- 'Is there anything that doesn't seem to fit with that thought?'
- 'How might someone else view the situation?'

- 'Is that so all of the time, or are there occasions when things are different?'
- 'Before you were depressed, what would have gone through your mind at that point?'
- 'If you were responding to your best friend, what would you say?'

Once clients have reviewed why they hold a belief (even though it might be an unhelpful cognition) and have looked at ways in which the belief might not stand up to scrutiny, then they can be guided towards generating alternative possibilities by questions such as:

- 'Now that you have looked at the bigger picture, how would you view your original concern?'
- 'Given what you've just described, how likely do you think it is that the worst will happen?'
- 'If you reflect on what we've discussed, what picture comes to mind now? And what message does that carry for you?'

In this way, you encourage your client to stand back and review the situation, reflecting on the bigger picture that has emerged. This is essential training in CBT if he is going to become his own CBT therapist (see Chapter 8).

Enquiry about the consequences of holding a current view (and an alternative view) will elicit the pros and cons of current beliefs and can provide a rationale for change that can motivate your client in taking the risk of changing their outlook and possibly their behaviours. This is often fundamental to engaging our clients.

- 'How helpful, or unhelpful, is it to hold this particular belief?'
- 'I'm curious, what good, if any, comes of holding this belief?'
- 'What is the downside of seeing things this way?'
- 'If you see the world this way, how do you feel, how do others react?'

It can be illuminating to write these pros and cons on a whiteboard, or to draw out a mini-formulation of the consequences of holding a belief so that your client can stand back and draw their own conclusions with minimal prompting. Whenever we set up situations that prompt clients to review *for themselves*, we are using a very powerful Socratic intervention because their conclusions will have credibility for them.

4 PROBLEM SOLVING AND WORKING OUT SOLUTIONS

CBT is, in many ways, all about problem solving. You can guide your clients towards effective problem solving by using the Socratic approach to encourage first precision and then creativity.

- 'So, just what is it that you fear will happen? Let's look at this in detail ...'
- 'That sounds like two issues – which do you want to focus on?'
- 'Have you dealt with this sort of problem in the past and if so, how?'
- 'How might your friend try to deal with such a dilemma? Let's brainstorm ...'
- 'Given that you have identified avoidance as an obstacle to gaining confidence, what might you try?'
- 'How would you advise a friend to go about dealing with this obstacle?'

This style of enquiry can then lead on to exploring as many coping options as necessary. You can also use the Socratic approach to tease out the pros and cons of a solution by asking your client to consider what might go well and what might go badly, and you can prompt him to devise back-up or reserve plans.

- 'Let's just take a moment to consider what is the worst-case scenario if this solution does not work?'
- 'How would you prepare for that? How might you guard against it happening? What could you do if it did happen?'

Thus, you can guide him through the stages of defining the problem, generating as many solutions as possible, planning to put a solution into action and devising contingency plans. This fits very well with relapse management planning (see Chapter 6).

5 DEVISING BEHAVIOURAL TESTS

Once the client has a new perspective, he needs to take it forward and check its validity. Thus, the insights that Socratic enquiries can generate often need to be followed by behavioural testing (see Chapter 9). For example, when working with a person with a phobia, we generally hypothesise that it will be helpful to face the fear. You can use the Socratic method to elicit the rationale for a behavioural experiment along these lines:

- 'What do you think would happen if you held your ground and did not run away?'
- 'What would go through your mind?'
- 'And if you were able to remain in the situation, what would go through your mind?'
- 'How would you feel? What would this mean to you?'
- 'How might you view the situation if you were able to stay rather than escape?'
- 'What might be the longer-term impact?'

This can lead on to questions that shape the behavioural experiment, such as:

- 'How might we set up a situation where we could try this out and see just what happens?'
- 'What would make it easier for you to take on the challenge?'
- 'What might we do in preparation?'
- 'How will you gauge your success?'

In this way, experiments can be evolved collaboratively. Similarly, trouble-shooting can become a collaborative venture, for example:

- 'What could go wrong?'
- 'Let's put our heads together and think what is the worst-case scenario …'
- 'How might you prepare yourself/deal with this if it happened?'
- 'How might a friend prepare herself/deal with it if it happened?'
- 'What would we learn from that?'

It is important that, as far as possible, experiments arise from the content of the session and are closely linked with the development of insight. Thus, if a man draws a new conclusion, for example 'If I could stay in that situation, like I used to do, then I'll get back my confidence', then you can ask, 'How might you check that out?'. Similarly, discoveries in session can be linked with behavioural change by asking the question: 'Given what we've covered today, how might you take things forward?'

After experiments, Socratic enquiry can be used to encourage analysis of what happened, highlight problems and doubts and then prompt clients to reconstruct new conceptualisations and further behavioural experiments.

6 IN SUPERVISION

A final note regarding the Socratic method is that it can be as useful in supervision as it is in therapy, a point that has been strongly promoted by Overholser (1991). All the arguments for using it as a therapeutic tool stand when using it as a supervisory tool: it enhances learning, fosters collaboration and tests hypotheses (see Chapter 19 on supervision and CBT). You may not be supervising others just yet – but your time will come and it will be helpful to remember that Socratic methods offer powerful training techniques.

WHEN DO WE USE SOCRATIC ENQUIRY?

By now, you will appreciate that a Socratic question is not the only 'good' question in CBT, that the Socratic approach is not the only 'good' style, although sometimes the Socratic route is by far the most productive on many levels.

We therapists have many tasks: establishing a collaborative relationship, gathering information, deriving a formulation, skills training and so on. Different approaches can yield different results, which can be useful at various points in therapy in achieving a range of goals. For example, information gathering might sometimes be best achieved through direct enquiry (e.g. 'Are you currently working?'), while establishing a warm and empathic relationship might merit a leading question (e.g. 'You seem distressed – is this too upsetting for you?') and understanding a fear might be best achieved Socratically (e.g. 'Just what do you think would happen if you touched that door knob?').

Whatever type of question we choose, Beck et al. (1979: 71) advise that 'Questions must be carefully timed and phrased so as to help the patient recognise and consider his notions reflectively – to weigh his thoughts with objectivity,' and they warn that a client 'may feel he is being cross-examined or that he is being attacked if questions are used to 'trap' him into contradicting himself'.

This reminds us that a good Socratic question is asked in the context of a good therapeutic relationship. Your aim is to communicate warmth, empathy and a non-judgemental attitude, whilst minimising client angst and hopelessness, so as to facilitate engagement, lateral thinking, creativity and recall. A client should feel that his perspective is interesting rather than 'wrong', and that his exploration of new possibilities will be valued and considered, rather than negatively judged. Clients need the knowledge, the time *and the confidence* to respond to a question.

HOW DO WE USE SOCRATIC METHODS EFFECTIVELY?

There is a common misconception that the effective cognitive therapist operates like a slick courtroom lawyer who never asks a question unless he knows the answer and, with two or three brilliant questions, reveals the 'truth'. It is interesting, therefore, that Beck has described the television detective Columbo as his role model. The gentle inquisitive style of the television hero – never pushy or omniscient – reflects a respectful and genuine enquiry. This attitude is crucial to 'good' Socratic style.

The style and purpose of Socratic questioning in CBT was most thoughtfully reviewed by Padesky (1993). She highlighted the important difference between using a Socratic approach to *change minds* and using it to *guide discovery*. In summary, she argued that the therapist who 'changes minds' illustrates that the client's thoughts are illogical, while the therapist who 'guides discovery' reveals new possibilities. She argued that genuine curiosity was key to achieving the latter. Teasdale (1996), commenting on Padesky's view, has suggested that, at a psychological level, 'changing minds' invalidates specific thoughts or meanings, while 'guiding discovery' creates alternative mental frameworks. Consider the impact on your client: 'You are wrong' versus 'There are other possibilities'.

The cognitive therapist should strive to guide discovery not only by adopting a position of curiosity but also one of humility. Humility enables us to anticipate that we might learn from the client, rather than assuming that we always have (or should have) the answer. In this way, we can avoid falling into the 'changing minds' trap.

Metaphor and analogy can aid Socratic enquiry. Each encourages your client to imagine a parallel situation so that the focus is temporarily shifted from his original view. By doing so, the strong emotion of the personal situation is tempered and your client may be able to think more productively. Clients can be encouraged to develop their own metaphors to help them discover more about their problems and solutions. For example:

Therapist: You say that it feels as if you have a pigeonhole in your mind that collects and stores all the hurt and betrayal from the past. What would it mean if you also had a pigeonhole that collected memories of good relationships?

Client: I would be able to recall good times and positive relationships.

Therapist: How might we begin to build a pigeonhole for the positive memories?

Client: I have no idea!

Therapist: Well let's think about it. If you were trying to help a friend hold on to memories of good times and positive relationships, how might you do it?

Client: I would encourage them to keep a notebook – or perhaps to keep a record on their mobile phone.

Therapist: Is that an idea which would work for you? And if so, how?

Client: Well – if I remember something, or if one of my friends recalls something positive, I could write it down so that I don't forget quite so easily. Then I'd have a record.

Therapist: Yes, you would have created a pigeonhole. How might we try to ensure that you checked that pigeonhole regularly?

Client: I'd have to look at my notes regularly – I could try to review them at night before I go to bed. I could try to get into a routine of doing that.

Examining analogies can also prompt the client to stand aside from his own situation and consider a parallel one. For example, a question like 'How would you advise your son, if he faced a similar dilemma?' can shift the client into a more hopeful and practical mindset, which enables him to begin to generate new ideas for coping. Similarly, questions such as 'How might a friend view the situation?' or 'How might a detective go about collecting evidence?' can help the client step into another 'mindset' and view things differently and more productively.

The skill of Socratic enquiry is one that might come more naturally if you do not try too hard. You are very likely to be using it in your everyday life without even realising it. There is a good chance that in many social interactions you formulate hypotheses and ask questions that facilitate but don't lead, and that you are flexible, eliciting genuine responses from those around you. It's that easy. Drew Westen, in his introductory psychology text (1996), gave the mundane example of meeting someone at a party – a situation where there might be much Socratic action. Imagine a man walking into a party and being greeted by an attractive, warm and friendly person. He hypothesises: 'She is interested in me'. It is very unlikely that he would just approach this guest and ask for a date, it is more likely that he will use a line of enquiry that will enable him to collect information to support or refute his hypothesis and which will give the other person an opportunity to feed back her intentions in greeting him. He might begin with a friendly statement and simple question:

- 'Hello, I'm Billy – a colleague of the host. Lovely setting for the party, don't you think?'

He will listen closely and, depending on the responses that he gets, he will try to gauge this person's romantic interest and ask further questions to clarify her intentions. For example, he might ask:

- 'The band here is excellent and local – do you ever go out and listen to them?'

If the guest continues to be friendly and replies that she often goes to listen to them and always enjoys the occasion, he then might maintain his hypothesis and continue with the gentle line of questioning. He will also listen for what the guest doesn't say – and if there is no mention of a partner, he will note this. However, at some point a response or behaviour might challenge his hypothesis and then he would revise it without having jumped to a premature conclusion (which could have resulted in embarrassment). For example, he might ultimately conclude:

> She is a member of the host's family and is helping the party run smoothly. She is polite and sociable rather than interested in a date with me. (Adapted from Westen, 1996)

So, if you can hold a social conversation and develop your ideas about a person without jumping to premature conclusions, then you probably already have what it takes to adopt the right style.

DOWNWARD ARROWING

'Downward arrowing' refers to a type of systematic questioning that aims to help clients elaborate on, or 'unpack', their experience or ATs and perhaps identify the more fundamental meanings underlying an unwanted reaction. In some texts it is called 'vertical arrow restructuring'.

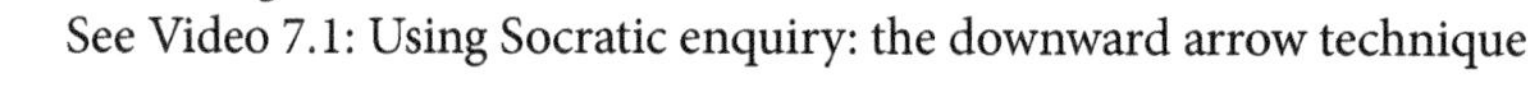

See Video 7.1: Using Socratic enquiry: the downward arrow technique.

Bea stated that she had to return to the house repeatedly to check that the door was locked. It was not immediately apparent to her why she needed to do this, but gentle, systematic questioning by her therapist gradually revealed that she felt rather incompetent and did not trust herself to lock the door properly. She feared that she would be burgled and would carry the blame for the loss to her family. This conclusion made sense of her drive to return again and again to make sure that the door was locked.

If you use the downward arrow technique, your questions should be paced and phrased so that your client never feels interrogated, but rather that you are taking a genuine interest. You might begin a line of enquiry with questions like:

- 'I wonder, just how did you feel at the time?'
- '... and what was going through your mind?'
- 'Any particular thoughts or pictures?'
- 'That's interesting – could you say a bit more?'
- 'That sounds really relevant – could you expand on just how you felt? What you thought?'

Such questions help clients re-activate the affect of the moment and focus on relevant cognitions. In the example above, Bea reported:

'I felt anxious, really nervous and tense and I was sure that the only way I could deal with these feelings was to go back again and check. I was thinking: I've got to make sure, I've got to make sure.'

Your initial line of enquiry might be followed by further questions to gently tease out or 'unpack' the personal relevance of a thought or an image – questions such as:

- 'I wonder what seems so bad about that?'
- 'In your view, what does that mean?'
- 'What does that say about you?'
- 'What would that mean about your life/your future?'
- 'What do you imagine others would think of you?'
- 'How would you label that?'
- 'Can you describe the worst thing that could happen?'
- '... and if that were true – then what?'

This way, you and your client can discover more about the belief system relating to a particular problem.

When first asked what would be so bad about being burgled and what it meant to her, Bea was reluctant to think about it and there was a period of silence. Her therapist acknowledged that this was difficult for her and suggested she take her time. Eventually, Bea revealed:

'It would be terrible because it would be all my fault ... It would prove how useless I am and no one would trust me again. They wouldn't respect me within my own family. I would feel so ashamed and unworthy.'

Like many of our clients, Bea found downward arrowing an emotionally charged challenge. For this reason it should be used thoughtfully, only if we can justify it, and then we need to pace it sensitively, accept periods of silence, look for ways of making the task easier, and we must be prepared to stop the exploration if a client finds it too distressing. Once the relevant cognitions have been identified, they can be examined and tested using cognitive testing and behavioural experiment.

It is worth remembering that during this exercise you can also discover more positive beliefs, such as 'On the whole, people seem to like me' or 'If I put in the effort, I can get things done'. Sometimes more positive beliefs are simply revealed as part of the course of enquiry, but we can increase the likelihood of uncovering them if we ask questions such as: 'What would be so good about that? How might that help you? What positive things does that suggest?' Positive beliefs can enhance progress: for example, someone who believes himself likeable and capable is likely to engage well with you, can probably take on quite challenging social assignments and would be motivated to engage in homework tasks, so it is useful to identify them. They can also contribute to the positive aspects of formulations (see Chapter 4).

Through downward arrowing, the client's fundamental belief system is often revealed (as in Bea's case). This is sometimes referred to as 'the bottom line' (Fennell, 1999), although it is often more akin to a 'bottom triangle', comprising the elements of Beck et al.'s (1979) cognitive triad: beliefs about the self, others and the world, and the future. These elements relate to each other, and finding yourself going round the triangle is often an indication that the 'bottom line' has been reached:

Therapist: ... and what might that say about you?

Client: That I am bad. [*Self*]

Therapist: ... and what would that mean to you?

Client: That no one is going to want to know me. [*Others*]

Therapist: ... and if that were the case, what would that mean to you?

Client: That I will always be alone and miserable. [*Future*]

In trying to determine whether or not the bottom line has been reached, ask yourself: 'Would anyone feel the way my client does if they held this view and believed it as much as he does?' If your answer is 'Yes', then you have probably uncovered a core belief.

It can take several sessions before the core belief system is revealed, and sometimes it is simply not accessible. In fact, it is not always necessary to reach the bottom line (or triangle) in order to carry out effective CBT, and much productive work can be, and should be, carried out at the level of an AT or with the rules and assumptions associated with core beliefs. This is how Beck and his colleagues envisaged CBT working (1979). However, there can be advantages in uncovering core beliefs. First, an understanding of core beliefs can aid a client in understanding persistent vulnerabilities: 'It's no wonder that I have no social confidence and am depressed if I feel so bad and undesirable'. Second, identifying core beliefs paves the way for schema-focused work, *if necessary*, as core beliefs are a key component of many schemata (see Chapter 17).

There is always a danger that if you have a strong belief in a hypothesis you may use the downward arrow technique simply to pursue its confirmation (to 'change minds'). It is crucial to remember that however well informed we might be, we are sometimes wrong. A great strength of Socratic dialogue, provided that it is coupled with curiosity and humility, is that it can lead us to conclusions that we did not anticipate. A useful rule when using the technique is to devise questions that might *refute* your hypothesis. When you think that you have confirmed your hunch, ask another question or two designed to disprove your theory. This both helps you refute an incorrect hypothesis and also guards against your being too narrow in focus.

See Video 7.2: Stages of Socratic method in action.

STAGES IN SOCRATIC METHOD

We have said several times now that Socratic method reflects a process, and Padesky (1996a) has defined four stages in this process:

1. *Concrete questioning*: structured, information-gathering questions, which begin to inform your hypotheses about the client's difficulties. For example:
   - How long have you felt low in your mood?
   - How often do you binge?
2. *Empathic listening*: careful, non-judgemental attention both to what the client is saying and to how it is said. The client can communicate a great deal through tone of voice or facial expression, which can further impact on your hypotheses and influence subsequent questions.
3. *Summarising*: feeding back a synopsis in order to check hypotheses, clarify information or reiterate a point. For example:
   - You say that you have felt depressed for the past three months, but that for several years you have felt rather low.
   - You seem to be saying that you probably binge every evening, but you are sometimes unsure whether or not you have actually binged.
4. *Synthesising or analysing questions*: these encourage either the development and expansion of an idea or a theme (synthesising), or the refinement of key information (analysing). For example:
   - When we review the past few years, your lowest points seem to be: when you split up from Paul; after the birth of Karen; when you feel that your marriage is not going well. Is there anything that links these events? (Synthesising)
   - Although there are many circumstances in which you binge, on what evenings are you most likely to? (Analysing)

Socratic enquiry helps the client review relevant evidence as widely as possible. You are more likely to obtain this 'bigger picture' by maintaining curiosity and not being too constrained by your own expectations and beliefs, and by frequently asking 'and is there anything else?'. If you get bound by rigid expectations, then you might terminate your enquiry before a wide enough data base has been uncovered. Consider the following example of different ways of approaching Jon, an anxious and miserable 14-year-old referred to the school psychologist because of poor performance in some subjects.

Approach 1: The psychologist asked about Jon's schoolwork and concluded that the issue was indeed study-related. She hypothesised that Jon was experiencing specific academic difficulties and her questions were focused on this hypothesis:

- 'Tell me more about the subjects that you're not doing so well in.'
- 'Maths and physics: have you always struggled with these topics?'
- 'So maths and physics have always been difficult for you, and now it's even harder to keep up. [*Summary*]'
- 'If a friend of yours was struggling with a subject, what would you suggest in order to help him out?'

In this way, the therapist efficiently progressed to her target of developing more efficient studying strategies. However, they didn't make much progress over the course of a few weeks.

Approach 2: This time the psychologist developed the hypothesis that Jon was experiencing specific academic difficulties and initially asked similar questions. However, she followed these focused questions with an exploratory enquiry:

- 'I can probably help you with your study technique, and we'll talk through some of the strategies later – but first, I was wondering if there is anything else on your mind when you find yourself struggling in class?'

It then transpired that Jon felt judged by the maths and physics teacher, Mr Smith. The psychologist focused her enquiry, finding out more about the relationship with the teacher. It became clear that Jon struggled in class because he felt especially anxious and self-conscious with this particular teacher. The psychologist then constructed a new hypothesis, that Jon had specific interpersonal difficulties with Mr Smith. Again she asked more exploratory questions, ascertaining the nature of their relationship:

- 'How do you imagine Mr Smith views you? What goes through your mind?'

Jon then revealed that he believed that this particularly conventional and religious teacher was blaming him for his parents' impending separation. Jon blamed himself for his parents' marital problems and felt guilty, even sinful.

By now you will appreciate that the revised formulation was fundamentally different from the initial hypothesis. Jon was insecure and distressed because his parents were going to separate. Increasingly, he felt responsible for this, but he also felt isolated and could not discuss it with his parents. Shame inhibited him from sharing his troubles with his friends.

He soldiered on. In lessons with Mr Smith, however, he felt judged and was reminded of his guilt. This interfered with his ability to perform in the class and his classroom difficulties were beginning to generalise to other classes. The psychologist's curiosity had paid off and Jon felt understood for the first time in a long time.

Having too narrow a focus is not necessarily a therapeutic disaster, as the limitations of the intervention will become apparent and you can reformulate. However, there are advantages to building the bigger picture as early as possible, as it communicates empathy – the therapist really 'gets it'– and this can inspire hope, particularly in the more cynical or pessimistic client. Also, the formulation will be better informed and will lead to more relevant interventions or more sensitive prioritisation of issues.

CAUTIOUS AND COMPASSIONATE SOCRATIC ENQUIRY

A skilled therapist can become increasingly adept at 'unpacking' cognitions and identifying key, fundamental beliefs. However, this can become anti-therapeutic if you become overly focused on getting to the bottom of a problem without empathic pacing, a practice a colleague of ours calls 'psycho-bulldozing'. It can leave clients feeling that you are insensitive, which will strain your alliance, and can result in your missing opportunities to teach them about the role and management of cognitions. There is useful material to be worked with en route to the 'bottom line', and we all need to be careful not to miss opportunities to explore this. It goes without saying that it can help the therapeutic dialogue if such exploration is sensitively paced and punctuated by summaries.

Maria is a depressed, 30-year-old divorced woman who, despite an impressive academic background, never remained employed for more than a few weeks. She tended to start jobs with great hope and enthusiasm but never sustained them. She was well defended emotionally and tended to minimise emotional responses, often appearing rather composed. However, the downward arrow procedure distressed her unless it was paced very carefully indeed. Her therapist felt justified in wanting to understand Maria's core beliefs because he was struggling to appreciate her inability to sustain work. However, because of her fragility, he did not proceed directly to the bottom line but achieved this over several sessions.

In such cases, it is always prudent (and respectful) to ask:

- Is it alright for me to continue with these questions?
- Do you need a bit of a break? Let me know if you do.

Clients like Maria may have spent a long time trying to avoid the pain that is provoked by a core belief, and a therapist must not underestimate the fear and distress that uncovering it might elicit. In summary, this is the course that Maria's therapist followed (although in reality it was paced over several sessions):

Therapist: Why did you give up the project?

Client: I was not good enough.

Therapist: And that means?

Client: There was no point. I have to be the best, or else I've achieved nothing.

Therapist: Can you tell me more about the importance of being the best?

Client: If I'm not superior, I'm wasting my time.

Therapist: What is so bad about wasting time?

Client: Time wasting is failure.

Therapist: Let's imagine that you did waste time and you felt like a failure. What would that mean to you?

Client: If one is a failure, one is pathetic.

Therapist: Are you able to tell me what that means to you personally?

At this point, Maria revealed a painful core belief. Before this, however, many assumptions, ripe for further exploration, had been revealed. The assumptions that Maria disclosed gave opportunities to address thinking biases; to look at the pros and cons of holding a particular assumption; to construct vicious circles explaining the maintenance of the assumptions; to look at evidence for and against them; to challenge beliefs; to set up behavioural experiments; and to introduce techniques such as continuum work (see Chapter 8 for descriptions of cognitive techniques). For example, the statement 'There was no point. I have to be the best, or else I've achieved nothing', gave an opportunity to highlight dichotomous thinking and unrelenting high standards and to explore the behavioural, emotional and occupational consequences of having such thoughts. Such opportunities for taking stock and teaching the skills of CBT should be considered before continuing with the downward arrow technique, otherwise we risk not equipping clients with basic techniques and we risk exposing painful cognitions before they have means of understanding and managing them.

When Maria disclosed her core belief, she was tearful and it was clearly a brave and difficult thing for her to say. Her worst fear was that she would be revealed as the 'candy floss' that she believed she was. As it was not obvious why this might be so upsetting, the therapist asked her to describe a person who was 'candy floss'. She reported that this was her family's term for the most despicable sort of character: soft, vulnerable and sensitive. As she elaborated, she completed the triangle when she said that 'candy floss' people end up despised, rejected and lonely. Interestingly, as she said this, she became less upset. The words 'soft, vulnerable, sensitive, despised, rejected and lonely' did not provoke the emotion that was triggered by 'candy floss'.

This is a reminder of the importance of uncovering the idiosyncratic meaning for the client: the image, word or phrase that holds the client's distress, and which helps the therapist make sense of the problem.

It might seem obvious, but the tone you use when posing Socratic questions will communicate messages to the client. Consider the commonly used downward arrow phrase 'What is so bad about that?'. If delivered in a brusque manner, a client might infer that you are suggesting that he is making a fuss about nothing, thus compromising the therapeutic relationship. If you pose the question in a gentle, inquisitive manner, perhaps prefaced with 'This might sound like a silly question, but …', then it is more likely that the client will feel able to respond without fear of being criticised or judged. Gilbert (2005) has studied the role of the 'compassionate voice' in CBT and argues for the advantages of clients developing a compassionate inner voice. You can be a good role model for promoting this voice. By using phrasing and a tone of voice that communicate support and non-judgement, you are leading by example.

SOCRATIC METHOD AND SELF-HELP

Ultimately, clients must become both Socrates and his pupil. They need to stand back, review and then develop new perspectives. An invaluable aid in learning to do this is the thought record (DTR) (see Chapter 8). This record of key events guides the user through the stages of identifying key emotions/cognitions, exploring the validity of the cognitions and then synthesising a new perspective. With rehearsal, this procedure can become second nature.

Some authors have produced annotated DTRs that prompt the user with salient Socratic questions at each stage in the log's completion (Greenberger & Padesky, 1995; Gilbert, 2005). For example:

- 'What is going through my mind and how much do I believe it?'
- 'What supports this?'
- 'What contradicts my conclusions?'
- 'How might someone else view this situation?'
- 'What would I advise someone else?'
- 'What evidence is there to support alternatives?'
- 'What thinking biases can I identify?'
- 'How does my thinking help or hinder me achieving my goals?'
- 'What effect would believing an alternative have?'
- 'What's the worst thing that could happen?'
- 'How would I cope?'
- 'Can the problem situation be changed?'
- 'What can I do differently?'
- 'How can I check this out?'

Others have produced lists of key questions for clients to use as prompts (Fennell, 1989), and clients can be encouraged to keep their own log of questions that have been particularly productive for them, such as:

- 'What line of enquiry has helped me in the past?
- 'What do I imagine a therapist asking at this point?'

WHEN NOT TO OPT FOR SOCRATIC METHODS

At the risk of repetition, we'd remind you of the earlier message that just as important as knowing when to use Socratic methods is knowing when not to. An effective clinician is one who gets the right balance. In this chapter we've highlighted some occasions when a direct question or a didactic approach will better progress therapy, for example:

- *Mind the gap*: when your client does not have the basic knowledge to benefit from Socratic methods.
- *Risk*: when you need swift and unambiguous information.
- *Information gathering*: when nothing is to be gained by using a Socratic approach, be direct.

There are other occasions when it is wise to consider your therapeutic style, namely when a Socratic approach risks colluding with avoidance, or encouraging worry and rumination, or reflects reassurance-giving.

Consider the following examples:

Rhiannon and her therapist had prepared for the behavioural experiment (BE) had understood Rhiannon's fears and had come up with good reasons – and a good plan – for testing them. Now at the doorway of the supermarket, Rhiannon began to express a fear that she would have a panic attack. Her therapist simply asked if Rhiannon could carry on, she did not explore the NAT. They had been over this very thoroughly and further exploration was unlikely to reveal any new understanding or solution and there was the risk that more discussion at this point would elevate Rhiannon's fear. The therapist also knew that Rhiannon was avoidant when stressed and the therapist did not want to collude in avoiding the BE – however, she did check with Rhiannon that it was OK to continue with the experiment.

Gerard's catastrophic thoughts and images just seemed to expand as his therapist probed more. Asking him questions like 'What could happen? What could go wrong?' and 'What would that mean to you?' seemed to take them deeper into catastrophisation. So he and his therapist agreed that it was more productive to look at the process of worry and coping with worry rather than try to clarify the content of his fear and search for specific solutions.

Paula found that unpacking her thoughts and feelings with her therapist gave her a sense of order and safety so she welcomed their verbal explorations. Knowing this, her therapist encouraged Paula to look at the pros and cons of being more 'Socratic-like' at times.

PROBLEMS WHEN USING THE SOCRATIC APPROACH

Although a generally easy strategy to use, here are some of the more common difficulties in adopting Socratic methods, with suggestions for managing them.

THE CLIENT CANNOT ACCESS THE KEY THOUGHTS OR IMAGES IN THE SESSION

Encourage clients to record relevant cognitions at or near the time of the problem occurring. It can also be useful to discuss a recent experience, using imagery or role play if necessary, in order to evoke the emotional state related to key cognitions: stronger emotions are likely to make relevant cognitions more accessible. As suggested in Chapter 8, it is also helpful to look out for clear changes in emotions within the session, as these can reflect 'hot cognitions' that might be relevant, and can be explored very close to the event. Encourage exploration of affect ('How do you feel emotionally?') and/or sensation ('How are you feeling in your body?') as this can give your client a more accessible starting point for exploring cognitive experiences.

THE CLIENT INVALIDATES DISTRESSING COGNITIONS

Some clients might invalidate key cognitions as they emerge: '… but I know that is silly', '… although I am sure that I'll be fine', '… but that doesn't really upset me'. This is sometimes a means of avoiding distressing cognitions (see below), but this minimisation can reflect a failure to recognise the impact of a 'hot cognition' after the event. If this is the case, ask your client if the thought or the image felt true at the time it crossed their mind, stressing the importance of that moment.

THE CLIENT IS AVOIDANT OF DISTRESSING COGNITIONS

A good starting point is working on your therapeutic relationship. Discover what your client needs in order to feel 'safe' and try to identify his fears. Take things slowly and make clear the rationale for unpacking potentially upsetting cognitions. Be aware that some clients might invalidate key cognitions as they emerge in order to avoid experiencing the 'hot thought'. Acknowledge this pattern and try to uncover the client's fears about staying with an emotionally laden thought or image. Such fears will have to be addressed before you can move on in therapy. Also remember that behavioural experiments (see Chapter 9) can help your client test out the negative predictions underlying the avoidance.

KEY COGNITIONS ARE FLEETING IN NATURE

Sometimes it is difficult to identify important cognitions because they seem inaccessible or 'slippery' and easily forgotten (see Chapter 8 for a full description of the nature of cognitions). You can help by encouraging clients to carry a DTR or thought log so that they are better able to catch key cognitions as they arise. Again, attend to mood shifts in session, as these can give insights into thoughts and images relating to the problem. And again, try evoking a recent experience so that the relevant cognitions might be accessible in the session.

CRUCIAL MEANINGS ARE HELD IN A NON-VERBAL FORM

When clients seem to be unable to express key meanings verbally, try exploring sensations: 'Where is it in your body, does it have a shape or texture? Colour? Temperature?', 'Can you picture it in your mind's eye?' This might provoke descriptions such as 'It's red and it is a hard ball in the pit of my stomach' and 'It's a soft, purple sensation that gradually spreads throughout my body.' Accept that some non-verbal meanings are going to be metaphorical rather than literal, for example: '... my body is full of red, boiling jelly with metal shards cutting through my skin' (pain) or 'I feel nausea, and a black tidal wave inside me is pulling me away' (disgust). It is still possible to incorporate this information into a formulation and to work towards developing alternative meanings. It is also possible – and sometimes necessary – to construct alternative 'meanings' in the form of more tolerable felt senses (see Chapter 8).

THE CLIENT INVALIDATES NEW PERSPECTIVES

Some clients seem to collaborate with guided discovery only to dismiss new conclusions with a 'yes but'. This might indicate that you have slipped into giving advice rather than posing Socratic questions: self-monitor to see if this is true. Alternatively, the client might need to substantiate his new perspective by engaging in behavioural change. Behavioural experiments can be really effective in achieving 'gut-level' changes in beliefs. 'Yes but's might also indicate that a robust undermining belief system is at work, which can be revealed through further Socratic enquiry. Sometimes such a belief system reflects a problem schema and schema-focused interventions might be appropriate (see Chapter 17).

THE THERAPIST QUESTIONS WITHOUT DIRECTION, OR IN AN UNFRUITFUL DIRECTION

Although the importance of curiosity has been stressed, Socratic enquiry should remain hypothesis-led and guided by a formulation. Without this underpinning, you might well collect information but be unable to structure it, struggle to remain focused on the presenting problem or find yourself in blind alleys, hopping from one topic to another without getting closure on any. In each of these situations, referring back to a working formulation will provide the necessary structure to make sense of new information and to keep you on track. Having said that, apparent blind alleys can sometimes give useful further information about a problem, provided there exists a conceptualisation that can incorporate it.

THE THERAPIST LECTURES

It is possible to lapse into lecturing, particularly if you have a clear idea of where you want to lead the client or what you think the client should know. Although there will be times when didactic presentation is in the best interest of the client, you need to have considered this carefully. The need for collaboration, curiosity and humility have already been discussed, and session recordings can help you identify when you lose these qualities. It is important to identify an unhelpful lecturing style early on, before the therapeutic relationship is put at risk. On occasion, you might find yourself unable to sustain a 'good' Socratic style because of tensions in the therapeutic alliance. It is crucial to keep the therapeutic relationship in mind and to address problems swiftly (see Chapter 3).

THE THERAPIST EXPLORES BUT DOES NOT SYNTHESISE AND DRAW CONCLUSIONS

Therapy should be regularly punctuated by summaries that draw together information and link it to the case conceptualisation. You might need to devise a reminder to summarise regularly, or to ask a client to synthesise new conclusions, say every 10 minutes. It can be helpful to ensure that a copy of the working formulation is always accessible for reference – better still, actually on view during the sessions, so that it is constantly there as a structure to guide both you and your client.

THE THERAPIST ASKS QUESTIONS ONLY TO VALIDATE A HYPOTHESIS

This can lead to a very biased 'unpacking' of information and, ultimately, a misleading conclusion. If you are exploring the hypothesis that your client has panic attacks, you need to ask questions that would allow for the possibility of your clinical hunch being wrong. After all, if you want to test the hypothesis that all swans are white, you need to look for a black swan. However, this is counter-intuitive for most of us so it does tend to require additional effort. Often, a little curiosity is helpful: 'Can you tell me more? Is there anything else? Do you have any other thoughts/feelings/urges?' Such questions will open up the field of exploration and prevent your enquiry from becoming too narrow.

THE THERAPIST LIMITS SOCRATIC ENQUIRY TO VERBAL GUIDED DISCOVERY

Although verbal guided discovery is an invaluable tool, it needs to be supplemented by other forms of Socratic method – creative development of assignments, curious devising and debriefing of behavioural experiments – and sharing a DTR can result in independent discoveries in your clients, for example. Try not to limit your use of Socratic methods but rather think how its many formats might help you and your clients get more out of a range of CBT approaches.

See Video 7.3: Multiple applications of Socratic method.

SUMMARY

- Socratic method is a technique fundamental to CBT which we can use to:
    - help clients discover things for themselves;
    - get a better understanding of their problems;
    - help them devise new ways of dealing with difficulties.
- It is a skill that is versatile and can be used in all aspects of therapy and in supervision. Even so, you should not strive to use Socratic questions exclusively – sometimes other forms of enquiry are more appropriate. For example, when carrying out a risk assessment or simply collecting demographic information, you could ask direct questions.
- Sometimes information-giving is a more effective means of teaching than Socratic methods. For example, informing someone of the physical dangers of self-starvation, or memory processes following psychological trauma. Remember, Socratic enquiry is only possible if a person has the knowledge to answer the question.
- To be most effective in a therapy setting remember to be:
    - *Curious* and humble: You don't have to know all the answers and you need to be prepared to learn from your client.
    - *Cautious*: Downward arrowing in particular can be a powerful technique.
    - *Compassionate*: This is not only a good stance for a therapist, but you are modelling an attitude for your clients to adopt.
    - *Confident*: You are an intuitive scientist so you know how to review, hypothesise and check out your hunches.
- Remember also that Socratic methods are used in context. Make sure that you try to get the most out of them by creating a collaborative relationship and by respecting your clients' needs.

LEARNING EXERCISES

These learning exercises are available to download from the companion website.

REVIEW AND REFLECTION:

- Consider what you have learnt from reading about Socratic method: what is new to you? What has been clarified for you? Are there aspects of Socratic methods that still puzzle you?
- Consider how Socratic methods fit with your practice: do you use this approach but could refine it? Do you need to start from scratch in improving your technique? Do you know the theory but are inconsistent in using Socratic methods? If so, what patterns can you identify?
- Consider what parts of the chapter fitted particularly well with your way of working or your approach to CBT – you will find these easy to build on. Think about what parts of the chapter seemed less familiar or clashed with your current style – it will take more effort to remember and use these sections and you will need to put more effort into taking things forward.
- When would you use didactic teaching or direct questions?

TAKING IT FORWARD:

- Once you have decided what you want, or need, to build on, consider how this will be best achieved. Be realistic in your planning and take into account your resources – how much funding is available to support your further training? How much time do you have? How much experience in Socratic methods does your supervisor have?
- Try to find workshops and literature that will help you develop your Socratic skills.
- Recording sessions is essential for improving your use of Socratic methods: you can then review recordings yourself and/or ask your supervisor or a colleague to critically appraise your Socratic ability.
- You need to think how you will evaluate your progress – this might require regular reviewing of session recordings and maintaining some form of rating.

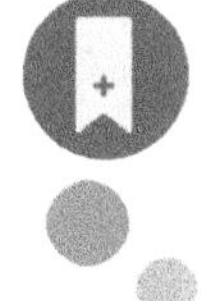

FURTHER READING

Kennerley, H. (2007). *Socratic method.* OCTC essential guides. Available from www.octc.co.uk

This is a brief text which considers how best we use Socratic methods in CBT. It is succinct, readable and covers the use of Socratic methods in assessment, testing beliefs and problem solving.

Padesky, C. (1993). *Socratic questioning: changing minds or guiding discovery?*

This was a landmark keynote address delivered at the European Association for Behavioural and Cognitive Therapies conference in London. In it Padesky challenged some of the conventional thinking about Socratic questioning in CBT, and her views on optimising its use remain as relevant today as they were in 1993. The keynote is available from www.padesky.com

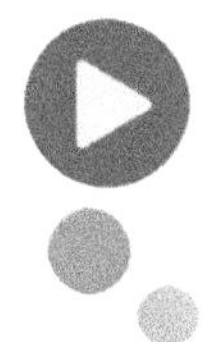

VIDEO LINKS

- **7.1 Using Socratic enquiry: the downward arrow technique**
- **7.2 Stages of Socratic method in action**
- **7.3 Multiple applications of Socratic method**

8 COGNITIVE TECHNIQUES

- Introduction
- Presenting a rationale for cognitive work
- Identifying cognitions
- Using distraction in CBT
- Identifying cognitive biases
- Appraising automatic thoughts and images
- Developing new perspectives
- Testing automatic thoughts and images
- Modifying core beliefs
- Problems
- Summary
- Learning exercises
- Further reading
- Video links
    - 8.1 Thought diary
    - 8.2 Distraction
    - 8.3 Dealing with worry and rumination
    - 8.4 Dichotomous thinking
    - 8.5 Imagery and role play
    - 8.6 Drawing new conclusions

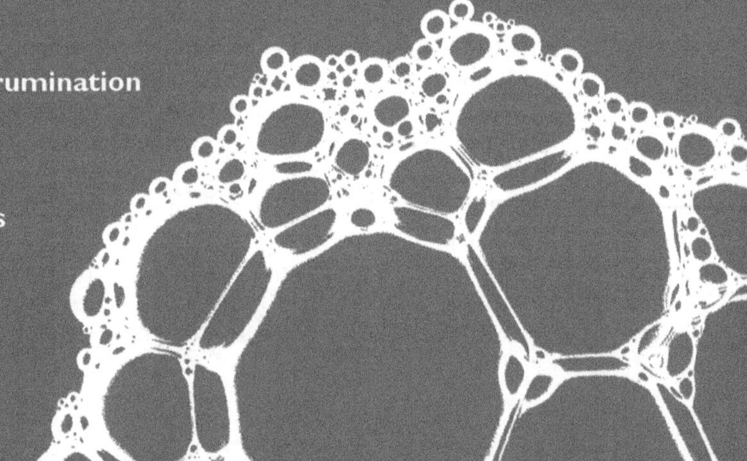

INTRODUCTION

This chapter introduces a range of cognitive techniques that are used to review and reappraise problem thoughts and images. As with any of the CBT interventions, their use must be part of a coherent plan and they should only be introduced with a genuine rationale that follows from a shared formulation. Even when following an empirically based treatment protocol, it is essential that you continue to ask: 'Is this an appropriate intervention for this person at this time? Given the formulation of this person's problem, can I justify introducing this intervention?'

Remember that not all distressing thoughts are inappropriate. For example, a man might attend a session feeling tremendously upset because he has to take exams in a day or two and is not fully prepared. He might believe that his chances of failure are high, and that he will therefore lose a postgraduate position. These thoughts *might* be realistic, and if so, your job is not to introduce unrealistic positive thoughts. Instead you might help him use problem-solving skills to minimise the likelihood of failing, or you might help him look at the *meaning* of losing his position and how he could cope with it.

Timing is also important. For example, Beck et al. caution that 'many depressed patients are so preoccupied with negative thoughts that further introspection may aggravate the perseverating ideation' (1979: 142). Beck and colleagues advocate focusing on goal-directed activities that change the negative estimates of capability, before directly focusing on the cognitions associated with depression. We are again reminded that a cognitive intervention is part of a larger cognitive behavioural treatment plan.

PRESENTING A RATIONALE FOR COGNITIVE WORK

Clients need to understand the rationale for cognitive work, because you will often be asking them to focus on the most frightening, most depressing or most shameful aspects of their lives and on cognitions that have been ignored or avoided for years. Fundamentally, that rationale rests on an individual's formulation, which demonstrates the links between his thoughts and his feelings and behaviours. He also needs to know that you are not going to require him immediately to share the worst thing he can imagine and to dwell on it. Although he is likely to need to face difficult-to-tolerate thoughts or images eventually, this will be in the context of a respectful, supportive, collaborative relationship and will be taken at an appropriate pace.

It might sound obvious, but it is also important that your client understands what is meant by the term 'cognition'. Beck et al. describe a cognition as 'either a thought or a visual image that you may not be very aware of unless you focus your attention on it' (1979: 147). This description nicely introduces the idea that cognitions can be ephemeral and that the client might have to work quite hard to identify them. It also reminds us that images are as relevant as thoughts.

You must guard against your clients identifying unhelpful cognitions as 'wrong' or 'irrational'. This can feed into negative beliefs such as 'I'm stupid' or 'I always get things wrong'. Even if a belief is currently *unhelpful*, that might not always have been the case.

For example, the firmly held belief that 'It is dangerous to trust' might have been a useful and adaptive belief for an abused child, even though in adulthood and away from an abusive environment it might be unhelpful. Alternatively, a cognition might only be unhelpful because it is held with too much conviction, not because it is 'wrong' – certain fears and phobias are good examples of this.

IDENTIFYING COGNITIONS

A fundamental task of the cognitive therapist is helping clients observe and record the thoughts and the images that run through their minds. It is not uncommon for people to struggle with this, sometimes reporting that they do not have cognitions or confusing thoughts and feelings. You cannot assume that you can leap in with a couple of well-constructed Socratic questions and discover the cognitive essence of a problem. Your first step is to help your client learn to 'catch' relevant reactions, to discriminate between feelings and thoughts and then to link them so that feelings become a cue for cognitive exploration. Table 8.1 gives some examples.

As the table illustrates, a good general rule for distinguishing thoughts and feelings is that feelings can often be expressed – at least crudely – by a single word, whilst cognitions demand a lengthier description. People often find it easier to notice feelings first, rather than thoughts or images. This can provide a useful stepping stone for accessing thoughts. If you encourage clients to begin by focusing on feelings, exploring and elaborating them, you will find that they tend to 'drift' into identifying cognitions.

Client: I don't know what was going through my mind.

Therapist: Can you see yourself back there? Get a picture in your mind's eye?

Client: Yes.

Therapist: Can you now try to remember how you felt at the time?

Client: Yes – physically sick. Tense.

Therapist: Stay with that image and those feelings and see if you can tell me more about your experiences that evening.

Client: Well I felt really tense, anxious. My heart was pounding and I was scared, really scared that he would come back and hit me. I thought that he was going to attack me.

Table 8.1 Feelings with commonly associated thoughts

Feeling	**Thoughts**
Depressed	I am hopeless. The future is bleak and I can't change it.
Anxious	I am in danger. Something bad is going to happen. I cannot cope.
Angry	I have been disrespected. People are mean to me and I won't stand for it.

In this example, the client first tapped into his physical state, then identified his mood and finally clarified his cognitions. Those who have difficulty in verbalising cognitions, or claim to have none, can often be helped by focusing on physical sensations.

'HOT' COGNITIONS

Beck et al. (1979) emphasised the importance of capturing *hot cognitions*, i.e. those that seem to be most directly linked to the client's most significant emotions. Cognitive interventions will be most effective if they target these hot thoughts or images. When trying to uncover these key cognitions, it can be helpful to ask: 'Would anyone feel as my client does if they had that thought and believed it as much as he does?' If the answer is 'No' then you might need to keep looking.

DIARY-KEEPING

Records of cognitions are most likely to be accurate if they are made at or near the time they occur. The records can range from simply counting thoughts or visual intrusions, perhaps using a golf counter, to quite complicated thought and/or image records (see Chapter 5).

When we ask people to keep records, we are not simply asking them to collect useful examples: we are also introducing a basic skills training exercise. We are encouraging them to tune into relevant thoughts, stand back from them and, ultimately, evaluate them. That is a challenging task: just as foreign vocabularies are best learnt by repeatedly writing them out, or piano-playing skills developed by playing arduous scales over and over, this fundamental skill of CBT is learnt through practice.

Such records are not filled in at random. You should ask clients to record cognitions at times that will cast light on their problems. For example, the following specific cues might be negotiated as prompts for recording:

- the urge to self-harm exceeding 5 on a 10-point scale;
- a mood rating of fewer than 4 on a 10-point scale;
- an urge to check exceeding 5 on a 10-point scale;
- a binge-eating episode (where the term 'binge' has been defined);
- a self-consciousness rating of more than 6 on a 10-point scale;
- a contentment rating of more than 6 on a 10-point scale;
- specific times of the day;
- particular environments.

Typical guidance would include:

- Each time you have an urge to cut or burn yourself which exceeds 5 on a 10-point scale, note the date, time and place and what went through your mind at that time.

- When your mood drops below 4, write down what you were doing at the time and what thoughts or images were going through your mind.
- As soon as you can after a binge, record what you ate, the place and time, and what was going through your mind before, during and after the binge.
- Whenever you take a bus/are in the supermarket/are alone in the house in the evening, pay attention to how you are feeling. If you are feeling anxious, rate how high this is and note what is going through your mind.

Remember that records need to be tailored to the individual. Although some excellent thought-record templates exist (Beck et al., 1979; Greenberger & Padesky, 2015), and an example of a thought record is given in Figure 8.1, it is crucial that any record you use reflects (a) the person's ability to gather information, and (b) the type of information that you and he need in order to understand the problem better. It is also crucial that the client fully understands *how* to fill in the record. It is advisable to carry out a dry run in the session, when he can reflect on a recent example and fill in the form with you.

See Video 8.1: Sharing a thought diary with your client.

Below you will meet Judy, who struggled with feelings of panic. This is her therapist's introduction to the assignment of diary-keeping.

It seems that we have two tasks immediately ahead of us. First, we need to get a better idea of just what is happening for you when you feel so uncomfortable – and keeping this record of events at the time will help us to do this. Second, you described the panicky feelings coming out of the blue and we agreed that we need a way to help you become more aware of what triggers the panic, and feel less overwhelmed by it – tracking your feelings using the diary should help you start to achieve that. But remember, this is our first trial, so we are experimenting really – see how it goes and we'll see if we have to modify the task at all. Why don't we run through it now, using the example that you described at the beginning of the session, and see how that would fit in?

Figure 8.2 is an example of Judy's first thought record, which she completed as a between-session assignment. This was drawn up with her in the session where it had become clear that she could readily articulate her thoughts if she 'anchored' herself in the way she was feeling physically. For her, reflecting on her physical feelings served as a powerful reminder of the time at which she was distressed, and her thoughts became accessible. She was also able to evaluate her experiences and put a rating on the severity of both her feelings and thoughts. Had she been very apprehensive about using a rating scale, the thought record could have omitted this and incorporated it later when she felt more confident. Had she not been able to access thoughts, the record could have comprised columns 1 and 2, with column 3 being introduced as she became able to catch her ATs. Had she found the thought of diary-keeping overwhelming, she could have started by simply keeping a tally of the times she felt panicky each day. If clients are to gain confidence in therapy, it is important that they feel capable of the task that you negotiate with them.

Date and time	Emotion(s)	Thoughts
	What emotion(s) did you feel? Also rate the strength of the feelings from 0 (none at all) to 10 (the strongest possible)	What went through your mind? Also rate how much you believed the thoughts at the time you had them, from 0 (did not believe at all) to 10 (absolutely sure they were true)

Figure 8.1 Example of a daily thought record

This figure is available to download from the companion website.

(1) Situation	(2) Feelings	(3) Thoughts
Tuesday lunch break: I was at the check-out, waiting to pay. It was a large shop with many customers milling around.	Hot and a bit jittery. Light-headed and it felt as though my heart was racing. **Discomfort:** 8/10	I am going to have a panic attack and all these eyes are upon me. They will think I'm crazy. **Belief in these thoughts:** Panic attack 7/10 Everyone is looking 9/10 Think I'm crazy 9/10
Saturday morning: filling car with petrol.	Nervous, dizzy, hot, shaking. **Discomfort:** 9/10	People on the forecourt are noticing that I'm a wreck. I am a wreck. I'm going to have a panic attack. **Belief in these thoughts:** People looking 9/10 Panic attack 9/10

Figure 8.2 Judy's first thought record

The advantage of rating the degree of physical, emotional or cognitive response was that it helped Judy develop a better ability to discriminate key reactions and it provided a method of quantifying changes over time.

It goes without saying that you must review diaries. Although some find diary-keeping fascinating, to others it can be tedious or distressing. Without a sense of achievement or progress, the client can easily stop completing records, so it is particularly important that you pay attention to them. Record-keeping is another therapeutic task that you should set up as 'no lose'. If the records are completed, then you have useful information to work with; if the records are not fully completed, then you can explore and work with what prevented your client from being able to complete them.

TURNING QUESTIONS INTO STATEMENTS

It is not uncommon for thoughts to take the form of questions. These can be rhetorical questions such as 'Why am I so stupid?', or they might be phrased as 'What if' questions: 'What if I fail?', 'What if it's bad news?'. Questions do not lend themselves to reappraisal and testing, so they should be turned into clear statements, with associated belief ratings. Thus, 'Why am I so stupid?' might lead to your asking 'How would you answer that?' The reply might be 'Why am I so stupid? Because it's my nature, it's what I am. I am very stupid.' Now we have identified a definite statement that can be rated for belief and eventually tested.

Similarly, you can explore 'What if' questions with an enquiry such as 'What if that did happen – what would be the consequences?' or 'What would be the worst answer to that question?'. A typical reply might be 'If I failed, then I would never get a proper job and I wouldn't be able to make a living' or 'If it's bad news then I won't be able to cope – I'll go to pieces'. You can then explore these statements further in order to make sense of your client's fears.

Sometimes people are reluctant to answer their own questions because the question feels less distressing to them than the statement that lies beneath it. This is a form of cognitive and/or emotional avoidance and, of course, unpacking this distress needs to be done sensitively.

ENHANCING RECALL THROUGH IMAGERY AND ROLE PLAY

Not everyone is as able as Judy to catch their ATs. For others, it may be helpful to use evocative interventions such as imagery and role play in order to recreate a key situation vividly enough for cognitions to become accessible. Possibly the most widely used technique is asking a client to recount a recent experience of the problem in detail (or, if the focus is a unique experience, to recall that specific event). The vividness of recall can be enhanced by questions such as 'Try to see this in your mind's eye: can you describe to me what is going on around you, what you felt, how you reacted?'

Judy had some difficulty describing her experiences verbally when she first came to therapy, and imagery helped her to appreciate why she experienced such powerful reactions:

Therapist: Can you recall when you last felt panicky?

Judy: In the waiting room here, just a few minutes ago.

Therapist: Perhaps we could explore that further. Can you imagine yourself back there for a moment? Can you see it in your mind's eye?

Judy: Yes.

Therapist: If you can, stay with that image and tell me as much as you can about the way you felt. Just focus on that feeling of being there and observe as many of your reactions as you can. See if you can describe things in the present tense.

Judy: I am okay but then another person joins me. I feel myself flush and I feel tense and a bit dizzy. I'm thinking that she reckons I'm a lunatic sitting in this place. I get hotter and I know that she's looking at me and I know that I am going to make a spectacle of myself. Then she gets up and walks out – she can't bear to be in the same room as such a weirdo.

Judy was asked to describe things in the present to increase the chance of catching the hot thoughts that make sense of her panicky feelings. Earlier in the session it had been difficult to target the hot thoughts because Judy rationalised them with phrases like 'I thought that she was looking at me but she might have been thinking of something else'. Although this is a useful perspective when reviewing her cognitions, at this point it does not help us explain Judy's extreme reaction.

Imagery need not be confined to visual images: 'visceral' or 'felt sense' reactions can also be relevant.

A woman with restrictive anorexia could not put into words why she was unable eat an objectively small amount of food. However, questions prompting her to imagine eating revealed that, although her mind was aware that she would not gain weight, she experienced a rapid sensation (a bodily image or felt sense) of bloating and feeling fat that made eating aversive.

A man who went to great pains to avoid touching certain shared objects like door handles, maintained that nothing went through his mind at these times. So his therapist supported him in imagining that he was reaching out to a door handle and the man physically recoiled. Realising that this was a 'hot' moment, she asked: 'What happened then – what did you feel?' The man replied that he felt physically contaminated and that this had been a very visceral, bodily sensation and not a thought.

Recall through imagery can be particularly pertinent for survivors of trauma who suffer from flashbacks or other unwanted mental intrusions, whether this relates to adult or childhood trauma (e.g. Arntz & Weertman, 1999; Ehlers & Clark, 2000; Holmes, Grey & Young, 2005).

However, the use of imagery can be a very powerful technique, and for some it can be *too* evocative. For example, a person who has been through a very traumatic experience might not be able to explore imagery without being overwhelmed by traumatic memories. In such cases, it can be prudent to gradually introduce imagery work, be it at assessment or in treatment. The first step would be to discuss the reasons for considering imagery work, then to establish the client's resilience. An alternative to using the first-person, present tense for recall is to begin with a third-person account in the past tense and gradually move towards capturing a more personal here-and-now account as the client becomes more robust (Resick & Schnicke, 1993).

Role play can also be used to evoke key feelings and cognitions.

Judy had recently felt panicky when she tried to pay for petrol, but she could not pinpoint what made sense of these feelings. When her therapist took on the role of cashier and Judy re-enacted the scene, she was able to identify the thoughts: 'I'm going to do something that makes me look stupid; she's going to think that I'm stupid; everyone will see that I am stupid'.

USING MOOD SHIFTS DURING SESSIONS

Therapy sessions can be a useful source of hot cognitions, so monitor changes in position, facial expression and tone of voice that may indicate negative thoughts.

Judy presented as a jovial and humorous character, but there were moments in sessions when her face grew serious and her posture stiffened. Asking 'What happened just then? Did something go through your mind?' frequently resulted in her identifying frightening hot cognitions. In Judy's case, it was crucial to catch them quickly, as otherwise she tended to trivialise and dismiss them.

John had the occasional brief moment of losing concentration and disengaging from the session. Asking what happened at this time revealed that he was experiencing flashbacks of a childhood trauma.

Opportunities for catching hot cognitions during a session are significantly enhanced when using imagery, role play or in-session behavioural experiments.

CLARIFYING GLOBAL STATEMENTS

Negative thoughts are often not very specific, which makes them hard to evaluate. In such cases, it will be useful to ask your client to specify what he means by a particular word or expression. Take, for example, a student who states 'I am useless'. This invites questions such as:

- 'In what way 'useless'?'
- 'What sort of things do you feel that you cannot accomplish?'

- 'What sort of things can you achieve?'
- 'How do you assess your success?

By reflecting on such questions, she might realise that, rather than being globally 'useless', she is achieving in many areas of study, but has not been able to achieve her rather high standards in English language.

In response to someone who believes 'It always goes badly for me', you might ask such questions as:

- 'Can you tell me more about the incident that prompted that thought?'
- 'What else ran through your mind at that time?'
- 'Have there been times when, in a similar situation, things have gone smoothly?'
- 'In your review of the last week, can you recall things that went well?'
- 'What good fortune have you had in your life?'

It might become apparent that, although this person felt profoundly pessimistic, things were going reasonably well in many ways. However, with regard to relationships he did seem to have difficulties, and each time a problem arose, he was beset by memories of other failed relationships and felt overwhelmingly negative.

USING DISTRACTION IN CBT

This very basic cognitive strategy rests on the idea that we can only concentrate on one thing at a time, so that if we actively focus on something neutral or pleasant, we can avoid getting caught up with negative thoughts and urges. This can serve two purposes:

- Breaking unhelpful cycles of thoughts or images that might otherwise result in negative moods, increasing preoccupation. This can offer temporary respite, but it sometimes results in problem management because of,
- Changing attitudes towards negative cognitions. Instead of getting caught up in them, distraction can help your client achieve distance from them and to see them as 'just thoughts' rather than convincing truths about themselves or the world.

You will find that distraction is a particularly invaluable strategy for giving relief to those who are caught up in worry (common in anxiety) or rumination (common in depression) or who struggle to ignore unhelpful mental intrusions. Distraction is a rather ubiquitous technique and has been shown to have direct therapeutic benefit both physically and psychologically. For example, in pain and anxiety management (Hudson, Ogden & Whiteley, 2015; and see Koller & Goldman, 2012, for a review of paediatric research), and reducing rumination in depression (Nolen-Hoeksema, 1991). It has even been suggested that it can improve the therapeutic alliance in CBT for depression (Teismann, Michalak, Willutzki & Schulte, 2012) and Grezellschak, Lincoln and Westermann (2015) have recently shown distraction to be helpful in enhancing emotional regulation and reappraisal of experiences in a group of people with schizophrenia. Research suggests that distraction is more effective than thought suppression in reducing unwanted cognitions (Wenzlaff & Bates, 2000) and that it is more effective when clients devise a positive distraction that is unrelated to their unwanted thoughts (Wenzlaff, Wegner & Klein, 1991).

Thus, thinking about something positive is more distracting than trying *not* to think about something negative. This is a general finding – we are more successful if we set out to think about something than if we set out not to think about something. You can easily try this out for yourself – try *not* to think about pink balloons, for example, and your mind will probably fill with pink balloons and you will fail to keep your mind free of them. If, on the other hand, your goal is to think about pink balloons and you try to do this, you will find that you succeed. Furthermore, you can probably manipulate the balloons in your imagination – you can make them rise or fall as you wish or have them explode, for example. This reminds us of the potential control that we have over images, a universal talent that we can use therapeutically.

Distraction techniques include:

- *Physical exercise*: This is particularly useful when a person is so preoccupied that it is very difficult to come up with mental challenges, or with children and adolescents who might be more physically predisposed than psychologically minded. Physical activities can be overt (e.g. going for a run), discreet (e.g. pelvic floor exercises), challenging (e.g. difficult yoga exercises) or mundane (e.g. household chores). The important thing is that they are engaging for your client.
- *Refocusing*: This usually means paying attention to the external environment, and objects or people within it, rather than one's internal world. Clients are encouraged to describe to themselves qualities of the surroundings such as shapes, colours, smells, sounds, textures and so on. The more detailed the description, the more distracting the task will be. The simple action of focusing outside the mind and realising that this is possible can give enormous relief to those who are preoccupied with painful cognitions or emotions.
- *Mental exercise*: Mental exercises include tasks such as counting backwards in 7s from 100, or reciting a poem, or reconstructing in detail a favourite piece of music or scene from a movie. Your client should choose one or two mental distractors that they enjoy – this way it will be easier to engage with them. Another effective distraction is a self-created mental image of a place where one would like to be (e.g. a beach, a beautiful garden, a ski slope), whatever appeals to your client. In order for this to be an effective distraction, the image should be attractive, filled with sensory details and well-rehearsed.
- *Counting thoughts*: Simply counting the thoughts can create a distance from them – not paying any other attention to them, just counting them, with the same attitude one might have to spotting how many pigeons there are in one's neighbourhood: 'There's one … and another … oh, and there's another!'

When devising distraction exercises, remember to do this collaboratively and with the following in mind:

- The exercise must suit the client. For example, mental arithmetic and a beach image would not be effective for a person who hates mathematics and is allergic to sand. Your client will only be able to engage in distraction if the exercise is readily accessible and attractive. Build on a person's interests and strengths.
- Clients might need several techniques to use under different circumstances. For example, tasks need to be discreet in a public place, whilst in private they can be more overt; physical strategies can be most accessible when a person is highly preoccupied, and mental strategies more usable at lower levels of preoccupation.
- Distraction can be used in behavioural experiments to test predictions such as 'I can't stop thinking about x' or 'I cannot get the worries out of my head'.
- Distraction will be counter-productive if used as a long-term avoidance or safety-seeking behaviour. If your client develops a belief that he is only coping because he uses distraction, rather than building up confidence that he can take command of his problems, then distraction will be of limited benefit and could actually undermine his confidence.
- Often distraction does not fundamentally change the unhelpful cognition, so it is not necessarily a good strategy for the long term: hence the need for the other strategies described in the remainder of this chapter.

Once distraction has been used, debrief. This is crucial to:

- establish whether or not its successful application is as a *coping strategy* or as a *safety behaviour*, and
- re-formulate and assess if you need to progress beyond distraction.

See Video 8.2: Introducing distraction to your client.

Judy experienced occasions when she felt trapped and immobilised by panicky thoughts. Recently she had experienced this at work (when it stopped her from completing a report that was urgent), at home (where she found herself so preoccupied that she failed to get ready for a social event) and in the street (when she couldn't rid herself of catastrophic thoughts and she wandered aimlessly). Judy said that sometimes she simply needed respite from panicky thoughts so that she could 'think straight and make a plan'. A repertoire of distractions gave her the mental break that she needed. Her chosen strategies embraced her interest in gardening and love of reading as well as her ability to run for several miles (see Figure 8.3). A person with different interests and abilities would generate a different list of physical and mental distractions.

Judy tried out her strategies and realised that she needed to refine her ideas – for example, when she was in public and very panicky, it was impossible for her to count backwards from 100 in multiples of 7 – so she abandoned this and opted for a less demanding (but very absorbing)

	At home	At work	In public
Low–moderate panic	Read my novel (keep it on my phone for easy access). Sing along to pop music: dancing helps, too. Plan the garden: go out and work on it if I can.	Read my novel. Look at the pictures of gardens that I keep on my phone: imagine walking through them. Review my calendar and my 'to do' list. In a meeting: make verbatim notes of what's being said.	Try to remember the plot of my novel and talk myself through it. Imagine walking through a beautiful garden. Listen to pop music through earphones.
High-level panic	Go out for a run if possible Walk to the garden centre. Watch something easy and entertaining on the internet, e.g. *Gardeners' World*.	Take a walk to the canteen or go for a lunch-time run. Work through the puzzle magazine in my drawer. In a meeting: doodle.	Describe what I can see: what is in shop windows/the number of red cars/people carrying handbags, etc. Count down from 100 in multiples of 7.

Figure 8.3 Judy's distraction repertoire

task of trying to walk as her childhood ballet teacher had taught her, being aware of keeping upright and positioning her feet carefully. These sorts of changes are necessary in order make the strategies sufficiently 'bespoke'.

Judy found that simply breaking the cycle of panicky thoughts often gave her enough relief to be able to put her concerns to one side and get on as normal. Just knowing this reduced her anxiety levels because she became less afraid of being afraid. There were times, however, when her concerns returned and so she developed strategies for focusing on and reviewing problem cognitions (see later).

See Video 8.3: Dealing with worry and rumination. Having a good repertoire of distraction techniques can also help those who struggle in managing excessive rumination (see Chapter 12) and extreme worry (see Chapter 14).

GROUNDING STRATEGIES

These are simply elaborations of distraction techniques (see Kennerley, 1996) that can be helpful in managing mental or physical intrusions (e.g. unwanted images or bodily sensations) and urges. The intention is to 'ground' a person back in the present if they are dissociated for time, or to 'ground' them in a pleasant or safe 'place-in-mind' or body if they are distressed, particularly if they have the urge to hurt themselves or others.

Grounding strategies generally need to be rehearsed very frequently if they are to successfully combat dissociation and urges and, like all distraction strategies, they are more likely to be engaging if they represent something that interests your client.

Below are some simple grounding strategies:

- *Imagining a safe 'place-in-mind'*: You can build on the power of distracting images by helping your clients elaborate one or more images into vivid mental pictures of somewhere that they feel safe and/or soothed. There are three things that really help make the image work: (i) making the image as full of sensory experiences as possible: sounds, sights, physical sensations and so on; (ii) making it somewhere enjoyable to think about; and (iii) making it active, perhaps with a pathway to follow (e.g. walking through a beautiful city if there are good memories of that place) or a routine to follow (e.g. all the necessary stages in making cake for someone who enjoys baking) – this will help engagement with the image. You really do need to encourage clients to create an appealing image and not just one that you both think should work. For example, there would be little point in a keen cyclist who hated the sensation of sand between his toes imagining 'walking bare-foot along a tropical beach' as his soothing image, it just wouldn't work and he would have far more success imagining himself cycling along on a particularly satisfying route.
- *Imagining and creating a safe or strong position*: Our body responds to emotion: this is the basis of embodied cognition theories first proposed by William James in the 1890s. So, for example, if we feel depressed we tend to slump and if we feel anxious we tend to cower, but it goes beyond that because our emotions also respond to our bodies. If we adopt a confident position we tend to feel more confident and if we smile we tend to feel more cheerful. This can be very helpful when developing 'grounding positions', postures that convey the emotions that a person needs to feel. Fearful clients might benefit from practising a confident posture, the submissive person an assertive stance and so on. This practice is often enhanced by also considering shapes and colours and temperatures, and it can be productive to ask questions like 'If you were feeling confident and good about yourself what colour might you 'feel', where would it be in your body, what shape would it take?' When asked this, one man replied: 'When I stand tall and feel in control, strong and in command of my anger, the colour in me is blue. It's a cool misty blue that descends from my head, displacing all the red anger.'
- *Using pleasurable and soothing smells*: Smell can be very powerful in triggering emotions and we can use this to advantage if a scent is really meaningful in a positive way. You could encourage your client to check out perfumes, aftershaves and familiar smells such as fresh coffee, cinnamon, vanilla and so on to discover which can give them a 'therapeutic feeling'. When they find something effective, help them develop ways of making it accessible. For example, one woman carried a little bottle of rose oil as this took her back to her wedding day and filled her with joy and hope; a man carried around coffee beans that made him feel 'grown up' and thus stronger; another man carried a cedar wood ball because the smell was a soothing reminder of safe, happy days in his grandfather's house.

- *Using grounding objects*: These are portable objects that distract and then cue the person to find the safe or soothing place-in-mind. Sometimes they have a scent, and that makes them even more potent. For example, the man above fixed a wooden cedar ball to his key chain so that it was always with him. When it was in his pocket he could simply hold it and the shape of it immediately triggered a mental picture that reminded him of his grandfather's house (which was also the subject of his safe place-in-mind image). If he took out the cedar ball, the smell ensured that he was transported back to this safe place. Some people use their smartphones to carry pictures and music that distract and remind them of their strengths, connectedness and safety – it is not unusual for a person to have a series of images that represent 'I'm loved', 'I can do', 'I am safe', 'I have achieved' for example.

Again, we must stress that once you have encouraged clients to use grounding strategies, you need to debrief and discover what they conclude from the experience. You need to establish as soon as possible if a technique is being used as a safety-seeking behaviour rather than a coping strategy.

IDENTIFYING COGNITIVE BIASES

As people become adept at identifying relevant images or thoughts, they can usefully learn to look out for cognitive biases (see Table 8.2). These are exaggerations in thinking that we all experience from time to time when we are emotionally aroused or depressed. They reflect normal fluctuations in our information-processing styles, and only become a problem when the bias is chronic or too extreme. For example, the first bias in Table 8.2 is 'dichotomous thinking' – an 'all or nothing' style which fails to incorporate the possibility of 'shades of grey'. This type of information-processing style increases with stress levels (Kischka, Kammer, Maier, Thimm & Spitzer, 1996), and, indeed, it may be appropriate when we are under threat. If a car swerves towards me, it is appropriate that I think 'life or death!' and swiftly manoeuvre out of the way – it would be inappropriate for me to lose valuable time considering the many less dramatic options. If, however, this was my habitual way of responding to moderately stressful situations, I would probably very quickly develop an anxiety-related problem.

Table 8.2 contains four groups of cognitive biases: extreme thinking, selective attention, relying on intuition and self-reproach. Note that the specific categories within these groups are not mutually exclusive.

Judy was given a copy of the summary of cognitive biases in Table 8.2, and she smiled and said: 'I can achieve something: I can tick all these!' Like many clients, she readily recognised a tendency towards cognitive biases or 'crooked thinking' (Butler & Hope, 2007). Her amusement at realising this helped her to stand back or 'decentre' (see next section) and, as it was difficult to maintain a fearful 'mindset' when she laughed, she was much better placed to see alternative, more positive possibilities. Figure 8.4 is an extract from her diaries, identifying the cognitive biases pertinent to her.

Table 8.2 Common cognitive biases

Extreme thinking	
Dichotomous thinking	Viewing things in 'all or nothing' terms without appreciating the spectrum of possibilities between the two extremes. Things are 'good or bad', 'successes or failures'. Typically, the negative category is more readily endorsed. Examples: *Nothing is ever going to go right for me. I can trust no one. I am a total failure.*
Unrealistic expectations/high standards	Using exaggerated performance criteria for self and/or others. Using 'shoulds', 'oughts' and 'musts'. Examples: *Unless it's the best, it doesn't count. I should get full marks. Mistakes are unacceptable. I must please everyone.*
Catastrophisation	Predicting the very worst, sometimes from a benign starting point. This may happen very rapidly so that it seems that the client has immediately leapt to the most awful conclusion. Examples: *I made a mistake. My boss will be furious. My contract won't be renewed. I will lose my job. I will lose my home. My wife will leave me. I will be poor and lonely.*
Selective attention	
Over-generalisation	Seeing a single negative event as an indication that everything is negative. Examples: *I have failed an interview – I'll never get a job. This relationship is going badly – I'll never find a partner. She let me down – I can trust no one.*
Mental filter	Picking out and dwelling on a single negative feature without reference to other, more benign events. Focusing on the one thing that went badly in an otherwise successful day. Forgetting achievements and compliments but dwelling on a single criticism. Example: *One of my exam marks is low – this is terrible – I'm really no good at anything.*
Disqualifying the positive	Rejecting, downgrading or dismissing as unimportant any positive event. Examples: *He is only saying that to be nice. She is probably trying to get something out of me. This was a small achievement – others do better.*
Magnification and minimisation	Exaggerating the importance of negative events and underestimating the importance of positive events. Examples: *What a mess up I made of that deal. Yes, I got the terms that my boss wanted but I didn't handle it well.*

Relying on intuition

Jumping to conclusions	Making interpretations in the absence of facts to support them. Examples of jumping to conclusions divide into two categories: (i) Mind-reading: *I just know that they were all laughing at me behind their friendly faces.* (ii) Fortune-telling: *When I meet him, he will dislike me.*
Emotional reasoning	Assuming that feelings reflect fact. Examples: *I feel as though I can't cope, so I'll have a couple of drinks first. I feel awful when I get angry, so it must be bad to get angry. I feel unattractive so I must be.*

Self-reproach

Taking things personally	Assuming responsibility if something (perceived as) bad happens. Examples: *The dinner party did not go well: it was my fault for being tense and causing others to feel uncomfortable. Two students left my lecture early; I must have been boring.*
Self-blame or self-criticism	Seeing oneself as the cause of a bad event or criticising oneself without cause. Examples: *I feel ill; I must have brought it on myself. I can't catch up with my work; I must be stupid and lazy.*
Name-calling	Attaching harsh and demeaning names to oneself. Examples: *Idiot! I am so stupid. What a fool I am.*

Thoughts	***Cognitive biases***
I am going to have a panic attack …	Catastrophising
… and all eyes are upon me.	Jumping to conclusions
They will think I'm crazy.	Mind-reading
People on the forecourt are noticing that I'm a wreck.	Mind-reading
I am a wreck.	Name-calling
I'm going to have a panic attack.	Catastrophising

Figure 8.4 Judy's extreme thinking

In summary, so far we have outlined the need to help your client to:

- understand and identify cognitions, using Socratic enquiry coupled with imagery and role play if necessary;
- record cognitions;
- link situations, thoughts and feelings, so that you are both able to say 'It's no wonder that ...';
- use distraction for short-term coping (although this will sometimes have longer-term impact);
- become aware of cognitive biases.

Now your client is ready to appraise the ATs and images that are causing problems.

APPRAISING AUTOMATIC THOUGHTS AND IMAGES

TAKING A STEP BACK, OR 'DECENTRING'

Beck et al. (1979) described decentring, or the ability to view cognitions as mental events rather than as expressions of reality, as a core component of CBT. Rather than buying into the emotionally laden content of a cognition, one stands back and observes it, recognising that a thought is an opinion, not necessarily a fact. Decentring is also termed 'meta-cognitive awareness', meta-cognition being defined as any knowledge or process that is involved in the appraisal, monitoring or control of cognition (Flavell, 1979). Clients may be able to achieve this if they are able to label the thinking *process* rather than dwell on the content. You might hear phrases like 'There's my all-or-nothing thinking again' or 'I'm catastrophising here' or 'It's my abandonment fear kicking in'. Such responses indicate that your client has achieved meta-cognitive awareness. Decentring has played an increasingly important part in CBT since the introduction of mindfulness meditation into CBT practice – see Chapter 17, which reviews such developments.

UNDERSTANDING THE ORIGIN OF A COGNITION

In CBT we look for the reasons why what seems like an unhelpful reaction or response is actually understandable. When clients are first learning to view their cognitions objectively, they can easily label themselves as 'stupid' or 'silly'. You need to help them appreciate why it makes sense that they have such unhelpful thoughts, or why it made sense at some time in their lives. One way of doing this is to ask them to consider the evidence or experience that supports a hot thought or image. Problem cognitions rarely, if ever, come out of the blue. There is usually an earlier experience that renders them understandable. Aim to help your client recognise that there might be good reason why they drew certain conclusions, so that they can begin to conclude 'It's no wonder that ...' or 'I can understand why ...' when they review their ATs.

The student in the earlier example, who believed 'I am useless', had attended a very demanding school where the pupils had been encouraged to excel in all subjects. Holding high standards at that time both helped her to cope with the culture of the school and, because she was academically able, to achieve and gain a great deal of reinforcement for doing so. Later, at a different time in her life, these same high standards proved stress-provoking and often unattainable, thus promoting the belief 'I am useless'.

The young man who felt that 'It always goes badly for me' had indeed had a number of broken relationships, so it was understandable that he might be pessimistic. He believed that he could protect himself against major hurt by anticipating the break-up of a relationship, and so it was not surprising that he had maintained a pessimism within relationships. However, he now discovered that this attitude diminished his enjoyment of, and commitment to, relationships.

Below are Judy's explanations for her ATs. When appraising 'They will think I'm crazy', the therapist asked:

- Can you recall a time when you did not feel like this, when getting panicky did not make you assume that others would think that you were crazy?
- Can you recall when you began to hold this view?
- Can you be more specific?

It transpired that Judy's attitude had very much been influenced by her mother telling her not to show emotions publicly, lest people assume that she was weak and strange (see Figure 8.5).

(3) Thoughts	(4) Why I draw this conclusion
I am going to have a panic attack and all these eyes are upon me. They will think I'm crazy. **Belief in these thoughts:** Panic attack 7/10 Everyone is looking 9/10 Think I'm crazy 9/10	I can understand why I anticipate having a panic attack, I've had them in the past. It is no wonder that I think everyone is looking at me because that is what it feels like. If I saw someone having a panic attack and I didn't know what was happening, I might think they were weird, especially as my mother has indoctrinated me over the years.
People on the forecourt are noticing that I'm a wreck: I am a wreck. I'm going to have a panic attack. **Belief in these thoughts:** People looking 9/10 Panic attack 9/10	It is no wonder that I think everyone is looking at me because that is what it feels like. No wonder I feel a wreck, I'm so distressed. I can understand why I anticipate having a panic attack, I've had them in the past.

Figure 8.5 Judy's automatic thoughts

WEIGHING UP PROS AND CONS

In looking for the reasons why a reaction or response makes sense we often ask our clients to consider the *advantages* of holding cognitions that are, ultimately, not in their best interests. It is useful to encourage them to explore the pros (as well as the cons) both in the short and the long terms, as some cognitions might only have limited advantages; some give short-term relief but long-term disadvantage; some give short-term discomfort but perceived long-term advantage. For example, permission-giving thoughts like 'I'm useless so I might as well give up' give a good deal of short-term relief by encouraging avoidance, but may compound problems in the long term; in eating disorders, the thought 'I am not giving into the hunger pangs' might create short-term discomfort but can confer a sense of control in the long term. An advantage of negative thoughts is often a perceived protection: for example, 'If I anticipate having a panic attack, it won't take me by surprise' or 'If I expect the worst from people, I won't be disappointed'. When the pros and cons of cognitions are considered in detail, the resilience of a negative thought often becomes more understandable. Some clients will explain to you that an advantage of holding certain negative beliefs is that they reflect the truth ('I could have a panic attack'; 'I am alone'; 'I'm hopeless in social situations'). Although there may indeed be a grain of truth in some negative cognitions, it is often exaggerated and we can help our clients appreciate this.

Next, we enquire about the *disadvantages* of having the thoughts or beliefs (again in both the short and long terms). This step helps loosen up a conviction that the negative thought is somehow protective and this can sometimes improve the client's motivation to change. In Judy's case, the disadvantages of predicting that she would have a panic attack were that she increased her physical discomfort, she made it more likely that she would have a panic attack, and she was always miserable in challenging situations. The disadvantages of assuming that others judged her negatively were again that she was always distressed in challenging situations, and she was inhibited about doing many things that she might otherwise enjoy.

Sometimes referred to as a cost–benefit analysis, balancing pros and cons is an approach that encourages a widening of perspectives, which is particularly useful when it is not possible to conclude whether something is true or not but, rather, what is most useful on balance. You will probably recognise that this is a Socratic technique as it draws on clients' own inner worlds and then prompts them to review.

Another related strategy is 'reframing', which facilitates the development of a wider perspective by prompting reflection about the 'other side of the coin'. Consider, for example, the ambitious father who spends most of his evenings at work and missing out on time with his children: the uncomfortable prospect of 'reducing my workload' could be reframed as 'making more time for my children'. Or consider the extreme dieter who, in striving for control of her weight and shape, is functioning less well in her social and work life because of her preoccupation with dietary restriction: she could reframe the apparent benefit of extreme dieting as the enemy of her work and social life.

When exploring the pros and cons, and reframes, you should, of course, be non-confrontational, empathic and collaborative. Such exercises are aimed at enabling and enlightening rather than illustrating how wrong your client might be. Carried out in this way, the approach is a particularly helpful one in engaging and motivating clients who are ambivalent about change (Miller & Rollnick, 2002).

WHAT IS THE WORST THING AND HOW WOULD YOU COPE?

Although it is a difficult prospect for some clients, asking them 'What is the very worst thing that could happen?' can be an extremely valuable question. It prompts them to name the fear (which cannot otherwise be tackled), and the answer clarifies the ultimate problem that needs to be resolved. The corollary question '... and how would you cope?' then kicks off the process of problem solving. When a solution for the worst-case scenario has been devised, it often takes the heat out of catastrophic predictions.

Judy's worst fear was that she would have a panic attack in public. The enquiry about how she might cope was, in itself, a revelation to her. She had never contemplated coping, and she had never viewed the panic attack as having an end – her projected fear had been too vague. Now, with the help of her therapist, she was able to generate some ideas for managing the situation: she would try to find somewhere discreet, she would try to talk herself through the experience, and she would rehearse a statement to explain her predicament to anyone who approached her. Through this exercise, Judy became more confident that she could cope with the worst outcome, and it frightened her less.

IDENTIFYING COGNITIVE THEMES

It is usual to find themes of either process or content running through thought records. Process themes might include dichotomous thinking as the most prominent form of information processing, or withdrawal as the reaction to perceived interpersonal conflict. Themes reflecting the content of cognitions might include rejection, threat, shame, anger and so on. Some themes are more common in particular disorders: for example, the need for control and perfectionism is often associated with eating disorders, loss and shame with depression, threat with anxiety disorders. The value of identifying such themes is twofold.

First, recurrent themes can be tackled thematically: that is, developing a repeatable counter statement for addressing, for example, pervasive shame or recurring sense of loss. This is much more efficient than having to generate a novel response to each problem cognition. Second, themes can give insight into pervasive core beliefs. Studying Judy's diaries revealed two dominant themes, one concerning the self (I am crazy) and one focusing on others (they are judgemental). Managing the latter core belief is illustrated later in this chapter.

In summary, we have so far described how you can help your client learn to:

- identify unhelpful cognitions;
- identify cognitive biases;

- stand back from them and view them as unhelpful but understandable thoughts;
- question their utility and validity;
- consider the worst outcome, and develop solutions for this.

At this point, your client can develop a more objective and wider perspective on unhelpful thoughts and beliefs.

DEVELOPING NEW PERSPECTIVES

The groundwork done, now it is time to reflect on problem cognitions and reappraise them where necessary: the notion of there being alternative, less-discomforting possibilities can be entertained. There are several techniques that can be used to develop new perspectives.

REVIEWING EVIDENCE FOR AND AGAINST: GETTING A BALANCED VIEW

Armed with an enhanced perspective on the situation, your client can now review what supports, and what undermines, his initial conclusion. This is illustrated in the example from Judy's diary in Figure 8.6, where she reviews why it is understandable that she draws a negative conclusion and then she goes on to counter-balance this with evidence that does not support that conclusion.

A useful strategy for gathering information to inform a more balanced view is an elaboration of decentring, in which you ask your clients to distance themselves from the thought or image enough to imagine a number of different perspectives. This can be prompted by questions such as:

- 'Can you think of other possibilities? Other explanations?'
- 'What does not fit with your initial conclusion?'
- 'If someone you cared about had this thought, what would you want to say to them?'
- 'If someone who cared about you knew that you had this thought, what might they say to you?'
- 'If someone you knew had this thought, or struggled with this situation, what might they say to themselves? How might they cope?'
- 'Are there things that you are overlooking when you are distressed?'
- 'Have you been in similar situations and not felt or thought like this?'
- 'Have there been times when you have felt like this and coped?'
- 'When you are away from this situation, what do you think?'
- 'If you 'fast-forwarded' five years from now, how would you view this situation?'

(3) Thoughts	(4) Why I draw this conclusion	(5) What conflicts with my conclusion
I am going to have a panic attack and all these eyes are upon me. They will think I'm crazy. **Belief in these thoughts:** Panic attack 7/10 Everyone is looking 9/10 Think I'm crazy 9/10	I can understand why I anticipate having a panic attack I've had them in the past. It is no wonder that I think everyone is looking at me because that is what it *feels* like. My mother has indoctrinated me over the years.	Feeling as though I will panic does not mean that I will. I've felt like this and not had a panic attack before. I know that calming myself helps. Even if I panic it won't last forever and I have some ways of coping. **Belief in this thought: 9/10** My *feeling* that others are looking does not make it fact. **Belief in this thought: 10/10** Even if I had a panic attack, it is unlikely that people would think that I was crazy. Even if they did, so what? They don't know me. **Belief in this thought: 10/10**
People on the forecourt are noticing that I'm a wreck. I am a wreck. I'm going to have a panic attack. **Belief in these thoughts:** People looking 9/10 Panic attack 9/10	It is no wonder that I think everyone is looking at me because that is what it feels like. No wonder I feel like a wreck, I'm so distressed. I can understand why I anticipate having a panic attack I've had them in the past.	My *feeling* that others are looking or that I am a wreck does not make it fact. **Belief in this thought: 10/10** Feeling as though I will panic does not mean that I will. I've felt like this and not had a panic attack before. I'm only here for a minute or two, so I'll be fine. **Belief in this thought: 9/10**

Figure 8.6 Judy's diary

The 'best' sort of evidence is factual and objective. So, although conclusions such as 'I think that a friend would say that there was nothing to worry about' might begin to shift a person's perspective, objective experience such as 'I have been in this situation at least 15 times and never had a panic attack' or 'I get light-headed every day and I have not once fainted' or 'In my entire school experience I have never failed an exam' will carry more weight.

Prompting for a broader range of possibilities can elicit coping statements and even plans for action.

When Judy was asked these questions in therapy, she readily generated helpful self-statements (see her diary, Figure 8.6) as well as strategies such as self-calming. She remembered that a friend had once told her that adopting a Pilates posture helped her to combat stress. Judy had attended Pilates classes but then neglected her practice – she decided to revise them and found it helpful.

This reminds us that familiar, comfortable strategies that have validity for the client will be most readily adopted and maintained.

ADDRESSING COGNITIVE BIASES

See Video 8.4: Addressing dichotomous thinking.

Dichotomous thinking is readily moderated by introducing the notion that there is a *range* of possibilities between the extremes. This technique is also described in Chapter 17 under 'Schema-focused work', as it is a really useful strategy for both 'straightforward' and more 'complex' clients.

In order to combat dichotomous thinking styles, first identify the relevant extremes.

Judy tended to assume that she felt calm or panicky (which meant that if she did not feel calm she anticipated that a panic attack was imminent).

Next, encourage your client in entertaining the idea that there might be stages between the extremes and in doing so generate examples that illustrate different points on the spectrum.

Below is Judy's new perspective of her emotional experience: she was able to recognise different stages in growing panicky.

1	2	3	4	5	6	7	8	9	10
Calm		Mildly nervous Might even be excitement				Panicky but not actually panicking			Panic attack

This exercise was helpful in several ways. It illustrated the range of possibilities, which curbed her tendency to jump to the most catastrophic conclusion; it provided assurance that she could feel panicky without progressing to a panic attack; and, in discussing the variations in her feelings of nervousness, she realised that she might misinterpret excitement as the warning signs of panic.

A different client, Alan, tended to view himself as a 'success' (i.e. he completed a piece of work to a very high standard) or a 'failure' (i.e. he did not regard his work as the very best that he could achieve). This made him very vulnerable to mood swings as he felt really good about himself when he had met his exacting standards but very bad about himself when he failed to do so. It also had an impact on his behaviour as he tended to withdraw and drink when he felt bad about himself and this, in turn, fuelled his depression.

In therapy he was able to construct a continuum of performance which helped him become more flexible in his appraisal of his work.

1	2	3	4	5	6	7	8	9	10
Unacceptable		Barely satisfactory		Satisfactory		Good but not perfect			Excellent work

He then considered what he would find acceptable in others and he realised that he would be quite happy if those around him were performing at a 'Good but not perfect level' and that he would consider 'Excellent' to be a bonus. He also realised that he could accept the occasional poor piece of work from colleagues, as long as this was not habitual. When he had completed this piece of continuum work, he found that his attitude towards himself was more lenient.

Sara had a different issue from Judy or Alan – she was dichotomous in trusting others. She tended to trust people absolutely until they let her down (or she perceived that they had let her down). At that point they became 100 per cent untrustworthy in her view. As you can imagine she had difficulty in maintaining relationships and this was a source of great distress to her. In therapy Sara devised two useful continua: one reflected the degree of trustworthiness of those in her social and occupational circle, and the second reflected information that was appropriate to share with people of different levels of trustworthiness.

1. Who I can trust (based on how well I know a person and what I know of their behaviour so far)?

0%	10%	20%	30%	40%	50%	60%	70%	80%	90%	100%
Tom (hardly know him) Janice (let me down a lot)			Sue (just getting to know her) Jim (wait and see)			Robin (probably OK) Joyce (OK but not with secrets)			Celia (always fair) Aunt Jane	

2. What I will share depends on how trustworthy a person is.

0%	10%	20%	30%	40%	50%	60%	70%	80%	90%	100%
Name, but no personal details		Maybe where I work, but nothing about my home life or feelings				Personal contact details, my likes and dislikes			My feelings, my problems and my history	

The first continuum helped Sara learn to review how well she knew a person and what she knew about them before considering how well she might trust them. The second helped remind her not to be either too open or too secretive. This helped her establish more balanced relationships where she shared information about herself with trusted friends.

Selective attention to the worst possibilities can be tackled by encouraging your client to search for other possibilities by asking himself questions such as:

- 'Are there other ways of looking at this?'
- 'Do I have strengths/assets/resources that I am ignoring?'
- 'What other possibilities might a friend see?'
- 'Am I missing something?'

Such questions prompt decentring – standing back and viewing the bigger picture.

By doing this, Judy was able to appreciate that not all unpleasant sensations heralded a panic attack, that not all eyes were upon her and that she had previously shown a composure and resilience which stood her in good stead. Alan learnt to consider his previous performances (which were generally very good) rather than always noting the one that disappointed him, while Sara learnt to give herself a little time to review the situation before drawing too rapid a conclusion about a person's trustworthiness.

Relying on intuition can be curbed if we accept that feelings or unsubstantiated beliefs do not necessarily represent reality. There are many non-clinical examples that clients can consider to support this idea: for example, children's strong belief in Father Christmas does not mean he is real; our ancestors' belief that the world was flat did not stop it being spherical; an emotionally deprived child's feeling that he is bad does not mean he *is* bad; and 'feeling ten feet tall today' does not mean that you need to duck when you go through doors! Whether mind-reading, fortune-telling or assuming that a feeling reflects a fact, clients can begin to question the truth of such intuitions and ask 'Is this supported by some evidence?' or 'Do I have experiences that suggest that this is the case?' or simply 'How do I know?'. One simple strategy that Judy worked out for herself was *asking* friends what they felt or what they intended by a remark, instead of ruminating on what her friends *might* feel or think; Alan began to routinely ask trusted colleagues to appraise his work and Sara carried around copies of her continua to which she would refer in order to remind herself of the reality of her relationships.

Self-reproach can be very undermining – just as it would be if severe criticism came from someone else. However, it can be moderated by questions such as:

- 'Is it really so bad?'
- 'Am I blaming myself unfairly? Who else might be responsible?'
- 'Whose voice is this? … and are they an expert?'

When Judy reflected on her thought 'They will think that I am crazy', she realised that this was [the memory of] the voice of her mother, who restricted emotional expression within the family and warned her children that others would view them as weak and silly if they were not in control of their emotions. She quickly realised that her mother was not an expert in social psychology and that her view was extremely unhelpful. As a result, Judy was able to dismiss this thought altogether.

Alan realised that his inner critic was driven by a fear of being seen to be flawed and weak and that this had arisen as a way of coping with the self-doubts he had developed at school when he was bullied. He had for years blamed himself for this, assuming that he had brought it on himself by being 'geeky and weak'. In therapy, he considered who (or what) else might have contributed to the bullying. He came up with quite a list: the particular girls and boys who chose to pick on him; the schoolteachers who did not notice or help him when he tried to ask for help; the school itself because it supported a culture of brutality amongst the children; his parents for never offering him a shoulder to cry on. By the time he had compiled this list, he perceived his own role in the bullying had diminished and he was more compassionate towards himself.

USING IMAGERY AND ROLE PLAY

The more experiential strategies of imagery and role play can be invaluable in shifting and manipulating unhelpful cognitions. Excellent reviews of the use of imagery in therapy can be found in Hackmann and Holmes (2004), Hackmann, Bennett-Levy and Holmes (2011) and Pearson, Naselaris, Holmes and Kosslyn (2015), who consider brain mechanism and its clinical relevance.

Rehearsal of new possibilities can be carried out in imagination. This has been shown to increase the perceived plausibility of an event happening (Szpunar & Schacter, 2013), which means that it can enhance confidence, and it has been shown that mental images can evoke similar physiological and emotional responses to the real thing (Pearson, Clifford & Tong, 2008). Thus we can usefully integrate imagery into therapy in order to:

- *build confidence*, step by step in those not yet ready to face challenges in real life: for example, a boy with a fear of snakes holding increasingly challenging mental images of snakes as a prelude to visiting the local zoo and handling one;
- *substitute* when it is not possible to practise in real life: for example, a woman with a fear of flying repeatedly imagining herself travelling by plane – for financial and practical reasons it would not have been possible to repeat this experience in real life;
- *prepare* to take on a challenge: for example, Judy imagined herself walking into a public area and feeling calm – reviewing this image helped her to feel more calm and confident when she took on a social task for real.

See Video 8.5: Using imagery and role play.

Transforming problem images can also be helpful. The horror of recurrent nightmares can be diminished through repeatedly imagining a new and bearable (or even pleasant) ending (Krakow et al., 2001); a predicted negative social encounter can be transformed to a hopeful possibility (Hirsch, Clark, Mathews & Williams, 2003); traumatic memories can be rescripted so that the meaning of a present threat is removed (Layden, Newman, Freeman & Morse, 1993; Ehlers & Clark, 2000); a hostile self-image can be transformed into a compassionate one (Gilbert, 2005); a simply unpleasant mental picture can be changed into one that is bearable, and clients can be encouraged to develop soothing, comforting images that can help them calm themselves.

As well as constructing such new narratives and/or mental pictures, you can help people overcome problem images via image manipulation techniques, such as envisaging the unwanted image on a TV screen and then manipulating it by changing the volume, fading the picture and so on, or 'morphing' characters in the image to make it more tolerable.

Judy had an unhelpful image of people looking at her judgementally, but she reduced its impact by shrinking the onlookers in her imagination. Alan had a similar image and he was able to transform the expression on the faces of the onlookers to that of acceptance and warmth.

An approach advocated by Padesky (2005) is to ask clients to create a vision of how they would *like* things to be. They are encouraged to make this mental picture as vivid as possible and to identify the assumptions that they would have to live by in order to realise the vision. Behavioural experiments can then further establish confidence in the new image.

For example, Judy's image might be walking into a public area and feeling calm. The assumptions that would facilitate this might be 'People who know me accept that I am basically OK, and strangers are not that interested in me'.

Imagery can be incorporated into role play. Beck et al. (1979) described client and therapist taking on critical and supportive inner voices and creating a dialogue to strengthen the supportive voice; Padesky (1994) described using 'historical role play' or 'psychodrama' to rework or reconstruct earlier unhelpful interpersonal interactions; Gilbert (2005) advocated using the Gestalt two-chair technique as the basis for building up an image of a compassionate self and diminishing the inner critic.

When Judy realised just how unhelpful her mother's influence had been, she felt less anxious, but she was angry and these feelings were uncomfortable. She resolved them in session by first imagining her mother in an empty chair. She then 'told' her mother of the consequences of her mother's attitudes and the anger that she now felt. In this exercise, she also agreed to take on the role of her mother responding to Judy's statement. In this role, 'her mother' explained that she had been trying to protect Judy from being victimised as she once was. This was the first time that Judy had considered her mother's perspective and it helped her to dissipate her anger.

DRAWING NEW CONCLUSIONS

By this point, your client has viewed the original negative thoughts from several angles, has built up a wider perspective (possibly including imagery work) and has entertained new possibilities. Now it is time to condense this awareness into pithy, memorable and *believable* new conclusions. Judy's new conclusions are shown in Figure 8.7, along with her ratings of belief in each statement.

It is interesting that the predominantly intellectual task of analysing her cognitions had resulted in her developing a 100 per cent belief that feeling was not fact, and that it was unlikely that others would think that she was crazy; however, her belief that the sensations of panic would not lead to a panic attack was not so compelling (80 per cent). It is also interesting that, although she developed a new conclusion ('My *feeling* that others are looking does not make it fact'), which she believed in the session, she was not wholly confident that she would be so convinced when in a challenging situation.

This reminds us that therapy does not end with the intellectual achievement of shifting cognitions. There is also scope for behavioural testing both to establish their veracity and to consolidate realistic new attitudes. Therefore, we would always ask questions like:

- 'And how could you check that out?'
- 'What might help your confidence in this new belief?'

This often leads neatly into behavioural work and behavioural experiments (see Chapter 9).

In summary then, in reappraising cognitions and developing new perspectives, we encourage:

- de-centring, standing back from the emotionally loaded cognition;
- addressing cognitive biases through tackling extreme thinking, selective attention, relying on intuition and self-reproach;
- using imagery and role play to enhance this process;
- drawing new conclusions, which can then be reality-tested.

6) New conclusion
Feeling as though I will panic does not mean that I will have a panic attack. I've felt like this before and not had a panic attack.
Belief in this conclusion: 8/10
My feeling that others are looking does not make it fact.
Belief in this conclusion: 10/10. (I know this but I don't know if I will feel confident when I'm outside).
Even if I had a panic attack, it is unlikely that people would think that I was crazy. Even if they did, so what? They don't know me.
Belief in this conclusion: 10/10

Figure 8.7 Judy's conclusions

See Video 8.6: Drawing new conclusions.

TESTING AUTOMATIC THOUGHTS AND IMAGES

The importance of testing out new possibilities or perspectives is elaborated in Chapter 9, which describes the role of behavioural experiments in CT. The validity of a new cognition is usually enhanced if it stands up to 'road testing'. In addition, the new possibility will be more memorable if a client takes it from a conceptualisation or a possibility through to an active experience.

Judy decided to 'research' her new conclusions by collecting information that could confirm or disconfirm them. With regard to her new prediction that the feelings of panic would not necessarily herald a panic attack, she planned to provoke panicky feelings and record what happened. She had begun to appreciate that panic was not 'all or nothing', and she devised a scale of her panicky sensations to assess degree of change. She also planned to involve her friends in her research, for example by asking them to observe the reactions of others and to note if Judy was the subject of much attention (see Figure 8.8).

(6) New conclusion	(7) Researching it
Feeling as though I will have a panic attack does not mean that I will. I've felt like this before and not had a panic attack.	I will go into difficult situations and instead of focusing on the times that I feel panicky and anticipating having a panic attack, I'll start to note the times that I move along my 'panic' spectrum without having a panic attack.
My feeling that others are looking does not make it fact.	I will ask my friends to check this out for me when I feel panicky. Then I'll see if there is justification for my thought.
Even if I had a panic attack, it is unlikely that people would think that I was crazy. Even if they did, so what? They don't know me.	I will ask friends if they think that panicking people are crazy people. However, since I realised where this thought came from, it really does not bother me anymore.

Figure 8.8 Judy researches her new conclusions

MODIFYING CORE BELIEFS

There is some confusion in the literature between 'core beliefs' and 'schemata'. The terms are not interchangeable because a schema is generally considered to be more complex than a core belief, but the latter can reflect a 'summary label' for a schema. For example, the core belief 'I am stupid' is a useful cognitive label which summarises the thoughts, feelings and physical sensations associated with believing that one is truly stupid. This section will focus on core beliefs; in Chapter 17 we discuss the nature of schemata.

We should not assume that core beliefs are always difficult to identify, as they may be expressed as ATs. In the earlier example, the student readily identified 'I am useless' as a key cognition, which might well be a core belief. If a core belief is not expressed as an AT, then guided discovery and the downward arrow technique can often uncover it, if it seems necessary to identify the core cognition.

It is also important not to assume that a core belief is necessarily resistant to change. Judy rapidly shifted a long-standing core belief ('I am crazy') when she realised that her mother was not an expert in character analysis; it is not uncommon for core beliefs to shift as a consequence of therapy that targets automatic cognitions (Beck et al., 1979). However, some belief systems are more rigid, and augmented techniques have developed to specifically target them (see Chapter 17).

In their self-help book, Greenberger and Padesky (1995) describe a collection of strategies aimed at modifying *core beliefs*. They emphasise that, because core beliefs can be robust, these strategies are likely to have to be used over several months before they have significant impact. They therefore need to be negotiated carefully so as to avoid disappointment and demoralisation. The strategies include:

- carrying out behavioural experiments to test the predictions of core beliefs;
- recording evidence that a core belief is not 100 per cent true;

- identifying alternative (more helpful) core beliefs;
- carrying out behavioural experiments to test the predictions of *alternative* core beliefs;
- recording evidence that supports an alternative core belief;
- historical tests of new core beliefs;
- rating confidence in new core beliefs.

Judy felt that she needed to work on a core belief that others were judgemental. The behavioural experiment that she devised was a data-collection task. Over several weeks she asked friends what they thought of people who had made a mistake or appeared 'silly' to her. Her prediction was that her friends would judge others badly. Figure 8.9 shows two examples from her record.

Judy then made a log of such findings, which she headed 'Evidence that my belief is not 100 per cent true'. On occasion, her opinion polls supported her prediction, but she was now able to put this in the context of the data that showed that this was not true 100 per cent of the time.

Of course, you might discover that your client's prediction is repeatedly confirmed. If so, it merits investigation: is your client only mixing with like-minded people?

Sion's wife and family were highly critical of him and had always been so. Therefore it was no wonder that his predictions of criticism were confirmed – he had real experiences of being told that he was 'stupid' and 'a waste of space'.

Is your client filtering out disconfirming evidence before it can reach the page?

Genna did have good experiences, but before she could even note them a 'voice in her head' would tell her that this didn't really count.

Incident	Prediction	What happened
Harry got rather drunk at the department party and was over-talkative and danced too much.	Others will think that he is a weak and silly person and his authority in the department will be undermined.	Sue thought that it was endearing to see him a bit tipsy; Ron said that he was pleased that Harry could let his hair down because he was too serious about his work.
A middle-aged woman in the street fell and became quite hysterical even though she did not seem to be hurt.	Sue (who was with me) would think that she was silly and attention-seeking.	Sue said that she felt concern for this woman and wondered if she had injured herself internally.

Figure 8.9 Judy collects data

You might consider that schema-focused techniques could be more helpful if negative core beliefs seem particularly resilient (see Chapter 17).

Judy, however, reviewed the responses that she had collected, and concluded:

It is true that some people are judgemental, but most of my friends are actually quite generous in their opinions of others. Furthermore, I find that those who are more judgemental are not amongst the friends that I most value and I tended to dismiss their harsh appraisals.

She was then able to identify a new core belief: Some are harshly judgemental but most people are generous. At first, she believed this at a 50 per cent level. In order to strengthen this new, more comfortable belief, she began a log of evidence that supported her new belief. She was diligent in maintaining this log, and after a few weeks her rating of her conviction in the new statement was 98 per cent.

In order to strengthen a new core belief that is counter-balancing a less helpful one from the past, Greenberger and Padesky (1995) advocate the use of a historical appraisal of the new core belief, where the client reviews his life history looking for evidence consistent with the new belief.

Although Judy was already successful in developing a new fundamental belief, she was keen to reinforce her progress and chose to carry out this retrospective analysis. She was, by now, much more able to 'see' the evidence that supported her new belief and found that many of her earlier experiences strengthened her new conviction.

PROBLEMS

THE CLIENT SEEMS TO AVOID EXPLORING COGNITIONS

Sometimes a person simply wants to talk about feelings and experiences. In some such cases, supportive counselling may be more appropriate. For instance, when people are first coming to terms with loss or trauma and realising the scope of their problems, they may need time just to talk them through. Alternatively, clients who are ambivalent about therapy might need an approach that emphasises 'motivational interviewing' (Miller & Rollnick, 2002).

Others focus on exploring feelings because they believe that this is the best use of therapy, so they may need to be reminded of the method and strengths of CBT and how this approach differs from other forms of talking therapy.

Avoidance of exploring cognitions also occurs when clients fear the content of their thinking. Sometimes the cognitions are never properly reviewed, but the sufferer has a sense of their awfulness or is reluctant to revisit cognitions that trigger other painful feelings – the shame of the sexual-abuse victim, for example. In these instances, you need to invest time in creating a sense of safety in the sessions that will allow your client gradually to confront distressing thoughts.

THE COGNITIONS ARE SO FLEETING THAT THEY ARE DIFFICULT TO IDENTIFY

This is not uncommon and it is helpful if your client realises that it is in the nature of automatic cognitions to be elusive. Behavioural experiments, done to provoke negative cognitions rather than to test them, can be useful in making them more obvious (see Chapter 9). However, we sometimes simply have to allow time for the skill of catching cognitions to be learnt as not everyone can readily do this.

Some thoughts don't easily map onto language and are better described as a visceral 'felt sense' (Kennerley, 1996). For example, clients with body dysmorphic disorder might report 'feeling' disfigured, a person with OCD might describe 'feeling' dirty, or someone with disgust-based PTSD might 'feel' this physically. Such felt senses can be worked with and most can be verbally articulated, given encouragement and time.

REVIEWING AND TESTING BELIEFS HAS LITTLE OR NO IMPACT

In such cases, the first question you must ask yourself is: 'Is the focus of therapy correct?' This will require revisiting the formulation and revising it if necessary.

It is also important to check out with your client what keeps him believing the old thoughts, or what *stops* his believing new alternative thoughts. There may be pieces of evidence, safety behaviours or other blockages that have not been fully dealt with. Or you may not be focusing on the 'hot' thought. Behavioural experiments can often be critical in ensuring that new learning is felt at a gut level rather than just heard intellectually.

A final possibility is that the problem is driven by a particularly rigid and inflexible belief system and so a more schema-focused approach is called for; however, do not jump to this conclusion too soon – consider other possibilities first.

SUMMARY

- This has been a lengthy chapter because the cognitive techniques of CBT are both crucial and diverse. There are techniques for:
    - observing key cognitions;
    - distracting from problem cognitions;
    - analysing them; and
    - synthesising new possibilities …
    - … which can be evaluated through behavioural experiment.
- Your first step is identifying key cognitions – predominantly through the use of Socratic enquiry and thought records. Over time, records can be used to observe, analyse and to synthesise information but the use of them must be paced to match your client's needs and abilities.
- The cognitive strategies you use to help your client identify problem cognitions and later test them will be determined by your formulation. Each intervention

needs to be justified and a rationale shared with your client. It is important not to pull a technique 'out of the hat'.

- Although the predominant focus is in the present, we have also seen that some cognitive strategies review or even confront the past, and although the predominant focus is on ATs and UAs, cognitive techniques can be used to address core beliefs.
- Interventions can be verbal, visual and experiential and can focus on cognitive content or cognitive process. You can be creative with cognitive strategies – but always make sure that you can justify your decision.

LEARNING EXERCISES

These learning exercises are available to download from the companion website.

REVIEW AND REFLECTION:

- Cognitive techniques are, of course, central to CBT. In reading this chapter were you surprised by any of the sections or the statements made – if so what did you not expect to see? If you were surprised by something in this chapter, was it welcome or worrying?
- Overall, what is your reaction to reading about strategies to identify and test problem cognitions? Do the techniques seem to fit with your preferred style of working? Can you see how this chapter builds on the knowledge you have gleaned from earlier chapters? Are there aspects of identifying or testing problem cognitions which feel wrong to you – if so, with what are you uncomfortable? Try to tease out your doubts and uncertainties.
- Do you have doubts about your ability to use these techniques – if so, what are your worries? Are their certain aspects of this predominantly cognitivel work for which you need further training?

TAKING IT FORWARD:

- An excellent way of gaining experience of using cognitive techniques is to use them on yourself, so:
  - identify a problem issue for yourself, perhaps a common work-related issue such as being avoidant of certain topics or fearful

of certain responses from your client, or you could address worries which you have about using cognitive techniques;

- keep a record of the cognitions (thoughts and images) that are associated with your difficulty;
- try to 'stand back' and identify cognitive biases and review the content of your cognitions;
- then try to re-evaluate your troublesome cognitions.

- **Reflect on how you got on with doing this for yourself – what did you learn not only about your own difficulty but about taking on this task? Consider how your clients will feel when asked to do something similar. How can you make that task most acceptable and achievable for them?**
- **If you feel uncertain about the usefulness of the strategies described in this chapter or if you feel that you need further training, find out what courses, workshops, supervision and reading are available to you and make a concrete plan to make use of them.**

FURTHER READING

Beck, A.T., Rush, A.J., Shaw, B.F., & Emery, G. (1979). *Cognitive therapy of depression.* New York: Guilford Press.

Although we introduced this book in Chapter 1, we feel justified in bringing it in again here. Although there have been refinements of cognitive techniques over the years, the foundations for using cognitive interventions lie in this book.

Greenberger, D., & Padesky, C. (2015). *Mind over mood.* New York: Guilford Press.

This self-help book was published 20 years ago and is now in its second edition. It contains the most clearly described and systematic approach to identifying and testing problem cognitions. It is useful for both clients and practitioners – particularly novice practitioners who can benefit from using the book on themselves.

Burns, D. (1980). *Feeling good: the new mood therapy.* New York: Morrow.

This self-help book for depression is even older, but it has stood the test of time and remains an excellent resource for both practitioner and clients. It also guides the

(Continued)

(Continued)

reader through the stages of CBT but it is particularly helpful as Burns addresses some of the common assumptions that can fuel depression (and other problems). For example, perfectionism and assuming that performance equals worth are explored in detail and the reader is given many ideas for combating such unhelpful assumptions.

VIDEO LINKS

- **8.1 Sharing a thought diary with your client**
- **8.2 Introducing distraction to your client**
- **8.3 Dealing with worry and rumination**
- **8.4 Addressing dichotomous thinking**
- **8.5 Using imagery and role play**
- **8.6 Drawing new conclusions**

9

BEHAVIOURAL EXPERIMENTS

- **Introduction**
- **What are BEs?**
- **Efficacy of BEs**
- **Types of BE**
- **Planning and implementing BEs**
- **Common problems in BEs**
- **Summary**
- **Learning exercises**
- **Further reading**
- **Video links**
    - **9.1 Predictions in behavioural experiments**
    - **9.2 Spontaneous behavioural experiments**
    - **9.3 *In vivo* experiment**

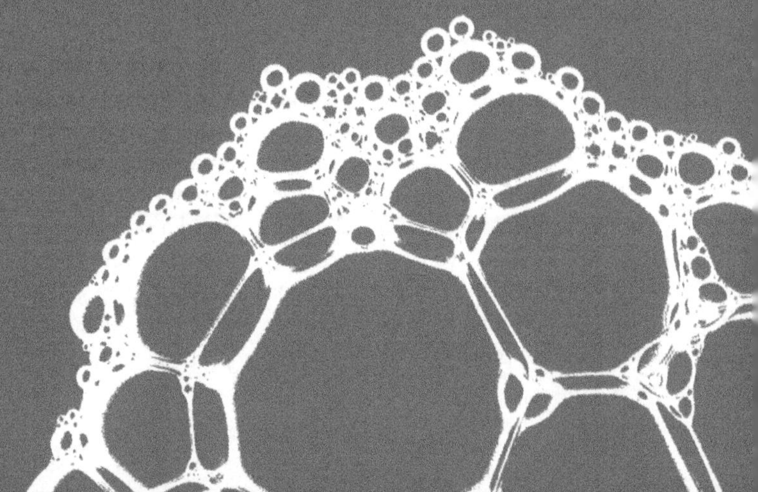

INTRODUCTION

At the 2004 conference of the European Association for Behavioural and Cognitive Therapies, there was a symposium entitled 'Where is the B in CBT?'. This chapter will address that question, that is, the place of behavioural methods in contemporary CBT. We shall focus on one specific area where behaviour change is crucial: behavioural experiments (BEs), a CBT strategy that can be used to great effect in most if not all problems. We have already seen (in Chapter 7) that Socratic methods can comprise BEs and another common behavioural technique/experiment that we have touched on is activity scheduling. However, activity scheduling is described fully in the chapter on depression (Chapter 12), because that is where it is most widely used.

WHAT ARE BEs?

The following discussion draws heavily on the comprehensive volume devoted to the use of BEs in CBT, to which all three of the present authors contributed (Bennett-Levy, Butler, Fennell, Hackmann, Mueller & Westbrook, 2004). We adopt Bennett-Levy et al.'s operational definition of BEs:

> Behavioural experiments are planned experiential activities, based on experimentation or observation, which are undertaken by patients in or between cognitive therapy sessions. Their design is derived directly from a cognitive formulation of the problem, and their primary purpose is to obtain new information which may help to:
>
> - test the validity of the patients' existing beliefs about themselves, others, and the world;
> - construct and/or test new, more adaptive, beliefs;
> - contribute to the development and verification of the cognitive formulation. (2004: 8)

This means that BEs are designed, like experiments in science, to generate evidence that will help us decide what hypothesis is best supported. But instead of testing scientific theories, BEs in CBT are designed to gather evidence that will test the predictions that follow from unhelpful cognitions or to test elements in a formulation. Chapters 7 and 8 have already addressed predominantly verbal methods for exploring cognitions and expanding the range of evidence to be considered. BEs offer us a way of taking this a step further, by exploring beliefs through action and observation rather than just through discussion, and by producing new evidence and new possibilities. BEs are therefore often used to follow up verbal discussion. Having explored a particular negative cognition and generated possible alternative views during a session, BEs may offer a useful way of testing out and even consolidating these conclusions. They can help gather more cogent evidence as to whether the original negative cognition or the new alternative offers the best (most accurate or most helpful) view of a situation.

A man with social anxiety had the belief that he looked 'peculiar' (and that others would therefore disapprove of him). One piece of evidence for this belief was that he noticed when he went into the canteen at work that other people 'stared at' him. His response was to look down so as to avoid their gaze, to sit and eat alone and to focus closely on his plate. During CBT sessions, an alternative account was developed, namely that perhaps people tended to look at anyone who entered the canteen, because they were curious, rather than this behaviour's being exclusive to him and due to his 'peculiarity'; furthermore, that maybe his subsequent avoidance of looking at other people meant that he had no opportunity to observe whether this was true. This discussion led on to a BE designed to gather evidence about which account was most convincing. It was agreed that he would enter the canteen as usual but this time try to keep looking up and count roughly how many people looked at him. Then after he sat down, he would make an effort to continue looking around and to count how many people looked at anyone else who entered the canteen. He was able to do this and, somewhat to his surprise, found the new alternative belief amply supported. Some people in the canteen seemed to look up at anyone who entered, and there was no evidence that he attracted more curiosity than anyone else. He found this helpful in beginning to question the belief that he was 'peculiar'.

Another client with social anxiety was worried about the consequences of blushing during social interactions. She believed that if she blushed, others would be bound to make negative judgements about her, for example that she was silly, or abnormal. Although she had occasionally been teased about her blushing, no one had ever actually expressed a negative evaluation because of it, but she tended to dismiss this on the grounds that they were just being kind to her. This client found it helpful to do a survey experiment. A question about reactions to people blushing was carefully constructed so that both she and the therapist agreed that it was reasonably unbiased (i.e. not obviously expecting either negative or positive responses, e.g. not starting off with 'Would you think badly of such a person?', but a more neutral 'Would blushing have any impact on your opinion of such a person?'). Then the therapist distributed the question sheet to a number of work colleagues and friends to collect their responses – for this client, it was important that the people surveyed did not know her and were therefore less likely to be 'kind' in their answers. She found that most people thought blushing was quite charming and that the worst anyone thought was that someone blushing might be anxious and that they would therefore tend to feel sympathetic.

HOW DO BEs COMPARE TO BEHAVIOUR THERAPY?

BEs are derived from CBT's behavioural legacy. If you are particularly interested in this evolution, we would urge you to read Rachman's (2015) extremely engaging and scholarly account of the shift in behavioural to cognitive behavioural emphasis in CBT.

Some BEs may look like traditional behavioural methods such as exposure *in vivo* to anxiety-provoking situations. However, it is important to remember that the aims of, and the conceptual framework surrounding, BEs are quite different from traditional behavioural therapy. In the latter, the most common conceptual model is of *exposure* leading to *habituation*. This can be graded or intense, brief or prolonged. To put it in very crude terms (with apologies to learning theorists, whose ideas are actually far more complex than this), the idea is that exposure to anxiety-provoking stimuli leads to the anxiety response gradually fading away as the person gets used to the situation. An analogy sometimes used is that if I suddenly make a loud noise, you will probably be startled, but if I repeatedly make a loud noise every 10 seconds for the next 10 minutes, then you will probably gradually stop being startled and react less. Craske, Treanor, Conway, Zbozinkek and Vervliet (2014) describe the mechanism of exposure therapy within CBT very clearly and from this comprehensive paper you can see that there is good reason to embrace this technique, particularly with anxiety disorders and especially with the less psychologically minded. Craske and co-workers describe how exposure therapies can be carried out in a very pure form but also modified in ways that involve more emphasis on review and learning consolidation. This very much reflects how we use BEs.

BEs in CBT are quintessentially a *cognitive* strategy, explicitly aimed at generating information and/or testing out beliefs, not at simply promoting habituation of anxiety responses. If we consider the treatment of someone with agoraphobia and panic who fears supermarkets, both traditional BT and CBT might suggest that it would be useful for this person to visit a supermarket, but the goals and thinking behind the strategy (and hence the exact procedure to be followed) would be quite different:

- Behavioural *exposure* would aim for the person to learn a new response to supermarkets, which would involve staying in the situation long enough (and repeating exposure often enough) for the anxiety response to die away and new learning to take place. No particular attention would be paid to thoughts or beliefs; all that would be thought necessary is for a client to overcome his avoidance for long enough for habituation to occur. In order to assist this, exposure would usually be graduated, that is, working up a hierarchy of increasing levels of anxiety, trying to make sure that he was not too anxious at any point (although there is also a form of exposure known as *flooding*, in which clients are exposed to the most fear-provoking situation from the beginning).
- If using a behavioural *experiment* within CBT, the visit to a supermarket would follow a cognitive understanding of the person's negative predictions about what might happen. The primary goal of the visit would be to help him test out these negative beliefs by seeing whether what he fears actually happens: does he actually collapse/die/pass out, or whatever it may be? His level of anxiety, although of course an important clinical concern, would not be the primary focus during the experiment – or at least not unless being anxious played a part in his negative beliefs (e.g. 'If I become very anxious I will lose control and go mad'). In the latter case, it might actually be important to an adequate BE that he *did* become very anxious, in order to test out this belief. Therefore, although it still might be clinically necessary to tackle the situation in a graded way, neither this nor repeated exposure is essential to a BE: the heart of the matter is simply to test out thoughts and beliefs as thoroughly and convincingly as possible, and this can sometimes happen with just one experiment.

Both these behavioural approaches can be effective, but one reason why you might consider using BEs is that they more overtly teach the 'scientist-practitioner' approach (generating and testing specific hypotheses) that underpins CBT. Another reason that BEs appeal to CBT therapists is that they offer a possible way of getting around a common obstacle in interventions that depend primarily on verbal methods, namely responses like 'Well I can see intellectually that this is a more logical way of looking at it, but it still *feels* like my negative thought is true'. By testing out thoughts and beliefs in action, rather than just through words, BEs can help to develop a more 'gut feel' kind of learning. They are also useful in almost every kind of psychological problem, in contrast to exposure, which is focused on anxiety problems.

EFFICACY OF BEs

The evidence on whether BEs are any more or less effective than exposure is limited at present. In a systematic review – the first on this topic – McMillan and Lee (2010) included 14 relevant studies, covering panic, social anxiety, OCD and specific phobias. Although they are appropriately cautious in their conclusions because of various methodological problems, their summary is that 'there was some evidence that behavioral experiments were more effective than exposure alone' (McMillan & Lee, 2010, last line of Abstract). Their perspective is supported in Rachman's review (2015). Thus, more and better evidence is needed, but this is the best we have at the moment.

TYPES OF BE

We can usefully distinguish two dimensions along which BEs may vary: hypothesis-testing versus discovery BEs; and active versus observational BEs (Bennett-Levy et al., 2004). Putting these together, we have a diagram of possible BEs (see Figure 9.1).

HYPOTHESIS-TESTING VERSUS DISCOVERY

Hypothesis-testing BEs are perhaps the closest to the classical scientific experiment. In such experiments we either start from one hypothesis, or from both of two relatively clear

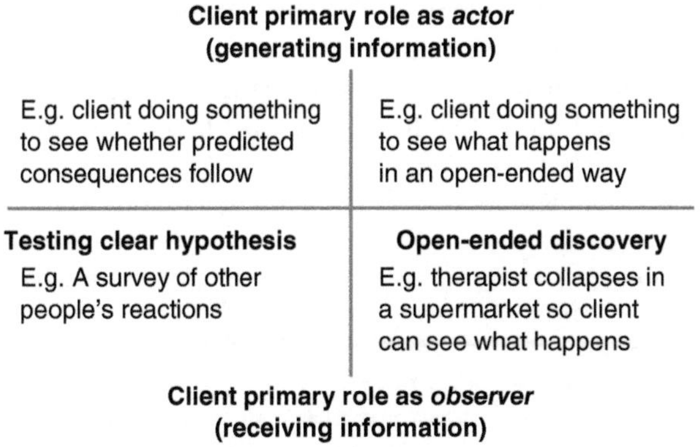

Client primary role as *actor*
(generating information)

E.g. client doing something to see whether predicted consequences follow	E.g. client doing something to see what happens in an open-ended way
Testing clear hypothesis E.g. A survey of other people's reactions	**Open-ended discovery** E.g. therapist collapses in a supermarket so client can see what happens

Client primary role as *observer*
(receiving information)

Figure 9.1 Types of behavioural experiment

hypotheses – often known as Theory A and Theory B. Theory A is the client's initial belief or explanation, for example 'People look at me because I look peculiar'. Theory B is the new, alternative belief, often based on the CBT formulation or perhaps worked out during a CBT session between client and therapist, for example 'People look at *anyone* coming into a room, out of curiosity – there is nothing special about me'. When we can state at least one of these hypotheses reasonably clearly, then we have the necessary conditions for a BE in which the aim is to find some clear evidence bearing on the hypothesis. We may either test Theory A or Theory B alone (the question to be tested is then 'Does this theory correctly predict what happens in this situation?'), or we may compare the two theories to see which one works best in predicting the observed outcomes – as in the canteen experiment above. The aim is to find some predicted consequence of the hypothesis that is in principle observable so that the client can tell whether his prediction comes true.

Hypothesis-testing experiments are the most common, and often the most useful, but clients sometimes have no clear hypothesis to test, perhaps because they have not yet worked out a clear statement of their negative cognitions or because they can't yet even conceive of an alternative. In such cases it may be useful to do *discovery BEs*, aiming to explore in a more open-minded way 'What would happen if I did X?': for example, 'What would happen if I were to talk a bit more openly about myself to other people? How would I feel? How would they react? Perhaps I can find out'.

ACTIVE VERSUS OBSERVATIONAL

The second distinction is between:

- BEs in which the client is an active participant, in the sense of going out and actively doing something to generate information – often something different to his usual behaviour; and
- BEs in which the client is observing events or gathering already available evidence rather than actively doing something different.

The canteen experiment is an example of an active experiment; the blushing survey is an example of an observational experiment.

Observational experiments can include therapist modelling, where the client observes the therapist doing something so that he can see what happens without too much 'risk' to himself.

A man who feared fainting in a public place found it useful to observe what happened when his therapist did collapse. After identifying the negative predictions: 'If I faint I will attract attention and be humiliated by the responses of others,' he and his therapist went into a busy supermarket together. Here the therapist pretended to collapse whilst the man observed at a pre-agreed distance. In this way he discreetly observed what actually happened and concluded that people responded with care, not ridicule, and no one made a fuss that attracted too much attention. In fact the whole thing was rather low-key and he was reassured by the concern of the strangers.

A teenage girl was very worried that she perspired heavily and that others would see this if she raised her arms. Furthermore, she was sure that they would judge her to be unclean and unacceptable if they did see sweat marks. She and her female therapist agreed that the therapist would put lots of water on the armpits of her own dark T-shirt and that they would go into town together where the therapist would take every opportunity to raise her arms whilst the girl observed the reaction of people around them. For about 40 minutes, the therapist stretched to the top shelves in supermarkets, pointed to notices high on the walls in cafés and so on. In this way she modelled revealing damp under-arms in several settings. She and the girl then debriefed what had been learnt. The teenager said that she was shocked that no one seemed to notice or even care and this made her feel far more relaxed. In fact she found it increasingly amusing as time went on and said that she wouldn't mind having a go herself – this was the basis of the next BE.

Many other kinds of information gathering are possible.

Feeling more confident, this same teenage girl carried out a survey of 12 of her classmates and she asked them what they would think of a girl who clearly perspired heavily. She found that all but one of her peers would not think badly of her and most would be sympathetic as they had experienced just those concerns. This enhanced her confidence and she also found it helpful to discover that others had similar worries. One person had been judgemental, but the teen now found herself countering the negative opinion of this person because she was feeling more confident and her own beliefs were shifting.

A man with social anxiety was worried about not having anything important or clever to say. He found it useful to observe how other people carry on conversations, which led to his realising that most ordinary conversations are pretty mundane, not necessarily containing profound topics or deep thoughts. He also picked up a few useful 'social phrases' and behaviours that would help him maintain the flow of conversation and this further increased his confidence.

It may also be useful to gather information from books or the Internet.

A client with claustrophobia found some detailed information on the Internet about the risks of suffocation in confined spaces, including a calculation of how long one might survive in an air-tight room! This assured him that he was safer than he had predicted.

A woman with PTSD found it helpful to read the literature that the therapist had given her about the condition. Using this material she was able to begin to shift her fear that her flashbacks were an indication of insanity to a realisation that this is a not uncommon response following trauma.

Most classic BEs fall into the top-left quadrant of Figure 9.1 (Theory A), but there are useful examples in the other quadrants as well. See Bennett-Levy et al. (2004) for a comprehensive collection. Using one or more of these approaches, the aim is to work out something the client can do, in or between sessions, that will help him generate or gather more evidence relevant to his negative cognitions.

PLANNING AND IMPLEMENTING BEs

PLANNING

Careful planning is a crucial preliminary to most successful BEs. Remember that, as therapists, we aim to make ourselves redundant so you are in the role of coach and trainer when devising BEs with your client. Sometimes we are able to carry out spontaneous experiments, experiments which evolve from the session and which can be carried out in that session. For example:

- A man who predicted that he would have a heart attack if his heart rate became elevated agreed to test this by jogging on the spot in the therapy room.
- A teenager who was certain that she would choke if she ate anything 'lumpy' agreed to eat a yoghurt containing pieces of fruit in the hospital canteen with her therapist.

A great advantage of spontaneous experiments is that anticipatory anxiety is often minimised. However, these BEs require just as much attention to planning.

There are several essential components to consider:

- Ensure that both you and the client clearly understand the purpose and rationale of the experiment, and always plan experiments collaboratively. BEs should not be unilaterally assigned in the last two minutes of a session, nor should they be done just because a protocol says you should be doing them! They should grow out of the session as a logical way to move things forward. Remember, it is desirable to involve the client in thinking about BEs and homework: 'Given what we've been discussing in this session, what do you think might be useful to take this further between now and the next session?'
- Particularly for hypothesis-testing experiments, spend time getting clear about what cognition(s) are to be tested and the client's negative predictions about what might happen. This step is crucial, because a BE aimed at a poorly defined cognition will rarely be effective. For example, your client may fear approaching a particular situation without safety-seeking behaviours, and his initial prediction may well be something vague, like 'It will be awful'. You are unlikely to be able to test this prediction, because it is not precisely defined. How can you or the client tell whether it is 'awful' or not? What exactly constitutes 'awful'? Furthermore, this kind of BE may indeed turn out to be 'awful', at least in the sense that the client feels anxious. It will usually be much better to work out a clear prediction, such as 'I will collapse' or 'People will laugh at me': something that (a) distinguishes between the belief to be tested and possible alternatives; and (b) can be developed into reasonably clear criteria that will enable both client and therapist to determine unambiguously whether it has happened.

See Video 9.1: Clarifying predictions when setting up a behavioural experiment.

- Having identified a clear cognition, have the client rate how strongly he believes it on a scale (e.g. from 0 to 100 per cent: 0 per cent = Not at all, to 100 per cent = Absolutely certain it's true) to provide a baseline against which any change can be measured.
- Choose the best type of experiment to test the cognition, for example an active experiment or an observational experiment. Partly this decision will depend on what point the client has reached in shifting his thinking and how threatening the experiment appears to him. Observational BEs are often less threatening and therefore may be a useful first step before moving on to active BEs.

A survey experiment for a man with body dysmorphic disorder involved getting a number of people who did not know him to look at photographs of him and several other people to see whether he was singled out – as he feared he would be – for the 'ugliness' of his nose. As is common in such experiments, the wording of the questions to respondents needed careful consideration so that the questions were meaningful without leading respondents to any particular response. In this case he agreed that he did not want respondents to be focusing especially on him or initially on noses, so early questions were framed along the lines of 'Do any of these people's faces seem unusual in any way? If so, in what way?'; only later did the survey ask respondents to rate noses specifically.

- In planning BEs you need to pay reasonable attention to safety and risk. This should be done in a balanced way, bearing in mind that CBT is about realistic thinking, not generalised positive or negative thinking; and that the risks of doing a particular BE need to be weighed against the risks of *not* doing it (in terms of potential reduced treatment efficacy and therefore an increased risk of continuing to have significant anxiety problems). It is important not simply to feed your client's anxiety by suggesting excessive caution, but it is equally important not to ignore significant risk. So, for example, you need to take care with experiments involving strenuous physical exercise if there is any reason to suppose your client has relevant physical problems (e.g. pulmonary or cardiac problems – if so, ask the GP or other doctor for a physical assessment); or if an experiment involves walking down the street to test a fear of being attacked, then you obviously need to be reasonably confident that it is in fact safe (e.g. it is a street where most people would not hesitate to walk). Keep a sense of proportion. We need to consider significant risks but we also need to remember the message we often give to clients: that not much in life is *absolutely 100 per cent* safe!

Grade BEs so that your client takes on a challenge at a rate that enables them to build on a series of successful activities. Although we can learn from them, try to avoid setbacks when you are planning. It can be useful to ask: 'Given that you can do X, what do you think you might be able to do if you now stretched yourself? Realistically, what might you be able to take on with some confidence even though we know it will stretch you?' This ensures that clients move in a forward direction but not too far too fast.

A trainee gardener, Lucas, was referred for help with his phobia of frogs as it was interfering with his ability to work outdoors. He had harboured this fear since he was three or four years old, when his older brother had dropped a frog down the back of his shirt. He had coped through long-term avoidance, and just the prospect of facing his fear made him feel nauseous in the session – he even tried not to say 'the other "f"-word', as he called it. With such a long-standing phobia and such high levels of avoidance, his BEs in facing his fear needed to be graded. He and his therapists began working on his ability to say 'the other "f"-word' without feeling sick. This involved first writing the letter 'f' then gradually building up the whole word, then saying the whole word whilst working on remaining relaxed. This took a couple of weeks, but once he could use the word 'frog' they could begin to discuss the rest of his graded programme in detail, always pacing it carefully.

- Ensure that the therapy end-goal is unambiguous and where possible operationalised if you are planning a graded approach to a problem. You and your client need to be able to monitor progress toward the goal and to recognise when it has been achieved. A vague notion of an end-point doesn't facilitate this, and worse, it is all too easy for a self-deprecating client to downgrade achievements if success has not been clearly defined. In the example above, the trainee gardener's ultimate goal was to 'Work in the boggy quadrant of the nursery, alone and using my hands to lift plants. If I am startled by a frog I will be able to remain where I am and calm myself enough to begin work again.'
- Design BEs so that as far as possible they are 'no lose', that is, whatever happens, you both will have gained something. If the experiment 'works' in the sense that negative predictions are not borne out, then that is useful; but equally if some part of the negative prediction is confirmed, that can still be useful if we have learned something and now need to think about what made that happen, which in turn can lead to further productive exploration and new BEs.
- For the same reason, try to be genuinely open-minded about the outcome of BEs. Do not approach them in a way that suggests to the client that you already know for sure what will happen. If the BE does not work out the way you predict, then the client may lose confidence in you and may also feel that he must have failed. It is much better to be genuinely curious: 'I really don't know for sure what will happen here, but maybe it won't be as bad as you fear – how about finding out?'
- Similarly, try to anticipate with the client what might be difficult or go wrong and then develop and rehearse strategies for coping with such setbacks. If you are doing a BE involving others' reactions, what will the client do if indeed he does get a negative response? If the BE involves a client with agoraphobia going into a supermarket alone, how will he cope if he does have a panic attack? BEs are much more likely to be helpful if you have considered such problems beforehand.
- Notwithstanding all of the above, do not ignore the potential for doing spontaneous BEs, prompted by something that has happened within a session. Sometimes people are more willing to try something on the spur of the moment, but this needs to be carefully done, and the client must be clear that he can refuse if he wants to.

See Video 9.2: Devising a spontaneous behavioural experiment.

THE EXPERIMENT ITSELF

Experiments may be carried out by clients independently, for example as part of homework, or carried out with you – in session or outside in the real world. The latter *in vivo* experiments can be very useful, both because you can support and encourage your client and because they offer invaluable opportunities for you to learn more about the problems: *in vivo* BEs frequently generate previously unknown thoughts and beliefs, safety-seeking behaviours and so on. If you are accompanying your client, there are several things you can be aware of in order to increase the chances of a successful outcome; if your client is trying a BE alone, then you can make him aware of these factors:

- Encourage your client to be fully engaged in the situation rather than just 'going through the motions'. He needs to understand that usually if a BE does not result in any anxiety (e.g. because he is distracting himself or not really pushing against his limits), then the BE is less likely to be useful.
- You and/or your client need to be continually monitoring his thoughts and emotions, both in order to be aware of any changes, whether positive or negative, and to be sure that the BE is going along the right lines. For example, it is unusual for a client to go through a BE without feeling at least some discomfort during it; if he remains completely unaffected, it would be wise to investigate whether he is subtly avoiding, or performing safety behaviours. On the other hand, if there is no positive change at all in the client's thoughts or emotional state during a BE, it may indicate that the cognitions have not really been touched, and it may be useful to think about taking it further, or doing something different.
- As noted above, BEs by their very nature are to some degree unpredictable, and the unexpected can and does happen. You and/or your client need to be flexible and ready to respond to unexpected events. If a BE goes in an unexpected direction, learn from this and modify your approach accordingly.

Lucas negotiated a series of BEs, working towards his ultimate goal. After gaining confidence in saying the word 'frog', he negotiated looking at a video recording of a frog in the session, alongside his therapist. He and his therapist planned this and together they viewed the film. Very quickly he was overwhelmed by anxiety. Clearly they had moved too far too fast. All was not lost as they had already discussed what they would do should this happen. The therapist simply switched off the film and prompted Lucas to relax. They had previously done some groundwork in the form of learning relaxation, so he achieved this quite quickly. They then reviewed his graded practice programme. They realised that they needed to scale down his steps and instead of looking at a video they planned a BE to look at simple drawings of frogs. If this went well, then they would look at more realistic pictures and eventually return to the BE looking at a video, with a view to ultimately carrying out BEs in real life, *in vivo*.

See Video 9.3: Carrying out an *in vivo* experiment.

Date	Target cognition(s)	Experiment	Prediction(s)	Outcome	What I learned
	What thought, assumption or belief are you testing? Is there an alternative perspective? Rate belief in cognitions (0–100%).	Design an experiment to test the cognition (e.g. facing a situation you would otherwise avoid, dropping precautions, behaving in a new way).	What do you predict will happen?	What actually happened? What did you observe? How does the outcome fit with your predictions?	What does this mean for your original assumption/belief? How far do you now believe it (0–100%)? Does it need to be modified? How?

Figure 9.2 Behavioural experiment record sheet

This figure is available to download from the companion website.

AFTER THE EXPERIMENT

In order to make the most of a BE, it is important to take time to 'debrief' and reflect on what happened:

- First, you need to go through with the client what actually happened. What were his thoughts/images? How did he feel? Did events go as predicted or were there significant differences to his predictions? If so, what were they? Did he still use any safety behaviours to prevent some disaster (if so, it may be important to try again with reduced or eliminated safety behaviours)?
- Second, it is important to encourage reflection on the meaning of the BE. What does this tell him that he didn't know before (about himself, or others, or the world in general)? How can he make sense of what happened? Does it have any implications for how he might tackle similar situations in the future? Are there any follow-up BEs that might be useful to extend or generalise his conclusions? Finally, have the client re-rate his belief in the cognitions tested so that both of you can see whether there has been any change.

This post-experiment reflection gains the maximum possible value from the experiment and may also help reduce the risk of his devaluing the results of the experiment as old habits reassert themselves.

Figure 9.2 gives a record sheet that you may find helpful for you and your client to record the planning and carrying out of BEs.

COMMON PROBLEMS IN BEs

BEs can be an extremely powerful way of modifying cognitions and emotions, but as noted above, their complexity and unpredictability also mean that there is plenty of scope for things to go in unexpected directions. Do remember that sometimes the 'unexpected direction' yields very valuable information and understandings, so always make the most of the debriefing stage when things don't go according to expectation (see below). Nonetheless, many unhelpful risks can be avoided by careful planning, and this section gives some further ideas about how to deal with some common problems.

EXPERIMENTS THAT 'FAIL'

Learn from setbacks. It is so very important to encourage an appreciation that there really is no such thing as a 'failed' experiment. No matter what the outcome, there is always something to be learnt about the client's strengths and needs or about your planning process. If negative predictions do come true, then we can still learn something useful by examining carefully what happened. Was it just an unlucky chance outcome, or did the client do something that produced that result? Is there some other aspect of ɔn or behaviour, the effect of which we have not fully taken into account? Are ,ubtle forms of avoidance or other safety-seeking behaviours that are reducing npact of the experiment? It is important to use such 'failures' constructively – . negative information can tell us something we can use to make therapy ultimately nıᴗre effective.

Find a graceful retreat. As we have said, even with the best planning in the world, sometimes things go awry: the test turns out to be harder than you or the client thought; other people react in precisely the 'wrong' way; or the client's nerve fails him. It is at these times that therapeutic skill and creativity are most needed, to find a way to retreat with grace in such a way that the client does not feel he has completely 'failed'. A good general rule is to try always to finish with a success, no matter how small. If the original aim is clearly too ambitious, try to find a smaller goal that the client can accomplish before finishing the exercise, as we saw with Lucas. It is always easier to make a graceful retreat if you have planned one! Always have a back-up plan prepared, and ensure that it has a behavioural component so you or your client will know what to *do* if things don't go according to plan (e.g. 'OK, this isn't going smoothly so my plan is to go back to the car where I will relax again and make some notes to discuss with my therapist') and a cognitive element so that your client will have something constructive to *say* (e.g. 'We considered that things might not go according to plan so it's good that I prepared a back-up strategy and I can give myself credit for giving this a go').

THERAPIST-CLIENT RELATIONSHIP

As we said in Chapter 3, there are different demands on the therapeutic relationship between a typical office-based therapy and BEs in CBT where, for example, you may be going to a supermarket with your client and falling over in the shop so that he can observe how others react. What professional issues does this raise? What kind of conversation is acceptable when you are outside the office and not 'on task'? It is important to reflect on these issues and discuss them with your client and in clinical supervision so that you can arrive at a way of relating that feels reasonably comfortable to both you and the client whilst respecting essential professional and ethical boundaries (see Chapter 3).

THERAPIST WORRIES

It is important to recognise that therapists, as well as clients, may have worries about BEs. If these become too intense, you may communicate your doubts and thus reinforce your client's fears. It is acceptable – maybe even desirable – for you sometimes to be pushing your own limits, for example by doing things in public that trigger your own social anxieties. But it is also important that you approach BEs in a positive and encouraging way: 'This may be a bit scary, but we've thought it through and planned carefully – so it's not going to be a catastrophe.' Use your supervision sessions to help you identify and overcome obstacles that you might have about carrying out certain BEs.

SUMMARY

- BEs involve the active gathering or generating of evidence that will help to test our clients' – or our own – thoughts and beliefs.
- BEs therefore offer a way to go beyond purely verbal examination of cognitions by testing them out in the real world. As such, they may lead to more 'gut-level' learning.
- There are different types of BE, including hypothesis-testing versus exploratory BEs, and active versus observational BEs.
- To help clients get the most out of BEs, it is usually best to plan and carry them out carefully – although there is also a useful role for occasional impromptu BEs, done on the spur of the moment in response to something that comes out of a session.
- BEs should have a clear goal and achieving this goal often needs to be graded.
- BEs sometimes demand an active role for therapists in doing activities with clients outside the therapy office. This can challenge therapists' fears, as well as clients'.

LEARNING EXERCISES

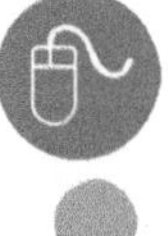

These learning exercises are available to download from the companion website.

REVIEW AND REFLECTION:

- **If you are new to BEs, then take a few minutes to think about your thoughts and feelings in relation to them. You might think particularly whether you have your own worries about doing BEs, as we mentioned above. If so, what could you do about that? Can you come up with any alternative views? Have you any evidence to support or contradict your worries? Remember this is one of those areas where our *own* susceptibility to negative thoughts and beliefs may be prominent, and may block us from trying out effective procedures.**
- **What are your own views about how to relate to clients when you are doing BEs together outside the therapy office? Reflect on these questions and perhaps discuss them with your supervisor.**

(Continued)

(Continued)

TAKING IT FORWARD:

- **If you are new to BEs, or have doubts about them as discussed above, perhaps you can do BEs about BEs. Review your caseload with your supervisor; think about which of your clients' beliefs you might be able to test through BEs; devise appropriate BEs; and then review the results with your supervisor.**
- **When you try out doing BEs, do they seem to offer any of the benefits to clients that we have suggested above? Do any disasters follow? On balance does the use of BEs seem useful or not?**

FURTHER READING

Bennett-Levy, J., Butler, G., Fennell, M., Hackmann, A., Mueller, M., & Westbrook, D. (Eds). (2004). *The Oxford guide to behavioural experiments in cognitive therapy*. Oxford: Oxford University Press.

The essential guide to BEs, with ideas about conceptualising them, guides to using them in different disorders, and many practical examples of actual BEs used with clients.

VIDEO LINKS

- **9.1 Clarifying predictions when setting up a behavioural experiment**
- **9.2 Devising a spontaneous behavioural experiment**
- **9.3 Carrying out an *in vivo* experiment**

10

PHYSICAL TECHNIQUES

- Introduction
- Relaxation
- Controlled breathing
- Physical exercise
- Applied tension
- CBT and sleep
- Summary
- Learning exercises
- Further reading
- Video links
    - 10.1 Relaxation exercise
    - 10.2 Controlled breathing

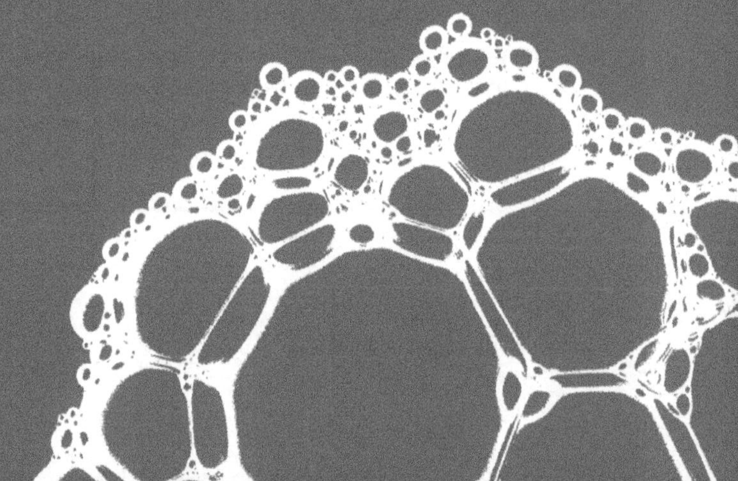

INTRODUCTION

This chapter reviews some of the physical approaches that supplement the cognitive and behavioural repertoire: specifically, relaxation, controlled breathing, exercise and applied tension. The management of sleep problems is also considered.

Physiological responsiveness is one of the interacting systems of the CBT model, along with cognition, emotion and behaviour. CBT may therefore include interventions focused on physiological symptoms, insofar as they are part of a maintenance cycle in the client's formulation. Of course, physiological problems can equally well be tackled using cognitive, behavioural or physical methods (e.g. tinnitus can be eased by changing catastrophic thinking), and by the same token, cognitive, behavioural or emotional problems can be tackled using physical methods. The important point is that the intervention, in whatever modality, should be derived from the formulation. We will look at a number of possible physical interventions, beginning with relaxation.

RELAXATION

Physical tension can be part of the maintenance cycle for many problems – anxiety disorders, depression and sleep problems, among others. It may be part of a more general increase in arousal, which includes other physical symptoms, such as increased heart rate, light-headedness, heavy legs and trembling. Such elevated arousal can be reduced by using relaxation, either via specific relaxation exercises or by building pleasurable, relaxing activities into the day, for example by having a soothing bath or a massage.

Relaxation has been used in its own right as a therapy approach, but CBT practitioners tend to incorporate it into CBT. Why? Well, there are good indications that pure relaxation training can indeed be as helpful as CBT in managing some anxiety disorders, but it can be associated with more drop-out (Norton, 2012). Other studies, such as Cuijpers and colleagues' GAD trial (2014), indicate that relaxation used *within* a CBT approach tends to be more effective than when used alone.

Thus the benefits of relaxation should never be discounted, but it is probably best used as part of our 'CBT tool kit', and it should be clear to both you and your client just how the relaxing activity fits into the formulation. We emphasise this point because in some treatment approaches relaxation training was almost 'prescribed' as part of an anxiety management programme, with little attention paid to rationale or the interactions of tension with thoughts and behaviour.

In the example below we see how the practice of relaxation has relevance within CBT and can be a powerful tool in testing out beliefs, as well as reducing symptoms directly.

A young man, Aaron, was experiencing anxiety symptoms across a range of situations and was finding some imminent exams highly stressful. Figure 10.1 shows the initial formulation of his problem, relating his beliefs about his work to his emotions, physical symptoms, his worrying thoughts and his behaviour. It is clear that if he could break into the cycle by reducing his physical symptoms, then he may be able to shift his beliefs, improve his concentration and work more productively, which in turn would allow him to feel less anxious.

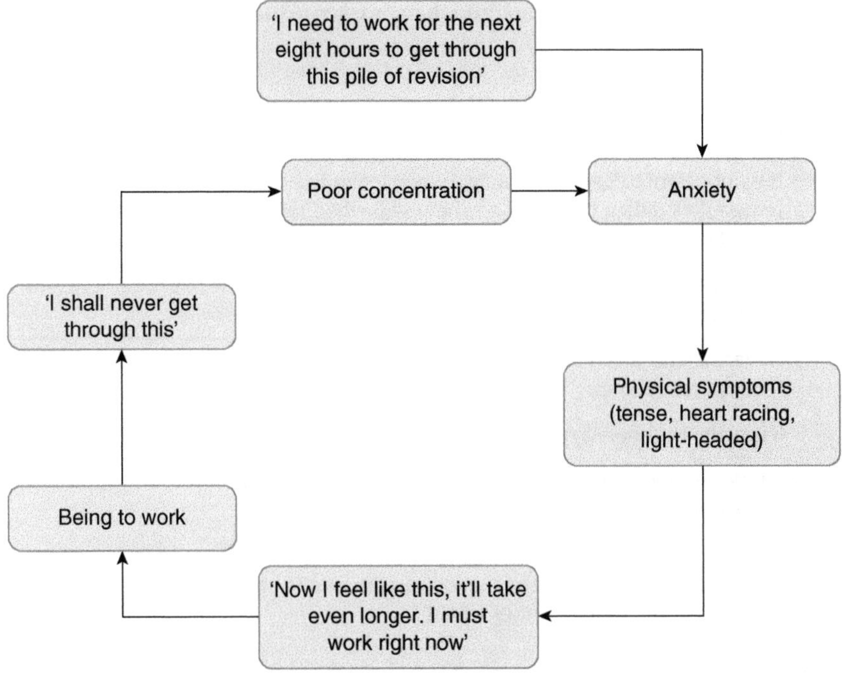

Figure 10.1 A maintenance cycle for anxiety about exams

There are a number of approaches to teaching relaxation, most of which rely on:

- systematic muscular relaxation, as by Jacobson's Progressive Muscular Relaxation technique (1970) or Öst's Applied Relaxation (1987); or
- the use of relaxing imagery; or
- meditation.

These three approaches are often combined to maximise the impact of relaxation as in the well-established 'relaxation response' (Benson, 1975). In this chapter, our main focus is on physical relaxation, but do bear in mind that the effect of the exercise can be enhanced by incorporating soothing images or meditations.

There is some evidence that matching relaxation method to the individual's pattern of symptoms (e.g. applied relaxation with clients with predominantly physiological symptoms) may improve outcome, but the evidence is by no means unequivocal (Michelson, 1986), and it is probably better to find out which approach suits your client by discussing it and trying it out. There are many forms of recorded relaxation instruction available, and we would suggest that you and your client find one you like. You can also make recordings for your own clients and they can make their own from scripts that are available in self-help books such as Kennerley (2014b).

Rather than describe a specific method, here are some general guidelines for acquiring relaxation skills:

- Explain that learning to relax is like acquiring any other skill, and that regular practice is required.
- It is important to begin to practise when feeling calm or only mildly anxious or tense – it is difficult to learn any new skill while tense, and this is particularly true of relaxation.
- It is better to begin to practise in a situation relatively close to ordinary life, for example sitting in a comfortable chair rather than lying down.
- Nevertheless, it is easier to begin practising with closed eyes, in order to reduce distractions.
- It is better to choose a quiet place to practise, with no phone or other distractions.
- It is better not to practise when feeling hungry, as this causes tension – or after a meal, which can promote sleep!
- Once some skill is acquired, it is helpful to monitor minor or moderate signs of anxiety or tension, so that relaxation can be used to combat symptoms before they have built up to stronger levels.

You can find relaxation scripts on the OCTC website: www.octc.co.uk/resources

If relaxation successfully reduces tension, your client's interpretation of its impact must be reviewed to ensure that it has not evolved into a safety-seeking behaviour. Although an audio-recording has been mentioned as a useful adjunct to learning to relax, the evidence suggests that it is better to go through the relaxation exercises with your client, rather than simply ask them to follow a recording (Borkovec & Sides, 1979). This is partly because you can then observe his practice and pick up on errors from the start: for example, if he is sitting with tightly crossed legs, or is tightening up his arms and shoulders once another area is focused on, you can comment on this and correct it from the outset. Also, you can invite questions or expressions of reservation so that together you can refine the relaxation practice. For example, many clients are concerned that they cannot focus continually on their muscle groups but find their minds wandering; you can assure them that this is to be expected and encourage them to simply note whatever thoughts come into their mind and to gently direct themselves to return to thinking about relaxation.

It is probably most useful to spend 10 or 15 minutes per session focusing on relaxation training, over perhaps five or six sessions if an approach like applied relaxation (Öst, 1987) is being used as a major component of treatment. The remainder of these sessions can then be used for other agenda items. In other cases, relaxation may play a more minor role, and you may only need to go over the relaxation procedure a couple of times. The effectiveness of the relaxation can be checked out by asking the client to monitor how relaxed he feels following his regular practice sessions and how he feels in whatever situations he applies relaxation. Figure 10.2 shows a possible diary for recording daily relaxation practice, and its effect.

Date	How relaxed before 0–10	How many minutes of practice	How relaxed afterwards 0–10
6th May	2	20	4
7th May	3	16	7
9th May	3	22	5

Scale: 0 = not relaxed at all; 10 = as relaxed as could possibly be.

Figure 10.2 Diary of relaxation practice, and its effect

Not all relaxation exercises are lengthy; Aaron learnt a brief relaxation exercise which he found very versatile.

Aaron's therapist first ensured that he was comfortable in his chair, breathing evenly. Then she suggested that he close his eyes – this was fine by Aaron, so they continued. The therapist prompted him to imagine his body feeling heavy and sinking into the chair whilst maintaining an even rhythm of breathing. She then asked him to focus on his feet and imagine them feeling so heavy that they 'sank' into the ground. Next, he was prompted to imagine his legs growing heavy and 'sinking' into the chair, followed by his torso and then his shoulders. Aaron was able to do this and finally he imagined his head feeling pleasantly heavy too. As it helped deepen the feeling of relaxation, he chose to bring to mind a soothing, calming memory of being with his partner enjoying a countryside walk. With regular practice at home, Aaron was able to use this strategy to diminish his physical tensions and develop a mental calm quite quickly. Then he was able to use this brief exercise whenever he needed to: on the train, in a waiting room, before exams. He learnt to respond to physical tension by letting it go.

See Video 10.1: Introducing a relaxation exercise.

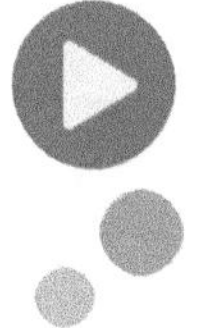

APPLICATIONS OF RELAXATION IN CBT

TO MANAGE EXCESSIVE AROUSAL AS IN ANXIETY, CRAVING OR ANGER

Once you have identified a physiological element to the maintaining cycles of anxiety (e.g. in phobia or panic) or arousal (e.g. in addictive behaviours) or anger problems, then you can use this as a basis for planning ways of disrupting the cycle by introducing the de-arousing activity of relaxation. In this way you both teach a skill and test the hypothesis that the client can take charge of and manage excess arousal.

WHERE THE CLIENT IS TOO SCARED TO CARRY OUT A BE

BEs often demand a great deal of courage, particularly if the prediction being tested includes elements such as 'If I do such-and-such, I will probably feel anxious, but I will not collapse/suffocate/jump over the edge' (or whatever other catastrophes the client fears). Relaxation can then be used as an aid to facing the feared situation (Rachman, Radomsky & Shafran, 2008), although often only as a temporary solution because of the risk of relaxation becoming established as a safety-seeking behaviour.

A man with a height phobia was planning to test out his prediction that he would be likely to jump off the cliff if he were to go onto a cliff path. He thought that he would be too anxious to do it 'cold turkey', so planned to use relaxation in the first instance as a way of getting himself onto the cliff path.

TO TEST OUT A BELIEF ABOUT WHETHER SYMPTOMS HAVE AN ORGANIC BASIS OR ARE ANXIETY-RELATED

If unhelpful beliefs are focused on the aetiology of symptoms, it may be possible to test out competing hypotheses by using relaxation.

A woman was fearful that her severe headaches were a symptom of a brain tumour. She practised relaxation on a daily basis and found that as she became more skilled at progressive relaxation, and gradually applied it in more stressful situations, the intensity and frequency of her headaches decreased. She recognised that this was more consistent with an anxiety explanation rather than a tumour explanation.

TO INTERRUPT VICIOUS CYCLES WHERE INCREASED AROUSAL INTERFERES WITH PERFORMANCE

There are a number of problems where physical anxiety symptoms have a direct effect on performance of a task or function (see Figure 4.8), and applying relaxation techniques may therefore be useful. For example, trembling whilst speaking in public, erectile problems, shaking whilst writing, tensions when swallowing can be eased in this way. In each of these areas, relaxation may make a contribution insofar as it reduces arousal and physical tension and allows the task to be performed without interference.

TO GIVE A BREAK FROM TENSION/AROUSAL

An obvious use of relaxation is where increased arousal is simply experienced as unpleasant in its own right. This can be the case with those who are chronically anxious and find the physical symptoms themselves intolerable. In such instances, it is important to check whether the symptoms have an idiosyncratic meaning for your client. For example, does your client believe that the presence of chronic tension means that he is harming his immune system, or is a sign that he is constitutionally deficient and ought not to have children, or that he can never hope to change? If the meaning of the symptoms seems to be distorted, then it can be tackled using well-planned BEs as described in Chapter 9. However, it may be that for your client the unpleasantness of the symptoms itself is stoking the problem, and that having a way to reduce this may increase a sense of mastery, which in turn boosts self-esteem, and onwards in a positive cycle. As ever, make sure that you and your client can make sense of what part the physical symptoms are playing in the problem: get out your diagram of the formulation, or draw it on your whiteboard, clarify how the physical symptoms fit in, and hence what role relaxation would have.

TO BEGIN OR END A STRESSFUL TREATMENT SESSION

If your client anticipates or has had a difficult and stressful session (e.g. prior to, or following restructuring traumatic images), then going through a relaxation exercise may calm him. At the beginning of the session this can enable him to engage, and at the end of a session it can help him to re-enter the everyday world before he leaves the session. Managing physical tensions like this can also enhance his confidence that he can experience, tolerate and cope with strong emotions, so it is worth reflecting on that with your client.

TO PROVIDE AN OPPORTUNITY FOR PLEASURE

Some of our clients have insufficient opportunities for pleasant and rewarding activities. Many people thoroughly enjoy muscular or other relaxation, and fitting it into a busy schedule, doing something for themselves, may result in improved mood and increased energy for other activities.

TO IMPROVE SLEEP

Relaxation can be a useful part of a programme to improve sleep, particularly if a person is in the habit of being active right up until bedtime (see the section below on sleep).

COMMON PROBLEMS ASSOCIATED WITH USING RELAXATION IN CBT

RELAXATION BECOMES A SAFETY-SEEKING BEHAVIOUR

Relaxation, as with many other strategies described as 'coping techniques', can become established as a safety-seeking behaviour. Typically, the client becomes trapped by the belief that success is due to the strategy. For example, 'If I had not relaxed, I would have panicked and then I would have lost control/passed out/gone mad, etc.' In essence, the client is left with the fear that he would have been overwhelmed by the problem if the relaxation had not allowed him to scrape through. The implication of this is that ultimately he has to face the problem without using relaxation in order to demonstrate that even in those circumstances, while he might feel bad, there is no catastrophic outcome. It is worth bearing in mind that safety-seeking behaviours are not unequivocally 'bad', there is some evidence that the judicious use of safety behaviours may facilitate exposure to phobic objects or situations during treatment, and that this may not necessarily result in poorer outcome (Rachman et al., 2008). Their use might give a person the courage to try out a challenging task and then their use can be systematically reduced, thus building confidence step-by-step.

INABILITY TO RELAX IF HIGHLY AROUSED

Past a certain level of arousal, it is very difficult to counter high arousal with relaxation. This can be an issue if the client is panicky, or is highly aroused for some other reason – as in PTSD, for example. In that case, it is more helpful to use a different strategy, for example a distraction (see Chapter 8) or a mindfulness approach (see Chapter 17) in which the symptoms are ignored or are viewed with disinterest. Of course, the ideal is that your clients sense and manage physical tensions before they reach this stage.

RELAXATION IS EXPERIENCED AS LOSING CONTROL

Some clients experience relaxation as anxiety-provoking rather than anxiety-reducing, often because it feels as though they are losing control or putting themselves in a position of vulnerability, as is the case with some survivors of trauma. If your client does fear letting go, it may be worth exploring the meaning of losing control and then using relaxation to test your client's predictions about what might happen.

Debbie had strong beliefs about the value of being in control, and this was associated with many intrusive thoughts about everyday financial issues that were not in her immediate control. She always tried to make sure that she stuck within the rules, and did not like to give herself time to 'play' in case it went too far. She feared that if she did not keep herself under control, she might 'lose it' and become irresponsible. She agreed to experiment with giving herself time to practise relaxation, initially to find out whether she could choose how much control she retained.

Chaim had been physically abused in childhood and was chronically hypervigilant as a result. This caused him much physical tension but he was afraid to let go of the tension because relaxing felt like reducing his guard, something he had not dared to do for 20 years. He and his therapist discussed a graded approach to relaxing and they began with a very brief exercise. This simply required Chaim to let go of the tension in his neck and shoulders and to breathe evenly for a few seconds – he was fully aware of his surroundings during this time. This formed the foundation for a series of BEs that systematically tested the danger/safety of letting go by introducing longer and more distracting relaxation exercises. After a few weeks, Chaim had learnt for himself that he could relax without fear and this made it possible for him to use relaxation to combat his physical tensions.

HYPERSENSITIVITY TO SMALL BODILY CHANGES

When they first begin to practise relaxation, many clients pick up on small bodily changes of which they were previously unaware. This may occasionally create or increase an attentional bias towards bodily changes, which can be interpreted as indicating a risk to health of some kind (see Chapter 4). If this happens, it should be explored and tested in the same way as other distorted thinking, and hence may provide a useful opportunity to practise evaluating a negative cognition.

Charles became aware of tingling in his fingers when he was practising his relaxation, and was fearful that this may be an indication of the onset of a stroke. He investigated this with his therapist by initially doing some highly distracting arithmetic, counting backwards in 7s, and looking at the effect on the tingling, then focusing on the pressure in his elbow leaning against his chair and on what sensations he experienced (not tingling, but certainly sensations he had not been aware of until he paid attention to them). This was followed by a discussion about the effect of attention on the perception of benign physiological 'symptoms', and how that could apply to his tingling fingers.

Despite these possible drawbacks, there are many imaginative ways that relaxation can be used within CBT to disrupt maintenance cycles causing distress to clients.

CONTROLLED BREATHING

Rapid breathing is part of the body's preparation for action, so we all over-breathe when we are scared or excited. This change in breathing can trigger a number of benign sensations such as light headedness, feeling hot, unsteadiness and so on. Jumping to the conclusion that these sensations are dangerous or unbearable tends to fuel anxieties. Indeed, the catastrophic misinterpretation of benign physical symptoms is the central process of one well-established model of panic (Clark, 1986), and one of the benign symptoms often implicated in panic is hyperventilation (i.e. breathing at a high rate and volume). This can result in sensations that mimic the person's panic attacks and which are liable to be interpreted catastrophically as indicating imminent death, collapse, madness and so on. Although these physiological responses can seem overwhelming for the client, they can often be readily countered by controlled breathing.

The introduction of controlled breathing should have a clear rationale that is consistent with the client's formulation. The actual technique requires a person to:

- relax the thorax, the upper body region, as much as possible;
- breathe out slowly using the diaphragm and the nose (rather than the mouth) if possible (5 seconds or so);
- inhale slowly through the nose (if possible), filling the lungs right down to the diaphragm (5 seconds or so);
- exhale slowly using the diaphragm and the nose (5 seconds or so);
- repeat.

Salkovskis, Jones and Clark (1986) developed a strategy of using controlled breathing to allow the hyperventilating client to reattribute their unpleasant sensations to a more benign cause (namely, a symptom of anxiety), and hence break into the vicious circle of misinterpretation maintaining the panic attacks (see below).

This strategy can be used in order to develop a shared understanding of the impact of hyperventilation, which can then enhance the client's formulation. It can also be used in a graded approach to dealing with panic attacks.

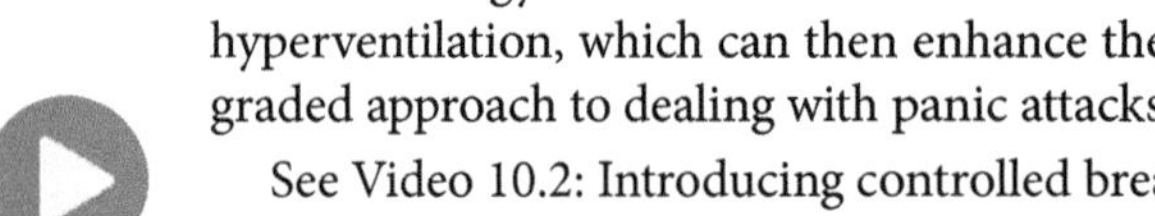

See Video 10.2: Introducing controlled breathing.

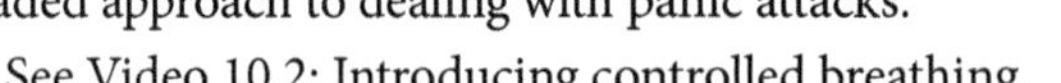

APPLICATIONS OF CONTROLLED BREATHING IN CBT

DEVELOPING A SHARED FORMULATION OF PANIC USING CONTROLLED BREATHING

The following steps can be used in developing a formulation with the client about the role of over-breathing in panic attacks:

1. Without explaining why, ask the client to over-breathe: *'What I would like you to do is to stand up, and to breathe like this* [demonstrating]*, as quickly and deeply as you can, for a few minutes. Just carry on breathing as deeply and quickly as you can.'*
2. When two or three minutes are up, or when the client stops and is unwilling to go on, ask him to reflect on his physical state and to describe the similarities to, and differences from, what he experiences in a panic attack. For example: *'Could you describe how you are feeling physically? What changes have you noticed? Can you tell me in what ways this is similar to how you feel in a panic attack, and how it feels different?'*
3. Ask him what he makes of that: what could explain it? How would he respond if he felt like that by himself?
4. Discuss whether panic feelings may be related to hyperventilation.

MANAGING PANIC SYMPTOMS THROUGH CONTROLLED BREATHING

Having derived a formulation involving the role of breathing, the client can then be taught to manage the symptoms. Initially, the therapist teaches controlled breathing, as we described earlier. The therapist then:

- asks the client to over-breathe and then to reduce the symptoms via controlled breathing;
- reviews the role of breathing in panic symptoms and repeats the exercise if necessary to enhance confidence;
- asks the client to consider what he has learnt from this (about his own ability to manage alarming sensations);
- asks him to practise controlled breathing at home, at least twice daily;
- then asks him to practise reversing the effects of hyperventilation through controlled breathing.

This approach is described in more detail in Clark (1989).

USING CONTROLLED BREATHING IN BEs WHEN THE CLIENT IS TOO SCARED TO CONTINUE

As with relaxation, controlled breathing can be used as a short-term coping strategy to allow a client to carry out a BE that he would otherwise be too scared to do. He could then move on in a graded way to do the experiment without controlled breathing.

PROBLEMS ASSOCIATED WITH USING CONTROLLED BREATHING IN CBT

DEVELOPING SAFETY-SEEKING BEHAVIOURS

Developing the habit of regular, smooth breathing is a good practice in its own right. However, as with relaxation, it is very important that the client does not misuse controlled breathing as a safety behaviour. If he always uses controlled breathing when he feels panicky or anxious, he may continue to believe that 'If I had not done my breathing, I would have collapsed/gone mad, etc.' Ultimately, he has to face the symptoms without using controlled breathing so that he can learn that while he might feel uncomfortable, the feelings are tolerable and there is no catastrophic outcome.

STRUGGLING TO USE CONTROLLED BREATHING WHEN FEELING ANXIOUS OR PANICKY

Some clients are unable to use controlled breathing when feeling very anxious or panicky but may learn to do so if they have more practice when they are not feeling anxious. It is important that there is a shared understanding of why this may be helpful, otherwise your client might not be motivated to practise controlled breathing in the absence of anxiety.

PRESENCE OF A CONTRA-INDICATIVE PHYSICAL DISORDER

Hyperventilation is not recommended in a number of physical conditions, unless medical supervision is available. These include atrial fibrillation, asthma and chronic obstructive pulmonary disease, epilepsy and pregnancy. Always ask about physical conditions and consult your client's family doctor if necessary (and with consent).

HYPERSENSITIVITY TO SMALL CHANGES IN BREATHING

The client may develop a heightened awareness of minor changes in his breathing, and so care must be taken to interpret these benignly and not as signs of dysfunction or precursors of panic (see e.g. the catastrophic misinterpretation shown in Figure 4.5, and the management of panic disorder described in Chapter 14).

BEING TOO TENSE TO BREATHE EVENLY

Some people will say that they are too tense to breathe properly. It is usually easier to start the cycle of controlled breathing if you suggest that the client focuses initially on the out-breath, as the lungs are then relatively 'empty' and the body naturally takes an in-breath.

PHYSICAL EXERCISE

Extensive research over the past 20 years has established the efficacy of exercise in the treatment of depression (Craft & Landers, 1998; Szuhany, Bugatti & Otto, 2015), and the NICE guidelines (2004a) on the treatment of depression recommend that all clients with mild depression should be advised of the benefits of a structured exercise programme. The effect of exercise on depression may be mediated by an increase in endorphins and other neurochemical changes (Szuhany et al., 2015), but it may be associated with other effects of increased exercise, many of which may also be important for clients with anxiety problems (Taylor, 2000). For example, exercise can provide distraction, or can increase self-esteem, as when engaging in a competitive sport or just simply feeling fitter.

For the CBT therapist, the question is whether intervening with exercise would disrupt a problem maintenance cycle for your client, and it is worth looking out for symptoms that could be addressed in this way, particularly as exercise can become self-maintaining once the basic skills are learned.

The choice of physical exercises is extensive: walking, swimming, cycling, running, individual exercise, team sport and so on. This means that a particular activity can be tailored to reflect a person's stamina, preferences, the choices available to them and so forth. The more 'bespoke' the activity, the more likely it is that your client will engage with it.

APPLICATIONS OF EXERCISE IN CBT

LOW MOOD

The best-established application of exercise is with depression, where apart from the direct effect of increased endorphins, exercise may also provide opportunities for pleasurable and satisfying activity, promoting improved mood. It is often helpful to begin in a graded way, as depressed clients may feel tired much of the time and may be doubtful that they have the energy for exercise – and may have given it up for that reason. This can be tested out in an experiment, and as it may be early in treatment, this can serve as an example of the empirical nature of CBT.

LOW SELF-ESTEEM

The sense of competence derived from exercise may be relevant for someone with low self-esteem (Fox, 2000).

CHRONIC FATIGUE SYNDROME (CFS)

Chronic fatigue syndrome (CFS) is a condition defined by persistent fatigue unrelated to exercise, not relieved by rest, and accompanied by other symptoms such as headache, and muscular and joint pains. Exercise can be central to a graded programme where the client can test out predictions about fatigue (Silver, Surawy & Sanders, 2004).

TENSION RELEASE

For those with chronic tensions or who are in chronically stressful situations, it can be helpful to test out the benefits of exercise on tension levels. This can be especially helpful with younger persons who may not take to relaxation.

SLEEP DISORDER

There is good evidence of the effects of exercise on sleep, as long as it is regular and is not used close to bedtime, when it tends to be arousing (see below).

HEALTH ANXIETY OR PANIC DISORDER

Many people with health anxiety or panic disorder have beliefs about the risks exercise poses to their health. For example, one man believed that if he exercised, his heart rate would increase, and this would increase his risk of a heart attack. It can be very important to discuss and then test out these beliefs via experiments focused on exercise.

ANGER MANAGEMENT

It can be helpful for those with anger problems to test out the effects of exercise on tension levels, particularly if this is followed by a soothing activity such as a relaxing bath or shower. Generally, for anger management it is best to avoid aggressive exercise, as this can fuel anger.

PROBLEMS ASSOCIATED WITH USING EXERCISE IN CBT

EXERCISE BECOMING OVERVALUED

In some disorders, such as eating disorders and body dysmorphic disorder, exercise is overvalued because of its perceived effect on body shape and weight control. In these cases, you should be circumspect about using it to tackle associated problems such as tension or low self-esteem.

PRESENCE OF PHYSICAL DISORDER

Exercise, or particular types of exercise, are not recommended in a number of physical conditions, such as cardiovascular problems. You should ask your clients whether they are aware of any condition that would be a contra-indication for exercise, and seek medical advice if necessary.

APPLIED TENSION

Although many anxious clients feel as though they are about to pass out, they usually don't because the physical tensions of anxiety keep them aware. However, some people, particularly those with phobic anxiety about blood or injury, frequently *do* faint in response to their anxiety (Öst, Sterner & Fellenius, 1989). This is because an initial increase in blood pressure (typical of anxiety) is followed by a sudden decrease, leading to fainting (Öst, Sterner & Lindhal, 1984). In applied tension, the client is taught to increase blood pressure by tightening the muscles in the arms, legs and torso for a few seconds and then to return the muscles to normal, without over-relaxing them. He is then taught to identify the signs of a drop in blood pressure (provoked, for example, by exposing him to photographs of blood or other injuries) and to reverse the decrease by using applied tension (Öst & Sterner, 1987).

PROBLEMS ASSOCIATED WITH USING APPLIED TENSION IN CBT

DEVELOPING A SAFETY-SEEKING BEHAVIOUR

Once again, the major risk of using applied tension is that it can function as a safety-seeking behaviour. It is important to help the client to view applied tension as a helpful thing to do when his blood pressure drops, just as it is helpful to look both ways before crossing the road (i.e. based on a reasonable caution about the consequences of not doing so).

PRESENCE OF PHYSICAL DISORDERS

Before using applied tension, therapists should seek medical advice about any client who is pregnant or has a known physical disorder, particularly hypertension or a cardiovascular condition.

CBT AND SLEEP

We will now turn to problems with sleep, implicated in many mental health problems as well as being common in the general population. In an extensive review, Morin et al. (2006) looked at evidence that psychological therapies can help those with sleep problems. They concluded that 'reliable changes' can be brought about and that CBT is amongst the effective approaches.

Insomnia is a problem experienced by 10 per cent of adults, and 20 per cent of those over 65 years of age at any one time (Espie, 2010) and can include delayed onset of sleep; difficulty staying asleep, with multiple awakenings; and waking too early. It can be secondary to a range of physical and psychiatric conditions, although most evaluations of psychological interventions have focused on insomnia as the primary condition.

Many of the early CBT treatments focused on relaxation as a way of reducing physical arousal levels, even though client reports about insomnia often emphasise *mental* arousal, for example, 'I lie calmly in bed, but my thoughts are racing' or 'All the worries of the day come into my mind'. Accordingly, there has been an increasing emphasis on cognitive approaches to sleep problems (Harvey, 2002), as well as attention to other physiological and behavioural aspects. We shall therefore look at the processes which are currently thought to be involved in poor sleeping, taking as an example Cara (see below), who was highly successful in business as well as being committed to her teenage children. She was chronically unable to fall asleep, and also woke repeatedly in the night and so she had relatively few hours' sleep.

PROCESSES IMPLICATED IN POOR SLEEPING

UNHELPFUL ATs AND BELIEFS IN BED OR BY DAY

Cara believed that if she did not have eight hours sleep then she would be unable to think productively or relate effectively to her family or colleagues; that she ought to be able to control her sleep, as she controlled other aspects of her life; and that any tiredness she experienced in the daytime was attributable to her insomnia (rather than a result of a busy day with no planned breaks and no time for relaxation).

SAFETY-SEEKING BEHAVIOURS, INCLUDING MONITORING INTERNALLY AND EXTERNALLY

When in bed, Cara repeatedly checked the clock; she wore ear-plugs and used a special cushion which she believed increased her control over falling asleep; she monitored her body for signs of wakefulness.

In the daytime, she tried to avoid complex work following a bad night; she monitored her body for signs of tiredness and for signs of poor concentration.

POOR STIMULUS AND TEMPORAL CONTROL OF SLEEP BEHAVIOUR

When she went to bed, Cara took a book and an iPod in case she could not sleep; she spent long periods of time wakeful in bed, reading and listening to music (poor stimulus control).

If she had a disturbed night, she would lie in, if possible, and go to bed early the next night, often when not sleepy (poor temporal control).

INCREASED MENTAL AROUSAL AND POSSIBLY PHYSICAL AROUSAL

As she lay in bed, Cara had many worrying thoughts and tried to work out solutions to them (mental arousal).

POOR SLEEP HYGIENE

In order to tire herself, Cara went to the gym after her evening meal; she had a glass of whiskey in order to settle herself before bed but then busied herself with household tasks.

DISTORTED PERCEPTION OF SLEEP

Cara significantly underestimated how long she slept, and judged how well she had slept in terms of how she felt on waking, at a time of 'sleep inertia' when very many people feel heavy and tired.

INTERVENTIONS FOR SLEEP PROBLEMS

As with other problems, interventions are planned on the basis of a detailed assessment and personalised formulation, taking account of whatever maintaining cycles seem most relevant for the particular client. The most common interventions are described below.

RE-EVALUATION OF UNHELPFUL OR DISTORTED THOUGHTS AND BELIEFS

Unhelpful cognitions can be tackled using verbal and behavioural testing.

Cara identified her thoughts about needing to be in control as particularly distressing, and reviewed these verbally by looking at alternative perspectives on controlling sleep (was it common for other people to be able to control when they slept? What was the evidence that they could/could not? What would she say to a friend who said that she should be able to control her sleeping? What were the pros and cons of thinking that way?)

Cara also tested the accuracy of the thought about needing eight hours sleep by doing a BE. For a number of days she recorded how many hours sleep she had, and then did ratings of how tired she felt at work, and rated how productive she had been in the morning and afternoon of each day. Although she was not 'blind' to the amount of sleep she had had, she still found that generally she was reasonably productive on most days at work. Although she felt tired on some days, the factor that made most difference to productivity was whether she was doing 'desk' work after lunch, when she concentrated poorly, whether she had had a good night or not. By contrast, she was highly effective if she was doing 'people' tasks, whether or not she had slept well.

REDUCTION IN SAFETY-SEEKING BEHAVIOURS

Insofar as safety-seeking behaviours often prevent the disconfirmation of unhelpful beliefs about sleep (e.g. 'I sleep so badly I could never manage without my ear-plugs'), they need to be removed so that beliefs about the importance of sleep can be softened.

Cara began by moving her clock out of sight, so that she could not check the time. She also stopped wearing her ear-plugs. Although it was initially difficult not knowing what the time was, she recognised that it reduced the pressure to get to sleep. Similarly, she found that she was not disturbed if she did not wear her ear-plugs, and felt that this further decreased her sense of being 'an insomniac'.

IMPROVED STIMULUS AND TEMPORAL CONTROL

This intervention has been extensively evaluated since Bootzin's (1972) paper. The approach was based on the notion that consistent cues are necessary to allow the client to clearly differentiate environmental and behavioural sleep cues from non-sleep cues, and to allow the body to acquire a consistent sleep rhythm. There are debates about whether this hypothesis is correct, but the approach has been shown to be effective in rapidly reducing sleep-onset latency. It can be difficult for clients to follow, because in the early stages of the procedure, tiredness may increase. Clients may need a great deal of encouragement to continue. A good description of the procedure can be found in Espie (1991, 2011) and in Morin et al. (2006) or via Espie's digital sleep improvement programme, Sleepio (www.sleepio.com). The main elements include the following:

1. Set up a stable, consistent sleep schedule: aim to develop a 'sleep habit', going to bed and rising at the same time each day. Set your alarm at the same time each morning and get up at that time regardless of how much sleep you have had.
2. Energise yourself earlier in the day (through exercise, stimulation, etc.) rather than later when it is best to develop a relaxing 'wind down' routine an hour or two before bed.
3. Reserve your bedroom only for sleep. The exception to this is sex.
4. If you do not fall asleep within 15–20 minutes, get up and go into another room. Have something relaxing waiting for you (e.g. magazines, a book, a blanket) and do this until you feel sleepy and then return to bed: keep your bedroom for sleeping.
5. If you do not fall rapidly asleep, simply return to your relaxing activity in another room. This may initially be required repeatedly during the night.
6. Do not nap during the daytime or evening, even for short periods.

DECREASE MENTAL AROUSAL

Insomnia may be maintained by a failure to 'tie up loose ends' before going to bed so that unresolved issues from the day rush into the mind. It may be helpful for your client to set aside time in the evening (though not immediately before going to bed) to experiment with writing down/thinking through issues from the day, including their emotional impact. If this is not sufficient, and there are themes that recur or are more troubling, then it may be helpful to rehearse cognitive re-evaluations of these thoughts (as outlined in Chapter 8) so that the client is prepared in advance.

A woman frequently worried about being an unsatisfactory parent, and the ways in which this would affect her children later in life. These thoughts were particularly pervasive when she went to bed. She found that she could never resolve her concerns and they often kept her awake. Therefore, one morning she systematically looked at the evidence for her being a bad parent, and at the determinants of her children's future success. She then summarised this in a phrase that she thought encapsulated the alternative view: 'I only have to be good enough, no one can be perfect; giving them love is the most important thing.' She kept the more detailed evidence recorded in her therapy notebook. When she then found her worries coming to mind at night, she simply repeated her coping phrase. This enabled her to then 'park' the worries and if necessary she then distracted herself by focusing on a soothing memory of a particularly good time in her life.

DECREASE PHYSICAL AROUSAL

Although the evidence for increased physical arousal in insomnia is unclear, many studies have shown that progressive muscular relaxation has some impact on sleep-onset latency, on total time slept and, importantly, on the perceived quality of sleep. Furthermore, many clients enjoy muscular relaxation. It seems to make no difference which relaxation approach is used. It can provide a soothing distraction in bed and people often drift off to sleep before they finish the exercise.

POOR SLEEP HYGIENE

For most clients, general information and advice would include:

- information about sleep patterns, stages and variability; the functions and effects of sleep; and facts and figures about insomnia (see Espie, 2010);
- advice about exercise (i.e. helpful as part of a regular programme aimed at fitness, but not near to bedtime), diet (i.e. avoidance of caffeine, unhelpfulness of chronic or heavy alcohol intake, benefit of warm, milky drinks);
- advice about a quiet comfortable bed and surroundings, with minimal distractions.

Although none of these elements would be sufficient to 'cure' chronic insomnia, they could each contribute to managing sleeping problems effectively.

PROBLEMS IN SLEEP MANAGEMENT

SAFETY-SEEKING BEHAVIOURS

Strategies that are initially useful for sleep hygiene can develop into safety-seeking behaviours. Review the *meaning* that your client is taking from success experiences: if it is a 'can do' conclusion, then all is well, but if your client believes that he only managed to get some sleep because he used a certain strategy in the right way, then this will need to be re-thought. Encourage him to experiment with using the strategies flexibly, to test the belief that the strategies themselves are essential for his wellbeing.

DRUG USE

Your client may not respond to psychological interventions if he is using drugs that promote wakefulness. Always ask about self-medication and prescribed drugs.

SLEEP PROBLEM SECONDARY TO ANOTHER PROBLEM, OR NOT INSOMNIA

A sleep problem may not respond to psychological interventions if it is secondary to another psychiatric or physical condition. In such cases, the primary disorder should be treated, using a cognitive behavioural approach if appropriate (e.g. with depression). Neither will it respond if it is a sleep disorder not classified as insomnia (e.g. sleep apnoea, nocturnal myoclonus or restless legs).

NIGHTMARES AND SLEEPWALKING

Nightmares and sleepwalking are often linked to stress, anxiety or trauma and so are best addressed using the approaches that directly tackle these difficulties (see Chapters 13 and 14).

SUMMARY

- It can be rewarding to pay attention to the role that physical interventions can have in problems, even those where cognitive factors are clearly implicated. Physical techniques may make a useful contribution in a range of disorders, as long as the interventions are planned with an eye on the formulation, and the maintenance cycles are being interrupted in ways that make sense to the client.
- Relaxation can often be helpful, and it does not seem to matter which method is used – including the use of pleasing and relaxing activities. If relaxation exercises are used, then there are sensible guidelines concerning the acquisition of skills that can be followed. Relaxation can be used, for example, to:
    - reduce general arousal;
    - provide pleasure;
    - facilitate exposure to anxiety-provoking situations.
- However, the use of relaxation in treatment is not problem-free, and the common problems include:
    - relaxation functioning as a safety-seeking behaviour;
    - relaxation being experienced as losing control;
    - hypersensitivity to small bodily changes.
- Controlled breathing has its primary role in the treatment of panic disorder but it can be relevant to other anxiety problems, too. A potential problem is its functioning as a safety-seeking behaviour.
- Physical exercise, creatively used, can often provide a direct way to interrupt a maintenance cycle.
- Applied tension can be used in the treatment of blood injury (and less commonly other) phobias.
- Finally, CBT can play a role in the management of sleep disorders. Physical, behavioural and cognitive strategies can be used to promote better sleep, but they should be clearly linked to a formulation.

LEARNING EXERCISES

These learning exercises are available to download from the companion website.

REVIEW AND REFLECTION:

- As you read through this chapter, what reactions have you had? Did any of the strategies stand out as particularly helpful? Did any strike you as alarming? Reflect on your reactions.
- As CBT is a psychological therapy, and emphasises cognitive and behavioural aspects, what do you understand to be the reasons for considering physiological variables, and physical interventions?
- In your previous psychological work, you may not have considered physiological variables like general arousal. If not, consider whether it would be helpful to read an introductory text in this area.

TAKING IT FORWARD:

- From your current case-load, draw a formulation diagram where breaking into a negative cycle with *relaxation* would be helpful.
- If you are not familiar with relaxation exercises, practise them yourself regularly for a week, and then try to apply them in mildly or moderately stressful situations. What do you learn from this that would be helpful in your work with clients? If you wanted to make sure throughout the day that you were maintaining a reasonable level of relaxation, how could you prompt yourself to remember? Could you use an everyday object or event as a cue? If you try to do that for two days, what do you learn from that?
- If you are not familiar with the *controlled breathing* procedure, go through it yourself, and notice what sensations you become aware of. How could you facilitate a client doing this in a way that might allow his panic symptoms to be replicated (i.e. not too defensively, and not too extremely)?

- **Role play with a peer/colleague how you could explain to a client that he should avoid using controlled breathing as a safety behaviour (i.e. when he should use it, how often, etc.).**
- **Try to fit *physical exercise* into two or three treatment plans for your current clients. Does it make sense in terms of the formulation? Did the clients carry it forward, and if not, why not?**
- **If you are unfamiliar with *applied tension*, go over the procedure with a peer/colleague. Get feedback on whether they understand how they are to use it. Practise it yourself, and note any difficulties that the technique presents. Brainstorm or consult a supervisor about how you could overcome those with a client.**
- **Complete one of the cognitive sleep questionnaires (Morin, 1993; Espie, 2010), and identify whether you have any distorted beliefs about sleep. If so, try to modify a thought verbally, and see how far the level of your belief changes as a result of that. See whether you can work out a BE to test out your distorted belief, and see how far the level of your belief changes as a result of that. What do you learn from that?**

FURTHER READING

Benson, H. (2000). *The relaxation response*. New York: Avon Books.

This is a revised edition of a 1970s classic guide to systematic relaxation and meditation. It offers ideas for developing a range of different relaxation exercises.

Espie, C.A. (2010). *Overcoming insomnia and sleep problems: a self-help guide using cognitive behavioural techniques*. London: Constable Robinson.

An easy to read self-help book which is based on practical applications of CBT.

VIDEO LINKS

- **10.1 Introducing a relaxation exercise**
- **10.2 Introducing controlled breathing**

11

THE COURSE OF THERAPY

- Introduction
- Overall pattern of sessions
- The early stages
- Offering time-limited CBT
- Summary
- Learning exercises
- Further reading
- Video links
  - 11.1 Introducing an agenda
  - 11.2 Mutually agreed agenda
  - 11.3 Initial goals
  - 11.4 Homework

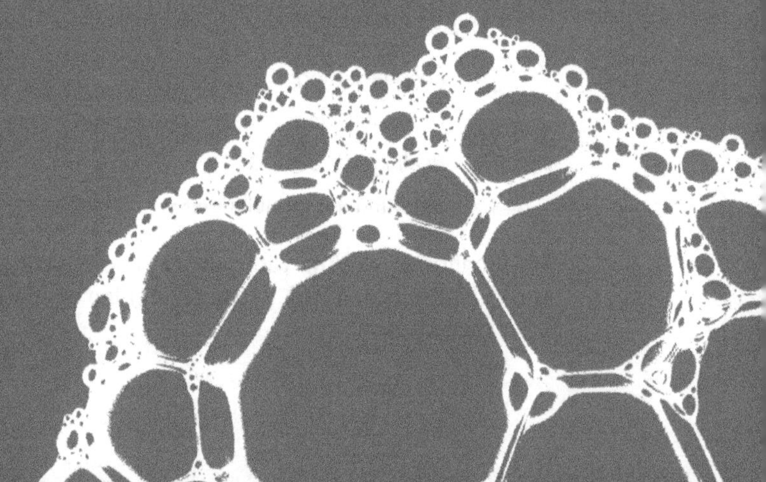

INTRODUCTION

So far we have introduced you to various elements of CBT but this chapter will present an overview of an entire course of therapy, drawing on what you have already learned. We will highlight the tasks and problems likely to arise at different stages.

OVERALL PATTERN OF SESSIONS

For most straightforward problems of the kind described in this book, a course of therapy typically takes 6–15 one-hour sessions. However, there are no hard and fast rules either about the length of each session or about the number of sessions. In the spirit of striving to tailor treatments to fit clients, the ideal CBT therapist is flexible enough to make the intervention 'bespoke'. For example, sessions may be shorter towards the end of treatment, when the client has become responsible for much of the treatment; on the other hand, if treatment demands lengthy in-session BEs, then those sessions may last considerably longer than 60 minutes. Similarly, the number of sessions may be extended if the problems are more complex or the client goes into crisis, or shortened if the problem is highly amenable to treatment. Sessions are usually weekly to begin with, and become gradually more spaced as treatment progresses, with a couple of follow-up sessions after the end of formal treatment.

Within certain services, the amount and type of intervention offered is directed by others. For example, an IAPT service or the setting where insurance companies dictate the level of intervention or the situation where a client can only afford a limited amount of therapy. You need to know how to use limited time wisely, and we will revisit this towards the end of this chapter. Others of you will be working in more autonomous settings and you will have the luxury of flexibility but the burden of making defensible decisions about the duration of therapy. What follows aims to help you make those decisions.

In the first two or three sessions, you will usually focus on assessing problem(s), with the aim of deriving a shared formulation. Running parallel with this, you will be attempting to educate your client about CBT and his expected role as an active, skilled collaborator in the therapeutic endeavour. Most of the active work on the target problems will be within sessions 2 to 12, and the final couple of sessions will be concerned with drawing up a blueprint for your client to take forward after discharge.

There are some features that appear throughout the course of treatment, and these include:

- agenda-setting;
- self-monitoring;
- dealing with setbacks;
- updating the formulation.

Self-monitoring, dealing with setbacks and updating the formulation are dealt with elsewhere (Chapters 5, 6 and 4 respectively) but we now need to elaborate on the important task of agenda-setting.

AGENDA-SETTING

The setting of a mutually agreed agenda at the beginning of each session is a key feature of CBT. As it is a relatively brief therapy, it is important to ensure that time is used effectively, and agenda-setting contributes to this goal by:

- allowing you and your client to prioritise the issues to be addressed in any given session;
- promoting the structure that is characteristic of CBT;
- helping you both to maintain a focus on relevant problems;
- helping to engage the client as an active participant in the therapeutic process.

To encourage the development of a collaborative relationship, it is helpful to address agenda-setting in the first session or two, by saying something like:

> It is important that the treatment sessions seem relevant and helpful to you, and given that we only have a limited time in each session, we usually find it helpful to decide at the beginning of the session what we will aim to cover. I usually have ideas about what I would like to include, but you will often want to discuss things that have happened in the week, or thoughts that have occurred to you, and so on. It is really important that we make time for those, and so it would be helpful if you would take a few minutes before each session just thinking over what you would like to include. We can then agree an agenda between us. Does that sound sensible? Would you be willing to have a go at that?

See Video 11.1: Introducing the idea of an agenda, and Video 11.2: Setting a mutually agreed agenda.

Follow this up by asking at the beginning of each session what the client wants to include on the agenda, and then, *following that*, suggest items that you want to include yourself (if you start with your own items, the client may be less likely to come up with his). Each item will need to be specific so that you both know what to focus on and you can review your progress in addressing an issue – vague notions of what to do in the session lend themselves to neither focus nor review! This process may take up to five minutes at the start of each session – this is time well spent, but you need to take account of it when working out how much time is available for other items.

The items you will usually include on the agenda are:

- *Brief review of the events of the past week*: This does not need to be extensive, and should only briefly identify matters that are determined as major agenda items. Clients may be unfamiliar with such a brief review, and go into too much detail. In that case you can model what is helpful by gently interrupting and summarising the main points, for example:

So what you seem to be saying is that for most of the week, your anxiety level was rather higher than it has been, and the major factor seems to have been your father's wedding plans. However, you have managed to go to work every day, and that has felt positive. You only need to give me an overall outline at this point, but have I got the general picture correct? Would it be helpful to put the wedding on our agenda?

- *Review of the last session*: This may include any problems with what was discussed, expansion on points made and so on. Many clients record their session to listen to as part of their homework, and new perspectives may have been gained as a result of that. If you have asked your client to keep notes about the session in a therapy notebook, he can also review that over the subsequent week. This process may raise issues that could be included on the agenda. For example, look out for whether he seems to be giving honest feedback, or saying what he thinks you would like to hear. In the latter case, you need to decide whether drawing attention to it at this point would weaken or strengthen the therapeutic relationship. If your client cannot remember what went on in the previous session, this should also be tackled as a problem, and ways of overcoming it need to be identified.

- *Assessment of current mood*: This can be formally assessed using a standardised measure such as a BDI (Beck, Ward, Mendelson, Mock & Erbaugh, 1961) or BAI (Beck, Epstein, Brown & Steer, 1988), or more informally via questioning: has the client's mood changed since last session? Does any aspect of it need to be included as an agenda item? It may be helpful to ask the client to rate his mood, using the same scale from week to week. For example, 'How would you say your mood has been over the past week from 0 to 10, where 0 is as low as it could be, and 10 is absolutely fine, no problems at all?', or for an anxious person it could make more sense to have a scale where 0 is no problem at all and 10 is as bad as you can imagine, highly anxious all of the time (see Chapter 5 for more discussion of how to devise measures). Make sure that you write down in your notes what scale you are using!

- *Review of homework:* This may heavily overlap with the major topics for the day (while this is often referred to as 'homework', some clients have bad associations with that word, e.g. from school experiences; alternative terms include 'assignment', 'behavioural experiment', 'tasks for next week', 'project', or a description of the specific task, like 'survey').

- *The session's main topics for discussion*: These may include symptoms (e.g. low mood, anxiety, sleeplessness), or current external problems (e.g. issues at work or relationship difficulties). You probably have plans to work on particular CBT skills (e.g. learning how to identify NATs, or the role of safety behaviours in the maintenance of a problem), and it is often possible to cover these at the same time as the client's symptoms or problems are being addressed.

- *Homework/assignment*: This should arise from the main topics discussed, and may already have been negotiated as part of that. However, it is worth bearing in mind that setting up homework can take 10 minutes.

- *Feedback*: How the client has experienced the session. You need to make sure you have left time on the agenda for this. For example, you could say:

> It would be very helpful if you would give me some feedback on how things have gone today: what has gone well and perhaps how things might have gone even better. It may be difficult at first to tell me if things have been disappointing, or if I have said something that has upset you, but as we try to work together on dealing with your problems, it is really important that you feel able to say whether things are helpful or not. What would you say are the take-home messages from today? Is there anything else that has been helpful? Is there anything I have said that is going to play on your mind, or has been unhelpful? Any other comments on today?

It will be apparent that, allowing for agenda-setting, agreeing homework and getting feedback, there is not much more than 35–40 minutes for the major topics for the day. This means that usually no more than two topics can be included, unless it is planned to allocate five minutes or so to an additional one.

In order to decide which issues to prioritise during agenda-setting, the following factors can be considered:

- issues of risk to the client or others, including children;
- urgent problems (e.g. possible job loss, imminent exams);
- level of distress;
- centrality to the formulation;
- potential for change;
- relevance to a skill that needs to be learned;
- whether the problem could be tackled with someone else outside therapy.

In the early stages, it is not usually helpful to tackle highly distressing and complex problems as it is unlikely that the client yet has the skills to deal with them effectively. Similarly, issues directly related to rigidly held or core beliefs should be avoided. This should, however, be balanced against the importance of dealing with issues seen as important by the client.

Once the agenda items are prioritised and agreed, you should consider roughly how much time you need to spend on each issue. Timing is not set in stone as we need to be responsive to unforeseen needs, but it is good to have a 'ballpark' idea of time allocation to guide you through the session, otherwise it is all too easy to run out of time.

Now the agenda is set, you should aim to follow it, and be explicit about any deviations from it. For example, if the client moves to a different topic, and perhaps becomes upset about it, you should not assume that the client would choose to prioritise the new topic. Instead, discuss the dilemma by saying, for example:

> This seems to be very upsetting for you, which makes me think it might be an important issue. Would you like us to spend some of our time thinking about this, or would you rather that we focus instead on …, as we agreed at the beginning of the session?

This allows the client to make a choice, sometimes with surprising results. Always be prepared to review the agenda if it becomes clear that an issue needs more (or less) time than anticipated. Similarly, if discussion brings up a topic related to risk, then you need to revise your agenda, and prioritise risk issues over other items, but again, be explicit that you intend to move away from the agenda.

The handling of the agenda needs to be sensitive, with respect for and understanding of the client's position. People may sometimes wish simply to ventilate feelings about a difficult situation, possibly without any expectation of problem resolution. This can be an entirely reasonable target for one or even two sessions, although it would probably need further exploration if your client wanted to take up a good proportion of each session in this manner.

In order to remain with the agenda, it is helpful if you either make, or request from your client, frequent summaries of the major points related to a topic or problem. A summary should cover the main points of a discussion in one or two sentences, and include, for example, important NATs, in the client's own words. This helps therapist and client to remain on the same wavelength, and it also serves as a useful break between topics on the agenda. In the first five or six sessions, it is helpful to summarise about every five to 10 minutes, and to ask the client whether he has understood accurately. For example:

- 'You seem to be saying ... and ... Have I got that right? Have I missed anything?'

or

- 'Could you put in your own words what you see as the main points of what we were discussing?'

COMMON DIFFICULTIES IN AGENDA-SETTING

Some common difficulties you might encounter in setting an agenda for the session are:

- *Setting a vague agenda*: This happens when the topic is described only in broad outline, rather than being operationalised in detail. For example, if a woman says that she wants to talk about her relationship with her family, you need to ask her to identify what aspects of the relationship she wants to discuss; or if a man wants to talk about his weight, you need to establish what aspect of his weight is concerning him, and to clarify if 'weight' is the key issue or if it is something that contributes to it, such as binge-eating.
- *Putting too many items on the agenda*: You will not usually manage more than two major items, and you and your client can be left feeling frustrated if you have to carry over items to the next session. If you and your client prioritise thoughtfully you will easily decide which are the one or two items you need to focus on.
- *Not prioritising which items to consider*: Tackle the major ones first, using the factors described above to guide your prioritising.

- *Dealing with issues prematurely*: Avoid dealing with issues as soon as they are mentioned, instead try to complete the agenda-setting and clarifying the item. Many clients need practice in setting agendas, and may launch immediately into a detailed discussion of the first item mentioned. Gently interrupt and remind them that it is important to agree explicitly about which issues to address, for example, you might say 'It looks as though this is a major topic for today. Can we just decide what else we want to include for this session, to make sure that we allocate enough time for everything?'
- *Not having genuine input from the client*: This runs the risk that he will introduce his preferred items 'off-agenda' later in the session, or not at all.
- *Misunderstanding the meaning of an issue for a client*: Continue to ask questions, use summaries to clarify meaning and make sure you have got it right, and ask your client for feedback.
- *Tackling issues not on the agenda without discussing it first*: The agenda can be flexible, but changes need to be overt and collaborative.
- *Skipping from one topic to another from session to session, without achieving closure on any of them*: Make sure that there is a broad strategy that will make progress across sessions.

It is helpful if you regularly review agenda-setting so that difficulties like these can be identified and dealt with. Although it may initially feel uncomfortable, especially if you are used to a less structured approach, it is worth experimenting to test out whether the consequences that you fear actually occur.

We will now go on to look at the stages in a course of therapy, beginning with the features of the early stages.

See Video 11.3 Working out initial goals.

THE EARLY STAGES

GOAL-SETTING

Another aspect of CBT that serves to maintain its efficiency as a time-limited therapy is the agreement to work towards mutually agreed and clearly specified goals. This helps to structure therapy sessions, and to maintain their focus. Goals are established as a joint effort, and this further emphasises the collaborative nature of CBT: the goals for therapy are those that are relevant for the client, with input from the therapist.

Goal-setting implies the possibility of change, and this helps to engender hope and reduce helplessness in the face of what may seem insurmountable problems. It also raises the prospect of an end to treatment, and so helps you negotiate in an open and explicit way when discharge may be approaching.

HOW TO SET GOALS

Goals should reflect your shared formulation. For example, if someone is depressed and you identify maintaining cycles of inactivity, rumination, your goals should embrace this. Sometimes, clients express goals such as 'to lose weight', 'to get on better with my partner'; before you both take these on board as goals, check that they are relevant to therapy, that they are indicated by the formulation. It could be that a person's low mood is genuinely exacerbated by weight gain that is driven by comfort-eating when depressed, and this would then be an appropriate issue to target. On the other hand, some expressions are simply 'wishes' that might be desirable for the client but not relevant to therapy. So, if a client is overweight but his eating patterns and weight do not actively contribute to the maintenance of depression, then weight loss needs to be tackled elsewhere.

Goals should also be 'SMART', that is, they should be:

- **S**pecific
- **M**easurable
- **A**chievable
- **R**ealistic
- and have a realistic **T**imeframe (i.e. a date for completion).

Setting out goals in *specific* detail can help clients feel more in control, because a global problem reduced to its component parts may feel more manageable. You can begin with general questions like:

- 'How would you like things to be at the end of treatment?'
- 'How would you know if treatment had been successful?'
- 'Let's imagine that therapy has been successful – what would be different? What changes would you see?'
- 'At the end of treatment, what would you like to be different?'

The so-called 'miracle question' is sometimes a good way of getting at goals:

- 'Suppose whilst you are asleep tonight a miracle happens, and all your problems disappear, just like that. But you don't know that it's happened, because you are asleep. When you get up the next morning and go through your day, how will you come to realise that the miracle has happened? What would you notice was different about you or about other people? What would *others* see that would tell them that the miracle had happened?'

A woman who was feeling that her life was controlled by her health worries had the following discussion with her therapist:

Therapist: How would you know if treatment had been successful? What would be different?

Client: I would stop checking myself for lumps … I wouldn't be thinking about cancer all the time, and boring the family with it.

Therapist: Is there anything else that would change?

Client: I suppose the main thing is I wouldn't get panicky every time cancer was mentioned.

This client's response demonstrates a common problem: she described how she would like *not* to be, rather than how she would *like* to be. This has been called the 'dead man's solution' (i.e. the goals could be achieved by a dead man – no more panicky feelings, no more checking lumps, no more talking to relatives about cancer). Ask your client to describe how he wants to be or what he wants to achieve, rather than what he wants to avoid.

The 'miracle question' helped the woman develop goals that were about achievements. She and the therapist eventually agreed that she would:

- carry out a full breast check on a monthly basis;
- discuss topics other than symptoms with her husband 95 per cent of the time;
- visit relatives (alone or with a companion) in hospital if they were admitted;
- respond calmly if she developed symptoms by relaxing (5/10 or lower on a 10-point scale) and re-assuring herself.

These are four specific goals: both she and the therapist are quite clear about what indicates a success. In order to measure her progress towards these goals, she was asked questions like 'Can we break this down into smaller, specific steps?' or 'What would be the first sign that you were making progress?'. This enabled her to create a hierarchy of achievement beginning with what was currently possible for her to do if she pushed herself. Her steps to her goal are shown in Figure 11.1.

Current behaviour: Daily full breast checks on rising and before going to bed. Mini-checks at odd times during the day.	
Step 1	Daily full breast checks on rising and before going to bed only.
Step 2	Daily full breast checks on going to bed only.
Step 3	Full breast checks every other day on going to bed.
Step 4	Full breast checks Monday and Thursday only (patient choice of timing).
Step 5	Full breast checks once per week (patient choice of timing).
Step 6	Full breast checks once per fortnight (patient choice of timing).
Goal	Full breast checks on a monthly basis.

Figure 11.1 Example of steps towards achieving goals

This series of tasks is not immutable. With each step the woman's confidence and perspectives would be reviewed and the steps might be refined and changed. However, to begin with, a breakdown of the goal can impart hope and improve motivation. It can make the impossible seem achievable.

Part of your role is to make sure that goals are *realistic*. Clients may have unrealistically extreme goals, such as a socially anxious person who wanted to find a life partner by the end of therapy; or the goals may be too limited, such as a man with obsessional disorder who wants to reduce his hand-washing to four hours a day. Occasionally it may be difficult for a client and therapist to agree on goals. For example, a client with anorexia nervosa may want help to lose weight; or a client with an OCD may want help to make his rituals more thorough. In these cases delicate negotiation is required, but the process allows you and your client to be explicit about what can and cannot be achieved through therapy.

A man with obsessional concerns about official forms identified that as one goal he wanted to learn how to be certain that he had filled in his tax form correctly. The session continued:

Therapist: That's interesting. You say that you would like to know how to be certain that you had made no errors in your tax form, so that your anxiety would fade. That sounds to me very much to be coming from the perspective of someone who still has an obsessional problem. Can you put yourself in the shoes of someone who no longer has OCD. What do you think things would be like then?

Client: Perhaps I could ask the accountant to check it with me?

Therapist: And if you had no worries about form filling, what effect would that have on your needing to check?

Client: I suppose I could be aiming not to be doing any checking at all, just filling in the form.

Therapist: Does that sound a reasonable goal to have? To fill in forms without checking them?

Client: I think everyone probably checks things like that once.

Therapist: OK. I guess that may be true. So what do you think would be a reasonable goal?

Client: I think I should aim at being OK if I fill the form in, and then only check it once, without going over it in my head or anything.

During treatment, it may be necessary for the man to submit a form without any checking at all, but his goal for successful treatment was in this case less rigorous but more realistic.

It is also important that the goals are *achievable* and involve change in things that are within a person's control: in particular, clients should focus on changing things about themselves, rather than other people. For example, it may be reasonable to have job-seeking as a goal, but obtaining a particular job is ultimately determined by someone else, and therefore

may not be an achievable goal. It is also worth considering whether the person has the resources – finance, skills, persistence, time, social support – to achieve the goals.

When considering the *timeframe*, the issue of which goals to tackle first can be approached by considering similar factors to those relevant for prioritising topics in a session. It is helpful to first tackle a goal where rapid change is possible, in order to increase hope and therefore engagement and motivation. Other factors to take into account include risk or urgency, importance to or level of distress for the client, and whether any particular goal logically needs to be approached before other ones can be tackled (e.g. you would need to be able to travel to an interview before you could apply for a post, and so you might need to tackle anxiety about travelling before you tackled anxiety about interviews). For the therapist, other considerations are the centrality of a goal in the formulation, and the ethical acceptability of the goal (e.g. one client wanted to reduce the distress felt when holding violent intrusive images about harming others, rather than address the images themselves; this person was encouraged to consider the personal meaning of the images and to focus on anger management instead).

HOMEWORK OR ASSIGNMENTS

There is clear evidence (Kazantzis, Deane & Ronan, 2002; Schmidt & Woolaway-Bickel, 2000) that those who complete homework tasks show greater improvement than those who do not, and this is presumably partly because they have more opportunity to generalise what they have learned from sessions into everyday life. Most problems are based outside the clinic rather than in it, and clients can use homework to collect information, test out new patterns of thinking and behaving, and learn through direct experience. As the general style of CBT involves handing skills over to clients, it is important that they have opportunities to practise the skills in real life, whether this involves identifying NATs, working out how to reduce safety behaviours, or how to increase assertiveness in particular situations.

Because between-session assignments are so central to CBT, it follows that time must be allocated to setting them up, which may need five or 10 minutes during or at the end of a treatment session. Homework will often follow on directly from the major topics on the agenda, and will be devised mid-session as part of that discussion. For example, if the agenda item concerned the role of negative thoughts in triggering anxious feelings, an obvious between-session task might be for the client to begin monitoring triggers and thoughts associated with anxiety in the following week. If there has been a discussion about the role of internal self-focus in a client with social anxiety, then homework may involve monitoring, or experimenting with an external focus and recording the effects on anxiety.

The range of possible assignments is boundless, and relies on the ingenuity of you and your client in setting up suitable tasks. It can include reading relevant material; listening to treatment recordings; self-monitoring feelings, thoughts or behaviours; carrying out BEs; practising new skills such as the use of thought records or assertive responses; doing a historical review of past experience; or activity scheduling. It is important that it makes sense to the client, and that it will be useful either for the subsequent treatment session, or for the achievement of a particular goal. For example, the elimination of a safety-seeking behaviour may feed directly into the next session, where the results may flesh out the formulation, and then lead on to the next manoeuvre. On the other hand, a client may be keeping a positive data log aimed at addressing low self-esteem as a long-term assignment; discussion of it from session to session may be minimal, unless it was identified as a major topic for the agenda.

Clients often do not do their homework. This can be for a number of reasons and you should always allow time for exploring why it is understandable that the assignment was neglected. More often than not, much can be learnt from this exploration. Nonetheless, these principles will help to increase the likelihood that homework is carried out and is useful:

- The homework should *follow logically* from what happened during the session. In fact, it can be devised during the session if it fits well there – you do not have to wait until the end of the session to discuss assignments.
- The assignment should be *relevant*, and be seen to be relevant by the client. Check this out with questions such as 'Does this make sense? Can you summarise for me how you think this would be helpful?'. This is less of an issue later in treatment as the client takes an increasing role in setting up between-session assignments, but may be more of a problem earlier on, when the therapist is likely to take the lead in suggesting suitable homework tasks.
- It is also worth bearing in mind that your *client has a life outside of therapy*. Although it is important that they prioritise treatment, there are limits to what they can be expected to do, and they will be less likely to complete the homework if they feel overburdened. Ask them if the demands of the assignment are reasonable.
- Homework should be *planned in detail*, spelling out what is to be done, when, where, with whom and so on. Pitfalls and difficulties must be identified and discussed, by asking carefully what could prevent the task not being carried through.

A woman was very concerned about being what she described as 'a doormat' in relation to her mother and sister. However, after a role play in the session, when an assertiveness task was being set up for a subsequent interaction with them, she mentioned that she was not likely to see either of the relatives in the next month or so! As a result, an alternative, more immediate assertiveness task was planned, and a homework opportunity was not missed.

See Video 11.4: Negotiating homework.

Difficulties may range from embarrassment at using a self-monitoring form at work, through to not having enough money to carry out a BE in a social situation. Be mindful of underlying beliefs that may interfere with completing homework assignments. For example, someone with perfectionist beliefs may find an activity schedule difficult to complete because he might think that none of his activities was challenging enough to include; a client with low self-esteem may find it difficult to do any task where the outcome could be construed as falling short of the therapist's 'wishes'. In the early stages of treatment, anticipated problems should be dealt with in the here and now, rather than attempting to modify such underlying beliefs.

- *Make sure that homework cannot be 'failed'*, but rather seen as a source of helpful information, whatever the outcome. For example, if a client is attempting to reduce avoidance of particular situations, set up homework so that he can collect useful information about anxious thoughts and feelings even if he cannot reduce the avoidance.
- *Provide relevant resources*, such as a diary form or reading material, at least early in therapy.
- The agreed assignments should be *written down*, by both you and the client. Although it may be quicker for you to write it down *for* the client, it is helpful to establish his active role in therapy and this kind of involvement can be an early step in that direction.
- *Homework review should always be included in the agenda of the subsequent session*. Partly this is because it should have been designed to be relevant for the session, but at a more general level, a client is highly unlikely to persist with homework assignments that you never follow up.

If the homework has been completed or nearly completed, then it should be reviewed in detail. For example, if the client has read a chapter of a book, what was helpful? What rang bells for him? Were there any sections that were difficult to understand? If he has completed an activity schedule, what was the pattern of pleasure and achievements? What did he learn? How can this be taken forward?

On the other hand, if the homework was not completed, it is important that this is explored and the reasons determined. There may have been practical reasons (e.g. someone was off sick at work so workload unexpectedly increased); the client may have misunderstood; it may not have been discussed in sufficient detail, or not written down so it was forgotten; it may be that the task was too difficult in some way. In all these cases, the task can be modified for a subsequent assignment, or perhaps carried out with assistance from you or someone else.

If underlying beliefs have interfered with the completion of the task then, as described above, this should be tackled pragmatically, at least early in treatment, rather than attempting premature belief change. For example, if it seems that the client has beliefs about control or autonomy that have been activated by a particular assignment, then the task could be modified to give him more control. This may not necessarily be spelled out unless the beliefs have been discussed in detail in the formulation, or unless the treatment has progressed to the point where such beliefs are the current focus.

A man did no homework on two consecutive weeks. When this was looked at in more detail, he raised concerns about the relevance of the tasks, although he had not mentioned this when the homework was agreed. The therapist wondered whether autonomy may be an issue for him, but did not raise it at this early stage in therapy, particularly as it did not seem to be related to the problems he had presented. Instead, it was agreed that the client would play a bigger role in setting up homework tasks. This meant that often homework tasks were weightier than the therapist would have suggested, but by and large they were completed.

The general point is that it is important to establish from the outset that homework is an integral part of therapy, and that it is difficult to proceed without the information and feedback that it provides. This is particularly true when the amount of treatment available is limited by resource constraints. Well-devised homework can mean that very limited treatment results in enormous changes for the client, as the majority of the work is done outside sessions.

PROBLEMS IN THE EARLY STAGES

LOW MOTIVATION FOR CHANGE

At the beginning of treatment it may appear that your client is not engaged with treatment, but it is helpful to understand this apparent reluctance to engage, rather than use a trait description like 'poor motivation'. This means that attempts should be made to analyse the problem in terms of thoughts, feelings and behaviours, so that ideas about management can follow on. The following possibilities should be considered:

- *Ambivalence about change*: Prochaska and DiClemente (1986) defined a spectrum of stages in a person's preparedness to change: pre-contemplation (no intention of changing, possibly no awareness of a problem), contemplation (aware of a problem and considering change), preparation (beginning to make changes), action (successful cognitive and behavioural change) and maintenance (working to prevent relapse). It is worth considering which of these stages best describes your client. This needs to be kept under review, as motivation can shift as therapy proceeds: it can increase as your client accrues more successful experiences; or it can diminish as he finds that he has to work harder for results, or if he encounters difficulties in treatment (e.g. if anxiety does not diminish as expected). A lack of self-efficacy can also be important, insofar as it affects what the client believes he can achieve; ways of dealing with this are discussed in Chapter 6.
- *Inaccurate expectations about the nature of the treatment approach*: This is particularly likely to be a problem with those who have had experience of different psychological treatment approaches, or who have a lack of faith in CBT. This reminds us that it is crucial to give clear information about CBT and a clear indication of what engaging in therapy involves.
- *Lack of understanding or acceptance of the formulation*: In our view, if a client and therapist have not agreed on a formulation or the cognitive behavioural approach by around session 4, it is less likely that treatment will be effective. It is therefore worth spending time on clarifying the formulation, asking for feedback, listening effectively to the client's concerns and trying to take account of them. If the client and therapist cannot come to a shared understanding, however simple the formulation, it is possibly not worth pursuing this treatment and other forms of therapy need to be reviewed.
- *Hopelessness*: Apart from the hopelessness that is common in depressed clients, hopelessness may also occur in clients who have had a history of unsuccessful psychological treatments. This can be approached using standard CBT techniques, including identifying and evaluating ATs and BEs focused on hopelessness.

'I DON'T HAVE ANY THOUGHTS'

It is difficult for clients to make sense of a formulation that focuses on cognitions if they are unaware of thoughts and/or images. It can be helpful for them to practise looking for thoughts, to look for images, or to try to identify what situations mean to them, even if they cannot easily identify ATs. Chapter 8 discusses ways of dealing with this problem, but as cognitions are central to this approach, it is important to deal with the issue rather than try to circumvent it.

HOLDING BELIEFS THAT MIGHT BE INCOMPATIBLE WITH CBT

Clients may have an understanding of their problems that is different from a cognitive behavioural view, and it is helpful to find a way of working with this as an experiment, without attacking the alternative explanation. For example, clients with somatic symptoms often construe them in terms of physical illness. It may be useful to try to negotiate using an alternative approach based on a CBT formulation, as an experiment for a specified time to see whether it works any better than the physical illness formulation (the so-called 'Theory A/Theory B' approach: see Chapters 9 and 13). Similarly, some clients with obsessional worries may explain their intrusions in terms of a religious framework, and a similar approach may be helpful. On the other hand, some may have differing beliefs about the roles and responsibilities of therapists and clients (e.g. 'It is your job to cure me'). Awareness of this can help the therapist devise assignments that could, for example, draw attention to the important contribution that the client can make to the process of change. A useful metaphor in this case is that of a road map: that the therapist's knowledge can put you on the right page of the map, but that you need the detailed information which only the client has to direct you along the right roads on that map. You then need to set up experiments that demonstrate that this approach can be helpful.

THE DISADVANTAGES OF THERAPY SEEM TO OUTWEIGH THE ADVANTAGES

We need to remember that therapy has costs as well as benefits: costs of emotional strain, investing time and possibly money, and (risky) implications for other changes in the client's life. Sometimes it is necessary to help clients think through the balance of costs and benefits, and we should always be prepared to carry out motivational work as necessary.

Reluctance to do a particular homework task should not be taken immediately as evidence of an unwillingness to change, but rather as indicating that perhaps the case for the task has not been made, or that there is a fear getting in the way. We often ask clients to make changes that require a great deal of bravery, and they are only likely to do that if, on balance, they see that the possible benefits outweigh the probable costs. Cost–benefit matrices can be very illuminating for the reluctant or ambivalent. They go beyond a simple listing of immediate pros and cons by prompting consideration of both short- and long-term implications.

Short-term costs	**Short-term benefits**
Would feel panicky at the time. Would feel anxious all day. Would feel nauseous. Might be sick. Would worry about the mess.	Would feel I was doing something for the problem. Would feel less weak and out of control.
Long-term costs	**Long-term benefits**
Might feel I had to do harder and harder things. Would have no excuse to avoid the places I don't want to visit!	Would gain confidence in my ability to cope with problems. Would have a better chance of overcoming my vomit phobia, and then I could: go out freely; travel more widely; eat more foods; not be anxious all the time; not be embarrassed at formal events; go abroad on holiday; eat in restaurants; feel more adult; relax about cleanliness in the home.

Figure 11.2 Cost–benefit matrix: exploring the consequences of giving up safety-seeking behaviours

A client with a severe vomit phobia was finding it very difficult to give up safety-seeking behaviours (such as carrying mints in her bag, driving with her car window open, carrying a moist flannel in her bag, and sleeping with the light on so that she could find her way to the bathroom if necessary), even though she understood the rationale for doing so. Her cost–benefit analysis for dropping the safety behaviours differentiating short-term from long-term effects is shown in Figure 11.2.

This analysis (set out in Figure 11.2), allowed the client to look beyond her short-term fears and consider the long-term benefits. This new perspective enabled her to begin to drop her safety-seeking behaviours. Although this type of analysis will often allow people to move forward, you should also remember that occasionally clients may decide that, on balance, the costs of therapy outweigh the benefits for them right now, and therefore not continue in treatment.

RELAPSE MANAGEMENT

You might wonder why this section is called *relapse management* rather than *prevention*, and why we have positioned it early in the course of treatment. We use the term 'management' because aiming for 'prevention' is often unrealistic. In general we find that people will have setbacks and that they need to learn the necessary skills to deal with them. Lapses can happen even early on in therapy and clients need to be well prepared. Relapse management is discussed in detail in Chapter 6.

REVIEW POINTS

Because CBT is time-limited, focused and structured, you need to carry out regular reviews throughout treatment. This helps to retain the focus of treatment, and to establish whether progress is sufficient to warrant continuing with treatment, or whether changes in the approach are required. The review should be related to the goals agreed at the beginning of treatment, and it is helpful if intermediate targets have been identified, as well as end-point goals. Any other measures that are being used, such as questionnaires or other self-monitoring, are also relevant for reviews.

It is prudent to agree at the outset that you will review progress after four or five sessions, in order to assess whether CBT is likely to be helpful. Although a decision not to continue with CBT may be dispiriting for someone who had high hopes of its efficacy, it is easier to deal with this at an early stage than after 20 sessions that have resulted in little change. After this initial review, further reviews should be carried out at five-session intervals, or 10-session intervals with long-term interventions.

The formulation developed in the first one or two sessions is tentative, so it is important to review it regularly to take account of any new information that becomes available as therapy progresses. This may be derived from homework assignments, BEs carried out in sessions and so on. Although the basic outline of the formulation may not change, the details of maintaining cycles are likely to be fleshed out during treatment, with implications for what interventions are likely to be helpful.

A man with agoraphobia was unclear about the content of his catastrophic thinking because he had for so long avoided situations that would trigger such thoughts. Once he had learnt to 'catch' cognitions it was established that he had thoughts about not being helped by other people, this could be built into the formulation, and experiments set up to test them out.

It is especially important to review progress if little change is being made, or if an impasse has been reached. This may be for many reasons, but it could mean that the formulation is not helpful or has significant omissions, so always review your shared conceptualisation. It is also worth looking at the therapeutic relationship to see whether there are problems interfering with the application of the formulation to the client's problems. Such problems may include your own blind spots, which should be discussed with your supervisor. If no solution can be found, you may conclude that treatment should be discontinued at this point and you can begin to explore alternative options with your client.

LATER STAGES

As treatment progresses, the focus moves increasingly onto intervention rather than assessment, but the results of any intervention should always be related to the initial formulation to see whether it needs modifying. The client becomes increasingly independent in determining what items go onto the agenda, how long is spent on each item, and what homework is taken away; and as more CBT skills are learnt the client takes the lead in, for example, evaluating negative thoughts and in devising BEs to test out new perspectives.

You will probably spend most of the time in treatment sessions on the details of automatic cognitions, feelings and behaviour in current situations, but as the end of treatment approaches you may begin to identify and evaluate unhelpful assumptions or core beliefs, particularly if you think that your client may be at risk of relapse if such beliefs are not modified. It is, however, not always necessary to modify underlying beliefs directly. If a person has worked successfully at re-evaluating NATs, both in sessions and *in vivo*, then very often there is an automatic re-evaluation of the more general beliefs, particularly to the level of DAs. Even so, one shouldn't assume this, so always ask your clients about their new rules for living and new general perspectives before discharging them.

A woman had strong beliefs about never expressing anger. In a range of situations, she experimented with being more assertive, including in situations where people were behaving unreasonably. During debriefing of her experiences it became clear that her beliefs about expressing anger were modified, although they were not directly addressed.

The emphasis on the portability of skills means that it is important for the client to reflect on what is taking place in therapy, so it is helpful to ask questions such as 'What were we doing there?', 'Can you identify the kind of crooked thinking you were showing there?', 'How could you use that in other situations?'. It is important that you attribute progress to the client's efforts, particularly if he is dependent and hence likely to attribute change to your attention and skill rather than his own efforts. This is discussed in more detail in Chapter 6.

As treatment progresses, the frequency of sessions may be reduced, perhaps moving to two-week gaps between two or three sessions, followed by perhaps a three- or four-week break before treatment ends.

ENDING THERAPY

It is relatively easy to work towards ending therapy if the treatment goals were well defined, and if there has been good progress towards them. Similarly, you can keep in mind the idea that treatment will be coming to an end through regular reviews of goals and progress, as this emphasises the short-term nature of the treatment process. The client should gradually have acquired confidence in his ability to apply a CBT approach to his problems, using the skills learned during therapy.

As the end of treatment approaches, it is important to review relapse management skills and it can be helpful to develop with your client a *blueprint* for dealing with problems that may emerge in the future, based on the relapse management work you have already done together (see Chapter 6). This could include:

- what has been learned during therapy;
- what strategies have been most helpful;
- what situations in the future may be difficult, or possibly lead to a recurrence of the problem;
- ways of responding to this, given what has been learned in treatment;
- how to handle a significant problem, including if necessary a brief review with the therapist.

The emphasis should be on the idea that the client is equipped to deal with most problems that are likely to arise, even if, in some circumstances, it would be reasonable for him to ask for your help.

Rather than having an abrupt end to treatment, it may make sense to plan a follow-up or booster session or two over the subsequent year. You can then review progress, reinforce the client's success at dealing with problems, check out how he dealt with problems that had been anticipated at previous sessions, check on the re-emergence of unhelpful patterns of thinking or behaviour (e.g. safety behaviours) and work together to trouble-shoot if necessary.

Despite the gradual withdrawal from therapy, and the emphasis on skills acquisition, some clients continue to worry that they will not cope by themselves after the end of treatment. This can be approached in a standard cognitive behavioural way, by identifying worrying thoughts and helping the client to deal with them. This could include setting up BEs to test out alternative perspectives. If a client has general beliefs about not being able to cope alone, the booster sessions over the year following the end of formal treatment can be used to test out the beliefs, perhaps via a positive data log.

A 59-year-old client who had been depressed as a result of a number of events, including his increasing difficulty with a rapidly changing job, had responded well to treatment, and had maintained his progress over a number of months. He nevertheless had thoughts like: 'If I am faced with a *real* problem, I shall not be able to deal with it, and everything will collapse round my ears.' As a homework task, he thought about what he would say to a friend in a similar position. He reminded himself of a number of situations over the preceding months when he had successfully tackled difficult situations, including getting a new job, coping with his wife's unexpected illness, and developing bad dreams as his medication was reduced. He discussed with his therapist the risk that he might focus excessively on times when he was struggling and, to counteract this, they agreed that he would for a couple of months keep a log of any examples of successful coping.

Some clients will not have benefited from treatment, and this can be especially difficult for them if they came to CBT having had little success with other treatment approaches. If the absence of progress was identified at an early review stage, it may be less dispiriting for the client to finish at that point, where the lack of progress could be attributed to a failure in CBT, rather than the client. For example, the therapist could say:

> It seems that we have not managed to make much difference to your problems. Cognitive therapy has been found to be useful with a lot of people, but there are instances when it does not seem to relieve the feelings, however committed the client is to working in this way. Research is still needed into how to find new ways of changing beliefs or behaviour, so that more people can benefit from it, but I think at this point we have to say that cognitive therapy does not deliver what you need. Perhaps we should look at what has been helpful, so that you can take away some strategies for helping you feel better. For example, we found that you were good at breaking problems down into different elements, and that then you could tackle difficult situations more easily. Is that something you can take away and use in the future?

While it may be difficult to end treatment with little in the way of gain, it is unfair to maintain false hopes for someone who is unlikely to benefit. If it seems that a different approach would be more useful, then this should be discussed as early on as possible: for example, if there are significant marital problems then couple therapy, or possibly systemic therapy, could be suggested; or it may be worth considering medication if this has not been exhausted previously. However, happily, the outcome of CBT with the majority of DSM Axis I disorders is good, and for most clients a plan based on the blueprint will be a more positive note on which to end treatment.

OFFERING TIME-LIMITED CBT

THE LONG AND THE SHORT OF IT

As you know, CBT was intended as a time-limited and focused intervention. Some of you might find that your service demands that you deliver very time-limited therapy indeed, perhaps to the extent that you feel unable to offer an appropriate intervention. On the other hand, some of you might work in systems that impose no limits. Both situations need to be given thought.

WORKING WITHIN A FRAMEWORK OF LIMITED SESSIONS

Since the instigation of IAPT (Department of Health, 2008), there has been a system in place in England and Wales for evaluating the impact of relatively brief, focused CBT. IAPT presents very clear guidelines for therapists who are required to work within a well-defined stepped-care framework. Similar boundaried structures might operate elsewhere, for example within private organisations where length and type of interventions is dictated by insurance companies.

In summary, the stepped system of IAPT looks like this:

- Step 1: **Primary care services**. Minimal intervention, assessment and watchful waiting.
- Step 2: **Low intensity (LI) services**. Computerised CBT, guided self-help, psychoeducational groups, behavioural activation.

- Step 3: **High intensity (HI) services.** CBT (also EMDR for PTSD; IPT and couples therapy for depression).
- Step 4: **Mental health specialist services.** Complex psychological treatments and combined treatments.
- Step 5: **In-patient mental health services.** Complex psychological treatments and combined treatments.

One of the many strengths of IAPT is the clarity of guidance for working at each step, and another is conscientious outcome data collection. The data from IAPT reviews has been illuminating and might well have relevance for other services and practitioners. The early evaluations showed enormous regional variation in recovery rates and closer scrutiny shed light on this (see Layard & Clark, 2014 for a review). In summary, the best rates of recovery were seen when:

- there was good fidelity to the empirically recommended CBT approach;
- therapists were more experienced/more highly trained;
- clients receive more sessions (for a 50 per cent recovery rate, an average of eight or more sessions was required in many services);
- there is good referral on to more specialist services when initial interventions are insufficient;
- NICE guidelines are closely followed.

Thus a relatively brief intervention can be effective if we are conscientious about developing therapist competency, respecting treatment fidelity and client need. At a recent OCTC Congress (Clark, 2015), Professor David Clark, one of the main instigators of IAPT, made a plea that IAPT interventions be guided by client-sensitive CBT formulation and that clients receive the level of therapy that they need, not an arbitrary number of sessions dictated by a service. Sound advice, indeed.

OFFERING LONG-TERM INTERVENTIONS

There is no doubt that some clients need more sessions than others, and again Professor Clark's appeal to formulate sensitively are relevant. Once engaged in CBT, people are likely to need longer if they have:

- complex presenting problems (by virtue of chronicity, co-morbidity or there being a personality disorder), and
- poor resources (*inner resources* such as good problem-solving skills or *external resources* such as social support).

Your formulation will not only give you insights into this but will also begin to direct your work together – that is, if CBT is suitable for your client. Remember that virtually all clients have presenting problems that we can formulate but not all are ready for CBT.

Sometimes a lengthy course of CBT simply reflects a fruitless engagement phase. It is on occasion absolutely necessary to invest additional time in engaging a client, but this needs to be kept under close review. In fact, close review is the guideline for longer therapies. Progress towards clear goals should be scrutinised every six to 10 sessions. Don't fall into the trap of having a vague notion of targets and progress, as the 'goal posts' for imprecise targets can all too easily shift and make it difficult to properly assess whether or not continued CBT is in your client's best interest. It is possible to do a disservice by not discharging the client who needs to experience independence or by not referring on the person whose needs are better met elsewhere.

SUMMARY

As CBT is structured and focused, it is relatively straightforward to describe the probable typical course of therapy:

- It is likely to last between six and 15 sessions, longer for more complex problems.
- The length of sessions varies, but the average is 50–60 minutes.
- The first two or three sessions focus on assessment and deriving an initial formulation, at the same time as developing a working alliance, and encouraging the client to become an active and collaborative participant.
- The next sessions focus on trying to tackle the client's problems.
- The final sessions focus on revising relapse management and drawing up a blueprint about what to do if further problems develop.

Throughout treatment, each session will include:

- agenda-setting;
- self-monitoring;
- dealing with setbacks;
- updating the formulation;
- summaries for the client and therapist.

Agenda-setting is important because it facilitates the structuring of the sessions. An agenda typically includes:

- review of events since previous session;
- review of the previous session;
- assessment of mood;
- review of homework;
- work on current topics (about 35 minutes);

- homework/assignment;
- feedback on the session.

Difficulties with agenda-setting include:

- being too vague;
- not prioritising;
- have too full an agenda;
- no client input;
- digressing from the agenda;
- misunderstanding the client;
- beginning the session while setting the agenda;
- hopping around from topic to topic.

Goal-setting is important, and goals should be:

- specific;
- measurable;
- achievable;
- reasonable;
- timeframed.

Homework is highly valued because being engaged with it is known to relate to success in treatment. Homework is more likely to be carried out if it:

- emerges from the session;
- is relevant;
- is not too burdensome;
- is planned in detail with difficulties discussed;
- cannot be 'failed';
- is written down;
- is reviewed in detail.

'Poor motivation' is analysed within the CBT model. It may be a result of:

- being too early along the 'readiness to change' dimension;
- inaccurate expectations of treatment;
- lack of understanding/acceptance of formulation;

- hopelessness;
- beliefs that are incompatible with CBT;
- cons of change outweighing pros.

The middle phase of treatment is spent on discussing the details of current situations, in terms of the four systems – emotions, cognitions, behaviours and physiology – and the environment in which your client lives.

The latter phase is spent devising a blueprint for action in the event of future problems. Your hope by this stage is that your client is as competent in CBT for their problem as you are.

LEARNING EXERCISES

These learning exercises are available to download from the companion website.

REVIEW AND REFLECTION:

- If you have experience with a different kind of therapy, and if CBT is more structured than you are used to, how comfortable do you feel with imposing structure on treatment sessions?
- How comfortable would you feel discharging someone because CBT does not seem to meet their needs?
- Are there bridges that you feel you cannot cross – for example, being explicit if you are going to talk about something that is not on the agenda?
- What do you feel about the suggestions for shorter-term or longer-term CBT? In your clinical experience is it relevant to consider this?
- If you review the relevant section of the chapter, does that make you feel any more comfortable? Comfortable enough to try it out?

TAKING IT FORWARD:

- Take any of the points of possible discomfort from the review exercise, and try to adopt the suggested format for three or

four clients. Keep a thought record if you feel uncomfortable with the way you are trying to work at any time – you will probably only be able to note down key words/phrases to remind yourself what went through your mind, but you will need to pay attention to the NATs so that you can write them down more fully at the end of the session. Once the session is over, take some time evaluating your cognitions, either by yourself or with a supervisor/peer.

- **Think of something you would like to change in your own life, and see if you can do a goal-setting exercise for it, deriving SMART goals. Note down any points that you learn from the process of carrying out the exercise.**
- **With your next five therapy sessions with different clients, rate (with a rating scale you design yourself, see Chapter 5) how much you involved the client in the selection and design of homework. Was this at an acceptable level, and if not in a particular case, in what ways could you improve things? Look at how many of the clients actually carried out the homework, and think about how this could be improved.**

FURTHER READING

Beck, A.T., Rush, A.J., Shaw, B.F., & Emery, G. (1979). *Cognitive therapy of depression.* New York: Guilford Press.

This classic text gives a description of the structure and process of both the early and subsequent treatment sessions, and gives a good 'feel' for how therapy proceeds.

Padesky, C.A., & Greenberger, D. (2015). *Clinician's guide to mind over mood.* New York: Guilford Press.

This book provides a clear account of the treatment process, particularly if you also read the accompanying manual for clients.

- **11.1 Introducing the idea of an agenda**
- **11.2 Setting a mutually agreed agenda**
- **11.3 Working out initial goals**
- **11.4 Negotiating homework**

12 DEPRESSION

- Introduction
- Characteristics of depression
- Common maintenance processes
- Course of treatment
- Components of CBT for depression
- Activity scheduling
- Common problems in activity scheduling
- Common problems with graded task assignment
- Jacobson's dismantling study and the behavioural activation approach
- Cognitive strategies in depression
- Early-stage cognitive strategies
- Main cognitive strategies
- Medication
- Dealing with suicidality
- Structured problem solving
- Potential problems when working with depressed clients
- Summary
- Learning exercises
- Further reading
- Video links
  - 12.1 WAS
  - 12.2 Positive imagery (i)
  - 12.3 Positive imagery (ii)

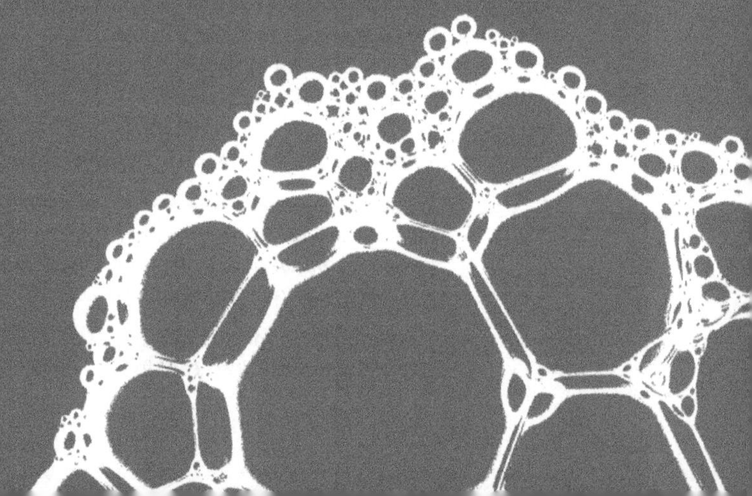

INTRODUCTION

CBT's early success arose largely from the impact of Beck et al.'s (1979) book on depression, coupled with research trials showing the effectiveness of this new approach. In this chapter, we will describe some of the classic CBT strategies for depression. See also Chapter 17 for a brief description of some of the later innovations in working with depression, including behavioural activation, rumination-focused therapy and mindfulness-based CBT.

You are very likely to find yourself working with clients with depression at some time in your career. There are various sources for prevalence and relapse figures, for example Centers for Disease Control and Prevention (CDC: no date), the Health and Social Care Information Centres (HSCIC: no date) and the Mental Health Foundation (MHF: no date), and they paint a pretty consistent picture of rather high prevalence – often estimated to be around 10 per cent, with women being more vulnerable to depression than men. Lifetime risk estimates are considerably greater. It is thought that 1.5 million people suffer from depression in UK at any one time. Rather shockingly, after one episode of depression the probability of suffering another is 50 per cent, and after two episodes this rises to 70–80 per cent. So it is wise to stress relapse management training in your work. As depression is commonly co-morbid with anxiety, it is particularly important that you are able to recognise the symptoms so that you can formulate the depression per se.

CHARACTERISTICS OF DEPRESSION

The literature on depression can seem overwhelming as, according to the American Psychiatric Association's *Diagnostic and Statistical Manual of Mental Disorders* (APA, 2013), there are several presentations of depressive disorders including: major depressive disorder, disruptive mood disorder, pre-menstrual dysphoric disorder, dysthymia and more. However, the APA also identifies common symptoms or factors underlying all depressive disorders, namely: loss of interest or enjoyment in activities; changes in weight and appetite; changes to sleep patterns; being either agitated or slowed up; loss of energy; feeling worthless or guilty; poor concentration and decision making; and suicidal thoughts and images. In CBT we work with presenting problems, it is these symptoms that we focus on and formulate. As a CBT therapist you can be confident that you can conceptualise the presenting problem whatever the presentation of the depressive disorder.

The classic Beck model of depression centres on the 'depressive cognitive triad', that is, a pattern of negative thinking about:

- oneself (guilt, blame, self-criticism) – 'I'm useless, worthless, inadequate, lazy ...';
- others/the world, and current and past experience (selective attention to the negative, global negativity, etc.) – 'Nothing is worthwhile, everything works out badly, no one cares about me ...';
- the future (pessimism, hopelessness) – 'It will always be like this, I'll never get better, there's nothing I can do ...'.

More recently depressive cognitions in the form of images have been the focus of research (see Holmes, Blackwell, Burnett-Heyes, Renner & Raes, 2016 for an outstanding review). Images take the form of negative views of past events and negative imagery of the future. When the latter are particularly intense and reflect suicidal ideation, we refer to them as 'flashforwards'. These have been associated with elevated risk of suicide, so do enquire about them in assessment. Holmes et al. (2016) also suggest that depression is associated with impoverished positive imagery and an inability to voluntarily generate specific images. Given that images are particularly emotionally evocative, the depressed person with few positive images would experience less positive affect and would struggle more to create them. A treatment implication might be that we should be conscientious in helping depressed clients not just to generate more positive statements, but to visually imagine the new possibility.

A depressed person not only has to battle with the negative *content* of their inner world, but also with unhelpful cognitive *processes*. Perception, interpretation and recall of events may all be negatively biased, so that depressed people are more likely to *notice* information that is consistent with their negative view, more likely to *interpret* any information negatively and more likely to *remember* negative events. Negative events are typically attributed to stable, global and internal factors and seen as having lasting consequences and implications for self-worth (Abramson et al., 2002), for example, 'This is my fault', 'I always mess up like this', 'It just shows how useless I am'. Positive events, on the other hand, are attributed to temporary, specific and external factors, with no lasting consequences – 'That was just a lucky break', 'It's the exception that proves the rule', 'It only worked out because my wife helped me'.

In addition, the cognitive process of rumination is characteristic of depression. Like worry, it can be a benign and even helpful cognitive process in small doses, but the depressed person gets locked into cycles of self-recrimination and doubt. This both deepens depression and impairs problem solving.

Alan became depressed shortly after his lover left him. He struggled with flashbacks of the ending of the relationship (which grieved him) and intrusions of their joyful times (which left him feeling bereft). Each memory triggered a preoccupation: 'If only I had been more attentive; If only I had seen this coming; Is there something wrong with me?; I'll never be happy again; I can't stop thinking about him with someone else.' These kinds of thoughts and images intruded throughout the day and night. Once one arrived it was as if it fed the next and he found himself caught in a spiral of increasing grief. When this happened, he lost sleep, he lost sense of time and he lost motivation to do anything.

The primary symptoms of depression are often exacerbated by secondary negative or self-defeating thoughts *about* the symptoms of depression, thus giving rise to further vicious circles. For example:

- Loss of energy and interest lead to thoughts such as 'It's not worth it, I'll wait until I feel better'.
- Poor memory, concentration and so on may lead the client to think 'I'm stupid' or 'I must be going senile'.
- Loss of sexual interest and irritability may be interpreted as indicating 'My marriage has major problems'.

COMMON MAINTENANCE PROCESSES

Figure 12.1 shows some of the common maintenance cycles in depressed people (as always, these are possibilities to explore, not rules to force your clients to obey!). First, there is a possible vicious circle linking depressed mood with negative biases and negative interpretations of symptoms, which leads to a negative view of the self, thus maintaining the depressed mood. Second, those negative biases and symptoms of depression may lead to reductions of activity ('I'm too tired, there's no point …'), which maintains the low mood because activities that previously gave pleasure or a sense of achievement are lost. Finally, the depressive biases and symptoms may lead to reduced attempts to cope and deal with problems, which leads to increased hopelessness and thus reinforces the depression.

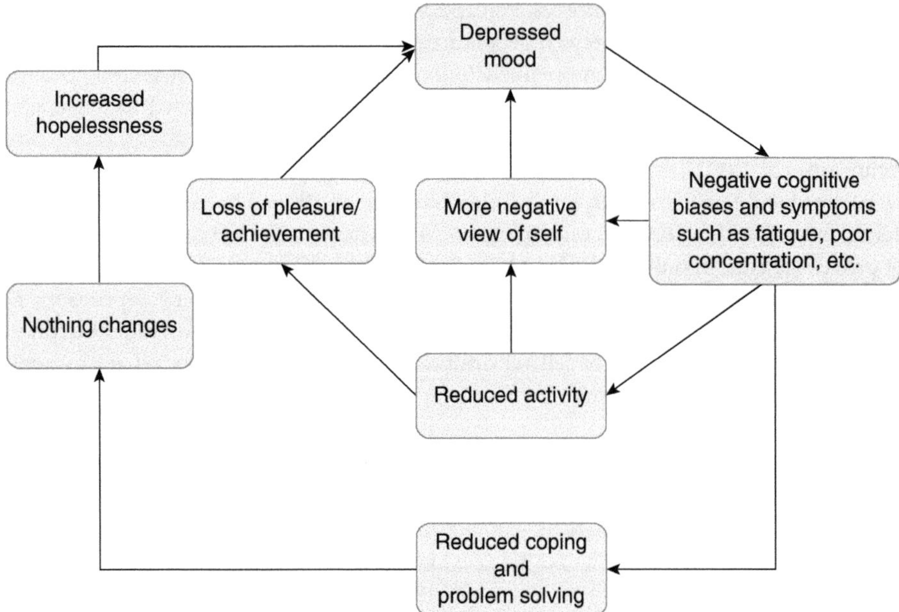

Figure 12.1 Common maintenance processes in depression

Moorey has established six maintenance cycles common to depression and he sees these as the basis for 'Growing a vicious flower' (2010), that is, devising a simple diagrammatic maintenance formulation similar to the 'vicious flower' described in Chapter 4. The cycles are:

- Automatic negative thinking.
- Rumination/self-attack.
- Withdrawal/avoidance.
- Unhelpful behaviour(s).

- Mood/emotion.
- Motivation/physical symptoms.

These form feedback loops around the central experience, 'Depression' forming a diagnosis-specific vicious flower. Although not all depressed clients will experience all of the 'petals' of this flower, these six cycles are worth exploring.

It follows from the above account that the goals of CBT for depression will usually include:

- helping your client identify and step back from negative cognitions;
- helping your client to counteract negative cognitive biases and develop a more balanced view of himself, the world and the future;
- restoring activity levels, especially activities that bring a sense of pleasure or achievement;
- increasing active engagement and problem solving.

As always, your task as therapist is to construct a formulation that makes sense for you and your client and then to devise cognitive behavioural strategies that will help to break maintaining cycles. The main approaches to cognitive strategies and BEs in depression are broadly similar to the standard approaches outlined in Chapters 7, 8 and 9, and therefore this chapter, after an outline of the broad approach to therapy, will focus on the interventions aimed at activity and problem solving, which are particularly characteristic of treatment for depression.

COURSE OF TREATMENT

CBT for depression usually contains the following elements, although, of course, this list needs adapting to the individual with whom you work. For instance, severely depressed clients may need more behavioural strategies, especially early in the course of therapy.

1. Identify the initial target problem list (i.e. a list of *specific* problems, not a general description such as 'depression'; a problem list might contain items such as 'Poor sleep', 'Difficulties in marital relationship', 'Lack of enjoyable activity', etc.).
2. Introduce the cognitive model and how it may apply to this client, through building a formulation (as in Chapter 4).
3. Begin work on reducing the symptoms, through behavioural or simple cognitive strategies. Introduce relapse management training as soon as you can.
4. In the central part of therapy, the main work is usually identifying and testing problem cognitions through thought records, discussion and BEs.
5. Towards the end of therapy, identify and modify unhelpful UAs and/or core beliefs as necessary, with a view to reducing the risk of relapse.

COMPONENTS OF CBT FOR DEPRESSION

CBT for depression usually contains the following components:

- Fundamental behavioural strategies, including activity scheduling and graded task assignments.
- Early-stage cognitive strategies, including distraction and counting thoughts.
- The main cognitive behavioural work of monitoring and testing ATs.
- Relapse management, including working with DAs and/or core beliefs, and revising earlier strategies (see Chapter 17's section on schema-focused work for ideas about how to work with more fundamental belief systems).

Beck et al. (1979) promoted a course of therapy lasting 15–20 sessions, with the first few sessions delivered at the rate of twice a week. Many ordinary clinical settings modify this to a standard weekly pattern and, perhaps, also reduce the total number of sessions. Clinical experience suggests that the protocol is sufficiently robust to withstand such modifications, but it is worth considering whether more frequent sessions are both desirable and feasible in particular cases.

ACTIVITY SCHEDULING

Activity scheduling is one of the core therapeutic techniques in CBT for depression (Beck et al., 1979). It is based on the ideas embodied in the 'Reduction of activity' vicious circle in Figure 12.1, that is, the notion that one maintaining factor for low mood is the reduction of activity that commonly accompanies it, which in turn leads to a loss of enjoyment and achievement, thus maintaining the low mood. Activity scheduling was derived from basic behavioural ideas about the need to build up reinforcing activities but has since developed into a sophisticated cognitive strategy. In fact, current conceptions would construe activity scheduling partly as a specialised form of BE (see Chapter 9, and Fennell, Bennett-Levy & Westbrook, 2004).

THE WEEKLY ACTIVITY SCHEDULE (WAS)

The weekly activity schedule (WAS), illustrated in Figure 12.2, is the essential tool for activity monitoring and management. It is basically a simple timetable grid with hours of the day down one side and days of the week across the top, so that there is a slot for every hour of the day. The version shown here has sufficient hourly slots to accommodate most clients but can be adapted if, for instance, your client has severe early morning waking, so that the grid might need to start at 4 a.m. [see p.122] instead of 6 a.m. Note also that if you are making a WAS template, it is best to (a) make it much bigger than this so that there is more space to

write (one A4 or letter page is usually sufficient); and (b) leave the days of the week blank so that a client you are seeing, for example, on a Wednesday can start his WAS on that or the following day, filling in the 'days' column headings appropriately.

	Days of the week						
Time of day	**Wed**	**Thu**	**Fri**	**Sat**	**Sun**	**Mon**	**Tue**
a.m. 6–7							
7–8							
8–9							
9–10							
10–11							
11–12							
p.m. 12–1							
1–2							
2–3							
3–4							
4–5							
5–6							
6–7							
7–8							
8–9							
9–10							
10–11							
11–12							
a.m. 12–1							

Figure 12.2 The weekly activity schedule (WAS)

This figure is available to download from the companion website.

USING THE WAS AS A RECORD

The first stage of activity scheduling is to use the WAS as a self-monitoring tool, to gather information about the client's activities. This information may be used in two ways, as in the two approaches to BEs described in Chapter 9:

- The WAS may be used in the sense of *discovery*, simply to find out what is happening, how the client is spending his time and what activities are giving any pleasure or achievement (see below).
- The WAS may also be used in a spirit of *hypothesis-testing*. For example, for a client whose negative thoughts lead him to dismiss his efforts at coping as 'useless' or 'pathetic', the WAS can be used to get a more accurate record of what he is actually doing, in order to test the client's belief that he is 'useless'.

In either case, typical guidance for clients using a WAS should contain the following points:

- Complete the record *at the end of each hour*, or as close as possible to it (to avoid the effects of negative memory bias if you do it later).
- Each hour slot should contain:
    - a brief description of how you spent the time during that hour;
    - two numbers, labelled P (for Pleasure) and A (for Achievement).
- Use these numbers to say how much you *enjoyed* what you did during that hour (Pleasure) and how much you felt you'd managed something it was *hard* for you to do (Achievement). These numbers can be anywhere from 0 (none at all) to 10 (the most possible). So P1 would mean it was only slightly enjoyable, P8 would mean it was very enjoyable. In rating your Pleasure and Achievement, remember to use your current activity level as the standard. When you are well, it might not be much of an achievement to get up and dressed (it might rate only A0 or A1), but it might well be a considerable achievement when you are depressed (maybe even A8 or A9 on some days).
- Note that 'P' and 'A' don't necessarily go together. Some activities are pleasurable but don't give much sense of achievement (e.g. eating a bar of chocolate); some are achievements but not necessarily pleasurable (e.g. doing a chore); some activities may give you both (e.g. going to a social occasion when you didn't feel like it but ending up enjoying it).

Since Beck's original guideline for rating the WAS, it has been shown that 'purposefulness', not simply pleasure, is significant in elevating mood (Lejuez, Hopko, Acierno, Daughters & Pagoto 2001; Lejuez, Hopko & Hopko, 2011) and we would recommend considering both.

Figure 12.3 shows part of a completed WAS.

Time of day	Monday	Tuesday	....
a.m. 7–8	Got up, dressed P0 A5 Purposefulness 2		
8–9	Breakfast for children, to school P1 A6 Purposefulness 8		
9–10	Walked the dog P3 A4 Purposefulness 6		

Figure 12.3 A sample WAS

USING WAS RECORDS

There are three main things for you and your client to look for when the completed WAS is returned:

1. You can get a better picture of how active the client really is. Sometimes it shows that a person is actually doing more than he initially indicated – maybe even overworking. On the other hand, the record may show that indeed he is doing very little (in which case, increasing activity will be useful later).
2. Second, the record can help you see which activities, if any, give the client at least *some* sense of achievement and purposefulness and pleasure. When you start to think about changes, these are the activities it may be worth increasing.
3. Finally, you can use the information to plan changes. What does it suggest needs to change? Is the client spending long periods doing very little except feeling low? Does it look as if there are lots of chores that must be done, but very little enjoyable activity? Are there any activities the client enjoys at least a bit, or which improve his mood even a little and which he might do more of?

See Video 12.1: Getting results from a WAS.

In addition to these activity-specific observations, the WAS provides an excellent laboratory in which you and the client can begin to observe ATs and images, noticing how cognitions and behaviour affect each other and using this to encourage the client to start spotting cognitions in action (e.g. those that block activity). You can watch out for this kind of thinking and work with it via discussion or BEs. For example, if attempts to do a particular task are blocked by predictions along the lines of 'I won't enjoy it' or 'I'll only make a mess of it', then you could set up a BE to see how true that is.

Maria's WAS immediately showed that her life was currently divided between hectic activity, almost all of which consisted of necessary but unrewarding chores, followed by what she called 'collapsing in a heap', when she would just sit and stare into space (often ruminating about how useless she was). This monitoring helped her and her therapist to identify (a) the need to find some activity that she found pleasant or enjoyable, and (b) the fact that despite her constant chores, she placed no value on this activity and still saw herself as 'useless'.

USING THE WAS AS A PLANNING TOOL

The next step is for you and your client to use what you have learned to plan future activity. There are three common ways to improve mood through activity:

1. To increase the overall level of activity if it is low.
2. To focus specifically on doing more of the things that give the client some sense of pleasure, purposefulness and achievement. If nothing is giving much pleasure at the moment, then it is worth thinking about things the client *used* to enjoy and plan to restart some of those.
3. Activity scheduling can be used as a way of doing BEs to test out negative cognitions about activity. For example, using a WAS to monitor and rate Pleasure, Purposefulness and Achievement may enable your client to combat 'all or nothing' thinking that tends to see Achievement as being either complete success or complete failure.

During this phase, instead of simply monitoring what he does, the client uses the WAS as a timetable to plan increases in activity and, specifically, activities identified as providing some pleasure or achievement. How much detail is needed, and how much activity should be aimed for, will depend on the individual client: in general, the more depressed the client, the more detailed planning he may need and the lower the initial goals for activity may need to be. Early on, you may need to be closely involved in planning, but later the client can take on more of this task for himself.

Maria agreed to construct with her therapist an activity plan (Figure 12.4) that still had time for necessary chores but which also started to build in some time for activities that she used to enjoy, such as watching movies on DVD. An important, although difficult, area for her was re-establishing social contacts. Although she was generally a sociable person who enjoyed contact with others, she had become almost completely socially withdrawn after her years of depression.

Time of day	Monday	Tuesday
...	...	...
p.m. 7–8	Make and eat supper: choose an easy ready meal that I used to like a lot.	
8–9	Ring sister to arrange to go out for somewhere. Chat and catch up.	
9–11	Watch movie: choose a DVD that I *want* to see.	
...	...	

Figure 12.4 Excerpt from Maria's activity plan

GRADED TASK ASSIGNMENT

The best general principle in planning activity is 'graded tasks'. In other words, aim to build up activity step by step, rather than attempting to go in one jump from low or no activity at all to being very busy. Because of a depressed person's extreme sensitivity to any possibility of failure, it will usually be counterproductive to agree over-ambitious tasks. If the task is not completed, it will be likely to be counted as a failure and taken as further reason to lose hope. It is usually better to agree a smaller but manageable task. For example, if your client wants to take up reading again after giving up because of concentration difficulties, then it is unlikely that he will be able to read a whole novel by next week. It will usually be better to negotiate a target he believes he can achieve, even if this is only to read one page by next week (but make sure that the target does not get so small that the client sees it as trivial).

Make sure that you have shared a rationale that will motivate your client to take part in an activity that will no doubt seem risky and challenging. Be clear about the starting point (what your client currently does) and the end point (ensuring that this is realistic). Then, together create a series of manageable steps linking the two. The general rule is that a step should stretch a person but not over-stress them. A useful question in agreeing the next step is: 'Given that you can do x, what do you imagine you could now do if you stretched yourself?' Then you need to plan taking this step (rehearsing in imagination or *in vivo* if appropriate) and to introduce trouble shooting and contingency plans, so that you maximise the experience being as manageable as possible.

Although Maria wanted to get back into social relationships, she was very anxious about how she would manage, and about how others would respond if she tried to make contact. A step-wise programme was therefore agreed, starting with making a brief phone call to her sister, with whom she still had some contact, and working up towards approaching friends with whom she had lost contact and trying to arrange to see them. Only one old contact failed to respond positively to Maria's approaches, and discussion in session allowed her to keep this in proportion to the many positive reactions she had.

EXERCISE

There is growing evidence that reasonably high levels of physical exercise may have a significant effect on depression, with some studies finding effects comparable to anti-depressants (Greist & Klein, 1985; Martinsen, Medhus & Sandvik, 1985). Current NICE guidance (2009) includes a recommendation for structured physical activity as a possible low intensity intervention for people with 'persistent sub-threshold depressive symptoms or mild to moderate depression', adding that such activity should:

- be delivered in groups, with support from a competent practitioner;
- consist typically of three sessions per week of moderate duration (45–60 minutes) over an average of 12 weeks.

It is therefore worth encouraging clients to make exercise sessions a part of their activity planning, particularly as it is often experienced as purposeful or pleasurable (see also

Chapter 10). It has been our experience that some clients initially engage more easily with physical activity than with some of the CBT interventions that require more intellectual application. For example, some adolescents or people with learning disabilities might more readily take to physical exercise and become engaged with CBT that way.

COMMON PROBLEMS IN ACTIVITY SCHEDULING

LACK OF PLEASURE

It is important to realise that in the early stages of fighting depression, people are not likely to enjoy anything as much as they did before the depression. It is important to forewarn clients that initially they will probably have to force themselves to do things even though they do not derive much pleasure from them. Persevering should at least give them some sense of achievement, and, eventually, the enjoyment should return as well. It is also important to convey the idea of pleasure as a continuum, not 'all or nothing'. We are looking for *some* increase in enjoyment, not an instant return to full enjoyment.

EXCESSIVE STANDARDS

It is also important to recognise that achievements do not have to be at the level of winning the Nobel Prize to be worthwhile. Spending 10 minutes tidying up a messy kitchen drawer can help a person feel he has done something useful today, and it may be a considerable achievement. It is important to encourage realistic standards in evaluating tasks and activities. What was easy when your client was well may be difficult (and therefore warrant a higher achievement score) when he is depressed.

VAGUE PLANNING

When planning activities, it is better to be specific. In other words, try to help the client move from vague goals like 'I must do more' to specific activities at specific times (e.g. 'Go and buy that birthday card on Wednesday morning'). If a goal or target is vague ('I must do more') it is all too easy for the depressed person to downgrade achievements or to 'move the goal posts': 'I didn't really do anything, I bought a few things in town. So what? Anyone can do that.' If buying the card is set up as a specific task, then there is no doubt that a particular goal has been achieved and it is more difficult to dismiss it.

COMMON PROBLEMS WITH GRADED TASK ASSIGNMENT

TOO MUCH TOO SOON

It is not unusual for clients to agree to rather ambitious steps. This can be because they expect too much of themselves, because they are trying to please their therapist or because dichotomous thinking has forced them into an extreme position. The outcome can be a sense of failure if the task is not achieved, or disappointment if it is achieved at great emotional or physical cost.

Make sure that your clients appreciate that there is a spectrum of activity that they can steadily work along and that this is fine by you. If they are over-ambitious and have a setback, take the opportunity to revise relapse management principles and learning from lapses.

TOO LITTLE

Sometimes the problem is that progress is held back by caution. If your client is avoidant, then it is crucial not to collude with this. If you (and your client) are uncertain of their capability, set up a behavioural experiment with sufficient contingency plans to accommodate possible over-ambition. In this way you might encourage a timid person to take a (safe) risk and learn more about his capabilities.

JACOBSON'S DISMANTLING STUDY AND THE BEHAVIOURAL ACTIVATION APPROACH

Anyone who might doubt the value of activity scheduling and behavioural methods in treating depression should read Jacobson et al.'s (1996) fascinating study comparing outcomes between three versions of CBT for depression, based on 'dismantling' the classic Beckian therapy. One treatment was normal Beckian therapy, and this was compared with two 'stripped down' versions: one in which therapists used only the behavioural components of CBT (including activity scheduling) and one in which they used both behavioural and cognitive methods but only at the level of ATs, with no direct targeting of assumptions or core beliefs. What they found was that all three treatments produced similar outcomes and *also similar changes on measures of negative cognitions*. One possible conclusion is that different methods may achieve the same end result of cognitive and emotional change by different pathways. Following on from this study, colleagues of Jacobson's elaborated their behavioural treatment into a new therapy for depression known as 'behavioural activation' (see Chapter 17).

COGNITIVE STRATEGIES IN DEPRESSION

There are two phases of cognitive work in classic CBT for depression. In the first phase the aim is to help the client get some symptom relief by using simple strategies to reduce the impact of negative cognitions on mood (with the useful secondary aim of providing evidence about how thoughts and images can influence mood). In the second phase, the unhelpful cognitions are tackled more directly, with the aim of helping the client consider them more carefully and, if appropriate, find alternative perspectives through the methods discussed earlier in this book: finding alternatives, looking for evidence, devising BEs and so on.

EARLY-STAGE COGNITIVE STRATEGIES

The goals of these strategies are to distract the client from his negative cognitions, and/or to change his attitude towards them. For example, rumination is a powerful cognitive process in depression, pulling a person deeper into depression, and the simple intervention of distraction (see Chapter 8) has been shown to reduce rumination in depression (Nolen-Hoeksema, 1991). This and other exercises are designed to promote a change of attitude towards NATs and negative images, too. Instead of getting 'swallowed up' by them, the aim is to get some distance from them, for the client to see them as 'just thoughts' or 'just images' rather than obvious truths about themselves or the world. Counting the cognitions can help – not paying any other attention to them, just counting them, with the same attitude one might have in spotting how many pigeons there are in one's neighbourhood: 'There's one … and another … oh, and there's another!' One metaphor to describe this approach is to imagine one's stream of thoughts as a rather dirty river, with all kinds of garbage in it. Initially, your client may be like someone who has fallen into the river and is being swept along by it, surrounded by all the garbage. The new attitude is like climbing out of the river and standing on the bank, watching it all go by; the garbage is all still there, but the client is likely to be less affected by it. This is similar to the mindfulness approaches outlined in Chapter 17.

MAIN COGNITIVE STRATEGIES

The bulk of a course of CBT for depression uses the approaches outlined in Chapters 8 and 9. Sessions will include, in varying proportions according to the stage of therapy and the client's reaction to therapy:

- identifying unhelpful cognitions, using self-monitoring, thought records, in-session mood changes and so on;
- verbal discussion of the cognitions, to examine their accuracy and helpfulness;
- identifying realistic alternatives;
- using BEs to gather evidence that will help the client to test out negative cognitions and the new alternative possibilities.

DEVELOPING COPING IMAGES TO SUPPORT COGNITIVE CHANGE.

See Video 12.2: Developing positive imagery: coping in the future and Video 12.3: Developing positive imagery: a safe body image.

Once Alan had learnt to use distraction to 'put the brakes on' his negative ruminations, his mood stabilised, his sleep improved and his agitation eased. He was still depressed but now he could engage better in therapy. Initially, activity scheduling also helped him to get active again and feel more in control and more purposeful. This alone helped him to combat the prediction that he would never feel happy again. Next, he began to keep thought and image logs and he and his therapist identified and addressed several cognitive biases and cognitions. Partly because his mood was improving and partly because he was being well coached by his therapist, he soon found he was able to stand back from his troubling thoughts and images and see them differently. He could distract himself from intrusions and he began to counter many of his depressing thoughts. His thoughts that he was unworthy of his partner were readily dismissed with: 'Now I realise that I gave a lot in this relationship and his demands were unreasonable – I've talked with friends and they saw this a long time ago.' A further NAT emerged that was harder to shift: that he could not trust his instincts about relationships because he had been so wrong about his ex-partner. Keeping a log of all those times his interpersonal instincts were right began to chip away at his self-doubt.

MEDICATION

CBT is, of course, not the only effective treatment for depression, and in particular, anti-depressant medication is helpful for many depressed clients. There is currently less concern about dependence and withdrawal for anti-depressants, compared to anxiolytics, and there is no conflict between pharmaceutical treatment and psychological therapy. In fact, there is some evidence that for people with more severe depression, the combination of both forms of treatment is better than either alone (e.g. Thase et al., 1997; NICE, 2009).

DEALING WITH SUICIDALITY

The risk of suicide in depressed clients should not be overestimated – the vast majority of depressed people do not commit suicide – but it clearly needs to be monitored and taken seriously. You should respond to any sign of suicidal ideation, sometimes even if it means breaking confidentiality. For this reason, you should always be very clear *at the outset* of treatment that you are bound by law to break confidentiality if you think that your client is a risk to themselves (or others). Do not delay telling your client this; it is less likely to disrupt your therapeutic relationship if you disclose your ethical obligations when you begin therapy.

Professional consensus is that amongst the risk factors for suicide are the following (Peruzzi & Bongar, 1999):

- acute suicidal ideation, particularly involving planning;
- a history of suicide attempts, or family history of suicide;
- the medical seriousness of any previous attempts;
- severe hopelessness;
- attraction to death;
- recent losses or separations;
- misuse of alcohol.

As we have already noted, suicidal imagery in the form of 'flashforwards' also heightens risk.

MANAGEMENT OF SUICIDAL CLIENTS

You need to have a basic management plan in place so that you can safely continue CT. The elements of such a plan might include:

- making sure that the client is either supervised or has immediate access to support whenever he needs it;
- taking steps to help the client or others to remove any easily accessible means of suicide (e.g. potentially toxic medication, poisons, ropes, guns, car keys, etc.);
- establishing ways of managing suicidal crises, should they occur: for example, arranging for the client to contact a friend or family member, or contact a crisis team if one is available. Ensure that plans are specific and clear and, perhaps, have a written copy for your client to carry around;
- working on building up the therapeutic relationship so that the client will see you as someone who is trustworthy and understanding and who can offer some credible hope;
- considering seeing if the client will agree at least to postpone suicide and not carry it out until a certain time has passed (e.g. not before your next meeting)
- using aspects of therapy to 'play for time' until the crisis has passed: for example, encourage engagement in therapy and curiosity about where it is going; 'build bridges' from the end of one session to the next session ('That's interesting – shall we explore that next time?').

EXPLORING AND WORKING WITH REASONS FOR SUICIDE

It is important to give clients a space in which to talk about suicidal thoughts and to approach the topic in an empathic and matter-of-fact way that gives the clear message that you understand and that the topic is not off limits. You will not make someone more likely to commit suicide by asking about their suicidal thoughts, and you may have a chance to prevent suicide if the topic is in the open. Important aspects of this discussion will include:

- exploring thoughts *and imagery*, remembering that 'flashforward' suicidal images increase risk;
- exploring the reason for suicide – there are two common main categories of reason:
    - to escape from an unbearable life (e.g. 'I can't go on – it's the only way out') – this is probably the most common reason for suicide, and the most dangerous;
    - to solve an external problem (e.g. to hold onto a relationship, take revenge or elicit care);

- building up with the client reasons for living versus reasons for dying, including past reasons for living which might become valid again in future;
- exploring the beliefs leading to hopelessness and using guided discovery to help elicit information that might be inconsistent with those beliefs;
- working on a problem area that has a high probability of being resolved fairly quickly, so as to decrease hopelessness – promoting realistic hope is crucial in suicide management;
- using problem solving for 'real-life' problems that are leading to hopelessness (see below).

STRUCTURED PROBLEM SOLVING

There is some evidence both that depressed people have deficits in social problem solving and that teaching structured problem solving can be an effective therapy for people with depression (see e.g. Nezu, Nezu & Perri, 1989; Mynors-Wallis, Davies, Gray, Barbour & Gath, 1997; Mynors-Wallis, Gath & Baker, 2000). This may be especially useful for those whose formulation includes something like the poor coping/hopelessness maintenance cycle outlined in Figure 12.1; it may also be helpful in dealing with suicidal ideas as outlined above.

The main steps in problem solving are:

- *Identify the problem to work on*: It is important to be clear about the exact nature of the problem. For example, not just 'Problems in my marriage' but something more precise, such as 'My wife and I don't talk together enough' or 'We never have any time to go out together'.
- *Brainstorm – possible ways of solving this problem*: This stage can be difficult, particularly with problems that have been around for a long time. Clients may have an immediate negative response to every solution they think of: 'That wouldn't work' or 'I've tried that'. To overcome this, it can be helpful to start with 'brainstorming', in other words the client tries to come up with as many ideas as he can, without any judgement at this stage as to whether they are useful, sensible or even possible. The aim is to generate lots of approaches, no matter how wild or impractical they may seem. The rule is to write down anything that comes into his mind as a possible solution, no matter how daft. The reason for this is that even wild solutions may generate other thoughts which might be useful. With more severely depressed clients, it may be helpful for the therapist to begin with some suggestions if the client is completely stuck.
- *After generating the list of possible solutions, work out which solution, or combination of solutions, seems to be the best*: Again, it is best to structure this process so that your client thinks carefully about each possible solution, without dismissing any of them too early. Only solutions that are clearly unacceptable should be disposed of immediately.

- *Weigh up solutions*: Think systematically about the pros and cons of each, making sure you consider both long- and short-term ones. Take the first possible solution and make a list of what the advantages and disadvantages of that solution would be. Then do the same for the next possible solution, then the next, and so on. Use this list of pros and cons to pick out and rank-order the best few solutions.
- *Pick the solution that seems to offer the most favourable balance*: Two problems can arise here:
  - It can sometimes be that no solution emerges as positive overall: they all have more negatives than positives. If that is the case, and you really have gone through every possible solution, then the client needs to accept that he has no choice but to pick the least bad one – it may not be good, but it is still better than the others.
  - You may find that when you go through the list, they all come out pretty much the same, with your client feeling that there is no clear winner. If that is so, and again if you really have gone through all possible solutions, then just pick one solution randomly and try that. Sometimes, the process of doing this will help the client realise that actually he does have a preference for one solution, because he finds himself wishing he had picked that one.
- *Use the principle of 'small steps' once a solution has been identified*: As always, small steps are usually better than giant leaps, because they are more likely to be successful and thus generate hope. Ask your client to think about what would be the first step towards carrying out his preferred solution. For instance, if he has decided a solution to a problem would be to find a new job, the first step might be to buy the local paper and look at what kind of job is available at the moment. It is probably much easier to do that first step than to imagine the whole process of ending up with a new job. Take it one step at a time.
- *Put into action whatever is the first step to a solution, and then review how it went*: Does this solution seem to be along the right lines? If not, why not? Do you need to modify the initial plan in the light of what has happened? Even solutions that look good on paper may turn out not to work in practice. Don't worry if this happens. By trying it out, your client will probably have learned something useful which may help him work out a better solution. If some major problem arises when he tries to put his solution into practice, you may need to identify that as a new problem. Then start the whole process again so that you can first find a solution to that problem.
- *Continue this process until the problem is solved or it is clear that there are no possible solutions*: You can go round and round the cycle of identifying problems, solutions and steps towards solutions until the problem improves. Of course, some problems may not have any practical solution – but beware of jumping to that conclusion too quickly. If there really is no solution, then you probably need to go back to cognitive strategies to help the client find a different way of reacting to the situation.

POTENTIAL PROBLEMS WHEN WORKING WITH DEPRESSED CLIENTS

THE NATURE OF DEPRESSION

It is obvious – but nevertheless important to remember – that a depressed person is often negative in his thinking, lacking in drive and energy, and hopeless about the possibility of change. Depression can also result in a 'depressing environment': for example, your client's depression leads to his losing his job, or to marital difficulties, which then tend to maintain his low mood. It is therefore hardly surprising that you may find yourself struggling to engage clients. They may find it difficult to take any action, greet every suggestion with 'That will never work' and be tempted to give up at every real or imagined 'failure'.

Therapists too may have difficulties in working with depression. You may find yourself 'infected' by the client's pessimism, silently thinking that he is right and things are indeed as bad as he thinks they are. Of course, that could be an accurate view, but you should be careful about buying into it too easily without a great deal of evidence. Although it may be the case that your client is facing genuine difficulties and at least some of his negative thoughts are accurate, there is usually still room for questioning and looking for alternatives. It may be bad, but it is usually not *so* bad that 100 per cent of people would feel as the client does, so there must be some room for alternative views. On the other hand, it is also important not to get so bound up with being so sceptical and positive that you come across as unempathic or impatient. Clients need to know that you understand where they're coming from before you start trying to help them see where they might go to. Kennerley, Mueller and Fennell (2010) have some ideas on managing the impact of such difficulties on yourself. The problems described here may be particularly difficult when working with chronic and severe depression (see Moore & Garland, 2003 for a useful guide to such work).

HOPELESSNESS AND 'YES, BUTS'

As we have just noted, most depressed clients will inevitably bring to therapy some of the negative thinking that pervades the rest of their lives. They will be hopeless about the possibilities of change and tend to have negative thoughts about therapy, with 'Yes, but' being a common reaction to attempts to broaden their thinking. For you, as a therapist, it is important not to be too influenced by this way of thinking but to remain (realistically) optimistic and to understand that your client's reactions to therapy are part of the depressive syndrome. Graded task assignments, as discussed earlier in this chapter, are a good way to get small successes that will help to build the client's confidence. BEs are also a good way to drive home verbal discussions so that new ways of thinking are not just vague theoretical possibilities but are tested out in action. Sometimes such 'Yes, buts' reflect extremely fixed fundamental beliefs, so it may be helpful to consider some of the schema-focused strategies in Chapter 17.

SLOW PACE

Depressed clients may be slowed up in their thinking and behaviour and, even if they are not, the pace of sessions and the speed of change early in treatment is likely to be slow.

It is helpful if you are prepared for this, and adapt to it, but do not become discouraged by it. Monitoring progress using some measure such as the BDI (Chapter 5) may also be useful in picking up small but steady changes.

FEEDBACK IN SESSIONS

As noted in Chapter 11, asking the client to give you feedback on a session is a standard part of CBT. However, it may be particularly important to encourage the depressed client to do this openly, because his negative bias makes it particularly likely that some words or behaviour on your part may be misinterpreted as being critical or rejecting of him. For the same reason, it is always worth noting and enquiring about any apparent decline in mood during a session: what went through your client's mind when that happened?

RELAPSE

As we have already noted, relapse is a particular problem in depression, with estimates that as many as 50 per cent of depressed clients will relapse within two years of the end of 'successful' treatment. It is therefore especially important to develop a relapse management plan (see Chapter 6) and perhaps also consider offering 'continuation' therapy at lower intensity to help maintain and consolidate gains as this has been shown to be effective for some (Vittengl, Clark & Jarret, 2010).

SUMMARY

- The key feature of cognition in depression is the 'cognitive triad', consisting of negative thinking about oneself, the world and the future:
    - perception, interpretation and recall of events all tend to be negatively biased.
- The main components of CBT for depression may include:
    - behavioural strategies such as activity scheduling;
    - early negative cognition management strategies such as distraction;
    - the main cognitive work of testing negative cognitions through discussion and BEs;
    - relapse management, including possible work on DAs and core beliefs.
- The weekly activity schedule (WAS) is a valuable tool in monitoring, and later counteracting, the loss of activity that is a common feature of depression, as well as providing useful data about negative thinking.
- Suicidal thoughts represent a particular challenge in depression and need to be tackled openly and carefully.
- Structured problem solving can be helpful in tackling genuinely negative situations.

LEARNING EXERCISES

These learning exercises are available to download from the companion website.

REVIEW AND REFLECTION:

- Therapists sometimes find working with severe depression challenging. What are your own reactions to working with depressed clients? What thoughts or beliefs affect your work with this group? What is your reaction when working with someone who could be suicidal – have you learnt anything here that might help you?
- Although there are of course significant differences between ordinary low moods and a clinical depression, nevertheless most of us have *some* experience of low mood, and the odds are that the high prevalence of depression means that some readers of this book will have experienced that as well. Thinking about your own experience of low mood or depression, what kind of thoughts and behavioural changes were most prominent for you? Did they fit well with the outline in this chapter? Were there any differences and if so, what were they?
- Some therapists tend not to use activity scheduling much in depression, thinking it is 'not cognitive enough' or 'too simplistic'. What are your thoughts about its value? What are the possible advantages of using it with depressed clients?
- Have you ever found yourself as a therapist being 'infected' by a client's depression, that is, becoming convinced that things are just as bad as your client thinks? What effect did this have on the therapy?

TAKING IT FORWARD:

- If you have not used activity scheduling or problem solving much before, what plans can you make to try it out with the next suitable client? How will you evaluate its usefulness with this client?
- If you have not routinely asked your depressed clients about images as well as thoughts – try it out. See what happens, see how it might

(Continued)

(Continued)

inform your formulations, and observe the effect it might have on your communication and therapeutic relationship.

- **What could you do differently or how would you need to think differently to prevent future 'depressive infection'?**
- **Try to make a point of asking *every* client for feedback at the end of every session, and see what emerges. What kind of feedback do you get from depressed clients? Are there any common themes? What lessons for the future can you take from this?**

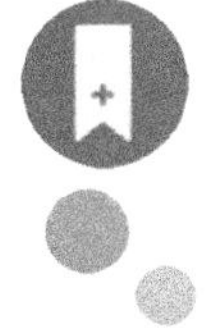

FURTHER READING

Beck, A.T., Rush, A.J., Shaw, B.F., & Emery, G. (1979). *Cognitive therapy of depression.* New York: Guilford Press.

As noted in Chapter 1, a classic of CT.

Martell, C., Addis, M., & Jacobson, N. (2001). *Depression in context: strategies for guided action.* New York: Norton.

The seminal book on the approach to depression known as 'behavioural activation', which grew out of the Jacobson dismantling study discussed in this chapter (see also Chapter 17 of this book).

Moore, R., & Garland, A. (2003). *Cognitive therapy for chronic and persistent depression.* Chichester: Wiley.

A very useful guide to adapting standard 'Beckian' CBT to the particular challenges of chronic, or treatment-resistant, depression, including helpful clinical examples.

Wenzel, A., Brown, G.K., & Beck, A.T. (2009). *Cognitive therapy for suicidal patients.* Washington, DC: American Psychological Association.

This is possibly the best CBT text for therapists working with suicidal clients: clearly written, very well informed and practical.

VIDEO LINKS

- **12.1 Getting results from a WAS**
- **12.2 Developing positive imagery: coping in the future**
- **12.3 Developing positive imagery: a safe body image**

13
ANXIETY DISORDERS

- Introduction
- Characteristics of anxiety and anxiety disorders
- Maintaining processes
- Treatment approaches
- Problems when working with anxious clients
- Summary
- Learning exercises
- Further reading
- Video links
  - 13.1 Graded practice plan
  - 13.2 Theory A versus Theory B

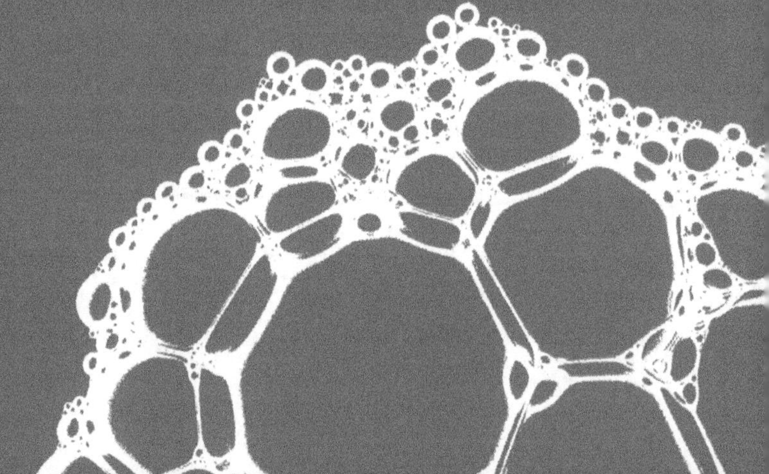

INTRODUCTION

The first treatment manual for CBT for *anxiety* disorders was published by Beck and his colleagues in 1985, and this was an exciting development in the world of CBT. It heralded the beginning of the revolution that has gradually applied CBT to an ever-wider range of problems.

The application of CBT to anxiety disorders was understandable given their prevalence (affecting 13.3 per cent of the US population – NIMH, 2001), and evidence of its efficacy in treating anxiety disorders has long been compelling (see e.g. Clark & Beck, 1988; Heimberg, 2002).

THE ANXIETY RESPONSE

It is important to remember that the anxiety *response* is a normal, vital reaction to threat. When we perceive danger, our bodies rapidly produce neurochemicals that prime us to respond to dangerous situations. The classic responses are 'fight' (challenging the fear directly) or 'flight' (escaping from or avoiding the fear), although 'freeze' (being physically or mentally immobile) is a third possible reaction. When faced with perceived threat, we feel fear and the mind and the body get ready to deal with it. The mind considers the worst-case scenario, and the body prepares to tackle it: breathing increases to provide more oxygen; the heart beats faster to get the oxygen-rich blood to key muscles; sweat glands become active to cool the body during activity; and blood is diverted away from the skin, which can result in uncomfortable sensations and paleness.

The response reflects the four systems referred to in Chapter 4: emotional, cognitive, physiological and behavioural. This quite complex response happens swiftly and efficiently every day.

A mother is standing at the side of the road close to her small son. A bus is heading towards them. The mother has a fleeting image of her son stepping into the road in front of the bus. She feels fear. Her adrenaline rises, she becomes tense, focused and primed for action. Swiftly, she takes her son's arm, despite his protestations, and holds him close to her as the bus passes them safely.

Thus, the anxiety response is a normal and largely unconscious process that regularly occurs in each of us and protects us. Anxiety only becomes a problem when the normal response is exaggerated or occurs in the absence of real threat.

Sally frequently had intrusive images and thoughts about her children being hurt on the street. Several times a day, she would feel very nervous about this. She never let them go out alone and she tried to take them everywhere in her car.

Geoff had suffered a panic attack and now lived in fear of having another. In order to minimise the likelihood, he tried not to vary his breathing for fear of hyperventilating; he moved slowly in order not to get light-headed; and he avoided situations which, he predicted, would be stressful. As a result, his life was very restricted.

In these examples, fears are exaggerated or dangers overestimated so that individuals feel compelled to take quite dramatic actions to alleviate their fears. They have each developed an anxiety disorder. It is important that your clients appreciate that their anxiety response is fundamentally normal but that it has become exaggerated so that it is no longer working well for them. The goal of therapy is not to eliminate the anxiety response but to manage it so that it works for a person not against him.

Sometimes the pathological fear arises because risk is overestimated:

- 'If I don't check the kitchen equipment something could over-heat and the house will catch fire.'
- 'The plane really could crash.'
- 'I'll be mugged.'
- 'I could have HIV.'

Sometimes it arises because ability to cope is underestimated:

- 'If the house burns down, I can't cope with the shame of having made my family homeless through my own stupidity.'
- 'I can't bear the thought of leaving my family alone – how will the children manage?'
- 'If I'm attacked it will bring back memories of when I was raped in my teens – I can't bear having flashbacks again.'
- 'If I have HIV, I don't think I could live with myself because I would have infected loved ones.'

Sometimes both sets of predictions occur in the same person – so do check this out in your assessment.

As interpretations of events determine responses, throughout this chapter you will note the use of the term '*perceived* danger' or '*perceived* threat'. This reminds us that two individuals can be in precisely the same situation but anticipate different consequences and, therefore, react in different ways.

Two musicians are waiting for the concert to begin. The first musician feels tense, her heart races and she concludes that these are bad signs. She is filled with dread: she fears that she will make a mistake, or that the audience will be hostile. This undermines her confidence further. The other musician feels tense, his heart races and he concludes that this is what will give him the energy necessary to perform. He is looking forward to the opportunity of performing, anticipating an enjoyable experience. Thus, in the identical situation, the first musician is worried and interprets her reaction as a bad thing, while the second is excited and assumes that his physical responses are helpful.

CHARACTERISTICS OF ANXIETY AND ANXIETY DISORDERS

Typically, dealing with anxiety is a linear process that comes to a natural conclusion. For example:

- Trigger → perceived threat → anxiety response → successful coping reaction → resolution of anxiety.
- A driver sees a child run out in front of a car → *production of adrenaline* → this promotes quick and focused thinking which enables the driver to brake and swerve in time → *resolution of anxiety.*
- A student learns of an impending assessment → *production of adrenaline* → the resulting focused thinking and raised energy levels enable the student to study efficiently → *resolution of anxiety.*

However, anxiety disorders are represented by a circular process (see Figure 13.1) in which cognitive and behavioural responses serve to maintain or worsen anxiety. For example:

- An anxious driver sees a child who he thinks is about to run out in front of his car → he is highly anxious and becomes physically tense and cannot think straight → he swerves to avoid a child who is not actually in the road and is reprimanded by another motorist for driving dangerously → this confirms that driving is hazardous and he remains a highly anxious driver.
- An anxious student learns of an impending oral assessment → she finds this threatening and experiences high levels of anxiety → her thinking becomes overly focused on the exam and she becomes so tense that she cannot study effectively → she does not perform well in the assessment; this promotes her belief that she is incapable, and she remains a highly anxious student.

The 'ultimate' fear cycle is probably 'fear of fear', where the experience of anxiety itself becomes aversive and is therefore avoided long after the original trigger for the anxiety has receded.

Roger thought that he had had a heart attack, but at the hospital he was reassured that he had experienced a panic attack. Roger was not totally relieved by this as he had found the panic attack so unpleasant. Now he lived in dread of it happening again. This of course elevated his fear, which made him feel more panicky and more prone to having a panic attack.

As we have seen, anxiety prepares the mind and body for dealing with danger: the mind is focused on the bad things that could happen, and the body is primed for action. Thus, anxiety comprises both psychological and physical symptoms, symptoms that become exaggerated and unhelpful in anxiety disorders. This is summarised in Figure 13.2.

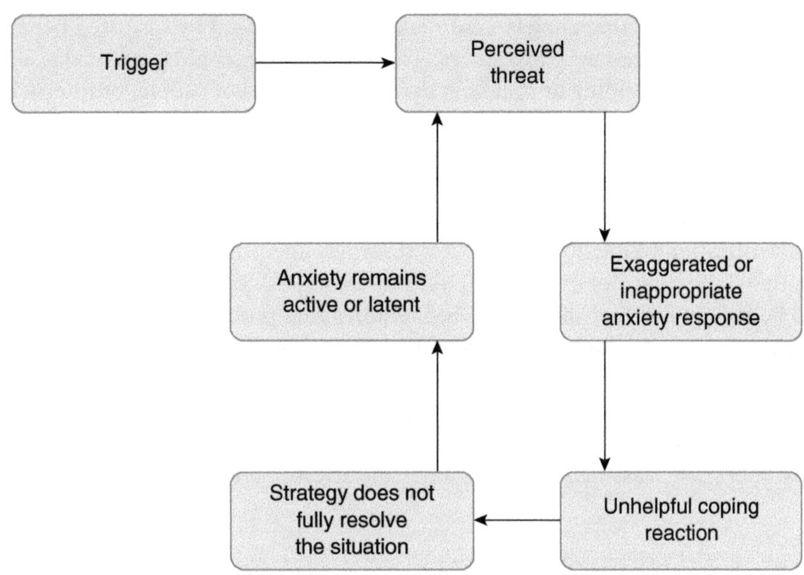

Figure 13.1 The cycle of problem anxiety

From anxiety	**To anxiety disorder**
A sense of threat	Overestimation of threat and/or overestimation of consequence; also underestimation of ability to cope, or available resources.
Focus on threat	Rumination, excessive worry, inability to think flexibly, persistent and threatening thoughts and images.
Apprehension	Fear of losing control, of going 'crazy' or of suffering health problems. Constant checking.
Temporarily exaggerated thinking	Habitual exaggerated thinking such as repeated catastrophisation, highly selective attention, pervasive 'all or nothing' thinking.
THE CONTINUUM OF PHYSICAL SYMPTOMS	
From anxiety	**To anxiety disorder**
Increased heart rate	Palpitations.
Muscular tension	Fatigue, trembling, muscular pain; e.g., chest, head.
Increased breathing rate	Dizziness, light-headedness, de-realisation or de-personalisation.
Changes in digestive system	Nausea, urge to go to the lavatory.
Changes in blood circulation	Blushing or paleness, unpleasant skin sensations.
Increased sweating	Excessive sweating.
In addition, chronic anxiety can be associated with sleep disorders and depression.	

Figure 13.2 Symptoms of anxiety

We have already noted that anxiety disorders are characterised by distorted beliefs about the dangerousness of certain experiences. They can be triggered by particular situations (e.g. being on a high building or speaking in front of a crowd of people) or internal stimuli (such as chest pains or an alarming thought).

There are many types of anxiety disorder, not always easily distinguished from each other. Below we look at the anxiety-related problems that you might encounter in your clinical practice. This list reflects the *Diagnostic and Statistical Manual of Mental Disorders* (DSM) classification (APA, 2013) of anxiety disorders and other common anxieties, which is commonly (although not exclusively) used to distinguish the different presentations. In order to be recognised as a 'disorder', DSM requires that problem anxiety is present for at least six months. The list does not include substance/medication induced anxieties and anxiety due to another medical condition, but it does include hypochondriasis (now defined as 'somatic symptom disorder' or 'illness anxiety disorder'), OCD (now classified under 'Obsessive-compulsive and related disorders') and acute stress disorder and post-traumatic stress disorder (now classified under 'Trauma and stressor-related disorders').

DSM-V DIAGNOSES OF ANXIETY DISORDERS AND OTHER COMMON ANXIETIES

- **Specific phobia:** describes a persistent fear of an object or situation and, often, a fear of one's reaction to it. Although a person no longer has to recognise that their anxiety is excessive in order receive a diagnosis (APA, 2013) the fear is often recognised as exaggerated, yet sufferers still tend to avoid the phobic stimulus (overtly or covertly), and their ability to function optimally is disrupted.

- **Panic disorder:** describes the repeated experience of panic attacks (panic attacks are described as sudden increases in anxiety accompanied by symptoms such as palpitations, breathlessness and dizziness). Such symptoms are often experienced as terrifying and are typically misinterpreted as signs of impending or current ill health, like a heart attack or a stroke. Panic disorder can occur with or without agoraphobia and agoraphobia is now a separate disorder.

- **Agoraphobia:** is a persistent fear of being in a place where one is vulnerable and escape is difficult, coupled with avoidance of such situations or severe difficulty enduring them. As with other anxiety disorders, the fear must be excessive.

- **Hypochondriasis:** describes an anxiety that is characterised by a preoccupation with, and fears of, having a serious illness, either now or in the future. *Somatic symptom disorder* describes undue worrying about chronic somatic symptoms; *illness anxiety disorder* is a condition in those who may or may not have a medical condition but who have heightened somatic sensations and an intense anxiety about the possibility of undiagnosed illness.

- **Social phobia/anxiety disorder:** is characterised by a marked and persistent fear of social or performance situations in which a person feels scrutinised by others and fears embarrassment or humiliation. The fear is restricted to social situations and is very focused on physical symptoms and behavioural performance.
- **Generalised anxiety disorder (GAD):** manifests as persistent and excessive worries, fears and negative thoughts about the future which then lead to distress and/or impairment of performance. It is commonly associated with irritability, muscle tensions and sleep disturbances.
- **Obsessive-compulsive disorder (OCD):** is characterised by recurrent obsessions (persistent and intrusive thoughts, images or impulses) and/or compulsions (compelling repetitive behaviour or rituals or mental acts intended to put right or neutralise the obsession). Sufferers realise that their fears are probably unfounded but remain compelled to act on them, trying to ignore, suppress or 'neutralise' the obsession with some other thought or action.
- **Acute stress disorder (ASD):** is diagnosed when a person, who has been exposed to a traumatic event, develops anxiety symptoms, a sense of re-experiencing of the event and marked avoidance of stimuli that trigger recollections of the trauma. The disturbance occurs within four weeks of the traumatic event and if it persists for longer than this it is reclassified as PTSD.
- **Post-traumatic stress disorder (PTSD):** occurs following an event or series of events deemed seriously threatening to oneself (or others). Symptoms include intrusive memories of the traumatic events (e.g. nightmares, flashbacks), avoidance, negative cognitions and mood, and hyperarousal.

Labels are all very well, but what is it like to experience an anxiety disorder?

SPECIFIC PHOBIA

People with phobia also tend to be on the look-out for signs of 'danger': so someone with a spider phobia would always check out the corners of a room or someone with a fear of heights would be vigilant in spotting road signs indicating bridges. Phobias can focus on a range of things: animals, the natural environment, specific situations and so on. Specific fears will trigger an elevation in blood pressure – with the exception of blood phobia, which causes it to drop. Thus, blood phobia, unlike other phobias, can lead to fainting.

Lucas was afraid of frogs. Ever since his older brother had frightened him by dropping one down his shirt, he had found them unbearable – their slimy skin and, worst of all, their quick unpredictable movements. As his work took him into the countryside a lot, his fear presented a problem. It limited his ability to go into damp areas, he was so busy looking out for frogs that his concentration was impaired, his physical nervousness was unpleasant and it also distracted him from the job.

AGORAPHOBIA

A particular form of fear whereby the sufferer fears being away from a place of safety or a place where escape is easy. In DSM-IV it was not regarded as a diagnosis in itself but associated with panic disorder (see below) as agoraphobia is commonly linked with the fear of having a panic attack or panic-like symptoms whilst away from a safe base. However, agoraphobia has been recognised as an anxiety disorder in its own right in DSM-V. Agoraphobia-like behaviours can be associated with other fears such as social anxiety or PTSD (see below), where it can be a safety-seeking behaviour to avoid social embarrassment or to avoid the triggering of a flashback, for example.

PANIC DISORDER

Sufferers of panic disorder have an enduring tendency to misinterpret benign experiences as indicative of catastrophe (such as impending death or madness) and this leads to repeated panic attacks. Agoraphobia is commonly co-morbid as it is a means of avoiding the situations which the sufferer believes will trigger a panic attack.

Monika described herself as a sensitive and highly-strung woman, but until recently she had been confident in her career and seemed to be coping well. Several months ago work stress and uncertainly took its toll and she went to the doctor with palpitations, dizziness and nausea. Monika believed that she was having a heart attack. Her GP assured her that this was a panic attack. At first she found it hard to accept that her experience was not heralding a heart attack, especially as the symptoms worsened over time and her chest pains became more intense. Each 'attack' seemed worse and her fears grew. Gradually she began to consider that she was experiencing panic – but this gave her little consolation as she was now terrified of its awful sensations. She became very sensitive to the slightest discomfort in her chest, and awareness of chest pain would usually escalate into a panic attack. She tried not to attend to sensations in her chest and refused to talk about panic with her therapist in case this triggered an attack.

HYPOCHONDRIASIS, SOMATIC SYMPTOM DISORDER, ILLNESS ANXIETY DISORDER OR HEALTH ANXIETY

All these terms are used to describe fears associated with health. Sufferers tend to be hypervigilant for, and to misinterpret, benign bodily symptoms as indications of illness. However, the experience is different from panic disorder in that panic attacks are extremely acute and immediate, while those with health anxiety experience more chronic concerns and preoccupations. Sufferers of health anxieties also tend to seek reassurance very actively but, typically, the reassurance does not have an enduring effect and the health concerns return.

Maya worried about developing cancer. She regularly checked her body for outward signs of the disease and she noted any sensation that could indicate cancer. In particular she noted headaches, which she feared indicated a brain tumour, abdominal discomforts (ovarian cancer), and changes in her bowel movements (bowel cancer). She veered between avoiding reading articles about health (in case she developed new concerns) to spending hours on the Internet reading about cancer symptoms. She visited her GP practice regularly to discuss her 'symptoms'. Typically she felt initial relief when reassured that she was healthy, but this soon wore off and doubt and worry would set in again. She tried not to turn to friends for reassurance because she knew that this now irritated them.

SOCIAL PHOBIA OR SOCIAL ANXIETY

The description of social anxiety disorder in DSM is specific, but extreme shyness can also be a problem in those who do not meet DSM diagnostic criteria (Butler & Hackmann, 2004). Avoidance is a common coping strategy in both social anxiety disorder and pathological shyness (including subtle avoidance such as using alcohol to cope in a social setting or avoiding eye-contact) and this helps to maintain the problem. It is sometimes also maintained because symptoms of anxiety impair performance (e.g. not being able to think clearly or shaking) and this enhances self-consciousness and social fears.

Lilia was perfectly confident and able in her work as long as she did not have to speak to a group of her peers or present herself to prospective customers. She went out of her way to avoid public speaking. If she knew that she would have to address her colleagues she would begin to worry that they would realise she was incompetent, and she would become so tense that she was unable to concentrate or sleep properly. She would first try to delegate the task to someone else, and if she was unable to do this she then tended to 'stick her head in the sand' and ignore the challenge. As a result, she was often ill-prepared for presentations and they never went as well as she had hoped. This confirmed to her that she had been incompetent and that it was now public knowledge! If she needed to meet a new customer, she had similar fears.

GENERALISED ANXIETY DISORDER (GAD)

Typically, sufferers of GAD are beset with 'What if' worries, pervading many aspects of their lives: 'What if I miss my connection?', 'What if I can't answer the questions?', 'What if my child is harmed?'. Worry is the main cognitive feature and it is not uncommon for sufferers to worry about worry, thinking that they are going mad. On the other hand, some clients attribute positive qualities to their worrying, such as 'Worrying means that I will be prepared'. However, worrying gets in the way of problem solving and so people with GAD tend not to deal well with challenges. They also tend to be intolerant of uncertainty, and this underpins reassurance-seeking behaviours.

Colin experienced high levels of worry and anxiety sometimes amounting to panicky feelings, physical tension and shortness of breath. He woke 'with a feeling of dread' and described 'worrying about everything: one worry just seems to merge into the next'. He worried about his daughter's health and academic progress, about financial matters and whether he will be made redundant and fail to meet the mortgage repayments, about his own health. He found it difficult to make decisions at work and frequently sought reassurance from his boss. He feared that his worry would lead to a 'mental breakdown'. He avoided watching the news and reading newspapers, especially anything to do with health and finance, to prevent himself from 'obsessing' about it.

OBSESSIVE-COMPULSIVE DISORDER (OCD)

OCD sufferers believe that they are responsible for the safety of themselves or others, and their fears centre, for example, on contamination (e.g. passing on germs by not washing hands sufficiently); disaster due to neglect to do something properly (e.g. switching off switches); behaving inappropriately as a consequence of having improper thoughts (e.g. thinking about swearing in church resulting in swearing). Some compulsions represent exaggerated helpful behaviours, such as washing excessively to avoid contamination, others represent more superstitious behaviours, such as ritualistic counting. In DSM-V, OCD is now grouped with disorders of preoccupation and repetitive behaviours such as body dysmorphia, hoarding, hair pulling and skin picking.

Joachin could not remember a time when he had not felt the urge to touch things in a ritualised way. He had an awful feeling of foreboding – that something bad would happen to him or a loved one – which was only relieved when he tapped a surface with his elbow or, if he was passing through a doorway, he rocked three times (in Joachin's mind this was like tapping the floor with his feet). He felt embarrassed by his actions as he knew that they were irrational and he had been teased at school for them; however, the sense that something bad might happen if he didn't was so strong and so very unpleasant that he always gave in to the urge in order to get mental and emotional relief.

ACUTE STRESS DISORDER (ASD)

ASD lasts for a maximum of four weeks. After this time, this presentation is diagnosed as PTSD (see below). The majority of cases of ASD remit naturally.

Alison had been sexually assaulted. Two weeks later she still could not sleep in her bedsit where it had happened even though she had redecorated the next day in order to try to eliminate the memory of her rape. She had taken leave from her studies because she found that she could not concentrate, was tearful and snapped at everybody. Being at home, though, made it worse: she was agitated and she couldn't eat or sleep properly. When she closed her eyes she saw her attacker's face and at night she was terrified by every noise and sometimes she felt as if he were there, as if she could smell him.

POST-TRAUMATIC STRESS DISORDER (PTSD)

In PTSD, concerns focus on an *enduring* sense of danger, although shame, disgust and anger are also reported. Typically, clients with PTSD can recall fragments of the traumatic event, or events, in detail, but the entire picture is misplaced, jumbled or incomplete (Foa & Riggs, 1993). A common and frightening traumatic memory is the very vivid 'flashback', which can give the sense of re-experiencing the traumatic event, but PTSD sufferers can also experience nightmares and other less vivid recollections. A common coping strategy is avoiding the triggers for these memories. DSM-V introduced a PTSD dissociative subtype, which is used when the condition has prominent dissociative symptoms.

Anton had witnessed a fatal shooting. Six months later he still had nightmares of the event and even in his waking hours he experienced brief 'flashbacks' to the killing. He felt as though he was in a constant state of physical tension and the slightest provocation made him jump. Anything that sounded like a shot would trigger a panic reaction and flashbacks. He could not walk past the shopping arcade where the shooting took place and more recently he had begun to avoid that part of the shopping district altogether – it brought back too many memories. He thought that he was going mad.

There are also anxiety disorders that fall outside a formal diagnostic category, and DSM-V uses the category 'Anxiety Disorder Not Otherwise Specified (Anxiety Disorder NOS)' (APA, 2013). This reminds us not to assume that clients will slip neatly into a category, and we should certainly not try to 'ease' them into one, but rather formulate or conceptualise each person's difficulties as they describe them.

MAINTAINING PROCESSES

Why do anxiety disorders persist? The key to this (and thus to managing problems) is identifying the maintaining cycles that explain their persistence.

There is a common pattern to the maintenance of anxiety problems (see Figure 13.3). In response to an internal or external trigger, the anxious person assumes threat or danger and either draws a catastrophic conclusion (something bad *has happened* and this has frightening implications for the future) or makes a catastrophic prediction (something bad *will happen*). Understandably, a person then tries to protect himself from the perceived threat. For example, someone with agoraphobia retreats to a 'safe' base or the client with health anxiety seeks reassurance. Such responses give immediate relief but do not challenge the validity of the belief. Thus, the person with agoraphobia fails to learn that it is possible to be in a public place without something terrible happening; the client with health anxiety does not learn to assure herself of her good health. In short, the original fears remain intact, ready to be triggered sometime later.

Essentially, anxiety disorders are perpetuated by how we feel, what we think and what we do. Clark (1999) has proposed that six processes maintain distorted beliefs about the

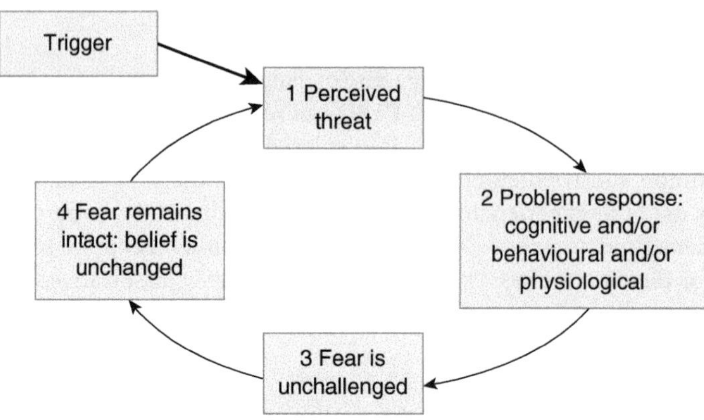

Figure 13.3 The maintaining cycle of anxiety

(irrational) dangerousness of certain situations, even in the face of evidence that the world is a safe place. These are summarised below and might give you some hypotheses about the nature of your clients' problem(s).

SAFETY-SEEKING BEHAVIOURS

Safety-seeking behaviours (Salkovskis, 1988) are behaviours or mental activities carried out in an attempt to minimise or prevent something bad from happening (see also Chapter 4). Of course, behaving in a safe way is not dysfunctional: looking both ways before we cross the road is a highly adaptive safety-seeking behaviour. However, standing at the kerbside repeatedly checking for cars, unable to take the risk of crossing, is an exaggerated and unhelpful safety-seeking behaviour – it is the latter that Salkovskis describes. In Figure 13.3, they fall into Box 2. These responses prevent a person from learning that they overestimate danger, because each 'safe' experience is attributed to the success of a safety-seeking behaviour (SB). The conclusion is that 'I only managed because of the behaviour' rather than 'I coped!'.

For example, a young woman with vomit phobia might get through the day without feeling nauseous and certainly without being sick. This should provide assurance that she is not at risk of vomiting. However, if she has been sucking mints as an SB, she will attribute her wellbeing to the sweets. Alternatively, a man with panic disorder who fears having a heart attack may move around slowly in order to remain safe; he may attribute his good health to slow movement rather than realise that he has a healthy heart. Colin and Maya, in the previous examples, both engaged in the unhelpful SBs of seeking reassurance, while Joachin's ritualised touching was his SB.

The distinction between 'helpful coping behaviour' and 'unhelpful safety behaviour' reflects the intention behind the behaviour and the perception of the outcome. For example, a man might relax his shoulders and slow his breathing in response to feeling tense and, subsequently, feel calmer. If he interpreted this as 'I'm only feeling better because I did my relaxation routine and if I had not done it something terrible would have happened', it is unlikely that he would develop confidence that he could manage tension and need not be afraid of it: the 'relaxation routine' would be an SB. However, if he concluded 'If I'm tense, there are things I can do about it – I relax', then relaxing is simply a functional coping behaviour, and he is likely to grow confident that he can cope. Rachman et al. (2008) remind us not to reject all SBs as anti-therapeutic because their judicious use, particularly in the early stages of therapy, can facilitate change by giving clients the confidence to take the first steps of engaging in treatment. Over time they can be encouraged to systematically drop unhelpful behaviours as their adaptive coping repertoire grows.

FOCUS OF ATTENTION

Focus of attention falls into two categories: attention directed *towards* threat cues, and attention directed *away* from them. Examples of the former would include Lucas who, because of his frog phobia, scans for signs of undergrowth or wet areas that could conceal a frog, or Lilia, with her social anxiety, who ruminates on her behaviour at work, concentrating on all the dissatisfying aspects of it. Increased focus of attention serves to emphasise the fear, as it is constantly in mind and because anyone who scans for threat is vulnerable to assuming the worst: thus a clump of moss 'is' a frog, bubbles on the water's surface 'is' frogspawn. In these ways, an inappropriately increased amount of fear is experienced.

Examples of attention being directed away from threat cues would include Lilia's 'head in the sand' strategy or the socially anxious person who avoids eye contact, or the road-traffic-accident victim who averts his gaze when nearing the site of the accident. In doing this, the fundamental fears are not faced, not even named in some instances, and it becomes impossible to review and test the beliefs about the perceived threat.

SPONTANEOUS IMAGERY

Several studies indicate that mental images can enhance the sense of threat (Ottavani & Beck, 1987; Clark & Wells, 1995). For example, the person with social phobia might hold a vivid mental picture of himself looking incompetent, or the client with panic disorder might have a catastrophic image of herself losing control. Such images appear to heighten anxiety. Imagery is particularly relevant in the maintenance of PTSD, where vivid traumatic intrusions are thought to maintain a sense of *current* threat to the individual and thus prevent anxieties from remitting.

EMOTIONAL REASONING

Emotional reasoning refers to the process of believing that 'If I feel it, then it must be so' (see also Chapter 8). As far back as 1995, Arntz, Rauner and van den Hout showed that anxious clients rate situations as being more dangerous than control subjects do – even when given information that assured them of safety. Anxious people conclude that there must be a threat because they feel anxious. Thus, based on her feelings, a highly nervous woman might not be able to identify danger but would *assume* it existed; or a man might feel anxious about his thoughts and thus *assume* that his thoughts are dangerous. Often, such assumptions further heighten anxiety.

MEMORY PROCESSES

Clark (1999) suggests that there are distortions of memory that account for the perpetuation of problem anxiety: namely, selective recall of threat and anxiety-provoking situations. 'Selective recall' means having a limited and blinkered recollection of how things were. Anxious individuals tend to have the capacity for more negative and traumatic recall of their own past experiences than do non-anxious individuals (Mansell & Clark, 1999). This, of course, helps maintain a view of the world as personally threatening. Selective recall also prevents someone from being able to appraise the bigger, more balanced, picture. Without this, fears cannot be put into perspective. The most striking example of this process is in PTSD, where sufferers have intense recollections or flashbacks that maintain a sense of current threat, whilst having an imprecise recall of the entire event – which would otherwise help to put the intense recollection into context and combat the impression of danger being current.

INTERPRETATION OF REACTIONS TO A THREAT EVENT

The conclusions that a person draws when experiencing anxiety symptoms can exacerbate the problem. For example, if someone with a perfectly normal initial response to threat jumps to the catastrophic conclusion 'This means that I'm going crazy!' or 'This means that I'm going to pass out!', then fear is heightened, anticipatory anxieties are provoked and this results in the use of avoidant strategies, which are likely to prolong the fears.

Another psychological process that has been associated with protracted or exaggerated anxiety is worry (Borkovec, 1994). Although a brief period of worrying is helpful as it guides our attention to potential threats (Davey & Tallis, 1994), prolonged worrying is unproductive and can even be undermining. For example, whilst on holiday, I might worry about losing my passport. This focuses my thinking: I check that I have my passport and I consider where I might put it for safety. A more anxiety-prone person might worry about losing his passport but continue this cycle of worry even though he had checked that he was carrying it. He might keep thinking 'but what if …' and increase his anxiety levels with each repetition of this (usually unanswered) question. This is unhelpful in several ways: worrying itself can be distracting and cause problems (in worrying about the passport, a traveller might forget his tickets, not note a gate change, leave behind some luggage); worry is an obstacle to problem solving (preoccupations about the passport could undermine the traveller's ability to focus on and sort out a minor problem arising at security); worry often exacerbates difficulties because it prevents more central concern(s) being addressed (worrying about the passport gave the traveller some respite from facing his marital problems and he again put off considering the state of his relationship).

Tom came to therapy for help with his concern about contracting a sexually transmitted disease (STD) back in his village in Eastern Europe. Exploration and reconsideration of his fear always ended in 'but what if I have caught it and it will show itself later?'. Over several sessions, he began to talk about the shame that he would experience if he had an STD and later spoke of his shame for having run from his village when he saw military police vehicles. He had later discovered that several members of his family had been shot by the military police that day and his active concerns about infection helped him to avoid the pain of dwelling on this. However, it also prevented his grieving and the resolution of that pain and shame.

Clearly, the groups of thinking biases described in Chapter 8 (selective attention, extreme thinking, relying on intuition, self-reproach) can also play a part in the maintenance of problem anxiety, so you need also to bear them in mind when understanding your clients' problems.

In summary, understanding the maintaining cycles that drive problem anxiety is fundamental to managing it. What implications does this then have for therapy? The beauty of identifying maintaining cycles is that we can then plan interventions to break these unhelpful patterns, and in the next section we will look at this.

TREATMENT APPROACHES

As we indicated earlier in this chapter, it is essential that you carry out a thorough assessment before attempting to classify your client's problem. You can find detailed guidelines on assessment in Chapter 4, and McManus (2007) and Butler et al. (2008) provide brief, but useful, guides to the assessment of anxiety. In those cases where it becomes clear that the difficulty does indeed fall into a recognisable DSM category, you are urged to use the established cognitive model and treatment protocols for that disorder. These are elaborated in the next chapter.

Earlier we outlined the generic anxiety cycle: a trigger taps into a fear, a person responds in a self-protective way (usually a form of avoidance), the fear is unchallenged and remains intact, ready to be triggered in the future.

John is so scared of confined spaces that he can no longer travel by air or public transport, he cannot use lifts and he will not ride in another person's car. His alarming prediction is that, in a confined space, he will not be able to get sufficient air and will suffocate. John protects himself as best he can: for example, if he has to travel, he will use his own car; he will choose a route that allows him to stop as he feels necessary; he will have the windows open to ensure that he gets enough air. The consequence of his use of safety behaviours is that he avoids the lack of air that he fears and thus his belief that something dreadful will happen remains intact.

Pamela fears contamination of herself and loved ones and has a catastrophic prediction that someone might die as a result of contamination. Like John, she does her best to deal with her fear and engages in quite elaborate cleaning rituals and uses plastic covers on her furniture to repel dirt. She also asks her family to remove their shoes outside the house, immediately go into the cloakroom by the door and to 'scrub up' before entering the main living areas. Each of these strategies ensures that Pamela avoids facing her fear and, as a result, she never gains confidence that she can relax her standards for cleanliness. Her problem is further enhanced by her family members colluding with the avoidance, and the problem is steadily getting worse.

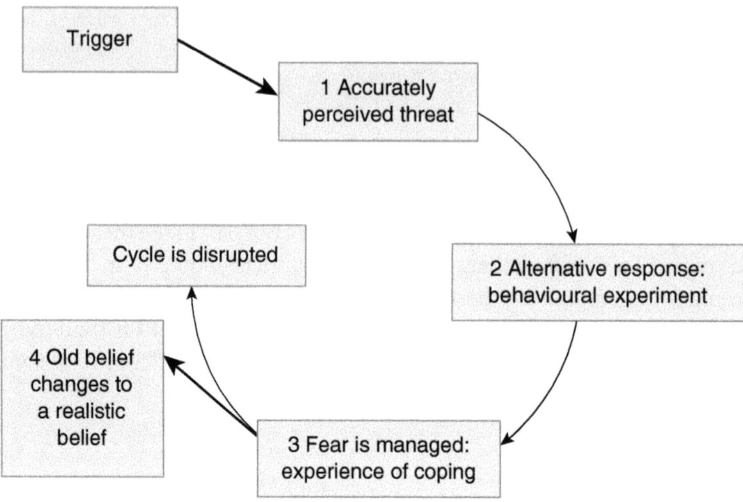

Figure 13.4 Breaking maintaining cycles

Essentially, if John and Pamela are to overcome their anxieties, they need to break the cycles by tackling their fears (see Figure 13.4).

John, with the help of his therapist, agreed to let go of some of his SBs (giving up all of them was too threatening to begin with), and he began driving with his window closed. He found that he had ample air and the only times that he felt short of breath were when his anxiety increased because of a driving challenge and not because of a shortage of air in his car. This began to undermine his fear-related beliefs and he dared to relinquish more of his unhelpful behaviours. He and his therapist worked out a programme of BEs, and he began to drive on motorways where he might have to stay on a stretch of road for miles before being free to take a break. He gradually took on increasingly challenging tasks and soon became comfortable driving on any stretch of motorway. By now his fearful predictions of catastrophe were significantly undermined and the maintenance cycle for his fear broken. As a result, he was able to begin to use public transport with relative ease.

In John's case, the results of behavioural changes facilitated cognitive change: his behavioural achievements challenged his earlier beliefs with very little input from the therapist.

Pamela's excessive cleaning and her demands on her family members eventually became intolerable, and her husband and children persuaded her to seek therapy. At first, Pamela was both sceptical of therapy and very frightened of making changes. It seemed improbable that she would begin to change her behaviours without some compelling assurance that it would be worth the risk. Thus, therapy began with a cognitive emphasis (see Chapter 8) and data-gathering, using a survey method of BE (see Chapter 9). She made a checklist for her friends, asking them what precautions they took to avoid contamination in their homes. She gave options such as: covering the furniture with plastic, asking family members to leave their shoes outside and so on. She also asked how often they or their family members were sick. Using this approach, she first discovered that not only did her friends not engage in elaborate precautions, but that they and their loved ones were rarely ill and never fatally. This helped her feel less afraid of changing her own behaviours and she was then able to engage in a series of BEs that systematically helped her to drop her SBs.

See Video 13.1: Devising a graded practice plan.

When aiming to break unproductive cycles, you are always faced with the question of what interventions to use. As cognitive behavioural therapists, we have a collection of cognitive, behavioural and physical strategies at our disposal (see Chapters 8, 9 and 10). The key is in identifying relevant components of the maintaining cycle and 'matching' the techniques accordingly.

The physical strategies, such as relaxation, are particularly useful when the physical consequences of being anxious impair performance (e.g. shaking) or when physical activity becomes aversive, because of physical discomfort, and is avoided. The behavioural techniques are invaluable in tackling avoidance head on and can also be used in self-monitoring and planning, as with activity scheduling. The cognitive approaches are relevant for helping clients 'stand back' from their problems and identify the components of a maintenance cycle, for helping them evaluate the usefulness of certain ways of processing information and in helping them re-evaluate unhelpful perspectives.

See Video 13.2: Theory A versus Theory B in practice.

An additional adaptable technique is the 'Theory A versus Theory B' strategy. This collaborative intervention, developed by Salkovskis and Bass (1997), promotes therapy as a BE offering the opportunity for testing two opposing theories. Essentially, one theory is 'There is danger', and the other is 'I am worrying too much about danger'. As a therapist, you need to adopt a curious, experimental approach to considering the two theories. Rather than proposing that the client is incorrect in holding a particular belief, instead you suggest that *perhaps* the client is right but *perhaps* there is another possibility. These alternatives are then explored in therapy: Theory A reflects the client's predicted belief (e.g. 'I am seriously ill'), while Theory B states an alternative explanation (e.g. 'These symptoms are due to anxiety'). You and your client can test the theories both retrospectively (by reviewing past beliefs, behaviours and outcomes) and prospectively (by setting up behavioural tests). This both brings the benign theory into the client's awareness and potentially collects data to support it.

In summary, anxiety disorders reflect a normal reaction to stress or threat, one which has become exaggerated by heightened physical reactions, skewed thinking and/or problem behaviours. This sets up unhelpful cycles that can be broken by introducing techniques to counter problem sensations, cognitions and behaviours. Table 13.1 shows several examples of CBT techniques and type of problems for which they would be relevant.

Table 13.1 Problems and techniques

Examples of problems	Examples of techniques
	Physical
Muscular tension impairing sleep or public speaking.	Relaxation
Avoidance of exertion because of a prediction of threat to health.	Exercise
	Behavioural
Avoidance of perceived threat.	Graded practice
Unawareness of relevant patterns or fluctuations in anxiety. Limited engagement in soothing, relaxing activities.	Activity scheduling
Focusing on the worst prediction. Avoiding behavioural challenges.	Behavioural experiment (Theory A versus Theory B)
	Cognitive
Poor insight into the processes maintaining anxiety. An inability to see 'thoughts' as 'thoughts'.	Decentring
Chronic and unproductive worry cycles.	Distraction
Skewed beliefs or images which perpetuate anxiety.	Cognitive testing
Inability to define difficulties, to make decisions, to plan ahead.	Problem solving

PROBLEMS WHEN WORKING WITH ANXIOUS CLIENTS

SELF-FULFILLING PROPHECIES: COGNITIVE

It is not unusual for the mental effects of heightened anxiety to get in the way of clear thinking. We have all probably encountered the client who describes his mind 'going blank' or who complains that so many concerns race through his mind that he cannot think straight. A graded approach to facing difficult situations, backed up by strategies to reduce stress levels (such as constructive self-talk), can help your clients learn to manage their anxiety levels, thus managing their ability to think clearly, at a realistic pace. In this way they can systematically test their predictions and face their fears.

SELF-FULFILLING PROPHECIES: PHYSICAL OR BEHAVIOURAL

Similarly, we often encounter those who report that the physical effects of anxiety impair their performance: struggling to articulate words during public speaking, shaking while writing in public and so on. Again, helping them learn self-calming strategies to minimise the physical effects of anxiety, followed by facilitating them through a series of graded and systematic BEs, can build a body of positive data that will help to consolidate their confidence.

THE POWER OF AVOIDANCE

Avoidance is the most compelling SB. It often represents the path of least resistance, providing tremendous short-term reward. Avoidance can be passive, as with clients who simply do not engage with their fears (e.g. not leaving the house, not using public transport, not attending social events), or it can be active, when a client puts much active effort into avoiding facing their fears (e.g. the person with OCD who carries out elaborate or time-consuming rituals in order to avoid facing a fear of contamination or a fear of causing harm). Avoidance can also be subtle: for example, a person carrying out a frightening task but drinking a unit or two of alcohol first; or a socially anxious person helping with 'hostess duties' to avoid having to engage in proper conversations; or someone with agoraphobia appearing to get out and about but using a mobile phone as a constant link to his safe base. A thorough assessment is needed to clarify the complexities of avoidance – remember to ask questions such as: 'And is there anything else that helps/that you use to get you through such times?', 'What do you do that you wouldn't do if you did not have this problem?', 'What do you not do as a result of having this problem?'.

In order to help clients reappraise the usefulness of avoidance, we can:

- encourage self-monitoring, including monitoring the longer-term consequences of avoidance;
- share a formulation, clearly illustrating the disadvantages of this choice of coping;
- negotiate a graded reduction in the use of avoidance for the particularly reluctant client (using a series of BEs); the positive feedback of success will then support further reductions.

'I'M ANXIOUS ALL OF THE TIME'

This common statement rarely stands up to self-monitoring. Although a retrospective appraisal might be 'I have the headache all of the time' or 'The images are with me all of the time', both daily thought records (see Chapter 8) and activity grids (Chapter 9) can reveal a variation in levels of physical tension and visual intrusions. Once these variations are clear, patterns and correlates can be established and cycles understood and ultimately managed.

'I DO ALL THE THINGS THAT WE AGREE, AND MY ANXIETY DOES NOT DECREASE'

If this is the case, look for subtle forms of avoidance and SBs, including superstitious behaviours such as doing or saying things so as 'not to tempt fate'. This can include the misuse of distraction, which results in the conclusion 'I only got through this because I distracted myself', rather than 'I took my mind off my worries and calmed myself'. In addition, you might find it helpful to consider the rate at which the feared situation is faced: although graded practice can be helpful, if it is too gentle and cautious, the client will gain little sense of achievement. Also check if others are helping to maintain the problem: a doctor reassuring his patient, a partner being critical and undermining, a 'helpful' neighbour shopping for your client.

NOT ACTUALLY FACING THE FEAR

This can apply to both you or your client. When your client is reluctant to tackle a demanding challenge, you need to ask 'Is this an appropriate task for this person at present?'. Although it is important to encourage engagement in challenging tasks, clients should not be *over*-stretched, as this can cause demoralisation and drop-out. However, it is possible that the task is appropriate yet the client cannot overcome reluctance to take it on. This might be because of inhibiting beliefs about feeling anxious, such as 'Feeling anxiety is bad or dangerous and I must avoid it'. Ensure that he appreciates that feeling anxious is not synonymous with failing or mental or physical threat and that it is to be expected during a behavioural assignment geared to facing fears. Also, make sure that you have shared a rationale that makes clear the advantages of tolerating the discomfort of the task. Similarly, you may need to address unhelpful assumptions concerning behavioural assignments (e.g. 'This won't work for me – my anxieties are different from others', or 'What's the point – I know the theory and that should be enough'), perhaps including specific BEs to test such assumptions.

As therapists we too need to check that we are not holding obstructive beliefs such as: 'This won't work for my client – her anxieties are different from others,' or 'What's the point, we've covered the theory and it's not making a difference.' As a therapist you also need to consider your own beliefs with regard to tasks that involve discomfort – are you sometimes simply assuming that your client will not be able to tolerate the stress? Do you sometimes collude with client avoidance? Are you occasionally avoidant yourself?

RELIANCE ON MEDICATION TO MANAGE ANXIETY

This is a problem if your client really invests his confidence in medication so that the CBT intervention holds little credibility for him and his motivation to engage is low. In addition, there is some evidence that some anxiolytics interfere with CBT for anxiety (Westra & Stewart, 1998). If you feel that your client is over-reliant on medications, explore his assumptions about drugs and CBT to see if it is possible to engage him in BEs that might help him develop more confidence in a psychological approach. It is not unusual for even well-motivated clients to be taking anxiolytic medication when they begin therapy, but they often readily learn cognitive behavioural techniques and then systematically reduce their medication – however, this should always be done with medical supervision.

SUMMARY

- Anxiety disorders reflect a normal reaction to stress or threat which has become exaggerated by heightened physical reactions, skewed thinking and/or problem behaviours.
- Problem anxiety is maintained by unhelpful cycles driven by cognitive biases and, usually, avoidant behaviours.
- There are many presentations of anxiety disorder and careful assessment will tell you which disorder best describes your client's condition. Some anxiety presentations, however, do not fit neatly into a diagnostic group and some

clients will present with one or more types of anxiety disorder: you need to be prepared for this.

- As a cognitive therapist you have a range of interventions that can be used to help your clients manage their anxiety-related problems. These include physical, behavioural and cognitive strategies. Deciding on the appropriate intervention depends on developing an appropriate formulation, which will be based on a sound assessment.
- The anxiety with which your clients struggle can sometimes hinder therapy, but this is often readily overcome by attending closely to unhelpful thoughts and behaviours.

LEARNING EXERCISES

These learning exercises are available to download from the companion website.

REVIEW AND REFLECTION:

- **Do you recognise your own clients in the description of anxiety disorders? In what ways are your clients similar or different?**
- **Does the description of anxiety disorders being an unhelpful development of 'normal' anxiety fit with your experience? How could you use this understanding to better help your clients?**
- **Do you see the cognitive biases described in this chapter in your own clients? Can you bring to mind examples from your own work?**
- **Look through the summary of strategies for managing anxiety-related problems – are you familiar with them? Are there gaps in your knowledge?**

TAKING IT FORWARD:

- **Review your anxious clients and reformulate their difficulties in the light of having read this chapter.**
- **Consider how you will share an understanding of the development of problem anxiety.**

(Continued)

(Continued)

- **Check that your maintaining cycles make sense for you and for your client. Ensure that you have considered the cognitive, the behavioural, the physical and the systemic factors that could be fuelling vicious cycles.**
- **Read more about the strategies for managing anxiety – go back to source materials to ensure that you properly understand them.**
- **Keep your formulation updated. Anticipate that there might be some difficulties when working with the very anxious and be ready to revise your formulation and to understand why these difficulties make sense rather than assuming that the therapy is not working or that your client is not complying.**

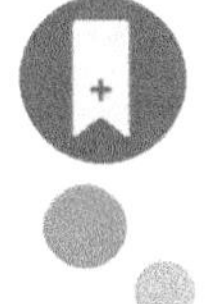

FURTHER READING

Butler, G., Fennell, M., & Hackmann, A. (2008). *Cognitive-behavioural therapy for anxiety disorders: mastering clinical challenges.* New York: Guilford Press.

A wise and excellent formulation-based approach to treating anxiety disorders which remains evidence-based. It is extremely readable yet avoids oversimplifying the management of anxiety disorders.

Clarke, D.A., & Beck, A.T. (2009). *Cognitive therapy of anxiety disorders.* New York: Guilford Press.

A comprehensive, integrative text which combines theoretical and clinical wisdom. It provides an overview of models of anxiety and an easy-to-read summary of the empirical literature. It is an accessible, up-to-date and practical text.

VIDEO LINKS

- **13.1 Devising a graded practice plan**
- **13.2 Theory A versus Theory B in practice**

14 ANXIETY DISORDERS

SPECIFIC MODELS AND TREATMENT PROTOCOLS

- **Introduction**
- **Specific phobia**
- **Panic disorder**
- **Hypochondriasis or health anxieties**
- **Social anxieties**
- **Generalised anxiety disorder (GAD)**
- **Obsessive-compulsive disorder (OCD)**
- **Post-traumatic stress disorder (PTSD)**
- **Co-morbidity**
- **Conclusion**
- **Potential problems when working with specific models and treatment protocols**
- **Summary**
- **Learning exercises**
- **Further reading**
- **Video links**
    - **14.1 Explaining traumatic memories**

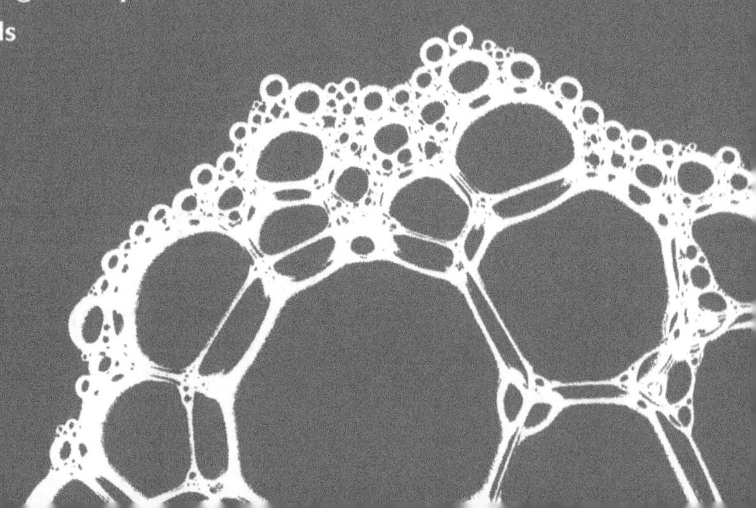

INTRODUCTION

Many anxiety presentations will fall into diagnostic categories, for which there are specific cognitive models and treatment protocols evolved from clinical trials. Major references for key models and protocols are summarised in Table 14.1. The publication dates for some of these references will show you that many of these models are long established and based on diagnostic groups that pre-date the current DSM-V (APA, 2013), therefore we have maintained some pre-DSM-V labels.

In this chapter, we will introduce the cognitive model for each of these disorders along with the associated treatment guidelines. You will probably notice similarities across models, but it is important to note the sometimes subtle differences between them. Empirically, the subtle differences matter, as you will see later when we review treatment protocols that are based on the different models.

Table 14.1 Key models and protocols for anxiety disorders

Anxiety disorder	References
Specific phobia	Kirk & Rouf (2004)
Panic disorder and agoraphobia	Clark (1986, 1999); Wells (1997)
Health anxiety	Salkovskis & Warwick (1986); Warwick & Salkovskis (1989)
Social anxiety	Clark (2002); Clark & Wells (1995); Wells (1997)
Generalised anxiety disorder (GAD)	Borkovec & Newman (1999); Borkovec, Newman, Pincus & Lytle (2002); Wells (1997, 2000)
Obsessive-compulsive disorder (OCD)	Salkovskis (1985, 1999); Wells (1997)
Post-traumatic stress disorder (PTSD)	Ehlers & Clark (2000)

SPECIFIC PHOBIA

There is, as yet, no evaluated 'cognitive model' of specific phobias, although a preliminary model has been proposed by Kirk and Rouf (2004). In brief, they suggest that those with specific phobias (e.g. of a particular animal or situation or of blood) are hypervigilant for threat cues. Thus, the cycle begins with:

- focusing on the perceived threat with selective attention for fear cues. This increases the likelihood of
- perceiving a threat, whether this is actually what they fear (e.g. a spider or blood) or a misinterpretation (e.g. a piece of fluff on the carpet or a splash of

tomato ketchup). This triggers the phobic response, which has both psychological and physiological elements. This, in turn, reinforces

- over-estimating the probability of harm and under-estimating ability to cope (Beck et al., 1985), which then maintains the fear that drives hypervigilance.

The primary cognitions (fear of an object or a situation) exacerbate:

- physiological arousal, which can be further interpreted as threatening; and
- SBs, such as overtly avoiding certain places (e.g. shops, zoos) or situations (e.g. writing in public) or covertly avoiding feared situations (e.g. wearing excessive amounts of insect repellent to ward off spiders). These then prevent anxious predictions from being disconfirmed, the fear remains unchallenged and the sufferer remains hypervigilant.

Beliefs about the meaning of the phobia (secondary cognitions) can also heighten anxiety, with beliefs such as 'I am foolish' or 'I am going mad' (see Figure 14.1).

Katya had always been fearful of wasps. The thought of them made her shudder, and the sight of one triggered panic. If she saw one, she could not think straight and would run away – recently she had left her youngest child outside a shop when she ran for cover. She coped by doing all she could to avoid wasps: never going into the garden during the summer months; not allowing her children to eat sweets outdoors in case this attracted wasps; keeping the doors and windows closed in her home. It was hard for her to verbalise what made her so afraid, but she had an image of being unable to escape angry wasps caught in her hair.

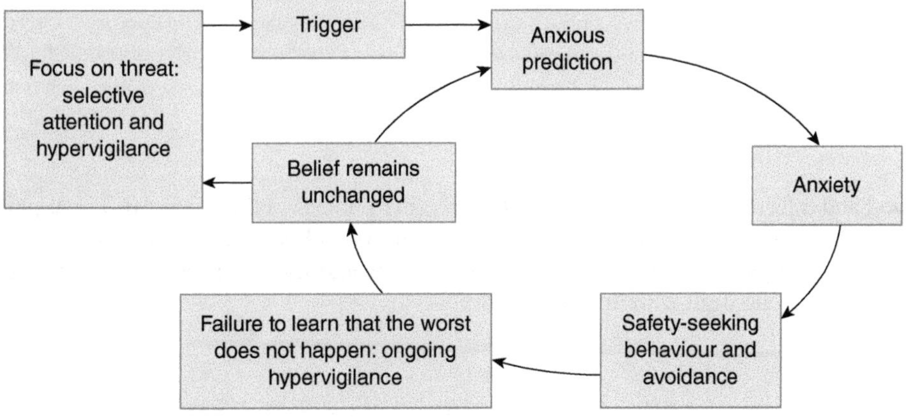

Figure 14.1 A cognitive model of specific phobia

Overcoming a specific phobia involves:

- *Exposure*: a person can only overcome a fear by facing it. This can be done in imagination as well as in reality – although exposure in reality is usually more effective. Facing fears is typically carried out in a graded way so that the client is challenged but not overwhelmed by the task, and in CBT, exposure is followed by debriefing so that the client and therapist can make the most of the cognitive and emotional opportunity for re-evaluation and change that exposure affords.
- *Decreasing focusing on the perceived threat*: this can be achieved by using distraction (see Chapter 8) and also by setting up BEs (see Chapter 9) to evaluate the consequences of reducing the amount of time spent checking or anticipating the worst. Many clients will hold beliefs such as 'If I don't keep a look out for spiders, I'll be taken by surprise by one' and very often the thought continues in a catastrophic direction: 'I won't cope'. They can be encouraged to test this prediction using BEs and in this way can often gain confidence that it is unnecessary to remain hypervigilant.
- *Reducing SBs*: this can also be achieved through BEs (often graded) to test the predictions of harm.
- *Addressing misinterpretations*: by teaching decentring and cognitive reappraisal of situations. This is relevant to both primary and secondary cognitions.

Katya wanted to tackle her phobia 'head on' and was prepared to try to confront a wasp. She and her therapist devised a hierarchy of graded BEs and made predictions about her probable responses to increasingly challenging wasp-related tasks. The experiments began with looking at photographs of wasps and progressed through to releasing a wasp from a jar into the garden. When she got as far as releasing wasps, she realised that they flew from rather than to her: her images of the wasps caught in her hair then diminished. This success gave her courage to work towards dropping her safety behaviours. Each SB lent itself to behavioural testing, and, through this, she discovered that her anxiety was heightened by her excessive hypervigilance. She also learned that if she left windows open, or let her children eat sweets outdoors, she encountered wasps, but far fewer than she had predicted, and that she coped better than she had anticipated.

Blood and injection phobias are different from other phobias as they have a different physiological maintaining pattern. As blood pressure drops in both these disorders, the client experiences unpleasant bodily and mental sensations and the prospect of fainting is real. These phobias are dealt with in Chapter 10.

PANIC DISORDER

A prominent cognitive model of panic disorder (see Figure 14.2) is that of Clark (1986), which identifies the maintaining factors as:

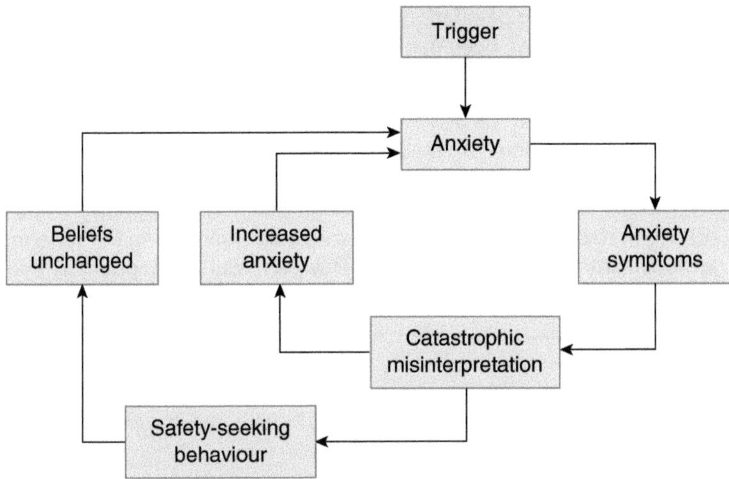

Figure 14.2 A cognitive model of panic disorder

- Catastrophic misinterpretation of bodily sensations (particularly those associated with anxiety) as indicative of impending mental or physical harm, such as an imminent stroke or heart attack.
- SBs employed in order to reduce the likelihood of catastrophe. These include frank avoidance, such as not going to certain places or events, and subtle avoidance, such as holding on to someone to avoid collapse or sucking ginger to avoid vomiting.
- Selective attention as sufferers become highly sensitised to 'dangerous' sensations or situations, and their attention becomes biased towards them.

When Wendy had a panic attack, her chest tightened, she fought for breath and she trembled. She felt pain in her chest and arms and experienced tunnel vision. She thought she was having a heart attack and could die. She avoided any situation where she anticipated she might exert herself as she feared provoking a heart attack. For example, she no longer did the weekly supermarket shop, nor took her children to the park. She knew that she was becoming physically unfit, and this heightened her fears.

The management of panic disorder typically involves:

- *Generating less catastrophic explanations*: for the origin of feared symptoms and less catastrophic predictions of the consequences, for example, attributing chest pains or a racing heart to anxiety, which is not harmful.
- *Setting up BEs*: (i) to discover the benign origin of an unpleasant sensation: for example, asking a client to exert himself to trigger feared sensations such

as muscular pains or palpitations; and (ii) to establish the validity of the new perceptions that have been generated through cognitive testing, such as 'I'm feeling the symptoms of anxiety and this will pass'.

- *Reducing SBs:* this can be achieved through cognitive and behavioural work. Cognitive interventions can be used to generate and explore new hypothetical ways of coping that are not SBs. These, in turn, can be reinforced through behavioural testing. For example, through preliminary cognitive work, a client began to consider it possible that she could walk around the supermarket without leaning on a trolley for safety. However, real-life shopping without the trolley actually consolidated her confidence.

Wendy's therapist raised the question of whether her muscular pain and difficulty breathing could result from the muscular tension associated with her state of heightened anxiety. Wendy was eventually convinced of this when she agreed to exercise in the session – even though the prospect had frightened her and had initially provoked the predicted symptoms. Once she had exercised in the session and discovered that she was a bit breathless but otherwise okay, her belief changed to 'I am not having a heart attack but I am highly anxious and it will pass'. Once she had gained this new perspective, she engaged in increasingly physically demanding activity. She began by exercising in the session and then between sessions, and grew confident that a racing heart or muscular tension was not harmful to her. Ultimately, she attended a gym regularly and ceased avoiding situations that she feared would over-exert her.

HYPOCHONDRIASIS OR HEALTH ANXIETIES

The cognitive understanding of health anxieties centres on the enduring catastrophic predictions concerning future health issues and preoccupation with physical symptoms (i.e. focus of attention towards the perceived threat). In itself, the fear of developing physical illness can exacerbate alarming physical symptoms, for which there is also likely to be selective awareness. This leads to high levels of anxiety. Sufferers of health anxieties tend to engage either in reassurance-seeking behaviours or in avoidance of situations they predict will heighten their anxiety.

Reassurance-seeking is ineffective in changing any anxiety as it reflects a reliance on external support. Sufferers fail to learn to *assure* themselves, and health concerns remain intact; there is always room for doubt – 'Maybe I didn't fully explain my symptoms to my doctor', 'Maybe I didn't fully understand what he said – maybe he said that I could have cancer!'. Furthermore, it is not unusual for a person who repeatedly complains of potentially harmful physical symptoms to be subjected to various tests, which can be interpreted as proof of real ill-health.

Maintaining cycles can take several forms:

- *Avoidance of situations* that trigger health fears, which means that the sufferer does not learn that there is no need to be over-concerned, that such situations are tolerable.

- *Turning to others*, such as medical specialists or family members, for comforting reassurances (safety-seeking).
- *Scanning*: *focusing on the perceived threat* with hyper-awareness of physical sensations such as heart rate, numbness, pain and so on. This means that benign sensations can be misinterpreted and can feed the health concerns.
- *Checking*: this can be related to the sufferer's body (e.g. looking for moles, lumps, etc.) or to external information (e.g. reading medical literature). Either way, it is then all too very easy to discover things that can fuel alarm.

Tina woke each morning with thoughts that she might have breast cancer. She tried unsuccessfully to avoid the media and, because of her heightened concern, noticed every article about cancer. Each day she felt compelled to check her breasts, armpits and neck for signs of lumps or enlarged glands. She believed that it would be dangerous not to check, as a missed tumour could become malignant. She always found something that gave her concern, so she persuaded her partner to 'double-check' for her. The relief each time she was reassured was exhilarating, although short-lived.

As with GAD, the *interpretation* of the preoccupation needs to be explored too, as some clients hold beliefs about their continued concern, such as 'If I am vigilant for signs of illness I will be OK' or 'If I think about my illness I will bring it on'.

Figure 14.3 illustrates how health anxiety can be maintained through:

- avoidance;
- reassurance-seeking;
- scanning.

The treatment approaches for health anxieties reflect these maintaining cycles and incorporate:

- *Defining and testing the content of the catastrophic prediction*. As therapist, you will need to tease out the anticipated worst outcome for your client (e.g. abandonment or protracted physical or mental torment). For some, the worst scenario is not simply illness or even death, but the nature and consequences of the illness or of death – so it is important to understand what illness or death means to your client. For example, he may not be worried about dying from a heart attack (perceived as rapid and dignified) but may be preoccupied with the fear of dying slowly from a neurological disorder, needy and incontinent, or he may not be worried about dying from a heart attack as much as he is worried about surviving a heart attack only to be left disabled.
- It is also wise to explore possible *superstitious thinking* (meta-cognition) such as 'If I don't think/do think about the illness, I will be protected from it'.

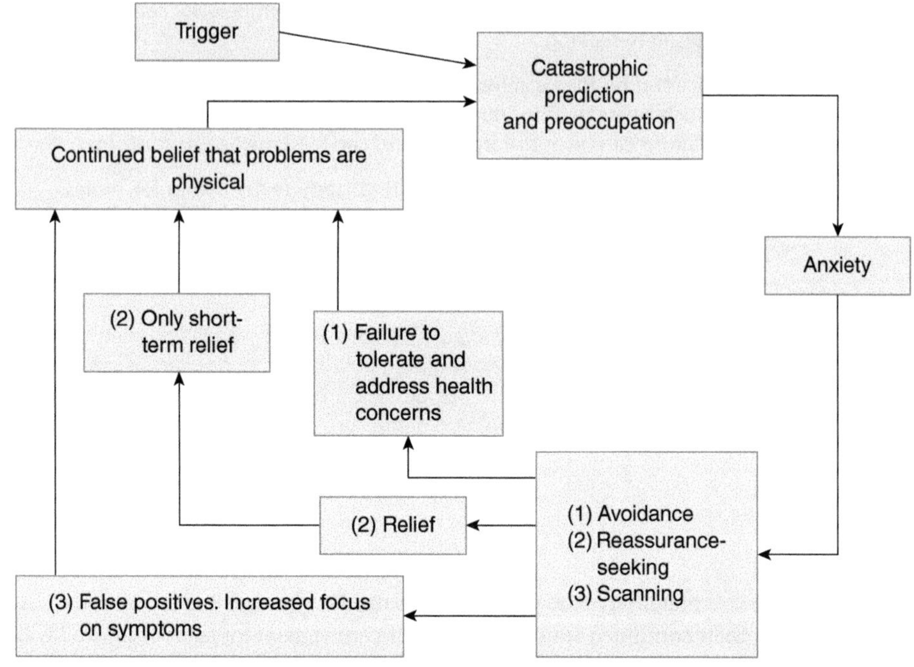

Figure 14.3 A cognitive model of health anxiety

- *Testing unhelpful health-related beliefs*, such as 'Chest pain means my heart is weak' or 'Every worrying symptom has to be checked by my doctor'. This can be achieved through cognitive interventions and BEs.
- *Reducing SBs* (reassurance-seeking, scanning and avoidance). Sometimes, an explanation of the role of these behaviours allows the client to reduce them; in other instances, it is necessary to test beliefs concerning safety behaviours, possibly via BEs. This can also be relevant to carers who collude with unhelpful behaviours.
- *'Theory A versus Theory B'* is a useful approach to gaining an alternative perspective (see Chapters 9 and 13).

Tina's most awful thought was that she would die a lingering death that would torment both her and her loved ones. With help, she was able to review this prediction, but her relief stemmed less from the statistical data about her risk of dying of cancer than from her re-appraisal of her coping resources. Once she believed that she could tolerate a protracted death (however undesirable this might be), she focused less on her health and her preoccupation diminished.

She also believed that if she did not get reassurance, she would be unable to withstand the uncertainty, and this would undermine her ability to function. She refined her definition of 'to function', specifying what activities would be impaired and how. She then conducted BEs to test the validity of her predictions and learnt that she could use distraction to help her with any tasks that she needed to complete and that she often functioned better when she kept her health worries at bay. She then built on this series of BEs by testing her prediction that she would become uncontrollably preoccupied by thoughts of cancer if she read or watched the media. She discovered that she could cope.

In addition, Tina's partner agreed to stop giving her reassurance and, although Tina initially felt uncomfortable about this, she quickly learnt to reassure herself.

At her first review session, Tina reflected on her beliefs in Theory A (that she would get breast cancer and would be unable to cope) and Theory B (that her preoccupation and safety-seeking kept health concerns foremost in her mind). She concluded that she now felt that Theory A was unlikely and she believed 80 per cent in Theory B.

SOCIAL ANXIETIES

As we said in Chapter 13, social anxieties can be in the more severe form of social phobia or the milder 'shyness'. Some social anxieties are quite specific, only arising when meeting a new person or an attractive person, for example, or only when carrying out particular tasks such as writing or eating in public. Sometimes the anxiety is more pervasive.

Cognitive models for social phobia have been developed (see Figure 14.4), most notably by Clark and Wells (1995), which, suggest Butler and Hackmann (2004), are readily applicable to 'shyness'. Models of social phobia incorporate the following:

- *Perceived social danger*: Typical assumptions and predictions of the socially anxious person are 'If I talk to them they will find me boring and reject me' or 'If I don't get this just right, I will be humiliated'. Essentially, these are fears centring on being negatively judged and on not coping.
- *Self-focused attention*: The social anxiety cycle is propelled by intense self-awareness, which can also manifest as self-referent *imagery* (Hackmann, 1998). This heightened self-consciousness is distracting and, thus, disabling as it is not possible to properly review a situation and engage in productive problem solving. For example, someone who is preoccupied with their ability to perform in front of friends might not be able to deal with a minor crisis, as all their attention is taken up in self-evaluation. Being so focused on self also prevents the sufferer from reviewing situations objectively, and then it is all too easy to (negatively) misinterpret the reactions of others.
- *Emotional reasoning*: The intense introspection about the sensations of anxiety renders the sufferer acutely aware of symptoms such as shaking and blushing. This heightens his self-awareness and he feels increasingly self-conscious. Because he feels self-conscious, he assumes others can see his symptoms as clearly as he feels them – and he assumes that others will judge him negatively.
- *Safety-seeking behaviours (SBs)*: Understandably, the socially anxious person will attempt to avoid predicted humiliation or embarrassment by avoiding social contact, for example, focusing on a task such as helping out in the kitchen during a party or avoiding eye contact during conversation. Of course, in doing so the social fear is not addressed and remains intact, ready for the next social challenge. In some instances, the safety behaviour is doubly counter-productive. For example, spending the evening in the kitchen at a party or avoiding eye-contact might well give the impression that a person *is* rather odd.

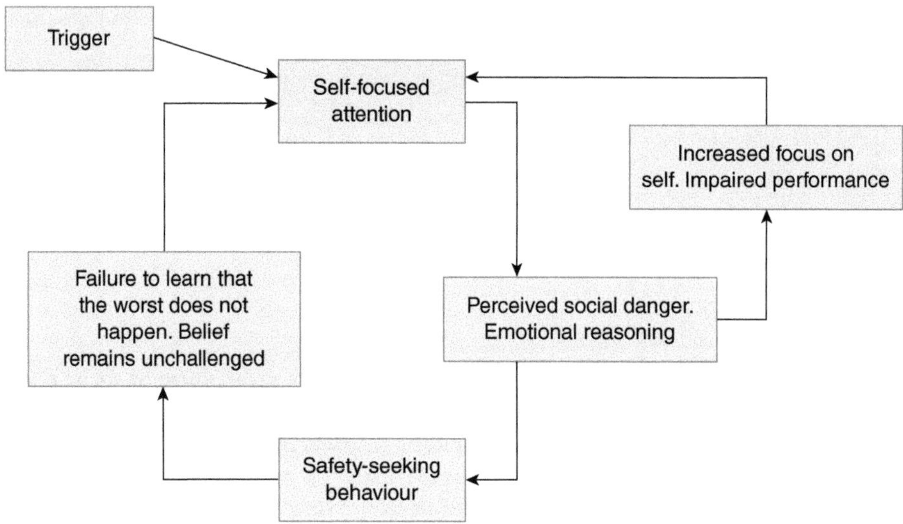

Figure 14.4 A cognitive model of social anxiety

Bette anticipated rejection. Her prediction in social situations was that others would realise that she had nothing to offer and would not want to know her. If someone did show interest, she discounted it: 'They don't know the real me' or 'They were just being polite'. As far as possible, she avoided social gatherings, and when she attended them, avoided eye contact but could 'feel' the critical gaze of others. She tended to busy herself attending to the practical needs of guests. If she became involved in conversation, the intensity of her negative intrusive thoughts rendered her unable to chat.

Interventions for social phobia involve:

- *Re-focusing attention away from introspection.* This strategy was particularly elaborated and evaluated by Wells and Mathews (1994) and involves switching attention between different sources of sensory information (auditory, visual, sensory, etc.). This is first practised in sessions, then between sessions until the client becomes adept at shifting his attention away from himself.
- Developing an *assertive or compassionate inner voice* to combat the harsh criticism that sufferers predict from others (Padesky, 1997; Gilbert, 2005). Thus, you would encourage your clients to address themselves in an empathic and understanding way, for example: 'It is understandable that I feel like this, I am not very confident yet. It's okay to pace myself – I don't have to be able to tackle the most difficult situations right now.'
- *Cognitive re-evaluation* of the cognitions relating to perceived social danger and emotional reasoning, including BEs. Particularly useful are (i) the use of videoed sessions, which allow clients to evaluate the severity of their overt anxiety symptoms, and (ii) modelling of feared consequences by the therapist. The latter means that you, the therapist, might have to appear to have blushed,

sweated or even wet yourself in a public place – but be comforted that this seems to go unjudged by the general public (see Chapter 9).

- There is also a useful series of questions often used to help the socially anxious person gain a more balanced perspective on problems like blushing, shaking, stammering and so on:
    - Are the symptoms you fear actually as likely to happen as you predict?
    - Even if they do happen, will it actually be as severe as you imagine?
    - Even if it is, will other people actually notice?
    - Even if they do notice, will they interpret it in the way that you fear they will?
    - Even if they do see it that way, so what? Is it possible you can survive it and get on with your life?

Bette learnt several strategies to combat her social anxiety. First, she described her worst-case scenario and tested her predictions that (i) she would almost certainly be criticised and ostracised, and (ii) that she would not cope with criticism but would accept it and become deeply depressed. Cognitive restructuring, developing a strong but caring inner voice and role play with her therapist helped her to conclude that she was unlikely to be openly criticised, but even if she were, she could stand up for herself and not spiral into despair. She also learnt strategies to refocus attention from her negative, self-referent thoughts. In addition, she carried out behavioural tests: she allowed her therapist to log the number of people who looked at her critically when they attended a social gathering – to her surprise, the therapist noted no one. Finally, she engaged in a series of assignments focused on not tending to guests' practical needs (i.e. dropping her major SB). As she progressed through the hierarchy of assignments, she built her confidence that she could mix socially.

GENERALISED ANXIETY DISORDER (GAD)

As described in the previous chapter, GAD is defined in DSM-V as chronic, excessive anxiety and worry pertaining to a number of events or activities (APA, 2013).

Sam was 64 years old and felt he should be looking forward to his retirement – his wife certainly was. However, as usual, he was beset with worries about it: What if he and his wife did not get on? What if their financial planning had been insufficient? He found his worrying shameful but familiar, and he could not remember a time when he had been free of it, just times when it was slightly better or worse.

Cognitive models of GAD give prominence to worry as a key cognitive factor. There are several possible mechanisms for persistent worry:

- Focusing attention towards the perceived threat can be an attempt to avoid addressing a more distressing fear, as 'What if?' statements are superficial to the real concern. The real concern would be revealed by answering the 'What if' question (Borkovec & Newman, 1999).

- It can also reflect an attempt to avoid facing uncertainty which is felt to be intolerable, even in small amounts (Ladouceur et al., 2000; Dugas, Buhr & Ladouceur, 2004).
- The *meaning* of the worry itself (the meta-cognition) can perpetuate worry (Wells, 1997, 2000). Wells calls this 'Type II worry' to distinguish it from worries about everyday concerns (Type I worry). Type I worries, such as 'What if I don't have enough money!' can be perpetuated by Type II worries. Type II worries can be positive, such as the superstitious: ('If I worry, bad things won't happen') or a misconception about worry ('If I am worrying, I am doing something useful'). Such beliefs would increase the likelihood of engaging in worry and continuing to worry could become a SB. In Sam's case, he believed that worry would better prepare him to cope – that he would not be 'caught out' by bad luck. So, uncomfortable as it was, he felt compelled to worry. Type II worries can also be negative and alarming (e.g. 'I will go crazy'), which can trigger more worry (Wells, 1997, 2000). Again, in Sam's case he was ashamed by his tendency to worry, he felt that it was weak and unmanly. This therefore worried him, raised his anxiety levels and increased his vulnerability to worry. A very vicious cycle.
- Worry undermines the ability to problem solve, so that a person loses confidence in their problem-solving ability, which supports further worry (Dugas et al., 2004).

Treatment for GAD focuses on breaking the worry cycle by understanding and eliminating unhelpful worry and then addressing the underlying fears. See Figure 14.5 for a cognitive model of GAD.

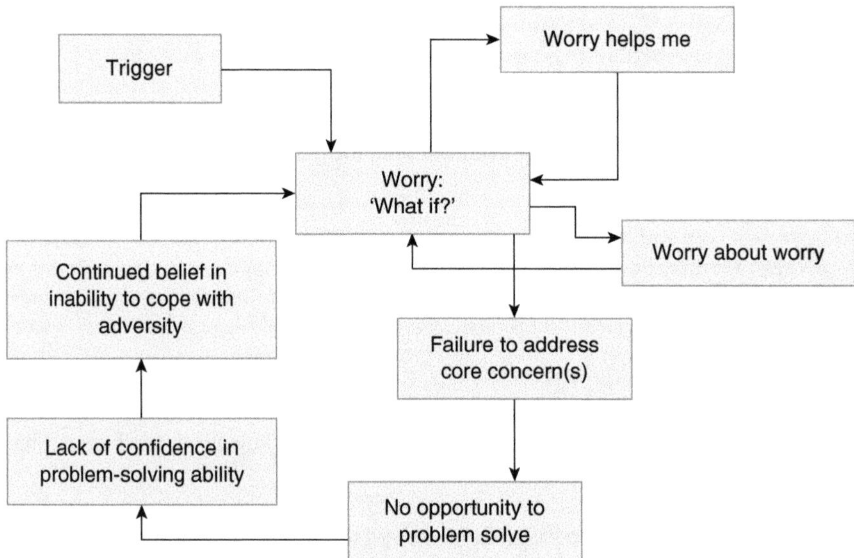

Figure 14.5 A cognitive model of GAD

The required steps include:

- *Normalising worry and worry awareness training.* The former means helping your client understand that a degree of worry is normal and even helpful but that their level of worry has probably become unhelpfully exaggerated. Worry awareness training is particularly useful for those for whom worrying has become habitual. It simply involves self-monitoring so that frequencies, triggers and patterns of worry become clear.
- *Overcoming avoidance* by encouraging articulation of the fear (e.g. personal harm or harm to loved ones) beneath the 'What if?' question, and then helping your client address these fears.
- *Accepting uncertainty.* Butler and Rouf (2004) recommend focusing on testing the cognitions that reflect intolerance of uncertainty rather than trying to review the likelihood of the feared events actually happening. Therefore they stress the importance of helping clients simply accept uncertainty. This means that, as a therapist, you focus on clarifying the alarming answer to 'What if?' rather than debating the probability of the worst-case scenario. BEs involving clients testing out their negative predictions about enduring uncertainty can then be used to help them accept doubt or ambiguity (see Butler & Rouf, 2004).
- *Identifying and testing unhelpful cognitions* concerning worry. This would involve first identifying meta-cognitions, such as 'Worrying will damage my heart' or 'I must worry so that I am never caught unprepared', followed where appropriate by behavioural testing. The aim of the BEs is not to control the worry but to change beliefs about it.
- *Teaching alternative responses* to worrying, such as problem solving or distraction, or limiting the time permitted for worrying, where the aim is to help your client have the experience of disengaging from worry and learning that all is well. For example, a client who typically spent five hours in the evening worrying about events in the next day might develop a plan to worry only during the 30 minutes between getting home and supper, with other worrying thoughts 'held over' until the following day. Distraction could be a useful strategy to help her resist engaging in worrying, and thus she would have the experience of learning that she could get through the evening without being so caught up with her concerns. Another useful strategy for helping clients 'put worries aside' is writing worries on a paper which is then destroyed (Butler & Rouf, 2004). Close debriefing is needed to ensure that these strategies are not being used as SBs.
- *The Worry Decision Tree* (Butler & Hope, 2007) elegantly brings together these strategies as a structured means of managing worry. It guides one through a branching series of questions beginning with 'What am I worried about?' (this pinpoints the fear) followed by 'Is there anything I can do about this?'. If the answer is no, then distraction is the best option; if the answer is yes, then a third question is: 'Is there anything I can do right now?' Again, if the conclusion is no, distraction is in order; if the conclusion is yes, then it's time to get problem solving and planning. Once the plan is made, distraction can stave off further worrying.

Sam was encouraged to articulate his fears: he said that he was terrified that his wife would realise that he had nothing to offer her and would leave him; that they would run out of money and be unable to afford decent health care; that his wrong decision in taking retirement would cost him his marriage, his security and, worst of all, would prove that he was useless. By using cognitive strategies, he was able to both decatastrophise specific negative thoughts and to appreciate his resilience (he had managed many personal and business crises in the past), and that enabled him to tolerate the uncertainty of his future. Throughout, there was a theme of shame, worthlessness and responsibility, and these general negative themes were also reappraised.

Sam carried out a BE comparing his ability to problem solve when he focused on his worries with his ability to do so when he distracted himself from them. He learned that worrying was counterproductive and recognised that it had become both a habit and a source of comfort, as he believed that he could ward off bad luck by worrying. Once he understood this, he readily distracted himself from worrying, thus breaking an unhelpful pattern.

OBSESSIVE-COMPULSIVE DISORDER (OCD)

Unwanted intrusive thoughts, in the form of words, images or impulses, are not in themselves pathological (Rachman & de Silva, 1978), so we would not attempt to challenge them, but the response to them can be unhelpful. Cognitive models of OCD share the basic premise that intrusive thoughts are in themselves normal but become a problem when they are interpreted as indicating that something bad might happen and that the sufferer is responsible for preventing it. To manage this fear, people engage in SBs (avoidance, reassurance-seeking and cognitive or motor rituals), which prevent them from learning that the worries are not accurate or that anxiety will actually decline without performing rituals. The aim of CBT is for the client to learn that such intrusive thoughts do not indicate a need for action and can safely be ignored.

The most common obsessional worries relate to:

- fears of contamination (e.g. infection from touching a dirty cloth or surface), leading to washing or cleaning rituals;
- fears of missing something potentially dangerous (e.g. electric switches which have been left on, or an unlocked front door), leading to checking and/or repeating rituals;
- over-concern with orderliness and perfection, leading to repeating actions until things 'feel right';
- fears of uncontrollable and inappropriate actions (e.g. swearing in public, or sexual or aggressive behaviour), leading to unhelpful attempts to control thoughts.

The most common SBs are:

- behavioural rituals (e.g. cleaning, checking and repeating actions);
- cognitive rituals: neutralising 'bad' thoughts by thinking other thoughts (e.g. prayers or 'safe' incantations, or other 'good' thoughts);

- avoidance of situations, people or objects that trigger the obsessional worries;
- seeking reassurance about the worries from family, doctors or others;
- thought suppression.

Most OCD sufferers have behavioural or motor rituals, but some have predominantly cognitive rituals with few, if any, motor rituals (so-called 'pure obsessions' – a presentation that may be harder to treat).

Vince had always been very cautious and was proud of his high standards for safety. However, since a promotion (with responsibility for ensuring departmental security), his safety checks had become exaggerated and he was now struggling to leave the building at night. He often returned five or six times to recheck – occasionally driving in from his home. He tried unsuccessfully to put the worrying thoughts out of his mind. His fear was that insufficient caution would result in a catastrophe for which he would shoulder the blame. He thought that the shame of this would destroy him.

It has been suggested by the Obsessive-Compulsive Cognitions Working Group (1997) that the key cognitions in OCD are:

- *thought–action fusion*: the idea that having a 'bad' thought can result in 'bad' consequences (e.g. if I think about harm coming to someone, that may make that harm happen in reality), or that having a thought about something 'bad' is morally just as bad as carrying out a bad action;
- *inflated responsibility*: an assumption that one has the power and the obligation to prevent bad things from happening;
- *beliefs about the controllability of thoughts*: for example, the belief that one ought to be able to control 'bad' thoughts;
- *perfection*: the dichotomous assumption that only the best is effective or acceptable;
- *overestimation of threat*, which is often related to
- *intolerance of uncertainty*: a belief that things can and must be certain (e.g. 'I ought to be able to be *sure* that an action is safe').

As with other anxiety disorders, thoughts about negative thoughts (e.g. 'There must be something fundamentally wrong with me for having such thoughts') can heighten anxiety (Wells, 2000). Emotional reasoning (the assumption that feelings are a reliable source of information about a situation, e.g. 'I feel anxious, therefore this must be a dangerous situation') is also common amongst sufferers of OCD (Emmelkamp & Aardema, 1999) (see Figure 14.6).

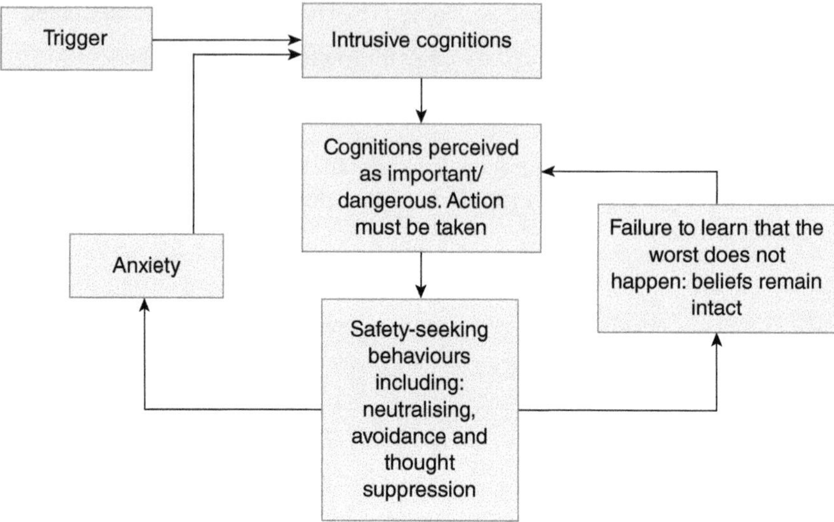

Figure 14.6 A cognitive model of OCD

Interventions for OCD incorporate:

- *Exposure and response prevention (ERP)*: This is the best-established intervention for OCD. The aim is for the sufferer to expose himself to the feared situation (e.g. something 'contaminated') without engaging in his usual safety behaviour (e.g. washing). Although originally conceived as a behavioural intervention, ERP is readily adapted to a cognitive approach in which it is seen as a BE through which the client learns that his obsessional predictions of disaster are not justified and that he can tolerate distress. Rituals are essentially SBs and therefore ERP is exactly analogous to reducing SBs in any other anxiety disorder. It is possible that family, friends or professionals collude or assist with the unhelpful behaviours, and it may therefore be necessary to involve them in this aspect of therapy.
- *Testing unhelpful thoughts and beliefs* related to the intrusions, such as 'If I think it, it will happen' or 'I am responsible for the welfare of others', by using the cognitive and behavioural strategies described in earlier chapters. The continuum method, or scaling, can be particularly helpful in addressing the extreme perspective of the perfectionist (see Chapters 13 and 17). In OCD, the intrusive thoughts themselves are *not* directly challenged in this way (since they are seen as normal phenomena) – it is the negative thoughts *about* intrusions that need testing.
- *Theory A versus Theory B*: As with health anxiety, this intervention can be useful in highlighting a benign perspective. The aim is to learn that OCD is not about the need to prevent a real threat but rather about being excessively *worried* about such a threat.

Vince's most unhelpful belief was: 'I am wholly responsible for any crisis that arises at work.' He tested this by recognising the cognitive biases in his thinking and by constructing a 'responsibility pie' (see Chapter 17), which helped him to apportion responsibility more realistically. However, he also had to work on the dichotomous thinking that underpinned his unrealistically high standards: continuum work (see Chapter 17) helped him to become more flexible. He addressed other key beliefs such as 'I will be destroyed if I am to blame' using standard cognitive interventions.

Feeling more confident that he could tolerate the worst-case scenario, he agreed to a programme to reduce his SBs. This incorporated an agreement that his wife would not reassure him when he was at home feeling uneasy about his department's security. He struggled initially with refocusing his thoughts away from catastrophic possibilities. He kept (meticulous) diaries of his experiences, and these showed clearly that he felt less anxious and more content on the days that he reduced safety behaviours and catastrophic thinking. He also recognised that catastrophes never ensued at these times, giving him evidence that his safety behaviours were not necessary.

POST-TRAUMATIC STRESS DISORDER (PTSD)

PTSD is a curious diagnostic category as DSM-V (APA, 2013) defines what constitutes 'trauma': this makes the diagnosis particularly specific. DSM-V defines traumatic stressors as events involving *actual or threatened death or serious injury or a threat to the physical integrity of self and others*. This does now include vicarious trauma. If an event does not meet the DSM-V criteria for 'trauma', the diagnosis of PTSD cannot be made, regardless of how distressed a person appears or how they might have construed a distressing event.

Several cognitive models for PTSD have been developed over the past decade, but the most prominent is probably that of Ehlers and Clark (2000) and it is based on the DSM-IV (APA, 2000) criteria for PTSD. Cognitive models tend to put an emphasis on:

- the emotion of fear or horror as the main affective component of the model (consistent with DSM-IV), although DSM-V (APA, 2013) recognises that emotions such as guilt, grief, disgust, anger and shame can be prominent too;
- vivid memories that promote the experience of the danger still being current;
- these memories being disconnected from an intellectual understanding of the trauma which might otherwise put them into perspective and enable the sufferer to better tolerate them;
- memories being intrusive, usually visually, although recollections of a traumatic event can also be experienced in other sensory modalities (e.g. as sounds, physical sensations and smells);
- memories also being experienced as nightmares.

The vivid memories of trauma are emotionally highly provocative and remain so for several reasons:

- *SBs*: in an attempt to manage high anxiety, PTSD sufferers often use behavioural and mental avoidance to inhibit the memories.
- This *prevents processing of the memory* (i.e. reviewing the traumatic content so that it can be linked with information about time, place and outcome and therefore put in the past), so the memory remains a disconnected, emotionally charged recollection which, in itself, triggers high levels of distress and arousal.
- *Neurological inhibition of memory processing*: over-arousal of the emotion-generating part of the brain (limbic system) during a flashback can in itself prevent the natural processing of memory. Thus the recollection remains emotionally over-intense and disconnected with current reality (for a simple review, see Kennerley & Kischka, 2013).
- *Misinterpretations*: unhelpful appraisals of the traumatic experience (e.g. 'This proves that no man can be trusted', 'I brought this on myself through carelessness') or of the PTSD symptoms (e.g. 'I am weak', 'I am going crazy') can further worsen the distress associated with the intrusions and can therefore lead to increased arousal and more safety behaviours.

In addition, the cycle of PTSD can be maintained by:

- spontaneous and vivid imagery which can be powerfully aversive, thus sufferers will try to avoid situations that trigger them;
- selective memory processes, which distort recollections such that they are biased towards negative aspects of the trauma, thus heightening distress;
- overestimation of danger: it is not unusual for trauma victims to overestimate current threats to their safety – in turn further promoting both heightened arousal and safety behaviours.

See Figure 14.7 for a cognitive model of PTSD.

Alistair had been involved in a road-traffic accident when his car tyre exploded at high speed. He had had a lucky escape. Eight months later, he still experienced vivid memories of his car flipping over, memories of the sights, sounds and smells as if it were happening again. For him, everything went black again, he smelled fuel, he heard metal scraping along the road, sounding like an old train braking; he felt as if he were hanging upside down, and each time he again had the thought 'I'm going to die'. He was particularly likely to have flashbacks when he smelled petrol or when he returned to the area where the accident took place. Therefore, although he still drove his car, his partner would always refuel it, and he never drove near the site of the crash.

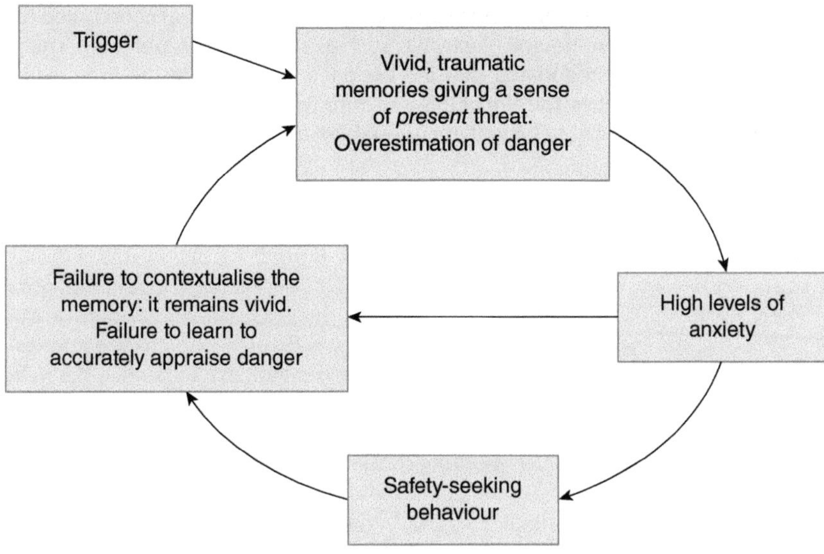

Figure 14.7 A cognitive model of PTSD

Treatment for PTSD based on the cognitive models involves addressing:

- *Spontaneous imagery*: Strategies are introduced to diminish the very high levels of arousal associated with the images, so that they can be processed and contextualised. This means that they form memories that are subject to rational appraisal. The sense of *present* threat is then eliminated, by placing the image in context of time, place and longer-term outcome. This is often achieved by using cognitive restructuring while 'reliving' the trauma (Grey, Young & Holmes, 2002) or cognitive processing therapy (Resick & Schnicke, 1993; Ehlers et al., 2003) where the client writes a detailed account of the traumatic experience for cognitive review. Along with constructing more helpful interpretations of the traumatic memory, clients are encouraged to expose themselves to real-life situations linked to the trauma so that they might manage their anxiety-provoking cognitions *in vivo*.
- *SBs* can be reduced by reviewing unhelpful beliefs and field-testing new possibilities, as with other anxiety disorders.
- *Misinterpretations* can be reappraised by reviewing these conclusions and generating plausible alternatives, again using 'standard' CBT interventions.
- *Selective memory processes* can be usefully addressed, as can all of the cognitive biases, by teaching the technique of decentring, or standing back and viewing the cognitions at a distance. This allows the sufferer to gain a wider, more balanced perspective, which is less distressing.

- *'Reclaiming your life'*: Many trauma victims neglect activities that contributed to their wellbeing pre-trauma – activities such as socialising or exercising. Thus, assignments are negotiated that are designed to re-engage survivors with meaningful activities; the aim of this is to improve the quality of their lives and their mood as well as helping them re-establish a more normal life style.

Alistair's intrusive memories responded well to cognitive restructuring: in short, he 'updated' his recollections. Ultimately, his therapist helped him to talk through his experience as if it were currently happening, pausing at the emotional 'hot spots' to review his cognitions in the light of what he now knew. By doing this, Alistair was able to counter his most salient thought: 'I am about to die'. He was able to remind himself that he got out of the crashed car with few injuries and, in doing so, he reduced the intensity of the flashbacks. He was also able to revise a shameful belief that had developed after the accident, namely that he was responsible for the incident. This further reduced the anxiety that the memories evoked.

He was gradually able to revisit the site of the crash – first with his partner and later alone – and to talk and read about accidents. His predictions that he would have flashbacks were not borne out, and his confidence returned. His avoidance of smelling petrol was more difficult to tackle, as fears associated with smells are particularly resilient, but because he had learnt to be less afraid of flashbacks, he tolerated the occasional vivid memory without undue distress, and he no longer felt the need to avoid the smell of petrol.

The precipitants of PTSD may be impersonal, such as a natural disaster, or perceived as highly personal, for example when a person has been assaulted in some way. In cases of personal attack, there is likely to be a need for greater sensitivity to interpersonal relationships both within and outside the therapy setting. Some clients will have experienced sexual assault and, clearly, there needs to be sensitivity when discussing this and other sexual relationships.

See Video 14.1: Sharing a simple neuropsychological explanation of traumatic memories.

CO-MORBIDITY

Anxiety disorders can present as discrete problems, in combination with other anxiety disorders or as co-morbid with other problems: for example, the high standards and perfectionism of the person with OCD might predispose her to an eating disorder, the chronicity of an anxiety problem might give rise to depressed mood, while coping strategies such as comfort eating or drinking can develop into difficulties in their own right. Remember to take this into account during your assessment, and throughout treatment remain aware that other problems might exist.

With regard to co-morbid anxiety disorders, a preliminary evaluation of a trans-diagnostic intervention was recently published by McManus, Clark, Shafran and Muse (2015). Although based on only a small case series, it clearly indicated that trans-diagnostic approaches can be beneficial to those with co-morbid anxiety disorders.

CONCLUSION

The previous chapter reviewed a generic understanding of anxiety disorders, while this chapter has focused on specific models and the treatment approaches linked to them. In your practice, you will need to be aware of both the generic and specific approaches so that you can be flexible and responsive to your client's needs. The models give an elegant and invaluable understanding of particular anxiety disorders, while the generic overview provides you with the 'first principles' that you can fall back on if the models and protocols do not meet your client's needs.

POTENTIAL PROBLEMS WHEN WORKING WITH SPECIFIC MODELS AND TREATMENT PROTOCOLS

ASSUMING THE VALIDITY OF A DIAGNOSIS WITHOUT CARRYING OUT A FULL ASSESSMENT AND THEN ADHERING TO A TREATMENT PROTOCOL

Although many of your clients will fulfil criteria for a particular diagnostic group and will benefit from a protocol-driven approach, do not presume this without first carrying out a proper assessment. There will be times when the referrer's diagnosis or your first impressions are wrong.

TRYING TO FORCE A CLIENT'S EXPERIENCES INTO A SPECIFIC MODEL

Keep a curious and open mind during your assessments. If your client's presentation does not fit neatly into the model that you anticipate being relevant, perhaps the model is invalid for this person. In such instances, a generic formulation (Beck et al., 1979) will be appropriate and this will guide you in deciding which interventions might be best.

STICKING TOO RIGIDLY TO A PROTOCOL WHEN THE CLIENT IS NOT RESPONDING WELL

While it is important to follow a protocol, there will be individual differences amongst your clients and aspects of their presentation which, at some point, may not fit with the protocol. In some instances, the deviation will be sufficiently marked for you to have to reassess your client and consider if the protocol offers the optimum approach. At other times, staying with the protocol will be in your client's best interest, but you may need to adapt it slightly: for example, introducing a session on specific skills training (assertiveness, time management, etc.) or temporarily diverting to tackle an issue that appears to obstruct progress, issues such as excessive anger, unresolved grief or flashbacks.

SUMMARY

- In general, there are well-established and very specific models for understanding the different presentations of anxiety disorders and there are tried and tested protocols for managing them.
- Where possible, the use of protocols should be the first choice of intervention. Therefore you need to be familiar with them.
- You also need to be familiar with the 'first principles' of anxiety. This means that you need to have:
    - a generic understanding of the factors that contribute to, and maintain, anxiety-related difficulties so that you can formulate the problems of your clients who do not fit the standard models; and
    - an appreciation of the range of management strategies you can apply to breaking the cycles that maintain anxiety disorders so that you can be flexible in your approach when this is necessary.

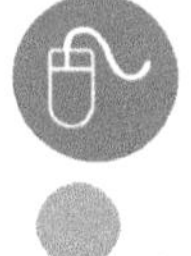

LEARNING EXERCISES

These learning exercises are available to download from the companion website.

REVIEW AND REFLECTION:

- What is your reaction to seeing the models underpinning anxiety disorders? Do they fit with your experience? Do they make sense for you? If not, what is the difficulty you have in linking this theory to your clinical experience?
- What about the protocols? Again, do they make sense to you? Can you think of clients who might benefit from your applying them more vigorously? Do you have problems in seeing how they could work for your clients? If so, what difficulties do you foresee?

TAKING IT FORWARD:

- Read more about models and protocols – go back to source materials to ensure that you properly understand them.

- **Review your anxious clients in the light of understanding more about the cognitive models that underpin anxiety disorders. Review your formulations of their difficulties.**
- **If your client fits a model, check that you are making the most of there being a protocol to guide you.**
- **If you are not used to closely following a protocol, try out a 'test case'. Really familiarise yourself with the relevant intervention and stick as closely to the protocol as possible. Discover how this works for your client and for you. If you have difficulties adhering to a protocol that is working for your client, then explore your own assumption about models and protocols.**
- **If your client does not fit a model, consider how you will formulate, and help your client manage, the problem, given what you understand about the nature of anxiety disorders and the strategies available to you.**
- **Use your supervisor's support and, if necessary, ring-fence time for discussing your questions and difficulties in working with your anxious clients.**

FURTHER READING

Wells, A. (1997). *Cognitive therapy of anxiety disorders: a practical guide.* London: Wiley Blackwell.

A well-established 'basic' text, which addresses the various anxiety disorders in a practical and informative way. It is comprehensive and successfully marries theory and practice.

Butler, G., Fennell, M., & Hackmann, A. (2008). *Cognitive-behavioural therapy for anxiety disorders: mastering clinical challenges.* New York: Guilford Press.

A wise and excellent formulation-based approach to treating anxiety disorders which remains evidence-based in its recommendations for intervention. It is extremely readable yet avoids oversimplifying the management of anxiety disorders.

VIDEO LINKS

- **14.1 Sharing a simple neuropsychological explanation of traumatic memories**

15 WIDER APPLICATIONS OF CBT

- Introduction
- Eating disorders
- Psychological trauma
- Anger
- Psychotic symptoms
- Relationship difficulties
- Substance misuse and addictive disorders
- Other applications of CBT
- Learning exercises
- Video link
    - 15.1 Motivating your client

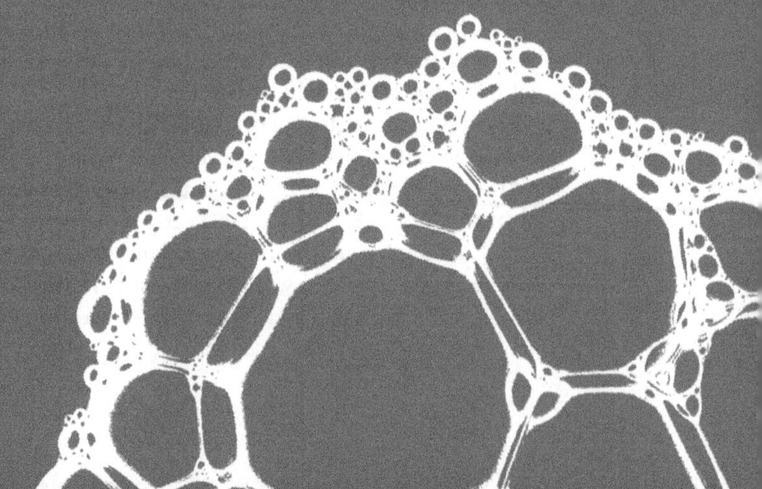

INTRODUCTION

Over the past 35 years, CBT has been applied to an ever-widening range of psychological problems beyond anxiety and depression. This chapter will briefly review the application of CBT to some of those other problems. Our intention is twofold:

- to highlight salient aspects of the disorders to help you recognise them;
- to outline what might be involved in the management of such problems so that you can decide whether to refer on or to take a client yourself. Remember that additional training and supervision may be required to work with these disorders.

At the end of each section, we will refer you to further reading.

We are not attempting to address all the psychological disorders to which CBT has been applied, but we will briefly review perhaps the most common:

- eating disorders;
- psychological trauma;
- anger;
- psychosis;
- relationship difficulties;
- substance misuse.

EATING DISORDERS

There has been a long *behavioural* tradition of working with people with eating disorders. These interventions have been relatively effective in achieving weight reinstatement and stability and improved eating patterns. However, gains were poorly maintained, and in the 1980s emphasis moved towards modifying cognitions (e.g. Fairburn, Kirk, O'Connor & Cooper, 1986).

CBT has been the most exhaustively researched form of cognitively focused treatment for eating disorders (EDs), particularly bulimia nervosa, and there is reasonable evidence that it remains a defensible treatment (see Hay, 2013 for a review), that good results can be achieved in routine clinical practice and that successful management of EDs can impact on co-morbid difficulties (Turner, Marshall, Wood, Stopa & Waller, 2016). Over time, cognitive therapists have developed a trans-diagnostic understanding of the EDs (Waller, 1993; Fairburn, Cooper & Shafran, 2003) and refined models and approaches, but the main focus for CBT therapists has been anorexia nervosa, bulimia nervosa and binge-eating disorder. Despite common features, there are distinct differences in the presentations of these conditions, differences that must be taken into account in their understanding and treatment.

DSM-V (APA, 2013) defines them under 'Feeding and eating disorders' and now recognises binge-eating disorder (BED) which was formerly a provisional category.

- *Anorexia nervosa (AN)*: is defined as being of low weight, with an over-concern with weight and shape, and a disturbance in body image. There is a sub-classification of restricting AN (pure restriction of caloric intake) and of binging/purging AN (episodes of over-eating with extreme compensation for this). Excessive exercise is not uncommon in AN.
- *Bulimia nervosa (BN)*: criteria include an over-concern with weight and shape, but an essential criterion is recurrent episodes of binge-eating (rapid consumption of a large amount of food in a discrete period of time, experienced as being uncontrollable). In BN, there is significant compensation for binge-eating: for example, self-induced vomiting, purging, fasting or excessive exercise.
- *Binge-eating disorder (BED)*: this describes recurring episodes of binge-eating without extreme compensation. This may or may not be associated with being overweight, but it is linked with feeling out of control and it is often associated with emotions such as disgust or feelings of shame.
- *Other diagnosable EDs*: DSM-IV-TR (APA, 2000), had a category of 'Eating disorders not otherwise specified', or 'EDNOS'. It was notable that EDNOS was found to be the most common diagnosis used in eating-disorder services (Palmer, 2003). Now it has been revised extensively for DSM-V and EDNOS no longer exists. Other EDs are more exactly defined as: pica, rumination disorder, avoidant/restrictive food intake disorder (ARFID), other specified feeding or ED (OSFED) and unspecified feeding or ED (UFED).
- *Obesity:* although often included in psychiatric conditions, obesity refers only to a medical state of overweight – a state that can result from psychological or non-psychological factors.

EDs commonly occur in young women, but take care not to overlook them in men and older women, and take care not to confuse them with other disorders such as the 'true' anorexia of depression or high anxiety, or an OCD that focuses on excessive control of food intake.

In clinical practice, body mass is estimated by using the body-mass index (BMI = kg/m^2). Classification of under- and overweight can be seen in Table 15.1.When working with someone with an ED, it is usually necessary to keep track of their BMI, especially when it is low or particularly high. Some clients weigh themselves excessively, and this should be tackled as a form of reassurance-seeking; others are reluctant to do so – a potential obstacle to treatment, which needs early intervention. The use of BEs is limited if a client is unable to weigh herself, the therapeutic alliance can be compromised, and, most importantly, extreme weight carries health risks and must be monitored. This can be done by you as therapist, by a GP, or by another member of a multidisciplinary team. Do not be persuaded that your client can make an accurate estimate of her size – felt sense of fatness is notoriously unreliable.

Features shared by the EDs are summarised below.

[illegible]ass index

[illegible]	WHO classification
[illegible]	Underweight
[illegible]	Healthy weight
[illegible]–29.9	Grade I overweight
30–39.9	Grade II overweight (obesity)
≥40	Grade III overweight (morbid obesity)

1 INTERPLAY OF COGNITION, EMOTION AND BEHAVIOUR

Identifying such patterns is fundamental to helping those with EDs, whatever the diagnosis or presentation. When your client's difficulties do not fall into a clear diagnostic category, a cognitive behavioural maintenance cycle will be your guide to treatment. Three examples are illustrated in Figure 15.1: a cycle of self-starvation; a cycle of over-compensation for eating; and a cycle of over-eating.

2 COMMON CORE THEMES

As you know, ATs often beg the question 'What is so bad about that?'. EDs are unlikely to be driven purely by concerns about shape and weight, so we have to ask, what does it mean to have a normal body weight/be overweight/be top-heavy/and so on. Themes that emerge from clinical report and research include:

- *Social and interpersonal issues*: these include fears of being abandoned, of social evaluation, shame and low self-esteem (see Waller & Kennerley, 2003, for a review). Thus, systemic (particularly family) factors need consideration at assessment, and partners or parents might be usefully involved in treatment.
- *Control*: this has long been recognised as a powerful factor in the aetiology and maintenance of EDs, and its role has been elaborated (Fairburn, Shafran & Cooper, 1999), but typically clients try to exert over-control and become at risk of losing control.

3 COGNITIVE PROCESS

Extreme cognitive processes are as pertinent to the development and maintenance of EDs as they are to other psychological problems. Specifically, perfectionism and dissociation have been identified as playing a powerful role in their maintenance.

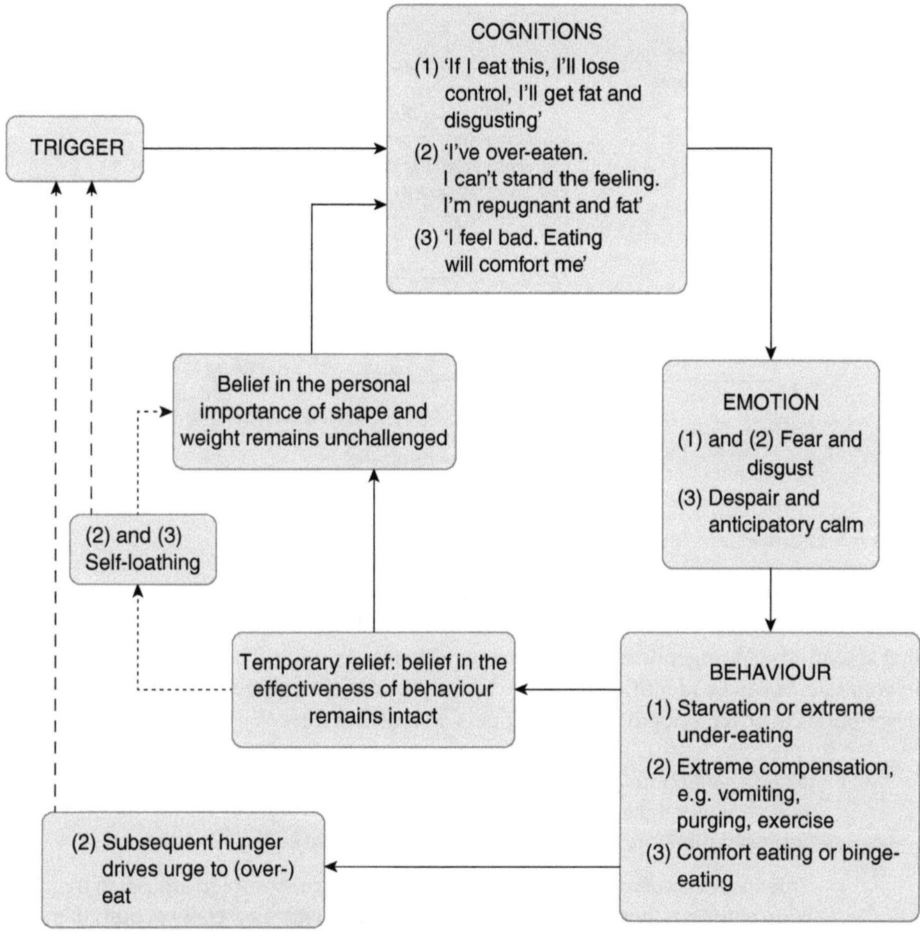

Figure 15.1 Maintaining cycles in eating disorders

- *Dichotomous thinking*, the 'all or nothing' view, is common and tends to be expressed as perfectionism. This is apparent in extreme goals for thinness and in extreme over- or under-eating, for example. It is often underpinned by negative self-evaluation, which drives a compensatory behaviour of attempting to overachieve. Perceived 'success' usually fuels the belief that performance equals worth, and the negative self-view is unchallenged; perceived 'failure' feeds the low self-esteem (see Figure 15.2).
- *Dissociation*, namely mental processes of 'tuning out' or disassociating from current emotional or cognitive experience, has been linked with EDs, as it can be induced by self-starvation or by over-eating (Vanderlinden & Vandereycken, 1997). Repeated dissociation in the face of perceived negative emotions results in a person failing to learn that the emotions can be tolerated, and thus dissociation through misuse of food remains a major coping strategy.

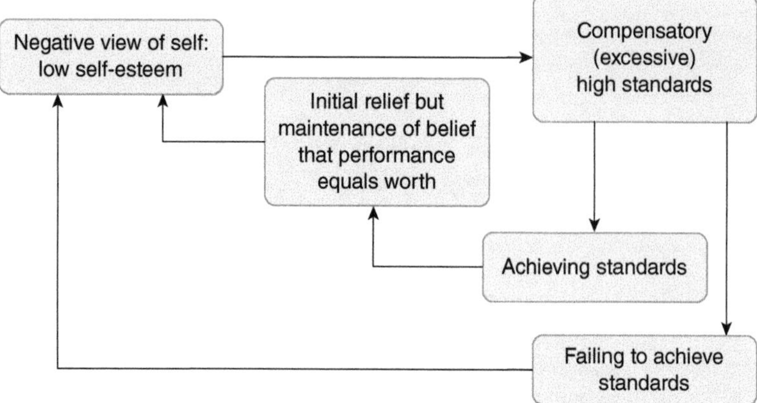

Figure 15.2 Perfectionism maintaining an eating disorder

4 AFFECT

There is substantial evidence for the role of emotion in driving eating behaviours (e.g. Waters, Hill & Waller, 2001). This is relevant to both over- and under-eating, and research suggests that sensations of hunger or satiation are overridden by emotion. The precise role of emotion in your clients will be identified through close analysis of thought records which incorporate descriptions of affect, but put simply, you need to look out for:

- *Mood or affect intolerance*: where bingeing or restrictive eating serve to moderate emotions clients find intolerable. This can be very effective in the short term and therefore a compelling reason for extreme eating behaviours.
- *Emotions overriding the sensations of hunger or of satiation*: high arousal in the form of anxiety, anger or excitement can interfere with awareness of both the need to eat and the need to stop eating.
- *Emotions being mistaken for hunger*: clients who mislabel anger, anxiety, thrill or misery as hunger typically eat in response to this. As eating has a soothing effect, they experience the sensations diminishing, which then reinforces the belief that they were, indeed, hungry.

5 MOTIVATION

People with EDs frequently show an ambivalence about, or even overt resistance to, change, with therapists often having to focus on enhancing motivation. This costs time, and currently there is little evidence that adding a motivational element to CBT improves outcome (Treasure, Katzman, Schmidt, Troop, Todd & de Silva, 1999). However, clients with EDs – particularly those with restricting anorexia nervosa – can be very ambivalent about changing their behaviour, and this has to be acknowledged. Waller et al. (2007) have set out clear guidelines for understanding the client's position and helping them through their ambivalence in a compassionate and effective way.

6 HEALTH RISKS

Severe physical consequences are possible with both acute and chronic EDs. Therefore therapy should be conducted with caution and managed in consultation with a physician. For most therapists practising in the UK, this will be your client's GP. The main concerns include:

- *Starving, bingeing and/or purging*: malnourishment and its consequences, cardiovascular complications, gastrointestinal problems, deficiencies in the immune system, biochemical abnormalities, central nervous system changes, amenorrhoea, osteoporosis, renal failure.
- *Obesity*: metabolic complications, cardiovascular complications, respiratory problems, osteoarthritis.

USING CBT WITH THE EDs

Whatever the diagnosis, you know by now that we will always advocate that you carry out a thorough assessment. Your resulting formulation will guide you towards appropriate cognitive and behavioural interventions. This is especially important if you discover that your client does not fit one of the established models relating to DSM diagnoses. The characteristic dichotomous thinking style of those with EDs can be addressed using continuum work (see Chapter 8), and relapse management is particularly relevant in helping manage powerful cravings and the absolute thinking style that can put someone at risk of binge-eating or self-starvation (see Chapter 6).

As with other problems, treatment involves breaking the cycles that maintain the problem. The most prominent CBT protocols for managing EDs are based on very specific 'maintenance models' (see Vitousek, 1996); generic models and models that encompass schema-level meanings have also proved relevant (see Waller & Kennerley, 2003, for a review). Clinically, you need to be aware of the particular needs of eating-disordered clients and to ask yourself if you are sufficiently resourced to help them.

Treatments for AN need to take into account:

- the consequences of prolonged low body weight – there is general agreement that those with anorexia should have regular medical screening (Zipfel, Lowe & Herzog, 2003);
- the effects of starvation, including behavioural and cognitive changes that reduce motivation and impair the ability to engage in CBT;
- a client's denial or lack of an appreciation of the medical dangers of anorexia, reducing their ability to engage in treatment.

Engagement is further undermined when our clients feel that their behaviour is appropriate and not at all dysfunctional.

Treatments for BN need to take into account:

- the medical risks of extreme compensation for perceived over-eating (vomiting, purging, etc.).

Treatments for binge-eating and obesity need to take into account:

- the medical risks of over-eating and being overweight.

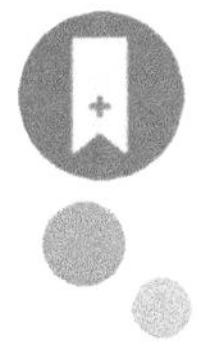

RECOMMENDED READING

Treasure, J., Schmidt, U., & van Furth, E. (2003). *Handbook of eating disorders* (2nd ed.). Chichester: Wiley.

Waller, G., Cordery, H., Corstorphine, E., Hinrichsen, H., Lawson, R., Mountford, V., & Russell, K. (2007). *Cognitive behavioural therapy for eating disorders: a comprehensive treatment guide.* New York: Cambridge University Press.

Vitousek, K.B., & Brown, K.E. (2015). Cognitive-behavioural theory of eating disorders. In L. Smolak & M.P. Levine (Eds.), *The Wiley handbook of eating disorders*. Chichester: Wiley-Blackwell.

PSYCHOLOGICAL TRAUMA

Psychological trauma can take many forms: it can be acute or chronic, it can be of varying levels of severity, it can take place in childhood or adulthood and it can be evoked by many incidents (e.g. witnessing atrocities, being in a natural disaster, sexual assault). In some instances the outcome for the survivor will be PTSD. Even when trauma experiences are complex we should always first consider PTSD rather than something more diagnostically complicated, as PTSD is commonly experienced and we have well-established models and protocols to guide us in supporting sufferers. But PTSD is not always the outcome of a traumatic experience and clinicians need to appreciate that the sequelae of trauma can be very diverse. We see clients who have not experienced 'trauma' as defined by DSM and yet who struggle to cope with the psychological consequences of bad experiences. We also see those who have endured a recognisable 'trauma', but they do not fulfil other DSM criteria for PTSD, such as re-experiencing the trauma and emotional numbing. The psychological legacy of trauma can extend far beyond PTSD, and this is reflected in the attempts of clinicians and researchers to distinguish more categories of post-traumatic responses. For example: 'complex PTSD' (Herman, 1992), 'complex trauma' (Courtois, 2004), 'developmental trauma disorder' (Van der Kolk, Roth, Pelcovitz, Sunday & Spinozzol, 2005).

Terr (1991) made a highly relevant distinction when she recognised two types of trauma victim:

- Type I: those who have experienced a single traumatic event.
- Type II: those who have been repeatedly traumatised.

Terr originally made this distinction with regard to children, but the division has been applied to adults. Rothschild (2000) has suggested further refinements to the adult Type II classification, in order to distinguish those with and without stable backgrounds and to distinguish those who can recall discrete traumatic events from those who have a generic recall of trauma. Scott and Stradling (1994) have proposed a further category, that of *prolonged duress* stress disorder (PDSD), which describes the response to ongoing stress such as chronic illness or emotional cruelty during childhood, rather than specific, tangible trauma.

These distinctions remind us that trauma survivors are not a homogenous group and that PTSD is not the only clinically significant response to trauma. However, research cognitive therapists have tended to focus on trauma victims who have PTSD, and for this population there are well-developed treatments (see Chapter 14). If you are working with survivors of trauma who do not fulfil criteria for PTSD, you will have to work from first principles: formulations leading to interventions, rather than assuming that PTSD protocols fit all trauma survivors.

It is well established that those who have suffered childhood trauma are more likely to experience psychological difficulties in adulthood (Mullen, Martin, Anderson, Romans & Herbison, 1993). Survivors of developmental trauma can present with any combination of psychological problems, such as EDs, depression or interpersonal difficulties. Thus, many of the presenting difficulties of survivors of childhood trauma are familiar to cognitive therapists, and a cognitive understanding of the problem(s) already exists.

There are several key issues that need to be considered when working with survivors of trauma. These are discussed below and further elaborated by Kennerley (in press).

1 MEMORY OF TRAUMA

As we have already said, presentations of non-PTSD trauma are diverse. One manifestation of this is the range of available memories of traumatic experience(s).

- *Lack of memories of trauma*: Some people simply do not have accessible memories of trauma. Sometimes a victim is so distracted or dissociated that full memories are never laid down. Clients will say things like 'My mind froze, I don't remember what he said/did' or 'I can see the knife but I can't recall anything else'. In such cases, there might be no more memory to retrieve. You should not try to force recall because of the danger of creating false memories (see below). It has also been suggested that traumatic memories can be repressed (British Psychological Society, 1995): there will be stored recollections of the trauma, but again, do not force recollection because of the danger of encouraging distortions.
- *Intrusive memories*: Although it is not inevitable, many survivors of trauma have intrusive memories that can involve any, or all, of the senses. For some, these memories will have the quality of flashbacks. Some memories will reflect specific incidents reasonably accurately; some will have become inaccurate over time (a normal phenomenon, to which we are all subject), while some will be a composite of several events which creates a 'representative recollection' where the meaning of the events will be maintained but the specificity of a particular event will be lost. The empirically based methods of managing intrusive memories in Type I PTSD (e.g. Ehlers & Clark, 2000) may not be the best option for managing Type II and/or developmental trauma intrusions – we do not yet know.
- *False memory*: This has been well-researched, and is recognised to exist (British Psychological Society, 1995). All memories are vulnerable to distortion, as they are not stored in the brain like a video-recording, but more like a collection of jig-saw pieces which are reformed each time a memory is recalled. This means that there is a risk of 'misplacements of pieces' each time we remember something and the more we recall a situation the more likely it is that details can get a bit distorted. However, we also know that while memory for detail is rather unreliable, general memories are not. Thus, we might accurately recall that we enjoyed or hated a holiday, even though our recollection of the detail of it would be considerably less reliable. Clinically, the guideline is not to get too obsessed with the detail in remote memories as it can be inaccurate, instead focus on the *meaning* that your client is left with.

2 SENSE OF SELF (AND OTHER SCHEMA-DRIVEN BELIEFS)

Childhood trauma, especially if chronic, can impact on a person's fundamental sense of self, of others and of the future, which can result in the development of powerful belief systems (or schemata) which, by adulthood, can be both rigid and unhelpful, particularly as these belief systems tend to be negative. Schemata and schema therapy are described in Chapter 17, so suffice to say that you need to hold in mind the possibility that your client may express a wide range of difficulties underpinned by inflexible (predominantly negative) belief systems about themselves, the world around them and their future.

Other self-related consequences of developmental trauma can be a fragmented or even absent sense of self. For example, one man described himself as 'constantly flipping from one "me" to another. Sometimes I know that I'm being mean but I can't stop myself; other times, I feel quite comfortable in my own skin and then the next minute I'm feeling scared and vulnerable.' A woman who had experienced chronic childhood neglect described a different experience when she said 'I never feel as if I'm really here, I'm just a shell. I get on with life but I don't really feel I have purpose or identity.' The message for therapists is to be sensitive to the possibility that a trauma survivor might not have a robust sense of self. A first step would be building confidence in her awareness of who she is before trying to unpack belief systems about the self. As our colleague Dr Gillian Butler says, 'How do I know what I think if I don't know who I am?'

3 INTERPERSONAL AND SYSTEMIC ISSUES

Many survivors of interpersonal trauma have difficulty in developing a trusting relationship with others, including you as therapist. It is not unusual to have to 'invest' in sessions to build up your working alliance in preparation for the CBT per se (see Chapter 3). Survivors of accidents, impersonal attack and natural disasters may, however, find it much easier to establish rapport.

Survivors of interpersonal trauma often develop difficulties in their real-life relationships, and a systemic overview of your client's situation can be helpful. This means frequently updating your understanding of their relationship with their children (Are the children at risk of neglect or abuse?) or with significant others (Is your client at risk of harm? Is their partner at risk?). You may find it relevant to take this a step further and consider occupational, institutional and cultural factors in the maintenance of difficulties.

A further consideration is that repeated early life trauma has often been linked with personality disorders (Terr, 1991; Layden et al., 1993; Beck, Freeman, Davis & Associates, 2004), and having a personality disorder is commonly associated with interpersonal difficulties.

As a clinician, you need to be prepared for these various possibilities and then consider what we might call the 'bigger picture' beyond the cognitions and behaviours of the individual. This will stretch your formulation skills, but the basic principles of formulation (see Chapter 4) apply however complex the presentation.

4 COMPLEXITY OF PRESENTATIONS

Sometimes, when working with survivors of complex or chronic trauma, you may find that the 'bigger picture' is complicated. It is not unusual for clients to present with a collection of problems: many suffer from several psychological difficulties, some have concurrent physical difficulties that are a legacy of their trauma, many live in dysfunctional environments, all of which undermines therapy. You are again reminded to formulate the 'bigger picture' by asking questions that will elicit more information: 'Are there other difficulties in your life?', 'Is there anything else that you do that might affect this?', 'Are there other occasions when ... ?', 'And in your work life?', 'And in your home life?'.

CBT WITH SURVIVORS OF TRAUMA

With the exception of research focused on PTSD, evaluation of CBT with survivors of trauma in a wider sense has not been profuse and systematic, and sadly there remains a paucity of RCTs. However, there are guidelines from highly experienced practitioners to help you develop your approaches to working with survivors of trauma who have personality disorders (e.g. Layden et al., 1993; Davidson, 2000; Beck et al., 2004; Arntz & van Genderen, 2009). There is increasing research supporting the theory behind Gilbert's compassionate mind therapy (CMT), and it may be an effective intervention with those who have been left with fixed self-blaming and self-attacking beliefs (see Gilbert & Irons, 2005, for a review). There is also evidence that supports the use of cognitive techniques for specific aspects of a client's presentation (e.g. Arntz & Weertman, 1999; Geisen-Bloo et al., 2006) and for interventions for particular categories of trauma (e.g. Resick & Schnicke, 1993).

A very key development in our appreciation of how best to offer cognitive and behavioural therapies to those with complex trauma and developmental trauma is the emergence of graduated or 'phased therapy' (Herman, 1992; Chard, Weaver & Resick, 1997; Cloitre, Koenen, Cohen & Han, 2002). This advocates beginning with a period of stabilisation before shifting to trauma-focused work. The stabilisation phase often includes learning basic mood and stress management skills, working with thematic (unhelpful) schemata, developing interpersonal skills. In our experience of supervising CBT therapists, we frequently found that practitioners preferred this more stepped, cautious approach with clients who were less emotionally and cognitively robust. More recently, outcome studies have indicated that it does have therapeutic advantage for clients with more complex trauma-related presentations (e.g. Cloitre et al., 2010).

In summary, with Type II and/or developmental trauma there is no single well-established protocol to follow, and you will have to call on the generic skills of CBT, informed by the theory and research that is currently available. However, we would promote the following guidelines:

- Formulate the *big* picture, think interpersonally, systemically and even culturally in order to appreciate the full impact of trauma, particularly chronic and childhood trauma.
- Remember the qualities of memory and don't force recollections.
- Focus on the accessible DSM Axis I problems as far as possible, using treatment protocols where appropriate.
- Bear in mind the possibility of your having to accommodate interpersonal difficulties, schema-driven problems and multi-problem presentations.
- Consider a stepped approach with an early focus on the mood, stress and interpersonal skills that your client will need to 'stabilise' himself if he becomes emotionally overwhelmed.
- Keep risk assessment on your agenda.

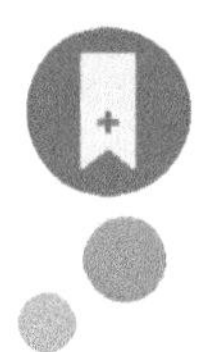

RECOMMENDED READING

Beck, A.T., Freeman, A., Davis, D., & Associates (2004). *Cognitive therapy of personality disorders* (2nd ed.). New York: Guilford Press.

Cloitre, M., Stovall-McClough, K.C., Nooner, K., Zorbas, P., Cherry, S., Jackson, C.L., Gan, W., & Petkova, E. (2010). Treatment for PTSD related to childhood abuse: a randomized controlled trial. *American Journal of Psychiatry*, *167*, 915–924.

Grey, N. (2009). *A casebook of cognitive therapy for traumatic stress reactions*. Hove: Routledge.

Kennerley, H. (in press). Special Issue of *the Cognitive Behaviour Therapist* on the theme of Complexity within Cognitive Behavioural Therapy, Supervision and Services.

Layden, M.A., Newman, C.F., Freeman, A., & Byers-Morse, S. (1993). *Cognitive behaviour therapy of borderline personality disorder*. Needham Heights, MA: Allyn & Bacon.

McNally, R.J. (2003). *Remembering trauma*. Cambridge, MA: Harvard University Press.

Petrak, J., & Hedge, B. (2002). *The trauma of sexual assault: treatment, prevention and practice*. Chichester: Wiley.

ANGER

Anger is an emotion, and, like other emotions, it is not *necessarily* a problem. However, anger may become a problem when it is excessive in frequency or severity and when it leads to behaviour that is dangerous to self or others, or that hinders rather than helps people in achieving their goals. It can be at the heart of a range of interpersonal problems such as domestic violence (physical or emotional) or aggressive outbursts in the workplace, on the road, in social settings and so on. It can also be a post-traumatic reaction – sometimes the emotional theme of a flashback is rage, or the predominant feeling in bereavement is an angry one.

Although anger has received less attention than other emotions, there is evidence that CBT can be an effective treatment for anger problems (Beck & Fernandez, 1998; Naeem,

Clarke & Kingdon, 2009; Henwood, Chou & Browne, 2015), so there is good reason to use quite 'standard' approaches to understanding and managing this problem. The Beckian approach sees anger as arising in situations where people feel that important 'rules' about how others should behave are violated, or as a defensive reaction when there is a perceived threat: Beck has said that behind anger is often hurt or fear (Beck, 1999). So use your Socratic skills to discover the meaning behind irritation and rage and then formulate the consequences, but bear in mind that your client might be particularly sensitive to perceived criticism so pay extra attention to adopting a non-judgemental position and keep a close eye on your interpersonal interchange.

A Beckian approach to anger management is clearly articulated for the client by Greenberger and Padesky (2015), who also address guilt and shame as these responses are so often linked to an angry outburst. When guilt and shame are prominent, consider looking at Gilbert's guidelines on incorporating a compassionate focus into CBT (Gilbert, 2005). Assertiveness training is also highly relevant in managing anger. There are very many assertiveness texts on the market, particularly self-help guides, but an overtly cognitive behavioural approach can be found in Kennerley (2014b). This is a very short guide to being assertive, but it is a simple starting point and it can easily supplement your CBT work.

However, the best-known CBT approach to anger control was developed by Novaco (1979, 2000) and derives more from Meichenbaum's (1975) stress inoculation training than from Beckian cognitive models. In brief, the therapy typically consists of three stages:

- *Preparation*: the client is helped to identify patterns of anger, including triggers and typical thoughts, feelings and behaviours, through the usual assessment and formulation.
- *Skills acquisition*: the client learns techniques to help him lower his arousal when provoked. These may include relaxation and 'self-instructional techniques' (see below).
- *Application training*: the client rehearses the techniques in progressively more difficult situations, perhaps starting off with practising in imagination and progressing through role play to *in vivo* application.

The self-instruction central to Novaco's approach teaches management of different stages of a potentially anger-provoking situation. These stages include cognitive and physical approaches that you will recognise from what has gone before in this book:

- preparing for the provocation (e.g. recognising situations that may be difficult; reducing excessive expectations of other people);
- coping with physical arousal (e.g. through relaxation and/or breathing control);
- coping with cognitive arousal (using self-instruction statements such as 'Getting angry won't help me');
- post-confrontation reflection (evaluating the outcome and working out how to move forward).

This can only be helpful, of course, if we have collaboration with our client. Unfortunately, a common difficulty in therapy for anger is a strained working alliance. Your client might be ambivalent about engaging because they are ambivalent about modifying their aggressive responses. Anger has often been perceived as useful to them in the past and it can be rewarding in the short term. This reminds us of the importance of carrying out an assessment that explores the meaning and not just the consequence of angry outbursts. Asking questions such as 'What does this feeling mean to you?' or 'What's the up-side of being angry?' can be revealing and help us better understand the attractiveness of anger:

- 'I lived in fear as a child, but when I get this whoosh of anger, I feel no fear and it's just the best feeling – I feel safe.'
- 'I see the red mist and I feel as though I'm untouchable: I don't feel fear and I don't feel pain.'
- 'The only time I feel confident is when I'm angry – then I feel strong and sure of myself.'

It is understandable that any of these clients might be reluctant to give up the experience of feeling safe and strong and confident. The goals themselves are excellent goals so we would want to preserve them, but we would need to help clients develop the means of achieving them in other ways. Once a person has the ability to feel safe, strong and confident by other means, then they might more willingly take the risk of letting go of the angry outbursts.

Some people may have been referred to therapy because someone *else* thinks their anger is a problem (e.g. their families or the courts). In these instances, motivating clients can be especially difficult and we would direct you back to Chapters 7 and 11 for more guidance on taking a motivational approach. Of course, formulations should embrace the 'bigger picture' of interpersonal and social interactions to illustrate how anger undermines relationships. However, sometimes (but not always) a person prone to anger perceives this as a criticism ('So it's my fault, is it?'), and you might find that beginning with a positive formulation of the *virtuous cycles* of anger management, thus showing the co-operative patterns that your client can forge, might usefully illustrate the advantages of change without it seeming confrontative.

A further reason for engagement difficulties can be therapist reactions. Some of us are unnerved by heated outbursts or discomforted when hearing harsh and critical appraisals of others, and we might find ourselves losing our Rogerian stance and our cognitive curiosity. If you find yourself in this situation, try to discover what personal meanings explain your response and take this issue to supervision if necessary. Do this before a therapeutic impasse is established because you will make little progress without an authentic working alliance and, even worse, your client might find more to anger them.

It probably goes without saying that all work needs to be carried out with a keen awareness of risk – to those around your client and to you, yourself. So do ensure that you practise in conditions that maximise your safety: let colleagues know if you are seeing a person with anger issues, have access to an alarm, have a clear exit, have a contract with your client that sets out the expectations of behaviour within a session. When you begin therapy do the 'groundwork' of establishing what the early signs of anger might be and how you will both respond. For example, you might agree that as soon as your client begins to feel anger that he or she will tell you and you will take a break to carry out controlled breathing and distraction to restore a sense of calm and control, or perhaps you might agree that your client can take a minute or two break walking outside with or without you.

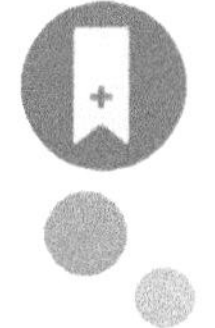

RECOMMENDED READING

Beck, A.T. (1999). *Prisoners of hate*. New York: HarperCollins.

Henwood, K.S., Chou, S., & Browne, K.D. (2015). A systematic review and meta-analysis of the effectiveness of CBT informed anger management. *Aggression and Violent Behaviour, 25*, 280–292.

Novaco, R.W. (1979). The cognitive regulation of anger and stress. In P.C. Kendall & S.D. Hollon (Eds.), *Cognitive-behavioral interventions: theory, research, and procedures*. New York: Academic Press.

Novaco, R.W. (2007). Anger dysregulation. In T. Cavell & K. Malcolm (Eds.), *Anger, aggression, and interventions for interpersonal violence*. Mahwah, NJ: Erlbaum.

PSYCHOTIC SYMPTOMS

Psychotic symptoms are common in several mental illnesses, particularly schizophrenia and bipolar disorder. Schizophrenia is characterised by delusions, hallucinations, disorganised speech and behaviour and other symptoms that cause social or occupational dysfunction. Relapse rates are high, with sufferers often experiencing multiple relapses over their lifetime. For a DSM diagnosis, symptoms must have been present for six months and include at least one month of active symptoms (APA, 2013). It affects just under 1 per cent of the population and sufferers have an elevated risk of suicide (Birchwood et al., 2014). Bipolar disorder is characterised by periods of depression alternating with periods of mania, that is, an unusual sense of elation, excitement, subjective racing of thoughts and sense of over-optimism. For a diagnosis of mania to be made, this must last at least a week and cause marked impairment in social or occupational functioning or to require hospitalisation (APA, 2013). About 2 per cent of the population experiences bipolar disorder and it has a high relapse rate – 60 per cent within two years (Geddes & Miklowitz, 2013).

Most of the earlier work on CBT for psychosis (CBTp) focused on medication-resistant symptoms in schizophrenia, although there was a gradually increasing interest in CBT for bipolar disorder (see e.g. Basco & Rush, 1996; Lam, Jones, Bright & Hayward, 1999; Scott, 2001).

Although effect sizes from first generation psychological treatments for psychosis yielded only modest outcomes of approximately 0.4 (Wykes, Steele, Everitt & Tarrier, 2008), the adoption of a 'precision-medicine paradigm', focusing on specific, independent psychotic symptoms rather than on diagnoses such as 'schizophrenia', is beginning to yield much greater effect sizes (Freeman et al., 2015). As a close colleague of ours says, 'It's early days but exciting times!'

An encouraging and recent review of CBTp and bipolar disorders (Thase, Kingdon & Turkington, 2014) concluded that many important questions remained to be answered but the evidence to date suggested that adjunctive CBT conveyed clinical and statistically significant benefits. People with psychosis or bipolar disorder often receive CBT as an adjunct to pharmacotherapy, thus you need to routinely ask about medications and to be familiar with their effects and side-effects. It is also worth being aware of the implications of them reducing medications without medical advice (as this sometimes happens).

Researchers and clinicians recognise that *appraisals* of actual experiences (mental and/or physical) are key; that having an anomalous experience such as hearing voices or derealisation or racing thoughts does not in itself indicate psychosis or bipolar disorder, but rather it is the appraisal that is made of those experiences, together with the associated levels of distress or dysfunction, and behavioural consequences that are important. Furthermore, the experience of over-valued ideas, hallucinations and delusions are cognitions and as such not 'all or nothing' phenomena. They sit along a continuum causing differing degrees of distress to different clients. Once again we are reminded that each person's difficulties need to be assessed sensitively so that we, the clinicians, don't fall into the trap of jumping to conclusions.

It is important to appreciate that CBT with people who suffer from psychoses or bipolar disorder can help with a range of difficulties – which often go beyond the expected symptoms of psychosis or bipolar disorder:

- hallucinations, particularly auditory hallucinations (i.e. experiencing unusual or distorted sensory perceptions which do not seem to exist outside one's perception);
- delusions (false beliefs that persist despite a lack of evidence and which are not explained by cultural norms);
- problems of mood, such as depression or anxiety, which can so commonly develop as a result of suffering hallucinations, delusions or the psycho-social sequelae of psychoses or bipolar disorder;
- other related difficulties such as sleep problems, substance misuse, low self-esteem, relationship problems and social withdrawal.

In addition, there may be an important role for working with families or other carers; for useful reviews, see Pilling et al.'s (2002) account of CBT and family therapy for schizophrenia and Geddes and Miklowitz's (2013) account relating to bipolar disorder.

Given that people who experience psychosis or bipolar disorder often struggle with difficulties that go beyond delusion, hallucination and mania there is much the CBT therapist can offer. Even if you do not feel equipped to help someone who is experiencing a current episode, you can still usefully aid that person in remission – a person who is likely to continue to struggle with other psycho-social difficulties.

Nonetheless, this work has sufficient risks and complications that we would urge you to make sure you are very familiar with using CBT with more straightforward presentations and that you have recourse to suitable supervision and psychiatric support. Almost all trials of CBTp and bipolar disorder use CBT as part of a care package which also includes medication and mental health team support, rather than using CBT as a stand-alone treatment.

Psychological treatments for psychosis and bipolar disorder have steadily moved away from targeting diagnoses and instead have focused on specific symptoms and maintaining cycles, with particularly good evidence that CBT is effective for persecutory delusions (Freeman, 2016) and command hallucinations in schizophrenia (Birchwood et al., 2014), and growing indications that CBT is effective in managing anxiety-related difficulties, such as GAD and PTSD, in bipolar disorders (Stratford, Cooper, Di Simplicio, Blackwell & Holmes, 2015).

As with other CBT work, the over-arching aim is to help clients achieve the shared goal of overcoming obstacles to their wellbeing, and the targets of treatment are a person's appraisal of their experiences and the maintaining patterns for unhelpful appraisals.

Key processes thought to maintain extreme appraisals (i.e. delusions in psychosis and over-valued ideas in bipolar disorder) include:

- reasoning biases;
- SBs;
- worry;
- poor sleep;
- negative self-cognition;
- strong imagery.

As ever, your task as a CBT practitioner is to establish a relationship, build a formulation and apply CBT therapeutic strategies to the maintaining factors in that formulation.

The aim is to help clients achieve their own valued goals by working to reduce the distress and disability caused by symptoms and to reduce the risk of relapse. Some of the standard features of CBT described earlier in this book are particularly relevant to this work. Building a collaborative relationship and a formulation that can give an alternative, non-threatening and non-stigmatising account of the symptoms is vital. The formulation is then used to identify and test cognitions about the source, meaning and controllability of symptoms. BEs can be a key part of this exploration (see Close & Schuller, 2004) but need to be planned and carried out with particular sensitivity.

Other factors that may need special care include engaging clients who may be suspicious and who sometimes perceive themselves, rightly or wrongly, as having been abused by psychiatric systems; the pleasurable experience of mild mania, which can prevent a sufferer from wanting to manage it; idiosyncratic thought processes, which may make it difficult for you to keep track of the client's thinking; and the sometime neediness of the client's family or carer.

All these complications mean that CBTp may be a longer-term treatment, taken at a relatively slow pace, and that you need skilled supervision and support.

RECOMMENDED READING

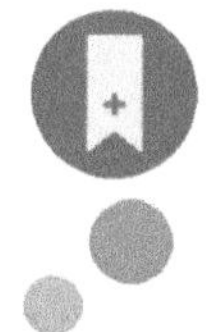

Chadwick, P., Birchwood, M., & Trower, P. (1996). *Cognitive therapy for delusions, voices and paranoia*. Chichester: Wiley.

Birchwood, M., Michail, M., Meaden, A., Tarrier, N., Lewis, S., Wykes, T., Davies, L., Dunn, G., & Peters, E. (2014). Cognitive behaviour therapy to prevent harmful compliance with command hallucinations (COMMAND): a randomised controlled trial. *The Lancet Psychiatry, 1*, 23–33.

Deckersbach, P., Eisner, L., & Sylvia. L. (2016). Cognitive behavioural therapy for bi-polar disorder. In T. J. Petersen, S.E. Sprich, & S. Wilhelm (Eds.), *The Massachusetts General Hospital handbook of cognitive behavioural therapy*. New York: Springer.

Freeman, D. (2016). Persecutory delusions: a cognitive perspective on understanding and treatment. *The Lancet Psychiatry, 3*, 685–692.

Geddes, J. R., & Miklowitz, D.J. (2013). Treatment of bipolar disorder. *Lancet, 3813*, 1672–1682.

Kingdon, D., & Turkington, D. (2004). *Cognitive therapy of schizophrenia*. New York: Guilford Press.

Lam, D., Jones, S., & Hayward, P. (2010). *Cognitive therapy for bipolar disorder: a therapist's guide to concepts, methods and practice* (2nd ed.). Chichester: Wiley.

Larkin, W., & Morrison, A. (2006). *Trauma and psychosis*. Hove: Routledge.

Morrison, A.P., Renton, J.C., Dunn, H., Williams, S., & Bentall, R.P. (2004). *Cognitive therapy for psychosis: a formulation-based approach*. Hove: Brunner-Routledge.

Scott, J., Colom, F., & Vieta, E. (2006). A meta-analysis of relapse rates with adjunctive psychological therapies compared to usual psychiatric treatment for bipolar disorders. *International Journal of Neuro-psychopharmacology, 10*, 123–129.

RELATIONSHIP DIFFICULTIES

Difficulties in relationships are common in clients who ask for help. Sometimes this is the main problem, or at least the identified difficulty, but sometimes you will find that your client's anxieties or depression or ED has also taken a toll on relationships. This is true for people with recent-onset discrete disorders, as well as with people with long-standing problems, perhaps even a personality disorder.

For example, a man with social anxiety may have difficulties in asserting himself; someone with low self-esteem may be overly dependent on others; a depressed client may have become socially withdrawn; a woman with exaggerated health concerns might be stressing her husband and children, as might the man with chronic OCD. A cognitive behavioural formulation allows issues such as these to be approached in similar ways to other problems, by looking at the inter-linkages between cognitions and emotions, behaviours and physical state, where the cognitions and behaviours will be concerned with relationships.

A woman who had been depressed for a number of months had gradually reduced the amount of time she spent with her friends. If she were invited to see someone, her AT would be 'I am boring and have nothing to say. If I see my friends in this state, I shall lose them'. She therefore turned down most invitations, with the result that her friends made less contact with her and her mood suffered.

With someone like this, where the ATs were typical of her depressed state but not of her thinking in general, the problem could successfully be approached at the level of ATs. For people with a personality disorder, the difficulties in relationships are likely to be more pervasive and enduring, and a central feature of the disorder. However, the CBT approach still emphasises the central role of cognitions about self, other people and relationships, and their linkages with behaviour and emotions, though it is likely to be more necessary to also tackle underlying beliefs.

A man with a history of emotional neglect had a powerful and pervasive belief that 'No one is there for me'. In response to this, he had developed a rule that 'If I am honest about my failures, I shall be rejected', and as a result, frequently chose lying as a way of protecting himself. In the short term this allayed his fears, but in the medium term presented him with real difficulties as he had to weave more and more complicated stories to cover his lies. Treatment partly involved experiments with confessing to small failures, and keeping careful notes of the responses that this drew from others, particularly from his wife.

One setting where relationship problems can be viewed as they occur is the therapeutic relationship. Safran and Muran (1995) have written about how interactions in the therapeutic relationship can be used to invalidate unhelpful beliefs about relationships (see Chapter 3).

Safran and Segal (1990) proposed that the ways that other people respond can play an important role in the maintenance of dysfunctional thinking about relationships. They suggested that a client's interpersonal behaviour towards others may 'pull' a predictable response from the other person, which then confirms the client's original belief.

A woman who was bullied at school had a belief that she was not easy to be with, and that if she tried to join in, she would be rejected, and feel isolated and desolate. As she assumed that she would not be welcome in groups, she acted in an aloof and arrogant manner when she was in group situations (e.g. at professional conferences), on the basis that 'If you don't want me, I am not going to demean myself by looking as though I want you'. Her colleagues responded to this by turning to others who were easier to approach, thus confirming her belief that she was not welcome.

If an unhelpful belief has been identified, then in the therapy setting the therapist can experiment with *not* being 'pulled' into responding in the predicted way, and therapist and client can reflect on the impact that this has on the client's beliefs. The client can then experiment with using different interpersonal behaviours based on his modified belief.

This same woman's therapist needed to change the regular time for appointments because of a teaching commitment, and as the woman interpreted this as indicating that the therapist was trying to find a way not to be with her, she became aloof and rigid about alternative dates. The therapist rejected the 'pull' to respond with 'Well, it's up to you!', and instead was warm and concerned about their difficulty with rescheduling, and showed non-verbally that she very much wanted to find a solution so that she could see the client. After the practical problem was dealt with, the therapist asked the client to reflect upon how she had construed the situation, and what implication the therapist's response had for her original belief (which in this case had been extensively discussed in earlier sessions).

Beck et al. (2004, 2015) and Young, Klosko and Weishaar (2003) have also written creatively about ways of dealing with interpersonal problems (see Chapter 17), and Linehan, Heard and Armstrong (1993) have developed a group programme called 'dialectical behaviour therapy' (DBT) for helping clients with borderline personality disorders (BPDs) (see Chapter 16). The programme is lengthy, taking up to a year, but the outcome data so far are encouraging, with significant impacts on interpersonal and social adjustment.

Finally, there are many useful ideas about working with relationship problems incorporated in Dattilio and Padesky's (1990) work with couples. Indeed, there is now a wealth of theory and research on cognitive behavioural couple therapy (CBCT) and a growing interest in systemic CBT. Baucom and Boeding (2013) present a popular approach to couples work that is building a compelling evidence base and in their article they describe how to maximise success and minimise relapse. Koch, Stewart and Stuart (2010) describe systemic aspects of CBT, illustrating just how and when this might facilitate recovery.

RECOMMENDED READING

Baucom, D.H., & Boeding. S (2013) The role of theory and research in the practice of cognitive-behavioral couple therapy: if you build it, they will come. *Behaviour Therapy*, *44*, 592–602.

Dattilio, F.M., & Padesky, C.A. (1990). *Cognitive therapy with couples*. Sarasota, FL: Professional Resource Exchange.

Koch, C., Stewart, A., & Stuart, A. (2010). Systemic aspects of CBT. In M. Mueller, H. Kennerley, F. McManus, & D. Westbrook (Eds.), *The Oxford guide to surviving as a CBT therapist*. Oxford: Oxford University Press.

Safran, J.D., & Muran, J.C. (1995). Resolving therapeutic alliance ruptures: diversity and integration. *In Session: Psychotherapy in Practice*, *1*, 81–92.

Safran, J.D., & Segal, Z.V. (1990). *Interpersonal process in cognitive therapy*. New York: Basic Books.

SUBSTANCE MISUSE AND ADDICTIVE DISORDERS

When people talk about substance misuse, they are generally thinking about misuse of alcohol, psychoactive drugs and possibly smoking. It is worth bearing in mind that other behaviours such as gambling, over-eating and compulsive spending have also been viewed as 'addictive', so may be amenable to the management outlined for substance misuse.

DSM-IV (APA, 2000), distinguished two categories:

- *Substance abuse* refers to a maladaptive pattern of use leading to significant impairment or distress (e.g. failure to fulfil responsibilities, legal or interpersonal problems).
- *Substance dependence* is more severe, and includes increased tolerance, withdrawal symptoms, use of increasing amounts of a substance, and a persistent desire for the substance even though the person recognises the negative consequences of its use.

DSM-V (APA, 2013) combines these into a single disorder measured on a continuum from mild to severe while adding the condition 'Addictive disorders'. This grouping of 'Substance-related and addictive disorders' reflects research findings that gambling disorder is similar to substance-related disorders in clinical expression, brain origin, co-morbidity, physiology and treatment. Kennerley's clinical model for self-injurious behaviours (2004) also recognises such similarities.

WHY ENGAGE IN SUBSTANCE MISUSE OR ADDICTIVE AND HARMFUL BEHAVIOURS?

In the face of the negative consequences, why do people do things that inevitably backfire? Among the most common reasons are rapid management of feelings (physical or emotional), for example:

- mood regulation, either to control depression or anxiety, or to enhance positive moods like happiness;
- to manage cravings, which can be physiological or psychological;
- to cope with adverse circumstances (e.g. abusive relationships, poverty);
- to contain severe psychiatric symptoms.

It is very difficult for people to give up behaviours that have such an immediate impact, partly because they often report that nothing competes with the positive effects of the substance (thrill, mood enhancement, blanking out problems). This is exacerbated when there is a *physical dependence*, where *withdrawal symptoms* are experienced.

Some clients can be helped with short-term interventions, but many will require longer-term input, particularly those with dependency. Ideally, treatment should address the client's associated problems, and not just the substance misuse or addiction. Many programmes involve more than one treatment modality, typically medication and psychosocial help, as well as psychological input. There is then good evidence of effectiveness (see e.g. Hubbard, 2005). The CBT approach to substance misuse emphasises the additional role of unhelpful thinking in the maintenance of the behaviour (Beck, Wright, Newman & Liese, 1993; Marlatt & Gordon, 1985) and this will now be considered.

THE COGNITIVE BEHAVIOURAL APPROACH TO SUBSTANCE MISUSE AND ADDICTIVE BEHAVIOURS

Liese and Franz's (1996) developmental model for substance misuse is similar to the general CBT model of development (see Chapter 4), with the specific addition of exposure to, and experimentation with, addictive behaviours (e.g. family members who use drugs, friends who encourage drug use), and consequent development of drug-related beliefs ('If I use drugs I shall feel less anxious', 'I will fit in more easily if I use drugs').

The general CBT approach is similar to that used with other kinds of problems, including socialisation to the model, structured sessions, and the range of cognitive, behavioural and physical techniques described in Chapters 8, 9 and 10; there are useful clinical examples in Daley and Marlatt (2006) and an excellent guide to be found in Mitcheson et al. (2010).

With this group of clients there is a very strong emphasis on building a non-blaming conceptualisation, whilst encouraging the development of a sense of autonomy and responsibility. Given the challenges of this work, it is particularly helpful to emphasise client assets such as adaptive coping styles or strong social supports. A collaborative therapeutic alliance is clearly important, and relates to compliance in treatment (Petry & Bickel, 1999). This can be difficult in the face of frequent relapses and, sometimes, antisocial and illegal behaviour, dishonesty and so on. Thus a significant challenge for us is maintaining a genuinely compassionate and empathic stance. This is facilitated by truly understanding difficult behaviours in terms of the formulation, being prepared to work at an interpersonal level and taking supervision as necessary.

It is often productive to consider a broader systemic formulation that embraces the interpersonal, social, domestic, institutional or cultural factors that could drive the problem behaviour. For example, it is very difficult for a young person to give up drug misuse if she is constantly mixing with a crowd who offer access to drugs and endorse their use.

An important concept, highly relevant for any client with marked ambivalence about change, is that of *preparedness for change* (Prochaska et al., 1994) (see Chapter 11), and the importance of working with them to change their position on this continuum. Readiness to risk changing behaviour can fluctuate, depending on the level of urge or craving a person experiences. Powerful physiologically driven urges to engage in misuse can undermine commitment to therapy, and you need to anticipate this and to encourage clients to develop substitute behaviours that can help take the edge off the craving: for example, monitoring internal and external triggers for craving, and then using forms of self-soothing or distraction, physical activity, social interaction or 'urge surfing' (Daley & Marlatt, 2006; Mitcheson et al., 2010).

Preparedness to change often goes hand in hand with motivational work. By motivating a person to consider that it is worth taking the risk of changing, you can move them along the spectrum of preparedness to change (again see Chapter 11 and see also Video 15.1: Motivating your client). This is sometimes the key to working with those who struggle to resist certain behaviours, and it is worth visiting the work of Bill Miller, the father of MI. He likens this compassionate, empathic and encouraging approach to 'horse whispering' (Miller, 2000) – a reminder that it's not about heavy-handed persuasion but about understanding and guiding in a non-judgemental fashion.

The issue of whether you should encourage control of the problem behaviour or total abstinence (advocated by major influences such as Alcoholics Anonymous) has continued to divide people who work in this area. It is possible that controlled behaviour is more relevant for the very large group with less severe problems (Sobell & Sobell, 1993). The *harm reduction approach* is one attempt to circumvent this issue, while accepting the need to take account of the stage that the client has reached. The goals of therapy are to limit the impact of the behaviour rather than aim for total abstinence (Marlatt, Larimer, Baer & Quigley, 1993).

The cognitive behavioural approach emphasises the individual's capacity to exercise control. Another important aspect of this is *relapse minimisation* (Daley & Marlatt, 2006), including the identification and avoidance of high-risk situations, exploration of the decisions that lead to problem behaviours, lifestyle changes and learning from relapses in order to reduce future ones (see also Chapter 6).

Some of the problems of working with people who feel very compelled to engage in harmful behaviours have already been identified: marked ambivalence about change, and difficult behaviours such as non-compliance and dishonesty. Some problem behaviours may also be difficult to identify because the manifestations may be hard to recognise (e.g. a person who still functions well despite nocturnal drug misuse; the woman who is not in financial difficulties (yet) through her gambling) or easily not attributed to substance misuse (e.g. sleep disturbance, panic attacks). It is important to bear this in mind as a hypothesis when clients present for help with other problems.

RECOMMENDED READING

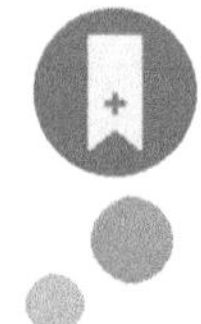

Beck, A.T., Wright, F.D., Newman, C.F., & Liese, B.S. (1993). *Cognitive therapy of substance abuse.* New York: Guilford.

Daley, D.C., & Marlatt, G.A. (2006). *Overcoming your alcohol or drug problem. Effective recovery strategies: therapist guide.* Oxford: Oxford University Press.

Liese, B.S., & Franz, R.A. (1996). Treating substance use disorders with cognitive therapy: lessons learned and implications for the future. In P.S. Salkovskis (Ed.), *Frontiers of cognitive therapy.* New York: Guilford.

Miller, W.R. (2000). Motivational interviewing: some parallels with horse whispering. *Behavioural and Cognitive Psychotherapy, 28*, 285–292.

Mitcheson, L., Maslin, J., Meynen, T., Morrison, T., Hill, R., & Wanigarantne, S. (2010). *Applied cognitive and behavioural approaches to the treatment of addiction.* Chichester: Wiley-Blackwell.

OTHER APPLICATIONS OF CBT

Clearly, the application of CBT extends beyond the few described here. It is used with diverse clinical populations: children and adolescents, older adults, those with learning disabilities, or sexual problems, in settings that are forensic, physical health, occupational and so on. However, interesting as these applications are, it is beyond the scope of this book to describe them, though we want to alert you to the versatility of CBT. There will be training events, specialist supervision and textbooks to guide you if a client has specialist needs, and we strongly urge you to make use of them. However, remember that the principles described in this book are relevant to *every* CBT intervention, and the methods that we have described will be useful across client groups. The foundation set out in Chapters 1 to 11 will stand you in good stead for carrying out a cognitive assessment, offering a formulation and, where appropriate, beginning work with a range of clients.

LEARNING EXERCISES

These learning exercises are available to download from the companion website.

REVIEW AND REFLECTION:

- Which of these approaches would fit well with your way of working and your client group?
- Even if you work in a generic CBT service (rather than within a specialist service), are you inspired by the developments in CBT summarised in this chapter? If so, how might you use this to inform your more generalist practice?
- Are there any possible *disadvantages* to any of these approaches? What are they, and how much of a problem do they represent?

TAKING IT FORWARD:

- Is there scope for trying any of these approaches in your own clinical practice or in the service for which you work?
- What would you need to do to make this happen? With whom do you need to discuss CBT approaches? How can you best make your case?
- How will you evaluate the impact of introducing any of the ideas in this chapter into your practice?

VIDEO LINK

- **15.1 Motivating your client**

16

ALTERNATIVE METHODS OF DELIVERY

- Introduction
- Modes of delivery for CBT
- Self-help
- Large groups
- Conventional groups
- Couple therapy
- Pair therapy
- Summary
- Learning exercises
- Further reading

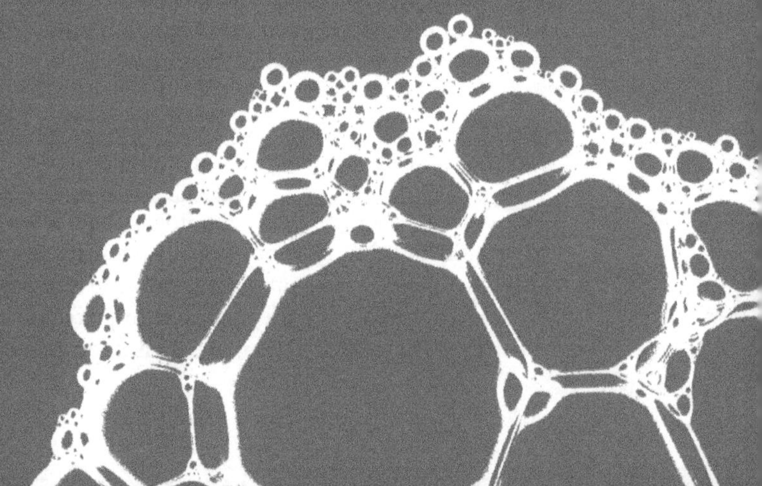

INTRODUCTION

Traditionally, 'classic' psychotherapy comprises weekly sessions of a 50-minute 'therapeutic hour' of face-to-face contact between therapist and client. CBT has often followed this style but has also investigated whether other modes of therapy may have advantages over traditional models. These alternative approaches are usually motivated by the desire to achieve one or more of the following goals.

MAKING THERAPY MORE COST-EFFECTIVE

This is a sound goal. In private practice we want to give 'value for money' and in most publicly funded health care systems there is the perennial problem that the resources available for psychological therapy are insufficient to meet demand, with the inevitable result that long waiting lists for treatment are common.

It is fairly easy to derive a common-sense 'equation' for waiting time, as follows:

$$\text{Waiting time} \propto \frac{\text{Number of referrals} \times \text{Average therapist hours per referral}}{\text{Available therapist hours}}$$

This is not a true mathematical equation, nevertheless, it helps us to remember that in principle we can reduce waiting times by:

- reducing the number of people seeking therapy (e.g. by limiting referrals or by improving the general psychological wellbeing of a population so that fewer referrals arise);
- increasing the amount of therapist time available (e.g. by providing more therapists or by increasing the proportion of their time therapists spend doing therapy);
- decreasing the average number of therapist hours taken by each client (e.g. by seeing clients for shorter times or seeing more clients at one time in groups).

Some of the approaches we shall consider reflect the last of these variables: by reducing the amount of therapist contact per client, they anticipate increasing the throughput of clients and hence offer more or faster treatment.

IMPROVING THE ACCESSIBILITY AND/OR CONVENIENCE OF THERAPY

This is yet another good goal. Finding an hour a week during the working day (plus possibly lengthy travel time) is not easy for many clients. They may have jobs that do not easily allow them to take time off or that lead to loss of pay if they do so; they may have children or others to care for; or they may live in places that make getting to therapy difficult and expensive. These difficulties make it hard for many people to access therapy, and we need to think of ways to overcome them. A classic paper summarising the arguments for greater flexibility about modes of delivery was written by Lovell and Richards (2000), where they coined the acronym 'MAPLE', standing for Multiple Access Points and Levels of Entry. In essence, they argued that CBT should offer the mode of treatment that best combines effectiveness, accessibility and economy for that individual.

IMPROVING THE EFFECTIVENESS OF THERAPY

Some 'non-standard' ways of delivering therapy have as their main aim the harnessing of extra resources, which the clinician believes will increase the effectiveness of therapy. Thus, practitioners of group or pairs therapy (see below) believe that these approaches are not just economical or convenient but also that they allow the clinician to tackle problems in ways that are not available in conventional one-to-one therapy.

IAPT LOW INTENSITY INTERVENTIONS

As well as discussing some of the specific strategies under the above headings, we will also briefly cover the programmatic approach that has become known as low intensity (LI) CBT within the UK's Improving Access to Psychological Therapies (IAPT) project.

MODES OF DELIVERY FOR CBT

We consider five main alternatives to traditional therapy in this chapter: self-help, large groups, conventional groups, couple therapy and pair therapy (see Table 16.1).

Table 16.1 Main goals of different delivery methods

Method	Cost	Accessibility	Effectiveness
Self-help	✓	✓	
Large groups	✓	✓	
Conventional groups	✓		✓
Couple therapy			✓
Pair therapy		✓	✓

SELF-HELP

Here we refer to a range of approaches where clients use media to teach themselves CBT therapeutic strategies, with therapist contact being either entirely absent or much reduced, compared to traditional therapy. Thus we include under 'self-help' the following approaches:

- *Bibliotherapy*: that is, client use of CBT books to carry out their own therapy. Although CBT books are frequently used by therapists as an *adjunct*, we shall focus here on the use of bibliotherapy as a more or less complete *substitute* for traditional therapy, where an important aim is to reduce the amount of therapist contact time. Bibliotherapy can be used without *any* actual contact with a therapist, in what we might call *pure* self-help (either because a clinician recommends they use a book instead of therapy or because they just pick up a book in a shop); or they may still see a therapist, but for a reduced amount of time (*assisted self-help*). Although we shall concentrate here on books that are specifically about therapy, we recognise that novels or other books that do not directly offer therapeutic advice might nevertheless assist in the process of therapy.
- *Computerised CBT (CCBT)*: that is, the use of computer programs, delivered either by CD- or DVD-ROM or via the Internet, aimed at teaching people how to use CBT. Such programs often use a multimedia approach, including, for example, video clips, written text, user-completed questionnaires or diaries and so on. There is a rapidly increasing choice of mental health apps and, although there is a clear need for more research, there is already evidence that smartphone assisted therapy can be effective (see Donker et al., 2013 for a review). But before we get too excited about their use it is wise to reflect on Lawlor-Savage and Prentice's (2014) ethical concerns and to hold in mind Wiederhold's observation 'Behavioural health apps abundant, but evidence-based research nearly nonexistent' (2015: 309).
- Recently developed approaches to self-help include the use of so-called *book prescription* schemes. In this approach, developed by Frude (2005), the public libraries in a locality stock a list of self-help books that people can borrow on extended loan by getting a 'book prescription' from a primary care health worker. Another 'light' approach is the assisted self-help clinic in primary care, in which clients have brief appointments with a mental health worker who guides and supports their use of CBT bibliotherapy materials (Lovell, Richards & Bower, 2003).

The evidence on these approaches is at least modestly hopeful, suggesting that both bibliotherapy and CCBT can give outcomes in primary care settings which are superior to treatment as usual (TAU). One review of guided self-help concluded that it may be as effective as face-to-face therapy (Cuijpers, Donker, van Straten, Li & Andersson, 2010), and a more recent trial concluded that guided self-help was significantly superior to TAU (Williams et al., 2013). However, the evidence is still relatively limited, findings conflicting and the quality of studies is often not high, so further evaluation is needed (Bower, Richards & Lovell, 2001; Lewis et al., 2003; Richardson & Richards, 2006). For example, although an early uncontrolled pilot study on assisted self-help clinics was very promising (Lovell et al., 2003), more recent controlled trials have not shown the same advantages (Richards et al., 2003). In addition, it should be noted that most research findings to date come from primary care, so there is less evidence to support the use of such approaches with more severe or complex problems in secondary or tertiary care.

Despite these uncertainties, self-help approaches continue to be developed and recommended as one stage in a stepped-care programme (e.g. NICE, 2004a). As well as their benefits in terms of cost-effectiveness and accessibility to a wide range of people who might not come to conventional therapy, self-help approaches may have other advantages. They help clients avoid extensive involvement in psychiatric systems, perhaps minimising stigma and dependence; they promote self-efficacy; and they provide a form of help that is permanently available to the client for future revision. There are, of course, also some potential negative effects. Apart from the possibility that they do not work, some people have suggested that 'failed' self-help attempts may 'inoculate' clients against CBT: they may conclude that CBT is useless and then miss out on what might have been an effective treatment (we know of no evidence about whether this theoretical risk is significant in actual clinical practice).

Our view is that self-help approaches are well worth trying, particularly in primary care, but whenever possible their efficacy should be evaluated. Clinical experience suggests that the main guidelines for using such approaches as total or partial substitutes for conventional therapy are:

- Clients need to be literate and comfortable with reading (or using computers for CCBT) and not have physical or mental disabilities that prevent reading.
- Self-help should be used as the first step in a CBT approach (not for clients who have already had CBT, except perhaps as a 'top-up' for those who merely want to be reminded of CBT strategies).
- Clients need to be willing to give self-help a try; it is probably wise always to check clients' thoughts about self-help and to help them think through significant doubts.
- Self-help may be more likely to succeed with relatively mild and circumscribed problems, rather than complex and enduring problems (but may still be of some help in some aspects of the latter).
- At least some therapist contact (i.e. 'assisted' or 'guided' self-help) seems to increase the chances of success (see e.g. Gellatly, Bower, Hennessy, Richards, Gilbody & Lovell, 2007). This contact might be very limited: for example, Lovell's self-help clinic used 15-minute appointments, and the average total therapist contact time in a course of 'therapy' was just over one hour. Such limited contact is usually focused on suggesting appropriate literature, supporting and encouraging clients' attempts at self-help and helping them to problem solve when difficulties arise.
- In bibliotherapy, there is insufficient evidence to compare the relative efficacy of different books, but the book prescription schemes described above can guide you towards books with some consensus of support from clinicians (see e.g. the list available on the Internet from the Devon Book Prescription Scheme, 2004). For CCBT, the National Institute for Health and Clinical Excellence recommends 'Beating the Blues' for depression and 'FearFighter' for panic and phobias (NICE, 2006).

Therapists must view the material before recommending it. This might sound obvious, but we simply can't trust an enthusiastic 'blurb' advertising a book or an app. Some materials are at best confusing and at worst misleading and upsetting.

See Williams (2001) for further discussion of some of these points.

USING IT INTERFACES

Increasingly, clients have access to computers, tablets, smartphones, any of which could be used to conduct virtual face-to-face therapy, although Prentice and Dobson (2014) quite rightly urge careful consideration of the risks and benefits of this mode of therapy.

In some instances, an entire course of therapy might be carried out using this type of interface, but possibly more common is using it when someone might otherwise have had to cancel an appointment (e.g. because of unexpected childminding or transport difficulties). It can also be a relevant medium for BEs: for example, a therapist could communicate with a client or observe a behaviour being carried out *in vivo* when that client cannot be accompanied.

LARGE GROUPS

Another approach to 'economical CBT' is White's stress-control programme for anxiety (White, Keenan & Brooks, 1992; White, 1998, 2000). White's approach is delivered to groups of 20–50 clients, who also receive a written version of the course content which they can work on during and after the course.

Although calling this approach 'large group' conveys one of its distinctive features – the sheer number of people involved – it may in other ways be misleading since it is not group therapy in the usual sense, but is educational, more akin to an evening class. The course consists of six two-hour sessions, usually held in the evenings, in a primary care or non-health care setting, and clients are encouraged to bring their partners if they wish. Outcome studies suggest that the programme can result in good outcomes for anxiety disorders, and that improvements are well maintained in follow-up (White et al., 1992; White, 1998). White (2000) gives a comprehensive account of the approach, including practical advice on how to set up and run classes.

Possible advantages of this format include its obvious capacity to provide help to large numbers of people in a way that is very economical of time, both for clinicians and for clients. Its approach to anxiety problems, conceptualised as 'stress' that can be managed using teachable skills, may also appeal to populations who would be less likely to access conventional psychological therapies – White originally developed the approach partly to appeal to such groups. Apart from the size of the large group, which means that no one stands out unless they want to, one of the course's guidelines is that members are discouraged from discussing their particular problems in any detail, a rule that some clients find very reassuring. There may also be non-specific and destigmatising benefits from the sheer size of the class: 'I can't be that weird if 40 other people have the same kind of problem!' On the other hand, of course, there are clients who will not respond to such a relatively impersonal approach and who might find it difficult to cope with such a large number of people – although bringing a partner along may counteract this.

LOW INTENSITY INTERVENTIONS

As noted in Chapter 1, a major development of the past few years has been the IAPT project in England and Wales, which aims to improve the availability of psychological therapies for common mental health problems in NHS primary care settings. The first stage of IAPT contains two different CBT approaches: high intensity (HI) treatment (which is essentially what most of this book is about); and low intensity (LI) treatment, which we cover briefly in this section. We do not have enough space to cover LI in depth, so if you are interested we would advise consulting the sources in the 'Further reading' section of this chapter.

The LI approach contains several of the features already described above. It is an explicitly 'high volume, low intensity' approach to CBT, whose goal is to increase the accessibility of CBT by providing it in ways that minimise both the restrictions on clients and the use of scarce and expensive professional resources. The main characteristics of IAPT-style LI interventions are:

- It uses a *stepped-care* model, in which a client making contact with services is triaged and allocated to the form of treatment that is least restrictive, whilst still being effective. Clients are routinely monitored on outcome measures, and can be 'stepped up' to more intensive forms of therapy if necessary.
- It uses *collaborative care* to ensure that different professional contributions are co-ordinated and to maintain contact assertively with clients.
- It uses many of the ways of delivering *economical* therapy that have been described above. Richards (2010) describes LI clinically as 'characterised by fewer sessions; more emphasis on self-management; the structured and central use of written material as a core strategy, rather than merely an adjunct to therapy; [and] variation in administration methods, such as delivery via the telephone or computer'.

Typical LI interventions include guided self-help in CBT strategies such as working with thoughts or exposure to anxiety-provoking situations (often using brief telephone contacts rather than full-length face-to-face sessions); a brief form of behavioural activation (see Chapter 17); medication support; and CCBT. See the IAPT website (IAPT, 2010) for downloadable resources and the curriculum for the training of LI workers. In the first academic publication on IAPT outcomes, Clark et al. (2009) provide some data suggesting that LI is capable of achieving both good outcomes for clients and impressively high capacities for services treating those clients, with a mean of 2.6 hours of treatment contact.

Two other points about LI work are worth remembering: (1) it should not be thought of as a kind of 'diluted' version of conventional CBT – rather, both the therapy and the therapists are *different* from standard CBT and standard CBT practitioners in important ways; (2) because of the different therapeutic approach and the high volume of clients (with caseloads of 50 per worker not uncommon), the approach to supervision has to be different from that described in Chapter 19 of this book. For instance, it is recommended (Richards, 2010) that client cases are monitored and automatically flagged up for supervision by computer systems. For both these reasons, it is not necessarily the case that conventional CBT therapists make good LI therapists or supervisors.

CONVENTIONAL GROUPS

Another way of reducing costs while maintaining a more active clinical relationship with one's clients is to develop a CBT group, by generalising the CBT approach used with individuals to a small-group format but without mimicking the principles of psychodynamic groups. There are various established group protocol programmes that have been developed for specific disorders (Bieling, McCabe & Antony, 2006). The CBT structure of agenda-setting; monitoring of affect, thoughts and behaviour; re-evaluation of dysfunctional beliefs; homework tasks; and BEs has been maintained in group settings (Freeman, 1983). Initially the focus was on groups for depressed clients (e.g. Hollon & Shaw, 1979), but this has gradually been extended to a wide range of other disorders (see Ryder, 2010 for a review). Apart from economic considerations, there are other advantages of working in this way, including:

- economy of therapist time (but see discussion below);
- normalising group members' experiences, as the symptoms and problems of others are shared;
- clients often spot in others what was not obvious in themselves, for example increased ability to recognise links between thoughts and feelings or others' cognitive distortions (Rush & Watkins, 1981);
- group support for doing difficult tasks, for example BEs where courage is demanded;
- development of a culture of homework completion and so on;
- potential for group members acting as co-therapists for each other, facilitating skills acquisition (Hope & Heimberg, 1993), for example in tracking 'hot thoughts';
- capacity for doing BEs within the group, particularly (but not exclusively) for social anxieties.

However, the advantages need to be offset against a number of possible disadvantages (Tucker & Oie, 2007), including:

- reduced ability to tailor the sessions to the idiosyncratic beliefs/behaviours of each client;
- possible reluctance to disclose shameful beliefs;
- risk of one or a few individuals monopolising the sessions or not really engaging;
- different improvement rates among the group may be discouraging for some;

- drop-outs may have a dispiriting impact on the group;
- potential for unhelpful culture to develop (off-target discussion or non-compliance with homework).

We would also add that crisis management for a specific group member is sometimes compromised. Nevertheless, the potential saving in therapist time has proved very tempting, and a number of different kinds of groups have been developed.

FORMAT OF CBT GROUPS

Groups have been developed for different purposes (e.g. in-patient versus out-patient), and Morrison (2001) has differentiated them as follows:

- *Open-ended*: clients can join for a number of sessions at any point. Such groups may have a strongly educational tone. They necessarily focus on broad issues, for example links between affect and cognition, with less opportunity to consider individual issues.
- *Open, rotating theme* (e.g. Freeman, Schrodt, Gilson & Ludgate, 1993): there is a prearranged programme so not all sessions may be appropriate for any individual client. They are often at a higher frequency than usual (e.g. three times a week).
- *Programmed*: highly didactic and the least interactive – similar to the large group format described above.
- *Closed*: everyone joins the group at the same time and goes through the whole programme, so all are at a similar level of skill with CBT.

MEMBERSHIP OF GROUPS

This is largely dependent on the function of the group. If the group is designed to deal with problems like panic disorder or BPD, then there would need to be a screening process. If, on the other hand, the group is intended to increase skills in the management of problems across diagnoses, as may be the case with an open-ended in-patient group, then it would be more likely that a wide range of clients would be included, independent of diagnosis. The relevant questions are what the aim of the group is and who would be most likely to benefit. As the success of a group depends partly on its membership, the issue of who to take in is crucial, and Ryder (2010) has useful suggestions for inclusion criteria (e.g. socially able to benefit from the group) and exclusion criteria (e.g. actively suicidal) which could be considered if you were planning to set up a group.

THERAPIST INPUT

The general view (e.g. Freeman et al., 1993) is that it is easier to run a group with more than one therapist, partly because of the twin tasks of providing the technical input (e.g. teaching how to use a thought record) at the same time as attending to interactions between group members. Hollon and Shaw (1979) suggest that six group members is about the maximum an individual therapist can handle unless a co-therapist is available. Ryder (2010) indicates that a greater number can be included as long as the number of therapists is increased, so that group process can be attended to (Yalom, 1995), in addition to teaching technical skills. The roles of the therapists should be differentiated and agreed between them so that there is neither duplication nor gaps. A useful division of labour is where one therapist attends to the 'content' (the overt tasks) of the group while the other keeps an eye on 'process' (interpersonal interactions, over- or under-involvement). These roles need not be fixed over the course of the session, therapists can switch. Although we do not 'use' process therapeutically as would be the case in a psychodynamic group, catching possible interpersonal issues and addressing them early can improve the productivity of the group.

One therapist noted that Shia was saying less as the group session progressed and she mentioned this to her co-therapist. Their hunch was that the topics were getting more demanding as the content of the sessions shifted from relatively simple skills training to exploring the personal issues underlying the problem. They planned to test out their hypothesis by adding an item to the agenda the following meeting: 'How do I feel now that the sessions are becoming more personal and is there anything that can make it easier for me?' In this way they gave Shia the opportunity to voice his difficulties without obviously singling him out and, should others share his feelings, they would be able to raise their concerns.

FREQUENCY

Open groups can continue for an indefinite period, but closed groups tend to run for between 12 and 20 sessions, usually on a weekly basis in out-patient settings, more frequently with in-patients. They generally last for one and a half or two hours, which allows sufficient time for group discussion in addition to the didactic and technical elements. Group members in sessions that run for a couple of hours might benefit from having an agreed break half way though.

GROUP RULES

It is helpful for group members to know what rules should be followed, for example about confidentiality, attendance, punctuality, respect for other members, dealing with crises and so on. A useful opening exercise is establishing ground rules, where all group members have an opportunity to contribute their thoughts on what would be necessary for them to feel safe enough to properly use the group setting. This can often lead on to a group problem-solving exercise, which emphasises collaboration, shared responsibilities, develops skills and can be a bonding experience.

WHAT OUTCOME CAN BE EXPECTED FROM GROUP CBT?

Morrison (2001) looked at the outcome studies for different kinds of groups, across diagnoses and formats, and these are summarised succinctly in her paper. Overall, it was difficult to demonstrate advantages for group over individual treatment, largely because the studies were inadequate for the purpose: in many studies, the samples were too small (e.g. Rush & Watkins, 1981, for depression; Scholing & Emmelkamp, 1993, for social phobia); or the outcomes for individual treatments were lower than in other published studies concerning the same problem (e.g. Telch, Luxcas, Schmidt, Hanna, Jaimez & Lucas, 1993, for panic); or the group programme offered was not consistently CBT (e.g. Enright, 1991, with OCD). Nevertheless, Morrison concluded that outcome studies generally support the efficacy of CBT offered in groups, although it seems probable that clients with more serious disorders, those with serious depression, or OCD, do better with individual treatment.

A review of group CBT for depression states, rather disappointingly, that even by 2012 'The quality of evidence is poor' (Huntley, Araya & Salisbury, 2012: 184). Overall, there did seem to be some superiority for group CBT over TAU, but this was not sustained at three-month follow-up. An even more recent review of group CBT for psychosis (CBTp) (Owen, Speight, Sarsam & Sellwood, 2015) draws the conclusion that, although the approach shows promise, there is still not enough evidence to draw strong conclusions. These reviews are pretty representative of more recent evaluations of the literature and it seems that we continue to be faced with that old cliché, 'further research needed'.

COST-EFFECTIVENESS OF GROUP CBT

Much of the argument in favour of group CBT lies in its cost-effectiveness, but this may be more apparent than real, for the following reasons:

- group sessions usually last one and a half or two hours rather than the single hour typical of individual therapy;
- the screening process may be very time-consuming, with referrers taking a chance on clients likely to be unsuitable for the group;
- there is often a lot of preparation of materials for groups, such as hand-outs, questionnaires/ratings and so on;
- time is taken for preparation of the group programme, probably with a co-therapist;
- time is required for debriefing with a co-therapist after each session;
- it may be more difficult for clients to take two hours plus travel time off work; Antonuccio, Thomas and Danton (1997) argued that this cost needs to be factored in when looking at comparative costs;
- there may be less treatment gain for each individual in the group, and the gain per unit of therapist time may need to be considered.

By all means, go ahead and develop CBT groups, but it is important to evaluate the progress made by individuals in the group and to compare this with the progress made by similar clients seen individually in your own practice or in published research. As long as your clients make progress, you may consider that it is more equitable to offer more people a group, with less expected gain, than it is to offer a smaller number of clients individual therapy, even if you know the small number are likely to do better if seen individually. Morrison (2001) suggested that it may be useful to offer clients two or three individual sessions before moving them into a group, to identify idiosyncratic features for attention in the group and to socialise them to the CBT approach. You may then get the best of both worlds.

COUPLE THERAPY

Working with couples is another way of increasing the effectiveness of therapy when it is apparent that their relationship is central to the problems presented by one or both clients. The CBT approach to therapy with couples assumes that the beliefs of each client about themselves, their relationship and relationships in general are crucial in understanding how they feel about their own relationship and each other and how they behave towards each other. These beliefs may have been learned early in life and may not be verbally articulated, so a major task is to help the couple identify those beliefs (Beck, 1988). It is important to pay *equal attention* to each partner's expectations about relationships and how those expectations may distort their perceptions of their current relationship.

The general principles and characteristics of CBT apply to this kind of working, with an emphasis on structured sessions and inter-session assignments. The assessment includes a joint session, plus individual sessions with each of the partners, where ground rules are laid down about, for example, telephone calls outside the session and arguing within the session (see Dattilio & Padesky, 1990). Having developed a problem list and formulation, therapy is likely to focus on three broad areas, as described below.

1 MODIFYING UNREALISTIC EXPECTATIONS

Modifying unrealistic expectations is done following the principles and techniques described for individuals in earlier chapters.

A woman who felt hopeless about her marriage held the belief 'Unless I am the centre of his life, our relationship means nothing' and had ATs such as 'We never do anything together' whenever her partner engaged independently in an activity. Therapy involved looking at the evidence for each partner's NATs and gradually worked towards jointly defining a belief that took account of their experience of current relationships: for example, 'Our lives can interconnect and overlap in important areas and be separate in other areas; and our relationship can still be meaningful.'

Beck (1988) gives good examples of typical cognitive distortions and how to tackle them.

2 MODIFYING FAULTY ATTRIBUTIONS OF BLAME

It is common for couples to be locked in a vicious cycle of mutual recrimination and blaming, with neither partner accepting responsibility for the difficulties in the relationship. It is a priority to help them identify and re-evaluate their beliefs about responsibility so that they can collaborate in working on their problems.

3 COMMUNICATION TRAINING AND PROBLEM SOLVING

Couples typically need help in developing new skills to help them reduce destructive interactions. Communication training emphasises good listening skills, clearly stating one's needs and taking responsibility for one's feelings and is well described in Burns (1999). It is important that couples learn how to deal with intense anger while they are learning to communicate effectively, and this can usefully be rehearsed in treatment sessions.

Once they can communicate more effectively, many couples need to learn to problem solve to deal with areas of disagreement. Jacobson and Margolin (1979) set out general principles for problem solving in couples, including:

- specifically defining the problem;
- focusing on solutions rather than blame;
- learning to compromise.

Behavioural approaches to couple therapy (e.g. Stuart, 1980) emphasise the exchange of positive behaviours, where each partner acted in specific ways to please the other. Within CBT, this strategy can be used to identify dysfunctional beliefs and incorporated into BEs.

Issues that need special attention within couple therapy include crises, such as recently divulged infidelity or newly developed violence within the relationship. Defusing a crisis would take priority at the early stages of treatment. Other problem areas are where one partner wants the relationship to end; where one partner has a secret (e.g. infidelity) he does not want to disclose; where one partner has another ongoing relationship; and where one partner has a significant psychiatric disorder. Problems such as these are addressed in Dattilio and Padesky (1990) and should be discussed with a supervisor, ideally one experienced in couple work.

Baucom has been developing evidence-based approaches to couples work for many years and most recently has refined a couples CBT approach that combines working with the relationship distress and individuals' own psychological difficulties (Baucom, Belus, Adelman, Fischer & Paprocki, 2014). This is proving a compelling and popular intervention but Baucom does, rightly, emphasise the importance of being properly training in using this population specific approach (Baucom & Boeding, 2013).

PAIR THERAPY

This describes therapy delivered simultaneously to two clients with similar difficulties. To our knowledge, pair therapy in CBT was first presented by Kennerley (1995), who described offering it to trauma victims who wanted to share their difficulties with others in a structured and therapeutic setting but who were unable to join a CBT therapy group. The main reasons for wanting to work with other trauma survivors were to destigmatise the experience of childhood abuse and to discover how others coped, objectives that would have been met in a therapy group. The predominant reasons for not joining a group were: being too socially anxious to participate in a group; having personality disorders that precluded them from the group therapy on offer; or facing a lengthy wait for the next group.

Pairs were matched according to similarities in their traumatic history and current difficulties, and then a single therapist took them through the same programme used in a group intervention (see Kennerley, Whitehead, Butler & Norris, 1998/2014). Norris (1995) gives a detailed account of two women's experience of pair therapy and you can find a summary of the approach on the OCTC website (www.octc.co.uk/innovations). Although pair therapy for managing problems related to childhood trauma has not been used in a controlled trial, the preliminary indications were that clients found it acceptable, gained the social benefits of sharing their problems without having to join a group, and did as well in treatment as those in group therapy.

Pair therapy might worth considering if it could benefit any of your clients.

SUMMARY

- CBT can be delivered in a variety of ways beyond the traditional format of 'one client and one therapist for one hour'.
- This chapter reviews variations including:
    - self-help
    - IT interfaces
    - large groups
    - the IAPT low intensity approach
    - small groups
    - couples
    - pairs.
- All these variations may be useful in improving costs, accessibility or effectiveness compared to conventional one-to-one CBT.

The pros and cons of a particular format need to be considered carefully.

LEARNING EXERCISES

These learning exercises are available to download from the companion website.

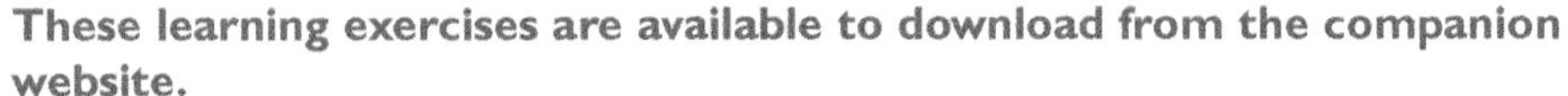

REVIEW AND REFLECTION:

- Are there any possible *disadvantages* to any of these approaches? What are they and how much of a problem do they represent?
- One often-cited objection to some of these approaches is that they might 'inoculate' clients against 'proper' CBT – in other words, that if a low intensity approach or a group approach is not effective, clients might be resistant to trying full-blown CBT and hence miss out on a treatment that might help them. We know of no evidence to support or refute this idea: how likely does it seem to you?
- Which of these approaches would fit well with your way of working and your client group?

TAKING IT FORWARD:

- Is there scope for trying any of these approaches in your own clinical practice, or in the service for which you work?
- What would you need to do to make this happen? With whom do you need to discuss CBT approaches? How can you best make your case?
- If the 'inoculation' worry seems significant to you, how could you go about checking out how much of a problem it really is in practice?
- In general, how will you evaluate the impact of adopting a different CBT approach?

FURTHER READING

Bennett-Levy, J., Richards, D., Farrand, P., Christensen, H., Griffiths, K., Kavanagh, D., Klein, B., Lau, M., Proudfoot, J., Ritterband, L. White, J., & Williams, C. (Eds.). (2010). *The Oxford guide to low intensity CBT interventions*. Oxford: Oxford University Press.

IAPT (2010). Web page: *Training resources for low intensity therapy workers*. Retrieved 27 January 2010 from www.iapt.nhs.uk/2009/01/20/training-resources-for-low-intensity-therapy-workers/

Richards, D. (2010). Low intensity CBT. In M. Mueller, H. Kennerley, F. McManus, & D. Westbrook (Eds.). *The Oxford guide to surviving as a CBT therapist*. Oxford: Oxford University Press.

Ryder, J. (2010). CBT in groups. In M. Mueller, H. Kennerley, F. McManus, & D. Westbrook (Eds.). *The Oxford guide to surviving as a CBT therapist*. Oxford: Oxford University Press.

Useful sources of self-help materials for clients include:

The Robinson 'Overcoming' series of self-help books by leading CBT therapists. See: www.constablerobinson.com/?section=books&series=overcoming

Oxford Cognitive Therapy Centre's booklets for clients. See: www.octc.co.uk/product-category/booklets (accessed 22 May 2016).

Chris Williams's Five Areas approach, with downloadable resources: www.fiveareas.com/ (accessed 22 May 2016).

17

DEVELOPMENTS IN CBT

- Introduction
- Why consider moving outside the framework of traditional CBT?
- Schemata in therapy
- Schema-focused work
- Compassion-based therapy
- Mindfulness-based cognitive therapy (MBCT)
- Other meta-cognitive therapies
- The radical behavioural interventions
- Neuroscience
- Conclusion
- Problems
- Summary
- Learning exercises
- Further reading
- Video links
    - 17.1 Dichotomous thinking
    - 17.2 Historical review
    - 17.3 Responsibility pie

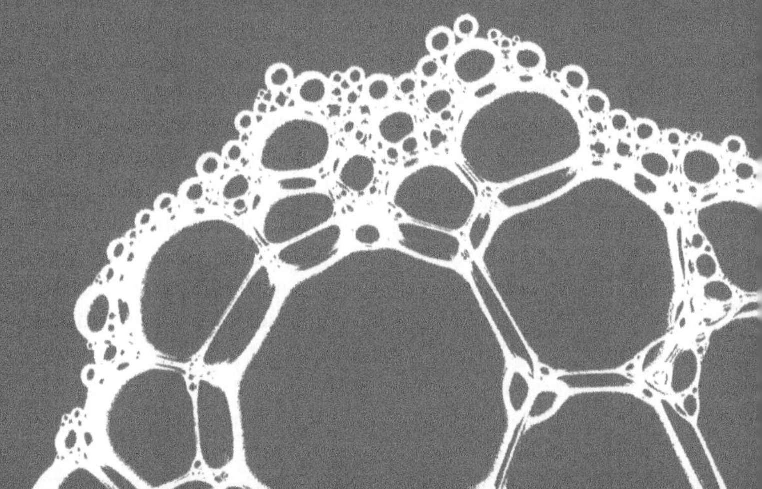

INTRODUCTION

CBT was originally developed to help those suffering from clinical depression and has gradually been extended to a wide range of psychological disorders. By the 1990s, the model had been elaborated to include the cognitive, emotional and behavioural processes that might underpin the difficulties of those who experience more complicated problems, including personality disorder.

The most clinically prominent models for complex problems emphasise the role of schemata (or schemas) in cognitive and behavioural difficulties, and these have given rise to approaches to CBT that are overtly schema-focused (Beck et al., 2004; Young, 1990) and those that indirectly target problem schemata (Gilbert, 2005; Linehan, 1993). These schema-focused developments will be given prominence in this chapter, as well as other important models and theories that have given rise to exciting possibilities for enhancing or shifting the emphasis of interventions. These include the interacting cognitive subsystem (ICS) model (Teasdale & Barnard, 1993), which underpins mindfulness-based cognitive therapy (MBCT) (Segal, Williams & Teasdale, 2002); and relational frame theory (Hayes, Barnes-Holmes & Roche, 2001), which provides the theoretical basis for acceptance and commitment therapy (ACT).

The past decade has also seen the emergence of behavioural activation (BA) (Jacobson, Martell & Dimidjian, 2001), a therapy that focuses on a single component of CBT for depression (see also Chapter 12).

Each of these developments can only be briefly reviewed in this chapter, therefore the reader is advised to refer to the available training manuals or publications for detailed guidance.

WHY CONSIDER MOVING OUTSIDE THE FRAMEWORK OF TRADITIONAL CBT?

First, on an ad hoc basis, traditional CBT might require modification or elaboration to be effective. This may mean extending treatment sessions beyond the number indicated by a treatment protocol or 'adding' an extra intervention to supplement the protocol when the client has, for example, to deal with an unforeseen life event.

Furthermore, CBT is not the optimum therapy for all psychological problems and is not accessible to all people. In some instances, other forms of psychotherapy are more helpful, for example family therapy in the treatment of anorexia nervosa (see Eisler, le Grange & Asen, 2003; Watson & Bulik, 2013 for reviews).

Second, some practitioners have elaborated CT in a substantial way in order to increase its accessibility to and effectiveness for those with chronic and complicated problems. This includes the expansion of interest in long-standing low self-esteem (Fennell, 1997), interpersonal processes in CT (Safran & Segal, 1990), the development of schema-focused cognitive therapy (SFCT) (Beck et al., 2004), schema therapy (Young et al., 2003) and MBCT (Segal et al., 2002), which combines CBT with mindfulness training.

Third, some practitioners have streamlined traditional CBT by focusing on specific aspects of it. For example, BA (Jacobson et al., 2001) de-emphasises the cognitive components of traditional CBT in the treatment of depression.

A therapist might consider moving outside the traditional framework of CBT when the 'classic' approach seems to be insufficient yet the client seems suited to CBT and the formulation of the client's problem appears to support a cognitive behavioural intervention. In some instances, there are guidelines to indicate who might be helped in this way. For example, MBCT is advocated as a treatment for recurrent depressive disorder, compassionate mind training for those whose progress seems arrested by self-criticism and shame, and SFCT for clients who are 'stuck' because of the resilience of long-standing negative belief systems. These approaches are discussed later in this chapter.

SCHEMATA IN THERAPY

WHAT IS A SCHEMA?

There is agreement that a schema is more than a belief: it is an information-processing structure that enables us to classify incoming information and to anticipate events. Some authors argue that it is a purely cognitive structure, while others argue that it is more complex and multi-modal. We all have schemata, about ourselves, about categories of events and so on. These knowledge structures enable us to process, with speed, what is happening and help us render the environment predictable. It is accepted that, in general, schemata develop from early childhood and subsequently predispose a person to interpret themselves, the world and the future in a particular way.

Williams, Watts, McCleod and Mathews give a succinct description of a schema as 'a *stored body of knowledge* which interacts with the encoding, comprehension and/or retrieval of new information within its domain, by guiding attention, expectancies, interpretation and memory search …[a] consistent internal structure, used as a template to organise new information' (1997: 211). You might ask 'What does this mean in practice?' Consider the following brief passage:

> Mary walked down the aisle, the congregation was silent and her mother looked on proudly.
>
> She readjusted her mortarboard slightly.

You probably quickly concluded that this was Mary's graduation ceremony even though there is no mention of graduation. Your previous knowledge of ceremonies furnished you with the information that you needed to 'read between the lines' and to anticipate what was happening. This body of knowledge resides in a schema. Thus, schemata are highly functional – and flexible (there is a reasonable chance that you were holding out for a wedding until you read 'mortarboard' and switched to an alternative possibility). This ability to make a rapid deduction on the basis of limited information generally serves us well, but problems arise when the content of a schema is biased or is inflexible. When this happens, a person can 'read between the lines' inaccurately.

Rosie's boss had barely finished saying 'You look well today!' when she felt overwhelming distress and had to get out of the room. The thought running through her mind was 'He thinks I look fat!' and the feelings that she experienced were fear and self-loathing.

Rosie's self-schema was so biased towards the negative that when her boss commented on her appearance, she 'read between the lines' and, instead of perceiving a compliment, she believed that she had been criticised.

Beck et al. (1979) recognised the position of schemata in the cognitive model of depression. Beck acknowledged that ATs are coloured by 'deeper' mental structures (schemata). For example, a self-schema represented by the label 'hopeless' could well underpin ATs such as 'There's no point in trying' or 'Things will never go well for me'; an interpersonal schema, represented by 'mistrust', might explain ATs such as 'He's only saying that to manipulate me' or 'Others will leave me in the end'.

Although schemata have long been recognised as 'enduring structures of knowledge' (Neisser, 1976), they are flexible to varying degrees, enabling us to change our attitudes and expectations as we have new experiences. For example, with managerial experience, a person's view of self might shift from 'I can't handle people', laced with apprehension and predictions about interpersonal conflict to 'I can manage others', infused with self-confidence and a hopeful outlook; following a traumatic experience, a person's view of themselves within the world might shift from 'basically safe' to self being 'vulnerable' and the future being 'threatening and dangerous', accompanied by fear and apprehension. CBT exploits this flexibility by working in the here and now, offering clients new possibilities, encouraging new experiences which might have an impact at the schema level.

We all have schemata and your clients' problems will be underpinned by these deeper structures; however, this does not mean that schemata have to be targeted directly. Consistent changes in current experiences generally impact on and moderate schemata, so testing automatic cognitions and carrying out BEs will usually do the trick. Revisiting the site of a trauma and discovering that this event is manageable will often be sufficient to shift a schema that previously led to fear and avoidance; having repeated successful ventures is often enough to shift a 'can't do' to a 'can do' schema. In most of our work, the underlying schemata respond without direct focus and for this reason one should first try the 'classic' and better established approaches.

SCHEMA-FOCUSED WORK

Some clients, however, present with fundamental beliefs that seem resistant to change even in the face of new evidence. This is seen to be pivotal in the maintenance of chronic psychological problems, including those associated with personality disorders. Typically, clients with change-resistant schemata cannot embrace the positive experience that counters a negative belief. Instead, they *repeatedly* dismiss it with comments such as 'Yes but he's only saying that out of pity' or 'Yes but that was down to luck'. Some people, such as Rosie, never get as far as appreciating the compliment; they rapidly distort it to a negative comment that sits comfortably with their inner, negative perspective.

This is the client group for whom schema-focused, or 'second generation', CBT (Perris, 2000) was developed. The resilience of unhelpful schemata demanded the development of strategies that could more directly target them and an approach that could facilitate this. Thus, schema-focused work is an elaboration of traditional CBT with a shift of emphasis – it is not a distinct, new approach.

The approach puts greater emphasis on understanding the childhood and adolescent origins of psychological problems and on the client–therapist relationship, placing the formulation in a greater historical and interpersonal context. As far back as 1979, Beck et al. suggested that 'the use of childhood material is not crucial in treating the acute phase of depression or anxiety, but it is important in the chronic personality disorders'.

Practitioners have emphasised using the client–therapist interaction to more readily uncover sensitive or elusive core themes, to engage clients with interpersonal difficulties or profound hopelessness and to use the relationship as a mediator of change (Perris, 2000; Beck et al., 2004). In CBT, transference is not assumed to be operating but is a possibility to be explored. In their particular practice of schema therapy, Young et al. (2003) particularly emphasise the therapeutic value of 'partial re-parenting' and 'empathic confrontation', both of which assume that the therapeutic relationship represents a medium for change.

Beck's schema-focused CBT (SFCT) and Young's schema therapy (ST) share a common goal: to develop functional and balanced schemata that will enable the client to overcome his problems. Both are formulation driven and as transparent as possible, and both use cognitive and behavioural interventions. However, the therapeutic approaches are different in two fundamental ways. First, SFCT takes the stance of collaborative empiricism (as does 'classic' CBT), whereas ST initiates a relationship of 'partial re-parenting'. Second, SFTC tends to be more phased in its approach to schema-focused work, first using conventional CBT strategies, whereas the ST approach is more likely to introduce schema-focused interventions early on. There are manuals to guide practitioners and we would urge you to use these so that you maintain treatment fidelity. Schema work is about developing new, helpful belief systems that will be to the client's advantage and will compete with old perspectives – simply demolishing old beliefs can leave a client in something of a cognitive-emotional void. Many of these strategies are elaborations of 'classic' CBT techniques as you can see for yourself (see Table 17.1). As this section simply presents a brief overview of schema-focused work, we highlight just a few of the more ubiquitous techniques. However, some of you will wish to learn more about the wider range of strategies and the use of schema-focused therapies with clients with complex difficulties, and if this is so we strongly recommend that you first become very familiar with 'classic' CBT and then we would refer you to the texts of Young et al. (2003), Riso, du Toit, Stein & Young (2007) and Beck et al. (2015).

POSITIVE DATA LOGS

Positive data logs (Padesky, 1994) are systematically compiled lists of experiences that serve to build new, more constructive belief systems and that counter old, less helpful perspectives.

Rosie collected information that was consistent with a new possibility: 'I am an attractive person'. First, she compiled a list of qualities she found attractive in others:

- a ready smile;
- genuine warmth;
- kindness;
- tolerance;
- fairness.

Rosie was interested to see that her list did not contain descriptions of physical appearance, and she reflected that others might share similar views. She used this list as a checklist and noted each time she became aware that she fulfilled one of her criteria, or when someone paid her a compliment indicating that she was attractive. At first, it was difficult to recognise the positives and she needed encouragement to continue to keep the log, but, with practice, Rosie became more adept at noticing compliments and achievements. In this way she both collected information to help her construct a new belief system and she developed the skill of noticing positive events.

This technique is not a fundamentally new strategy but more an elaboration of the data-collecting exercises that we use in traditional CBT. However, it is generally more effortful for your client and will span a longer period.

CONTINUUM WORK OR 'SCALING'

Continuum work or 'scaling' (Pretzer, 1990) is a strategy for combating an unhelpful dichotomous thinking style. In classic CBT, we often help clients recognise their 'all or nothing' thinking and prompt them to take stock of the range of possibilities linking the extremes. Continuum work elaborates this and involves drawing out the spectrum that lies between the extremes, discussing and weighing up the validity of an 'all or nothing' perspective (this is also discussed in Chapter 8).

In Rosie's case, she held a dichotomy of 'ugly or attractive' and, unless she was given a very unambiguous message that she was attractive, she perceived comments as confirming that she was ugly. In therapy, she began to realise a continuum of attractiveness existed and that it included more than physical appearance.

See Video 17.1: Addressing dichotomous thinking.

HISTORICAL LOGS

Historical logs (Young, 1984) are essentially retrospective thought records. Key incidents from the past are re-evaluated in a systematic way, reviewing the historical reasons why a belief might have seemed compelling and why its validity might now be doubted.

Rosie dated her belief that she was ugly to several incidents from her past, including an incident at age eight when a group of children surrounded her and chanted that she was 'repulsive'. She reflected on why it was that she believed them at the time:

> 'I was overweight and my parents never did anything but criticise me.'

Now, however, she could use her 'wise mind' to challenge the conclusion she drew as an eight-year-old:

> 'I was a regular-looking, slightly overweight girl who was scapegoated by a group of kids who knew no better.'

She then drew a new conclusion:

> 'I was vulnerable to believing criticism because of my home life, but I can now see that those kids were being superficial and cruel, which reflects badly on them rather than on me.'

See Video 17.2: Historical review with a client.

RESPONSIBILITY PIES

The *responsibility pie* technique (Greenberger & Padesky, 2015) encourages people to consider who or what else might have contributed to a difficult situation. Sometimes our clients assume that they are predominantly, if not totally, responsible for bad things that have happened and they feel painfully ashamed.

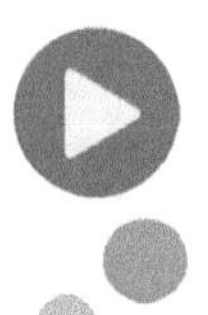

See Video 17.3: Using a responsibility pie chart.

In Rosie's case, she blamed herself for being overweight, which fuelled self-loathing, shame and depressed mood. Her therapist prompted her to think who or what else might have contributed to her being overweight. At first she struggled, but slowly generated a list:

1. The food industry, which packages and advertises food to make it so appealing.
2. My depression, which leads me to comfort eat.
3. My parents, who were unsupportive so that I turned to comfort eating.
4. My mother, who was always dieting but fed me the food she craved, which made me an overweight child.
5. The children who teased me for being 'fat', which triggered my obsession with weight.
6. My dance school, which indoctrinated us with the idea that only thin is acceptable and contributed to my obsession with weight.

(Continued)

(Continued)

7. My obsession with weight: I am preoccupied with food.
8. My aunt, though I love her dearly, who tried to cheer me up with chocolate treats, which is probably why I find chocolate particularly tempting.

When she had exhausted all possibilities, she added her name to the bottom of the list.

Making this list is an excellent Socratic vehicle and for some clients, this alone is sufficient to modify an extreme view of responsibility, as they now realise that there were many contributors to their problem. However, Greenberger and Padesky suggest taking the exercise further and asking clients to estimate *how much* each person/thing contributed and then to convert this to a pie chart. While this is too demanding for some clients, it can be helpful to others.

In Rosie's case, her ratings were as follows:

1. The food industry 5%
2. My depression 10%
3. My parents 40%
4. My mother 10%
5. The children 10%
6. My dance school 5%
7. My weight obsession 15%
8. My aunt 1%
9. Myself 4%

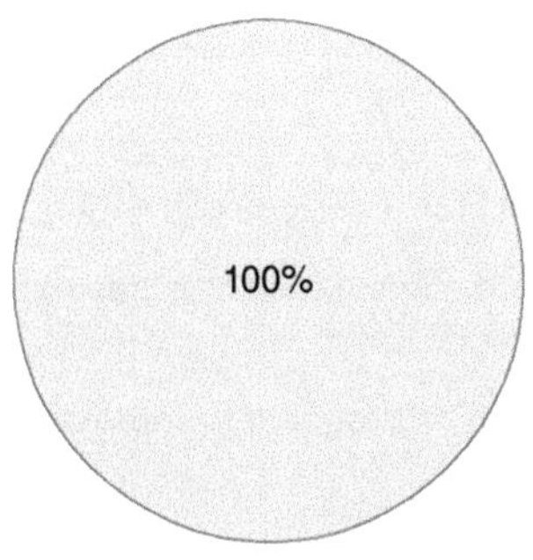

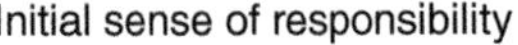
Initial sense of responsibility

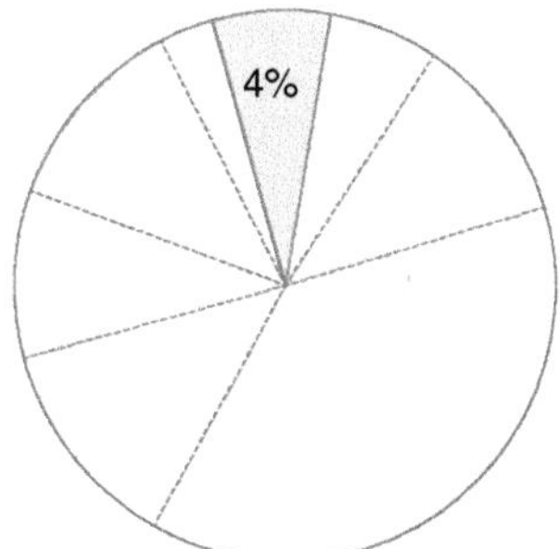

Personal blame after the exercise

Figure 17.1 Rosie's responsibility pie charts

When she reached the bottom of the list, Rosie discovered that she only had 4 per cent left to apportion to herself, and, as a consequence, felt less shameful and angry with herself. Her pie charts are shown in Figure 17.1.

If your client thinks that this is a trick and you have manipulated the figures, you can ask them to review their estimates and change the figures with which they are not happy. In general, your client will still end up with a responsibility figure for themselves that is less than they had originally expected.

It is important that you discourage the conclusion 'I am not responsible, therefore there is nothing I can do about it'. Although a person no longer feels overly responsible for something happening to them, they can take responsibility for moving on. You might not be responsible for your central heating breaking down, but you can take responsibility for getting it fixed.

EXPERIENTIAL TECHNIQUES

Schema change strategies have also involved the development of 'experiential techniques', reflecting the role plays and visualisations used in classic CBT while also drawing on Gestalt techniques and complex imagery exercises. For example, Rosie benefited from what Padesky calls 'psychodrama' (Padesky, 1994), a role play of an interaction with her dead father which enabled her to confront him about his emotional and physical abuse. She was also helped by engaging in image restructuring (Layden et al., 1993), where she reviewed the image of being ridiculed by schoolchildren, reconsidered her responses and conclusion and then rescripted an ending with positive connotations.

For Rosie, this new image was of her walking away feeling tall and attractive (rather than cowed and ugly), confident in her knowledge that they were wrong and that she was morally superior. She particularly focused on the physical sensations of feeling tall and attractive, as this challenged her 'felt sense' of ugliness.

Such body-image transformation can be particularly helpful in those with a long-standing 'sense' of being unattractive or uncomfortable (Kennerley, 1996).

SCHEMA DIALOGUE

Another experiential technique is schema dialogue (Young et al., 2003), where a client conducts a dialogue between the old, unhelpful belief system and the more adaptive one.

In a session, Rosie's therapist played the part of her assumption that she was ugly, and Rosie rehearsed responding with compassionate, positive statements that supported the belief that she was attractive. Initially, the therapist modelled arguments to undermine the validity of the negative perspective, but Rosie was soon able to take on this role and, in debate, became adept at generating convincing arguments that she was attractive.

SCHEMA FLASHCARDS

To help the client in the early stages of schema review, Young et al. (2003) advise the use of schema flashcards that summarise the process. These essentially prompt a client to use a problem feeling (anger, angst, urges, etc.) to cue reflection on what makes sense of the feeling, and what they might do about it.

Rosie's schema flashcard reflects a modified, brief version of Young's format.

- Right now I feel:................................
- It is no wonder because:.......................
- However:...
- Therefore I will:.................................

Rosie carried her card with her and when she was distressed she used it as a reminder to pause, recognise what was happening and think what would be best for her. For example, she was very agitated driving home one evening and headed off to the garage to buy (a lot of) chocolate. She pulled into a parking bay and took out her schema flashcard.

- Right now I feel: Agitated and fragile. I want to binge this feeling away.
- It is no wonder because: I think I really messed up at work and I'm so ashamed. It makes me hate myself.
- However: This is my negative schema kicking in, making me assume the worst and feel bad. It's my old view of myself and I have begun to learn to appreciate that I am a reasonably capable and okay person.
- Therefore I will: Not try to eat my way through this distress. I'll put on some lively music, remind myself of my achievements and I'll see if I can get through this without resorting to a binge.

By doing this, Rosie decentred, became aware of the schema activation that was driving her feelings and urges, so that she was able to counter her unhelpful ATs and set up an experiment for herself.

The techniques used to address fundamental beliefs are predominantly developments of 'classic' CBT strategies and are summarised in Table 17.1.

The experiential techniques have been shown to be particularly effective in achieving schema-level changes (Arntz & Weertman, 1999; Giesen-Bloo et al., 2006). However, they can be very evocative of strong emotion and should be used with caution: that is, only when clearly justified and when you are confident that your client can tolerate the consequent affect.

The more ambitious aims of schema-focused work often make it necessary to offer longer therapy – sometimes several years (Young et al., 2003). Thus, you need to ask not only 'Have I the skills to engage in a schema-focused therapy?' but also 'Can both the client and I commit to a long-term intervention?'.

Table 17.1 'Classic' and schema-focused CBT strategies

'Classic' CBT	Schema-focused CBT
Collecting data as part of a behavioural experiment	Positive data logs
Identifying dichotomous thinking and recognising	Continuum or scaling technique gradations
Thought records	Historical log
Questioning blame	Responsibility pies
Role play	Psychodrama
Simple imagery transformation	Transformation of meaning of early memories; complex imagery transformation
Physical techniques	Body-image transformation
Challenging unhelpful thoughts	Schema dialogue
Progress review	Core belief logs
Aides-memoire	Schema flashcards

It is striking that schema-focused therapy achieved popularity in the world of CBT, and across a range of disorders (Riso et al., 2007), without a substantial empirical foundation. There have been single case reports (e.g. Morrison, 2000), examination of specific schema-change methods (e.g. Arntz & Weertman, 1999) and open clinical trials (Brown, Newman, Charlesworth, Crits-Christoph & Beck, 2004), but only relatively recently have we seen the outcome of randomised controlled trials (RCTs). In 2006, Giesen-Bloo et al. published a study which showed that, over a three-year period, Young's ST was superior to transference-focused psychotherapy with clients with borderline personality disorder (BPD). In the same year Davidson and co-workers published the results of a shorter study (one year treatment and one year follow-up) where schema-focused CBT was combined with TAU. Again, this study concentrated on clients with BPD and the results showed superiority for the combined intervention over TAU. Although the two interventions were different – in that one used Young's ST (Young et al., 2003) while the other combined a more Beckian schema-focused CBT approach (as outlined in Beck et al., 2004) – they each produced compelling results. However, it has to be borne in mind that both studies focused on a very specific population, so we cannot assume that the results would generalise to non-BPD populations. The same can be said for a more recent RCT that has also concentrated on clients with BPD (Farrell, Shaw & Webber, 2009). This study investigated the impact of adding 30 sessions of schema-focused group therapy (SFT) to TAU. The results again indicated significant improvement in functioning of participants in the SFT-TAU group over the TAU group.

In summary, although schema-focused interventions might be theoretically justifiable and clinically defensible with BPD clients, schema-focused approaches should be used with thoughtful caution with non-BPD populations. We would suggest that traditional CBT should be the first choice for a client who has been assessed and considered suitable for CBT.

COMPASSION-BASED THERAPY

WHAT IS IT?

A commonly reported emotion among those seeking psychotherapy is shame (Gilbert & Andrews, 1998). For example, it has long been associated with depressive disorder (Gilbert, 1992), and EDs and childhood abuse (Andrews, 1997). There is evidence that those who are highly self-critical do less well with traditional CBT (Rector, Bagby, Segal, Joffe & Levitt, 2000), and the explanation might lie in the nature of long-standing negative schemata. Compassion-based therapy aims to help those with internal shame, self-criticism and self-condemnation develop compassion towards themselves and thus reduce or eliminate their feelings of shame.

Shameful clients often adopt the techniques of CBT but fail to feel an emotional shift, because shame and self-criticism pervade their responses. One reason might be that they use a harsh tone when trying to counter unhelpful cognitions. This can perhaps be likened to a parent 'comforting' a child by saying 'Don't be afraid' in a stern tone, as though fear is ridiculous, and contrasting this with a parent who uses the same words but with a tone of empathy and genuine caring.

Gilbert's (2005) approach combines familiar cognitive behavioural interventions with *compassionate mind training* directed at addressing self-criticism and shame. This combines the technical aspects of cognitive reappraisal with developing an attitude of caring and concern.

SOCIAL MENTALITY THEORY

Compassionate mind training is based on Gilbert's social mentality theory (1989), which proposes that self-relevant information is often processed through systems (social mentalities) that were originally evolved for social relating. Thus, each of us has an internal relationship with the self, and our thinking and feelings can reflect this 'self-to-self' relating. For example, a person can be self-attacking and feel attacked, or a person can feel needy for care and be self-soothing. Compassion-based therapy focuses on this internal relationship, training clients to develop inner compassion and warmth so that they might self-soothe and counter self-attack effectively.

COMPASSION-BASED THERAPY IN PRACTICE

Compassion-based therapy shares many similarities with classic CBT. A sound therapeutic relationship is crucial to therapy. The therapist uses guided discovery and thought-monitoring to identify key cognitive-emotional processes that relate to feelings of shame and to self-criticism. A formulation is shared and, through this, patterns are identified, as well as blocks to therapy such as beliefs like 'Self-criticism is good for me: it is character building'. The shared understanding of how the problem developed and why it persists allow what Gilbert calls 'de-shaming and de-guilting' (2005: 287), which is not dissimilar to Linehan's (1993) concept of *validation*. He advocates using imagery to capture the experience of being cared for, thus promoting feelings of acceptance, safeness and self-soothing. This compassionate state of mind is then used to promote a *compassionate reframe* of unhelpful ATs.

Compassion-based therapy uses experiential interventions, many similar to those employed in the schema-focused treatments. Techniques include promoting imagery of the compassionate self and restructuring past, traumatic experiences; achieving a detachment from the emotional impact of NATs by learning to name the critical process; and developing inner dialogues with the hostile self – sometimes using the Gestalt two-chairs technique. Compassionate meditations are also advocated, with similarities in form and purpose to the mindfulness exercises of DBT and MBCT (see below).

Compassionate mind training's popularity has steadily grown and each year there are more excellent texts and opportunities for training. The website www.compassionatemind.co.uk is an ideal starting place if you wish to pursue CMT. The approach has been adapted for the treatment of depression (Gilbert, 2005), PTSD (Lee, 2005) and anxiety disorders (Bates, 2005; Hackmann, 2005). Arguments for adopting compassionate approaches have always been theoretically strong, and gradually the empirical argument for a compassion-focus in clinical practice is building. There are uncontrolled trials (e.g. Gilbert & Proctor, 2006), case series (e.g. Mayhew & Gilbert, 2008) and RCTs (e.g. Neff & Germer, 2013) to support its use. Nonetheless, it should be employed with the cautions and reservations previously suggested when considering schema-focused approaches.

MINDFULNESS-BASED COGNITIVE THERAPY (MBCT)

WHAT IS IT?

The novel treatment approach of MBCT was developed as a relapse-prevention intervention for depression (Segal et al., 2002). It combines elements of classic CBT with 'mindfulness' training, a therapeutic meditation approach developed by Kabat-Zinn, who described mindfulness as 'paying attention in a particular way: on purpose, in the present moment and non-judgementally' (1994: 4).

As far back as 1995, Teasdale, Segal and Williams proposed an alternative to the assumption that CBT was effective because of changes in belief in the *content* of negative cognitions. They suggested that CBT might work because, by prompting clients to pause, identify cognitions and evaluate the accuracy or usefulness of their content, it helps them 'stand back' from problem cognitions. This allows 'distancing' or 'decentring'. Teasdale, Moore, Hayhurst, Pope, Williams & Segal (2002) highlighted the importance of decentring and increased *meta-cognitive* awareness as an effective intervention in reducing relapse in depression.

This raises the possibility that relief from psychological distress might be achieved by helping clients switch to a state of mind in which unhelpful thoughts and feelings are viewed from a decentred perspective. As the meditative stance of mindfulness training enhances decentring, mindfulness was incorporated into CBT, and MBCT was developed.

INTERACTING COGNITIVE SUBSYSTEMS (ICS)

MBCT is based on a model of information-processing known as interacting cognitive subsystems (ICS), which regards the mind as a collection of interacting components (Teasdale & Barnard, 1993). Each of these components receives information from the senses or from other components of the mind. Each component then processes this information and passes the transformed information to other components. Thus, there is an *interacting network* within which recurring patterns appear in response to certain stimuli. In particular, those with previous experiences of depressive disorder get caught up in escalating self-perpetuating cycles of cognitive–affective ruminations more readily than those without a history of major depression. This pattern of rumination increases the likelihood of relapse into depression (Teasdale, 1988).

Teasdale calls the recurring patterns of interaction between mental components 'modes of mind' and likens them to the gears of a car:

> Just as each gear has a particular use (starting, accelerating, cruising, etc.), so each mode of mind has a characteristic function. In a car, change of gear can be prompted either automatically (with an automatic transmission, by a device that detects when the engine speed reaches certain critical values) or intentionally (by the individual consciously choosing to rehearse a particular intention or to deploy attention in a particular way). (2004: 275)

He goes on to say that, just as with a car, the mind cannot be simultaneously in two gears or modes. Thus, operating in one mode of mind precludes a person from being in another state of mind at the same time. MBCT aims to help clients recognise a 'mental gear' which is unhelpful, to disengage from it and to shift to a more functional cognitive mode. Mindfulness is seen as an alternative and helpful cognitive mode, as it is the antithesis of rumination. Depressive rumination is characterised by repeatedly and automatically thinking about negative material, and mindfulness appears to decrease the likelihood of relapse into depression by putting the client into a state of mind that is incompatible with rumination, namely:

- *intentional*: focusing on present experience rather than processing thoughts about the past or the future;
- *regards thoughts as mental events*, rather than valid reflections of reality;
- *non-judgemental*: viewing events as events, rather than 'good' or 'bad';
- *fully present*: that is, experiencing the moment, which reduces cognitive and experiential avoidance.

MBCT IN PRACTICE

MBCT is a manualised group skills training programme for clients in remission from recurrent major depression (Segal et al., 2002). It integrates mindfulness with compatible elements of CBT. However, there is little emphasis on *changing* unhelpful thoughts but rather on cultivating greater mindfulness with respect to them. The key to this is achieving a stance of non-judgement and radical acceptance. MBCT aims to help people become more aware of, and to relate differently to, their cognitive, emotional and physical experiences. Clients are taught to disengage from habitual and dysfunctional cognitive routines as a way to reduce future relapse and recurrence of depression.

Groups meet weekly for eight two-hour sessions, with homework assignments between meetings. These take the form of awareness exercises and tasks designed to integrate the application of awareness skills into daily life. Following the initial eight meetings, follow-up sessions are scheduled at increasing intervals.

Two early RCTs evaluated the effects of MBCT for recurrent depression, and showed a 50 per cent reduced risk of relapse. In a more recent randomised controlled study, Kuyken et al. (2008) showed that, over a 15-month follow-up period, MBCT is as effective in preventing relapse as anti-depressant medication, and a later RCT established both the effectiveness *and* the cost-effectiveness of MBCT (Kuyken et al., 2015). There are also small studies (e.g. Barnhofer, Crane, Hargus, Amarasinghe, Winder & Williams, 2009) that show that it is also effective in reducing symptoms in clients with chronic depression and suicidal ideas (Barnhofer et al., 2015). So far, the results of trials indicate that MBCT is a cost-efficient preventative programme that can reduce the risk of relapse and recurrence in those with three or more previous episodes of depression.

MBCT is also being used to help sufferers of other problems such as bipolar disorder, chronic fatigue, insomnia, GAD and cancer. It has been introduced into schools and perinatal settings, and we can look forward to a continued refinement of the model and further clinical trials.

OTHER META-COGNITIVE THERAPIES

WHAT ARE THEY?

As we have seen, in earlier chapters, meta-cognitive awareness is the capacity to experience thoughts and images as cognitions, as processes, simply events in the mind, and its therapeutic advantages have been applied to other developments of CBT in addition to MBCT. It is part of ACT and DBT (see below), and in 1995 Wells introduced the idea of meta-cognitive therapy (MCT) for anxiety disorders and later (2008) for both anxiety and depression. Other interventions that focus on cognitive process rather than cognitive content are worry-focused therapies that go beyond those outlined in Chapters 8 and 14, such as Freeman's worry intervention trial (WIT) for delusions (Freeman et al., 2015) and rumination-focused therapies (RFCT) for residual symptoms of depression (see Watkins et al., 2007). These approaches generally remain grounded within the core principles and techniques of CBT, but particularly attend to formulating and targeting cognitive processes.

The empirical status of these meta-cognitive approaches is extremely encouraging (see e.g.: Watkins et al., 2007; Freeman et al., 2015; Normann, Van Emmerik & Morina, 2014).

META-COGNITIVE THERAPY (MCT)

The theoretical grounding for this clinical approach is the self-regulatory executive function model (S-REF: Wells & Mathews, 1994), which proposes that psychological disorder is underpinned by cognitive attentional syndrome (CAS), which comprises:

- worry and rumination;
- threat monitoring;
- unhelpful coping behaviours.

The MCT approach teaches:

- detached mindfulness;
- attention training;
- situational attentional refocusing.

These strategies aim to enhance a person's meta-awareness of cognitions, change the relationship with the cognition, and address beliefs *about* the utility and necessity of worry, rumination and threat monitoring. Rather than attempting to modify the content of the automatic cognition or schema by considering its validity, it addresses the content of the meta-cognition and the way in which thoughts are experienced and regulated.

MCT has been evaluated in several open trials, case series and in RCTs where it proved superior to a no-treatment waiting period and in some instances appears superior to CBT (see Wells, 2008 for a review, and Normann et al., 2014). However, Normann et al. (2014) urge a cautious interpretation of the studies that indicate its superiority to classic CBT as it is not yet well proven.

THE RADICAL BEHAVIOURAL INTERVENTIONS

WHAT ARE THEY?

Some practitioners and researchers have developed cognitive behavioural interventions that have a clear cognitive component but emphasise the importance of the behavioural aspect of treatment. These include Linehan's dialectic behaviour therapy (1993), ACT (Hayes, Strosahl & Wilson, 1999) and Jacobson's BA (Martell, Addis & Jacobson, 2001). Below is a brief summary of each of these increasingly popular approaches.

DIALECTICAL BEHAVIOUR THERAPY (DBT)

Linehan et al. (1993) devised this intervention specifically for para-suicidal women diagnosed as having BPD, a diagnosis associated with poor treatment outcome. DBT comprises a broad array of cognitive and behavioural strategies, tailored to address problems associated with BPD, including suicidal behaviours. The core skills taught were:

- emotion regulation;
- interpersonal effectiveness;
- distress tolerance;
- mindfulness;
- self-management.

Treatment required both individual and group sessions to run concurrently.

The defining characteristic of DBT is an emphasis on 'dialectics' or the reconciliation of opposites: for example, achieving self-acceptance whilst recognising the need to change, or balancing the alternating high and low aspirations which are common in those with BPD. Together with this focus on dialectical processes, there is more emphasis on process than on structure and content.

DBT differs from CBT in several other respects. Rather than aiming to test the validity of cognitions, it promotes acceptance and validation of the client's behaviour and reality. The therapeutic relationship is deemed central to DBT, and there is an emphasis on identifying and addressing therapy-interfering behaviours.

DBT has now been evaluated in several trials, usually comparing it with TAU (see e.g. Bohus et al., 2004, and Burmeister et al., 2014 for a review of two recent meta-analyses of RCTs). Overall, it is associated with better retention rates and is effective in reducing self-harmful behaviours. Although DBT appears to diminish a particularly dangerous behaviour in those with BPD, its effectiveness has seemed quite specific until recently. Now, we see it being used with increasingly diverse populations, for example with adolescents (MacPherson, Cheavens & Fristad, 2012) and with people with EDs (Bankoff et al., 2012). Interestingly, simply using DBT skills (employed in the absence of other DBT modalities) is also showing promise as a stand-alone intervention (see Valentine, Bankoff, Poulin, Reidler & Pantalone, 2015, for a useful review).

ACCEPTANCE AND COMMITMENT THERAPY (ACT)

ACT assumes that psychological problems are due to a lack of behavioural flexibility and effectiveness, and the goal of therapy is to help clients choose effective behaviours even in the face of interfering thoughts and emotions. Therapy is based on Hayes et al.'s (2001) relational frame theory, which views psychological problems as a reflection of psychological inflexibility and experiential avoidance. The model has two main components: *acceptance and mindfulness processes* and *commitment and behaviour change processes* – hence 'acceptance and commitment therapy'. In ACT, these processes are balanced to produce greater 'psychological flexibility' (which Hayes et al. view as the ability to experience the present moment fully as a conscious, historical being) and, depending on the situation, changing or persisting in behaviour in the service of chosen values.

Therapists are advised to adopt a compassionate attitude towards the client, echoing Gilbert's therapeutic guidelines. Hayes also emphasises the importance of being in the present moment, advocating the therapeutic use of mindfulness, echoing MBCT and DBT.

To support ACT, there are several randomised controlled studies indicating its efficacy with, for example, psychotic symptoms (Bach & Hayes, 2002) and specific anxiety disorders (Zettle, 2003).

BEHAVIOURAL ACTIVATION (BA)

BA emerged as a stand-alone treatment for depression following a component analysis study of CBT (Jacobson et al., 1996). BA was found to equal in efficacy a more complete version of CT, which also incorporated coping skills to counter depressive thinking.

BA helps depressed people re-engage in their lives through focused activation strategies. This counters patterns of avoidance, withdrawal and inactivity that may exacerbate depressive episodes by generating additional secondary problems. BA is also designed to help clients reintroduce positive reinforcement in their lives, which can have an antidepressant effect. This approach is also mentioned in Chapter 12, which more fully details the role of activity scheduling in the management of depression. See Martell et al. (2001) for a full account of BA, and Chartier & Provencher (2013) for a recent review.

There is also a brief version of BA which has demonstrated effectiveness for depression (Lejuez et al., 2011).

NEUROSCIENCE

WHAT IS IT?

Neuroscience is the study of brain function, and interestingly, in the past decade or so it has made an increasing appearance in the CBT literature (see Frewin, Dozois & Lanius, 2008 for an empirical and methodological review of studies of the impact of CBT on the brain).

Theorists and practitioners seem to have become more interested in understanding emotional and cognitive reactions at a fundamental level. For example, Brewin (2001), and also Ehlers and Clark (2000), referred to brain mechanisms in describing their understanding of the formation of traumatic memories and in developing their models of PTSD. Gilbert's social mentality theory (1989) incorporates neurochemistry, Young et al. (2003) cite the importance of understanding the neurobiology of the 'emotional brain' and make reference to LeDoux's (1999) neurological findings. Researchers in MBCT are increasingly studying the neurophysiological effects of the training (e.g. Barnhofer, Duggan, Crane, Hepburn, Fennell & Williams, 2007). Beck published a cognitive model of depression and its neurobiological correlates in 2008 and a neurophysiological model of Beck's CBT two years later (Clark & Beck, 2010). More recently a neuroscience-informed CBT model (n-CBT) has been proposed (Field, Beeson & Jones, 2015). So you can see there is a growing interest in the brain and CBT.

WHY IS THIS INTERESTING?

Cognitive therapists are fascinated by emotions and emotional processing: it is what we assess, address and monitor in our CBT sessions. It has long been known that basic emotional responses are generated by the primitive limbic system in the brain and in particular by the amygdala. Links from the limbic system to the cortices help to inform our emotional responses by 'contextualising' them (cross-referencing with previous knowledge) and different links to the highly developed pre-frontal areas help us recognise and moderate our emotions. In 2008, Beck called for a better understanding of the neuroscience of depression and McNally (2007) for a better appreciation of the neuropsychology of the anxiety disorders. Both argued that an improved understanding of brain function can improve psychological treatments by giving us a more comprehensive understanding of psychological problems. But how?

A better understanding can inform our interventions. For example, we know that diminished pre-frontal cortex (PFC) functioning correlates with poor emotional management. It is also associated with BPD (Berlin, Rolls & Iversen, 2005). It is no wonder, therefore, that clients with BPD can be impulsive and have difficulties recognising and managing emotions, and as therapists we need to take this into account and have realistic expectations of ourselves and our clients. Poor frontal lobe functioning is associated with developmental trauma and this might help us better appreciate why some of our clients with traumatic childhoods struggle to cope with the very emotionally evocative imagery work or role play. We also know that enhanced functioning of these areas of the brain is associated with meditation (Lazar et al., 2005) and exercise (Colcombe et al., 2003), and that physical exercise also increases levels of the monoamines that can moderate mood and anxiety (Chaouloff, 1989), thus we can confidently encourage these activities in clients who are having initial difficulty engaging with the standard cognitive elements of treatment. It has been shown that fear circuitry (McNally, 2007) and depressive circuitry in the brain is robust (Bhagwagar & Cowan, 2008), which can help us understand a client's vulnerability to relapse and help us appreciate the importance of relapse management work (see Chapter 6).

Chronic stress causes shrinkage of the hippocampus and this impairs memory formation and recall – something you can compensate for by introducing memory aids into sessions.

Brain function is crucial to learning, and we can facilitate this. You might remember that, in Chapter 7, we noted that complex alterations within neural networks create enduring memories and the harder the brain works, the more likely it is that a memory will be robust.

This was mentioned in Chapter 7 because Socratic methods (including BEs) stimulate the brain to work harder and thus create deeper learning. Your ability to remember that will reflect how active your neural networks were after you had read it.

For over a century, neurological models of recollection have proposed and shown that memory stabilises (or consolidates) over time and until it has achieved this state, is very vulnerable to disruptions that can lead to forgetting or distortions. More recent theories posit that memory recovery is an active, reconstructive process (for a review see Hardt, Einarsson & Nader, 2010). This requires the PFC to reassemble fragments of recollections stored, or localised, in different parts of the association cortex. The visual fragments will have been stored in the visual cortex, the motor fragments in the motor cortex and so on. The PFC is the 'jig-saw puzzle mat' where different pieces of memory are gathered and reconstructed to create coherent recall. This localisation of memory fragments and the reconstructive nature of memory is efficient, but we should be aware that it does render remembering vulnerable to distortion and suggestion.

What this means is that memory can be distorted both when we first develop a novel memory and again when we recollect it. Although not inevitable, these are times when 'false' memories or confabulations can occur, especially if a third party supplies erroneous material during the consolidation phase. In therapy we frequently ask clients to remember, so we should be vigilant in avoiding leading questions or making suggestions. A great strength of Socratic methods is that they prompt the clients to generate their own material so we minimise the likelihood of facilitating distorted recollections.

We also exploit this natural phenomenon of reconsolidation by encouraging clients to 'update' recollections in the light of new material. This enables them to develop more functional and tolerable meanings linked to memories which had previously been troublesome.

For researchers, understanding more about the different brain mechanisms for different disorders can inform pharmacological, psychological or combination treatments – particularly in the more severe psychiatric disorders.

These are just a few examples of how understanding some 'first principles' of brain functioning can help you enhance your psychotherapy. There is a rapidly growing body of research if you are drawn to learn more about CBT, memory and the brain, but for a simple overview, see Kennerley & Kischka (2013).

CONCLUSION

Since CBT emerged in the 1970s, researchers and clinicians have been striving to apply it more effectively and to a wider population. As a result we have now a range of CBT-based interventions we can adopt when working with a range of clients with differing needs and problems. However, we would urge you to consider carefully any departure from the evidence-based interventions and ensure that your understanding of your client's difficulties justifies it.

PROBLEMS

THE THERAPIST IS NOT COMPETENT TO OFFER THE THERAPY

Clinicians not only need to be familiar with the basic principles of CBT and the augmentations of it, but also need to be able to work with clients who might have challenging interpersonal difficulties and who might present with a range of problems – some dangerous to themselves and others. Thus, as a therapist, you need to be prepared to gain additional training and to ensure that this is combined with good supervision and support.

THE THERAPIST IS STRESSED BY THE COMPLEXITY AND THE DEMANDS OF THE THERAPY

The therapies described in this chapter tend to be reserved for those with more complex problems and this can be taxing on the therapist's skills and resources. As indicated above, supervision is essential for therapists working with complex difficulties and additional peer support can also offset some of the stress (although support should be in addition to supervision and not instead of supervision). Nevertheless, therapists need to be realistic and only take on cases when they are reasonably confident that they can provide long-term or intensive care when necessary. It is also important to have a caseload with a 'balance' of clients that matches the therapist's skills and resources. Kennerley et al. (2010) have written a useful and practical chapter that addresses coping with therapist stresses.

THE CASE SEEMS NEVER-ENDING

Clients with complex needs can require 'longer-term' therapy, which, in the literature, can mean anything from 20 sessions to several years. In order to guard against unnecessarily prolonging therapy and to guard against fostering dependence, you are advised to use supervision and to review progress regularly with a view to ending therapy if there is little indication that CBT is helpful or necessary.

VICARIOUS TRAUMA

Some of the more complex case-work invariably involves working with clients who will describe traumatic events, and vicarious traumatisation can occur in therapists exposed to this (McCann & Pearlman, 1990). Good supervision and support can help you identify the early signs of vicarious trauma, such as experiencing traumatic intrusions or taking actions to avoid triggering them – actions such as drinking to numb emotions or suppress images. Good supervision and support can also be helpful in guiding you towards developing ideas for coping, and again, the recent chapter by Kennerley et al. (2010) mentioned above gives some advice on managing vicarious trauma.

SUMMARY

- CBT has been used with an increasing variety of clinical populations and with client groups of increasing complexity and/or chronicity. This has demanded developments in cognitive therapies and augmentations of CBT and we have seen the rise of:
  - schema-focused approaches: Young's schema therapy (ST) and the 'Beckian' schema-focused cognitive therapy (SFCT);
  - the meta-cognitive approaches of CMT, MBCT and MCT;
  - the radical behaviour therapies of DBT, ACT and BA.
- It is interesting (and reassuring) that there are themes common to several of the newer approaches, including the relevance of schemata, of meta-cognitive awareness and of acceptance. There is also a zeitgeist of understanding the neurological processes underlying psychological functioning.
- There can be no doubt that these developments have been exciting and have been met with enthusiasm. In general, however, the empirical status of some of the interventions is still poor and where there is empirical support some of the treatment trials are highly specific: for example, for BPD in the case of schema-focused approaches and for para-suicidal women with BPD in the case of DBT. Until there is further evidence, we cannot assume that the approaches will generalise to other populations and so they should be used with appropriate reservation.

These learning exercises are available to download from the companion website.

REVIEW AND REFLECTION:

- **There are several distinct parts to this chapter, and each is very much a brief overview, so there is much scope for you to take your interests further. So, first consider which aspects are most relevant to you and take some time to review that section, making notes if you find it helpful.**
- **When you have identified what interests you, ask yourself questions such as:**
  - **'How does this actually relate to my clinical practice and my clients' needs?'**

  - 'How does this fit with my way of working?'
  - 'How does this relate to my supervision or research opportunities or interests?'
  - 'Can this new approach really enhance my client's treatment?'
  - 'What advantages will this approach have over classic CBT?'
- Ask yourself: 'Is there enough theoretical support or empirical data to justify my adopting a new way of working?' and review your client's formulation to see if your case conceptualisation indicates novel approaches.
- Are you sure that you have used 'classic' CBT to the best of your ability – have you given it a reasonable chance?
- Be critical and realistic in your thinking: don't be tempted to adopt a new approach just because it seems attractive.

TAKING IT FORWARD:

- If you have decided that you will take up some of the ideas in this chapter, consider how you will ensure that you develop your knowledge and skills. The first step might be more reading or attending training or finding a specialist supervisor. This will require some groundwork as training opportunities might be relatively rare. You also need to find the time (and the money) to do this. So make some concrete plans for securing the resources and set yourself deadlines for starting this project and for taking stock of your progress.
- It can be helpful to see if a colleague is also interested in learning more about the developments in CBT as you can 'buddy' with each other and provide support and encouragement.
- Evaluate your interventions. It is always good practice to develop ways of assessing the impact of your therapy and it is even more important to do this when you are using approaches that are relatively new or, as yet, have little empirical foundation.

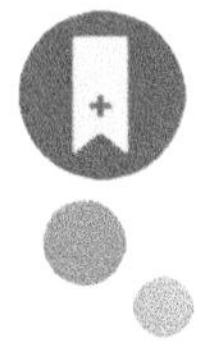

FURTHER READING

The *CBT Distinctive Features* Series (Ed. Windy Dryden). Hove: Routledge.

This series includes recently published texts covering all the developments that have been mentioned in this chapter, with the exception of neuroscience.

Gilbert, P. (2005). *Compassion: conceptualizations, research and use in psychotherapy*. Hove: Routledge.

The first CMT 'manual' which invites expert contributors to detail CMT interventions within specific clinical areas. This text contains a great deal of clinical wisdom and practical guidance.

Riso, L.P., du Toit, P.L., Stein, D.J., & Young, J.E. (2007). *Cognitive schemas and core beliefs in psychological problems*. Washington, DC: American Psychological Association.

This is a useful comprehensive volume which considers the application of schema-focused interventions across a range of psychiatric presentations. The contributors to the book are experts in specific fields and describe the potential for using schema-focused approaches with wise caution. The text is rich in clinical illustration.

Segal, Z.V., Williams, M.J.G., & Teasdale, J. (2001). *Mindfulness-based cognitive therapy for depression: a new approach to preventing relapse*. New York: Guilford Press.

This is the basic text for MBCT practitioners. It is very clinician-friendly, thoughtfully and clearly presented with a systematic overview of a course of MBCT for recurrent depression.

VIDEO LINKS

- **17.1 Addressing dichotomous thinking**
- **17.2 Historical review with a client**
- **17.3 Using a responsibility pie chart**

18 EVALUATING CBT PRACTICE

- Introduction
- Types of evaluation
- Some frequently used questionnaires
- Clinical significance statistics
- Difficulties in evaluation
- Summary
- Learning exercises
- Further reading

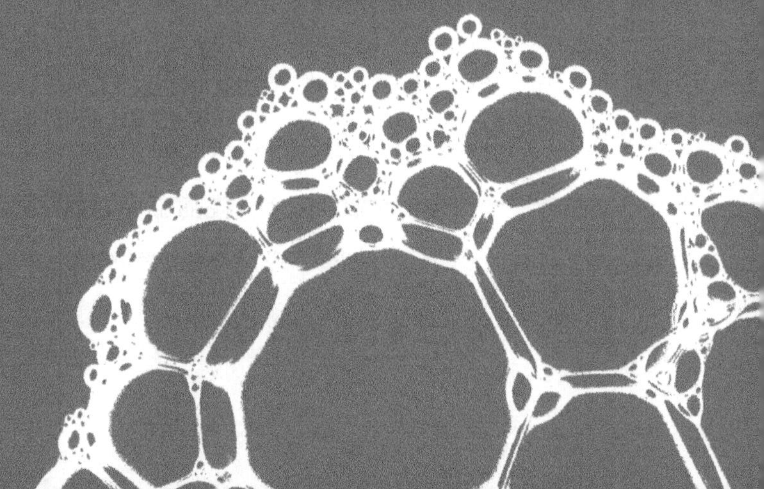

INTRODUCTION

WHAT IS EVALUATION AND WHY SHOULD WE DO IT?

By evaluating practice, we mean gathering data with the aim of determining how well therapy is working or whether one form of therapy is better than another. We believe that CBT practitioners should attempt to evaluate the effectiveness of their therapy for several reasons:

1. It places us in the great tradition of 'scientist-practitioners' (Committee on Training in Clinical Psychology, 1947; Raimy, 1950), aiming to expand knowledge through 'real world' research by practitioners. (See also Salkovskis, 1995, 2002; Margison et al., 2000.) The idea behind these approaches is that although traditional, university-based, controlled research is essential to progress, some questions are best answered through research based in clinical practice and carried out by ordinary clinicians.
2. It allows us to give both clients and purchasers more accurate information about what kind of outcomes clients can expect. Such evaluation is, therefore, an important part of accountability to our commissioners and of informed consent for our clients. It also allows both our clients and ourselves to see whether we are doing as well as expected and, therefore, whether there are areas that we need to improve.
3. It gives us a baseline of data against which we can compare changes we introduce in running our services. For instance, if we introduce a change hoping to reduce the proportion of people who drop out of therapy, then it is helpful to know what the original proportion was; if we do some training, hoping to improve outcomes with depression, then we need to know what our outcomes were before the training. This kind of routine data can be an enormously useful support for clinical audits.

Thus, some system for routinely evaluating therapy is important, and while one short chapter can only cover a fraction of the issues of research design that arise in this area, we hope we can give you some useful pointers.

TYPES OF EVALUATION

There are two main foci for evaluation:

- individual clinical case outcome (including evaluating a single group);
- whole clinical service outcome (whether provided by one clinician or 100).

We shall look at each of these in turn.

EVALUATING INDIVIDUAL CLINICAL CASES

The major purposes of evaluating individual outcomes are: to allow you and your client to see what, if any, changes have occurred in therapy; and in some cases to look more closely at the effects of a clinical intervention, perhaps using what has been called *single-case experimental designs*.

The first of these is fairly straightforward: we take some relevant measures, perhaps at the beginning and end of therapy, and see whether and by how much they change. Used at this level, such evaluation is straightforward good clinical practice. It gives both therapist and client a clear view of how much difference therapy has made to target problems.

Specific single-case research designs are probably less familiar to many readers, and we shall briefly introduce some of the ideas behind these approaches, although we cannot do more than scratch the surface. The interested reader is directed to classic texts such as Barlow, Andrasik and Hersen (2006) and Kazdin (2010).

The aim of these designs is to allow us to be more confident about evaluating the impact of treatment or some component of treatment. The most common approaches to single-case design rely on regularly repeated measures. The basic logic is that we establish some measure of the problem in which we are interested and then repeat that measure sufficiently often to establish a trend – the so-called *baseline* – against which we can compare subsequent changes when we introduce an intervention. The baseline gives us some protection against the likelihood that changes we observe are actually due to chance or some other factor, rather than our intervention. If we take just one measurement before therapy and one after, with only one individual, then it is impossible to rule out the chance that something external to therapy (e.g. that our client won the lottery, or fell in love, or got a wonderful new job) caused any changes we see. If we have larger numbers of measurements, it becomes much less plausible that an external change happened to occur at exactly the time when we changed our intervention.

Figure 18.1 illustrates this logic. Imagine that the vertical axis here represents some relevant measure: score on a depression questionnaire, or number of obsessional thoughts in a day, or ratings of fear in a particular situation. In the left-hand part of this figure, with a single measurement before and after treatment, there is nothing to assure us that the

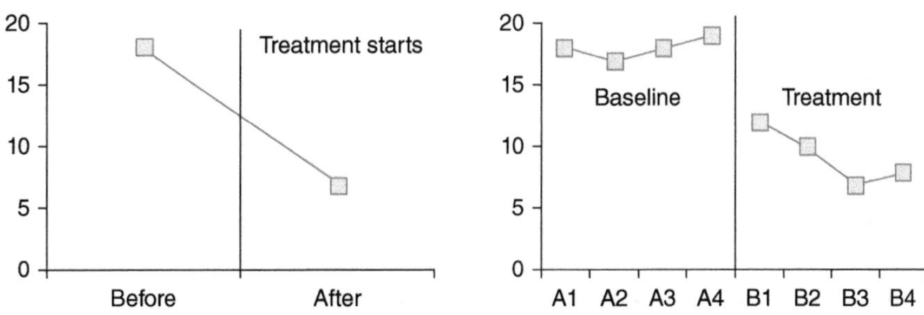

Figure 18.1 'Before and after' versus 'Repeated measurements'

reduction in score is not due to some external cause unrelated to therapy. We have only two measurements – anything could have happened in the intervening time and had an impact on whatever the measure is. In the right-hand chart, however, the frequent repeated measures give us greater reason to believe that the treatment has caused the change because it is less likely that a sequence of repeated measurements should happen to respond to such an event *just at the specific time* that the treatment is introduced.

The basic logic of many single-case designs follows this principle. We look at the *pattern* of measurements to see whether changes coincide with changes of treatment: if they do, that gives us some reason to believe that the treatment was responsible for the change (but we still cannot be *sure* that some coincidental event has not caused the change).

The simple design on the right-hand side of Figure 18.1, consisting of a baseline before treatment and a continuation over the course of treatment, is often known as an A–B design: the baseline is Condition A and treatment is Condition B. If the treatment is one that we would expect not to have a lasting effect but only to work whilst it is being implemented (e.g. perhaps a sleep hygiene programme), then there is scope for extending the A–B design to variations such as A–B–A, in which we first introduce the treatment and then withdraw it; see Figure 18.2 for an illustration of this.

The basic logic is strengthened here by the measure's responding not just to the introduction of the treatment but also to its withdrawal. The likelihood that such opposite responses should coincide with treatment changes just by chance is even smaller, and thus our conviction that the treatment caused a change is stronger. Of course, if the treatment is one that we would expect to have a persisting effect (e.g. CBT for depression leading to improved mood), then this A–B–A model is not usable: we do not expect the client's mood to drop as soon as the treatment is withdrawn.

We shall briefly describe two further common designs. The first, the *alternating treatments design*, is a way of determining in a single case which of two treatments is more effective (but requires that the treatment's effect will be measurable rapidly). During each segment (e.g. a treatment session, or some other unit of time), one of the two treatments is chosen randomly, and the measure is repeated for each segment. If the measure shows a clear separation of the two conditions, as in Figure 18.3, then we have some evidence that

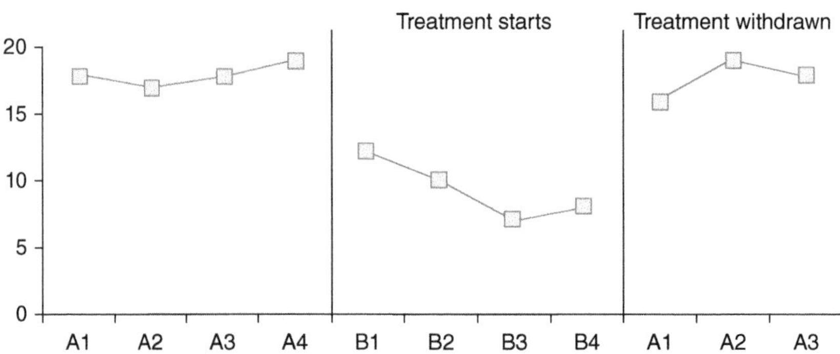

Figure 18.2 A–B–A design

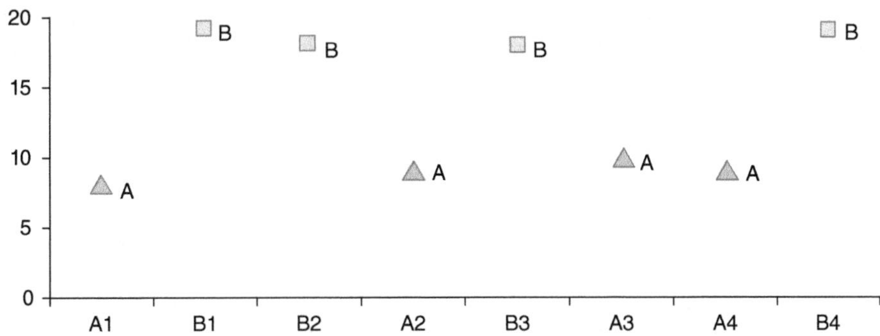

Figure 18.3 Alternating treatments design

one treatment is more effective than the other. For example, suppose we wanted to test the hypothesis that talking about a particular topic makes our client anxious. Then we could agree with the client to decide randomly in some sessions to talk about the topic; and in other sessions not to; and to take ratings of anxiety. In Figure 18.3, if A marks the 'avoiding' sessions and B marks the 'talking' sessions, then the pattern suggests that avoiding leads to lower scores on our measure than talking does.

This design can also usefully be adapted for clients' BEs (Chapter 9), for example to help an obsessional client decide whether repeated checking of the front door actually causes more or less anxiety than doing one quick check and walking away.

Finally, there is the *multiple baseline design*, where we look at several different measurements at the same time, hence the name. There are several variations: multiple baseline across *behaviours*, across *settings* or across *subjects*. Consider this simple example of multiple baselines across behaviours. A client has two different obsessional rituals, both of which we monitor regularly during the baseline period (see Figure 18.4, where the triangles represent

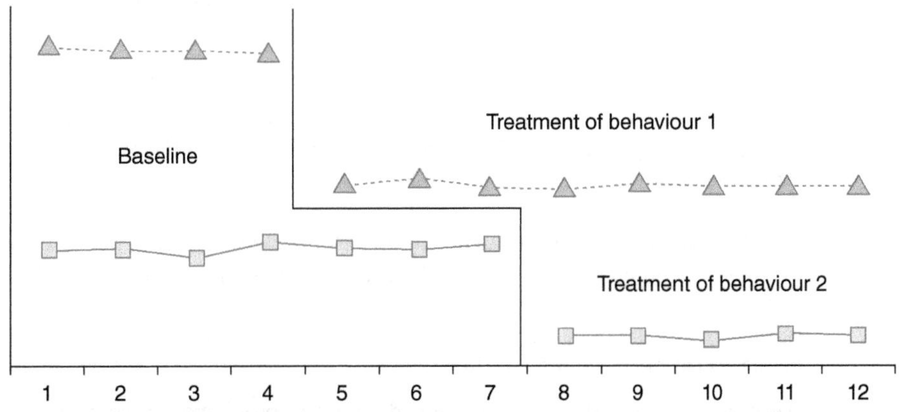

Figure 18.4 Multiple baselines across behaviours

the frequency of one ritual and the squares the other ritual). Then we introduce the treatment for one behaviour only (one ritual in this case). After a delay, we introduce the treatment for another behaviour (the second ritual in this case). If we get a pattern like Figure 18.4, where each behaviour shows a change *just at the time treatment was introduced for that behaviour*, then this gives us some reason to believe it was the treatment that caused the change (see Salkovskis & Westbrook, 1989 for an example of this design's being used to evaluate treatment for obsessional thoughts).

The same principles apply to multiple baseline designs across subjects or settings: of course, the number of different baselines does not have to be two, as in our example above, but can be any number. In the example in Figure 18.4, each set of data represents one *behaviour* (a ritual in our example); in the case of multiple baseline across *subjects*, each set of data represents a person, to whom we introduce the treatment at different times after baseline; in the case of multiple baseline across *settings*, each data set represents one situation (e.g. a programme for disruptive behaviour that is introduced first in the school setting and then later at home). Note that this design can only work when we would expect some independence between the behaviours, subjects or settings: if the treatment is likely to generalise from one of these to the others, then the synchronised change we are looking for will not happen.

Finally, note that we have described here the common approach of analysing the results of such single case designs by *visual inspection*: that is, by looking at the pattern of results and seeing what they seem to show. Over the past 20 years, there have also been developments in the statistical analysis of single-case designs, but such statistics are not yet straightforward enough for most ordinary clinicians to use.

EVALUATING SERVICES

The other common form of evaluation is the collection of data about whole services and, therefore, larger numbers of clients. The main purposes of such evaluations are:

- to describe the client population (e.g. age, sex, chronicity of problems, etc.);
- to describe the nature of the service (e.g. drop-out rates, average number of treatment sessions, etc.);
- to establish the effectiveness of the service's treatments, using outcome measures;
- to use routinely collected data as a baseline against which changes of service can be evaluated (e.g. does this change result in better outcomes, or greater client satisfaction?).

It is impossible to specify what kind of data should be collected, as that depends on your own service's interests and goals, but most services collect various forms of data, including:

- client outcome data (e.g. mental health questionnaire measures, administered before and after treatment – see below);
- client demographic data (e.g. age, sex, duration of problems, employment status, etc.);

- service parameters, such as dates of referral and so on (from which waiting times can be calculated);
- service outcomes such as dropping out of treatment or not attending appointments.

Several years ago the service in which all the authors then worked decided to implement a limit of 10 sessions on treatment in an attempt to reduce waiting lists. Because this change naturally aroused some worries, it was agreed that its effects should be evaluated. Several different aspects of the new procedure were included in the evaluation:

1. *Did the limit have an effect on client outcomes?* The service had been collecting routine outcome data for many years, so those existing data could be used as 'historical controls' against which to compare the outcomes obtained under the new regime.
2. *Did it change client satisfaction?* Again, we had previous data using the client satisfaction questionnaire (Larsen, Attkisson, Hargreaves & Nguyen, 1979) that were used as a comparison.
3. *How did therapists respond to the limits?* We used ad hoc rating scales to evaluate whether they found it easier or harder, how it affected therapy and so on.

The results were that broadly the 10-session limit did not result in different outcomes; clients were just as satisfied; and therapists had a 'swings and roundabouts' response in that they found some things harder but some easier. The exception to the finding of broadly similar outcomes was that there was some evidence that clients with 'personality disorders' did less well with the brief treatment, so this was investigated further.

In England and Wales, evaluating CBT services has been carried out at a level never seen before via the IAPT initiative. This systematic service delivery and evaluation of evidence-based psychotherapies, including CBT, was implemented in 2008 (Department of Health, 2008). By 2013 it was treating nearly 400,000 people per year – and collecting data on the progress of every client at every session (Layard & Clark, 2014). These data have shown how many people have been seen, for how long, in what service, by whom and so on. All of which is valuable information in itself, but perhaps even more importantly, the data have yielded pointers for improving services.

Analyses of client outcome indicated that there was a huge variation of performance in different parts of the country (for a readable overview of IAPT outcomes, see Layard & Clark, 2014), but that was not where evaluation ended. Whether one is appraising the progress of the client with whom you meet each week or assessing the performance of a national service, we should look at the initial outcome and ask ourselves further questions, Socratic questions actually:

(Continued)

(Continued)

- 'What else is this telling me?'
- 'What more can I learn from this?'
- 'How can I take this forward?'

Professor David Clark did just that and found the outcome data highly instructive. It was apparent that success rates were better when the IAPT model and NICE guidelines were followed, when therapists were more experienced and highly trained, where clients received more sessions and where they were 'stepped-up' to more intensive therapy if needed. Recovery rates were also better in the larger services, which offered more comprehensive care. This has contributed to refining IAPT training and delivery to improve services – further data collection will reveal if this is effective.

If you work in IAPT, this type of evaluation will be going on around you, but if you don't you might consider what you can learn from this initiative. No matter how modest your service, it will benefit from regular and meaningful evaluation and that will benefit your clients.

SOME FREQUENTLY USED QUESTIONNAIRES

Which outcome measures to use is again a matter for each service to decide according to its needs, but the following are suitable for routine clinical use in that they (a) do not take too long for a client to complete; (b) are widely used, so that comparisons can be made with other services and/or research trials; and (c) assess aspects of mental health that are common in most populations:

- The Beck Depression Inventory (BDI: Beck et al., 1961) is probably the best-known measure of depression. The latest revision is the BDI II (Beck, Brown & Steer, 1996), although the original version is still sometimes used in research in order to retain comparability with earlier work.
- The Beck Anxiety Inventory (BAI: Beck et al., 1988) is a similar measure of anxiety.
- The Clinical Outcomes in Routine Evaluation – Outcome Measure (CORE–OM: Evans et al., 2002; Barkham, Mellor-Clark, Connell & Cahill, 2006; Mullin, Barkham, Mothersole, Bewick & Kinder, 2006 – see also the website at www.coreims.co.uk) is an increasingly popular general measure of mental health in the UK, especially in primary care settings. Mullin et al. (2006) provide some useful national benchmarking standards, by giving mean CORE scores for a sample of over 10,000 clients from many different services across the UK.
- The Hospital Anxiety and Depression Scale (HADS: Zigmond & Snaith, 1983), is, despite the name, suitable for community settings. The name arose because it was originally designed for use in general hospital settings and, therefore, aimed to avoid confounding mental health problems with physical health problems. This characteristic makes it particularly useful for settings where one might expect a significant proportion of clients to have physical health problems as well as mental health problems.

- The PHQ-9 (Kroenke, Spitzer & Williams, 2001) is the depression module of a larger diagnostic instrument for common mental disorders. It is used for monitoring depression and for making a tentative diagnosis in at-risk populations. It is routinely used in IAPT services (see above). It is brief, which is an advantage when a measure is frequently used, and it has good psychometric properties.
- The GHQ-12 (Goldberg & Williams, 1988) is also a staple of the IAPT services and a brief questionnaire. It is a screening device for identifying minor psychiatric disorders in non-psychiatric settings. The questionnaire is available in lengthy versions (e.g. GHQ-60), but the brief GHQ-12 has been established as a reliable and valid form, and because it is so brief it is not too demanding or intrusive.

A literature search will quickly turn up other measures suitable for almost any specific mental health problem.

However, always choose your psychometric tools thoughtfully. Consider if they are justifiable for your client: is there a shorter, less intrusive option? Is your chosen questionnaire actually valid for this client (who may be younger or older or culturally different from the population that the questionnaire was meant for)? Can you confidently repeat the measure? Does this measure actually target this person's rather idiosyncratic presentation? There are many such questions to ask yourself in order to be confident that your assessment is reasonable and meaningful. We can't just assume that using psychometrics will be in the best interests of our client, or our service (Gilbody, House & Sheldon, 2001). Routine measurement is costly of time and can take its toll on your therapeutic alliance if it is not credible or sensitive.

OTHER MEASURES

Standardised questionnaires are often supplemented by other measures, such as individual problem ratings, belief ratings for particular cognitions, problem frequency counts or duration timings and so on (see Chapter 5).

CLINICAL SIGNIFICANCE STATISTICS

Service-evaluation data can be analysed using any of the standard statistical approaches. However, an approach known as 'clinical significance' analysis is particularly suited for clinical services, and especially an approach developed by Jacobson (Jacobson & Revenstorf, 1988; Jacobson, Roberts, Berns & McGlinchey, 1999). The aim of clinical significance analysis is to deal with the problem in conventional statistical testing that almost any change in average scores, even a tiny one, will emerge as significant if the number of participants in the study is large enough. Conventional testing tells us that such a change is 'significant' in the sense that it is unlikely to have emerged by chance but does *not* tell us that it is significant in the sense of being important. Thus, given large enough numbers, a change in clients' mean BDI score of a couple of points from start to end of treatment might be statistically significant – and rightly so, in the sense of being 'not due to chance'. But clinicians would not regard such a change of score as *clinically* significant, in the sense that their clients would not be happy if this was the kind of benefit they could expect.

Jacobson's approach to testing for clinical significance looks at each participant in a study individually and asks two questions:

1. Did this person's score on a particular measure change sufficiently for it to be unlikely to be due to chance? A 'reliable change' index, dependent on the reliability of the measure and its natural variation in the population, is calculated. If a client's change score is greater than the calculated criterion, then that client may be described as reliably improved (or deteriorated) on the measure.
2. If the client *has* reliably changed, has the change also taken them across a cut-off point into the normal range for this measure? If so, we may consider the person not just improved but also 'recovered'. Jacobson et al. set out different possible ways of setting this 'normal cut-off' criterion, for example by calculating the point beyond which a client is statistically more likely to belong to a normal population than a dysfunctional population.

Figure 18.5 shows the possible outcomes resulting from this analysis for each client. Depending on the above two calculations, every client is classified as: reliably deteriorated; no reliable change; reliably improved (but not recovered); or recovered. The results of the analysis are reported as the proportion of clients falling into each of these categories.

The advantages of this approach are twofold:

- it gives us more meaningful statistics to report: most clinicians would agree that a client who meets both of the Jacobson criteria has truly made clinically significant progress;
- the resulting figures are more comprehensible to clients and/or service commissioners: it is much easier for most people to understand 'On average 56 per cent of clients recover' than 'On average, clients' scores on the BDI move from 17.3 to 11.2' (Westbrook and Kirk, 2005 give an example of this kind of analysis for routine clinical data).

Incidentally, it is worth noting that although such 'benchmarking' strategies (see also Wade, Treat & Stuart, 1998; Merrill et al., 2003) typically find that CBT is an effective treatment in clinical practice as well as in research trials, clinical significance analysis is sobering for

		1. Change score larger than reliable change criterion?		
		Yes, for the worse	*No*	*Yes, for the better*
2. Score crossed cut-off into normal range?	*No*	**Reliably deteriorated**	**No reliable change**	**Reliably improved (but not recovered)**
	Yes			**Recovered**

Figure 18.5 Classification of change scores for clinical significance

anyone who believes that CBT (or any other kind of psychological therapy) is a panacea that can help all clients: most such analyses find that only around one-third to a half of clients achieve recovery by these criteria.

DIFFICULTIES IN EVALUATION

KEEPING IT SIMPLE

There is always a temptation to gather more data. It is easy to think 'Whilst we're at it, let's find out about this … and this … and this …'. The result can be an unwieldy mass of data that overburdens the client, is too time-consuming to collect reliably and is even more time-consuming to analyse. In general, it is better to have a small number of data items which can be collected and analysed reasonably economically.

REPEATING MEASURES

Sometimes clients become over-familiar with regularly used measures and begin to complete them on 'automatic pilot'. Always spend a minute or two discussing questionnaire results with your client so that you can assess how valid the responses are.

KEEPING IT GOING

Most routine data collection starts enthusiastically, but this cannot be sustained. We suggest two factors are important in keeping data collection going. First, having a 'champion' at a reasonably senior level – someone who will support data collection and analysis and make sure that people are prompted if they forget about collecting data. Second, it is crucial that clinicians collecting data see that something is done with it and that results are fed back to them periodically. Data that are never analysed are useless anyway, and the chances are low that people will continue to collect it when no results appear.

RESEARCH DESIGN

Clinical service evaluation usually cannot reach the highest standards of research design, such as RCTs. All research designs involve some compromise between (a) the tightly controlled research that eliminates as much uncertainty as possible but, in doing so, may end up not resembling real clinical practice; and (b) the more 'real-world' research that is very close to clinical practice but, as a result, leaves room for ambiguity about causal factors. Service evaluation therefore often works on the principle that some evidence is better than nothing and accepts some lack of rigour for the sake of being able to describe everyday outcomes. Robson's (2002) book on 'real-world research' is a useful resource to look further at these issues.

SUMMARY

- One of CBT's strengths is its commitment to empiricism, that is, to evaluating whether there is good evidence to support its theories and the effectiveness of its treatments. This commitment is not just for academics but can and should be incorporated into clinical services.
- One common form of evaluation looks at individual clinical cases in order to tell, more reliably than mere subjective opinion, whether therapy (or some component of therapy) is effective. So-called *single case designs* are particularly useful here, and can be implemented without a great deal of change to ordinary CBT practice.
- The other common form of evaluation takes a broader view and aims to evaluate whether a clinical service as a whole is in some relevant sense 'doing a good job': obtaining good outcomes, doing as well as some relevant comparison service, obtaining outcomes better than it used to, or whatever. There are many measurement tools available to assess outcomes, some of which enable comparisons with other services or with research trials.
- *Clinical significance* analysis can be a useful tool for summarising outcomes in a way that is meaningful and understandable, both to clinicians and to clients.

LEARNING EXERCISES

These learning exercises are available to download from the companion website.

REVIEW AND REFLECTION:

- Does your service currently do any form of routine evaluation? If so, how well does it work? What could be improved? If not, what might be the pros and cons of doing some? How might you persuade your colleagues and/or managers that it would be a good idea?
- What about your own individual clients? Could you do more to evaluate their progress in therapy? How might that be useful, for you or for them? What challenges would arise if you were to do more?

TAKING IT FORWARD:

- **Many interesting ideas for research and evaluation arise from thinking about questions that come up in clinical practice: 'It seems to me that treatment technique X works better than Y for this problem', or 'Clients seem to be less likely to drop out of treatment if I do Z', or whatever. Perhaps you could keep a note of thoughts like that, and see whether there is any way to gather some relevant evidence.**
- **If your service does not currently collect routine data, could you talk to colleagues about whether it would be useful, what data to collect and so on?**
- **If you have data but have not analysed it or collated it, maybe you could book some time out some way ahead in order to do so.**

FURTHER READING

Robson, C., & McCartan, K. (2016). *Real world research* (4th ed.). Chichester: Wiley.

As the title suggests, this is an excellent and comprehensive introduction to doing research in the 'real world', i.e. outside academic settings.

Field, A. (2009). *Discovering statistics using SPSS* (3rd ed.). London: Sage.

Statistics is always going to be intimidating for many of us, but Field does as good a job as possible in making it interesting and practical, with many detailed examples of how to do statistical tests using the popular statistics software package, SPSS.

Westbrook, D. (2010). Research and evaluation. In M. Mueller, H. Kennerley, F. McManus, & D. Westbrook (Eds.), *The Oxford guide to surviving as a CBT therapist*. Oxford: Oxford University Press.

A brief introduction to some of the issues around doing evaluation research in clinical practice.

19 USING SUPERVISION IN CBT

- Introduction
- Goals of supervision
- Modes of supervision
- Choosing a supervisor
- Negotiating supervision arrangements
- Preparing for a supervision session
- During a supervision session
- Problems with supervision
- Summary
- Learning exercises
- Further reading
- Video link
    - 19.1 Supervision agenda

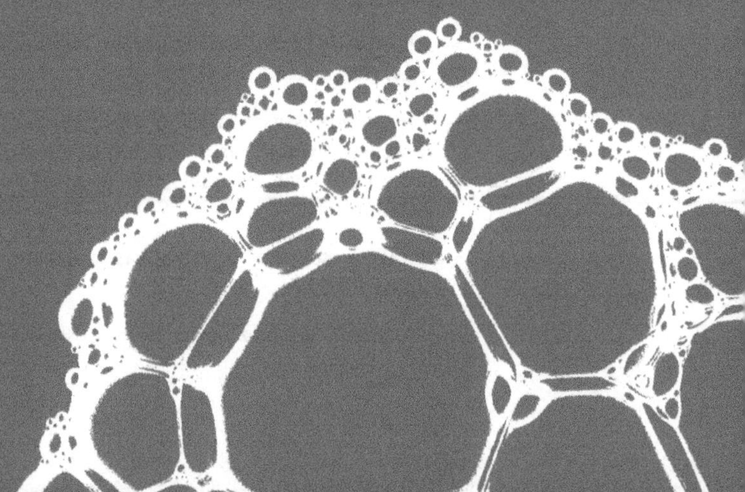

INTRODUCTION

As anyone who tries it soon discovers, the practice of good therapy is not something you can learn quickly or easily. You cannot just read a book, or attend a workshop, and then go off and do good CBT: effective clinical training demands a much longer process of learning, in which you bring together what you have learned about theory and therapeutic strategies with the complex reality of the clients you see. Clinical supervision is one of the main ways in which this continued learning can occur. It can take different forms (see below), but the basic idea is that by having someone else to discuss or directly observe your therapy, you can examine how well it is going, identify problems, find solutions, develop your skills and ensure that your client receives best treatment. The need for supervision applies to CBT practitioners at any level, but most crucially for novices.

These views of the positive value of supervision would probably gain support from most CBT practitioners. However, embarrassingly for an approach that values empiricism as CBT does, there is not yet a significant body of evidence about whether CBT supervision actually makes a difference, either to the supervisee's skills or to the outcomes for clients. One important study (Mannix et al., 2006) found that clinicians receiving continued supervision after six months training in CBT did better in maintaining and improving their CBT skills than those whose supervision ceased after six months, but much more evidence is needed. What follows is, therefore, based mostly on the clinical experience and beliefs of ourselves and others, rather than on a compelling evidence base. Much of what we have to say can and should be challenged as new evidence emerges.

There are guidelines for good practice for CBT supervisors (see e.g. Padesky, 1996a; Pilling & Roth, 2008; Gordon 2012), but in this chapter we consider supervision from the consumer's point of view and how best to *use* it.

GOALS OF SUPERVISION

Each of you needs to consider your goals for your supervision experience. Although we are unaware of any single agreed definition of clinical supervision in CBT, there is agreement that 'good' clinical supervision can help achieve any or all of the following goals:

- *Developing therapist skills*: honing and improving existing skills, and learning new skills.
- *Protecting clients*: providing a form of quality control for therapy, both at the practical level of ensuring appropriate strategies are being used and at the emotional level of enabling an external, more objective view of therapeutic relationships.
- *Providing support* for therapists in dealing with the difficulties therapy may cause for them.
- *Monitoring and evaluating* therapist skills and practice.

The balance between these different components will vary according to factors such as the characteristics and experience of you (the therapist) and your supervisor, and the context of the supervision and so on.

In thinking about the last of the goals (i.e. evaluation), it is worth considering the distinction between *summative* and *formative* evaluation:

- *Summative evaluation* refers to evaluation whose primary aim is to arrive at a summary judgement: is the subject of evaluation 'good enough' in some sense (e.g. is the trainee good enough to pass the course)?
- *Formative evaluation* refers to evaluation whose primary aim is to help the subject to improve: that is, where the main point is not 'Is X good enough?' but rather 'How can we make X better?'. Almost all clinical supervision contains elements of formative evaluation, but summative evaluation is usually only important in the context of a training course, therapist accreditation or similar processes.

Useful tools to evaluate cognitive therapy skills for both summative and formative purposes are the Cognitive Therapy Scales (CTS: Young & Beck, 1980; Dobson, Shaw & Vallis, 1985; or a revised version, the CTS-R – see Blackburn et al., 2001) and the assessment of core CBT skills (ACCS: Muse & McManus, 2013; see www.accs-scale.co.uk).

MODES OF SUPERVISION

We can distinguish two important dimensions of supervision: first, whether the supervision is for an individual therapist or a group; second, whether the supervision is from one person considered to be more expert to another considered less expert or is between people of roughly equal expertise. Combining these categories gives us four modes of supervision, which we have given arbitrary names and is illustrated in Table 19.1.

It is sometimes thought – wrongly, in our view – that all supervision must have an identified leader. We feel that peer supervision can be very useful, even if none of the participants is highly expert. We would draw an analogy with CBT therapy: just as the therapist may be able to help the client in an area about which she knows little, through a process of guided discovery, so peers may be able to use the same processes to open up new ways of thinking for the therapist in supervision. Although there is a danger of 'the blind leading the blind', if *none* of the participants has any CBT experience, such supervision can be better than nothing at all in situations where access to expert supervision is limited.

Table 19.1 Modes of supervision

	Individual	**Group**
Identified leader	1 'Apprenticeship'	2 'Led group'
No identified leader	3 'Consultation' (mutual or one-way)	4 'Peer group'

There are pros and cons to each of these modes and if you have options available to you, you should consider which best meets your needs.

1 APPRENTICESHIP

This is probably what most people think of as typical supervision: a skilled and experienced practitioner meeting a relative novice, one to one, to develop the novice therapist's skills. It is undoubtedly a good model, with excellent scope for detailed examination and rehearsal of therapy skills, finely tuned to the supervisee's needs. The main disadvantages are that it is relatively extravagant in its use of the leader's time (and thus expensive); and because there is only one supervisor, the range of views and expertise available to the supervisee is limited.

2 LED GROUP

The main selling point of the led group is that it has the advantages of the apprenticeship model in terms of offering expertise, whilst being more economical and therefore more practical in many settings. Another advantage is that supervisees can learn from hearing about other practitioner's cases as well as their own. Possible disadvantages include the possibility that each person in the group gets less individual time and that it can sometimes become more like a seminar – with a bias towards the didactic – although this too can sometimes be helpful.

3 CONSULTATION

We use the term 'consultation' to refer to a similar set-up to apprenticeship (i.e. two individuals meeting for supervision), but in this case they are roughly equally skilled, so neither one is an 'apprentice'. For very experienced practitioners, this may well be the only available mode of supervision, since there may be no one with more expertise available. Consultation can either be one-way – one of the pair consults the other for supervision – or can be mutual, where each supervises the other.

4 PEER GROUP

The advantages of the peer group include its being relatively cheap and easy to set up; that it allows vicarious learning; and that by being more egalitarian it may encourage less experienced participants to be creative and to share their ideas. Disadvantages include the risk that 'the blind can lead the blind', with no one really knowing what they are talking about; that, as with any form of group supervision, each supervisee perhaps gets less time; and that there is no leader to take responsibility for group dynamics.

ALTERNATIVE CHANNELS FOR SUPERVISION

In addition to the above modes, it is worth considering that some of them can be practised using other means of communication, such as telephone, video-conferencing and e-mail.

These alternative channels probably work best with individual supervision: managing group interactions without any face-to-face contact is not easy! Such methods may lose some of the subtleties of face-to-face communication, especially when it comes to emotional issues, and there are possible technical difficulties in playing audio- or video-recordings and sharing materials, and you must be mindful of data-governance laws if you play clinical material over the Internet. Nevertheless, they can offer a useful alternative if no face-to-face supervisor is available to meet your needs.

The authors have several supervisees who get clinical supervision from us by phone or via the Internet (usually because they have no appropriate supervisor within a reasonable travelling time – many are overseas supervisees). In many cases we have never actually met the supervisee face-to-face. Such supervisory relationships can work well despite the restrictions of this format. As with any mode that excludes some non-verbal aspects of communication, the potential for misunderstanding is increased, so it may need particular attention from both parties to ensure clear summarising and feedback in order to avoid such problems. This need is reduced if supervision is carried out over the Internet such that the parties can both see and hear each other. Some such systems even allow recordings to be played. This approach can work well, but it does need reasonably powerful technology and a fast and reliable Internet connection at both ends.

SUPERVISION OR THERAPY?

It is recognised in all forms of therapy that there may be times when the therapist's own problems or beliefs may impinge on therapy. Is such material suitable for exploration in supervision, or should it be considered as personal therapy that should take place in another setting? Is there a limit to the personal material dealt with in supervision sessions? If so, where will you go with material that it is agreed should not be part of supervision? There are no right answers to these questions, but most CBT practitioners would say that such material should only be part of supervision to the extent that it has a direct impact on your work with your clients (e.g. Padesky, 1996b). If one of your own beliefs (e.g. 'I must never do anything that clients will find distressing' or 'I am solely responsible for my clients' progress') is blocking you from implementing a therapeutic strategy that appears relevant in other respects, then it may be appropriate to look at that in supervision. If it appears that the belief is part of a wider problem, it probably cannot be dealt with in the limited time available in supervision. If it is not something that directly affects your work with clients, then it should probably be taken elsewhere.

USE OF RECORDINGS

The use of audio or video recordings of client sessions has always been a distinctive feature of CBT supervision. Instead of the supervisor having to rely on the supervisee's account of therapy, the supervisee records sessions and plays back (parts of) the recordings during supervision so that the supervisor can observe what happens more directly. Although almost everyone initially feels anxious about presenting their therapy openly to others in this way, it gets easier and is extremely useful once initial inhibitions have been overcome. We therefore strongly advise using recordings. Advantages include:

- *Self-reflection*: Although not always comfortable, it is good practice to listen to your therapy sessions and critically appraise your performance. In addition, you can better prepare your supervision question and identify the most relevant parts of the recording to share with your supervisor.
- *Avoiding omissions and distortions* (positive or negative) in the therapist's view and account of clients. It could be that what is important in the sessions is something you have not noticed or are reluctant to report – and recordings give you and the supervisor a chance to spot that.
- It therefore allows a *depth and precision of supervision* that is almost impossible if supervision is based only on the therapist's account. Instead of an inevitably partial account from the therapist, the supervisor can hear or see more of the full complexity of the interaction. Think how long it would take you to give a detailed verbal *description* of a therapeutic interaction, compared to what can be gleaned from listening to a couple of minutes of recording! It is difficult for most people to convey a full sense of what a client is like through verbal description. Via recordings, the supervisor can get a much better impression of your client, as well as what is happening in the therapy, and may therefore be better able to offer useful suggestions for how to manage the client's behaviour.
- If you are intending to work towards accreditation as a therapist by the British Association for Behavioural & Cognitive Psychotherapies (BABCP), then bear in mind that a certain amount of what they call 'live supervision' (i.e. your supervisor hearing or seeing actual client sessions, directly or through recordings) is now a requirement. See www.babcp.com for more information about this.

If you are using recordings, then you need to consider the practicalities of how to do so effectively and ethically:

- Clients must give full informed consent before sessions are recorded. You therefore need to establish processes to obtain and record consent. Your hospital or other organisation may have a policy that you need to follow. If not, you should think about developing a policy of your own that includes informing clients what will be done with the recordings, who will hear them and what arrangements will be made for storing them, and for destroying or securely wiping them after supervision. Many professional agencies nowadays demand that digital recordings are kept in an *encrypted* format, so that they cannot be listened to by anyone else if they are lost or stolen.

- If you have decided to use recordings, then it is usually much easier if you get into the habit of recording *all* your sessions rather than thinking about it only when something has gone wrong or a specific need has arisen. It is usually much easier to get clients' consent to a routine procedure at the start of therapy rather than negotiating recording with the client when some particular difficulty has come up.

CHOOSING A SUPERVISOR

In some situations, particularly when training, you may have no choice about who your supervisor is because he or she is allocated to you, but if you have a choice then you may want to consider the following:

- Is the supervisor someone you think you can trust and be comfortable with? You need to be able to form a good working relationship that is as important – and sometimes as demanding – as a therapeutic relationship.
- Does the supervisor have the skills that you need to learn from? For example, you might want someone who is expert in treating certain problems, or someone who can work more with the therapeutic process. It may be difficult to judge initially how well someone will meet your needs, hence the importance of agreeing an initial trial period (see below).
- Is the supervisor motivated to supervise you and willing to commit to the agreed period of supervision?
- Is the supervisor receiving supervision? It is increasingly common for supervisors to seek supervision of their practice.
- BABCP now offers a pathway for accredited therapists to be accredited as supervisors as well. The number of people with this additional qualification is relatively small at the time of writing, so having an accredited supervisor is not yet a requirement, but you may want at least to enquire whether a potential supervisor is accredited as such. Roth and Pilling, whose competence framework for CBT we mentioned in Chapter 1, have developed a similar set of competences for supervision, which you or your supervisor may find of interest (Roth & Pilling, 2009).

NEGOTIATING SUPERVISION ARRANGEMENTS

Whether you are choosing a supervisor or have one allocated to you, it is always important to have a preliminary meeting in order to clarify hopes and expectations. You may want to consider:

- Practical arrangements: when supervision will take place, where, how long will sessions be, how often and so on?
- Confidentiality issues.

- Is the supervision to be 'general' or are there specific objectives (e.g. to get better at formulating, or dealing with clients with OCD, or managing clients who are self-harming)? If you have specific objectives, does the supervisor feel she has the necessary skills to help?
- Do you or the supervisor have priorities regarding the possible aims of supervision outlined above? For example, are you on a training course where summative evaluation is an important part of supervision?
- Although it is often impossible to predict in advance what will happen during a course of supervision, it is worth considering your views and the supervisor's about the boundaries between supervision and personal therapy.
- It is usually wise to have a trial period and then review so that if it is not working well the arrangements can be changed.

A reviewable contract that defines the parameters of your supervision agreement is an essential foundation. Many institutions have their own frameworks for this or you may have to devise a 'bespoke' contract with your supervisors. A useful pro-forma for devising a contract can be found in the Appendix to this chapter: this is the template for a supervision agreement, provided by the BABCP (2005).

For any kind of group supervision, similar questions will arise, and there will also be others unique to the group setting. For example, how will the available time be divided between the group members? Options include equal time for all group members in every session; or one person presenting at each session (with possibly long intervals between supervision sessions for any one individual); or a combination of these, in which one person takes a larger chunk of time in a session but others also take smaller amounts of time. There may be more need for explicit feedback from the supervisee(s) to the group and/or the leader about their experience of supervision. If, as sometimes happens, most or all of the group members disagree with a supervisee's approach, the supervisee can be left feeling very exposed and isolated. Careful attention to defining a group contract and to group process may be needed to avoid excessively painful and off-putting experiences for supervisees.

PREPARING FOR A SUPERVISION SESSION

You will get the most out of supervision if you prepare carefully for it with:

- a clear supervision question;
- a parsimonious formulation or overview.

This does not need to take hours, but it needs more than taking two minutes to think before supervision starts, grabbing the client's notes and running off to meet the supervisor! We would always recommend that you identify a clear and specific *supervision question* for each client you will discuss. So rather than a vague 'What do I do now?' or 'Where do I go from here?', aim to ask questions that address the very particular issue or point that you need to address. The potential range of questions is limitless, but might include:

- 'How can I develop a maintenance formulation for this client with bulimia nervosa?'
- 'What might I do to manage this client's tendency to get dependent on me, given that she has no social support?'
- 'What BEs could I usefully do with this client who is very phobic?'
- 'I've kept a record of my own thoughts – can we formulate what makes me get angry with this client?'
- 'Where can I learn more about treating OCD in adults with learning difficulties?'

You will get the most out of limited supervision time if you supplement your specific question with the minimum of information that your supervisor needs in order to set your question in context. Often, this simply amounts to a parsimonious formulation or, if you have not yet derived one, a very brief overview of the situation. Much time can be lost by recounting details that are not necessary – if more information is needed, the supervisor can ask for it.

In preparing for your own supervision, Padesky's (1996b) exploratory questions for supervisors can be helpful to you, too. Working through this 'roadmap', as Padesky calls it, will often illuminate the best question for you to take to supervision and sometimes this systematic reappraisal will guide you such that you can resolve the problem yourself (and therefore use precious supervision time only for issues that you really can't manage alone!).

Padesky's questions include the following sequence of factors that might contribute to difficulties in therapy:

1. Is there a CBT formulation and consequent treatment plan for this client? If not, developing one may be a supervision question.
2. Is the formulation and consequent treatment plan being followed? If not, the supervision question might be thinking about what is stopping you from following the formulation and treatment plan – either something in your own beliefs or some characteristic or behaviour of the client.
3. Do you have the knowledge and skills to implement the required treatment? If not, you might want to use supervision to gain knowledge, practise skills or get advice on where you can go to achieve those goals.
4. Is the client's response to therapy as expected? If not, you might want to use supervision to consider what client beliefs, life circumstances, developmental history and so on might be blocking progress.
5. If all the above have satisfactory answers, what else might be interfering? Supervision might need to consider therapist factors, problems in the therapeutic relationship, whether the formulation needs modifying, whether a different treatment approach is needed and so on. See Westbrook, Mueller, Kennerley and McManus (2010) for further thoughts about common difficulties in therapy.

Michael found it useful to go through this checklist in relation to a client with whom he was struggling. By doing so he realised that the problem seemed to be around Step 4: he had what looked like a reasonable formulation and treatment plan, and he was following them, but it just did not seem to be working. The client's dominant emotions were depression and anger, and she seemed preoccupied with justifying her anger, rather than working towards any of her other overt treatment goals. Having identified this point, Michael recognised that something was missing in the formulation, because this preoccupation with 'justified anger' was not currently adequately explained. This prompted him to begin exploring further with his client, without his having to take this therapy issue to supervision. Michael soon learned that she had beliefs that meant that the only way she could assert her needs was to get angry; and that recognising that her anger might sometimes be excessive therefore seemed to her like subjugating herself to the other person. With this reformulation, they could explore other ways in which the client might assert herself. However, Michael was unconfident in his knowledge and skill in assertiveness training and so he took this to supervision, his question being: 'What assertiveness skills will be relevant to my client given her tendency towards anger and her fear of subjugation?'

Preparation is also important in using recordings for supervision. It is almost impossible for supervisors to listen to complete sessions for all your clients, as that would take many hours. It is therefore best to make this a two-stage process. First, listen to your recordings yourself. This alone will provide you with useful insights about how you might improve. As you listen, make a note of any points where problems seem to emerge: those are the issues you might want to take to supervision. Select segments of a few minutes that illustrate the points you want to discuss, then, before the supervision session, have your recording ready to run from those points. With this kind of preparation, time can be used effectively and economically.

Remember also that supervisors welcome hearing both about successes and about sessions that have not gone so well. It helps them get a more rounded picture of your practice, your strengths and your needs, than they would if you only brought your 'success' cases or your most difficult ones.

DURING A SUPERVISION SESSION

The form of a supervision session can usefully follow the model of a CBT session, as outlined in Chapter 11. Thus, supervision might go through the same sequence:

- *Agenda-setting*: What are today's main topics and how will we divide the available time between them? Both parties should be able to raise topics for the agenda, and the supervisee should take increasing responsibility for the agenda as she becomes more experienced. Reviewing homework should always be on the agenda and there should be the opportunity to review the clinical consequences of the previous session's supervision if this is not covered in reviewing homework.
- *Bridging items*: Is there anything to be carried over from the previous session? Loose ends? Follow-up information? Belated feedback? And so on.

- *Main topics*: The bulk of the session will be taken up with going through the agreed main agenda items. Many of these items will be in the form of specific supervision questions.
- *Homework*: Supervisees will often leave supervision with some agreed list of tasks to be carried out, ranging from reading a particular article to trying out a particular strategy with a client.
- *Review*: What feedback do you have about the session, what has been learned, what was particularly useful, what was difficult and so on. You should ask yourself whether your supervision question has been answered; whether the supervisor made it easy for you to use supervision; whether the balance of informality and rigidity, being didactic and being non-directive, or support and constructive criticism, was right. Try to give positive feedback and constructive criticism.

See Video 19.1: Setting an agenda in supervision.

Other aspects of your contribution to successful supervision include: keeping on track; being as open as possible, rather than feeling you have to show only competence; and not being defensive about admitting difficulties. You will not learn much from supervision if you say everything is OK and your supervisor says that sounds fine! Everyone does imperfect therapy, and your best chance of getting more skilled is through openness about what goes wrong.

Finally, remember that supervision can involve a range of techniques beyond straightforward verbal discussion of cases. It is useful to use role play, in either of two ways: either you play the client and the supervisor models how you might respond to that client; or the supervisor plays the client whilst you rehearse a particular strategy as therapist (recordings come in useful here – it is much easier for supervisors to play your clients if they have heard or seen them). There may also be times when straightforward didactic teaching or recommended reading is a useful part of supervision.

PROBLEMS WITH SUPERVISION

NOT BEING ABLE TO FIND A SUPERVISOR

Although we must stress the importance of securing regular, competent supervision, you might sometimes find yourself between supervisors or unable to contact your supervisor. We would then suggest that you first consider self-supervision. Set aside time to listen to your therapy recordings and to review your supervision question (perhaps using the Padesky guidelines above) and critically reflect on your practice and resources – in short, discover whether you can resolve the difficulty yourself. If you cannot, you could consider trying to obtain a one-off consultation from a colleague or external 'expert'. Do not simply resign yourself to not having supervision.

PROBLEMS WITH THE SUPERVISOR

A well thought through and regularly reviewed contract will go a long way in minimising problems within the supervisory relationship, and a good contract should have clearly defined steps that can be taken in the event of the supervisory relationship breaking down (see Kennerley and Clohessy, 2010 for a brief account of the supervisory relationship and contracting in CBT supervision).

Common problems include a lack of commitment from the supervisor (e.g. regularly being late or interrupting supervision sessions to take phone calls, etc.); or feeling poorly supported by the supervisor. It is possible that such problems arise because a supervisor and supervisee are not well matched and an alternative arrangement is needed. However, it is worth considering if the working relationship can be improved. Is the supervisor aware of your needs? If not, why not? Did you ensure that your goals and needs were clearly articulated in your contract? Are your expectations of your supervisor realistic, or do you need to supplement your supervision with further support or personal therapy? Do you need to review and revise your contract? Investing time in establishing a mutually agreeable contract can often prevent or minimise problems arising in the supervisory relationship.

FEELING UNABLE TO BRING ALONG RECORDINGS OF SESSIONS FOR EVALUATION

Try to discover what is handicapping you. Perhaps you need to think through the reasons for using recordings; or perhaps you need to do a BE to see whether the pros or cons are as you imagine them to be.

Is the problem performance anxiety or fears of being 'found out' as incompetent? That kind of worry is extremely common, even in experienced therapists, and it is important to try to work with it. Use guided discovery to help you unpack the reason(s) for your reluctance, formulate what is happening and consider taking the problem along to supervision.

AGREEING STRATEGIES THAT ARE NOT CARRIED OUT

Again, you need to understand the thoughts and beliefs that account for this. For example, is it over-compliance with your supervisor, agreeing to take actions that you do not really agree with? If so, what makes it difficult for you to tell your supervisor that you disagree?

Or is it that you genuinely think the plans are good, but then in your therapy sessions you get sidetracked? Again, try to understand what leads to that. Therapy recordings may be very helpful in looking at where therapy sessions go off track. And, as always, you can take these questions to supervision.

NEGATIVE BELIEFS ABOUT SUPERVISION

We have occasionally come across therapists who have negative views about supervision. For instance, the primary purpose of supervision may be seen as 'overseeing' or making sure that it is done 'right', and it may therefore be perceived as an aversive experience in which you are likely to be subjected to managerial control or trenchant criticism. On review, it might well become apparent that the primary purpose of supervision is usually to help you get better at what you do and to be able to help your clients more effectively. Supervision

could therefore be seen as an opportunity to learn, not as a threat. As in our clinical work, it is crucial to identify the negative beliefs that interfere with progress. Thus, you need to be aware of your own unhelpful beliefs and use your CBT skills to evaluate them.

SUMMARY

- Although we need more research evidence, there is an almost universal consensus that adequate clinical supervision is an essential part of becoming a competent CBT therapist (or indeed any other kind of therapist).
- Supervision can be done in different formats (pairs, groups, etc.), via different channels (face-to-face, phone, etc.) and with or without a recognised leader. Although what we have called the 'apprenticeship' mode is probably the most common, all have their pros and cons, depending on individual circumstances.
- In CBT, 'live' supervision (i.e. the supervisor having direct access to the session, by sitting in or by listening to recordings) is highly valued and is also now required for BABCP accreditation as a therapist.
- If you have a choice, give some thought to who would be the best supervisor for you, and agree the terms of the supervision contract.

Supervision is most useful if you prepare for it: identify beforehand what your supervision question is (i.e. what you want to get out of the supervision session) and prepare some minimal contextual information. Take a range of cases to your supervisor so that you showcase your strengths and your needs.

LEARNING EXERCISES

These learning exercises are available to download from the companion website.

REVIEW AND REFLECTION:

- **Spend a little time reflecting on your current supervision (and perhaps arrange to reflect together with your supervisor as well). What is working well? What not so well? What are the main learning points you have got out of it? Is there anything you and/or your supervisor need to do differently to get more out of it?**

(Continued)

(Continued)

- **Are you currently using session recordings? If not, think about what combination of factors is stopping you: technological difficulties, problems stemming from a lack of confidence, particular beliefs about what might happen, or whatever else it might be.**
- **Are you sharing both material that indicates your strengths and achievements *and* information that illustrates your needs? If not, why not?**
- **Are you getting enough supervision? If not, why not?**

TAKING IT FORWARD:

- **Could you make better use of supervision time if you do more preparation? Perhaps you could use the Padesky supervision questions described above as a framework, and see whether it is helpful.**
- **If you currently have fears that stop you from playing session recordings to your supervisor, perhaps you could think about doing a BE to see how it goes if you try it out? Is it as bad as you feared? What are the actual advantages and disadvantages?**
- **If you are starting out with CBT and you do not yet have a CBT supervisor, then get one as soon as possible!**

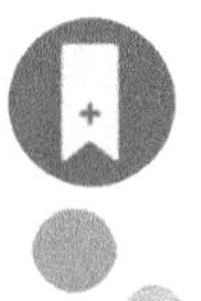

FURTHER READING

We are not aware of any other significant texts on *receiving* supervision, as opposed to *doing* supervision. The following are therefore suggested as useful references on the general topic of CBT supervision.

Bennett-Levy, J. (2006). Therapist skills: their acquisition and refinement. *Behavioural and Cognitive Psychotherapy*, *34*, 57–78.

An interesting and influential attempt to build a model of how therapists become more skilled and how different aspects of skill may need different learning methods.

Kennerley, H., & Clohessy, S. (2010). Becoming a supervisor. In M. Mueller, H. Kennerley, F. McManus, & D. Westbrook (Eds.), *Oxford guide to surviving as a CBT therapist*. Oxford: Oxford University Press.

A guide for new supervisors on the challenges that arise and the skills that are needed for good supervision.

Milne, D. (2009). *Evidence-based clinical supervision: principles and practice*. Chichester: Wiley-Blackwell.

Derek Milne, one of the leading UK researchers in supervision, provides a summation of the available evidence about supervision, and a guide to best practice based on that evidence.

Padesky, C. (1996). Developing cognitive therapist competency: teaching and supervision models. In P. Salkovskis (Ed.), *The frontiers of cognitive therapy*. New York: Guilford Press.

In this chapter Padesky argues that CBT supervision can usefully parallel the approach of CBT therapy; and she also outlines the useful 'supervision checklist' referred to earlier in this chapter.

VIDEO LINK

- **19.1 Setting an agenda in supervision**

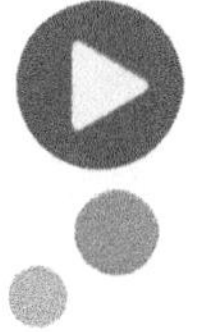

APPENDIX TO CHAPTER 19: EXAMPLE SUPERVISION AGREEMENT FROM THE BRITISH ASSOCIATION FOR BEHAVIOURAL & COGNITIVE PSYCHOTHERAPIES (BABCP, 2005)

Supervision Agreement between .... & ....

CONFIDENTIALITY

- All professional and clinical issues discussed are confidential and are not to be discussed outside the supervision session. The exceptions to this are where professional malpractice may be evident, or if requested to release information by a Court of Law, Coroner's Office or professional body.
- All cases or professionals discussed during supervision must be made anonymous.
- Where recording of sessions takes place this must be agreed with and have the informed consent of the service user, carer or professional. Arrangements must also be made to destroy/wipe any recordings. The supervisee is responsible for ensuring this process is followed.

COMMENTS

____

____

____

____

CONTENT OF SUPERVISION

- Content of supervision will focus on the acquisition of knowledge, conceptualisation and clinical skills within a cognitive behavioural model(s).
- Associated issues will also be discussed when it is relevant to do so, e.g. medication, hospitalisation, case management.
- Identification (and collaborative change of these if appropriate) of supervisee thoughts, attitudes, beliefs and values and the impact of these on therapeutic and professional behaviour.
- Discussion and working through relationship and process aspects of supervision.
- There will be an equal split between the time spend on each of the above in the time available.

COMMENTS

____

____

____

____

PRACTICALITIES

- One session each ………………… for …………….. hours/minutes
- The venue the session (s) will take place at is …………………………..
- The person responsible for booking the accommodation is ……………………..
- Fees for supervision are …………………………………..
- Cancellation arrangements …………………………………

COMMENTS

____

____

____

____

SUPERVISION METHODS AND CONTENT

- Discussion of therapeutic relationship and engagement issues.
- Case conceptualisation/formulation.
- Rehearsal of therapeutic techniques, e.g. simulation, role-play.
- Discussion about therapeutic strategies.
- Case presentations.
- Homework.
- Review of audio and videotapes (at least one per month).
- Direct observation of practice – at least once in a month per supervisee.
- Identification of supervisee thoughts, attitudes, beliefs with exploration of the impact of these on therapeutic and professional behaviour.
- Review of risk and therapist/service user safety.
- Review of clinical guidelines/manuals.
- Review of psycho-educational material.
- Experiential exercises.
- Other strategies as agreed.

COMMENTS

____

____

____

____

AIMS OF SUPERVISION

The primary focus of supervision is the welfare of the client through the supervisee's learning process, in terms of knowledge attainment, attitude refinement, and skills development.

GOALS FOR SUPERVISION

1. ____________________________________
2. ____________________________________
3. ____________________________________
4. ____________________________________

COMMENTS

___

___

___

___

ANTI DISCRIMINATORY PRACTICE

Practice will follow the policy of .... [employer/ professional body]

COMMENTS

___

___

___

___

STEPS IN THE EVENT OF A BREAKDOWN IN THE ARRANGEMENTS FOR CLINICAL CBT SUPERVISION

In the event of inappropriate behaviour by the supervisor/supervisee this should be discussed together initially.

If this is unsuccessful or the behaviour is of a serious and immediate nature then .... should be informed IMMEDIATELY.

In the unlikely event that the relationship between the supervisee and supervisor deteriorates, each person is responsible for attempting to work together to resolve the problem.

COMMENTS

___

___

___

___

CHANGES TO THIS AGREEMENT AND TIMESCALE

Changes to this agreement can be negotiated at any time.

This agreement covers the period ....
Signed ______________________ Supervisor __________________ Date ____________
Signed ______________________ Supervisee __________________ Date ____________

(With thanks to Michael Townend. Please feel free to circulate and edit the document as you wish.)

GLOSSARY

ACCS	Assessment of Core CBT Skills
ACT	acceptance and commitment therapy
AN	anorexia nervosa
ASD	acute stress disorder
ATs	automatic thoughts
AVE	abstinence violation effect
BABCP	British Association for Behavioural & Cognitive Psychotherapies
BAI	Beck Anxiety Inventory
BDD	body dysmorphic disorder
BDI	Beck Depression Inventory
BED	binge-eating disorder
BEs	behavioural experiments
BN	bulimia nervosa
BPD	borderline personality disorder
BT	behaviour therapy
CAS	cognitive attentional syndrome
CBT	cognitive behaviour therapy
CBTp	CBT for psychosis
CCBT	computerised cognitive behavioural therapy
CFS	chronic fatigue syndrome
CMT	compassionate mind therapy
CORE	clinical outcomes in routine evaluation
CT	cognitive therapy
CTS	Cognitive Therapy Scale
CTS-R	Cognitive Therapy Scale-revised
DAs	dysfunctional assumptions
DBT	dialectical behaviour therapy
DSM-IV	*Diagnostic and Statistical Manual*, 4th edition
DSM-V	*Diagnostic and Statistical Manual*, 5th edition

EDs	eating disorders
ERP	exposure and response prevention
GAD	generalised anxiety disorder
HADS	Hospital Anxiety and Depression Scale
HI	high intensity
IAPT	Improving Access to Psychological Therapies
ICS	interacting cognitive subsystem
IPT	intensive psychological intervention
LI	low intensity
LTM	long-term memory
MAPLE	multiple access points and levels of entry
MBCT	mindfulness-based cognitive therapy
MCT	meta-cognitive therapy
NATs	negative automatic thoughts
n-CBT	neuroscience-informed CBT
NHS	National Health Service
NICE	National Institute for Health and Care Excellence
NIMH	National Institute of Mental Health
OCD	obsessive-compulsive disorder
PFC	pre-frontal cortex
PTSD	post-traumatic stress disorder
PWPs	psychological wellbeing practitioners
RCT	randomised controlled trial
RFCT	rumination-focused therapies
SB	safety-seeking behaviour
SFCT	schema-focused cognitive therapy
STM	short-term memory
TAU	treatment as usual
UAs	underlying assumptions
WAS	weekly activity schedule
WIT	worry intervention trial

REFERENCES

Abramson, L.Y., Alloy, L.B., Hogan, M.E., Whitehouse, W.G., Donovan, P., Rose, D.T., Panzarella, C., & Raniere, D. (2002). Cognitive vulnerability to depression: theory and evidence. In R.L. Leahy & E.T. Dowd (Eds.), *Clinical advances in cognitive psychotherapy: theory and application*. New York: Springer.

Ackerman, S.J., & Hilsenroth, M. (2003). A review of therapist characteristics and techniques positively impacting the therapeutic alliance. *Clinical Psychology Review, 23*, 1–37.

Andrews, B. (1997). Bodily shame in relation to abuse in childhood and bulimia. *British Journal of Clinical Psychology, 36*, 41–50.

Antonuccio, D.O., Thomas, M., & Danton, W.G. (1997). A cost-effective analysis of cognitive behaviour therapy and fluoxetine (Prozac) in the treatment of depression. *Behaviour Therapy, 28*, 187–210.

APA (American Psychiatric Association) (2000). *Diagnostic and statistical manual of mental disorders*, (4th ed., text revision) (DSM-IV). Washington, DC: American Psychiatric Association.

APA (American Psychiatric Association) (2013). *Diagnostic and statistical manual of mental disorders*, (5th ed.) (DSM-V). Washington, DC: American Psychiatric Publishing.

Ardenne, P., & Farmer, E. (2009). Using interpreters in trauma therapy. In N. Grey (Ed.), *A casebook of cognitive therapy for traumatic stress reactions*. Hove: Routledge.

Arntz, A., Rauner, M., & van den Hout, M.A. (1995). 'If I feel anxious there must be a danger': ex-consequentia reasoning in inferring danger in anxiety disorders. *Behaviour Research & Therapy, 33*, 917–925.

Arntz, A., & van Genderen, H. (2009). *Schema therapy for borderline personality disorder*. Chichester: Wiley-Blackwell.

Arntz, A., & Weertman, A. (1999). Treatment of childhood memories: theory and practice. *Behaviour Research & Therapy, 37*, 715–740.

BABCP (British Association for Behavioural & Cognitive Psychotherapies) (2005). BABCP supervision template. Retrieved 28 March 2006 from www.babcp.org.uk/downloads/supervision_agreement_ 2004.pdf

Bach, P., & Hayes, S.C. (2002). The use of acceptance and commitment therapy to prevent the re-hospitalization of psychotic patients: a randomised controlled trial. *Journal of Consulting & Clinical Psychology, 70*, 1129–1139.

Baddeley, A. (2004). *Your memory: a user's guide* (2nd ed.). London: Carlton.

Baldwin, S., Berkerjon, A., Atkins, D., Olsen, J., & Nielson, S. (2009). Rates of change in naturalistic therapy: contrasting dose-effect and good-enough level models of change. *Journal of Consulting and Clinical Psychology, 77*, 203–211.

Bankoff, S.M., Karpel, M.G., Hope, E.F., & Pantalone, D.W. (2012). A systematic review of dialectical behaviour therapy for the treatment of eating disorders. *Eating Disorders: the Journal of Treatment & Prevention, 20*, 196–215.

Barkham, M., Mellor-Clark, J., Connell, J., & Cahill, J. (2006). A core approach to practice based evidence: a brief history of the origins and applications of the CORE-OM and CORE System. *Counselling and Psychotherapy Research, 6*, 3–15.

Barlow, D.H., Andrasik, F., & Hersen, M. (2006). *Single case experimental designs* (3rd ed.). Boston, MA: Allyn & Bacon.

Barlow, D.H., Hayes, C.H., & Nelson, R.O. (1984). *The scientist practitioner: research and accountability in clinical and educational settings*. Oxford: Pergamon.

Barnhofer, T., Crane, C., Brennan, K., Duggan, S.D., Crane, S.R., Eames, C., Radford, S., Silverton, S., Fennell, M., & Williams, M. (2015). Mindfulness-based cognitive therapy (MBCT) reduces the association between depressive symptoms and suicidal cognitions in patients with a history of suicidal depression. *Journal of Consulting and Clinical Psychology*, *83*, 1013–1020.

Barnhofer, T., Crane, C., Hargus, E., Amarasinghe, M., Winder, R., & Williams, J.M.G. (2009). Mindfulness-based cognitive therapy as a treatment for chronic depression: A preliminary study. *BRAT*, *47*, 366–373.

Barnhofer, T., Duggan, D., Crane, C., Hepburn, S., Fennell, M., & Williams, J. (2007). Effects of meditation on frontal alpha-asymmetry in previously suicidal individuals. *Neuroreport*, *18*(7), 709–712.

Barrett, A.M., Crucian, G.P., Schwartz, R.L., & Heilman, K.M. (2000). Testing memory for self-generated items in dementia: method makes a difference. *Neurology*, *54*, 1258–1264.

Bartlett, F. (1932). *Remembering*. Cambridge: Cambridge University Press.

Basco, M., & Rush, A. (1996). *Cognitive behavioural therapy for bipolar disorder*. New York: Guilford Press.

Bates, A. (2005). The expression of compassion in group therapy. In P. Gilbert (Ed.), *Compassion: conceptualisations, research and use in psychotherapy*. Hove: Brunner-Routledge.

Baucom, D.H., Belus, J.M., Adelman, C.B., Fischer, M.S., & Paprocki, C. (2014). Couple-based interventions for psychopathology: a renewed direction for the field. *Family Process*, *53*, 445–461.

Baucom, D.H., & Boeding, S. (2013). The role of theory and research in the practice of cognitive-behavioral couple therapy: if you build it, they will come. *Behaviour Therapy*, *44*, 592–602.

Beck, A.T. (1963). Thinking and depression, 1: Idiosyncratic content and cognitive distortions. *Archives of General Psychiatry*, *9*, 324–333.

Beck, A.T. (1964). Thinking and depression, 2: Theory and therapy. *Archives of General Psychiatry*, *10*, 561–571.

Beck, A.T. (1988). *Love is never enough*. New York: Harper & Row.

Beck, A.T. (1999). *Prisoners of hate*. New York: HarperCollins.

Beck, A.T. (2008). The evolution of the cognitive model of depression and its neurobiological correlates. *American Journal of Psychiatry*, psychiatryonline.org, 1–9.

Beck, A.T., Brown, G., & Steer, R.A. (1996). *Beck Depression Inventory II manual*. San Antonio, TX: The Psychological Corporation.

Beck, A.T., Davis, D., & Freeman, A. (2015). *Cognitive therapy of personality disorders* (3rd ed.). New York: Guilford Press.

Beck, A.T., Emery, G., & Greenberg, R.L. (1985). *Anxiety disorders and phobias: a cognitive perspective*. New York: Basic Books.

Beck, A.T., Epstein, N., Brown, G., & Steer, R.A. (1988). An inventory for measuring clinical anxiety: psychometric properties. *Journal of Consulting & Clinical Psychology*, *56*, 893–897.

Beck, A.T., Freeman, A., Davis, D., & Associates (2004). *Cognitive therapy of personality disorders* (2nd ed.). New York: Guilford Press.

Beck, A.T., Rush, A.J., Shaw, B.F., & Emery, G. (1979). *Cognitive therapy of depression*. New York: Guilford Press.

Beck, A.T., Ward, C.H., Mendelson, M., Mock, J., & Erbaugh, J. (1961). An inventory for measuring depression. *Archives of General Psychiatry*, *4*, 561–571.

Beck, A.T., Wright, F.D., Newman, C.F., & Liese, B.S. (1993). *Cognitive therapy of substance abuse.* New York: Guilford Press.

Beck, R., & Fernandez, E. (1998). Cognitive-behavioral therapy in the treatment of anger: a meta-analysis. *Cognitive Therapy & Research, 22,* 63–74.

Bennett-Levy, J. (2003). Mechanisms of change in cognitive therapy: the case of automatic thought records and behavioural experiments. *Behavioural and Cognitive Psychotherapy, 31,* 261–277.

Bennett-Levy, J. (2006). Therapist skills: their acquisition and refinement. *Behavioural and Cognitive Psychotherapy, 34,* 57–78.

Bennett-Levy, J., Butler, G., Fennell, M., Hackmann, A., Mueller, M., & Westbrook, D. (Eds.). (2004). *The Oxford guide to behavioural experiments in cognitive therapy.* Oxford: Oxford University Press.

Bennett-Levy, J., Richards, D., Farrand, P., Christensen, H., Griffiths, K., Kavanagh, D., Klein, B., Lau, M., Proudfoot, J., Ritterband, L., White, J., & Williams, C. (Eds.). (2010). *The Oxford guide to low intensity CBT interventions.* Oxford: Oxford University Press.

Benson, H. (1975). *The relaxation response.* New York: Morrow.

Berlin, H.A., Rolls, E.T., & Iversen, S.D. (2005). Borderline personality disorder, impulsivity, and the orbitofrontal cortex. *American Journal of Psychiatry, 162,* 2360–2373.

Bhagwagar, Z., & Cowan, P.J. (2008). It's not over when it's over; persistent neurobiological abnormalities in recovered depressed patients. *Psychological Medicine, 38,* 307–313.

Bieling, P.J., & Kuyken, W. (2003). Is cognitive case formulation science or science fiction? *Clinical Psychology: Science & Practice, 10,* 52–69.

Bieling, P., McCabe, R., & Antony, M. (2006). *Cognitive behavioural therapy in groups.* New York: Guilford Press.

Birchwood, M., Michail, M., Meaden, A., Tarrier, N., Lewis, S., Wykes, T., Davies, L., Dunn, G., & Peters, E. (2014). Cognitive behaviour therapy to prevent harmful compliance with command hallucinations (COMMAND): a randomised controlled trial. *The Lancet Psychiatry, 1,* 23–33.

Blackburn, I.M., James, I.A., Milne, D.L., Baker, C., Standart, S., Garland, A., & Reichelt, K. (2001). The revised cognitive therapy scale (CTS-R): psychometric properties. *Behavioural & Cognitive Psychotherapy, 29,* 431–446.

Bohus, K., Haaf, B., Simms, T., Limburger, M.F., Schmahl, C., Unckel, C., Lieb, K., & Linehan, M.M. (2004). Effectiveness of inpatient dialectical behavioural therapy for borderline personality disorder: a controlled trial. *Behaviour Research & Therapy, 42,* 487–499.

Bootzin, R.R. (1972). Stimulus control treatment for insomnia. *Proceedings of the American Psychological Association, 7,* 395–396.

Bordin, E.S. (1979). The generalisation of the psychoanalytic concept of the working alliance. *Psychotherapy, 16,* 252–260.

Borkovec, T.D. (1994). The nature, functions and origins of worry. In G.C.L. Davey & F. Tallis (Eds.), *Worrying: perspectives on theory, assessment and treatment.* Chichester: Wiley.

Borkovec, T.D., & Newman, M.G. (1999). Worry and generalized anxiety disorder. In P. Salkovskis (Ed.), *Comprehensive clinical psychology, Vol. 6.* Oxford: Elsevier.

Borkovec, T.D., Newman, M.G., Pincus, A.L., & Lytle, R. (2002). A component analysis of cognitive-behavioral therapy for generalized anxiety disorder and the role of interpersonal problems. *Journal of Consulting and Clinical Psychology, 70,* 288–298.

Borkovec, T.D., & Sides, J.K. (1979). Critical procedural variables related to the physiological effects of progressive relaxation: a review. *Behaviour Research & Therapy, 17*, 119–125.

Bower, P., Richards, D.A., & Lovell, K. (2001). The clinical and cost effectiveness of self-help treatments for anxiety and depressive disorders in primary care: a systematic review. *British Journal of General Practice, 51*, 838–845.

Braun, J.D., Strunk, D.R., Sasso, K.E. & Cooper, A.A. (2015). Therapist use of Socratic questioning predicts session-to-session symptom change in cognitive therapy for depression. *Behaviour Research and Therapy, 70*, 32–37.

Brewin, C.R. (2001). A cognitive neuroscience account of post-traumatic stress disorder and its treatment. *Behaviour Research and Therapy*, 39, 373–393.

British Psychological Society (1995). *Recovered memories: the report of the working party of the BPS.* Leicester: BPS Publications.

Brown, G.K., Newman, C.F., Charlesworth, S.E., Crits-Christoph, P., & Beck, A.T. (2004). An open clinical trial of cognitive therapy for borderline personality disorder. *Journal of Personality Disorders, 18*, 257–271.

Brown, G.W., & Harris, T.O. (1978). *The social origins of depression: a study of psychiatric disorder in women*. London: Tavistock.

Brown, G.W., Harris, T.O., & Bifulco, A. (1986). Long-term effects of early loss of parent. In M. Rutter, L. Izard, & P. Read (Eds.), *Depression and childhood: developmental perspectives.* New York: Guilford Press.

Bruch, M., & Bond, F.W. (1998). *Beyond diagnosis: case formulation approaches in CBT*. Chichester: Wiley.

Burmeister, K., Höschel, K., von Auer, A.K., Reiske, S., Schweiger, U., Sipos, V., Philipsen, A., Priebe, K., & Bohus, M. (2014). Dialectical behavior therapy (DBT) – developments and empirical evidence. *Psychiatrische Praxis, 41*, 242–249.

Burns, D. (1980). *Feeling good: the new mood therapy.* New York: Morrow.

Burns, D. (1999). *The feeling good handbook*. New York: Plume.

Butler, G. (1998). Clinical formulation. In A.S. Bellack & M. Hersen (Eds.), *Comprehensive clinical psychology*. New York: Pergamon.

Butler, G. (2008). *Overcoming social anxiety and shyness: a self-help guide using cognitive and behavioural techniques*. London: Constable and Robinson.

Butler, G., Fennell, M., & Hackmann, A. (2008). *Cognitive behaviour therapy for anxiety disorders: mastering clinical challenges*. New York: Guilford Press.

Butler, G., & Hackmann, A. (2004). Social anxiety. In J. Bennett-Levy, G. Butler, M. Fennell, A. Hackmann, M. Mueller, & D. Westbrook (Eds.), *Oxford guide to behavioural experiments in cognitive therapy.* Oxford: Oxford University Press.

Butler, G., & Hope, T. (2007). *Manage your mind.* Oxford: Oxford University Press.

Butler, G., & Rouf, K. (2004). Generalized anxiety disorder. In J. Bennett-Levy, G. Butler, M. Fennell, A. Hackmann, M. Mueller, & D. Westbrook (Eds.), *Oxford guide to behavioural experiments in cognitive therapy.* Oxford: Oxford University Press.

Butler, G., & Surawy, C. (2004). Avoidance of affect. In J. Bennett-Levy, G. Butler, M. Fennell, A. Hackmann, M. Mueller, & D. Westbrook (Eds.), *Oxford guide to behavioural experiments in cognitive therapy.* Oxford: Oxford University Press.

Carey, T.A., & Mullan, R.J. (2004). What is Socratic questioning? *Psychotherapy: Theory, Research, Practice, Training, 41*, 217–226.

Centers for Disease Control and Prevention (CDC) (no date). *Mental health: data and statistics*. Retrieved 31 March 2016 from www.cdc.gov/mentalhealth/data-stats.htm

Centre for Economic Performance, Mental Health Policy Group (2006). *The depression report: a new deal for depression and anxiety disorders*. London: London School of Economics.

Chaddock, A. (2013). The therapeutic relationship. Big deal or no deal? In M. Papworth, T. Marrinan, & B. Martin, with D. Keegan & A. Chaddock (Eds.). *Low intensity cognitive behavior therapy: a practitioner's guide*. London: Sage.

Chadwick, P., Birchwood, M., & Trower, P. (1996). *Cognitive therapy for delusions, voices and paranoia*. Chichester: Wiley.

Chaouloff, F. (1989). Physical exercise and brain monoamines: a review. *Acta Physiologica Scandinavica, 137*, 1–13.

Chard, K.M., Weaver, T.L., & Resick, P.A. (1997). Adapting cognitive processing therapy for child sexual abuse survivors. *Cognitive Behaviour and Practice, 4*, 31–52.

Chartier, I.S., & Provencher, M.D. (2013). Behavioural activation for depression: efficacy, effectiveness and dissemination. *Journal of Affective Disorders, 145*, 292–299.

Clark, D.A., & Beck, A.T. (2009). *Cognitive therapy of anxiety disorders*. New York: Guilford Press.

Clark, D.A., & Beck, A.T. (2010). Cognitive theory and therapy of anxiety and depression: convergence with neurobiological findings. *Trends in Cognitive Science, 14*, 418–424.

Clark, D.A., Beck, A.T., & Alford, B. (1999). *Scientific foundations of cognitive theory and therapy of depression*. New York: Wiley.

Clark, D.M. (1986). A cognitive approach to panic. *Behaviour Research & Therapy, 24*, 461–470.

Clark, D.M. (1989). Anxiety states: panic and generalised anxiety. In K. Hawton, P. Salkovskis, J. Kirk, & D. Clark (Eds.), *Cognitive-behaviour therapy for psychiatric problems: a practitioner's guide*. Oxford: Oxford University Press.

Clark, D.M. (1999). Anxiety disorders: why they persist and how to treat them. *Behaviour Research & Therapy, 37*, S5–S27.

Clark, D.M. (2002). A cognitive perspective on social phobia. In W.R. Crozier & L.E. Alden (Eds.), *International handbook of social anxiety*. Chichester: Wiley.

Clark, D.M. (2015). *Disseminating CBT: science, politics and economics*. Keynote presented at the OCTC Congress, Oxford.

Clark, D.M., & Beck, A.T. (1988). Cognitive approaches. In C. Last & M. Hersen (Eds.), *Handbook of anxiety disorders*. New York: Pergamon.

Clark, D.M., Layard, R., Smithies, R., Richards, D., Suckling, R., & Wright, B. (2009). Improving access to psychological therapy: initial evaluation of two UK demonstration sites. *Behaviour Research & Therapy, 47*, 910–920.

Clark, D.M., & Wells, A. (1995). A cognitive model of social phobia. In R. Heimberg, M. Liebowitz, D.A. Hope, & F.R. Schneier (Eds.), *Social phobia: diagnosis, assessment and treatment*. New York: Guilford Press.

Clark, G.I., & Egan, S.J. (2015). The Socratic method in cognitive behavioural therapy: a narrative review. *Cognitive Therapy and Research, 39*, 863–879.

Cloitre, M., Koenen, K.C., Cohen, L.R., & Han, H. (2002). Skills training in affective and interpersonal regulation followed by exposure: a phase-based treatment for PTSD related to childhood abuse. *Journal of Consulting and Clinical Psychology, 70*, 1067–1074.

Cloitre, M., Stovall-McClough, K.C., Nooner, K., Zorbas, P., Cherry, S., Jackson, C.L., Gan, W., & Petkova, E. (2010). Treatment for PTSD related to childhood abuse: a randomized controlled trial. *American Journal of Psychiatry, 167*, 915–924.

Close, H., & Schuller, S. (2004). Psychotic symptoms. In J. Bennett-Levy, G. Butler, M. Fennell, A. Hackmann, M. Mueller, & D. Westbrook (Eds.), *Oxford guide to behavioural experiments in cognitive therapy.* Oxford: Oxford University Press.

Colcombe, S.J., Erickson, K., Raz, N., Webb, A.G., Cohen, N.J., McAuley, E., & Kramer, A.F. (2003). Aerobic fitness reduces brain tissue loss in aging humans. *Journal of Gerontology Biological Science Medical Science, 58*(2), M176–M180.

Committee on Training in Clinical Psychology (1947). Recommended graduate training program in clinical psychology. *American Psychologist, 2*, 539–558.

Courtois, C.A. (2004). Complex trauma, complex reactions: assessment and treatment. *Psychotherapy: Theory, Research, Practice, Training, 41*, 412–425.

Craft, L.L., & Landers, D.M. (1998). The effect of exercise on clinical depression and depression resulting from mental illness: a meta-analysis. *Journal of Sport and Exercise Psychology, 20*, 339–357.

Craske, M.G., Treanor, M., Conway, C.C., Zbozinkek, T., & Vervliet, B. (2014). Maximising exposure therapy: an inhibitory learning approach. *Behaviour Research and Therapy, 58*, 10–23.

Cuijpers, P., Donker, T., van Straten, A., Li, J., & Andersson, G. (2010). Is guided self-help as effective as face-to-face psychotherapy for depression and anxiety disorders? A systematic review and meta-analysis of comparative outcome studies. *Psychological Medicine, 40*, 1943–1957.

Cuijpers, P., Sijbrandij, M., Koole, S., Huibers, M., Berking, K., & Andersson, G. (2014). Psychological treatment of generalized anxiety disorder: a meta analysis. *Clinical Psychology Review, 34*, 130–140.

Daley, D.C., & Marlatt, G.A. (2006). *Overcoming your alcohol or drug problem. Effective recovery strategies: therapist guide.* Oxford: Oxford University Press.

Dattilio, F.M., & Padesky, C.A. (1990). *Cognitive therapy with couples.* Sarasota, FL: Professional Resource Exchange.

Davey, G.C.L., & Tallis, F. (Eds.). (1994). *Worrying: perspectives on theory, assessment and treatment.* Chichester: Wiley.

Davidson, K. (2000). *Cognitive therapy for personality disorders: a guide for clinicians* (2nd ed.). Hove: Routledge.

Davidson, K., Norrie, J., Tyrer, P., Gumley, A., Tata, P., Murray, H., & Palmer, S. (2006). The effectiveness of CBT for borderline personality disorder: results from the BOSCOT trial. *Journal of Personality Disorders, 20*, 450–465.

Deckersbach, P., Eisner, L., & Sylvia. L. (2016). Cognitive behavioural therapy for bi-polar disorder. In T.J. Petersen, S.E. Sprich, & S. Wilhelm (Eds.), *The Massachusetts General Hospital handbook of cognitive behavioural therapy*. New York: Springer.

Department of Health (2008). *Improving access to psychological therapies – implementation plan; national guidelines for regional delivery*. London: Department of Health.

Devon Book Prescription Scheme (2004). Book list. Retrieved 18 February 2006 from www.research.plymouth.ac.uk/pei/projects/selfhelpbookspresc/booklist.htm

Dobson, K., Shaw, B., & Vallis, T. (1985). Reliability of a measure of the quality of cognitive therapy. *British Journal of Clinical Psychology, 24*, 295–300.

Donker, T., Petrie, K., Proudfoot, J., Clarke, J., Birch, M.R., & Christensen, H. (2013). Smartphones for smarter delivery of mental health programs: a systematic review. *Journal of Medical Internet Research, 15*, e247.

Dryden, W. (Ed.) (no date). *The CBT Distinctive Features*. Hove: Routledge.

Dugas, M.J., Buhr, K., & Ladouceur, R. (2004). The role of intolerance of uncertainty in etiology and maintenance. In R.G. Heimberg, C.L. Turk, & D.S. Mennin (Eds.), *Generalized anxiety disorder: advances in research and practice*. New York: Guilford Press.

Durham, R.C., & Turvey, A.A. (1987). Cognitive therapy vs behaviour therapy in the treatment of chronic general anxiety. *Behaviour Research & Therapy, 25*, 229–234.

Ehlers, A., & Clark, D.M. (2000). A cognitive model of post-traumatic stress disorder. *Behaviour Research & Therapy, 38*, 319–345.

Ehlers, A., Clark, D.M., Hackmann, A., McManus, F., Fennell, M., Herbert, C., & Mayou, R. (2003). A randomised controlled trial of cognitive therapy, a self-help booklet, and repeated assessments as early interventions for posttraumatic stress disorder. *Archives of General Psychiatry, 60*, 1024–1032.

Eisler, I., le Grange, D., & Asen, E. (2003). Family interventions. In J. Treasure, U. Schmidt, & E. van Furth (Eds.), *Handbook of eating disorders* (2nd ed.). Chichester: Wiley.

El-Leithy, S. (2014). Working with diversity in CBT. In A. Wittington & N. Grey (Eds.). *How to become a more effective CBT therapist: mastering metacompetence in clinical practice*. Chichester: Wiley.

Emmelkamp, P.M.G., & Aardema, A. (1999). Metacognitive, specific obsessive-compulsive beliefs and obsessive compulsive behaviour. *Clinical Psychology and Psychotherapy, 6*, 139–146.

Enright, S.J. (1991). Group treatment for obsessive-compulsive disorder: an evaluation. *Behavioural Psychotherapy, 19*, 183–192.

Erdelyi, M., Buschke, H., & Finkelstein, S. (1977). Hypermnesia for Socratic stimuli: the growth of recall for an internally generated memory list abstracted from a series of riddles. *Memory & Cognition, 5*, 283–286.

Espie, C.A. (1991). *The psychological treatment of insomnia*. Chichester: Wiley.

Espie, C.A. (2010). *Overcoming insomnia and sleep problems: a self-help guide using cognitive behavioural techniques*. London: Constable Robinson.

Espie, C.A. (2011). *An introduction to overcoming insomnia and sleep problems*. London: Constable Robinson.

Evans, C., Connell, J., Barkham, M., Margison, F., McGrath, G., Mellor-Clark, J., & Audin, K. (2002). Towards a standardised brief outcome measure: psychometric properties and utility of the CORE-OM. *British Journal of Psychiatry, 180*, 51–60.

Eysenck, H.J. (1952). The effects of psychotherapy: an evaluation. *Journal of Consulting & Clinical Psychology, 16*, 319–324.

Fairburn, C.G., Cooper, Z., & Shafran, R. (2003). Cognitive behaviour therapy for eating disorders: a 'transdiagnostic' theory and treatment. *Behaviour Research & Therapy, 41*, 509–528.

Fairburn, C.G., Kirk, J., O'Connor, M., & Cooper, P.J. (1986). A comparison of two psychological treatments for bulimia nervosa. *Behaviour Research & Therapy, 24*, 629–643.

Fairburn, C.G., Shafran, R., & Cooper, Z. (1999). A cognitive-behavioural theory of anorexia nervosa. *Behaviour Research & Therapy, 37*, 1–13.

Farrell, J.M., Shaw, I.D., & Webber, M.A. (2009). A schema-focused approach to group psychotherapy for outpatients with borderline personality disorder: a randomized controlled trial. *Journal of Behaviour Therapy and Experimental Psychiatry, 40*, 317–328.

Fennell, M. (1989). Depression. In K. Hawton, P. Salkovskis, J. Kirk, & D. Clark (Eds.), *Cognitive-behaviour therapy for psychiatric problems: a practitioner's guide*. Oxford: Oxford University Press.

Fennell, M.J. (1997). Low self-esteem: a cognitive perspective. *Behavioural and Cognitive Psychotherapy, 25*, 1–26.

Fennell, M. (1999). *Overcoming low self esteem: a self-help guide using cognitive-behavioural techniques*. London: Constable Robinson.

Fennell, M. (2016). *Overcoming low self esteem: a self-help guide using cognitive-behavioural techniques* (2nd ed.). London: Constable Robinson.

Fennell, M., Bennett-Levy, J., & Westbrook, D. (2004). Depression. In J. Bennett-Levy, G. Butler, M. Fennell, A. Hackmann, M. Mueller, & D. Westbrook (Eds.), *The Oxford guide to behavioural experiments in cognitive therapy*. Oxford: Oxford University Press.

Field, A. (2009). *Discovering statistics using SPSS* (3rd ed.). London: Sage.

Field, T.A., Beeson, E.T., & Jones, L.K. (2015). The new ABCs: a practitioner's guide to neuroscience-informed cognitive-behavior therapy. *Journal of Mental Health Counseling, 37*, 206–220.

Flavell, J.H. (1979). Metacognition and cognitive monitoring: a new area of cognitive developmental inquiry. *American Psychologist, 34*, 906–911.

Foa, E.B., & Riggs, D.S. (1993). Post-traumatic stress disorder in rape victims. In *American Psychiatric Association, Annual review of psychiatry*. Washington, DC: APA.

Fox, K.R. (2000). The effects of exercise on self-perceptions and self-esteem. In S.J.H. Biddle, K.R. Fox, & S.H. Boutcher (Eds.), *Physical activity and psychological well-being*. London: Routledge.

Freeman, A. (1983). *Cognitive therapy with couples and groups*. New York: Springer.

Freeman, A., Schrodt, R., Gilson, M., & Ludgate, J.W. (1993). Group cognitive therapy with inpatients. In J.H. Wright, M.E. Thase, A.T. Beck, & J.W. Ludgate (Eds.), *Cognitive therapy with inpatients*. New York: Guilford Press.

Freeman, D. (2016). Persecutory delusions: a cognitive perspective on understanding and treatment. *The Lancet Psychiatry, 3*, 685–692.

Freeman, D., Dunn, G., Startup, H., Pugh, K., Cardwell, J., Mander, H., Černis, E., Wingham, G., Shrivell, K., & Kingdon, D. (2015). Effects of cognitive behaviour therapy for worry on persecutory delusions in patients with psychosis (WIT): a parallel, single-blind, randomised controlled trial with a mediation analysis. *Lancet Psychiatry, 2*, 305–313.

Freud, S. (1909). Analysis of a phobia in a five-year-old boy. *Standard Edition*, Vol. X, 5–149.

Frewin, P.A., Dozois, D.J.A., & Lanius, R.A. (2008). Neuroimaging studies of psychological interventions for mood and anxiety disorders: empirical and methodological review. *Clinical Psychology Review, 28*, 228–246.

Frude, N. (2005). Prescription for a good read. *Counselling & Psychotherapy Journal, 16*, 28–31.

Gabbard, G.O. (1991). Psychodynamics of sexual boundary violations. *Psychiatric Annals, 21*, 651–655.

Garfield, S.L. (1986). Research in client variables in psychotherapy research. In S.L. Garfield & A. Bergin (Eds.), *Handbook of psychotherapy and behaviour change* (3rd ed.). New York: Wiley.

Geddes, J. R., & Miklowitz, D.J. (2013). Treatment of bipolar disorder. *Lancet, 3813*, 1672–1682.

Gellatly, J., Bower, P., Hennessy, S., Richards, D., Gilbody, S., & Lovell, K. (2007). What makes self-help interventions effective in the management of depressive symptoms? Meta-analysis and meta-regression. *Psychological Medicine, 37*, 1217–1228.

Ghaderi, A. (2006). Does individualization matter? A randomized trial of standardized (focused) versus individualized (broad) cognitive behavior therapy for bulimia nervosa. *Behaviour Research & Therapy, 44*, 273–288.

Giesen-Bloo, J., Van Dyck, R., Spinhoven, P., Van Tilburg, W., Dirksen, C., Van Asselt, T., Kremers, I., Nadort, M., & Arntz, A. (2006). Out-patient psychotherapy for borderline personality disorder: randomised clinical trial of schema-focused therapy vs. transference-focused psychotherapy. *Archives of General Psychiatry, 63*, 649–658.

Gilbert, P. (1989). *Human nature and suffering*. Hove: Lawrence Erlbaum.

Gilbert, P. (1992). *Depression: the evolution of powerlessness*. New York: Guilford Press.

Gilbert, P. (2005). *Compassion: conceptualisations, research and use in psychotherapy*. Hove: Brunner-Routledge.

Gilbert, P. (2009). *Overcoming depression: a self-help guide using cognitive-behavioural techniques* (rev. ed.). London: Constable Robinson.

Gilbert, P., & Andrews, B. (1998). *Shame: interpersonal behaviour, psychopathology and culture*. New York: Oxford University Press.

Gilbert, P., & Irons, C. (2005). Focused therapies and compassionate mind training for shame and self-attacking. In P. Gilbert (Ed.), *Compassion: conceptualisations, research and use in psychotherapy*. Hove: Brunner-Routledge.

Gilbert, P., & Leahy, R. (Eds.). (2007). *The therapeutic relationship in the cognitive behavioural psychotherapies*. Hove: Routledge.

Gilbert, P., & Proctor, S. (2006). Compassionate mind training for people with high shame and self-criticism: overview and pilot study of a group therapy approach. *Clinical Psychology and Psychotherapy, 13*, 353–379.

Gilbody, S., House, A., & Sheldon, T. (2001). Routinely administered questionnaires for depression and anxiety: systematic review. *British Medical Journal, 332*, 406–409.

Goldberg, D.P., & Williams, P. (1988). *A user's guide to the general health questionnaire*. Basingstoke: NFER-Nelson.

Gordon, P.K. (2012). Ten steps to cognitive behavioural supervision. *The Cognitive Behaviour Therapist, 5*, 71–82.

Gottlieb, M.C. (1993). Avoiding exploitative dual relationships: a decision-making model. *Psychotherapy, 30*, 41–48.

Graham, P. (1998). *Cognitive behaviour therapy for children and families*. Cambridge: Cambridge University Press.

Grant, A., Townend, M., & Mill, J. (2009). *Assessment and case formulation in cognitive behavioural therapy*. London: Sage.

Greenberger, D., & Padesky, C. (1995). *Mind over mood*. New York: Guilford Press.

Greenberger, D., & Padesky, C. (2015). *Mind over mood* (2nd ed.). New York: Guilford Press.

Greist, J.H., & Klein, M. (1985). Running as treatment for depression. *Comprehensive Psychiatry, 20*, 41–54.

Grey, N. (2009). *A casebook of cognitive therapy for traumatic stress reactions*. Hove: Routledge.

Grey, N., Young, K., & Holmes, E. (2002). Hot spots in emotional memory and the treatment of post-traumatic stress disorder. *Behavioural & Cognitive Psychotherapy, 30*, 37–56.

Grezellschak, S., Lincoln, T.M., & Westermann, S. (2015). Cognitive emotion regulation in patients with schizophrenia: evidence for effective reappraisal and distraction. *Psychiatry Research, 229*, 434–439.

Hackmann, A. (1998). Cognitive therapy with panic and agoraphobia: working with complex cases. In N. Tarrier, A. Wells, & G. Haddock (Eds.), *Treating complex cases: the cognitive behavioural approach*. Chichester: Wiley.

Hackmann, A. (2005). Compassionate imagery in the treatment of early memories in Axis I anxiety disorders. In P. Gilbert (Ed.), *Compassion: conceptualisations, research and use in psychotherapy*. Hove: Brunner-Routledge.

Hackmann, A., Bennett-Levy, J., & Holmes, E. (2011). *Oxford guide to imagery in cognitive therapy*. Oxford: Oxford University Press.

Hackmann, A., & Holmes, E. (2004). Reflecting on imagery: a clinical perspective and overview of the special issue of *Memory* on mental imagery and memory in psychopathology. *Memory, 12*, 389–402.

Haddock, G., Barrowclough, C., Shaw, J., Dunn, G., Novaco, R., & Tarrier, N. (2009). Cognitive-behavioural therapy vs social activity therapy for people with psychosis and a history of violence. *British Journal of Psychiatry, 194*, 152–157.

Hardt, O., Einarsson, E.O., & Nader, K. (2010). A bridge over troubled water: reconsolidation as a link between cognitive and neuroscientific memory research traditions. *Annual Review of Psychology, 61*, 141–167.

Harvey, A.G. (2002). A cognitive model of insomnia. *Behaviour Research & Therapy, 40*, 869–893.

Hawton, K., Salkovskis, P., Kirk, J., & Clark, D. (Eds.). (1989). *Cognitive-behaviour therapy for psychiatric problems: a practitioner's guide*. Oxford: Oxford University Press.

Hay, P. (2013). A systematic review of evidence for psychological treatments in eating disorders: 2005–2012. *International Journal of Eating Disorders, 46*, 462–469.

Hays, P.A. (2006). Integrating cognitive-behavioural therapy with Alaskan native people. In P.A. Hays & G.Y. Iwamasa (Eds.), *Culturally responsive cognitive behaviour therapy: assessment, practice and supervision*. Washington, DC: American Psychological Association.

Hays, P.A., & Iwamasa, G.Y. (Eds.). (2006). *Culturally responsive cognitive behaviour therapy: assessment, practice and supervision*. Washington, DC: American Psychological Association.

Hayes, S.C. (2004). Acceptance and commitment therapy, relational frame theory, and the third wave of behavioral and cognitive therapies. *Behavior Therapy, 35*, 639–665.

Hayes, S.C., Barlow, D.H., & Nelson-Gray, R.O. (1999). *The practitioner: research and accountability in the age of managed care*. Boston, MA: Allyn & Bacon.

Hayes, S.C., Barnes-Holmes, D., & Roche, B. (2001). *Relational frame theory: a post-Skinnerian account of human language and cognition*. New York: Plenum.

Hayes, S.C., Strosahl, K., & Wilson, K.G. (1999). *Acceptance and commitment therapy: an experiential approach to behaviour change*. New York: Guilford Press.

Health and Social Care Information Centre (HSCIC) (no date) *Mental health*. Retrieved 31 March 2016 from www.hscic.gov.uk/

Heimberg, R.G. (2002). Cognitive behaviour therapy for social anxiety disorder: current status and future directions. *Biological Psychiatry, 51*, 101–108.

Henwood, K.S., Chou, S., & Browne, K.D. (2015). A systematic review and meta-analysis of the effectiveness of CBT informed anger management. *Aggression and Violent Behaviour, 25*, 280–292.

Herman, J. (1992). Complex PTSD: a syndrome in survivors of prolonged and repeated trauma. *Journal of Traumatic Stress, 5*, 377–391.

Hirsch, C.R., Clark, D.M., Mathews, A., & Williams, R. (2003). Self-images play a causal role in social phobia. *Behaviour Research and Therapy, 41*, 909–921.

Hollon, S.D., De Rubies, R.J., Shelton, R.C., Amsterdam, J.D., Salomon, R.M., O'Reardon, J.P., Lovett, M.L., Young, P.R., Haman, K.L., Freeman, B.P., & Gallop, R. (2005). Prevention of relapse following cognitive therapy vs medications in moderate to severe depression. *Archives of General Psychiatry, 62*, 417–422.

Hollon, S.D., & Shaw, B.F. (1979). Group cognitive therapy for depressed patients. In A.T. Beck, A.J. Rush, B.F. Shaw, & G. Emery (Eds.), *Cognitive therapy for depression*. New York: Guilford Press.

Holmes, E.A., Blackwell, S.E., Burnett-Heyes, S., Renner, F., & Raes, F. (2016). Mental imagery in depression: phenomenology, potential mechanisms and treatment implications. *Annual Review of Clinical Psychology, 12*, 249–280.

Holmes, E.A., Grey, N., & Young, K.A.D. (2005). Intrusive images and 'hotspots' of trauma memories in posttraumatic stress disorder: an exploratory investigation of emotions and cognitive themes. *Journal of Behavior Therapy and Experimental Psychiatry, 36*, 3–17.

Honey, P., & Mumford, A. (1992). *The manual of learning styles*. Maidenhead: Peter Honey.

Hope, D.A., & Heimberg, R.G. (1993). Social phobia and social anxiety. In D.H. Barlow (Ed.), *Clinical handbook of psychological disorders: a step-by-step manual* (2nd ed.). New York: Guilford Press.

Horvarth, A.O. (1995). The therapeutic relationship: from transference to alliance. *In Session: Psychotherapy in Practice, 1*, 7–17.

House, R., & Loewenthal, D. (Eds.). (2009). *Against and for CBT: towards a constructive dialogue?* Ross-on-Wye: PCCS Books.

Hubbard, R.L. (2005). Evaluation and outcome of treatment. In: J.H. Lowinson, P. Ruiz, R.B. Millman, & J.G. Langrod (Eds.), *Substance abuses: A comprehensive textbook* (4th ed.). Philadelphia, PA: Lippincott Williams & Wilkins.

Hudson, B.F., Ogden, M.S., & Whiteley, M.S. (2015). Randomised controlled trial to compare the effect of simple distraction and interventions on pain and anxiety experienced during conscious surgery. *European Journal of Pain, 19*, 1447–1455.

Huntley, A.L., Araya, R., & Salisbury. C. (2012). Group psychological therapies for depression in the community: systematic review and meta-analysis. *The British Journal of Psychiatry, 200*, 184–190.

IAPT (2010). Web page: *Training resources for low intensity therapy workers*. Retrieved 27 January 2010 from www.iapt.nhs.uk/2009/01/20/training-resources-for-low-intensity-therapy-workers/

Iwamasa, G.Y., Hsia, J., & Hays, P.A. (2006). Cognitive-behavioural therapy with Asian Americans. In P.A. Hays & G.Y. Iwamasa (Eds.), *Culturally responsive cognitive behaviour therapy: assessment, practice and supervision*. Washington, DC: American Psychological Association.

Jacobson, E. (1970). *Modern treatments of tense patients*. Springfield, IL: Thomas.

Jacobson, N.S., Dobson, K.S., Truax, P.A., Addis, M.E., Koerner, K., Gollan, J.K., Gortner, E., & Prince, S.E. (1996). A component analysis of cognitive-behavioural treatment for depression. *Journal of Consulting & Clinical Psychology, 64*, 295–304.

Jacobson, N.S., & Margolin, G. (1979). *Marital therapy: strategies based on social learning and behaviour exchange principles*. New York: Brunner/Mazel.

Jacobson, N.S., Martell, C.R., & Dimidjian, S. (2001). Behavioural activation treatment for depression: returning to contextual roots. *Clinical Psychology: Science & Practice*, *8*, 255–270.

Jacobson, N.S., & Revenstorf, D. (1988). Statistics for assessing the clinical significance of psychotherapy techniques: issues, problems, and new developments. *Behavioral Assessment*, *10*, 133–145.

Jacobson, N.S., Roberts, L.J., Berns, S.B., & McGlinchey, J.B. (1999). Methods for defining and determining the clinical significance of treatment effects: description, application and alternatives. *Journal of Consulting & Clinical Psychology*, *67*, 300–307.

James, I.A., Morse, R., & Howarth, A. (2009). The science and art of asking questions in cognitive therapy. *Behavioural and Cognitive Psychotherapy*, *38*, 83–93.

James, W. (1890). *The principles of psychology*. New York: Holt.

Kabat-Zinn, J. (1994). *Wherever you go, there you are: mindfulness meditation in everyday life*. New York: Hyperion.

Kazantzis, N., Deane, F., & Ronan, K. (2002). Homework assignments in cognitive and behavioural therapy: a meta-analysis. *Clinical Psychology Science and Practice*, *7*, 189–202.

Kazantzis, N., Whittington, C., & Dattilio, F. (2010). Meta-analysis of homework effects in cognitive and behavioral therapy: a replication and extension. *Clinical Psychology Science & Practice*, *17*, 144–156.

Kazdin, A.E. (2010). *Single-case research designs: methods for clinical and applied settings* (2nd ed.). New York: Oxford University Press.

Kelly, S. (2006). Cognitive-behavioural therapy with African Americans. In P.A. Hays & G.Y. Iwamasa (Eds.). *Culturally responsive cognitive behaviour therapy: assessment, practice and supervision*. Washington, DC: American Psychological Association.

Kennerley, H. (1995). Presentation at BABCP annual conference, Lancaster.

Kennerley, H. (1996). Cognitive therapy of dissociative symptoms associated with trauma. *British Journal of Clinical Psychology*, *35*, 325–340.

Kennerley, H. (2004). Self-injurious behaviour. In J. Bennett-Levy, G. Butler, M. Fennell, A. Hackmann, M. Mueller, & D. Westbrook (Eds.), *Oxford guide to behavioural experiments in cognitive therapy.* Oxford: Oxford University Press.

Kennerley, H. (2007). *Socratic method.* OCTC essential guides. Available from www.octc.co.uk

Kennerley, H. (2014a). Developing and maintaining a working alliance in CBT. In A. Wittington & N. Grey (Eds.), *How to become a more effective CBT therapist: mastering metacompetence in clinical practice*. Chichester: Wiley.

Kennerley, H. (2014b). *Overcoming anxiety: a self-help guide using cognitive and behavioural techniques*. London: Constable and Robinson.

Kennerley, H. (2015). The 'blobby' formulation. *OCTC Clinical Innovations*, www.octc.co.uk/innovations.

Kennerley, H. (in press). Special Issue of *the Cognitive Behaviour Therapist* on the theme of Complexity within Cognitive Behavioural Therapy, Supervision and Services.

Kennerley, H., & Clohessy, S. (2010). Becoming a supervisor. In M. Mueller, H. Kennerley, F. McManus, & D. Westbrook (Eds.), *The Oxford guide to surviving as a CBT therapist.* Oxford: Oxford University Press.

Kennerley, H., & Kischka, U. (2013). The brain, neuropsychology and dissociation. In F. Kennedy, H. Kennerley, & D. Pearson (Eds.), *Cognitive behavioural approaches to the understanding and treatment of dissociation*. Hove: Routledge.

Kennerley, H., Mueller, M.M., & Fennell, M.J. (2010). Looking after yourself. In M. Mueller, H. Kennerley, F. McManus, & D. Westbrook (Eds.), *The Oxford guide to surviving as a CBT therapist.* Oxford: Oxford University Press.

Kennerley, H., Whitehead, L., Butler, G., & Norris, R. (1998/2014). *Recovering from childhood abuse: therapy workbook.* Oxford: Oxford Cognitive Therapy Centre.

Kingdon, D., & Turkington, D. (2004). *Cognitive therapy of schizophrenia.* New York: Guilford Press.

Kirk, J., & Rouf, K. (2004). Specific phobias. In J. Bennett-Levy, G. Butler, M. Fennell, A. Hackmann, M. Mueller, & D. Westbrook (Eds.), *Oxford guide to behavioural experiments in cognitive therapy.* Oxford: Oxford University Press.

Kischka, U., Kammer, T., Maier, S., Thimm, M., & Spitzer, M. (1996). Dopaminergic modulation of semantic network activation. *Neuropsychologia, 34,* 1107–1113.

Koch, C., Stewart, A., & Stuart, A. (2010). Systemic aspects of CBT. In M. Mueller, H. Kennerley, F. McManus, & D. Westbrook (Eds.), *The Oxford guide to surviving as a CBT therapist.* Oxford: Oxford University Press.

Kolb, D. (1984). *Experiential learning: experience as the source of learning and development.* Englewood Cliffs, NJ: Prentice–Hall.

Koller, D., & Goldman, R.D. (2012). Distraction techniques for children undergoing procedures: a clinical review of paediatric research. *Journal of Paediatric Nursing, 27,* 652–681.

Krakow, B., Hollifield, M., Johnston, L., Koss, M., Schrader, R., Warner, T.D., Tandberg, D., Lauriello, J., McBride, L., Cutchen, L., Cheng, D., Emmons, S., Germain, A., Melendrez, D., Sandoval, D., & Prince, H. (2001). Imagery rehearsal therapy for chronic nightmares in sexual assault survivors with post-traumatic stress disorder. *Journal of the American Medical Association, 286,* 537–545.

Kroenke, K., Spitzer, R.L., & Williams, J.B. (2001). The PHQ-9: validity of a brief depression severity measure. *Journal of General Internal Medicine, 16,* 606–613.

Krupnick, J.L., Sotsky, S.M., Elkin, I., Simmens, S., Moyer, J., Watkins, J., & Pulkonis, P.A. (1996). The role of the therapeutic alliance in psychotherapy and pharmacotherapy outcome: findings from the NIMH treatment of depression collaborative research project. *Journal of Consulting and Clinical Psychology, 64,* 532–539.

Kuyken, W. (2006). Evidence-based case formulation: is the emperor clothed? In N. Tarrier (Ed.), *Case formulation in cognitive behaviour therapy: the treatment of complex and challenging cases.* Hove: Brunner-Routledge.

Kuyken, W., Byford, S., Taylor, R.S., Watkins, E., Holden, E., White, K., Barrett, B., Byng, R., & Evans, A. (2008). Mindfulness-based cognitive therapy to prevent relapse in recurrent depression. *Journal of Consulting and Clinical Psychology, 76*(6), 966–978.

Kuyken, W., Hayes, R., Barrett, B., Byng, R., Dalgleish, T., Kessler, D., Lewis, G., Watkins, E., Brejcha, C., Cardy, J., Causley, A., Cowderoy, S., Evans, A., Gradinger, F., Kaur, S., Lanham P., Marant, N., Richards J., Shah, P., Sutton, H., Vicary, R., Weaver, A., Wilks, J., Williams, M., Taylor, R., & Byford, S. (2015). Effectiveness and cost-effectiveness of mindfulness-based cognitive therapy compared with maintenance antidepressant treatment in the prevention of depressive relapse or recurrence (PREVENT): a randomised controlled trial. *The Lancet, 386,* 63–73.

Kuyken, W., Padesky, C.A., & Dudley, R. (2009). *Collaborative case conceptualization: working effectively with clients in cognitive-behavioural therapy.* New York: Guilford Press.

Ladouceur, R., Dugas, M.J., Freeston, M.H., Leger, E., Gagnon, F., & Thibodeau, N. (2000). Efficacy of cognitive behavioural therapy for generalized anxiety disorder: evaluation in a controlled clinical trial. *Journal of Consulting & Clinical Psychology, 68,* 957–964.

Lam, D., Jones, S., Bright, J., & Hayward, P. (1999). *Cognitive therapy for bipolar disorder: a therapist's guide to concepts, methods and practice*. Chichester: Wiley.

Lam, D., Jones, S., & Hayward, P. (2010). *Cognitive therapy for bipolar disorder: a therapist's guide to concepts, methods and practice* (2nd ed.). Chichester: Wiley.

Lambert, M.J., & Bergin, A.E. (1994). The effectiveness of psychotherapy. In A. Bergin & S. Garfield (Eds.), *Handbook of psychotherapy and behaviour change* (4th ed.). New York: Wiley.

Lang, P.J. (1968). Fear reduction and fear behavior: problems in treating a construct. In J.M. Shlien (Ed.), *Research in psychotherapy, Vol. I.* Washington, DC: American Psychiatric Association.

Larkin, W., & Morrison, A. (2006). *Trauma and psychosis*. Hove: Routledge.

Larsen, D.L., Attkisson, C.C., Hargreaves, W.A., & Nguyen, T.D. (1979). Assessment of client/patient satisfaction: development of a general scale. *Evaluation & Program Planning, 2*, 197–207.

Lawlor-Savage, L., & Prentice, J.L. (2014). Digital cognitive behaviour therapy (CBT) in Canada: ethical considerations. *Canadian Psychology/Psychologie Canadienne, 55*, 231–239.

Layard, R., & Clark, D.M. (2014). *Thrive: the power of psychological therapy*. Penguin.

Layden, M., Newman, C., Freeman, A., & Morse, S.B. (1993). *Cognitive therapy of borderline personality disorder.* Boston, MA: Allyn & Bacon.

Lazar, S.W., Kerrb, C.E., Wasserman, R.H., Gray, J.R, Greve, D.M., Treadway, M.T., McGarvey, M., Quinn, B.T., Dusek, J.A., Benson, H., Rauch, S.L., Moore, C.I., & Fischl, B. (2005). Meditation experience is associated with increased cortical thickness. *Neuroreport, 16*(17): 1893–1897.

LeDoux, J. (1999). *The emotional brain: the mysterious underpinnings of an emotional life*. London: Phoenix.

Lee, D.A. (2005). The perfect nurturer: a model to develop a compassionate mind within the context of cognitive therapy. In P. Gilbert (Ed.), *Compassion: conceptualisations, research and use in psychotherapy.* Hove: Brunner-Routledge.

Lejuez, C.W., Hopko, D.R., Acierno, R., Daughters, S.B., & Pagoto, S.L. (2011). Ten year revision of the brief behavioral activation treatment for depression: revised treatment manual. *Behaviour Modification, 35*, 111–161.

Lejuez, C.W., Hopko, D.R., & Hopko, S.D.A. (2001). Brief behavioural activation treatment for depression: treatment manual. *Behaviour Modification, 25*, 255–286.

Lewin, K. (1946). Action research and minority problems. *Journal of Social Issues, 2*, 34–46.

Lewis, G., Anderson, L., Aray, R., Elgie, R., Harrison, G., Proudfoot, J., Schmidt, U., Sharp, D., Weightman, A., & Williams, C. (2003). *Self-help interventions for mental health problems. Report to the Department of Health R&D Programme.* London: Department of Health.

Liese, B.S., & Franz, R.A. (1996). Treating substance use disorders with cognitive therapy: lessons learned and implications for the future. In P.M. Salkovskis (Ed.), *Frontiers of cognitive therapy*. New York: Guilford Press.

Linehan, M.M. (1993). *Cognitive-behavioural treatment for borderline personality disorder: the dialectics of effective treatment*. New York: Guilford Press.

Linehan, M.M., Heard, H.L., & Armstrong, H.E. (1993). Naturalistic follow-up of a behavioural treatment for chronically parasuicidal borderline patients. *Archives of General Psychiatry, 50*, 971–974.

Lovell, K., & Richards, D.A. (2000). Multiple access points and levels of entry (MAPLE): ensuring choice, accessibility and equity for CBT services. *Behavioural and Cognitive Psychotherapy, 28*, 379–391.

Lovell, K., Richards, D.A., & Bower, P. (2003). Improving access to primary mental health care: uncontrolled evaluation of a pilot self-help clinic. *British Journal of General Practice, 53,* 133–135.

MacPherson, H.A., Cheavens, J.S., & Fristad, M.A. (2013). Dialectical behavior therapy for adolescents: theory, treatment adaptations, and empirical outcomes. *Clinical Child and Family Psychology Review, 16,* 59–80.

Mannix, K., Blackburn, I., Garland, A., Gracie, J., Moorey, S., Reid, B., Standart, S., & Scott, J. (2006). Effectiveness of brief training in cognitive behaviour therapy techniques for palliative care practitioners. *Palliative Medicine, 20,* 579–584.

Mansell, W., & Clark, D.M. (1999). How do I appear to others? Social anxiety and biased processing of the observable self. *Behaviour Research & Therapy, 37,* 419–434.

Margison, F., Barkham, M., Evans, C., McGrath, G., Mellor-Clark, J., Audin, K., & Connell, J. (2000). Measurement and psychotherapy: evidence-based practice and practice-based evidence. *British Journal of Psychiatry, 177,* 123–130.

Marlatt, G.A., & Gordon, J.R. (1985). *Relapse prevention: maintenance strategies in the treatment of addictive disorders.* New York: Guilford Press.

Marlatt, G.A., Larimer, M.E., Baer, J.S., & Quigley, L.A. (1993). Harm reduction for alcohol problems: moving beyond the controlled drinking controversy. *Behaviour Therapy, 24,* 461–504.

Martell, C.R., Addis, M.E., & Jacobson, N.S. (2001). *Depression in context: strategies for guided action.* New York: Norton.

Martinsen, E.W., Medhus, A., & Sandvik, L. (1985). Effects of aerobic exercise on depression: a controlled study. *British Medical Journal, 291,* 109.

Mayhew, S.L., & Gilbert, P. (2008). Compassionate mind training with people who hear malevolent voices: a case series report. *Clinical Psychology and Psychotherapy, 15,* 113–138.

McCann, I.L., & Pearlman, L.A. (1990). Vicarious traumatization: a framework for understanding the psychological effects of working with victims. *Journal of Traumatic Stress, 3,* 131–149.

McManus, F.V. (2007). Assessment of anxiety. *Psychiatry, 6*(4), 149–155.

McManus, F., Clark, G., Shafran, R., & Muse, K. (2015). A preliminary evaluation of a transdiagnostic approach to treating co-morbid anxiety disorders. *Behavioural and Cognitive Psychotherapy, 43,* 744–758.

McMillan, D., & Lee, R. (2010). A systematic review of behavioral experiments vs. exposure alone in the treatment of anxiety disorders: a case of exposure while wearing the emperor's new clothes? *Clinical Psychology Review, 30,* 467–478.

McNally, R.J. (2003). *Remembering trauma.* Cambridge, MA: Harvard University Press.

McNally, R.J. (2007). Mechanisms of exposure therapy: how neuroscience can improve psychological treatments for anxiety disorders. *Clinical Psychology Review, 27,* 750–759.

Meichenbaum, D.H. (1975). A self-instructional approach to stress management: a proposal for stress inoculation training. In C.D. Spielberger & I. Sarason (Eds.), *Stress and anxiety, Vol. 2.* New York: Wiley.

Mental Health Foundation (MHF) (no date) *Statistics.* Retrieved 31 March 2016 from www.mentalhealth.org.uk/statistics

Merrill, K.A., Tolbert, V.E., & Wade, W.A. (2003). Effectiveness of cognitive therapy for depression in a community mental health center: a benchmarking study. *Journal of Consulting & Clinical Psychology, 71,* 404–409.

Michelson, L. (1986). Treatment consonance and response profiles in agoraphobia: the role of individual differences in cognitive, behavioural, and physiological treatments. *Behaviour Research & Therapy*, *24*, 263–275.

Middle, C., & Kennerley, H. (2001). A grounded theory analysis of the therapeutic relationship with clients sexually abused as children and non-abused clients. *Clinical Psychology and Psychotherapy*, *8*, 198–205.

Miller, W.R. (1983). Motivational interviewing with problem drinkers. *Behavioural Psychotherapy*, *11*, 147–172.

Miller, W.R. (2000). Motivational interviewing: some parallels with horse whispering. *Behavioural and Cognitive Psychotherapy*, *28*, 285–292.

Miller, W.R., & Rollnick, S.R. (2002). *Motivational interviewing: preparing people to change behaviour* (2nd ed.). New York: Guilford Press.

Milne, D. (2009). *Evidence-based clinical supervision: principles and practice*. Chichester: Wiley-Blackwell.

Mitcheson, L., Maslin, J., Meynen, T., Morrison, T., Hill, R., & Wanigarantne, S. (2010). *Applied cognitive and behavioural approaches to the treatment of addiction*. Chichester: Wiley-Blackwell.

Moore, R., & Garland, A. (2003). Cognitive therapy for chronic and persistent depression. Chichester: Wiley.

Moorey, S. (2010). The six cycles maintenance model: growing a 'vicious flower' for depression. *Behavioural & Cognitive Psychotherapy*, *38*, 173–184.

Morin, C.M. (1993). *Insomnia: psychological assessment and management*. New York: Guilford Press.

Morin, C.M., Bootzin, R.R., Buysse, D.J., Edinger, J.D., Espie, C.A., & Lichstein, K.L. (2006). Psychological and behavioural treatment of insomnia: update of the recent evidence (1988–2004). *Sleep*, *29*, 1398–1414.

Morrison, A.P., Renton, J.C., Dunn, H., Williams, S., & Bentall, R.P. (2004). *Cognitive therapy for psychosis: a formulation-based approach*. Hove: Brunner-Routledge.

Morrison, N. (2000). Schema-focused cognitive therapy for complex long-standing problems: a single case study. *Behavioural & Cognitive Psychotherapy*, *38*, 269–283.

Morrison, N. (2001). Group cognitive therapy: treatment of choice or sub-optimal option? *Behavioural & Cognitive Psychotherapy*, *29*, 311–332.

Mullen, P.E., Martin, J.L., Anderson, J.C., Romans, S.E., & Herbison, G.P. (1993). Child sexual abuse and mental health in adult life. *British Journal of Psychiatry*, *163*, 721–732.

Mullin, T., Barkham, M., Mothersole, G., Bewick, B., & Kinder, A. (2006). Recovery and improvement benchmarks for counselling and the psychological therapies in routine primary care. *Counselling and Psychotherapy Research*, *6*, 68–80.

Muse, K., & McManus, F. (2013). A systematic review of methods for assessing competence in cognitive-behaviour therapy. *Clinical Psychology Review*, *33*, 484–499.

Myhr, G., Talbot, J., Annable, L., & Pinard, G. (2007). Suitability for short-term cognitive-behavioral therapy. *Journal of Cognitive Psychotherapy*, *21*, 334–345.

Mynors-Wallis, L., Davies, I., Gray, A., Barbour, F., & Gath, D. (1997). A randomised controlled trial and cost analysis of problem-solving treatment for emotional disorders given by community nurses in primary care. *British Journal of Psychiatry*, *170*, 113–119.

Mynors-Wallis, L., Gath, D.H., & Baker, F. (2000). Randomised controlled trial of problem solving treatment, antidepressant medication, and combined treatment for major depression in primary care. *British Medical Journal*, *320*, 26–30.

Naeem, F., Clarke, I., & Kingdon, D. (2009). A randomized controlled trial to assess an anger management group programme. *The Cognitive Behaviour Therapist, 2*, 20–31.

Naeem, F., Phiri, P., Rathod, S., & Kingdon, D. (2010). Using CBT with diverse patients: working with South Asian Muslims. In M. Mueller, H. Kennerley, F. McManus, & D. Westbrook (Eds.), *Oxford guide to surviving as a CBT therapist*. Oxford: Oxford University Press.

Neff, K.D., & Germer, C.K. (2013). A pilot study and randomized controlled trial of the mindful self-compassion program. *Journal of Clinical Psychology, 69*, 28–44.

Neisser, U. (1976). *Cognition and reality: principles and implications of cognitive psychology*. San Francisco, CA: W.H. Freeman.

Newman, C.F. (1994). Understanding client resistance: methods for enhancing motivation to change. *Cognitive and Behavioural Practice, 1*, 47–69.

Nezu, A.M., Nezu, C.M., & Perri, M.G. (1989). *Problem-solving therapy for depression: theory, research and clinical guidelines*. New York: Wiley.

NICE (2004a). *Depression: management of depression in primary and secondary care*. Retrieved 9 May 2005 from www.nice.org.uk/page.aspx?o=235367

NICE (2004b). *Eating disorders: core interventions in the treatment and management of anorexia nervosa, bulimia nervosa and related eating disorders*. Retrieved 9 May 2005 from www.nice.org.uk/page.aspx?o=101246

NICE (2005a). *Post-traumatic stress disorder: guidance*. Retrieved 18 March 2016 from www.nice.org.uk/guidance/cg26/chapter/1-Guidance

NICE (2005b). *Obsessive compulsive disorder: core interventions in the treatment of obsessive compulsive disorder and body dysmorphic disorder*. Retrieved 25 January 2010 from www.nice.org.uk/nicemedia/pdf/cg031niceguideline.pdf

NICE (2006). *Technology appraisal 97: computerised cognitive behaviour therapy for depression and anxiety*. London: National Institute for Health & Clinical Excellence.

NICE (2007). *Chronic fatigue syndrome myalgic encephalomyelitis: guidance*. Retrieved 18 March 2016 from www.nice.org.uk/guidance/cg53/chapter/1-Guidance

NICE (2009). *Depression: the treatment and management of depression in adults*. Retrieved 25 January 2010 from www.nice.org.uk/nicemedia/pdf/CG91NICEGuideline.pdf

NICE (2011a). *Generalised anxiety disorder and panic disorder in adults: guidance*. Retrieved 18 March 2016 from www.nice.org.uk/guidance/cg113/chapter/1-Guidance

NICE (2011b). *Alcohol-use disorders: guidance*. Retrieved 18 March 2016 from www.nice.org.uk/guidance/cg115/chapter/1-Guidance

NICE (2014a). Psychosis and s*chizophrenia in adults: guidance*. Retrieved 18 March 2016 from www.nice.org.uk/guidance/cg178/chapter/1-Guidance

NICE (2014b). Antenatal and post natal mental health: guidance. Retrieved 18 March 2016 from www.nice.org.uk/guidance/cg192/chapter/1-recommendations

NIMH (National Institute of Mental Health) (2001). *Facts about anxiety disorders*. Retrieved 21 May 2006 from www.nimh.nih.gov/publicat/adfacts.cfm

Nolen-Hoeksema, S. (1991). Responses to depression and their effects on the duration of depressive episodes. *Journal of Abnormal Psychology, 100*, 569–582.

Normann, N.M., Van Emmerik, A.A.P., & Morina, N. (2014). The efficacy of metacognitive therapy for anxiety and depression: a meta-analytic review. *Depression and Anxiety, 31*, 402–411.

Norris, R. (1995). *Pair therapy with adult survivors of sexual abuse.* Thesis submitted for MSc in Clinical Psychology, University of Derby.

Norton, P.J. (2012). A randomized clinical trial of transdiagnostic cognitive behavioural treatments for anxiety disorder by comparison to relaxation training. *Behaviour Therapy, 43,* 506–517.

Novaco, R.W. (1979). The cognitive regulation of anger and stress. In P.C. Kendall & S.D. Hollon (Eds.), *Cognitive-behavioral interventions: theory, research, and procedures.* New York: Academic Press.

Novaco, R.W. (2000). Anger. In A.E. Kazdin (Ed.), *Encyclopedia of psychology.* Washington, DC: American Psychological Association and Oxford University Press.

Novaco, R.W. (2007). Anger dysregulation. In T. Cavell & K. Malcolm (Eds.), *Anger, aggression, and interventions for interpersonal violence.* Mahwah, NJ: Erlbaum.

Obsessive-Compulsive Cognitions Working Group (1997). Cognitive assessment of obsessive-compulsive disorder. *Behaviour Research & Therapy, 35,* 667–681.

Orlinsky, D., Grawe, K., & Parks, B. (1994). Process and outcome in psychotherapy. In A. Bergin & S. Garfield (Eds.), *Handbook of psychotherapy and behaviour change* (4th ed.). New York: Wiley.

Öst, L.G. (1987). Applied relaxation: description of a coping technique and review of controlled studies. *Behaviour Research & Therapy, 25,* 397–410.

Öst, L.G., & Sterner, U. (1987). Applied tension: a specific behavioural method for treatment of blood phobia. *Behaviour Research & Therapy, 25,* 25–30.

Öst, L.G., Sterner, U., & Fellenius, J. (1989). Applied tension, applied relaxation, and the combination in the treatment of blood phobia. *Behavior Research & Therapy, 27,* 109–121.

Öst, L.G., Sterner, U., & Lindhal, J.-L. (1984). Physiological responses in blood phobics. *Behaviour Research & Therapy, 22,* 109–127.

Ottavani, R., & Beck, A.T. (1987). Cognitive aspects of panic disorder. *Journal of Anxiety Disorders, 1,* 15–28.

Overholser, J.C. (1991). The Socratic method as a technique in psychotherapy supervision. *Professional Psychology: Research and Practice, 22,* 68–74.

Owen, M., Speight, T., Sarsam, M., & Sellwood, W. (2015). Group CBT for psychosis in acute care: a review of outcome studies. *The Cognitive Behaviour Therapist, 8,* 1–18.

Padesky, C. (1993). *Socratic questioning: changing minds or guiding discovery?* Keynote address delivered at European Association for Behavioural & Cognitive Therapies Conference, London.

Padesky, C. (1994). Schema change processes in cognitive therapy. *Clinical Psychology & Psychotherapy, 1,* 267–278.

Padesky, C., for Center for Cognitive Therapy and New Harbinger (co-producers) (1996a). *Guided discovery using Socratic dialogue* (DVD). Huntington Beach, CA: Center for Cognitive Therapy. Available from www.padesky.com.

Padesky, C. (1996b). Developing cognitive therapist competency: teaching and supervision models. In P. Salkovskis (Ed.), *Frontiers in cognitive therapy.* New York: Guilford Press.

Padesky, C. (1997). A more effective treatment focus for social phobia? *International Cognitive Therapy Newsletter, 11,* 1–3.

Padesky, C. (2005). *Constructing a new self: cognitive therapy for personality disorders.* Workshop presented in London, England, 23–24 May 2005.

Padesky, C., & Greenberger, D. (1995). *Clinician's guide to mind over mood.* New York: Guilford Press.

Padesky, C.A., & Mooney, K.A. (1990). Clinical tip: presenting the cognitive model to clients. *International Cognitive Therapy Newsletter*, *6*, 13–14.

Padesky, C.A., & Mooney, K.A. (2012). Strengths-based cognitive-behavioural therapy: a four-step model to build resilience. *Clinical Psychology and Psychotherapy*, *19*, 283–290.

Palmer, B. (2003). Concepts of eating disorders. In J. Treasure, U. Schmidt, & E. van Furth (Eds.), *Handbook of eating disorders* (2nd ed.). Chichester: Wiley.

Papworth, M., Marrinan, T. & Martin, B., with Keegan, D. & Chaddock, A. (2013). *Low intensity cognitive behavior therapy: a practitioner's guide*. London: Sage.

Pearson, J., Clifford, C.W.G., & Tong, F. (2008). The functional impact of mental imagery on conscious perception. *Current Biology*, *18*, 982–986.

Pearson, J., Naselaris, T., Holmes, E.A., & Kosslyn, S.M. (2015). Mental imagery: functional mechanism, and clinical applications. *Trends in Cognitive Sciences*, *19*, 590–602.

Perris, C. (2000). Personality-related disorders of interpersonal behaviour: a developmental-constructivist cognitive psychotherapy approach to treatment based on attachment theory. *Clinical Psychology & Psychotherapy*, *7*, 97–117.

Persons, J.B. (1989). *Cognitive therapy in practice: a case formulation approach*. New York: Norton.

Peruzzi, N., & Bongar, B. (1999). Assessing risk for completed suicide in patients with major depression: psychologists' views of critical factors. *Professional Psychology: Research and Practice*, *30*, 576–580.

Petrak, J., & Hedge, B. (2002). *The trauma of sexual assault: treatment, prevention and practice*. Chichester: Wiley.

Petry, N., & Bickel, W. (1999). Therapeutic alliance and psychiatric severity as predictors of completion of treatment for opioid dependence. *Psychiatric Services*, *50*, 219–227.

Pilling, G., & Roth, A. (2008). Supervision competencies framework. Retrieved 21 May 2016 from www.ucl.ac.uk/pals/research/cehp/research-groups/core/competence-frameworks/Supervision_of_Psychological_Therapies

Pilling, S., Bebbington, P., Kuipers, E., Garety, P., Geddes, J., Orbach, G., & Morgan, C. (2002). Psychological treatments in schizophrenia: I. Meta-analysis of family intervention and cognitive behaviour therapy. *Psychological Medicine*, *32*, 763–782.

Pope, K.S., & Bouhoutsos, J. (1986). *Sexual intimacy between therapists and patients*. New York: Praeger.

Pope, K.S., Tabachnick, B.G., & Keith-Spiegel, P. (1987). Ethics of practice: the beliefs and behaviours of psychologists as therapists. *American Psychologist*, *42*, 993–1006.

Prentice, J.L., & Dobson, K.S. (2014). A review of the risks and benefits associated with mobile phone applications for psychological interventions. *Canadian Psychology/Psychologie Canadienne*, *55*, 282–290.

Pretzer, J. (1990). Borderline personality disorder. In A.T. Beck, A. Freeman, D. Davis, & Associates, *Cognitive therapy of personality disorders*. New York: Guilford Press.

Prochaska, J.O., & DiClemente, C.C. (1986). Towards a comprehensive model of change. In W. Miller & H. Heather (Eds.), *Treating addictive behaviours: processes of change*. New York: Plenum.

Prochaska, J.O., Velicer, W.F., Rossi, J.S., Goldstein, M.G., Marcus, B.H., Rakowski, W., Fiore, C., Harlow, L.L., Redding, C.A., Rosenbloom, D., & Rossi, S.R. (1994). Stages of change and decisional balance for twelve problem behaviors. *Health Psychology*, *13*, 39–46.

Rachman, S.J. (2015). The evolution of behaviour therapy and cognitive behaviour therapy. *Behaviour Research and Therapy*, *64*, 1–8.

Rachman, S.J., & de Silva, P. (1978). Abnormal and normal obsessions. *Behaviour Research & Therapy*, *16*, 233–248.

Rachman, S.J., & Hodgson, R. (1974). Synchrony and de-synchrony in fear and avoidance. *Behaviour Research & Therapy*, *12*, 311–318.

Rachman, S., Radomsky, A.S., & Shafran, R. (2008). Safety behaviour: a reconsideration. *Behaviour Research and Therapy*, *46*, 163–173.

Raimy, V. (Ed.). (1950). *Training in clinical psychology*. New York: Prentice–Hall.

Raue, P.J., & Goldfried, M.R. (1994). The therapeutic alliance in cognitive-behaviour therapy. In A.O. Horvath & L.S. Greenberg (Eds.), *The working alliance*. New York: Wiley.

Rector, N.A., Bagby, R.M., Segal, Z.V., Joffe, R.T., & Levitt, A. (2000). Self-criticism and dependency in depressed patients treated with cognitive therapy or pharmacotherapy. *Cognitive Therapy & Research*, *24*, 571–584.

Resick, P.A., & Schnicke, M.K. (1993). *Cognitive processing therapy for rape victims*. Newbury Park, CA: Sage.

Richards, A., Barkham, M., Cahill, J., Richards, D., Williams, C., & Heywood, P. (2003). PHASE: a randomised controlled trial of supervised self-help cognitive behavioural therapy in primary care. *British Journal of General Practice*, *53*, 764–770.

Richards, D. (2010). Low intensity CBT. In M. Mueller, H. Kennerley, F. McManus, & D. Westbrook (Eds.), *The Oxford guide to surviving as a CBT therapist*. Oxford: Oxford University Press.

Richardson, R., & Richards, D.A. (2006). Self-help: towards the next generation. *Behavioural & Cognitive Psychotherapy*, *34*, 13–23.

Riso, L.P, du Toit, P.L, Stein, D.J., & Young, J.E. (2007). *Cognitive schemas and core beliefs in psychological problems*. Washington DC: American Psychological Association.

Robson, C. (2002). *Real world research*. Oxford: Blackwell.

Robson, C., & McCartan, K. (2016). *Real world research* (4th ed.). Chichester: Wiley.

Rogers, C. (1951). *Client-centred counselling*. Boston: Houghton–Mifflin.

Rollnick S., & Miller, W.R. (1995). What is motivational interviewing? *Behavioural and Cognitive Psychotherapy*, *23*, 325–334.

Rollnick, S., Miller, W.R., & Butler, C.C. (2008). *Motivational interviewing in health care: helping patients change behaviour.* New York: Guilford Press.

Roth, A., & Fonagy, P. (2005). *What works for whom?* (2nd ed.). New York: Guilford Press.

Roth, A., & Pilling, S. (2007). *The competences required to deliver effective cognitive and behavioural therapy for people with depression and with anxiety disorders*. London: Department of Health. Retrieved 22 April 2010 from www.dh.gov.uk/prod_consum_dh/groups/dh_digitalassets/@dh/@en/documents/digitalasset/dh_078535.pdf

Roth, A., & Pilling, S. (2009). *A competence framework for the supervision of psychological therapies*. Retrieved 26 May 2010 from www.ucl.ac.uk/clinical-psychology/CORE/supervision_framework.htm

Rothschild, B. (2000). *The body remembers: the psychophysiology of trauma and trauma treatment*. New York: Norton.

Rush, A.J., Beck, A.T., Kovacs, M., & Hollon, S.D. (1977). Comparative efficacy of cognitive therapy and pharmacotherapy in the treatment of depressive outpatients. *Cognitive Therapy & Research*, *1*, 17–37.

Rush, A.J., & Watkins, J.T. (1981). Group versus individual therapy: a pilot study. *Cognitive Therapy and Research, 5*, 95–103.

Ryder, J. (2010). CBT in groups. In M. Mueller, H. Kennerley, F. McManus, & D. Westbrook (Eds.), *The Oxford guide to surviving as a CBT therapist*. Oxford: Oxford University Press.

Safran, J.D. (1998). *Widening the scope of cognitive therapy: the therapeutic relationship, emotion, and the process of change*. New York: Aronson.

Safran, J.D., & Muran, J.C. (1995). Resolving therapeutic alliance ruptures: diversity and integration. *In Session: Psychotherapy in Practice, 1*, 81–92.

Safran, J.D., & Segal, Z.V. (1990). *Interpersonal process in cognitive therapy*. New York: Basic Books.

Safran, J.D., Segal, Z.V., Vallis, T.M., Shaw, B.F., & Samstag, L.W. (1993). Assessing patient suitability for short-term cognitive therapy with an interpersonal focus. *Cognitive Therapy & Research, 17*, 23–38.

Salkovskis, P.M. (1985). Obsessive-compulsive problems: a cognitive-behavioural analysis. *Behaviour Research & Therapy, 23*, 571–583.

Salkovskis, P.M. (1988). Phenomenology, assessment and the cognitive model of panic. In S.J. Rachman & J. Maser (Eds.), *Panic: psychological perspectives*. Hillsdale, NJ: Erlbaum.

Salkovskis, P.M. (1991). The importance of behaviour in the maintenance of anxiety and panic: a cognitive account. *Behavioural Psychotherapy, 19*, 6–19.

Salkovskis, P.M. (1995). Demonstrating specific effects in cognitive and behavioural therapy. In M. Aveline & D. Shapiro (Eds.), *Research foundations for psychotherapy practice*. Chichester: Wiley.

Salkovskis, P.M. (1999). Understanding and treating obsessive-compulsive disorders. *Behaviour Research & Therapy, 37*, S29–S52.

Salkovskis, P.M. (2002). Empirically grounded clinical interventions: cognitive-behavioural therapy progresses through a multi-dimensional approach to clinical science. *Behavioural & Cognitive Psychotherapy, 30*, 3–9.

Salkovskis, P.M., & Bass, C. (1997). Hypochondriasis. In D.M. Clark & C.G. Fairburn (Eds.), *Science and practice of cognitive-behaviour therapy*. Oxford: Oxford University Press.

Salkovskis, P.M., Jones, D.R.O., & Clark, D.M. (1986). Respiratory control in the treatment of panic attacks: replication and extension with concurrent measurement of behaviour and pCO2. *British Journal of Psychiatry, 148*, 526–532.

Salkovskis, P.M., & Warwick, H.M. (1986). Morbid preoccupations, health anxiety and reassurance: a cognitive-behavioural approach to hypochondriasis. *Behaviour Research & Therapy, 24*, 597–602.

Salkovskis, P., Warwick, H., & Deale, A. (2003). Cognitive-behavioral treatment for severe and persistent health anxiety (hypochondriasis). *Brief Treatment and Crisis Intervention, 3*, 353–367.

Salkovskis, P.M., & Westbrook, D. (1989). Behaviour therapy and obsessional ruminations: can failure be turned into success? *Behaviour Research & Therapy, 27*, 149–160.

Schmidt, N., & Woolaway-Bickel, K. (2000). The effects of treatment compliance on outcome in cognitive-behavioural therapy for panic disorder: quality versus quantity. *Journal of Consulting and Clinical Psychology, 68*, 13–18.

Scholing, A., & Emmelkamp, P.M.G. (1993). Exposure with and without cognitive therapy for generalised social phobia: effects of individual and group treatment. *Behaviour Research & Therapy, 31*, 667–681.

Schulte, D., & Eifert, G.H. (2002). What to do when manuals fail? The dual model of psychotherapy. *Clinical Psychology: Science and Practice, 9*, 312–338.

Schulte, D., Kuenzel, R., Pepping, G., & Schulte, B.T. (1992). Tailor-made versus standardized therapy of phobic patients. *Advances in Behaviour Research & Therapy, 14*, 67–92.

Scott, J. (2001). *Overcoming mood swings: a self-help guide using cognitive behavioural techniques.* London: Robinson.

Scott, J., Colom, F., & Vieta, E. (2006). A meta-analysis of relapse rates with adjunctive psychological therapies compared to usual psychiatric treatment for bipolar disorders. *International Journal of Neuro-psychopharmacology, 10*, 123–129.

Scott, M.J., & Stradling, S.G. (1994). Post-traumatic stress without the trauma. *British Journal of Clinical Psychology, 33*, 71–74.

Segal, Z.V., Williams J.M., & Teasdale, J.D. (2002). *Mindfulness-based cognitive therapy for depression: a new approach to prevent relapse.* New York: Guilford Press.

Silver, A., Surawy, C., & Sanders, D. (2004). Physical illness and disability. In J. Bennett-Levy, G. Butler, M. Fennell, A. Hackmann, M. Mueller, & D. Westbrook (Eds.), *The Oxford guide to behavioural experiments in cognitive therapy.* Oxford: Oxford University Press.

Simon, R.I. (1991). Psychological injury caused by boundary violation precursors to therapist–patient sex. *Psychiatric Annals, 21*, 616–619.

Smith, D., & Fitzpatrick, M. (1995). Patient–therapist boundary issues: an integrative review of theory and research. *Professional Psychology: Research and Practice, 26*, 499–506.

Sobell, M.B., & Sobell, L.C. (1993). *Problem drinkers: guided self-change treatment.* New York: Guilford Press.

Stenfert-Kroese, B., Dagnan, D., & Loumidis, K (1997). *Cognitive-behaviour therapy for people with learning disabilities.* London: Routledge.

Stratford, H.J., Cooper, M.J., Di Simplicio, M., Blackwell, S.E., & Holmes, E. (2015). Psychological therapy for anxiety in bipolar spectrum disorders: a systematic review. *Clinical Psychology Review, 35*, 19–34.

Stuart, G.L., Treat, T.A., & Wade, W.A. (2000). Effectiveness of an empirically based treatment of panic disorder delivered in a service clinic setting: 1-year follow-up. *Journal of Consulting & Clinical Psychology, 68*, 506–512.

Stuart, R. (1980). *Helping couples change: a social learning approach to marital therapy.* New York: Guilford Press.

Szpunar, K.K., & Schacter, D.L. (2013). Get real: effects of repeated simulation and emotion on the perceived plausibility of future experiences. *Journal of Experimental Psychology, 142*, 323–327.

Szuhany, K.L., Bugatti, M., & Otto, M.W. (2015). A meta-analytic review of the effects of exercise on brain-derived neurotrophic factor. *Journal of Psychiatric Research, 60*, 56–64.

Taylor, A.H. (2000). Physical activity, anxiety, and stress. In S.J.H. Biddle, K.R. Fox, & S.H. Boutcher (Eds.), *Physical activity and psychological well-being.* London: Routledge.

Teasdale, J.D. (1988). Cognitive vulnerability to persistent depression. *Cognition & Emotion, 2*, 247–274.

Teasdale, J.D. (1996). Clinically relevant theory: integrating clinical insight with cognitive science. In P. Salkovskis (Ed.), *Frontiers of cognitive therapy.* New York: Guilford Press.

Teasdale, J.D. (2004). Mindfulness-based cognitive therapy. In J. Yiend (Ed.), *Cognition, emotion and psychopathology: theoretical, empirical and clinical directions.* Cambridge: Cambridge University Press.

Teasdale, J.D., & Barnard, P.J. (1993). *Affect, cognition and change: re-modelling depressive thought.* Hove: Lawrence Erlbaum.

Teasdale, J.D., Moore, R.G., Hayhurst, H., Pope, M., Williams, S., & Segal, Z.V. (2002). Metacognitive awareness and prevention of relapse in depression: empirical evidence. *Journal of Consulting & Clinical Psychology, 70,* 275–289.

Teasdale, J.D., Segal, Z.V., & Williams, J.M.G. (1995). How does cognitive therapy prevent depressive relapse and why should attentional control (mindfulness) training help? *Behaviour Research & Therapy, 33,* 25–39.

Teismann, T., Michalak, J., Willutzki, U., & Schulte, D. (2012). Influence of rumination and distraction on the therapeutic process in cognitive behavioural therapy for depression. *Cognitive Therapy and Research, 36,* 15–24.

Telch, M.J., Luxcas, J.A., Schmidt, N.B., Hanna, H.H., Jaimez, T.L., & Lucas, R.A. (1993). Group cognitive-behavioural treatment of panic disorder. *Behaviour Research & Therapy, 31,* 279–287.

Terr, L.C. (1991). Childhood traumas: an outline and overview. *American Journal of Psychiatry, 148,* 10–20.

Thase, M.E., Greenhouse, J.B., Frank, E., Reynolds, C.F., Pilkonis, P.A., Hurley, K., Grochocinski, V., & Kupfer, D.J. (1997). Treatment of major depression with psychotherapy or psychotherapy–pharmacotherapy combinations. *Archives of General Psychiatry, 54,* 1009–1015.

Thase, M.E., Kingdon, D., & Turkington, D. (2014). The promise of cognitive behavior therapy for treatment of severe mental disorders: a review of recent developments. *World Psychiatry, 13,* 244–250.

Treasure, J.L., Katzman, M., Schmidt, U., Troop, N., Todd, G., & de Silva, P. (1999). Engagement and outcome in the treatment of bulimia nervosa: first phase of a sequential design comparing motivation enhancement therapy and cognitive behaviour therapy. *Behaviour Research & Therapy, 37,* 405–418.

Treasure, J., Schmidt, U., & van Furth, E. (2003). *Handbook of eating disorders* (2nd ed.). Chichester: Wiley.

Tucker, M., & Oie, T. (2007). Is group more cost effective than individual CBT? The evidence is not solid yet. *Behavioural and Cognitive Psychotherapy, 35,* 77–91.

Turner, H., Marshall, E., Wood, F., Stopa, L., & Waller, G. (2016). CBT for eating disorders: the impact of early changes in eating pathology on later changes in personality pathology, anxiety and depression. *Behaviour Research and Therapy, 77,* 1–6.

Valentine, S.E., Bankoff, S.M., Poulin, R.M., Reidler, E.B., & Pantalone, D.W. (2015). The use of dialectical behavior therapy skills training as stand-alone treatment: a systematic review of the treatment outcome literature. *Journal of Clinical Psychology, 71,* 1–20.

Van der Kolk, B., Roth, S., Pelcovitz, D., Sunday, S., & Spinozzol, J. (2005). The empirical foundation of a complex adaptation to trauma. *Journal of Traumatic Stress, 18,* 389–399.

Vanderlinden, J., & Vandereycken, W. (1997). *Trauma, dissociation and impulse dyscontrol in eating disorders.* Bristol, PA: Brunner/Mazel.

Vitousek, K.B. (1996). The current status of cognitive behavioural models of anorexia nervosa and bulimia nervosa. In P.M. Salkovskis (Ed.), *Frontiers of cognitive therapy.* New York: Guilford Press.

Vitousek, K.B., & Brown, K.E. (2015). Cognitive-behavioural theory of eating disorders. In L. Smolak & M.P. Levine (Eds.), *The Wiley handbook of eating disorders.* Chichester: Wiley-Blackwell.

Vittengl, J., Clark, L., & Jarret, R. (2010). Moderators of continuation phase cognitive therapy's effects on relapse, recurrence, remission, and recovery from depression. *Behaviour Research & Therapy, 48,* 449–458.

Wade, W.A., Treat, T.A., & Stuart, G.L. (1998). Transporting an empirically supported treatment for panic disorder to a service clinic setting: a benchmarking strategy. *Journal of Consulting & Clinical Psychology*, *66*, 231–239.

Waller, G. (1993). Why do we diagnose different types of eating disorder? Arguments for a change in research and clinical practice. *Eating Disorders Review*, *1*, 74–89.

Waller, G., Cordery, H., Corstorphine, E., Hinrichsen, H., Lawson, R., Mountford, V., & Russell, K. (2007). *Cognitive behavioural therapy for eating disorders: a comprehensive treatment guide*. Cambridge: Cambridge University Press.

Waller, G., & Kennerley, H. (2003). Cognitive behavioural treatments. In J. Treasure, U. Schmidt, & E. van Furth (Eds.), *Handbook of eating disorders* (2nd ed.). Chichester: Wiley.

Warwick, H.M.C., & Salkovskis, P.M. (1989). Hypochondriasis. In J. Scott, J.M.G. Williams, & A.T. Beck (Eds.), *Cognitive therapy in clinical practice*. London: Croom Helm.

Waters, A., Hill, A., & Waller, G. (2001). Bulimics' responses to food cravings: is binge-eating a product of hunger or emotional state? *Behaviour Research & Therapy*, *39*, 877–886.

Watkins, E., Scott, J., Wingrove, J., Rimes, K., Bathurst, N., Steiner, H., Kennell-Webb, S., Moulds, M., & Malliaris, Y. (2007). Rumination-focused cognitive behaviour therapy for residual depression: a case series. *Behaviour Research & Therapy*, *45*, 2144–2154.

Watson, H.J., & Bulik, C.M. (2013). Update on the treatment of anorexia nervosa: review of clinical trials, practice guidelines and emerging interventions. *Psychological Medicine*, *43*, 2477–2500.

Watson, J.C., & Greenberg, L.S. (1995). Alliance ruptures and repairs in experiential therapy. *In Session: Psychotherapy in Practice*, *1*, 19–31.

Wells, A. (1995). Meta-cognition and worry: a cognitive model of GAD. *Behavioural and Cognitive Psychotherapy*, *23*, 301–320.

Wells, A. (1997). Cognitive therapy of anxiety disorders: a practice manual and conceptual guide. Chichester: Wiley.

Wells, A. (2000). *Emotional disorders and metacognition*. Chichester: Wiley.

Wells, A. (2008). A metacognitive therapy: cognition applied to regulating cognition. *Behavioural and Cognitive Psychotherapy*, *36*, 651–658.

Wells, A., & Mathews, G. (1994). *Attention and emotion: a clinical perspective*. Hove: Lawrence Erlbaum.

Wenzel, A., Brown, G.K., & Beck, A.T. (2009). *Cognitive therapy for suicidal patients*. Washington, DC: American Psychological Association.

Wenzlaff, R.M., & Bates, D.E. (2000). The relative efficacy of concentration and suppression strategies of mental control. *Personality and Social Psychology Bulletin*, *26*, 1200–1212.

Wenzlaff, R.M., Wegner, D.M., & Klein, F.B. (1991). The role of thought suppression in the bonding of thought and mood. *Journal of Personality and Social Psychology*, *60*, 500–508.

Westbrook, D. (2010). Research and evaluation. In M. Mueller, H. Kennerley, F. McManus, & D. Westbrook (Eds.), *The Oxford guide to surviving as a CBT therapist*. Oxford: Oxford University Press.

Westbrook, D.J., & Kirk, J. (2005). The clinical effectiveness of cognitive behaviour therapy: outcome for a large sample of adults treated in routine practice. *Behaviour Research & Therapy*, *43*, 1243–1261.

Westbrook, D., Mueller, M., Kennerley, H., & McManus, F. (2010). Common problems in therapy. In M. Mueller, H. Kennerley, F. McManus, & D. Westbrook (Eds.), *Oxford guide to surviving as a CBT therapist*. Oxford: Oxford University Press.

Westen, D. (1996). *Psychology: mind, brain and culture.* New York: Wiley.

Westra, H., & Stewart, S. (1998). Cognitive behavioural therapy and pharmacotherapy: complementary or contradictory approaches to the treatment of anxiety? *Clinical Psychology Review, 18,* 307–340.

White, J. (1998). 'Stress control' large group therapy for generalized anxiety disorder: two year follow-up. *Behavioural & Cognitive Psychotherapy, 26,* 237–246.

White, J. (2000). *Treating anxiety and stress: a group psycho-educational approach using brief CBT.* Chichester: Wiley.

White, J., Keenan, M., & Brooks, N. (1992). 'Stress control': a controlled comparative investigation of large group therapy for generalized anxiety disorder. *Behavioural Psychotherapy, 20,* 97–114.

Wiederhold, B. (2015). Behavioral health apps abundant, but evidence-based research nearly non-existent. *Cyberpsychology, Behaviour and Social Networking, 18,* 309–310.

Wilkinson, P.W. (2002). Cognitive behaviour therapy. In J.N. Hepple, J. Pearce, & P.W. Wilkinson (Eds.), *Psychological therapies for older people. Developments for effective practice.* Hove: Brunner-Routledge.

Williams, C. (2001). Use of written cognitive-behavioural therapy self-help materials to treat depression. *Advances in Psychiatric Treatment, 7,* 233–240.

Williams, C., Wilson, P., Morrison, J., McMahon, A., Andrew, W., Allan, L., McConnachie, A., McNeil, Y., & Tansey, L. (2013). Guided self-help cognitive behavioural therapy for depression in primary care: a randomised controlled trial. *PLoS ONE, 8*(1): e52735.

Williams, J.M.G. (1997). Depression. In D.M. Clark & C.G. Fairburn (Eds.), *Science and practice of cognitive behaviour therapy.* Oxford: Oxford University Press.

Williams, J.M.G., Teasdale, J.D., Segal, Z.V., & Soulsby, J. (2000). Mindfulness-based cognitive therapy reduces overgeneral autobiographical memory in formerly depressed patients. *Journal of Abnormal Psychology, 109,* 150–155.

Williams, J.M.G., Watts, F.N., McCleod, C., & Mathews, A. (1997). *Cognitive psychology and emotional disorders* (2nd ed.). New York: Wiley.

Witkiewitz, K., & Marlatt, G.A. (2007). *Therapist's guide to evidence-based relapse prevention.* Burlington, MA: Elsevier.

Wittrock, M.C. (1978). The cognitive movement in instruction. *Educational Psychologist, 13,* 15–29.

Wolpe, J. (1958). *Psychotherapy by reciprocal inhibition.* Stanford, CA: Stanford University Press.

Wright, J.H., & Davis, D. (1994). The therapeutic relationship in cognitive-behaviour therapy: patient perceptions and therapist responses. *Cognitive and Behavioural Practice, 1,* 25–45.

Wykes, T., Steel, C., Everitt, B., & Tarrier, N. (2008). Cognitive behavior therapy for schizophrenia: effect sizes, clinical models, and methodological rigor. *Schizophrenia Bulletin, 34,* 523–537.

Yalom, I. (1995). The theory and practice of group psychotherapy. New York: Basic Books.

Young, J.E. (1984). *Cognitive therapy with difficult patients.* Workshop presented at the meeting of the Association for Advancement of Behavior Therapy, Philadelphia, PA.

Young, J.E. (1990). *Cognitive therapy for personality disorders: a schema focused approach.* Sarasota, FL: Professional Resource Exchange.

Young, J., & Beck, A.T. (1980). *Cognitive therapy scale: rating manual.* Unpublished MS, University of Pennsylvania, PA.

Young, J.E., Klosko, J., & Weishaar, M.E. (2003). *Schema therapy: a practitioner's guide.* New York: Guilford Press.

Zettle, R.D. (2003). Acceptance and commitment therapy (ACT) versus systematic desensitization in treatment of mathematics anxiety. *The Psychological Record*, *53*, 197–215.

Zigmond, A.S., & Snaith, R.P. (1983). The Hospital Anxiety and Depression Scale. *Acta Psychiatrica Scandinavica*, *67*, 361–370.

Zipfel, S., Lowe, B., & Herzog, W. (2003). Medical complications. In J. Treasure, U. Schmidt, & E. van Furth (Eds.), *Handbook of eating disorders* (2nd ed.). Chichester: Wiley.

INDEX

Page numbers with 'f' suffixes indicate figures and 't' suffixes tables.